France					
	Red Bordeaux		**White Bordeaux**		**Alsace**	
Vintage	Médoc/Graves	Pom/St-Ém	Sauternes & sw	Graves & dry		
2016	8–9	8–9	8–10	7–9	7–8	
2015	7–9	8–10	8–10	7–9	7–9	
2014	7–8	6–8	8–9	8–9	7–8	
2013	4–7	4–7	8–9	7–8	8–9	
2012	6–8	6–8	5–6	7–9	8–9	
2011	7–8	7–8	8–10	7–8	5–7	
2010	8–10	7–10	7–8	7–9	8–9	
2009	7–10	7–10	8–10	7–9	8–9	
2008	6–8	6–9	6–7	7–8	7–8	
2007	5–7	6–7	8–9	8–9	6–8	
2006	7–8	7–8	7–8	8–9	6–8	
2005	9–10	8–9	7–9	8–10	8–9	
2004	7–8	7–9	5–7	6–7	6–8	
2003	5–9	5–8	7–8	6–7	6–7	
2002	6–8	5–8	7–8	7–8	7–8	
2001	6–8	7–8	8–10	7–9	6–8	
2000	8–10	7–9	6–8	6–8	8–10	
1999	5–7	5–8	6–9	7–10	6–8	
1998	5–8	6–9	5–8	5–9	7–9	

	France continued				
	Burgundy			**Rhône**	
Vintage	Côte d'Or red	Côte d'Or white	Chablis	North	South
2016	7–8	7–8	7–8	7–9	7–9
2015	7–9	7–8	7–8	8–9	8–9
2014	6–8	7–9	7–9	7–8	6–8
2013	5–7	7–8	6–8	7–9	7–8
2012	8–9	7–8	7–8	7–9	7–9
2011	7–8	7–8	7–8	7–8	6–8
2010	8–10	8–10	8–10	8–10	8–9
2009	7–10	7–8	7–8	7–9	7–8
2008	7–9	7–9	7–9	6–7	5–7
2007	7–8	8–9	8–9	6–8	7–8
2006	7–8	8–10	8–9	7–8	7–9
2005	7–9	7–9	7–9	7–8	6–8
2004	6–7	7–8	7–8	6–7	6–7
2003	6–7	6–7	6–7	5–7	6–8

Beaujolais 2015, 14, 11. Crus will keep. **Mâcon-Villages** (white). Drink 15, 14.
Loire (sweet Anjou and Touraine) best recent vintages: 15, 10, 09, 07, 05, 02, 97, 96, 93, 90, 89; Bourgueil, Chinon, Saumur-Champigny: 15, 14, 10, 09, 06, 05, 04, 02. **Upper Loire** (Sancerre, Pouilly-Fumé): 15, 14, 12. **Muscadet**: DYA.

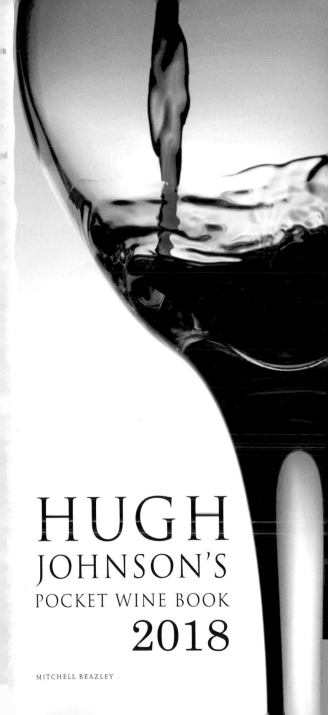

HUGH
JOHNSON'S
POCKET WINE BOOK
2018

MITCHELL BEAZLEY

Hugh Johnson's Pocket Wine Book 2018

Edited and designed by Mitchell Beazley,
an imprint of Octopus Publishing Group Limited,
Carmelite House, 50 Victoria Embankment
London EC4Y 0DZ
www.octopusbooks.co.uk

An Hachette UK Company
www.hachette.co.uk

Distributed in the US by Hachette Book Group
1290 Avenue of the Americas
4th and 5th Floors
New York, NY 10020
www.octopusbooksusa.com

ISBN (UK): 978-1-78472-293-7
ISBN (US): 978-1-78472-407-8

The author and publishers will be grateful for any
information that will assist them in keeping future editions
up to date. Although all reasonable care has been taken in
preparing this book, neither the publishers nor the author
can accept any liability for any consequences arising from
the use thereof, or from the information contained herein.

General Editor **Margaret Rand**
Commissioning Editor **Hilary Lumsden**
Senior Editor **Pauline Bache**
Proofreader **Jamie Ambrose**
Art Director **Yasia Williams-Leedham**
Designer **Jeremy Tilston**
Picture Research Manager **Giulia Hetherington**
Senior Production Manager **Katherine Hockley**

Printed and bound in China

Mitchell Beazley would like to acknowledge and thank the following
for supplying photographs for use in this book:

123RF.com Bertrand Iniesta 16; foodandmore 332; Iakov Filimonov 333;
Israel Hervás 326 left; Markus Mainka 14; miloszg 326 right. **Alamy Stock
Photo** Carlos Sánchez Pereyra/mauritius images GmbH 325; Christian
Guy/hemis.fr 334; Hendrik Holler/Bon Appetit 323; Jim Mires 1; Per
Karlsson - BKWine.com 331; Steve Race/Stockimo 321 left. **Dreamstime.
com** Flynt 7; Inna Paladii 4; Michele Ranchetti 11; Talita Nicolielo 6.
Shutterstock ksl 328. **SuperStock** Biosphoto/Biosphoto 336; Pixtal/Pixtal
321 right.

HUGH
JOHNSON'S
POCKET WINE BOOK

General Editor
Margaret Rand

2018

Acknowledgements

This store of detailed recommendations comes partly from my own notes and mainly from those of a great number of kind friends. Without the generous help and cooperation of innumerable winemakers, merchants and critics, I could not attempt it. I particularly want to thank the following for help with research or in the areas of their special knowledge:

Ian d'Agata, Helena Baker, Amanda Barnes, Lana Bortolot, Jim Budd, Michael Cooper, Michael Edwards, Sarah Jane Evans MW, Rosemary George MW, Caroline Gilby MW, Anthony Gismondi, Anne Krebiehl MW, James Lawther MW, Konstantinos Lazarakis MW, John Livingstone-Learmonth, Jordan Mackay, Campbell Mattinson, Adam Montefiore, Jasper Morris MW, Ch'ng Poh Tiong, André Ribeirinho, Margaret Rand, Ulrich Sautter, Eleonora Scholes, Stephen Skelton MW, Paul Strang, Sean Sullivan, Marguerite Thomas, Gal Zohar, Philip van Zyl.

Contents

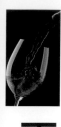

The top line of most entries consists of the following information:

1. Aglianico del Vulture Bas

2. r dr (s/sw sp)

3. ★★★

4. 05' 06 07 08 09' 10 (11)

1. Aglianico del Vulture Bas

Wine name and the region the wine comes from, abbreviations of regions are listed in each section.

2. r dr (s/sw sp)

Whether it is red, rosé or white (or brown/amber), dry, sweet or sparkling, or several of these (and which is most important):

r	red
p	rosé
w	white
br	brown
dr	dry*
sw	sweet
s/sw	semi-sweet
sp	sparkling

( ) brackets here denote a less important wine
* assume wine is dry when dr or sw are not indicated

3. ★★★

Its general standing as to quality: a necessarily rough-and-ready guide based on its current reputation as reflected in its prices:

★	plain, everyday quality
★★	above average
★★★	well known, highly reputed
★★★★	grand, prestigious, expensive

So much is more or less objective. Additionally there is a subjective rating:

★ etc.   Stars are coloured for any wine, which, in my experience, is usually especially good within its price range. There are good everyday wines as well as good luxury wines. This system helps you find them.

4. 05' 06 07 08 09' 10 (11)

Vintage information: those recent vintages that can be
recommended, and of these, which are ready to drink this year, and
which will probably improve with keeping. Your choice for current
drinking should be one of the vintage years printed in **bold** type.
Buy light-type years for further maturing.

05 etc.   recommended years that may be currently available
06' etc. vintage regarded as particularly successful for the property
          in question
07 etc.   years in bold should be ready for drinking (those not in bold
          will benefit from keeping)
08 etc.   vintages in colour are those recommended as first choice
          for drinking in 2018. (*See also* Bordeaux introduction, p.100.)
(11) etc. provisional rating

The German vintages work on a different principle again: *see* p.158.

Other abbreviations & styles

DYA	Drink the youngest available.
NV	Vintage not normally shown on label; in Champagne this means a blend of several vintages for continuity.
CHABLIS	Properties, areas or terms cross-referred within the section; all grapes cross-ref to Grape Varieties chapter on pp.16–26.
Foradori	Entries styled this way indicate wine especially enjoyed by Hugh Johnson (mid-2016–17).

Agenda 2018

Would you like wine to be a simple matter of red or white? Be honest. Nor would I. Sometimes when I browse through this book, and especially when I contemplate the task of updating it, I have felt a faint twinge of brain-fatigue. But then I start re-reading the entries, and a potent mix of thirst and curiosity takes over. "Is that so?" I say to myself. "Are they really planting Pinot Noir in Brazil? Why are this Meursault grower's prices zooming up? I've got to try that."

It was what got me into wine in the first place. Every label (well, an almighty multitude of labels – more than I'll ever meet) represents some individual's best shot at making, in his or her particular circumstances, something delicious, individual, memorable – to tempt you and me to pay them a wage. Every label, every cork, conceals an unknown, like Alice in Wonderland's bottles, saying "Drink me".

There is a kind of madness comes over people who take up wine as a way of life. Some believe farming grapes is an ideal existence close to nature; some delude themselves that they'll make a fortune; some feel what they see as an almost sacred commitment; others can't shake off the memory of a sublime glass and devote their lives to reproducing it. And then of course pride kicks in. The unhinged pride of an ex-pat determined to prove you can make sparkling wine in Mauritius, or the dynastic pride of an aristo deploying his ancestral coat of arms. These days, there is competition for Gold, Silver and Bronze as well – not to mention those bizarre scores out of a hundred.

Whatever the impetus, the results are all around us, clamouring not just for our money, but our respect, even affection, and best of all, loyalty. But who could be loyal, and give their custom to one supplier day after day, when there are 8695 others in these pages, singing away like sirens to seduce you?

I've written and rewritten this little book 41 times and the thirst and the curiosity have not gone away. In fact they're more insistent than ever. Why? Because there are five times more wines on offer, from a vast geographical range of places (half the vineyards listed here didn't exist when I began) and, crucially, because they are all, almost without exception, getting better at what they do.

Does all this sound rather pie in the sky when you wheel your trolley down an aisle hemmed in by bottles flaunting their USPs? Does the Discount Bin sing the sexiest song? What to do? If you haven't got a thread to follow, go by price (remembering that a good proportion of it goes on bottle, cork, label, tax, logistics and margins). Far better, find a thread.

Because I'm in the business of appreciating and investigating, my threads may sound a bit geeky; following a region, a producer, a grape variety or a vintage to make comparisons and glean information. Nor do I make my choices in a supermarket: I make them with proper wine lists in hand, printed ones from dedicated independent merchants (who offer the best values) and with my laptop at the ready. Winesearcher.com can tell me what different merchants are charging for the same wine. Cellartracker and many other websites will offer me an infinity of opinions – far too many to make sense of – and producers' own websites will show me their vineyards, cellars and family histories, all suspiciously ideal.

So where do I start? Most often with food or friends, or both. Wine is all about context, and context is first and foremost how you feel. Hungry? Busy? In love? You're on a beach, a ski slope, with a Wall Street wolf.... Let instinct be your guide – instinct, and the vintage charts on the front endpapers.

Is there a theme for 2018? A trend, an imperative, a sleeper, a star in the East, a revelation or something to avoid at all costs? Various hares I have started in these pages, I'm happy to say, have since been more publicly hunted, with generally benign results. We are most of us drinking fresher, more transparent wines than a few years ago, less clogged with oak, with flavours and dyes, less processed and pumped and filtered. And at least nominally less alcoholic – though I learn that certain wines rated as 14.5% alc (often in minuscule print up the corner of the label) may be as strong as 17%.

There is a general pressure on suppliers these days not to muck about with our comestibles. It can take many forms, from lists of ingredients (who reads them?) to brave experiments in non-intervention. "Natural" wine is an obvious debating point I needn't pursue here. "Orange" wine, which usually means a white wine left to macerate on its skin for an unconventionally long time, has its passionate adherents, who find authenticity in its consequent tannins and faintly oxidized character. It's not often for me, but then I don't wear torn jeans either.

Rosé, on the other hand, has been a valid idiom for many years without ever attaining much respect – unless it comes from Champagne, when it commands a surprising premium. How much more expensive are black grapes, or the processing of them, to add to white? A very pale Pinot Noir from Burgundy can be delicious too. Why is it never given serious consideration? Because in Burgundy we are looking for other characters – depth, structure, texture and longevity – that a fleeting maceration of the skins can't provide.

I wrote in my last edition that it is open season on alternatives. In fact wine professionals, sommeliers especially, are demanding them – whether from new regions, untried grape varieties or unconventional technologies. There used to be enough fascination in following, for example, *climat*-by-*climat* distinctions of terroir, the speed and effects of maturation, or stylistic changes as children take over the reins in the cellar. That's all a bit slow for restaurants that hire guest chefs in case anyone gets bored. Now every self-respecting grower has planted some edgy variety in a corner of his land, just to see.

It is against custom, if not actual law, to conclude any summary like this without a reference to climate change. Those on the warm fringes of wine-growing are alarmed by it. Some who can afford it are taking precautions: buying land in cooler spots. The owners of vineyards on the cool margins – Champagne, or Germany, where high acidity is essential to high quality – are apprehensive too. We may well see more Champagne houses buying land in England. Meanwhile, the net effect of fractionally higher temperatures and a longer ripening season has so far been benign. Wine is better than it used to be, in greater variety. It's frightening to think how fat this book will be in a few more years.

Hail, frost, floods... 2016 in Europe was a challenging year. In France, Alsace, Bordeaux and the Rhône came off best. In Alsace, Hugel was a bit surprised to see the quince tree in its orchard in bud-break on January 6; it did not, however, presage a particularly mild spring, and hot weather didn't really begin until August. Then, after heavy rain, there was (naturally) drought. Picking was quite late, the yield good for a change, but there was little botrytis, so few sweet wines. The dry wines are profound and elegant, with the Pinots looking especially good.

Summer drought was also the story in **Bordeaux**. The whites look very promising, says Jean-Christophe Mau of Château Brown, because, "ripening stopped in the heat, and when it started again the acidity was so high we could afford to wait". For the reds, quality looks close to the excellent 2010s, with ripeness and richness across the board; both Cabernet Sauvignon and Merlot seem to have succeeded brilliantly.

The **Rhône** was very good too. In the Southern Rhône they're even more pleased with their stylish 2016s than they are with their 2015s – and the latter are splendid. The north has made wines of lovely poise and concentration. 2016 will be yet another reason to buy these glorious wines.

So which regions had less luck? **Burgundy** had late frost from Chablis right down to the Mâconnais, and it was followed by hail. The **Loire** was also severely frosted; Sancerre escaped but nearby Menetou-Salon and Pouilly-Fumé were badly hit. Quality, however, is good: Anjou has produced beautiful Chenins, and reds are ripe and juicy. The **Languedoc** had unaccustomed April frost too and then August hailstones the size of golf balls in some places, especially Pic St-Loup. Over 1000 ha of grapes were destroyed in just half an hour, just a week or two away from harvest. **Champagne** also had frost, especially in the Aube, then rain, then mildew, and ended up with a yield probably lower than in roastingly hot 2003.

Italy was a game of two halves: floods in the south, and a very difficult year; in the north, wines of beautiful balance and fresh acidity. In Valpolicella it looks even better than 2015; Barolo had hail in late July, but because Nebbiolo is late-ripening the damage was less than it might have been.

In **Austria**, Steiermark and Burgenland were frosted but Niederösterreich was unscathed, and overall the wines have good aromas and good acidity.

Vintage report 2016

The summer in **Spain** was hot and dry after a wet spring; both Rioja and Ribera del Duero seem officially happy with the results. Alcohol levels are middling; quality will probably be patchy.

Germany suffered as well: frost, hail, downy mildew, drought, sunburn. But in the end it turned out well, and the wines are ripe, fresh and healthy. There was even a bit of botrytis in the later autumn, and there are some fine Spätlesen and Auslesen, though Beerenauslesen and Trockenbeerenauslesen are scarce. But there is some Eiswein.

In the **Douro**, the year followed the common pattern: a wet early summer, followed by drought and heat. (Any café with air-conditioning did well.) The vines took a long time to regain their balance after so many extremes. However, the wines look promising: fresh and structured. A potential vintage year.

California's long drought kept going, though flavours, according to Kendall Jackson, are "outstanding". **Chile** had rain, rain, rain. It was an El Niño harvest, like 1998 and 1983. The wines have less alcohol and less concentration than usual; they're elegant rather than powerful (which some will welcome). Maule was drier. **Australia** had a generally early vintage; dry in Barossa where growers are enthusiastic about the Shiraz and Grenache.

A closer look at 2015

Years when everybody is happy are rare: 2015 was one. Everybody was so happy, in fact, that one began to think that a little journalistic scepticism might be necessary; there's nothing like hyping a vintage for selling wine.

But mostly it does look very good. In the **Loire** the wines are lush and opulent, and earlier drinking than the saline, tight 2014s. Both are very good, and if you want to take a good look at Sancerre or Pouilly-Fumé, and see how producers are focusing on Sauvignon Blanc as a conduit for the terroir rather than as a means of offering explosive green flavours, then 2015 could be the vintage to do it.

In **Bordeaux** quality is good to really good. They know they'll be teased for having another Vintage of the Century, but it could be the year that brings people back to Bordeaux. In St-Émilion a radical reduction in oak combined with more gentle extraction has produced succulent, delicious wines of freshness and spicy aromas. They're forward and they may not last forever, but they display all the character that made us love St-Émilion before they started covering it in oak.

Champagne too, looks very good. Not outstanding, perhaps, and better for Pinot than Chardonnay, but the wines are ripe and expressive, big and flavoursome.

Burgundy is almost too big and flavoursome, especially the whites: there is almost a New World lushness to the Chardonnays of the Côte d'Or, and if you want typical Côte d'Or styles you might have to look in Chablis (or back at 2014). If you want typical Chablis steeliness, this is not your vintage. The reds are often equally plump and opulent. At the moment the vintage often dominates the terroir, but burgundy has a habit of changing as it ages.

The 2015s in **Germany** look terrific: they're very pure, with little or no botrytis, and will close up and then slowly re-emerge. August Kessler recommends that we drink the simple wines now, and leave the serious ones for five to ten years.

In **Spain**, there was rain just when they wanted to pick so they picked either before or after, and after meant dilute wines. So there are nice wines, but not the greatest. In Ribera del Duero it's officially "excellent" (which is not unusual) and more powerful than 2014.

In **Italy** the wines seem generally to be living up to expectations, and are therefore very good. Tuscan reds are approachable young and will age well, says Paolo di Marche of Isole e Olena; for him alcohol isn't as high as in some years, because he's been working on ways of using the vine canopy to slow sugar accumulation. Out on the coast at Bolgheri, Masseto is doing similar things, though there can never be anything other than relatively high-alcohol wines. Bolgheri's 2015 was slightly cooler than 2016; the reverse applied further inland. Most of Sicily had a close to ideal vintage.

Tokaj in 2015 was hot and dry, and better for dry wines than for sweet; what Aszú there is is good but there isn't much. The late autumn was wet, so the botrytized grapes were too dilute for Aszú. But late-harvest wines look good, and dry wines are fresh, with good acidity, without being aggressive.

Southern hemisphere wines, with six months' start on those of Europe, are developing well. In **New Zealand** Hawke's Bay reds are looking elegant, with Rhône-style Syrahs; **South African** reds and whites are concentrated and balanced.

In **Australia**, standout wines seem to be Riesling from Eden Valley and Clare, pretty well anything from Adelaide Hills, Chardonnay and Pinot Noir from Victoria, including Yarra and Mornington Peninsula, and Shiraz from New South Wales. Expect poise and elegance in the new Aussie style.

If you like this, try this

If you like red burgundy, try Mencía

It's hard not to love red burgundy: that glorious pure Pinot Noir fruit, those crunchy tannins, those fascinating aromas – and that precision, that layered complexity. But because everybody loves it the price is climbing, climbing... and is unlikely to come down any time soon. The truth is it's impossible to find that same flavour and structure anywhere except in other Pinots, but if you want to branch out you may like the acidity and juiciness of the Mencía grape of northwest Spain. It's becoming more and more popular for its raspberry and blackcurrant fruit and the attractive grip of its tannins, and it has a mouthwatering moreishness that Pinot-lovers will recognize. Bierzo is the trophy region, with rediscovered vineyards of old vines on schist slopes, but other regions – Ribera Sacra, Valdeorras and Monterrei – are also proud of the grape. Beware of high-alcohol versions, however; acidity can drop quickly at the end of ripening, putting the wine out of balance.

If you like Dolcetto, try Cabernet Franc

Dolcetto is the everyday wine of Piedmont – the red you might open on a Wednesday evening, while keeping the Barbaresco and Barolo for Saturday or Sunday. Its name suggests something sweet and diminutive, but this is relative: a good Dolcetto is not short of stuffing. But it also has plenty of freshness and hedgerow fruit, and unlike the two other star wines of the region, it's good young. Cabernet Franc, also often good young, is the fresher, lighter, more aromatic alternative to Cabernet Sauvignon, typically tasting of raspberries, and becoming increasingly popular in places just not warm enough to ripen the bigger grape. The Loire (Saumur-Champigny, Chinon, Bourgueil) is France's main region for it (in Bordeaux, where there's lots in St-Émilion, it's usually blended with Merlot and Cabernet Sauvignon) and elsewhere, Hungary, Washington State, Virginia and Canada are making very fair examples.

If you like Châteauneuf, try Garnacha

This seems obvious, doesn't it? Châteauneuf-du-Pape is based on Grenache, with the grower's choice of a dozen other grapes thrown in as well, so obviously, if you like that, you'll like the Spanish equivalent. Except that the Spanish equivalent takes you in different directions. In this year's supplement we look at how Garnacha is evolving, and it's all good. Even Priorat, which used to be a bit frightening to anyone who counted elegance as a virtue, is changing. There are now Priorats you can drink without taking a deep breath first. All we need now is for Châteauneuf to rediscover elegance. Some, of course, never abandoned it.

If you like Sancerre, try Albariño

Sancerre is one of the most iconic names in wine, and a white that non-winos often regard as a lifebelt when asked to navigate a tricky restaurant wine list. Sancerre is better than it's ever been, with a new generation of growers focusing on terroir and producing salty, citrus, pure wines infused with the chalk or flint of the local rock. It also ages with splendid results: five years on and the fruit will be edging towards honey, still with that refreshing lick of salt. Albariño is on the same flavour spectrum. Rías Baixas, its Spanish home on the Atlantic, is granite rather than chalk but the acidity is there, providing an elegant backbone for the salt and orange-peel flavours and sometimes an addictive wet-earth note – the smell of earth after rain. You're getting nicely textured, firm, precise, aromatic whites that will age for up to ten years and have only around 12.5% alc. Just a caution: some Albariños have been sweetened up recently to catch casual sales.

If you like Champagne, try English fizz

It's a no-brainer, of course. Same grapes, same winemaking method, same soil, sometimes. And same price, usually. How many tastings have there been demonstrating irrefutably that English fizz is even better than Champagne? Ignore them. Blind tastings prove everything and nothing. Instead, try for yourself: Champagne's keynote flavour is not fruit but the fresh-bread note of lees ageing, plus the tensile acidity that comes from chalk soil. To these you can add white flowers, confit fruit, mandarin peel, nuts.... Most English vineyards are not on chalk, and the acidity then is different, but still marked. Most English fizz is based on Chardonnay too, so expect a leaner profile, with quite low dosage. The talisman is orchard freshness; a very English garden message – which at best is wonderful. Quality is not even, and many producers are still on a learning curve, but the entries on pp.218–9 should help you sort the sheep from the goats.

If you like Gewurztraminer, try Torrontés

We're talking about heavily aromatic wines here, smelling of roses and face cream, lychees and sweet spice. Gewurztraminer is at its most aromatic in Alsace, where everything tastes of spice and everything has a touch of opulence; Gewurztraminer here can have a texture like oil of roses and unmistakeable complexity – as well as, ideally, enough acidity to balance. This is not a high-acid grape. Other Traminers are likely to be less perfumed; the absence of "Gewurz" in the grape name is a safe guide to less aroma. But even NZ, which is making some proper Gewurztraminer, seems a little reluctant to turn the power on full. Argentina's Torrontés is an alternative if you want aromas delivered in a slightly more girly way; it's a more obviously Muscatty grape with less weight behind it – more roses, a bit of air freshener and soap, in a good way. (Though there are some more macho ones too). Try it chilled on a summer's evening.

Grape varieties

In the past two decades a radical change has come about in all except the most long-established wine countries: the names of a handful of grape varieties have become the ready-reference to wine. In senior wine countries, above all France and Italy, more complex traditions prevail. All wine of old prestige is known by its origin, more or less narrowly defined – not just by the particular fruit juice that fermented. For the present the two notions are in rivalry. Eventually the primacy of place over fruit will become obvious, at least for wines of quality. But for now, for most people, grape tastes are the easy reference point – despite the fact that they are often confused by the added taste of oak. If grape flavours were really all that mattered, this would be a very short book. But of course they *do* matter, and a knowledge of them both guides you to flavours you enjoy and helps comparisons between regions. Hence the originally Californian term "varietal wine", meaning, in principle, made from one grape variety. At least seven varieties – Cabernet Sauvignon, Pinot Noir, Riesling, Sauvignon Blanc, Chardonnay, Gewurztraminer and Muscat – taste and smell distinct and memorable enough to form international wine categories. To these add Merlot, Malbec, Syrah, Sémillon, Chenin Blanc, Pinots Blanc and Gris, Sylvaner, Viognier, Nebbiolo, Sangiovese, Tempranillo. The following are the best and/or most popular wine grapes.

All grapes and synonyms are cross-referenced in small capitals throughout every section of this book.

Grapes for red wine

Agiorgitiko Greek; the grape of Nemea, now planted almost everywhere. Versatile and delicious, from soft and charming to dense and age-worthy. A must-try.

Aglianico S Italian, the grape of Taurasi; dark, deep and fashionable.

Alicante Bouschet Used to be beyond pale, now stylish in Alentejo, Chile, esp old vines.

Aragonez *See* TEMPRANILLO.

Auxerrois *See* MALBEC, if red. White Auxerrois has its own entry in White Grapes.

Băbească Neagră Traditional "black grandmother grape" of Moldova; light body and ruby-red colour.

Babić Dark grape from Dalmatia, grown in stony seaside v'yds round Šibenik. Exceptional quality potential.

Baga Portugal. Bairrada grape. Dark and tannic. Great potential but hard to grow.

Barbera Widely grown in Italy, best in Piedmont. high acidity, low tannin, cherry fruit. Ranges from barriqued and serious to semi-sweet and frothy. Fashionable in California and Australia; promising in Argentina.

Blauburger Austrian cross of BLAUER PORTUGIESER and BLAUFRÄNKISCH. Simple wines.

Blauburgunder *See* PINOT N.

Blauer Portugieser Central European, esp Germany (Rheinhessen, Pfalz, mostly for rosé), Austria, Hungary. Light, fruity reds: drink young, slightly chilled.

Blaufränkisch (Kékfrankos, Lemberger, Modra Frankinja) Widely planted in Austria's Mittelburgenland: medium-bodied, peppery acidity, a characteristic salty note, berry aromas and eucalyptus. Often blended with CAB SAUV or ZWEIGELT. Lemberger in Germany (speciality of Württemberg), Kékfrankos in Hungary, Modra Frankinja in Slovenia.

Doğazkere Tannic and Turkish. Produces full-bodied wines.

Bonarda Ambiguous name. In Oltrepò Pavese, an alias for Croatina, soft fresh *frizzante* and still red. In Lombardy and Emilia-Romagna an alias for Uva Rara. Different in Piedmont. Argentina's Bonarda can be any of these, or something else. None are great.

Bouchet St-Émilion alias for CAB FR.

Brunello SANGIOVESE, splendid at Montalcino.

Cabernet Franc [Cab Fr] The lesser of two sorts of Cab grown in B'x, but dominant in St-Émilion. Outperforms CAB SAUV in Loire (Chinon, Saumur-Champigny, rosé), in Hungary (depth and complexity in Villány and Szekszárd) and often in Italy. Much of ne Italy's Cab Fr turned out to be CARMENÈRE. Used in B'x blends of Cab Sauv/MERLOT across the world.

Cabernet Sauvignon [Cab Sauv] Grape of great character: slow-ripening, spicy, herby, tannic, with blackcurrant aroma. Main grape of the Médoc; also makes some of the best California, South American, East European reds. Vies with Shiraz in Australia. Grown almost everywhere, and led vinous renaissance in eg. Italy. Top wines need ageing; usually benefits from blending with eg. MERLOT, CAB FR, SYRAH, TEMPRANILLO, SANGIOVESE, etc. Makes aromatic rosé.

Cannonau GRENACHE in its Sardinian manifestation; can be v. fine, potent.

Carignan (Carignane, Carignano, Cariñena) Low-yielding old vines now v. fashionable everywhere from s of France to Chile; best: Corbières. Lots of depth and vibrancy. Overcropped Carignan is wine-lake fodder. Common in North Africa, Spain (as Cariñena) and California.

Carignano *See* CARIGNAN.

Cariñeña *See* CARIGNAN.

Carmenère An old B'x variety now a star; rich, deep in Chile (where it's pronounced *carmeneary*). B'x looking at it again.

Castelão *See* PERIQUITA.

Cencibel *See* TEMPRANILLO.

Chiavennasca *See* NEBBIOLO.

Cinsault (Cinsaut) A staple of s France, v.gd if low-yielding, wine-lake stuff if not. Makes gd rosé. One of parents of PINOTAGE.

Cornalin du Valais Swiss speciality with high potential, esp in Valais.

Corvina Dark and spicy; one of best grapes in Valpolicella blend. Corvinone, even darker, is a separate variety.

Côt *See* MALBEC.

Dolcetto Source of soft, seductive dry red in Piedmont. Now high fashion.

Dornfelder Gives deliciously light reds, straightforward, often rustic, and well-coloured in Germany, parts of the US and England. German plantings have doubled since 2000.

Duras Spicy, peppery, structured; exclusive to Gaillac and parts of Tarn Valley, Southwest France.

Fer Servadou Exclusive to Southwest France, aka Mansois in Marcillac, Braucol in Gaillac and Pinenc in St Mont. Redolent of red summer fruits and spice.

Fetească Neagră Romania: "black maiden grape" with potential as showpiece variety; can give deep, full-bodied wines with character. Acreage increasing.

Frühburgunder An ancient German mutation of PINOT N, mostly in Ahr but also in Franken and Württemberg, where it is confusingly known as Clevner. Lower acidity than Pinot N.

Gamay The Beaujolais grape: v. light, fragrant wines, best young, except in Beaujolais crus (*see* France) where quality can be high, wines for 2–10 yrs. Grown in the Loire Valley, in central France, in Switzerland and Savoie. California's Napa Gamay is Valdiguié.

Gamza *See* KADARKA.

Garnacha (Cannonau, Garnatxa, Grenache) Widespread pale, potent grape fashionable with *terroiristes*, because it expresses its site. Also gd for rosé and *vin doux naturel* – esp in s of France, Spain, California – but also the mainstay of beefy Priorat. Old-vine versions prized in South Australia. Usually blended with other varieties. Cannonau in Sardinia, Grenache in France.

Garnatxa *See* GARNACHA.

Graciano Spanish; part of Rioja blend. Aroma of violets, tannic, lean structure, a bit like PETIT VERDOT. Difficult to grow but increasingly fashionable.

Grenache *See* GARNACHA.

Grignolino Italy: gd everyday table wine in Piedmont.

Kadarka (Gamza) Makes spicy, light reds in East Europe. In Hungary revived esp for Bikavér.

Kalecik Karasi Turkish: sour-cherry fruit, fresh, supple. A bit like GAMAY. Drink young.

Kékfrankos Hungarian BLAUFRÄNKISCH.

Lagrein N Italian, dark, bitter finish, rich, plummy. DOC in Alto Adige (*see* Italy).

Lambrusco Productive grape of the lower Po Valley; quintessentially Italian, cheerful, sweet and fizzy red.

Lefkada Rediscovered Cypriot variety, higher quality than Mavro. Usually blended as tannins can be aggressive.

Lemberger *See* BLAUFRÄNKISCH.

Malbec (Auxerrois, Côt) Minor in B'x, major in Cahors (alias Auxerrois), the star in Argentina. Dark, dense and tannic, but fleshy wine capable of real quality. High-altitude versions in Argentina are the bee's knees. Bringing Cahors back into fashion.

Maratheftiko Deep-coloured Cypriot grape with quality potential.

Mataro *See* MOURVÈDRE.

Mavro Most-planted black grape of Cyprus but only moderate quality. Best for rosé.

Mavrodaphne Greek; the name means "black laurel". Used for sweet fortifieds;

speciality of Patras, but also found in Cephalonia. Dry versions on the increase, show great promise.

Mavrotragano Greek, almost extinct but now revived; found on Santorini. Top quality.

Mavrud Probably Bulgaria's best. Spicy, dark, plummy late-ripener native to Thrace. Ages well.

Melnik Bulgarian grape from the region of the same name. Dark colour and a nice dense, tart-cherry character. Ages well.

Mencía Making waves in Bierzo, Spain. Aromatic with steely tannins, lots of acidity.

Merlot The grape behind the great fragrant and plummy wines of Pomerol and (with CAB FR) St-Émilion, a vital element in the Médoc, soft and strong (and *à la mode*) in California, Washington, Chile, Australia. Lighter, often gd in n Italy (can be world class in Tuscany), Italian Switzerland, Slovenia, Argentina, South Africa, NZ, etc. Perhaps too adaptable for own gd: can be v. dull; less than ripe it tastes green. Much planted in Eastern Europe, esp Romania.

Modra Frankinja *See* BLAUFRÄNKISCH.

Modri Pinot *See* PINOT N.

Monastrell *See* MOURVÈDRE.

Mondeuse Found in Savoie; deep coloured, gd acidity. Related to SYRAH.

Montepulciano Deep-coloured grape dominant in Italy's Abruzzo, important along Adriatic coast from Marches to s Puglia. Also name of Tuscan town, unrelated.

Morellino SANGIOVESE in Maremma, s Tuscany. Esp Scansano.

Mourvèdre (Mataro, Monastrell) A star of s France (eg. Bandol), Australia (aka Mataro) and Spain (aka Monastrell). Excellent dark, aromatic, tannic grape, gd for blending. Enjoying new interest in eg. South Australia and California.

Napa Gamay Identical to Valdiguié (s of France). Nothing to get excited about.

Nebbiolo (Chiavennasca, Spanna) One of Italy's best red grapes; makes Barolo, Barbaresco, Gattinara and Valtellina. Intense, nobly fruity, perfumed wine with steely tannin; improves for yrs.

Negroamaro Puglian "black bitter" red grape with potential for either high quality or high volume.

Nerello Mascalese Characterful Sicilian red grape; potential for elegance.

Nero d'Avola Dark-red grape of Sicily, quality levels from sublime to industrial.

Nielluccio Corsican; plenty of acidity and tannin. Gd for rosé.

Öküzgözü Soft, fruity Turkish grape, usually blended with BOĞAZKERE, rather as MERLOT in B'x is blended with CAB SAUV.

País Pioneer Spanish grape in Americas. Rustic; some producers now trying harder.

Pamid Bulgarian: light, soft, everyday red.

Periquita (Castelão) Common in Portugal, esp round Setúbal. Originally nicknamed Periquita after Fonseca's popular (trademarked) brand. Firm-flavoured, raspberryish reds develop a figgish, tar-like quality.

Petite Sirah Nothing to do with SYRAH; gives rustic, tannic, dark wine. Brilliant blended with ZIN in California; also found in South America, Mexico, Australia.

Petit Verdot Excellent but awkward Médoc grape, increasingly planted in CAB areas worldwide for extra fragrance. Mostly blended, some gd varietals, esp in Virginia.

Pinotage Singular South African cross (PINOT N x CINSAULT). Has had a rocky ride, getting better from top producers. Gd rosé too. "Coffee Pinotage" is espresso-flavoured, sweetish, aimed at youth.

Pinot Crni *See* PINOT N.

Pinot Meunier (Schwarzriesling) [Pinot M] The 3rd grape of Champagne, scorned by some, used by most. Less acid than PINOT N; invaluable for blending. Found in many places, either vinified as a white for fizz, or occasionally (eg. Germany's Württemberg, as Schwarzriesling) as a still red. Samtrot is a local variant in Württemberg.

Pinot Noir (Blauburgunder, Modri Pinot, Pinot Crni, Spätburgunder) [Pinot N]
The glory of Burgundy's Côte d'Or, with scent, flavour and texture unmatched anywhere. Recent German efforts have been excellent. V.gd in Austria, esp in Kamptal, Burgenland, Thermenregion. Light wines in Hungary; mainstream, light to weightier in Switzerland (aka Clevner). Splendid results in Sonoma, Carneros, Central Coast, as well as Oregon, Ontario, Yarra Valley, Adelaide Hills, Tasmania, NZ's South Island (Central Otago) and South Africa's Walker Bay. Some v. pretty Chileans. New French clones promise improvement in Romania. Modri Pinot in Slovenia; probably country's best red. In Italy, best in ne and gets worse as you go s. PINOTS BL and GR are mutations of Pinot N.

Plavac Mali (Crljenak) Croatian, and related to ZIN, like so much round there. Lots of quality potential, can age well, though can also be alcoholic and dull.

Primitivo S Italian grape, originally from Croatia, making big, dark, rustic wines, now fashionable because genetically identical to ZIN. Early ripening, hence the name. The original name for both seems to be Tribidrag.

Refosco (Refošk) Various DOCs in Italy, esp Colli Orientali. Deep, flavoursome and age-worthy wines, particularly in warmer climates. Dark, high acidity. Refošk in Slovenia and points e, genetically different, tastes similar.

Refošk See REFOSCO.

Roter Veltliner Austrian; unrelated to GRÜNER V. Also Frühroter, Brauner Veltliner.

Rubin Bulgarian cross, NEBBIOLO x SYRAH. Peppery, full-bodied.

Sagrantino Italian grape grown in Umbria for powerful, cherry-flavoured wines.

St-Laurent Dark, smooth, full-flavoured Austrian speciality. Can be light and juicy or deep and structured. Also in Pfalz.

Sangiovese (Brunello, Morellino, Sangioveto) Principal red grape of Tuscany and central Italy. Hard to get right, but sublime and long-lasting when it is. Dominant in Chianti, Vino Nobile, Brunello di Montalcino, Morellino di Scansano and various fine IGT offerings. Also in Umbria (eg. Montefalco and Torgiano) and across the Apennines in Romagna and Marches. Not so clever in the warmer, lower-altitude v'yds of the Tuscan coast, nor in other parts of Italy despite its nr-ubiquity. Interesting in Australia.

Sangioveto See SANGIOVESE.

Saperavi The main red of Georgia, Ukraine, etc. Blends well with CAB SAUV (eg. in Moldova). Huge potential, seldom gd winemaking.

Schiava See TROLLINGER.

Schwarzriesling PINOT M in Württemberg.

Sciacarello Corsican, herby and peppery. Not v. tannic.

Shiraz See SYRAH.

Spanna See NEBBIOLO.

Spätburgunder German for PINOT N.

Syrah (Shiraz) The great Rhône red grape: tannic, purple, peppery wine that matures superbly. Important as Shiraz in Australia, increasingly gd under either name in Chile, South Africa, terrific in NZ (esp Hawke's Bay). Widely grown.

Tannat Raspberry-perfumed, highly tannic force behind Madiran, Tursan and other firm reds from Southwest France. Also rosé. Now the star of Uruguay.

Tempranillo (Aragonez, Cecibel, Tinto Fino, Tinta del País, Tinta Roriz, Ull de Llebre) Aromatic, fine Rioja grape, called Ull de Llebre in Catalonia, Cencibel in La Mancha, Tinto Fino in Ribera del Duero, Tinta Roriz in Douro, Tinta del País in Castile, Aragonez in s Portugal. Now Australia too. V. fashionable; elegant in cool climates, beefy in warm. Early ripening, long maturing.

Teran (Terrano) Close cousin of REFOSCO, esp on limestone (karst), Slovenia.

Teroldego Rotaliano Trentino's best indigenous variety; serious, full-flavoured wine, esp on the flat Campo Rotaliano.

Tinta Amarela *See* TRINCADEIRA.

Tinta del País *See* TEMPRANILLO.

Tinta Negra (Negramoll) Until recently called Tinta Negra Mole. Easily Madeira's most planted grape and the mainstay of cheaper Madeira. Now coming into its own in Colheita wines (*see* Portugal).

Tinta Roriz *See* TEMPRANILLO.

Tinto Fino *See* TEMPRANILLO.

Touriga Nacional [Touriga N] The top Port grape, now widely used in the Douro for floral, stylish table wines. Australian Touriga is usually this; California's Touriga can be either this or Touriga Franca.

Trincadeira (Tinta Amarela) Portuguese; v.gd in Alentejo for spicy wines. Tinta Amarela in the Douro.

Trollinger (Schiava, Vernatsch) Popular pale red in Germany's Württemberg; aka Vernatsch and Schiava. Covers a group of vines, not necessarily related. In Italy, snappy and brisk.

Vernatsch *See* TROLLINGER.

Xinomavro Greece's answer to NEBBIOLO. "Sharp-black"; the basis for Naoussa, Rapsani, Goumenissa, Amindeo. Some rosé, still or sparkling. Top quality, can age for decades. Being tried in China.

Zinfandel [Zin] Fruity, adaptable grape of California with blackberry-like, and sometimes metallic, flavour. Can be structured and gloriously lush, ageing for decades, but also makes "blush" pink, usually sweet, jammy. Genetically the same as s Italian PRIMITIVO.

Zweigelt (Blauer Zweigelt) BLAUFRÄNKISCH X ST-LAURENT, popular in Austria for aromatic, dark, supple, velvety wines. Also found in Hungary, Germany

Grapes for white wine

Airén Bland workhorse of La Mancha, Spain: fresh if made well.

Albariño (Alvarinho) Fashionable, expensive in Spain: apricot scented, gd acidity. Superb in Rías Baixas; shaping up elsewhere, but not all live up to the hype. Alvarinho in Portugal just as gd: aromatic Vinho Verde, esp in Monção and Melgaço.

Aligoté Burgundy's 2nd-rank white grape. Sharp wine for young drinking, perfect for mixing with cassis (blackcurrant liqueur) to make Kir. Widely planted in East Europe, esp Russia.

Alvarinho *See* ALBARIÑO.

Amigne One of Switzerland's speciality grapes, traditional in Valais, esp Vétroz. Total planted: 43 ha. Full-bodied, tasty, often sweet but also bone-dry.

Ansonica *See* INSOLIA.

Arinto Portuguese; the mainstay of aromatic citrus wines in Bucelas; also adds welcome zip to blends, esp in Alentejo.

Arneis Nw Italian. Fine, aromatic, appley-peachy, high-priced grape, DOCG in Roero, DOC in Langhe, Piedmont.

Arvine Rare but excellent Swiss *spécialité*, from Valais. Also Petite Arvine. Dry or sweet, fresh, long-lasting wines with salty finish. **Assyrtiko** From Santorini; one of the best grapes of the Mediterranean, balancing power, minerality, extract and high acid. Built to age. Could conquer the world....

Auxerrois Red Auxerrois is a synonym for MALBEC, but white Auxerrois is like a fatter, spicier PINOT BL. Found in Alsace and much used in Crémant; also Germany.

Beli Pinot *See* PINOT BL.

Blanc Fumé *See* SAUV BL.

Boal *See* BUAL.

Bourboulenc This and the rare Rolle make some of the Midi's best wines.

Bouvier Indigenous aromatic Austrian grape, esp gd for Beerenauslese and Trockenbeerenauslese, rarely for dry wines.

Bual (Boal) Makes top-quality sweet Madeira wines, not quite so rich as MALMSEY.

Carricante Italian. Principal grape of Etna Bianco, regaining ground.

Catarratto Prolific white grape found all over Sicily, esp in w in DOC Alcamo.

Cerceal *See* SERCIAL.

Chardonnay (Morillon) [Chard] The white grape of Burgundy and Champagne, now ubiquitous worldwide, partly because it is one of the easiest to grow and vinify. Also the name of a Mâcon-Villages commune. The fashion for overoaked butterscotch versions now thankfully over. Morillon in Styria, Austria.

Chasselas (Fendant, Gutedel) Swiss (originated in Vaud). Neutral flavour, takes on local character: elegant (Geneva); refined, full (Vaud); exotic, racy (Valais). Fendant in Valais. Makes almost 3rd of Swiss wines but giving way, esp to red. Gutedel in Germany; grown esp in s Baden. Elsewhere usually a table grape.

Chenin Blanc [Chenin Bl] Wonderful white grape of the middle Loire (Vouvray, Layon, etc). Wine can be dry or sweet (or v. sweet), but with plenty of acidity. Formerly called Steen in South Africa; many ordinary but best noble. California can do it well but doesn't bother.

Cirfandl *See* ZIERFANDLER.

Clairette Important Midi grape, low-acid, part of many blends. Improved winemaking helps.

Colombard Slightly fruity, nicely sharp grape, makes everyday wine in South Africa, California and Southwest France. Often blended.

Dimiat Perfumed Bulgarian grape, made dry or off-dry, or distilled. Far more synonyms than any grape needs.

Ermitage Swiss for MARSANNE.

Ezerjó Hungarian, with sharp acidity. Name means "thousand blessings".

Falanghina Italian: ancient grape of Campanian hills. Gd dense, aromatic dry whites.

Fendant *See* CHASSELAS.

Fernão Pires *See* MARIA GOMES.

Fetească Albă / Regală Romania has two Fetească grapes, both with slight MUSCAT aroma. F. Regală is a cross of F. Albă and GRASĂ; more finesse, gd for late-harvest wines. F. NEAGRĂ is dark-skinned.

Fiano High-quality grape giving peachy, spicy wine in Campania, s Italy.

Folle Blanche (Gros Plant) High acid/little flavour make this ideal for brandy. Gros Plant in Brittany, Picpoul in Armagnac, but unrelated to true PICPOUL. Also respectable in California.

Friulano (Sauvignonasse, Sauvignon Vert) N Italian: fresh, pungent, subtly floral. Used to be called Tocai Friulano. Best in Collio, Isonzo, Colli Orientali. Found in nearby Slovenia as Sauvignonasse; also in Chile, where it was long confused with SAUV BL. Ex-Tocai in Veneto now known as Tai.

Fumé Blanc *See* SAUV BL.

Furmint (Šipon) Superb, characterful. The trademark of Hungary, both as the principal grape in Tokaji and as vivid, vigorous table wine, sometimes mineral, sometimes apricot-flavoured, sometimes both. Šipon in Slovenia. Some grown in Rust, Austria for sweet and dry.

Garganega Best grape in Soave blend; also in Gambellara. Top, esp sweet, age well.

Garnacha Blanca (Grenache Blanc) The white version of GARNACHA/Grenache, much used in Spain and s France. Low acidity. Can be innocuous, or surprisingly gd.

Gewurztraminer (Traminac, Traminec, Traminer, Tramini) [Gewurz] One of the most pungent grapes, spicy with aromas of rose petals, face-cream, lychees, grapefruit. Wines are often rich and soft, even when fully dry. Best in Alsace; also gd in Germany (Baden, Pfalz, Sachsen), Eastern Europe, Australia, California,

Pacific Northwest and NZ. Can be relatively unaromatic if just labelled Traminer (or variants). Italy uses the name Traminer Aromatico for its (dry) "Gewürz" versions. (The name takes an Umlaut in German.) Identical to SAVAGNIN.

Glera Uncharismatic new name for Prosecco vine: Prosecco is now wine only.

Godello Top quality (intense, mineral) in nw Spain. Called Verdelho in Dão, Portugal, but unrelated to true VERDELHO.

Grasă (Kövérszölö) Romanian; name means "fat". Prone to botrytis; important in Cotnari, potentially superb sweet wines. Kövérszölö in Hungary's Tokaj region.

Graševina *See* WELSCHRIESLING.

Grauburgunder *See* PINOT GR.

Grechetto Ancient grape of central and s Italy noted for the vitality and stylishness of its wine. Blended, or used solo in Orvieto.

Greco S Italian: there are various Grecos, probably unrelated, perhaps of Greek origin. Brisk, peachy flavour, most famous as G. di Tufo. G. di Bianco is from semi-dried grapes. G. Nero is a black version.

Grenache Blanc *See* GARNACHA BLANCA.

Grillo Italy: main grape of Marsala. Also v.gd full-bodied dry table wine.

Gros Plant *See* FOLLE BLANCHE.

Grüner Veltliner [Grüner V] Austria's fashionable flagship white grape. Remarkably diverse: from simple, peppery everyday wines to others of great complexity and ageing potential. A little elsewhere in Central Europe, and now showing potential in NZ.

Gutedel *See* CHASSELAS.

Hárslevelü Other main grape of Tokaji, but softer, peachier than FURMINT. Name means "linden-leaved". Gd in Somló, Eger as well.

Heida Swiss for SAVAGNIN.

Humagne Swiss speciality, older than CHASSELAS. Fresh, plump, not v. aromatic. Humagne Rouge, also common in Valais, is not related but increasingly popular. Humagne Rouge is the same as Cornalin du Aosta; Cornalin du Valais is different. (Keep up at the back, there.)

Insolia (Ansonica, Inzolia) Sicilian; Ansonica on Tuscan coast. Fresh, racy wine at best. May be semi-dried for sweet wine

Irsai Olivér Hungarian cross of two table varieties, makes aromatic, MUSCAT-like wine for drinking young.

Johannisberg Swiss for SILVANER.

Kéknyelü Low-yielding, flavourful grape giving one of Hungary's best whites. Has the potential for fieriness and spice. To be watched.

Kerner Quite successful German cross. Early ripening, flowery (but often too blatant) wine with gd acidity.

Királyleányka Hungarian; gentle, fresh wines (eg in Eger)

Koshu Supposedly indigenous Japanese grape/wine, much hyped. Fresh, harmless.

Kövérszölö *See* GRASĂ.

Laski Rizling *See* WELSCHRIESLING.

Leányka Hungarian. Soft, floral wines.

Listán *See* PALOMINO.

Loureiro Best Vinho Verde grape variety after ALVARINHO: delicate floral whites. Also found in Spain.

Macabeo *See* VIURA.

Malagousia Rediscovered Greek grape for gloriously perfumed wines.

Malmsey *See* MALVASIA. The sweetest style of Madeira.

Malvasia (Malmsey, Malvazija, Malvoisie, Marastina) Italy, France and Iberia. Not a single variety but a whole stable, not necessarily related or even alike. Can be white or red, sparkling or still, strong or mild, sweet or dry, aromatic or neutral.

Slovenia's and Croatia's version is Malvazija Istarka, crisp and light, or rich, oak-aged. Sometimes called Marastina in Croatia. "Malmsey" (as in the sweetest style of Madeira) is a corruption of Malvasia.

Malvoisie See MALVASIA. A name used for several varieties in France, incl BOURBOULENC, Torbato, VERMENTINO. Also PINOT GR in Switzerland's Valais.

Manseng, Gros / Petit Gloriously spicy, floral whites from Southwest France. The key to Jurançon. Superb late-harvest and sweet wines too.

Maria Gomes (Fernão Pires) Portuguese; aromatic, ripe-flavoured, slightly spicy whites in Barraida and Tejo.

Marsanne (Ermitage) Principal white grape (with ROUSSANNE) of the Northern Rhône (Hermitage, St-Joseph, St-Péray). Also gd in Australia, California and (as Ermitage Blanc) the Valais. Soft, full wines that age v. well.

Melon de Bourgogne See MUSCADET.

Misket Bulgarian. Mildly aromatic; the basis of most country whites.

Morillon CHARD in parts of Austria.

Moscatel See MUSCAT.

Moscato See MUSCAT.

Moschofilero Pink-skinned, rose-scented, high-quality, high-acid, low-alcohol Greek grape. Makes white, some pink, some sparkling.

Müller-Thurgau [Müller-T] Aromatic wines to drink young. Makes gd sweet wines but usually dull, often coarse, dry ones. In Germany, most common in Pfalz, Rheinhessen, Nahe, Baden, Franken. Has some merit in Italy's Trentino-Alto Adige, Friuli. Sometimes called Ries x Sylvaner (incorrectly) in Switzerland.

Muscadelle Adds aroma to white B'x, esp Sauternes. In Victoria used (with MUSCAT, to which it is unrelated) for Rutherglen Muscat.

Muscadet (Melon de Bourgogne) Makes light, refreshing, v, dry wines with a seaside tang around Nantes in Brittany. Also found (as Melon) in parts of Burgundy.

Muscat (Moscatel, Moscato, Muskateller) Many varieties; the best is Muscat Blanc à Petits Grains (alias Gelber Muskateller, Rumeni Muškat, Sarga Muskotály, Yellow Muscat). Widely grown, easily recognized, pungent grapes, mostly made into perfumed sweet wines, often fortified, as in France's *vin doux naturel*. Superb, dark and sweet in Australia. Sweet, sometimes v.gd in Spain. Most Hungarian Muskotály is Muscat Ottonel except in Tokaj where Sarga Muskotály rules, adding perfume (in small amounts) to blends. Occasionally (eg. Alsace, Austria, parts of south Germany) made dry. Sweet Cap Corse Muscats often superb. Light Moscato fizz in n Italy.

Muskateller See MUSCAT.

Narince Turkish; fresh and fruity wines.

Neuburger Austrian, rather neglected; mainly in the Wachau (elegant, flowery), Thermenregion (mellow, ample-bodied) and n Burgenland (strong, full).

Olasz Riesling See WELSCHRIESLING.

Païen See SAVAGNIN.

Palomino (Listán) The great grape of Sherry; with little intrinsic character, it gains all from production method. As Listán, makes dry white in Canaries.

Pansa Blanca See XAREL.LO.

Pecorino Italian: not a cheese but alluring dry white from a recently nr-extinct variety. IGT in Colli Pescaresi.

Pedro Ximénez [PX] Makes sweet brown Sherry under its own name, and used in Montilla and Málaga. Also grown in Argentina, the Canaries, Australia, California and South Africa.

Picpoul (Piquepoul) Southern French, best known in Picpoul de Pinet. Should have high acidity. Picpoul Noir is black-skinned.

Pinela Local to Slovenia. Subtle, lowish acidity; drink young.

Pinot Bianco *See* PINOT BL.

Pinot Blanc (Beli Pinot, Pinot Bianco, Weißburgunder) [Pinot Bl] A cousin of PINOT N, similar to but milder than CHARD. Light, fresh, fruity, not aromatic, to drink young. Gd for Italian *spumante*, potentially excellent in ne, esp high sites in Alto Adige. Widely grown. Weissburgunder in Germany, best in s: often racier than Chard.

Pinot Gris (Pinot Grigio, Grauburgunder, Ruländer, Sivi Pinot, Szürkebarát) [Pinot Gr] Ultra-popular as Pinot Grigio in n Italy, even for rosé; top, characterful versions can be excellent (from Alto Adige, Friuli). Cheap versions are just that. Terrific in Alsace for full-bodied, spicy whites. Once important in Champagne. In Germany can be alias Ruländer (sw) or Grauburgunder (dr): best in Baden (esp Kaiserstuhl) and s Pfalz. Szürkebarát in Hungary, Sivi P in Slovenia (characterful, aromatic).

Počip Croatian; mostly on island of Korčula. Quite characterful, citrus; high yielding.

Prosecco Old name for grape that makes Prosecco. Now you have to call it GLERA,

Renski Rizling Rhine RIES.

Rèze Super-rare ancestral Valais grape used for *vin de glacier*.

Ribolla Gialla / Rebula Acidic but characterful. In Italy, best in Collio. In Slovenia, traditional in Brda. Can be v.gd, even made in eccentric ways.

Rieslaner German cross (SILVANER x RIES); low yields, difficult ripening, now v. rare (less than 50 ha). Makes fine Auslesen in Franken and Pfalz.

Riesling Italico *See* WELSCHRIESLING.

Riesling (Renski Rizling, Rhine Riesling) [Ries] Greatest, most versatile white grape, diametrically opposite in style to CHARD. Offers a range from steely to voluptuous, always positively perfumed, with far more ageing potential than Chard. Great in all styles in Germany; forceful and steely in Austria; lime-cordial and toast fruit in South Australia; rich and spicy in Alsace; Germanic and promising in NZ, NY State, Pacific Northwest; has potential in Ontario, South Africa.

Rkatsiteli Found widely in Eastern Europe, Russia, Georgia. Can stand cold winters and has high acidity, which protects it to some degree from poor winemaking. Also grown in ne US.

Robola In Greece (Cephalonia) a top quality, floral grape, unrelated to Ribolla Gialla.

Roditis Pink grape grown all over Greece, usually making white wines. Gd when yields are low.

Roter Veltliner Austrian; unrelated to GRÜNER V. There is also a Frühroter and an (unrelated) Brauner Veltliner.

Rotgipfler Austrian; indigenous to Thermenregion. With ZIERFANDLER, makes lively, lush, aromatic blend.

Roussanne Rhône grape of real finesse, now popping up in California, Australia. Can age many yrs.

Ruländer *See* PINOT GR.

Sauvignonasse *See* FRIULANO.

Sauvignon Blanc [Sauv Bl] Makes distinctive aromatic, grassy-to-tropical wines, pungent in NZ, often minerally in Sancerre, riper in Australia. V.gd in Rueda, Austria, n Italy (Isonzo, Piedmont, Alto Adige), Chile's Casablanca Valley and South Africa. Blended with SÉM in B'x. Can be austere or buxom (or indeed nauseating). Sauv Gris is a pink-skinned, less aromatic version of Sauv Bl with untapped potential.

Sauvignon Vert *See* FRIULANO.

Savagnin (Heida, Païen) Grape for *vin jaune* from Jura: aromatic form is GEWURZ. In Switzerland known as Heida, Païen or Traminer. Full-bodied, high acidity.

Scheurebe (Sämling) Grapefruit-scented German RIES x SILVANER (possibly), v. successful in Pfalz, esp for Auslese and upwards. Can be weedy: must be v. ripe to be gd.

Sémillon [Sém] Contributes lusciousness to Sauternes; decreasingly important for Graves and other dry white B'x. Grassy if not fully ripe; can make soft dry wine of great ageing potential. Superb in Australia; NZ and South Africa promising.

Sercial (Cerceal) Portuguese: makes the driest Madeira. Cerceal, also Portuguese, seems to be this plus any of several others.

Seyval Blanc [Seyval Bl] French-made hybrid of French and American vines. V. hardy and attractively fruity. Popular and reasonably successful in e US and England but dogmatically banned by EU from "quality" wines.

Silvaner (Johannisberg, Sylvaner) Can be excellent in Germany's Rheinhessen, Pfalz, esp Franken, with plant/earth flavours and mineral notes. V.gd (and powerful) as Johannisberg in the Valais, Switzerland. The lightest of the Alsace grapes.

Šipon *See* FURMINT.

Sivi Pinot *See* PINOT GR.

Spätrot *See* ZIERFANDLER.

Sylvaner *See* SILVANER.

Tămâioasă Românească Romanian: "frankincense" grape, with exotic aroma and taste. Belongs to MUSCAT family.

Torrontés Name given to a number of grapes, mostly with an aromatic, floral character, sometimes soapy. A speciality of Argentina; also in Spain. DYA.

Traminac Or Traminec. *See* GEWURZ.

Traminer Or Tramini (Hungary). *See* GEWURZ.

Trebbiano (Ugni Blanc) Principal white grape of Tuscany, found all over Italy in many different guises. Rarely rises above the plebeian except in Tuscany's Vin Santo. Some gd dry whites under DOCs Romagna or Abruzzo. Trebbiano di Soave or di Lugana, aka VERDICCHIO, is only distantly related. Grown in southern France as Ugni Blanc, and Cognac as St-Émilion. Mostly thin, bland wine; needs blending (and more careful growing).

Ugni Blanc [Ugni Bl] *See* TREBBIANO.

Ull de Llebre *See* TEMPRANILLO.

Verdejo The grape of Rueda in Castile, potentially fine and long-lived.

Verdelho Great quality in Australia (pungent, full-bodied); rare but gd (and medium-sweet) in Madeira.

Verdicchio Potentially gd, muscular, dry; central-e Italy. Wine of same name.

Vermentino Italian, sprightly with satisfying texture, ageing capacity. Potential here.

Vernaccia Name given to many unrelated grapes in Italy. Vernaccia di San Gimignano is crisp, lively; Vernaccia di Oristano is Sherry-like.

Vidal French hybrid much grown in Canada for Icewine.

Vidiano Most Cretan producers in love with this. Powerful, stylish. Lime/apricot fruit, gd acidity.

Viognier Ultra-fashionable Rhône grape, finest in Condrieu, less fine but still aromatic in the Midi. Gd examples from California, Virginia, Uruguay, Australia.

Viura (Macabeo, Maccabéo, Maccabeu) Workhorse white grape of n Spain, widespread in Rioja and Catalan Cava country. Also found over border in Southwest France. Gd quality potential.

Weißburgunder PINOT BL in Germany.

Welschriesling (Graševina, Laski Rizling, Olaszriesling, Riesling Italico) Not related to RIES. Light and fresh to sweet and rich in Austria; ubiquitous in Central Europe, where it can be remarkably gd for dry and sweet wines.

Xarel.lo (Pansa Blanca) Traditional Catalan grape, used for Cava, with Parellada and MACABEO. Neutral but clean. More character (lime cordial) in Alella (Pansa Blanca).

Xynisteri Cyprus's most planted white grape. Can be simple and is usually DYA, but when grown at altitude makes appealing, minerally whites.

Zéta Hungarian; BOUVIER X FURMINT. Used by some in Tokaji Aszú production.

Zierfandler (Spätrot, Cirfandl) Found in Austria's Thermenregion; often blended with ROTGIPFLER for aromatic, orange-peel-scented, weighty wines.

Wine & food

It's just as much about people, places, the occasion and the time of year as about food. Don't be paralyzed by rules, but bear some in mind: avoid vinegar with your food (*see* Salad, below). And dare to be conventional; drink white wines before red, dry before sweet and light before heavy. When God said white with fish and red with meat it was only His personal opinion – but He has lots of experience.

Before the meal – apéritifs

The conventional and most effective appetite-creating apéritif wines are either sparkling (epitomized by Champagne) or fortified (epitomized by Sherry in Britain, Holland, Scandinavia, or Port in France, vermouth in Italy, etc.). A glass of a light table wine before eating is the easy choice, but why not do better? **Warning** Avoid peanuts; they destroy wine flavours. Olives are too piquant for many wines. Don't serve them with Champagne; they need Sherry or a Martini. With Champagne nibble almonds, pistachios, cashews, cheese straws or succulent gougères straight from the oven.

First courses

Aïoli Its garlic heat demands a thirst-quencher. Cold young Rhône white, Provence rosé, VERDICCHIO, Loire SAUV BL. Beer, marc or grappa... you'll hardly notice.

Antipasti With the classic ham, olives and pickled bits, dry or medium white: Italian (ARNEIS, Soave, PINOT GRIGIO, VERMENTINO, GRECHETTO); light but gutsy red, eg. Valpolicella. Or Fino Sherry; sadly Italy doesn't know this.

Artichokes Not great for wine. An incisive dry white: NZ SAUV BL; Côtes de Gascogne or a modern Greek (precisely, 4-yr-old MALAGOUSIA, but easy on the vinaigrette); maybe Côtes du Rhône.
    with hollandaise Full-bodied crisp dry white: Pouilly-Fuissé, German Erstes Gewächs.

Asparagus Green or white are both difficult for wine, being slightly bitter (white is worse), so wine needs plenty of flavour. VIOGNIER has many adherents. Rheingau RIES is a classic (they have *Spargelfests* in those parts), but Ries generally gd to try. SAUV BL echoes the flavour. SÉM beats CHARD, esp Australian, but Chard works well with melted butter or hollandaise. Alsace PINOT GR, even dry MUSCAT can work, or Jurançon Sec.

Aubergine (*Melitzanosalata* or *Imam Bayaldi*) Crisp New World SAUV BL, eg. from South Africa or NZ; or modern Greek or Sicilian dry white. Baked aubergine dishes (eg. *Imam Bayaldi*) need sturdy reds: SHIRAZ, ZIN, or indeed Turkish. Or Mediterranean whites (incl Fino).

Avocado Not a wine natural. Dry to medium slightly sweet white with gd acidity. Rheingau or Pfalz Kabinett, GRÜNER V, Wachau RIES, Sancerre, PINOT GR; Australian CHARD (unoaked), or a dry rosé. With prawns: Premier Cru Chablis.
    with mozzarella and tomato Crisp but ripe white: Soave, Sancerre, Greek white.

Burrata Forget mozzarella; this is the crème de la crème. So a top Italian white, FIANO or Cusumano's Grillo. I'll try Sauternes one day.

Carpaccio, beef or fish The beef version works well with most wines, incl reds. Tuscan is appropriate, but fine CHARDS are gd. So are vintage and pink Champagnes. Give Amontillado a try.
    salmon Chard or Champagne.
    tuna VIOGNIER, California Chard or NZ SAUV BL.

Caviar Iced vodka (and) full-bodied Champagne (eg. Bollinger, Krug). Don't (ever) add raw onion.

Ceviche Australian RIES or VERDELHO, Chilean SAUV BL, TORRONTÉS. Manzanilla.

Charcuterie / salami Young Beaujolais-Villages, Loire reds (ie. Saumur), Chianti or young SANGIOVESE. LAMBRUSCO or young ZIN. Or of course Fino.

Crudités or raw veg Fino Sherry might be best. Light red or rosé: Côtes du Rhône, Minervois, Chianti, PINOT N.

Dim sum Classically, China tea. PINOT GR or classic German dry RIES; light PINOT N. For reds, soft tannins are key. Bardolino, Rioja; Côtes du Rhône. Also NV Champagne or gd New World fizz.

Eggs *See also* SOUFFLÉS. Not easy: they have a way of coating your palate. Omelettes: follow the other ingredients. With a truffle omelette, vintage Champagne. As a last resort I can bring myself to drink Champagne with scrambled eggs or eggs Benedict. Florentine, with spinach, is not a winey dish.

    quails' eggs Blanc de blancs Champagne; Viognier.

    gulls' eggs Push the luxury: mature white burgundy or vintage Champagne.

    oeufs en meurette Burgundian genius: eggs in red wine with glass of the same.

Escargots (or frogs' legs) A comfort dish calling for Rhône reds (Gigondas, Vacqueyras). In Burgundy white: St-Véran or Rully. In the Midi *petits-gris* go with local white, rosé or red. In Alsace, PINOT BL or dry MUSCAT. On the Loire, frogs' legs and semi-dry CHENIN BL.

Fish terrine or fish salad (incl crab) Calls for something fine. Pfalz RIES Spätlese Trocken, GRÜNER V, Premier Cru Chablis, Clare Valley RIES, Sonoma CHARD; or Manzanilla.

Foie gras Sweet white: Sauternes, Tokaji Aszú 5 Puttonyos, late-harvest PINOT GR or RIES, Vouvray, Montlouis, Jurançon *moelleux*, GEWURZ. Old dry Amontillado can be sublime. With hot foie gras, mature vintage Champagne. But never CHARD, SAUV BL, or red.

Goats cheese, cooked (eg. in a salad) SAUV BL, Loire (esp Sancerre) or New World.

    cold Chinon, Saumur-Champigny or Provence rosé. Or strong red: Chateau Musar, Greek, Turkish, Australian sparkling SHIRAZ.

Guacamole Mexican beer. Or California CHARD, NZ SAUV BL, dry MUSCAT or Sherry.

Haddock, smoked, mousse, soufflé or brandade Wonderful for stylish, full-bodied white: Grand Cru Chablis or Pessac-Léognan; Sonoma, S African or NZ CHARD.

Ham, raw or cured *See also* PROSCIUTTO. Alsace Grand Cru PINOT GR or Italian Collio white. With Spanish *pata negra* or *jamón*, Fino Sherry or Tawny Port. *See also* HAM, COOKED (MEAT, POULTRY, GAME).

Herrings, raw or pickled Dutch gin (young, not aged) or Scandinavian akvavit, and cold beer. If you must, try MUSCADET, but it's a waste.

Mackerel, smoked An oily wine-destroyer. Manzanilla, proper dry Vinho Verde or Schnapps, peppered or bison-grass vodka. Or lager. Or black tea.

Mayonnaise With lobster, Chablis Premier Cru, Pfalz RIES Erstes Gewächs; with chicken, Côte Chalonnaise whites (eg. Rully); with eggs ditto. Try NZ SAUV BL, VERDICCHIO. Or Provence rosé.

Mezze A selection of hot and cold vegetable dishes. Fino Sherry is in its element.

Mozzarella with tomatoes, basil Fresh Italian white, eg. Soave, Alto Adige. VERMENTINO from Liguria or Rolle from the Midi. *See also* AVOCADO.

Oysters, raw NV Champagne, Chablis, MUSCADET, white Graves, Sancerre, or Guinness. Experiment with Sauternes. Manzanilla is excellent. Flat oysters are worth good wine; Pacific ones drown it.

    stewed, grilled or otherwise cooked Puligny-Montrachet or gd New World CHARD. Champagne gd with either.

Pasta Red or white according to the sauce:

    cream sauce (eg. carbonara) Orvieto, GRECO di Tufo. Young SANGIOVESE.

    meat sauce MONTEPULCIANO d'Abruzzo, Salice Salentino, MALBEC.

pesto (basil) sauce BARBERA, Ligurian VERMENTINO, NZ SAUV BL, Hungarian FURMINT.

seafood sauce (eg. vongole) VERDICCHIO, Soave, Grillo, Cirò, unoaked CHARD.

tomato sauce Chianti, Barbera, Sicilian red, ZIN, South Australian GRENACHE.

Pastrami Alsace RIES, young SANGIOVESE or St-Émilion.

Pâté, chicken liver Calls for pungent white (Alsace PINOT GR or MARSANNE), a smooth red eg. light Pomerol, Volnay or NZ PINOT N, even Amontillado Sherry. More strongly flavoured pâté (duck, etc.) needs Gigondas, Moulin-à-Vent, Chianti Classico or gd white Graves.

Pipérade Navarra rosado, Provence or Midi rosé, dry Australian RIES. Red: Corbières.

Prawns, shrimps or langoustines MUSCADET is okay, but better a fine dry white: burgundy, Graves, NZ CHARD, Washington RIES, Pfalz Ries, Australian Ries – even fine mature Champagne.

Prosciutto (also with melon, pears/figs) Full, dry or medium white: Orvieto, FIANO, GRECHETTO, GRÜNER V, Tokaji FURMINT, Australian SEM, Jurançon Sec. SERCIAL Madeira.

Risotto Follow the flavour. **with vegetables** (eg. Primavera) PINOT GR from Friuli, Gavi, youngish SÉM, DOLCETTO or BARBERA d'Alba.

    with fungi porcini Finest mature Barolo or Barbaresco.

    nero A rich dry white: VIOGNIER or even Corton Charlemagne.

    seafood A favourite dry white.

Salads Any dry and appetizing white or rosé wine.

    NB Vinegar in salad dressings *destroys* the flavour of wine. Why don't the French know this? If you want salad at a meal with fine wine, dress it with wine or lemon juice instead of vinegar.

Salmon, smoked Dry but pungent white: Fino (esp Manzanilla), Condrieu, Alsace PINOT GR, Grand Cru Chablis, Pouilly-Fumé, Pfalz RIES Spätlese, vintage Champagne. Vodka, schnapps or akvavit.

Soufflés As show dishes these deserve ★★★ wines.

    cheese Mature red burgundy or B'x, CAB SAUV (not Chilean or Australian), etc. Or fine mature white burgundy.

    fish (esp smoked haddock with chive cream sauce) Dry white: ★★★Burgundy, D'R, Alsace, CHARD, etc.

    spinach (tough on wine) Mâcon-Villages, St-Véran or Valpolicella. Champagne (esp vintage) can also spark things with the texture of a soufflé.

Tapas Perfect with cold fresh Fino Sherry, which can cope with the wide range of flavours, hot and cold. Or sake.

Tapenade Manzanilla or Fino Sherry, or any sharpish dry white or rosé.

Taramasalata A Mediterranean white with personality, Greek if possible. Fino Sherry works well. Try Rhône MARSANNE.

Tortilla Rioja Crianza, Fino Sherry or white Mâcon-Villages.

Trout, smoked More delicate than smoked salmon. Mosel RIES Kabinett or Spätlese, Chablis or Champagne.

Whitebait Crisp dry whites, eg. FURMINT, Greek, Touraine SAUV BL, VERDICCHIO, Fino Sherry. Or beer.

Fish

Abalone Dry or medium white: SAUV BL, Meursault, PINOT GR, GRÜNER V. In Hong Kong: Dom Pérignon (at least).

Anchovies, marinated It scarcely matters. In eg. salade Niçoise: Provence rosé.

Bass, sea Weißburgunder from Baden or Pfalz. V.gd for any fine/delicate white, eg. Clare dry RIES, Chablis, white Châteauneuf-du-Pape. But rev the wine up for more seasoning, eg. ginger, spring onions; more powerful Ries, not necessarily dry.

Beurre blanc, fish with A top-notch Muscadet *sur lie*, a SAUV BL/SÉM blend, Premier Cru Chablis, Vouvray, ALBARIÑO or Rheingau RIES.

Brandade Premier Cru Chablis, Sancerre Rouge or NZ PINOT N.

Brill V. delicate: hence a top fish for fine old Puligny and the like.

Cod, roast Gd neutral background for fine dry/medium whites: Chablis, Meursault, Corton-Charlemagne, Cru Classé Graves, GRÜNER V, German Kabinett or Grosses Gewächs, or gd lightish PINOT N. Persuade the chef not to add chorizo.

  black cod with miso sauce NZ or Oregon Pinot N, Meursault Premier Cru or Rheingau RIES Spätlese. Vintage Champagne.

Crab Crab (esp Dungeness) and RIES together are part of the Creator's plan.

  Chinese, with ginger and onion German Ries Kabinett or Spätlese Halbtrocken. Tokaji FURMINT, GEWURZ.

  cioppino SAUV BL; but West Coast friends say ZIN. Also California sparkling.

  cold, dressed Top Mosel Ries, dry Alsace or Australian Ries or Condrieu.

  softshell Unoaked CHARD, ALBARIÑO or top-quality German Ries Spätlese.

  Thai crabcakes Pungent Sauv Bl (Loire, South Africa, Australia, NZ) or Ries (German Spätlese or Australian).

  with black bean sauce A big Barossa SHIRAZ or SYRAH. Even a tumbler of Cognac.

  with chilli and garlic Quite powerful Ries, perhaps German Grosses Gewächs or Wachau Austrian.

Curry A generic term for a multitude of flavours. Chilli emphasizes tannin, so reds need supple or silky ones. Any fruity, low-acid rosé can be a gd bet. Hot-and-sour flavours (with tamarind, tomato, eg.) need acidity (perhaps SAUV BL); mild, creamy dishes need richness of texture (dry Alsace RIES). But best of all is Sherry: Fino with fish, Palo Cortado or dry Amontillado with meat. It's revelatory.

Eel, smoked 1st choice is Fino Sherry. RIES, Alsace, or Austrian, or GRÜNER V. Vintage Champagne. Schnapps.

Fish and chips, *fritto misto,* **tempura** Chablis, white B'x, SAUV BL, PINOT BL, Gavi, Fino, Montilla, Koshu, sake, tea; or NV Champagne or Cava. Anything white goes.

Fish pie (with creamy sauce) ALBARIÑO, Soave Classico, German RIES Erstes Gewächs, Spanish GODELLO.

Gravadlax SERCIAL Madeira (eg. 10-yr-old Henriques), Amontillado, Tokaji FURMINT. Or NV Champagne.

Haddock Rich, dry whites: Meursault, California CHARD, MARSANNE or GRÜNER V.

Smoked as for KIPPERS, but see under EGGS, SOUFFLÉS.

Hake SAUV BL or any fresh fruity white: Pacherenc, Tursan.

  cold with mayonnaise fine CHARD.

Halibut As for TURBOT.

Herrings, fried / grilled Need a sharp white to cut their richness. Rully, Chablis, MUSCADET, Bourgogne ALIGOTÉ, Greek, dry SAUV BL. Or Indian tea. Or cider.

Kedgeree Full white, still or sparkling: Mâcon-Villages, South African CHARD, GRÜNER V, German Grosses Gewächs or (at breakfast) Champagne.

Kippers A gd cup of tea, preferably Ceylon (milk, no sugar). Scotch? Dry Oloroso Sherry is surprisingly gd.

Lamproie à la Bordelaise Glorious with 5-yr-old St-Émilion or Fronsac. Or Douro reds, with Portuguese lampreys.

Lobster, richly sauced Vintage Champagne, fine white burgundy, Cru Classé Graves. Alternatively, for its inherent sweetness, Sauternes, Pfalz Spätlese, even Auslese.

  cold with mayonnaise NV Champagne, Alsace RIES, Premier Cru Chablis, Condrieu, Mosel Spätlese or a local fizz.

Mackerel, grilled Hard or sharp white to cut the oil: SAUV BL from Touraine, Gaillac, Vinho Verde, white Rioja or English white. Or Guinness.

Monkfish A succulent but neutral dish; depends on the sauce. Full-flavoured white or red, depending.

Mullet, grey VERDICCHIO, Rully or unoaked CHARD.

    red A chameleon, tasty and delicate, adaptable to gd white or red, esp PINOT N.

Mussels marinières Muscadet *sur lie*, Premier Cru Chablis, unoaked CHARD.

    curried something s/sw; Alsace RIES.

    with garlic/parsley *see* ESCARGOTS.

Paella, shellfish Full-bodied white or rosé, unoaked CHARD. Or the local Spanish red.

Perch, sandre Exquisite fish for finest wines: top white burgundy, Grand Cru Alsace RIES or noble Mosels. Or try top Swiss CHASSELAS (eg. Dézaley, St-Saphorin).

Prawns with mayonnaise Menetou-Salon.

    with garlic keep the wine light, white or rosé, and dry.

    with spices up to and incl chilli, go for a bit more body, but not oak: dry RIES or Italian, eg. FIANO.

Salmon, seared or grilled PINOT N is the fashionable option, but CHARD is better. MERLOT or light claret not bad. Best is fine white burgundy: Puligny- or Chassagne-Montrachet, Meursault, Corton-Charlemagne, Grand Cru Chablis; GRÜNER V, Condrieu, California, Idaho or NZ CHARD, Rheingau Kabinett/Spätlese, Australian RIES.

    fishcakes Call for similar, but less grand, wines.

Sardines, fresh grilled V. dry white: Vinho Verde, MUSCADET or modern Greek.

Sashimi The Japanese preference is for white wine with body (Chablis Premier Cru, Alsace RIES) with white fish, PINOT N with red. Both need acidity: low-acidity wines don't work. Simple Chablis can be too thin. If soy is involved, then low-tannin red (again, Pinot). Remember sake (or Fino). As though you'd forget Champagne.

Scallops An inherently slightly sweet dish, best with medium-dry whites.

    in cream sauces German Spätlese, -Montrachets or top Australian CHARD.

    grilled or seared Hermitage Blanc, GRÜNER V, Pessac-Léognan Blanc, vintage Champagne or PINOT N.

    with Asian seasoning NZ Chard, CHENIN BL, GODELLO, GRÜNER V, GEWURZ.

Scandi food Scandinavian dishes often have flavours of dill, caraway, cardomom and combine sweet and sharp flavours. Go for acidity and some weight: GODELLO, FALANGHINA, VERDELHO, Australian, Alsace or Austrian RIES. Pickled/fermented/raw fish is more challenging: beer or akvavit. *See also* entries for smoked fish, etc.

Shellfish Dry white with plain boiled shellfish, richer wines with richer sauces. RIES is the grape.

    with *plateaux de fruits de mer* Chablis, MUSCADET de Sèvre et Maine, PICPOUL de Pinet, Alto Adige PINOT BL.

Skate / raie with brown butter White with some pungency (eg. PINOT GR d'Alsace or ROUSSANNE) or a clean, straightforward wine ie. MUSCADET or VERDICCHIO.

Snapper SAUV BL if cooked with oriental flavours; white Rhône or Provence rosé with Mediterranean flavours.

Sole, plaice, etc., plain, grilled or fried Perfect with fine wines: white burgundy or its equivalent.

    with sauce According to the ingredients: sharp, dry wine for tomato sauce, fairly rich for creamy preparations.

Sushi Hot wasabi is usually hidden in every piece. German QbA Trocken wines, simple Chablis, or NV Brut Champagne. Obvious fruit doesn't work. Or, of course, sake or beer.

Swordfish Full-bodied, dry white (or why not red?) of the country. Nothing grand.

Tagine, with couscous North African flavours need substantial whites to balance – Austrian, Rhône – or crisp, neutral whites that won't compete. Go easy on the oak. VIOGNIER or ALBARIÑO can work well.

Trout, grilled or fried Delicate white wine, eg. Mosel (esp Saar or Ruwer), Alsace PINOT BL, FENDANT.

Tuna, grilled or seared Best served rare (or raw) with light red wine: young Loire CAB FR or red burg. Young Rioja is a possibility.

Turbot The king of fishes (or "ambitious brill" in *HMS Pinafore*). Serve with your best rich, dry white: Meursault or Chassagne-Montrachet, Corton-Charlemagne, mature Chablis or its California, Australian or NZ equivalent. Condrieu. Mature Rheingau, Mosel or Nahe Spätlese or Auslese (not Trocken).

Meat, poultry, game

Barbecues The local wine: Australian, South African, Chilean, Argentina are right in spirit. Reds need tannin and vigour.

Beef (see also Steak), boiled Red: B'x (eg. Fronsac), Roussillon, Gevrey-Chambertin or Côte-Rôtie. Medium-ranking white burgundy is gd, eg. Auxey-Duresses. Mustard softens tannic reds, horseradish kills your taste: can be worth sacrifice.

roast Ideal partner for fine red wine of any kind. Even Amarone. *See* above for mustard. Silkier the texture of the beef (wagyu, Galician eg.) the silkier the wine.

steak Whole range of more or less tannic reds: relevant to time and place.

steak tartare NV Champagne, Swartland CHENIN BL or cru Beaujolais.

stew, daube Sturdy red: Pomerol or St-Émilion, Hermitage, Cornas, BARBERA, SHIRAZ, Napa CAB SAUV, Ribera del Duero or Douro red.

Beef stroganoff Dramatic red: Barolo, Valpolicella Amarone, Priorat, Hermitage, late-harvest ZIN. Georgian SAPERAVI or Moldovan Negru de Purkar.

Boudin blanc **(white pork sausage)** Loire CHENIN BL, esp when served with apples: dry Vouvray, Saumur, Savennières; mature red Côte de Beaune if without.

Boudin noir **(blood sausage)** Local SAUV BL, CHENIN BL, esp Loire. Or Beaujolais cru, esp Morgon. Or light TEMPRANILLO. Or Fino.

Brazilian dishes Pungent flavours that blend several culinary traditions. Sherry would add another. Rhônish grapes work for red, or white with weight: VERDICCHIO, Californian CHARD. Or Caipirinhas. And a ten-mile run afterwards..

Cabbage, stuffed Hungarian KADARKA; village Rhône; Salice Salentino, PRIMITIVO and other spicy s Italian reds. Or Argentine MALBEC (no oak, if you can find one).

Cajun food Fleurie, Brouilly or New World SAUV BL. **With gumbo** Amontillado.

Cassoulet Red from Southwest France (Gaillac, Minervois, Corbières, St-Chinian or Fitou) or SHIRAZ. But best of all Fronton, Beaujolais cru or young TEMPRANILLO.

Chicken Kiev Alsace RIES, Collio, CHARD, Bergerac rouge.

Chicken / turkey / guinea fowl, roast Virtually any wine, incl v. best bottles of dry to medium white and finest old reds (esp burgundy). The meat of fowl can be adapted with sauces to match almost any fine wine (eg. coq au vin; the burgundy can be red or white, or *vin jaune* for that matter).

Chilli con carne Young red: Beaujolais, TEMPRANILLO, ZIN, Argentine MALBEC, Chilean CARMENÈRE. Some drink beer.

Chinese food I often serve both whites and reds concurrently during Chinese meals; no one wine goes with the whole affair. Peking duck is pretty forgiving. Champagne becomes a thirst-quencher. Beer, too. But here are some observations.

Cantonese Rosé or dry to dryish white (Mosel RIES Kabinett or Spätlese Trocken). Ries should not be too dry; GEWURZ often suggested but rarely works; try GRÜNER V; This needs acidity in wine. Dry sparkling (esp Cava) works with the textures. Reds can work, but they should have worked off young tannins and not be too dry, or overtly oaky. PINOT N 1st choice; ★★St-Émilion or Châteauneuf-du-Pape.

Shanghai Richer and oilier than Cantonese, not great for wine. Shanghai tends to be low on chilli but high on vinegar of various sorts. German and Alsace whites can be a bit sweeter than for Cantonese. For reds, mature Pinot N is again best.

Szechuan style VERDICCHIO, Alsace PINOT BL or v. cold beer. Mature Pinot N can also work; but make sure the tannins are silky.

Choucroute garni Alsace PINOT BL, PINOT GR, RIES or lager.

Cold roast meat Generally better with full-flavoured white than red. Mosel Spätlese or Hochheimer and Côte Chalonnaise are v.gd, as is Beaujolais. Leftover cold beef with leftover vintage Champagne is bliss.

Confit d'oie / de canard Young, tannic red B'x, California CAB SAUV and MERLOT, Priorat cut richness. Alsace PINOT GR or GEWURZ match it.

Coq au vin Red burgundy. Ideal: one bottle of Chambertin in the dish, two on the table. *See also* under chicken.

Duck or goose Rather rich white, esp for the strong flavour of goose: Pfalz Spätlese or off-dry Grand Cru Alsace. Or mature, gamey red: Morey-St-Denis, Côte-Rôtie, Pauillac, Bairrada. With oranges or peaches, the Sauternais propose drinking Sauternes, others Monbazillac or RIES Auslese. Mature, weighty vintage Champagne is gd too, and handles red cabbage surprisingly well.

   Peking *See* CHINESE FOOD.

   wild duck Big-scale red: Hermitage, Bandol, California or South African CAB SAUV, Australian SHIRAZ – Grange if you can afford it.

   with olives Top-notch Chianti or other Tuscans.

   roast breast & confit leg with Puy lentils Madiran (best), St-Émilion, Fronsac.

Game birds, young, plain-roasted Best red wine you can afford, but not too heavy.

   older birds in casseroles Red (Gevrey-Chambertin, Pommard, Châteauneuf-du-Pape, Dão, or Grand Cru Classé St-Émilion, Rhône). Don't forget game birds can be even better cold the next day, esp with fine German wines.

   well-hung game Vega Sicilia, great red Rhône, Chateau Musar.

   cold game Best German RIES; or mature vintage Champagne.

Game pie, hot Red: Oregon PINOT N, St-Émilion Grand Cru Classé.

   cold Gd-quality white burgundy or German Erstes Gewächs, cru Beaujolais or Champagne.

Goulash Flavoursome young red: Hungarian Kékoportó, ZIN, Uruguayan TANNAT, Douro red, MENCÍA, young Australian SHIRAZ. Or dry white from Tokaj.

Grouse See GAME BIRDS – but push the boat right out. You need top burgundy.

Haggis Fruity red, eg. young claret, young Portuguese red, New World CAB SAUV or MALBEC or Châteauneuf-du-Pape. Or, of course, malt whisky.

Ham, cooked Softer red burgundies: Volnay, Savigny, Beaune; Chinon or Bourgueil; sweetish German white (RIES Spätlese); lightish CAB SAUV (eg. Chilean), or New World PINOT N. And don't forget the heaven-made match of ham and Sherry. *See* HAM, RAW OR CURED.

Hamburger Young red: Australian CAB SAUV, Chianti, ZIN, Argentine MALBEC, Chilean CARMENÈRE or SYRAH, TEMPRANILLO. Or full-strength cola (not diet). If you add cheese and stuff heaven help you; you're on your own.

Hare Jugged hare calls for flavourful red: not too old burgundy or B'x, Rhône (eg. Gigondas), Bandol, Barbaresco, Ribera del Duero, Rioja Res. The same for saddle or for hare sauce with pappardelle.

Indian dishes Various options: dry Sherry is brilliant. Choose a fairly weighty Fino with fish, and Palo Cortado, Amontillado or Oloroso with meat, according to the weight of the dish; heat's not a problem. The texture works too. Otherwise, medium-sweet white, v. cold: Orvieto *abboccato*, South African CHENIN BL, Alsace PINOT BL, TORRONTÉS, Indian sparkling, Cava or NV Champagne. Rosé is gd all-rounder. For tannic impact Barolo or Barbaresco, or deep-flavoured reds ie. Châteauneuf-du-Pape, Cornas, Australian GRENACHE or MOURVÈDRE, or Valpolicella Amarone – will emphasize the heat. Hot-and-sour flavours need acidity.

   Sri Lankan More extreme flavours, lots of coconut. Sherry, rich red, rosé or innocuous white.

Japanese dishes A different set of senses come into play. Texture and balance are key; flavours are subtle. Gd mature fizz works well, as does mature dry RIES; you need acidity, a bit of body, and complexity. Umami-filled meat dishes favour light, supple, bright reds: Beaujolais perhaps, or mature PINOT N. Full-flavoured *yakitori* needs lively, fruity, younger versions of the same reds. *See also* SUSHI, SASHIMI.

Kebabs Vigorous red: modern Greek, Corbières, Chilean CAB SAUV, ZIN or Barossa SHIRAZ. SAUV BL, if lots of garlic.

Kidneys Rather tannic red: St-Émilion or Fronsac, Castillon, Nuits-St-Georges, Cornas, Barbaresco, Rioja, Spanish or Australian CAB SAUV, Douro red.

Korean dishes Fruit-forward wines seem to work best with strong, pungent Korean flavours. PINOT N, Beaujolais, Valpolicella can all work: acidity is needed. Non-aromatic whites: GRÜNER V, SILVANER, VERNACCIA. But I drink beer.

Lamb, roast One of the traditional and best partners for v.gd red B'x, or its CAB SAUV equivalents from the New World. In Spain, finest old Rioja and Ribera del Duero Res or Priorat, in Italy ditto SANGIOVESE.
  slow-cooked roast Flatters top reds, but needs less tannin than pink lamb.
  shanks Young red burgundy: Santenay. Crozes-Hermitage. Montefalco SAGRANTINO.

Liver Young red: Beaujolais-Villages, St-Joseph, Médoc, Italian MERLOT, Breganze CAB SAUV, ZIN, Priorat, Bairrada.
  calf's Red Rioja Crianza, Fleurie. Or a big Pfalz RIES Spätlese.

Meatballs Tangy, medium-bodied red: Mercurey, Crozes-Hermitage, Madiran, MORELLINO di Scansano, Langhe NEBBIOLO, ZIN, CAB SAUV.

Keftedes **or spicy Middle-Eastern style** Simple, rustic red.

Moussaka Red or rosé: Naoussa, SANGIOVESE, Corbières, Côtes de Provence, Ajaccio, young ZIN, TEMPRANILLO.

Mutton Stronger flavour than lamb, not usually served pink. Needs a strong sauce. Robust red; top, mature CAB SAUV, SYRAH. Sweetness of fruit (eg. Barossa) suits it.

Osso bucco Low-tannin, supple red such as DOLCETTO d'Alba or PINOT N. Or dry Italian white such as Soave.

Ox cheek, braised Superbly tender and flavoursome, this flatters the best reds: Vega Sicilia, St-Émilion. Best with substantial wines.

Oxtail Rather rich red: St-Émilion, Pomerol, Pommard, Nuits-St-Georges, Barolo, or Rioja Res, Priorat or Ribera del Duero, California or Coonawarra CAB SAUV, Châteauneuf-du-Pape, mid-weight SHIRAZ, Amarone.

Paella Young Spanish: red, dry white, or rosé: Penedès, Somontano, Navarra, Rioja.

Pigeon or squab PINOT N perfect; young Rhône, Argentine MALBEC, young SANGIOVESE. Try Franken SILVANER Spätlese. With luxurious squab: top, quite tannic red.

Pork, roast A perfect rich background to a fairly light red or rich white. It deserves ★★★ treatment: Médoc is fine. Portugal's suckling pig is eaten with Bairrada Garrafeira; Chinese is gd with PINOT N.
  pork belly Slow cooked and meltingly tender, this needs a red with some tannin or acidity. Italian would be gd: Barolo, DOLCETTO or BARBERA. Or Loire red, or lightish Argentine MALBEC.

Pot au feu, bollito misto, cocido Rustic red wines from region of origin; SANGIOVESE di Romagna, Chusclan, Lirac, Rasteau, Portuguese Alentejo, Spain's Yecla, Jumilla.

Quail Succulent little chick deserves tasty red or white. Rioja Res, mature claret, PINOT N. Or a mellow white: Vouvray or St-Péray.

Rabbit Lively, medium-bodied young Italian red, eg. AGLIANICO del Vulture; Chiroubles, Chinon, Saumur-Champigny or Rhône rosé.
  with prunes Bigger, richer, fruitier red.
  with mustard Cahors.
  as ragu Medium-bodied red with acidity.

Satay McLaren Vale SHIRAZ; Alsace or NZ GEWURZ. Peanut sauce: problem with wine.

Sauerkraut (German) Franken SILVANER, lager or Pils. (But *see also* CHOUCROUTE GARNI.)

Sausages *See also* CHARCUTERIE, FRANKFURTERS. The British banger requires a young MALBEC from Argentina (a red wine, anyway) or London Pride (the city's great ale).

Singaporean dishes Part Indian, part Malay and part Chinese, this food has big, bold flavours that don't match easily with wine, not that that bothers the country's many wine-lovers. Off-dry RIES is as gd as anything. With meat dishes, ripe, supple reds: Valpolicella, PINOT N, DORNFELDER, unoaked MERLOT or CARMENÈRE.

Steak, *au poivre* A fairly young Rhône red or CAB SAUV.

    filet, ribeye or tournedos Any gd red, esp burgundy (but not old wines with Béarnaise sauce: top New World PINOT N is better).

    Fiorentina (bistecca) Chianti Classico Riserva or BRUNELLO. Rarer the meat, more classic the wine; the more cooked, the more you need New World, sweet/strong wines. Argentine MALBEC is perfect for steak Argentine style ie. cooked to death.

    Korean *yuk whe* (world's best steak tartare) Sake.

    tartare Vodka or light young red: Beaujolais, Bergerac, Valpolicella.

    T-bone Reds of similar bone structure: Barolo, Hermitage, Australian CAB SAUV or SHIRAZ, Chilean SYRAH.

Steak-and-kidney pie or pudding Red Rioja Res or mature B'x. Pudding (with suet) wants vigorous young wine.

Stews and casseroles Burgundy such as Nuits-St-Georges or Pommard if fairly simple; otherwise lusty, full-flavoured red: young Côtes du Rhône, Toro, Corbières, BARBERA, SHIRAZ, ZIN, etc.

Sweetbreads A rich dish, so grand white wine: Rheingau RIES or Franken SILVANER Spätlese, Grand Cru Alsace PINOT GR or Condrieu, depending on sauce.

Tagines Depends on what's under the lid, but fruity young reds are a gd bet: Beaujolais, TEMPRANILLO, SANGIOVESE, MERLOT, SHIRAZ. Amontillado is great.

    Chicken with preserved lemon, olives VIOGNIER.

Tandoori chicken RIES or SAUV BL, young red B'x or light n Italian red served cool. Also Cava and NV Champagne, or of course Palo Cortado or Amontillado Sherry.

Thai dishes Ginger and lemon grass call for pungent SAUV BL (Loire, Australia, NZ, South Africa) or RIES (Spätlese or Australian). Most curries suit aromatic whites with a touch of sweetness: GEWÜRZ is also gd

Tongue Gd for any red or white of abundant character, esp Italian. Also Beaujolais, Loire reds, TEMPRANILLO and full, dry rosés.

Veal, roast A friend of fine wine. Gd for any fine old red that may be fading with age (eg. Rioja Res, old Médoc); German or Austrian RIES, Vouvray, Alsace PINOT GR.

Venison Big-scale reds, incl MOURVÈDRE, solo as in Bandol or in blends. Rhône, B'x, NZ Gimblett Gravels or California CAB SAUV of a mature vintage; or rather rich white (Pfalz Spätlese or Alsace PINOT GR). With a sweet and sharp berry sauce, try a German Grosses Gewächs RIES, or a Chilean CARMENÈRE or SYRAH.

Vitello tonnato Full-bodied whites: CHARD; light reds (eg. Valpolicella) served cool. Or a southern rosé.

Wild boar Serious red: top Tuscan or Priorat. NZ SYRAH. I've even drunk Port.

Vegetarian dishes
(*See also* FIRST COURSES)

Baked pasta dishes *Pasticcio*, lasagne and cannelloni with elaborate vegetarian fillings and sauces: an occasion to show off a grand wine, esp finest Tuscan red, but also claret and burgundy.

Beetroot Mimics a flavour found in red burgundy. You could return the compliment.

    and goat's cheese gratin Sancerre, B'x SAUV BL.

Cauliflower Increasingly fashionable, with gd reason.

    roasted, etc: go by the other (usually bold) flavours. Try Austrian GRÜNER V, Valpolicella, NZ PINOT N.

Cauliflower cheese: Crisp, aromatic white: Sancerre, RIES Spätlese, MUSCAT, ALBARIÑO, GODELLO. Beaujolais Villages. No, go on; comfort wine wth comfort food.

Couscous with vegetables Young red with a bite: SHIRAZ, Corbières, Minervois; or well-chilled rosé from Navarra or Somontano; or a robust Moroccan red.

Fennel-based dishes SAUV BL: Pouilly-Fumé or NZ; SYLVANER or English SEYVAL BL; or young TEMPRANILLO.

Fermented foods *See also* SAUERKRAUT, CHOUCROUTE, KOREAN. Kimchi and miso are being worked into many dishes. Fruit and acidity is generally needed. If in sweetish veg dishes, try Alsace.

Grilled Mediterranean vegetables Italian whites; Brouilly, BARBERA, TEMPRANILLO, SHIRAZ.

Lentil dishes Sturdy reds such as Corbières, ZIN or SHIRAZ.

  dhal, with spinach Tricky. Soft light red or rosé is best, and not top-flight.

Macaroni cheese As for CAULIFLOWER CHEESE.

Mushrooms (in most contexts) A boon to many if not all reds. Pomerol, California MERLOT, Rioja Res, top burgundy or Vega Sicilia. On toast, best claret – even Port. Ceps/porcini: Ribera del Duero, Barolo, Chianti Rufina, Pauillac or St-Estèphe, NZ Gimblett Gravels.

Onion / leek tart / *flamiche* Fruity, off-dry or dry white: Alsace PINOT GR or GEWURZ is classic; Canadian, Australian or NZ RIES; Jurançon. Or Loire CAB FR.

Peppers or aubergines (eggplant), stuffed Vigorous red wine: Nemea, Chianti, DOLCETTO, ZIN, Bandol, Vacqueyras.

Pumpkin / squash ravioli or risotto Full-bodied, fruity dry or off-dry white: VIOGNIER or MARSANNE, demi-sec Vouvray, Gavi or South African CHENIN.

Ratatouille Vigorous young red: Chianti, NZ CAB SAUV, MERLOT, MALBEC, TEMPRANILLO; young red B'x, Gigondas or Coteaux du Languedoc. Fino Sherry can work too.

Root vegetables Sweet potatoes, carrots etc, often mixed with eg. beetroot, garlic, onions and others have plenty of sweetness. Rosé is a winner, esp one with some weight: Spanish, Italian, South American.

Seaweed Depends on the context. *See also* SUSHI. The iodine notes go well with Austrian GRÜNER V, RIES.

Spiced vegetarian dishes *See* INDIAN DISHES, THAI DISHES (MEAT, POULTRY, GAME).

Watercress, raw Makes every wine on earth taste revolting. Soup is slightly easier, but doesn't need wine.

Wild garlic leaves, wilted Tricky: a fairly neutral white with acidity will cope best.

Desserts

Apple pie, strudel, or tarts Sweet German, Austrian or Loire white, Tokaji Aszú, or Canadian Icewine.

Apples, Cox's Orange Pippins Vintage Port (and sweetmeal biscuits) is the Saintsbury [wine] Club plan.

Bread-&-butter pudding Fine 10-yr-old Barsac, Tokaji Aszú, Australian botrytized SEM.

Cakes & gâteaux *See also* CHOCOLATE, COFFEE, GINGER, RUM. BUAL or MALMSEY Madeira, Oloroso or Cream Sherry. Asti, sweet Prosecco.

Cheesecake Sweet white: Vouvray, Anjou, or Vin Santo – nothing too special.

Chocolate A talking point. Generally only powerful flavours can compete. Texture matters. BUAL, California Orange MUSCAT, Tokaji Aszú, Australian Liqueur Muscat, 10-yr-old Tawny or even young Vintage Port; Asti for light, fluffy mousses. Experiment with rich, ripe reds: SYRAH, ZIN, even sparkling SHIRAZ. Banyuls for a weightier partnership. Médoc can match bitter black chocolate, though it's a bit of a waste, and Amarone is more fun. Armagnac, or a tot of gd rum.

  and olive oil mousse 10-yr-old Tawny Port or as for black chocolate, above.

Christmas pudding, mince pies Tawny Port, Cream Sherry or that liquid Christmas pudding itself, PEDRO XIMÉNEZ Sherry. Tokaji Aszú. Asti, or Banyuls.

Coffee desserts Sweet MUSCAT, Australia Liqueur Muscats, or Tokaji Aszú.

Creams, custards, fools, syllabubs *See also* CHOCOLATE, COFFEE, RUM. Sauternes, Loupiac, Ste-Croix-du-Mont or Monbazillac.

Crème brûlée Sauternes or Rhine Beerenauslese, best Madeira, or Tokaji Aszú. (With concealed fruit, a more modest sweet wine.)

Ice cream, sorbets Fortified wine (Australian Liqueur MUSCAT, Banyuls). PEDRO XIMÉNEZ.

Lemon flavours For dishes like tarte au citron, try sweet RIES from Germany or Austria or Tokaji Aszú; v. sweet if lemon is v. tart.

Meringues (eg. Eton Mess) Recioto di Soave, Asti or top vintage Champagne, well-aged.

Nuts (incl praliné) Finest Oloroso Sherry, Madeira, Vintage or Tawny Port (nature's match for walnuts), Tokaji Aszú, Vin Santo, or Setúbal MOSCATEL.

salted nut parfait Tokaji Aszú, Vin Santo.

Orange flavours Experiment: old Sauternes, Tokaji Aszú, California Orange MUSCAT.

Panettone Jurançon *moelleux*, late-harvest RIES, Barsac, Tokaji Aszú.

Pears in red wine A pause before the Port. Try Rivesaltes, Banyuls, RIES Beerenauslese.

Pecan pie Orange MUSCAT or Liqueur Muscat.

Raspberries (no cream, little sugar) Excellent with fine reds which themselves taste of raspberries: young Juliénas, Regnié.

Rum flavours (baba, mousses, ice cream) MUSCAT – from Asti to Australian Liqueur, according to weight of dish.

Strawberries, wild (no cream) Serve with red B'x (most exquisitely Margaux) poured over.

Strawberries & cream Sauternes or similar sweet B'x; Vouvray *moelleux*; Vendange Tardive Jurançon.

Summer pudding Fairly young Sauternes of a gd vintage.

Sweet soufflés Sauternes or Vouvray *moelleux*. Sweet (or rich) Champagne.

Tiramisú Vin Santo, young Tawny Port, MUSCAT de Beaumes-de-Venise, Sauternes, or Australian Liqueur Muscat.

Trifle Should be sufficiently vibrant with its internal Sherry.

Zabaglione Light-gold Marsala or Australian bodyidzed SEM, or Asti.

Wine & cheese

The notion that wine and cheese were married in heaven is not borne out by experience. Fine red wines are slaughtered by strong cheeses; only sharp or sweet white wines survive. Principles to remember (despite exceptions): first, the harder the cheese, the more tannin the wine can have; second, the creamier the cheese, the more acidity is needed in the wine – and don't be shy of sweetness. Cheese is classified by its texture and the nature of its rind, so its appearance is a guide to the type of wine to match it. Below are examples, I always try to keep a glass of white wine for my cheese.

Bloomy rind soft cheeses, pure-white rind if pasteurized, or dotted with red: Brie, Camembert, Chaource, Bougon (goats milk "Camembert") Full, dry white burgundy or Rhône if the cheese is white and immature; powerful, fruity St-Émilion, young Australian (or Rhône) SHIRAZ/SYRAH or GRENACHE if it's mature.

Blue cheeses The extreme saltiness of Roquefort or most blue cheeses needs the sweetness of Sauternes (or Tokaji), especially old. Stilton and Port, (youngish) Vintage or Tawny, is a classic. Intensely flavoured old Oloroso, Amontillado, Madeira, Marsala and other fortifieds go with most blues.

Fresh, no rind: cream cheese, crème fraîche, mozzarella Light crisp white: Chablis, Bergerac, Entre-Deux-Mers; rosé: Anjou, Rhône; v. light, young, fresh red: B'x, Bardolino, Beaujolais.

Hard cheeses, waxed or oiled, often showing marks from cheesecloth: Gruyère family, Manchego and other Spanish cheeses, Parmesan, Cantal, Comté, old Gouda, Cheddar and most "traditional" English cheeses Hard to generalize; Gouda, Gruyère, some Spanish, and a few English cheeses complement fine claret or CAB SAUV and great SHIRAZ/SYRAH. But strong cheeses need less refined wines, preferably local ones. Sugary, granular old Dutch red Mimolette or Beaufort are gd for finest mature B'x. Also for Tokaji Aszú. But try whites too.

Natural rind (mostly goats cheese) with bluish-grey mould (the rind becomes wrinkled when mature), sometimes dusted with ash: St-Marcellin Sancerre, Valençay, light SAUV BL, Jurançon, Savoie, Soave, Italian CHARD.

Semi-soft cheeses, thickish grey-pink rind: Livarot, Pont l'Evêque, Reblochon, Tomme de Savoie, St-Nectaire Powerful white B'x, even Sauternes, CHARD, Alsace PINOT GR, dryish RIES, s Italian and Sicilian whites, aged white Rioja, dry Oloroso Sherry. The strongest of these cheeses kill almost any wines. Try marc or Calvados.

Washed-rind soft cheeses, with rather sticky, orange-red rind: Langres, mature Epoisses, Maroilles, Carré de l'Est, Milleens, Munster Local reds, esp for Burgundian cheeses; vigorous Languedoc, Cahors, Côtes du Frontonnais, Corsican, s Italian, Sicilian, Bairrada. Also powerful whites, esp Alsace GEWURZ, MUSCAT.

Food & finest wines

With very special bottles, the wine guides the choice of food rather than vice versa. The following is based largely on gastronomic conventions and newer experiments, plus much diligent and on-going research. They should help bring out the best in your best wines.

Red wines

Amarone Classically, in Verona, *risotto all'Amarone* or *pastissada*. But if your butcher doesn't run to horse, then shin of beef, slow-cooked in more Amarone.

Barolo, Barbaresco Risotto with white truffles; pasta with game sauce (eg. *pappardelle alla lepre*); porcini mushrooms; Parmesan.

Great Syrahs: Hermitage, Côte-Rôtie, Grange; Vega Sicilia Beef (such as the super-rich, super-tender, super-slow-cooked ox cheek I had at Vega Sicilia), venison, well-hung game; bone marrow on toast; English cheese (esp best farm Cheddar) but also hard goats milk and ewes milk cheeses such as England's Berkswell or Ticklemore. I treat Côte-Rôtie like top red burgundy.

Great Vintage Port or Madeira Walnuts or pecans. A Cox's Orange Pippin and a digestive biscuit is a classic English accompaniment.

Red Bordeaux: v. old, light, delicate wines, (eg. pre-59) Leg or rack of young lamb, roast with a hint of herbs (not garlic); *entrecôte*; simply roasted (and not too well-hung) partridge; roast chicken.

    fully mature great vintages (eg. 59 61 82 85) Shoulder or saddle of lamb, roast with a touch of garlic; roast ribs or grilled rump of beef.

    mature but still vigorous (eg. 89 90) Shoulder or saddle of lamb (incl kidneys)

Fail-safe face-savers

Some wines are more useful than others – more versatile, more forgiving. If you're choosing restaurant wine to please several people, or just stocking the cellar with basics, these will go with go with a wide range of dishes: (r) Alentejo, BARBERA d'Asti/d'Alba, BLAUFRÄNKISCH, Beaujolais, Chianti, GRENACHE/GARNACHA if not overextracted/overoaked, MALBEC (easy on the oak), PINOT N, Valpolicella; (w) Alsace PINOT BL, ASSYRTIKO, unoaked or v. lightly oaked CHARD, Fino Sherry, GRÜNER V, RIES from Alsace and Germany (dry and fruity), Sancerre, gd Soave, VERDICCHIO.

with rich sauce. Fillet of beef *marchand de vin* (with wine and bone marrow). Grouse. Avoid beef Wellington: pastry dulls the palate.

Merlot-based Beef as above (fillet is richest) or well-hung venison. In St-Émilion, lampreys.

Red burgundy Consider the weight and texture, which grow lighter/more velvety with age. Also the character of the wine: Nuits is earthy, Musigny flowery, great Romanées can be exotic, Pommard is renowned for its four-squareness. Roast chicken or (better) capon is a safe standard with red burgundy; guineafowl for slightly stronger wines, then partridge, grouse or woodcock for those progressively more rich and pungent styles. Hare and venison (*chevreuil*) are alternatives.

great old burgundy The Burgundian formula is cheese: Époisses (unfermented); a fine cheese but a terrible waste of fine old wines. *See* above.

vigorous younger burgundy Duck or goose roasted to minimize fat. Or *faisinjan* (pheasant cooked in pomegranate juice). Or lightly smoked gammon.

Rioja Gran Reserva, Pesquera... Richly flavoured roasts: wild boar, mutton, saddle of hare, whole suckling pig.

White wines

Beerenauslese / Trockenbeerenauslese Biscuits, peaches, greengages. Desserts made from rhubarb, gooseberries, quince, apples. But TBAs don't need food.

Condrieu, Château-Grillet, Hermitage Blanc V. light pasta scented with herbs and tiny peas or broad beans. Or v. mild tender ham. Old white Hermitage loves truffles.

Grand Cru Alsace: Ries *Truite au bleu*, smoked salmon, or *choucroute garni*.

Pinot Gr Roast or grilled veal. Or truffle sandwich (slice a whole truffle, make a sandwich with salted butter and gd country bread – not sourdough or rye – wrap and refrigerate overnight. Then toast it in the oven).

Gewurz Cheese soufflé (Münster cheese).

Vendange Tardive Foie gras or tarte tatin.

Old vintage Champagne (not Blanc de Blancs) As an apéritif, or with cold partridge, grouse, woodcock. The evolved flavours of old Champagne make it far easier to match with food than the tightness of young wine. Hot foie gras can be sensational. Don't be afraid of garlic or even Indian spices, but omit the chilli.

late-disgorged old wines have extra freshness plus tertiary flavours. Try with truffles, lobster, scallops, crab, sweetbreads, pork belly, roast veal, chicken.

Sauternes Simple crisp buttery biscuits (eg. *langues de chat*), white peaches, nectarines, strawberries (without cream). Not tropical fruit. Pan-seared foie gras. Lobster or chicken with Sauternes sauce. Château d'Yquem recommends oysters (and indeed lobster). Experiment with blue cheeses. Roquefort is classic, but needs a powerful wine.

Tokaji Aszú (5–6 puttonyos) Foie gras recommended. Fruit desserts, cream desserts, even chocolate can be wonderful. Roquefort. It even works with some Chinese, though not with chilli – the spice has to be adjusted to meet the sweetness. Szechuan pepper is gd. Havana cigars are splendid. So is the naked sip.

Very good Chablis, white burgundy, other top-quality Chards White fish simply grilled or *meunière*. Dover sole, turbot, halibut are best; brill, drenched in butter, can be excellent. (Sea bass is too delicate; salmon passes but does little for the finest wine.)

Vouvray *moelleux*, etc. Buttery biscuits, apples, apple tart.

White burgundy (ie. Montrachet, Corton-Charlemagne) or equivalent Graves Roast veal, farm chicken stuffed with truffles or herbs under the skin, or sweetbreads; richly sauced white fish (turbot for choice) or scallops as above. Or lobster or poached wild salmon.

France

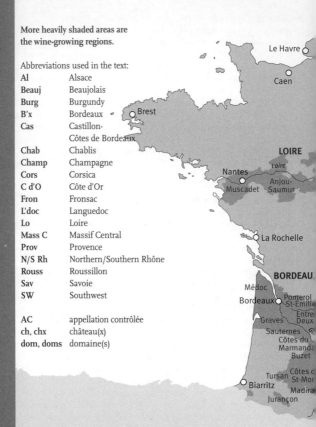

**More heavily shaded areas are
the wine-growing regions.**

Abbreviations used in the text:

Al	Alsace
Beauj	Beaujolais
Burg	Burgundy
B'x	Bordeaux
Cas	Castillon-Côtes de Bordeaux
Chab	Chablis
Champ	Champagne
Cors	Corsica
C d'O	Côte d'Or
Fron	Fronsac
L'doc	Languedoc
Lo	Loire
Mass C	Massif Central
Prov	Provence
N/S Rh	Northern/Southern Rhône
Rouss	Roussillon
Sav	Savoie
SW	Southwest
AC	appellation contrôlée
ch, chx	château(x)
dom, doms	domaine(s)

There's no hesitation about which country comes first in any book about the world's wines. France arrived first at fine wine and stays firmly in that position, with a greater variety even than the variety of its landscapes. The scenery, marvellously varied as it is, doesn't tell you what dramatic differences there will be in France's cellars.

Why, and how the country's far-from-tranquil history has produced so many delicious variations on a theme has always puzzled me. Italy has infinite variety too, but not (yet?) the polish, passion and professionalism that France brings to the arts of eating and drinking. I'm convinced it's in the Gallic genes. Hence the intricacy of the following pages, often tracing generations of obsessive farmers focused on tiny parcels of land. The names of their farms and fields,

and their complex families, form a sort of poetry that runs through even a summary list of the choices before you.

Quality, variety, value: you can't beat France for any of these three vital factors. They don't often meet in one wine, or in one region, but they're all here in these pages. Furthermore the French taste for wines with fresh flavours, balanced against headiness with the acidity of fruit, survives changes of fashion. America wanted strong, thick, oaky wines. France tried them and said no, we opt for finesse and elegance – and we have new ideas and new ways of achieving them – global warming or not.

France entries also cross-reference to Châteaux of Bordeaux

Recent vintages of the French classics

Red Bordeaux

Médoc / Red Graves For some wines, bottle age is optional: for these it is indispensable. Minor châteaux from light vintages need only 2 or 3 years, but even modest wines of great years can improve for 15 or so, and the great châteaux of these years can profit from double that time.

2016 Quality and quantity. Late harvest but healthy grapes. Cab Sauv with colour, depth, structure. Close to 2010.

2015 Excellent year for Cab Sauv but not the structure of 2005, 2010. Some variation. More rain at harvest in north Médoc than south.

2014 Saved by an Indian summer. Cab Sauv bright and resonant. Good to very good in terms of quality and quantity. Classic in style.

2013 Worst vintage since 1992. Patchy success at classed-growth level; some good wines have emerged.

2012 Erratic weather. Small crop. Difficulties ripening Cab Sauv. Some ready.

2011 Mixed quality but better than its reputation. Classic freshness with moderate alcohol. Modest crus ready to drink.

2010 Outstanding. Magnificent Cab Sauv, deep coloured, concentrated, firmly structured. At a price. To keep for years.

2009 Outstanding year, touted as "The Greatest". Structured wines with an exuberance of fruit. Don't miss this. Accessible or to keep.

2008 Much better than expected; fresh, classic flavours. Ageing potential.

2007 A difficult year. Some quite stylish but some are wearying. Be selective.

2006 Cab Sauv had difficulty ripening; best fine, tasty, nervous, long-ageing. Good colour, acidity. Starting to drink.

Fine vintages: 05 00 98 96 95 90 89 88 86 85 82 75 70 66 62 61 59 55 53 49 48 47 45 29 28.

St-Émilion / Pomerol

2016 Conditions as Médoc. Some young vines suffered in drought but overall excellent.

2015 Great year for Merlot. Perfect conditions. Colour, concentration, balance.

2014 More rain than Médoc so Merlot variable. Very good Cab Fr. Satisfactory.

2013 Difficult flowering (so tiny crop) and rot in Merlot. Modest to poor year.

2012 Conditions same as Médoc. Earlier-harvested Merlot was marginally more successful.

2011 Complicated, as Médoc. Good Cab Fr. Pomerol best overall? Don't shun it.

2010 Outstanding. Powerful wines again with high alcohol. Concentrated.

2009 Again, outstanding. Powerful wines (high alcohol) but seemingly balanced. Hail in St-Émilion cut production at certain estates.

2008 Similar conditions to the Médoc. Tiny yields helped quality, which is surprisingly good. Starting to drink, but best will age.

2007 Same pattern as Médoc. Extremely variable, but nothing to keep for long.

2006 Earlier-ripening Pomerol a success but St-Émilion and satellites variable.

Fine vintages: 05 01 00 98 95 90 89 88 85 82 71 70 67 66 64 61 59 53 52 49 47 45.

Red burgundy

Côte d'Or Côte de Beaune reds generally mature sooner than grander wines of Côte de Nuits. Earliest drinking dates are for lighter commune wines – eg. Volnay, Beaune; latest for Grands Crus, eg. Chambertin, Musigny. Even the best burgundies are more attractive young than equivalent red Bordeaux. It can seem magical when they really blossom years later.

2016 Catastrophe in April (frost), horrible May/June, then sun. If you had any
grapes left you could still make very good wine, in accessible, supple style.

2015 No hail! Very dense, concentrated wines, as 2005, but with the additional
juiciness of 2010. Well set to earn a stellar reputation.

2014 Beaune, Volnay, Pommard hailed once again. Attractive fresh reds of
medium density but lovely fragrance.

2013 Yet more horrific hail in Côte de Beaune. Small crop for Nuits, delicious
perfumed wines for those who waited, with crunchy energy.

2012 Very small crop of fine wines in Côte de Nuits. Côte de Beaune even
worse. Exuberant yet classy.

2011 Some parallels with 2007. But thicker skins in 2011 mean more structured
wine. Starting to be accessible

2010 Turning into a great classic, pure, fine-boned yet also with impressive
density. Start village wines, keep top wines to 2030.

2009 Beautiful, ripe, plump reds. Still adolescent, but some already accessible.
Beware overripe examples. Now to 2030?

2008 Fine, fresh wines from those who avoided fungal diseases; choose
carefully. Best show Pinot purity, opening up nicely. Now to early 2020s.

2007 Small crop of attractive, perfumed wines. Don't expect real density. Rather
good in Côte de Beaune. Start drinking up.

2006 Attractive year in Côte de Nuits (less rain), start looking at them now.
Côte de Beaune reds good now. Best to 2025.

Fine vintages: 05 03 02 99 96 (drink or keep) 95 93 90 88 85 78 71 69 66 64
62 61 59 (mature).

White burgundy

Côte d'Or White wines are now rarely made for ageing as long as they did
20 years ago, but top wines should still improve for up to 10 years. Most
Mâconnais (St-Véran, Mâcon-Villages) usually best drunk early (2–3 yrs).

2016 Frost damage widespread but vineyards that survived produced good
crop of juicily attractive wines.

2015 Rich, concentrated, from warm, dry summer. Most had sense to pick
early and have done well, later wines may be too heavy. Similar to 2009.

2014 Finest, most consistent vintage for a generation. White fruit flavours, ripe
but fresh, elegant and balanced. Successful whites throughout Burgundy.

2013 July hail mostly spared white vineyards. Those who picked early made
concentrated, lively wines but late-picked examples are flabby. Drink soon.

2012 Tiny production, poor flowering and repeated hailstorms. Decent weather
later very intense wines, beginning to show well.

2011 Fine potential for conscientious producers, some flesh and good balance,
but it was easy to overcrop. Attractive early and drinking well.

2010 Exciting wines with good fruit-acid balance, some damaged by September
storms. Starting to develop exotic aromatics. Now to 2020.

2009 Full crop, healthy grapes, two styles: first rate wines to keep from early
pickers, otherwise can be flabbily unbalanced.

2008 Small crop, ripe flavours, high acidity. Most reaching apogee, top to 2020.

Fine vintages (all ready): 05 02 99 96 93 92 85 79 73 59.

Chablis

Grand Cru Chablis of vintages with both strength and acidity can age superbly
for 10 years or more; Premiers Crus proportionately less, but give them 3 years
at least.

2016 Hail, frost, more hail, hardly any wine. Hurry up 2017, please.

2015 Hot, dry summer; rich, ripe wines with a concentrated core.
2014 Excellent early crop, happy vignerons. Saline, fresh; well worth keeping.
2013 Small crop, late harvest, rot issues. Mixed bag, some fine, drink up rest.
2012 Small crop, mostly very fine. Early pickers ultra-concentrated, classically
    austere; late pickers soft, low acid, after rain. Start to drink.
2011 Early season, large crop of attractive wines. Similar to 2002. Ready to drink.
2010 Harvested at same time as Côte d'Or; excellent results. Fine vintage: body,
    powerful mineral acidity. Great year for classical Chablis. Now to 2030.

Beaujolais

2016 Large crop of juicy wines, most escaped frost and hail. 15 Massive wines,
best may be outstanding, others alcoholic monsters. 14 Fine crop, enjoyable
now but keepable. 13 Late vintage with mixed results. 12 Tiny crop, economic
misery, vineyards abandoned. 11 Refined, classy wines, drinking well.
10 Compact and concentrated, maturing now.

Southwest France

2016 Long, mild, wet winter, cold showery spring, late flowering, widespread
    disease with local hail. Crop small, but long, hot, dry summer a tonic.
2015 Apart from some hail and storms, year of outstanding promise,
    overshadowing even 2014.
2014 Started with a cool winter, ended gloriously. Sweet whites outstanding.
2013 Initially thought to be disastrous, some good wines made by top growers.
2012 Good, though crop reduced by poor weather early on.
2011 Good, some Cahors, Madiran rather overstated. Excellent whites.
2010 First of run of Indian summers ensured good crop overall. Bigger reds
    especially now drinking well. Others OTT.

The Midi

2016 Very dry; ripe, healthy grapes, low quantity.
2015 Ripe fruit, balanced with elegant tannins, continuing to develop beautifully.
2014 Tricky year: hail in La Clape, Minervois; best have turned out very well.
    Picking before rain was key.
2013 Some lovely wines, developing nicely, some areas better than others.
2012 Quantity down, quality good; wines drinking well.
2011 Coolish summer, so fresher wines, nicely balanced. Quality, quantity good.

Northern Rhône

Depending on site and style, can be as long-lived as burgundies. White
Hermitage can keep for as long as red. Hard to generalize; don't be in a hurry.
2016 Good to very good, reds harmonious, hold pure fruit, made by marvellous
    Sept after much mildew. Good, clear whites.
2015 Excellent reds, wonderful Hermitage, Côte-Rôtie. Full, whites can be heady.
2014 Plump reds, depth over time. Excellent whites: content, style, freshness.
2013 Very good reds, with tight body, crisp tannin and freshness. 15–20 years
    life. Exceptional whites (Hermitage, St-Joseph, St-Péray).
2012 Very good Hermitage, open-book Côte-Rôtie. Fresh reds come together
    well, will last 15 years+. Whites have style, freshness (Condrieu).
2011 Gd Hermitage, Cornas. Côte-Rôtie more body recently. Whites satisfactory.
2010 Top notch. Reds: marvellous depth, balance, freshness. Long-lived. Côte-
    Rôtie as good as 78. Very good Condrieu, rich whites elsewhere.
2009 Excellent, sun-packed wines. Some rich Hermitage, very full Côte-Rôtie.
    Best Crozes, St-Joseph have aged well. Rather big whites: can live.

2008 Rain. Top names best. Good, clear whites. Reds: 8–12 years.

2007 Attractive depth, ageing well, if a little light. Best: 18 years+. Good whites.

Southern Rhône

2016 Very good, excellent for some (Châteauneuf). Rich, dense reds, great
length/style. Sun-filled whites, plenty of body; stash some away.

2015 Very good: rich, dark, lots of body, firm tannins, often enticing flair.
Quality high across board; cheap reds value. Very good, full whites.

2014 Good in places, aromatic finesse returns to Châteauneuf. Best names
best; dilution issue. NB Gigondas, Rasteau, Cairanne. Fresh whites.

2013 Tiny crop. Slow-burn reds, very low Grenache yields: atypical wines.
Châteauneuf best: old vines Gd-value Côtes du Rhône. Very good whites.

2012 Full reds, lively, good tannins. Open-book vintage. Food-friendly whites.

2011 Sunny; supple, can be fat, drink quite early. Alcohol issue. Decent whites.

2010 Outstanding. Full-bodied, balanced reds. Tiptop Châteauneuf. Clear-
fruited, well-packed tannins. Whites deep, long.

2009 Dense reds. Drought: some baked features, grainy tannins. Gd Rasteau.
Sound whites.

2008 Dodgy; life 12–15 years (top names). Very good, lively whites, to drink.

2007 Very good: Grenache-only wines intense. Exceptional Châteauneuf (top
names), especially with Mourvèdre.

Champagne

2016 Sunless, wet spring, warm July, hot Aug, saved vintage. Interesting
Pinot N; Chard variable. Very small crop: minimal in Aube, third down
in Marne. Reserve wines will be in demand.

2015 Warmest, driest summer for years. Great Pinots N/M: Chard more
uneven, some too broad. Jury still out.

2014 Challenging, variable. Chard best (as Chablis). Pinots N/M tainted by
Asian fruit fly. Better in Aube. Unlikely to be vintage year.

2013 Potentially brilliant for classic cool Chard of Côte des Blancs. Pinot N hit
and miss – glorious in Aÿ.

2012 Exquisite Pinots N/M, best since 1952? Chards less brilliant.

2011 Lack of proper maturity, structure. Against trend, some fine growers,
daring houses made decent wine.

2010 Difficult for Pinots N/M. Chard initially firm, tastes better and better,
good base for NV cuvées.

2009 Ripeness, elegance, perfect balance. Unfairly in shadow of 2008, can be
as fine: Louis Roederer Cristal, rich Bollinger, Côte aux Enfants still red.

Fine vintages: 08 07 05 04 02 00 98 96 95 92 90 89 88 82 76.

The Loire

2016 Complicated: April frost, then floods, mildew, sunburn; around a third
below average but quality good. Sancerre spared.

2015 Very dry summer then late rain, Pinot N survived. Good to very good
except Muscadet (August rain).

2014 Well-balanced dry whites, ripe reds. Outstanding Muscadet.

2013 Low sugar, high acidity. Some attractive, early drinking; a little Anjou sweet.

2012 Frost, widespread mildew. Melon de Bourgogne, Sauv Bl high quality plus
some reds, little sweet wine.

2011 Topsy-turvy. Rot in Muscadet. Quality very variable. Top sweet Anjou.

2010 Beautifully balanced dry whites, great Anjou sweet. Reds quite often
better than 2009. Long ageing potential.

Alsace

2016 Wet spring, dry July, some heat stress. Growers pleased, good volumes, all fine. Little botrytis.

2015 Rich vintage, one of driest ever. Top growers like wines across board more and more.

2014 Gewurz and Pinot Gr attacked by Suzuki fruit fly. Ries wonderful, generous, great acidity.

2013 Becoming a classic vintage, now opening up. Great potential, esp for Ries.

2012 Small crop of concentrated wines, in dry style of 2010.

2011 Round, fruity wines of charm, aroma; early drinking.

2010 Very small crop, excellent, some great, for long keeping, most naturally dry.

2009 Great Pinot Gr, Gewurz; some fine late-harvest wines.

AOP and IGP: what's happening in France

The Europe-wide introduction of AOP (*Appellation d'Origine Protegée*) and IGP (*Indication Géographique Protegée*) means that these terms may now appear on labels. AC/AOC will continue to be used, but for simplicity and brevity this book now uses IGP for all former VDP.

Abymes Sav w ★→★★ Hilly area nr Chambéry next to Aprémont. Fresh DYA Vin de SAV AC cru (300 ha). Jacquère grape (80% min) Growers: Ducret, Giachino, Labbe, Perrier, Ravier, Sabots de Venus.

Ackerman Lo r p w (dr) (sw) sp ★→★★★ Major pan-Lo, expansionist NÉGOCIANT. First SAUMUR sparkling firm (1811). Ackerman incl: Celliers du Prieuré (ANJOU), Donatien-Bahuaud and Drouet (Pays Nantais), Monmousseau (Montrichard), Perruche (Saumur), Rémy-Pannier, Varière (Anjou).

AC or AOC (Appellation Contrôlée) / AOP Government control of origin and production (but not quality) of most French wines; around 45 per cent of total. Now being converted to AOP (*Appellation d'Origine Protegée* – which is much nearer the truth than *Contrôlée*).

Agenais SW Fr r p w ★ DYA IGP of Lot-et-Garonne. DOMS such as Boiron, Lou Gaillot and Campet better than boring co-ops, but famous prunes (Agen Provocateurs) better, esp preserved in eau de vie.

Alain Chabanon, Dom L'doc ★★★ Once pioneering MONTPEYROUX producer. Campredon, Esprit de Font Caude, MERLOT-based Merle aux Alouettes. Delicious pair of whites, Le Petit Trélans and age-worthy Trélans are both VERMENTINO/ CHENIN BL, in differing proportions.

Allemand, Thiérry N Rh r ★★★ 90′ 91′ 94′ 95′ 98′ 99′ 00′ 01′ 02 03 04 05′ 06′ 07′ 08′ 09′ 10′ 11′ 12′ 13′ 14′ 15′ 16′ Wonderful CORNAS 5-ha DOM, low sulphur, organic. Intense wines, smokily fruited. Top is Reynard (mighty, complex; 20 yrs+), Chaillot drinks earlier.

Alliet, Philippe Lo r w ★★★→★★★★ 05′ 06 08 09′ 10′ 11 12 14′ 15′ (16) Excellent CHINON (17 ha) CAB FR. Ageability. Wines from low yields: Tradition VIEILLES VIGNES 50-yr-old+ vines planted on gravel. Two steep limestone v'yds e of Chinon: L'Huisserie and Coteau Noire. Joined by son Pierre.

Aloxe-Corton Burg r w ★★→★★★ 99′ 02′ 03 05′ 08 09′ 10′ 11 12′ 14 15′ (16) The n end of CÔTE DE BEAUNE, famous for GRANDS CRUS CORTON, CORTON-CHARLEMAGNE, but less interesting at village or PREMIER CRU level. Reds attractive if not overextracted. Best DOMS: Follin-Arbelet, Senard, Terregelesses, TOLLOT-BEAUT.

Alquier, Jean-Michel L'doc r w Stellar FAUGÈRES producer. White MARSANNE/ ROUSSANNE/GRENACHE Des Vignes au Puits. Also SAUV Pierres Blanches; red CUVÉES Les Premières (younger vines); Maison Jaune, only in gd Grenache yrs; Les

Bastides (old higher-altitude SYRAH); new Syrah-based Les Grandes Bastides d'Alquier with longer ageing in new oak.

Alsace (r) w (sw) (sp) ★★ →★★★★ 04 05 06 08' 09 10' 11 12 13 14 15' 16 Sheltered e slope of Vosges and 1800 sun hours make France's Rhine wines: aromatic, fruity, full-strength, drier styles back in vogue. Still much sold by variety (PINOT BL, RIES, GEWURZ). Yet rich diversity of 13 geological formations (incl granite, gneiss, limestone, marly clay) shapes best terroir-driven wines that age well, esp Ries, up to 20 yrs as GRAND CRU. Formerly fragile *Pinot N improving fast* (esp 10 12). *See* VENDANGE TARDIVE, SÉLECTION DES GRAINS NOBLES.

Alsace Grand Cru Al ★★★ →★★★★ 00 05 06 07 08' 09 10 11 12 13' 14 15' ★★★ AC. Restricted to 51 of best-named v'yds (approx 1600 ha, 800 in production) and four noble grapes (RIES, PINOT GR, GEWURZ, MUSCAT.) Production rules require higher min ripeness. Concept of local management allows extra rules specific to each cru. PINOT N's GC status still to be decided, but surely overdue.

Amiel, Mas Rouss r w sw ★★★ Leading MAURY estate combines innovation, tradition. Exemplary CÔTES DU ROUSS, MAURY, IGP. Look for Vol de Nuit from v. old CARIGNAN, GRENACHE-based Vers le Nord, Origine, Altaïr, others. Plus young grenat (Maury version of RIMAGE), venerable RANCIO VDN 20- to 40-yr-old Maury.

Amirault, Yannick Lo ★★★ →★★★★ 05' 06 08' 09' 10' 11 12 14' 15' (16) Organic. Yannick and son Benoît top growers in BOURGUEIL (20 ha)/ST-NICOLAS-DE-BOURGUEIL (10 ha). Best CUVÉES: La Petite CAVE, Le Grand Clos, Les Quartiers (Bourgueil); La Mine (St-Nicolas). La Source early drinking.

Angerville, Marquis d' C d'O r w ★★★★ Bio superstar in VOLNAY, esp legendary CLOS des Ducs (MONOPOLE), but Champans, Taillepieds also first rate. *See also* DOM DU PÉLICAN for Jura interests.

Anglès, Ch d' L'doc ★★★ Old LA CLAPE estate successfully transformed by Eric Fabre, ex-technical director of CH LAFITE, captivated by MOURVÈDRE. Unoaked Classique (r p w), age-worthy oaked *grand vin* (r w).

Anjou Lo r p w (dr) (sw) (sp) ★ →★★★★ Both region and AC encompassing ANJOU, SAUMUR. Often better than its reputation – can be v.gd value. CHENIN BL dry whites wide range of styles from light quaffers to complex repaying bottle aging; juicy reds, incl GAMAY; fruity CAB FR-based Anjou Rouge; age-worthy but tannic ANJOU-VILLAGES, incl CAB SAUV. Mainly dry SAVENNIÈRES; lightly sweet to rich COTEAUX DU LAYON Chenin Bl; rosé (dr s/sw), sparkling mainly CRÉMANT. Sweets: buy 2010, 11, 14, 15. Avoid 12. Frost reduced crop 16.

Anjou-Coteaux de la Loire Lo w sw s/sw ★★ →★★★ 05' 07' 09 10' 11' 14 15' (16) Small (30 ha) most w ANJOU AC for sweet CHENIN BL; not so rich but more racy than COTEAUX DU LAYON. Esp CH de Putille, Delaunay, Fresche, Musset-Roullier (v.gd).

Anjou-Villages Lo r ★ →★★★ 05' 06 08 09' 10' 11 12 14' 15' (16) Red AC for more structured ANJOU (CAB FR/CAB SAUV, a few pure Cab Sauv). Tannins need to be carefully managed; best given some bottle age. Top wines gd value, esp Bergerie, Branchereau, Brizé, CADY, CH Pierre-Bise, CLOS de Coulaine, Delesvaux, Ogereau, Sauveroy, Soucherie. Sub-AC Anjou-Villages-Brissac same zone as COTEAUX DE L'AUBANCE; look for Bablut, CH de Varière (now part of ACKERMAN), Haute Perche, Montigilet, Princé, Richou, Rochelles.

Aprémont Sav w ★★ Keep up to 5 yrs. Largest cru of SAV (378 ha, 28 per cent of production) just s of Chambéry. Jacquère only grape. Producers: Aphyllantes, Blard, Boniface, Masson, Perrier, Rouzan.

Arbin Sav r ★★ Deep-coloured, lively red from MONDEUSE grapes, rather like a Lo CAB SAUV. Ideal après-ski. Drink at 1–2 yrs.

Arbois Jura r p w (sp) ★★ →★★★ 05' 08 09 10' 12 14' 15' (16) AC of n Jura, birthplace (*see* museum) of Louis Pasteur. Gd CHARD, gamey SAVAGNIN whites, VIN JAUNE from eg. (terroir-driven) Stephane TISSOT, fresh "ouillé" styles from DOM DU

PÉLICAN (formerly Puffeney, now D'ANGERVILLE from VOLNAY), oxidative whites from Overnoy/Houillon, plus all-rounders AVIET, Pinte, Renardières. Poulsard and Trousseau reds usually bettered by PINOT N.

Ariège SW Fr r p w ★ **14 15** (16) Small but interesting IGP between Toulouse and Pyrénées. Bio DOM des Coteaux d'Engravies (esp varietal SYRAH) way ahead of field, but try Dom de Lastronques.

Arjolle, Dom de l' L'doc ★★★ Large CÔTES DE THONGUE estate, also PAYS D'OC single varietals. Z for ZIN, K for CARMENÈRE plus original blends, both L'DOC, B'X.

Arlaud C d'O r ★★★→★★★★ Leading MOREY-ST-DENIS estate energized by Cyprien Arlaud and siblings. Beautifully poised, modern wines with depth and class from exceptional BOURGOGNE Roncevie up to GRANDS CRUS CHARMES-CHAMBERTIN, CLOS DE LA ROCHE.

Arlay, Ch d' Jura r p w sw ★→★★ Ancient, aristocratic Jura estate based in imposing CH: Sound all-round offer of all colours incl VIN JAUNE.

Arlot, Dom de l' C d'O r w ★★→★★★ AXA-owned leading NUITS-ST-GEORGES estate, formerly (to 2011) closely identified with whole-bunch fermentation. Try CLOS des Forêts St Georges for haunting fragrance, also VOSNE-ROMANÉE Suchots, ROMANÉE-ST-VIVANT. Don't ignore whites.

Armand, Comte C d'O r ★★★ Sole owner of exceptional CLOS des Epeneaux in POMMARD and other v'yds in AUXEY, VOLNAY. Great wines, esp since 1999, poise, longevity, but tiny crops 2012–16.

Aube Champ S v'yds of CHAMP, aka Côte des Bar. V.gd PINOT N **12 14 15'**. Impressive new MOËT winery at Gyé-sur-Seine wholly devoted to rosé Champ, four million bottles/yr.

Aupilhac, Dom d' L'doc Early leader in MONTPEYROUX, now followed by several others. Sylvain Fadat favours old-vine Le CARIGNAN (his lst wine in 1989) and higher-altitude v'yds, as well as CINSAULT, Les Servières and L'DOC classics.

Auxey-Duresses C d'O r w ★★ **99' 02' 03 05' 08 09' 10' 11 12 14 15'** (16) CÔTE DE BEAUNE village in valley behind MEURSAULT. Fresh light-tasting *whites offer value*, reds now ripening more easily, so less rustic. Best: (r) COMTE ARMAND, COCHE-DURY, Gras, MAISON LEROY (Les Boutonniers), Moulin aux Moines, Prunier; (w) Lafouge, Leroux, ROULOT.

Aveyron SW Fr r p w ★ IGP DYA. ★★ Nicolas Carmarans, fan of rare grapes ie. Négret de Banyars, emerges as star of these country wines, raised alongside AOPS ENTRAYGUES, ESTAING, MARCILLAC. More orthodox ★ DOMS Bertau, Pleyjean.

Aviet, Lucien Jura Fine ARBOIS grower, nicknamed Bacchus. Gd-value, eg. attractive light Poulsard and tangy SAVAGNIN.

Avize Champ Fine Côte des Blancs CHARD village. Excellent growers' wines: Agrapart, Corbon, Selosse; great co-op Union Champagne.

Aÿ Champ Revered PINOT N village, home of BOLLINGER, DEUTZ. Mix of merchants and growers' wines, some made in barrel, eg. Claude Giraud, master of Argonne oak. *Gosset-Brabant* Noirs d'Aÿ (no wood) epitome of purity. Aÿ rouge (COTEAUX CHAMPENOIS) improving with climate change.

Ayala Champ Reborn ÄY house, owned by BOLLINGER. Fine Brut Zéro, Blanc de Blancs. Ace Prestige Perle d'Ayala **08' 09 12' 13 15'**. Precision, purity. Energy under Caroline Latrine, new chef de CAVE.

Bachelet Burg r w ★★→★★★ Widespread family name in Burg C D'O. Excellent whites from B-Monnot (MARANGES), Jean-Claude B (ST-AUBIN), improving Vincent B (CHASSAGNE). Denis B (heady GEVREY-CHAMBERTIN) no relation.

Bandol Prov r p (w) ★★★ **98 99 00 01 02 03 04 05 06 07 08 09 10 11 12 13 14 15 16** Compact coastal AC; PROV's finest. Superb barrel-aged reds; ageing potential enormous. MOURVÈDRE the key, with GRENACHE, CINSAULT; stylish structured rosé from young vines, drop of white from CLAIRETTE, UGNI BLANC, occasionally SAUV BL.

Stars incl: DOMS de la Bégude, de la Laidière, Gros'Noré, La Bastide Blanche, Lafran Veyrolles, La Suffrène, Mas de la Rouvière, Pradeaux, *Pibarnon*, TEMPIER, Terrebrune, Vannières.

Banyuls Rouss r br sw ★★→★★★★ Deliciously original VDN, based on old GRENACHES NOIR, BLANC, Gris. Young vintage RIMAGE is fresh, fruity. Traditional RANCIOS, aged for many yrs, more rewarding. Serious alternative to fine old Tawny Port. Best: DOMS du Mas Blanc (★★★), la Rectorie (★★★), la Tour Vieille (★★★), Les Clos de Paulilles, Coume del Mas (★★), Madeloc, Vial Magnères. *See also* MAURY.

Baronne, Ch La L'doc ★★★ Innovative bio family estate in CORBIÈRES, by Montagne d'Alaric; min intervention in cellar. IGP Hauterive (w); Corbières Alaric, Les Chemins, Les Lanes and (CARIGNAN planted 1892) Pièce de Roche. Sulphur-free Les Chemins de Traverse, and VERMENTINO/Grenache Gris (w).

Barrique B'X (and Cognac) term for oak barrel holding 225 litres. Used globally, but global mania for excessive new oak now mercifully fading. Average price €700/barrel.

Barsac Saut w sw ★★→★★★★ 89' 90' 95 96 97 98 99' 01' 02 03' 05' 07' 09' 10' 11' 12 13 14 15 16 Neighbour of SAUT with similar botrytized wines from lower-lying limestone soil; fresher, less powerful. Can label as Barsac or Saut. Top: CAILLOU, CLIMENS, COUTET, DOISY-DAËNE, DOISY-VÉDRINES, NAIRAC.

Barthod, Ghislaine C d'O r ★★★→★★★★ A reason to fall in love with CHAMBOLLE-MUSIGNY, if you haven't already. Wines of perfume, delicacy, yet depth, concentration. Impressive range of nine PREMIER CRUS incl Charmes, Cras, Fuées, Les Baudes.

Bâtard-Montrachet C d'O w ★★★★ 99' 00 02' 04' 05' 06 07' 08' 09' 10 11 12 13 14' 15 (16) 12-ha GRAND CRU downslope from LE MONTRACHET itself. Grand, hefty whites that should need time; more power than neighbours BIENVENUES-B-M and CRIOTS B-M. Seek out: BACHELET-Monnot, BOILLOT, CARILLON, DOM LEFLAIVE, Gagnard, FAIVELEY, LATOUR, Leroux, MOREY, Pernot, Ramonet, SAUZET, VOUGERAIE.

Baudry, Dom Bernard Lo r p w ★★→★★★ 05 06 08 09' 10' 11 12 14' 15' (16') 30 ha Cravant-les-Coteaux, gravel and limestone. V.gd CHINON across the range, from CHENIN BL whites to CAB FR (r p); early-drinking Les Granges to structured Les Grézeaux, CLOS Guillot, Croix Boissée. Organic; hand-harvested. 2016: half loss to frost, but high quality.

Baudry-Dutour Lo r p w (sp) ★★→★★★ 03 05' 06 08 09' 10' 11 14' 15' (16) CHINON's largest producer, incl CHX de St Louans, La Grille, La Perrière, La Roncée. Run by J-M Dutour, Christophe Baudry. Large modern winery in Panzoult. Reliable quality: light, early-drinking to age-worthy reds. Frost in 2016.

Baumard, Dom des Lo r p w sw sp ★★→★★★ 03 05' 06 07' (sw) 08 09 10 11 14 15 (16) Controversial producer of ANJOU, esp CHENIN BL whites, incl SAVENNIÈRES (CLOS St Yves, Clos du Papillon), Clos Ste Catherine. Believes in cryoextraction (freezing grapes) for QUARTS DE CHAUME.

Baux-de-Provence, Les Prov r p w ★★→★★★ 09 10 11 12 13 14 15 16 V'yds on dramatic bauxite outcrop of Alpilles by tourist village of Les Baux: sadly tourism can breed complacency. White from CLAIRETTE, GRENACHE BLANC, Rolle, ROUSSANNE. Reds CAB SAUV, SYRAH, GRENACHE. Most v'yds organic. Best estate remains TRÉVALLON: Cab/Syrah blend. Also CH Romanin, DOM Hauvette, Estoublon, Mas de la Dame, Milan, Ste Berthe, Terres Blanches, Valdition.

Béarn SW Fr r p w ★→★★ (r) 14 (15) (p w) AOP DYA. Pink wines are summer-popular. ★DOMS de la Callabère, Lapeyre/Guilhémas gd reds. Rare whites from Ruffiat de Moncade grape. Co-op at ★Bellocq now merged with JURANÇON.

Beaucastel, Ch de S Rh r w ★★★★ 78' 81' 85 88 89' 90' 95' 96' 97 98 99' 00' 01' 03' 04 05' 06' 07' 08 09' 10' 11' 12' 13' 14' 15' 16' organic CHÂTEAUNEUF estate: old MOURVÈDRE, 100-yr-old ROUSSANNE. Smoky, darkly fruited, recently smoother

New on the Beaujolais block

BEAUJ is one of greater Burg's most dynamic regions, where prices remain relatively affordable: so much so that many C D'O producers are investing in land down s: JADOT, Louis BOILLOT, Thibault LIGER-BELAIR in MOULIN-À-VENT; BOUCHARD, DROUHIN, LAFARGE-Vial in FLEURIE. Others sniffing around.... Alternatively look to hungry "new kid in town" producers ie. Julie Balagny or Julien Sunier in Fleurie, P-H Thillardon in CHÉNAS, Richard Rottiers in Moulin-à-Vent.

wines, drink at 2 yrs or from 7–8. Dense, top quality 60% Mourvèdre Hommage à Jacques Perrin (r). **Wonderful old-vine Roussanne**: enjoy over 5–25 yrs. Genuine, serious own-vines CÔTES DU RH Coudoulet de Beaucastel (r), lives 8 yrs+. Famille Perrin CAIRANNE, GIGONDAS (v.gd), RASTEAU, VINSOBRES (best) all gd, authentic. Gd organic Perrin Nature Côtes du Rh (r w). Gd, growing N Rh merchant venture, Nicolas Perrin (stylish). (*See also* Tablas Creek, California.)

Beaujolais r (p) (w) ★ DYA. Basic appellation of the huge Beauj region. Often dull but don't need to be – try those from hills around Bois d'Oingt. Can now be sold as COTEAUX BOURGUIGNONS.

Beaujolais Primeur / Nouveau Beauj More of an event than a drink. The BEAUJ of the new vintage, hurriedly made for release at midnight on the 3rd Wednesday in Nov. Enjoy juicy fruit but don't let it put you off real thing.

Beaujolais-Villages Beauj r ★★ 13 14 15' 16 Middle category between straight BEAUJ and ten named crus, eg. MOULIN-À-VENT. Often too simple but best sites around Beaujeu, Lantigné worth waiting for.

Beaumes-de-Venise S Rh r (p) (w) br ★★ (r) 09' 10' 12' 13' 15' 16' (MUSCAT) DYA. CÔTES DU RH village s of GIGONDAS, known for VDN Muscat apéritif/dessert. Serve v. cold: grapey, honeyed, can be fresh, fine eg. DOMS Beaumalric, Bernardins (musky, traditional), Coyeux, Durban (rich, long life), Fenouillet (brisk), JABOULET, Pigeade (fresh, v.gd), VIDAL-FLEURY, co-op Rhonéa. Also punchy, grainy reds, best in sunny yrs. CH Redortier, de Fenouillet, Doms Cassan, Durban, Ferme St Martin (organic), St-Amant (gd w). Leave for 2–3 yrs. Simple whites (some dry MUSCAT, VIOGNIER), lively rosés are Côtes du Rh.

Beaumont des Crayères Champ sp Côte d'Epernay co-op making model PINOT M-based Grande Rés NV. Vintage Fleur de Prestige top value 04 06 08' 10 12' 13 15'. Great CHARD-led CUVÉE Nostalgie 02' 06 09. New Fleur de Meunier BRUT Nature 09 12' 15'.

Beaune C d'O r (w) ★★★ 02' 03 05' 07 08 09' 10' 11 12 14 15' (16) Centre of Burg wine trade, classic merchants: BOUCHARD, CHAMPY, CHANSON, DROUHIN, JADOT, LATOUR, Remoissenet and young pretenders Gambal, Lemoine, Leroux, Roche de Bellène, plus iconic HOSPICES DE BEAUNE. No GRANDS CRUS v'yds but some graceful, perfumed PREMIER CRU reds eg. Bressandes, Cras, Vignes Franches; more power from Grèves, and some exciting whites, Aigrots, CLOS St Landry, and esp CLOS DES MOUCHES (Drouhin).

Becker, Caves J Al r w ★ →★★★ Organic estate, now certified bio. Stylish wines, incl poised, taut GRAND CRU Froehn in GEWURZ, RIES 06 09 10' 13 14' 15'. Fine Ries GC Mandelberg elegant in 10 13 14.

Bellet Prov r p w ★★ Minuscule AC; About 70 ha within city of Nice; rarely seen elsewhere. White from Rolle surprisingly age-worthy and delicious. Braquet, Folle Noire for light red (DYA). 15 valiant producers: CH de Bellet, oldest and under new ownership; also CLOS St Vincent, Collet de Bovis, DOM de la Source, Les Coteaux de Bellet, Toasc.

Bellivière, Dom de Lo r w sw (sp) ★★ →★★★ 05' 08 09' 10' 11' 14' 15' (16) 15-ha bio DOM of Christine and Eric Nicolas: outstanding CHENIN BL – JASNIÈRES and COTEAUX DU LOIR, peppery red Pineau d'Aunis.

Bergerac SW Fr r p w dr sw ★→★★★ 09' 10 11 12 14 (15) AOP adjoining B'x, wines for slender purses. Whites (dr sw) mostly from SÉM, reds mostly MERLOT. CH de la Jaubertie, ★★Ch Tour de Grangemont, ★★★CLOS des Verdots, DOM du Cantonnet, Fleur de Thénac, Jonc-Blanc, *Tour des Gendres*. For other gd growers, *see* sub-AOPS MONBAZILLAC, MONTRAVEL, PÉCHARMANT, ROSETTE, SAUSSIGNAC.

Berlioz, Gilles Sav V.gd boutique bio dom (3.5 ha) in CHIGNIN. Four small parcels planted: Altesse, MONDEUSE, Jacquère, Persan. Wines: Chez l'Odette (Jacquère), El Hem, Le Jaja, Les Filles, Les Fripons.

Berthet-Bondet, Jean Jura r w ★★ Ace maker of CH-CHALON VIN JAUNE and Côte de Jura Naturé: SAVAGNIN grape, not aged under flor yeast. Delicious Rubis (Trousseau, Poulsard, smidgin of PINOT N).

Bertrand, Gérard L'doc r p w ★★ Keenly ambitious grower now one of biggest in MIDI; Villemajou (CORBIÈRES cru Boutenac), Laville-Bertou (MINERVOIS-La Livinière), l'Aigle (LIMOUX), IGP Hauterive Cigalus, la Sauvageonne (Terrasses du Larzac); recently acquired CH de la Soujeole (Malepère), v'yds in Cabrières. Flagship: l'Hospitalet (LA CLAPE). Highly aspirational, expensive CLOS d'Ora (Minervois-La Livinière).

Besserat de Belfont Champ Épernay house specializing in gently sparkling CHAMP (old CRÉMANT style). Part of LANSON-BCC group. Respectable rising quality, always gd value, esp **13** 14.

Beyer, Léon Al r w ★★→★★★ Intense, dry wines often needing 10 yrs+ bottle age. Superb RIES Comtes d'Eguisheim **08** 10 13 14', actually GRAND CRU PFERSIGBERG (not mentioned on label). Ideal gastronomic, fully mature wines found in many Michelin-starred restaurants. Serious PINOT N **10' 12** (a '59 still in gd shape).

Bichot, Maison Albert Burg r w ★★→★★★ Major BEAUNE merchant/grower. Steadily more impressive wines in a powerful rather oaky style. Best wines from own DOMS, CLOS Frantin (NUITS), du Pavillon (Beaune), LONG-DEPAQUIT (CHAB), .

Bienvenues-Bâtard-Montrachet C d'O ★★★→★★★★ 02' 04 05 06 07 08 09 10 11 12 13 14' 15 (16) Fractionally lighter, earlier-maturing version of BÂTARD, with tempting creamy texture. Best: CARILLON, FAIVELEY, LEFLAIVE, Pernot, Ramonet.

Billecart-Salmon Champ Family-run house with new horsepower from financial partner, exquisite vintage CUVÉES fermented in wood. Superb CLOS St-Hilaire BLANC DE NOIRS **96** **98** **99** 02', NF Billecart 02' **98** 99 12', top BLANC DE BLANCS **08'**, BRUT **04** great value; fine, digestible Extra Brut ★★★NV. Oaked Cuvée Sous Bois. Exquisite ★★★★*Elizabeth Salmon Rosé* 02, 06.

Bize, Simon C d'O r w ★★★ Late Patrick Bize made exemplary range from BOURGOGNE (r W) to GRAND CRU by way of multiple bottlings of fine SAVIGNY-LÈS-BEAUNE, incl six PREMIERS CRUS (Aux Guettes, Vergelesses). Quality maintained.

Blagny C d'Or ★★→★★★ 99' 02' 03' 05' 08 09' 10' 11 12 13 14 15' (16) Hamlet on hillside above MEURSAULT and PULIGNY. Austere yet fragrant reds sadly out of fashion as growers replant with CHARD, sold as Meursault-Blagny PREMIER CRU. Best red v'yds: La Jeunelotte, Pièce sous le Bois, Sous le Dos d'Ane. Best growers (r): LEROUX, Martelet de Cherisey, Matrot.

Blanc de Blancs Any white wine made from white grapes only, esp CHAMP. Indication of style, not of quality.

Blanc de Noirs White (or slightly pink or "blush") wine from red grapes, esp CHAMP: generally rich, even blunt, in style. But change is in air, with ever more refined PINOT N and new techniques.

Blanck, Paul & Fils Al r w ★★→★★★ Grower at Kientzheim. Finest from 6-ha GRAND CRU Furstentum (RIES, GEWURZ, PINOT GR), Grand Cru SCHLOSSBERG (great Ries **08'** 10 12 13' 14 15). Excellent quality Classique generic range: tiptop, great value.

Blanquette de Limoux L'doc w sp ★★ Great-value bubbles from cool hills sw of Carcassonne; older history than CHAMP. 90% Mauzac with a little CHARD, CHENIN BL. AC CRÉMANT de Limoux, more elegant with Chard, Chenin Bl, PINOT N, and less

Mauzac. Large co-op with Sieur d'Arques and several other labels. Also Antech, Delmas, Laurens, RIVES-BLANQUES, Robert and newcomers DOMS La Coumje-Lumet, Les Hautes Terres, Jo Riu, Monsieur S.

Blaye B'x r ★→★★ 09' 10' 11 12 14 15 16 Designation for better reds (lower yields, higher v'yd density, longer maturation) from AC BLAYE-CÔTES DE B'X.

Blaye-Côtes de Bordeaux B'x r w ★→★★ 10' 12 14 15 16' Mainly MERLOT-led red AC on right bank of Gironde. A little dry white (mainly SAUV BL). Best CHX: Bel Air la Royère, Cantinot, des Tourtes, Gigault (CUVÉE Viva), Haut-Bertinerie, Haut-Colombier, Haut-Grelot, Jonqueyres, Monconseil-Gazin, Mondésir-Gazin, Montfollet, Roland la Garde, Segonzac. Also Charron and CAVE des Hauts de Gironde (Tutiac) co-op for whites.

Boeckel, Dom Emile Al Long-est estate in fairy-tale Mittelbergheim, now expanded to 23 ha in best marl and sandstone sites of Bas Rhin. Great RIES esp Wibbelsberg, Clos Eugenie 10 12 13. GRAND CRU Zotzenberg unique site for top SYLVANER. Exemplary CRÉMANT d'Alsace.

Boillot C d'O r w Interconnected Burg growers. Look for ★★★Jean-Marc (POMMARD), oaky reds and fine, long-lived whites; ★★→★★★★Henri (DOM/merchant in MEURSAULT), potent whites and modern reds; ★★★Louis (CHAMBOLLE, married to GHISLAINE BARTHOD) and his brother ★★→★★★★Pierre (GEVREY).

Boisset, Jean-Claude Burg Ultra-successful merchant/grower group created over last 50 yrs. Boisset label and own v'yds DOM DE LA VOUGERAIE excellent. Recent additions to empire are the brands VINCENT GIRARDIN (Burg) and HENRI MAIRE (JURA). Also projects in California (Gallo connection), Canada, Chile, Uruguay.

Boizel Champ Exceptional aged BLANC DE BLANCS NV and prestige Joyau de France 02' 08 09 12' 15', Joyau Rosé 04 06 08' 09 12'. Also Grand Vintage BRUT 04 06 08' 09 12, CUVÉE Sous Bois. Fine quality, great value.

Bollinger Champ Great classic house, ever-better quality. BRUT Special NV on top form since 12; Grande Année 09 08' 05 04 02 00 97 96). PINOT N; fine GA Rosé 06 04 02. Also v.gd NV Rosé. De luxe: RD 02' to drink or keep, VIEILLES VIGNES Françaises 02 69', La Côte aux Enfants AY 09' 12' 15'. Excavated secret cellar La Gallerie 1829 a must-visit: display of venerable bottles back to 1830s, res wines to 1892. *See also* LANGLOIS-CH.

Bonneau du Martray, Dom C d'O r w (r) ★★★ (w) ★★★★ Reference producer for CORTON-CHARLEMAGNE, bought 2016 by Stanley Kroenke, owner of Screaming Eagle (California) and Arsenal football club (UK). Intense wines designed for long (c.10 yrs) ageing, glorious mix of intense fruit, underlying minerals. Small amount of fine red CORTON.

Bonnes-Mares C d'O r ★★★→★★★★ 90' 91 93 95 96' 98 99' 00 02' 03 05' 06 07 08 09' 10' 11 12' 13 14 15' (16) GRAND CRU between CHAMBOLLE-MUSIGNY and MOREY-ST-DENIS with some of latter's wilder character. Sturdy, long-lived wines, less fragrant than MUSIGNY. Best: Bernstein, BRUNO CLAIR, Drouhin-Laroze, DUJAC, Groffier, JADOT, MUGNIER, ROUMIER, DE VOGÜÉ, VOUGERAIE.

Bonnezeaux Lo w sw ★★★→★★★★ 89' 90' 95' 96' 97' 03' 05 09 10' 11' 14 15' (16) 80 ha. Rich, almost eternal CHENIN BL from s-facing slopes in COTEAUX DU LAYON. Esp: CHX de Fesles (Grands Chais de France), La Varière (ACKERMAN) and DOMS Les Grandes Vignes, de Mihoudy, du Petit Val. 1947 is still iconic.

Bordeaux r (p) w ★→★★ 15 16 Catch-all AC for generic B'x (represents nearly half region's production). Mixed quality, but usually recognizable and often value. Most brands (DOURTHE, Michel Lynch, MOUTON CADET, SICHEL) in this category. *See also* CHX Bauduc, BONNET, Lamothe Vincent, Reignac, Tour de Mirambeau.

Bordeaux Supérieur B'x r ★→★★ 09' 10' 12 14 15 16 Superior denomination to above. Higher min alc, lower yield, longer ageing. Mainly bottled at property. Consistent CHX: Camarsac, Grand Verdus, Grand Village, Grée-Laroque,

Jean Faux, La France, Landereau, Parenchère, Penin, PEY LA TOUR (Rés), Pierrail, Reignac, THIEULEY.

Borie-Manoux B'x Admirable B'x shipper. CH-owner: BATAILLEY, BEAU-SITE, LA CROIX DU CASSE, TROTTEVIEILLE and DOM DE L'EGLISE. On-line wine sales.

Bouchard Père & Fils Burg r w ★★→★★★★ Largest v'yd owner in C D'O, based in CH de Beaune, quality v. sound all round. Whites best in MEURSAULT and GRANDS CRUS, esp CHEVALIER-MONTRACHET. Flagship reds: BEAUNE Grèves, CLOS VOUGEOT, CORTON, Vigne de L'Enfant Jésus, *Volnay Caillerets Ancienne Cuvée Carnot*. Part of HENRIOT Burg interests with WILLIAM FÈVRE (CHAB), Villa Ponciago (BEAUJ).

Bouches-du-Rhône Prov r p w ★ IGP from Marseille environs. Simple, hopefully fruity, reds from s varieties, plus CAB SAUV, SYRAH, MERLOT.

Bourgeois, Henri Lo r p w ★★→★★★ 05 07 08 10 11 12 13 14' 15 (16) Leading, v. impressive SANCERRE grower/merchant run by dynamic family always investing to improve. V'gd: CHÂTEAUMEILLANT, Coteaux du Giennois, MENETOU-SALON, POUILLY-FUMÉ, QUINCY, IGP Petit Bourgeois. Best: Jadis, La Bourgeoise (r w), MD de Bourgeois, Sancerre d'Antan. These can age beautifully. Also Clos Henri (r w) in Marlborough, NZ.

Bourgogne Burg r (p) w ★→★★ (r) 05' 09' 10' 12' 13 14 15' (16) (w) 12 14' 15 (16) Ground-floor AC for Burg, ranging from mass-produced to bargain beauties from fringes of C D'O villages, top tip for value. Sometimes comes with subregion attached, eg. CÔTE CHALONNAISE, HAUTES CÔTES or local would-be appellation, Chitry, Tonnerre, VÉZELAY etc. From PINOT N (r) or CHARD (w) but can be declassified BEAUJ crus (sold as Bourgogne GAMAY).

Bourgogne Passe-Tout-Grains Burg r (p) ★ Age 1–2 yrs. Burg mix of PINOT N (more than 30%), GAMAY. Fresh, sometimes funky. Can keep longer from top C D'O DOMS eg. CHEVILLON, Clavelier, LAFARGE, ROUGET.

Bourgueil Lo r (p) ★★→★★★ 96' 03 05' 06 08 09' 10' 11 12 14' 15 (16) Dynamic AC, 1400 ha, full-bodied TOURAINE reds, rosés based on CAB FR. Gd vintages age 50 yrs+. Esp AMIRAULT, Ansodelles, Audebert, Chevalerie, Courant, de la Butte, Gambier, Herlin, Lamé Delisle Boucard, Ménard, Minière, Nau Frères, Omasson, Rochouard, Severe 2016 frost, small crop.

Bouscassé, Dom SW Fr r w ★★★ 05' 09' 10' 11 (12) (14) (15) BRUMONT's Napa style base. Reds require even more patience than his MONTUS. Petit Courbu-based dry PACHERENC (little or no oak) gorgeous.

Bouvet-Ladubay Lo (r) p w sp ★★→★★★ SAUMUR and CRÉMANT DE LO now back in hands of Monmousseau family. Patrice Monmousseau (President) daughter Juliette (CEO). CUVÉE Trésor (p w) best, others: Cent Cinquantenaire, Island Antarctic (DEMI-SEC).

Bouzereau C D'O r w ★★→★★★ Shake a bush in MEURSAULT and a Bouzereau will fall out. Jean-Baptiste (DOM Michel B), Vincent B or B-Gruère & Filles all gd sources for whites.

Bouzeron Burg w ★★ 12 14' 15 (16) CÔTE CHALONNAISE village with unique AC for ALIGOTÉ, with stricter rules and greater potential than straight BOURGOGNE ALIGOTÉ. BOUCHARD PÈRE, Briday, FAIVELEY, Jacqueson gd; A & P DE VILLAINE outstanding.

Bouzy Rouge Champ r ★★★ 96 97 99 02 09 12 15 Still red of famous PINOT N village. Formerly like v. light burg, now with more intensity (climate change, better viticulture) also refinement. CLOS Colin and Paul Bara best producers.

Brocard, J-M Chab w ★★→★★★ Jean-Marc created dynamic business with ACS in and around CHAB. Son Julien added bio principles. Quality and commercial sense combined. Try DOM Ste Claire and exceptional GRAND CRU Les Preuses.

Brouilly Beauj r ★★ 09' 13' 14' 15' 16 Largest of ten BEAUJ crus: solid, rounded wines with some depth of fruit, approachable early but can age 3–5 yrs. Top growers: CH de la Chaize, Chermette, Dubost, Lapalu, Michaud, Piron, Ch Thivin.

Brumont, Alain SW Fr r w ★★★ Super-growths Le Tyre, Montus, Bouscassé command field, despite trend to easier-drinking MADIRAN, as reflected by Brumont's ★ Torus and range of quaffable IGPs. ★★★ PACHERENCS (dr sw) outstanding.

Brut Champ Term for dry classic wines of CHAMP. Most houses have reduced dosage (adjustment of sweetness) in recent yrs. But great Champ can still be made at 8/9g residual sugar.

Smash your Champ flutes: you get more Champ flavour in (big) wine glasses.

Brut Ultra / Zéro Term for bone-dry wines (no dosage) in CHAMP (also known as Brut Nature) back in fashion, mixed success. Needs ripe yr, old vines, max care, eg. Pol Roger Pur.

Bugey Sav r p w sp ★→★★ AC 2009 (380 ha) for sparkling, pétillant, still. Three sectors: Belley, Cerdon, Montagnieu. Eight associated Bugey ACs. Whites mainly CHARD also incl ALIGOTÉ, Jacquère, Roussette. Reds: GAMAY, MONDEUSE, PINOT N. Growers: Angelot, Lingot-Martin, Monin, Peillot, Pellerin.

Buxy, Caves de Burg r (p) w ★→★★ Leading CÔTE CHALONNAISE co-op for decent CHARD, PINOT N, source of many merchants' own-label ranges. Easily largest supplier of AC MONTAGNY.

Buzet SW Fr r (p) (w) ★★ 12 14 15 B'x with Gascon touch. AOP led by improving co-op, ★CHX de Salles, du Frandat, bio DOM Salisquet. Natural/bio ★★★ Dom de Pech best of all.

Cabernet d'Anjou Lo p s/sw ★→★★ DYA. DEMI-SEC to sweet rosé. Locally popular style, enjoyable summer quaffing, old vintages 47, 49 (★★★) v. rare but remarkable. Bablut, CADY, Chauvin, Clau de Nell, de Sauveroy, Grandes Vignes, Montgilet, Ogereau, CH PIERRE-BISE, Varière.

Cadillac-Côtes de Bordeaux B'x r ★→★★ 10' 12 14 15 16 Long, narrow, hilly zone on right bank of Garonne. Mainly MERLOT with CABS SAUV, FR. Medium-bodied, fresh reds; quality extremely varied. Wine tourism award in 2016. Best: Alios de Ste-Marie, Biac, Carignan, *Carsin*, CLOS Chaumont, Clos Ste-Anne, de Ricaud, Grand-Mouëÿs, Le Doyenné, Lezongars, Mont-Pérat, Plaisance, Puy Bardens, *Reynon*, Suau.

Cady, Dom Lo r p w sw sp ★★ →★★ 03 05' 07' (sw) 09 10' 11' 14' 15' (16') V.gd family in St Aubin de Luigné. Alexandre now taking over from parents. Full range ANJOU with accent on CHENIN incl COTEAUX DU LAYON esp Chaume, Les Varennes.

Cahors SW Fr r ★★ →★★★★ 09' 10 11 12' 14 (15) (16) AOP based on min 70% MALBEC. Some growers trying to copy Argentina rather than stick to local typicity. Three discernible styles: easy entry-level; bigger, sometimes with oak; blockbuster. All red (some white IGPs). Early-drinking from ★★CHX Paillas, CLOS Coutale. Wait for ★★★Ch Chambert, DOM de la Bérengeraie, Lo Domeni, ★★Chx Armandière, Clos Troteligotte, Croze de Pys, Gaudou, La Coustarelle, Nozières, Ponzac, Vincens. Longer still for ★★★*Clos de Gamot* (★★★★Vignes Centenaires), Clos Triguedina. Modern: ★★★CH DU CÈDRE, Clos d'Un Jour, DOM du Prince, Lamartine, La Périé, La Reyne, Les Croisille; ★★La Caminade, Eugénie. Cult ★★★★Dom Cosse-Maisonneuve straddles range.

Cailloux, Les S Rh r (w) ★★★ 78' 79' 81' 85' 89' 90' 95' 96' 98' 99 00' 01 03' 04' 05' 06' 07' 09' 10' 11' 12' 13' 14 15' 16' 18 ha CHÂTEAUNEUF DOM; elegant, profound GRENACHE, joyous handmade reds. Special wine Centenaire, oldest Grenache 1889 noble, costly. Also DOM André Brunel (esp gd value CÔTES DU RH red Est-Ouest), sound Féraud-Brunel Côtes du Rh merchant range.

Cairanne S Rh r p w ★★→★★★ 05' 07' 09' 10' 11 12' 13' 14 15' 16' Now cru, above Villages category, from 2015 vintage. Gd DOMS, wines of character, dark fruits, mixed herbs, smoky tannins, esp CLOS Romane, Doms Alary (stylish), Amadieu (pure, organic), Ameillaud (fruit), Brusset (deep), Escaravailles (flair), Féraud-

Brunel, Grosset, Hautes Cances (traditional), Jubain, **Oratoire St Martin** (detail, classy), Présidente, Rabasse-Charavin (punchy), **Richaud** (great fruit), Famille Perrin. Food friendly, 3D *whites*.

Cal Demoura, Dom L'doc r p w ★★★ Estate to follow in TERRASSES DU LARZAC. Meticulous winemaking: try L'Etincelle with six different grape varieties (w); L'DOC blends (r) Combariolles, predominantly GRENACHE Feu Sacré, L'Infidèle.

Canard-Duchêne Champ House owned by ALAIN THIÉNOT. BRUT Vintage 08 09 12', Charles VII Prestige multi-vintage. CUVÉE Léonie ★★. Improved Authentique Cuvée (organic) 09 12'. Single-v'yd Avize Gamin12 13.

Canon-Fronsac B'x r ★★→★★★ 05' 06 08 09' 10' 11 12 14 15 16 Small enclave within FRON, otherwise same wines. 47 growers. Best: rich, full, finely structured. Try CHX Barrabaque, Canon Pécresse, Cassagne Haut-Canon la Truffière, DU GABY, Grand-Renouil, Haut-Mazeris, La Fleur Cailleau, MOULIN PEY-LABRIE, Pavillon, Vrai Canon Bouché.

Carillon C d'O w ★★★ Classic PULIGNY producer, now separated between brothers. Jacques carries on old tradition; more ambitious François added new v'yds. Top sources for PREMIERS CRUS, eg. Combettes, Perrières, Referts. Reds less interesting.

Cassis Prov (r) (p) w ★★ DYA. Fashionable pleasure port e of Marseille best-known for savoury dry whites based on CLAIRETTE, MARSANNE, eg. CLOS Ste Magdeleine, DOM de la Ferme Blanche, Fontcreuse, Paternel. Growers fight with property developers, so prices high.

Castelnau, De Champ Est 1916, marque named for World War One general. Sleeping giant co-op: 900 ha on Montagne de Reims and Marne Valley. Longer lees-ageing since 2012. Top rosé NV, fine prestige Hors Categorie.

Castillon-Côtes de Bordeaux r ★★→★★★ 08 09' 10' 12 14 15 16 Appealing e neighbour of ST-ÉM; similar wines, usually less plump. Plenty of new investors incl owner of LE PIN. Top: Alcée, Ampélia, Cap de FAUGÈRES, CLOS Les Lunelles, Clos Louie, Clos Puy Arnaud, Côte Montpezat, D'AIGUILHE, DE L'A, Joanin Bécot, l'Aurage, La Clarière-Laithwaite, Montlandrie, Poupille, Robin, Veyry, Vieux CH Champs de Mars.

Cathiard C d'O r ★★★ Sylvain C made brilliant, perfumed VOSNE-ROMANÉE, esp Malconsorts and NUITS-ST-GEORGES Aux Thorey, Murgers, from 90s. Since 2011 son Sébastien continues: more tension, precision, less new oak, overt seduction.

Cave Cellar, or any wine establishment.

Cave coopérative Wine-growers' co-op winery; over half of all French production. Often well-run, well-equipped, and wines gd value for money, but many disappearing in economic crisis.

Cazes, Dom Rouss r p w sw ★★→★★★ Largest bio producer in ROUSS for 20 yrs, combining tradition and innovation. Among 1st to plant MERLOT, CAB SAUV. Now favours MIDI varieties. Le Canon du Maréchal incl SYRAH; Crédo CÔTES DU ROUSS-VILLAGES with Ego, Alter. Sensational aged RIVESALTES CUVÉE Aimé Cazes. CLOS de Paulilles for BANYULS, COLLIOURE. New sulphur-free Hommage, and Maury Sec. Now part of Advini, but still family-run. Great value.

Restaurants starting to decant old Champ. It loses fizz, but tastes more winey.

Cédre, Ch du SW Fr r w ★★→★★★ 09' 10 11' 12' 14 (15) Well-known leader of modern CAHORS school. ★★★Le Prestige is easier and of same quality as ★★oaky top growths. NB delicious ★★VIOGNIER IGP. Substantial NÉGOCIANT business.

Cépage Grape variety. See pp.16–26 for all.

Cérons B'x w sw ★★ 09' 10' 11 13 14 15 16 Tiny sweet AC next to SAUT. Less intense wines, eg. CHX de Cérons, Grand Enclos, Haura, Seuil.

Chablis w ★★→★★★ 10' 11 12' 14' 15 Scintillating CHARD from n Burg, infused with marine minerality. My default white when not overcropped or overoaked. Supply problems mean rising prices, though.

> **Chablis**
> There is no better expression of the all-conquering CHARD than the full but tense, limpid but stony wines it makes on the heavy limestone soils of CHAB. Best makers use little or no new oak to mask the precise definition of variety and terroir: Barat, B Defaix, Bessin★, Billaud-Simon★, Boudin★, C MOREAU★, Dampt family★, DOM des Malandes, Droin★, DROUHIN★, Duplessis, E Vocoret, G Robin, J Collet★, J DURUP, J-M BROCARD, J-P Grossot★, LAROCHE, LONG-DEPAQUIT, L Michel★, MOREAU-Naudet, N Fèvre, Picq★, Pinson★, Piuze, RAVENEAU★, Samuel Billaud★, Servin, Temps Perdu, Tribut, V DAUVISSAT★, W FÈVRE★. Simple, unqualified "Chab" may be thin, and PETIT CHAB thinner; well worth premiums for PREMIER CRU or GRAND CRU. Co-op, LA CHABLISIENNE, has high standards (esp Grenouille★) and many different labels. (★ – outstanding.)

Chablis Grand Cru Chab w ★★★→★★★★ 00' 02' 05' 07' 08' 09 10' 11 12' 13 14' 15 Contiguous block overlooking River Serein, most concentrated CHAB, needs age to show detail. Seven v'yds: Blanchots (floral), Bougros (incl Côte Bouguerots), CLOS (usually best), Grenouilles (spicy), Preuses (cashmere), Valmur (structure), Vaudésir (plus brand La Moutonne).

Chablisienne, La Chab r w ★★→★★★ Major player; many own-label CHAB supplied by this dynamic co-op. Sound wines across range; top is GRAND CRU Grenouilles.

Chablis Premier Cru Chab w ★★★ 02' 05' 08' 09 10' 11 12' 13 14' 15 Well worth premium over straight CHAB: better sites on rolling hillsides; more white-flower character on s bank of River Serein (Côte de Léchet, Montmains, Vaillons), yellow fruit on sw-facing n bank (Fourchaume, Mont de Milieu, Montée de Tonnerre).

Chambertin C d'O r ★★★★ 90' 93 95 96' 98 99' 01 02' 03 05' 06 07 08 09' 10' 11 12' 13 14 15' (16) Candidate for Burg's most imperious wine; amazingly dense, sumptuous, long-lived, expensive. Producers who match potential incl: Bernstein, BOUCHARD PÈRE & FILS, Charlopin, Damoy, DUGAT-Py, DROUHIN, DOM LEROY, MORTET, PRIEUR, ROSSIGNOL-TRAPET, ROUSSEAU, TRAPET.

Chambertin-Clos de Bèze C d'O r ★★★★ 90' 93 95 96' 98 99' 01 02' 03 05' 06 08 09' 10' 11 12' 13 14 15 (16) Splendid neighbour to CHAMBERTIN, slightly more accessible in youth, velvet texture, deeply graceful. Best Bart, CLAIR, Damoy, DROUHIN, Drouhin-Laroze, FAIVELEY (incl super-CUVÉE Les Ouvrées Rodin), Groffier, JADOT, Prieuré-Roch, ROUSSEAU.

Chambolle-Musigny C d'O r ★★★→★★★★ 90' 93 95' 96' 99' 02' 03 05' 07 08 09' 10' 11 12' 13 14 15' (16) Elegant, velvety wines from CÔTE DE NUITS: PREMIERS CRUS Amoureuses, Charmes for fragrance, silky texture, more chiselled from Cras, Fuées and majesty from GRANDS CRUS BONNES MARES, MUSIGNY. Superstars: BARTHOD, DE VOGÜÉ, Groffier, MUGNIER, ROUMIER; but try Amiot-Servelle, Bertheau, Digioia-Royer, DROUHIN, Felletig, HUDELOT-Baillet, RION.

Champagne Sparkling wines of PINOTS N, M and/or CHARD, and region (33,705 ha, c.90-miles e of Paris); made by *méthode traditionnelle*. Bubbles from elsewhere, however gd, cannot be Champ.

Champagne le Mesnil Champ Top-flight co-op in greatest GRAND CRU CHARD village. Exceptional CUVÉE Sublime 04 08' 12 13' 15' ★★★★ from finest sites. Impressive Cuvée Prestige 05 08 09 13. Real value.

Champs-Fleuris, Dom des Lo r p w sw sp ★★→★★★ 05' 08 09' 10 11 12 14' 15' (16') Gd-value 43-ha DOM in Turquant with age-worthy SAUMUR Blanc; SAUMUR-CHAMPIGNY, incl easy-drinking Audace; fine CRÉMANT, esp Prestige Zéro. COTEAUX DE SAUMUR CUVÉE Sarah. V.gd reports for complicated 2016.

Champy Père & Cie Burg r w ★★→★★★ BEAUNE-based NÉGOCIANT with ancient origins (1720). Sound rather than scintillating, strongest around hill of CORTON.

Chandon de Briailles, Dom C d'O r w ★★→★★★ DOM known for fine, lighter style yet perfumed reds, esp PERNAND-VERGELESSES, Île de Vergelesses, CORTON Bressandes. Bio farming, lots of stems, no new oak define style. Some sulphur-free wines.

Chanson Père & Fils Burg r w ★→★★★ An old name in BEAUNE, now one to watch for quality, fair pricing. Try any of its Beaunes (r w), esp CLOS des Fèves (r), CLOS DES MOUCHES (w). Great CORTON-Vergennes (w).

Chapelle-Chambertin C d'O r ★★★ 90' 93 95 96' 99' 01 02' 03 05' 08 09' 10' 11' 12' 13 14' 15' (16) Lighter neighbour of CHAMBERTIN, thin soil does better in cooler damper yrs. Fine-boned wine, less meaty. Top: Damoy, Drouhin-Laroze, JADOT, ROSSIGNOL-TRAPET, TRAPET, Tremblay.

Chapoutier N Rh ★★ →★★★★ Vocal, bio grower/merchant from base at HERMITAGE. Generally stylish wines, focus on low-yield, small plot-specific CUVÉES: thick GRENACHE CHÂTEAUNEUF: Barbe Rac, Croix de Bois (r); CÔTE-RÔTIE La Mordorée; Hermitage: L'Ermite (outstanding), Le Pavillon (deep, crunchy) (r), Cuvée de l'Orée, Le Méal (w). Also ST-JOSEPH Les Granits (r w). Complex, top-grade 100% MARSANNE N Rh whites. Gd value *Meysonniers Crozes*. V'yds in COTEAUX D'AIX-EN-PROV, CÔTES DU ROUSS-VILLAGES (gd DOM Bila-Haut), RIVESALTES. Michel Chapoutier bought BEAUJ house Trenel in 2015, CH des Ferrages (PROV) in 2016, has AL v'yds and Australian joint ventures, esp Doms Tournon and Terlato & Chapoutier (fragrant, fine); also Portuguese Lisboa project.

Charbonnière, Dom de la S Rh r (w) ★★★ 95' 98 99' 00 01' 03 04 05' 06' 07 09' 10' 11' 12' 13' 14 15' Progressive 17-ha CHÂTEAUNEUF estate run by sisters. Sound Tradition wine, distinguished, authentic Mourre des Perdrix, also Hautes Brusquières, new L'Envol, VIEILLES VIGNES. Open, tasty white. Also genuine, small production VACQUEYRAS red.

Chardonnay As well as a white wine grape, also the name of a MÂCON-VILLAGES commune, hence Mâcon-Chardonnay.

Charlemagne C d'O w ★★★★ 13 14' 15' (16) Almost extinct sister appellation to CORTON-CHARLEMAGNE, revived by DOM DE LA VOUGERAIE (2013). Same style, rules as sibling.

Charmes-Chambertin C d'O r ★★★★ 90' 93 95 96' 99' 01 02' 03 05' 06 07 08 09' 10' 11 12' 13 14 15' (16) 31 ha, incl neighbour MAZOYÈRES-CHAMBERTIN, middle-rank GRAND CRU, at best with explosive deep dark-cherry fruit, sumptuous texture, fragrant finish. Try ARLAUD, BACHELET, DUGAT, DUJAC, Duroché, Jouan, LEROY, Perrot-Minot, Roty, ROUSSEAU, Taupenot-Merme, VOUGERAIE.

Chassagne-Montrachet C d'O r w ★★→★★★★ (w) 02' 04 05' 06' 07 08' 09' 10 11' 12' 13 14' 15 (16) Large village at s end of CÔTE DE BEAUNE. Great whites from eg. Caillerets, La Romanée, Blanchots, GRANDS CRUS. Best reds: CLOS St Jean, Morgeot, others more rustic. Try: Coffinet, COLIN, GAGNARD, MOREY, Pillot families plus top CH de Maltroye and DOMS MOREAU, Niellon, Ramonet (reds too). But too much indifferent village white grown on land better suited to red.

Château (Ch) Means an estate, big or small, gd or indifferent, particularly in B'X (*see* p.100). Means, literally, castle or great house. In Burg, DOM is usual term.

Château-Chalon Jura w ★★★★ 96 99' 00 05' 08 09 Not a CH but AC and village, the summit of VIN JAUNE style from SAVAGNIN grape. Nutty sherryfied wines from flor with min 6 yrs barrel age. Difficult to make, so expensive. Ready to drink (or cook a chicken in) when bottled, but much more interesting with age. Fervent admirers search out BERTHET-BONDET, MACLE, Mossu. Bourdy for old vintages.

Château-Grillet N Rh w ★★ 91' 95' 98' 00' 01' 04' 05 06' 07' 08 09' 10' 11 12' 13 14'

Champagne growers to watch in 2018
Armand (Arnaud) Margaine, Anselme Selosse, J-L Vergnon, Lancelot-Pienne, Lilbert et Fils, Marie-Noëlle Ledru, Nicolas Maillart, Veuve Fourny, Vilmart, Yannick Doyard.

Châteauneuf as it should be

GRENACHE should be aromatic, tender, plump and beguiling, unlike many Châteauneufs in 90s to 2000s. Try CH des Tours VACQUEYRAS, CLOS du Caillou CÔTES DU RH Nature, DOMS Jean David SÉGURET Les Levants, de La Péquélette VINSOBRES Emile, du Val des Rois Côtes du Rh Les Allards au Naturel, Moulin de la Gardette GIGONDAS Tradition. Wispiness and beauty in glass.

15' 16' France's smallest AC. 3.7-ha amphitheatre v'yd nr CONDRIEU, loose, sandy granite terraces. Bought by F Pinault of CH LATOUR in 2011, prices up, wine in gear, albeit less deep than in past. Smooth, restrained VIOGNIER: drink at cellar temp, decanted, with new-wave food.

Châteaumeillant Lo r p ★ →★★ Dynamic 86-ha recent AC sw Bourges. Now 25 producers. GAMAY, PINOT N for light reds (75%), VIN GRIS (25%). Pinot N potentially best red but pure versions stupidly banned. Try BOURGEOIS, Chaillot, Gabrielle, Goyer, Joffre, Joseph Mellot, Lecomte, Nairaud-Suberville, Roux, Rouzé, Siret-Courtaud.

Châteauneuf-du-Pape S Rh r (w) ★★★ →★★★★ 78' 81' 83 85 88 89' 90' 95' 96 98' 99' 00' 01' 03' 04' 05' 06' 07' 08 09' 10' 11 12' 13' 14 15' 16' Nr Avignon, about 50 gd DOMS (remaining 85 inconsistent to poor). Up to 13 grapes (r w), headed by GRENACHE, plus SYRAH, MOURVÈDRE, Counoise. Warm, aromatic, textured, long-lived; should be fine, pure, but too many sweet, heavy, sip-only Parker-esque wines. Small, traditional names can be gd value, while prestige old-vine wines (worst are late-harvest, new oak, 16% alc) are often too pricey. Whites fresh, fruity, or sturdy, best can age 15 yrs. Top names: CHX DE BEAUCASTEL, Fortia, Gardine (lovely modern, also w), Mont-Redon, LA NERTHE, RAYAS (unique, marvellous), Sixtine, Vaudieu; DOMS de Barroche, Beaurenard, Bois de Boursan (value), Bosquet des Papes (value), LES CAILLOUX, Chante Cigale, Chante Perdrix, CHARBONNIÈRE, Charvin (terroir), CLOS du Caillou, Clos du Mont-Olivet, CLOS DES PAPES, Clos St-Jean (sip), Cristia, de la Janasse, de la Vieille Julienne, Font-de-Michelle, Grand Veneur (oak), Henri Bonneau, Marcoux (fantastic VIEILLES VIGNES), Pegaü, Pierre André (trad), P Usseglio, Roger Sabon, Sénéchaux (modern), St-Préfert (sleek), Vieux Donjon, VIEUX TÉLÉGRAPHE.

Chave, Dom Jean-Louis N Rh r w ★★★★ 85' 88' 89' 90' 91' 94 95' 96 97 98' 99' 00 01' 03' 04 05' 06' 07' 08 09' 10' 11' 12' 13' 14' 15' 16' Excellent family DOM at heart of HERMITAGE. Classy, fruit-laden, supple, long-lived reds (more plush recently), incl expensive, occasional Cathelin. V.gd white (mainly MARSANNE); marvellous, occasional VIN DE PAILLE. Deep, copious ST-JOSEPH red (incl Dom Florentin 2009 and new v'yds), fruity J-L Chave brand St-Joseph Offerus, jolly CÔTES DU RH Mon Coeur, sound merchant Hermitage Farconnet (r w).

Chavignol Lo r p w Leading SANCERRE village, two v. steep v'yds Cul de Beaujeu (largely white), Les Monts Damnés dominate enclosed village. Clay-limestone soil gives full-bodied, mineral whites and reds that age 15 yrs+; some v. fine young producers incl: Pierre Martin, Matthieu Delaporte (Vincent Delaporte). Others: Boulay (v.gd), BOURGEOIS, Cotat, DAGUENEAU, Paul Thomas, Thomas Laballe. Whites great match with goats cheese.

Chénas Beauj r ★★★ 09' 11' 12 13 14' 15' 16 Smallest BEAUJ cru, between MOULIN-À-VENT and JULIÉNAS, gd-value, meaty, age-worthy, merits more interest. Try: CH Bonnet, DUBOEUF, LAPIERRE, Pacalet, Piron, Thillardon (rising star), Trichard, co-op.

Chevalier-Montrachet C d'O w ★★★★ 99' 00' 02' 04 05' 06' 07' 08 09' 10 11 12 13 14' 15 (16) Just above MONTRACHET on hill, just below in quality, yet capable of brilliant crystalline wines. Long-lived but can be accessible early. Special CUVÉES Les Demoiselles from JADOT, LOUIS LATOUR and La Cabotte from BOUCHARD; top example is LEFLAIVE. Try: CH de Puligny, Dancer, Niellon, SAUZET.

Cheverny Lo r p w ★–★★★ 08 09′ 10 11 13 14 (15) LO AC (500 ha+) nr Blois. Dry white from SAUV BL/CHARD blend. Light reds mainly GAMAY, PINOT N (also CAB FR, CÔT). *Cour-Cheverny* (50 ha): Romorantin can be remarkable, age-worthy. Esp Cazin, CLOS Tue-Boeuf, de Montcy, Gendrier, Huards, Philippe Tessier; DOMS de la Desoucherie, du Moulin, Veilloux, Villemade.

Chevillon, R C d'O r ★★★ Top NUITS-ST-GEORGES address; fairly priced. Sensual style, though more structure from top v'yds eg. Cailles, Les St-Georges, Vaucrains.

Chidaine, François Lo (r) w dr sw sp ★★★ 08′ 09 10′ 11 13 14 15 Excellent v. precise MONTLOUIS, VIN DE FRANCE VOUVRAY stupidly barred from using AC Vouvray. Owns historic CLOS Baudoin (Vouvray). Concentrates on dry, DEMI-SEC AC TOURAINE at Chissay (Cher Valley). Again hit by April frost 2016. Bio champion. La CAVE Insolite (retail) in Montlouis.

Chignin Sav w ★ DYA. Light, soft white from Jacquère grapes for Alpine summers. Chignin-Bergeron (with ROUSSANNE grapes) is best and liveliest.

Chinon Lo r p (w) ★★–★★★★ 96′ 03 05′ 08 09′ 10′ 11 12 14′ 15′ (16′) 2400 ha (10% p, 2% w). Sand, gravel, limestone. light to rich TOURAINE CAB FR. Best age 30 yrs+. Parts badly hit by 2016 frost. A little dry CHENIN BL (some wood). Best: ALLIET, BAUDRY, BAUDRY-DUTOUR, Couly-Dutheil, Grosbois, JM Raffault, Jourdan-Pichard, Landry, L'R, Noblaie, Pain, Pierre & Bertrand Couly; CHX de Coulaine, de la Bonnelière. 2016: seven communes w of Chinon joined AC.

Chiroubles Beauj r ★★ 11′ 12 13′ 14 15′ 16 Rarely seen BEAUJ cru in hills above FLEURIE: fresh, fruity, silky wine for early drinking (1–3 yrs). Growers: Cheysson, Coquelet, DUBOEUF, Fourneau, Métrat, Passot, Raousset, Trenel.

Chorey-lès-Beaune C d'O r (w) ★★ 05′ 09′ 10′ 11 12 14 15′ (16) How many people have discoved joy of red burg through TOLLOT-BEAUT's Chorey? Pleasurable, affordable, accessible mini BEAUNE. Try also: Arnoux, DROUHIN, Guyon, JADOT.

Chusclan S Rh r p w ★★–★★★ 15′ 16′ CÔTES DU RH-VILLAGES with above-average Laudun-Chusclan co-op, incl gd crisp whites. Easy reds, direct rosés. Best co-op labels (r) Chusclan DOM de l'Olivette, LAUDUN Enfant Terrible (w), CÔTES DU RH Femme de Gicon, LIRAC DOM St Nicolas. Also full CH Signac (best Chusclan, can age), Dom La Romance, special CUVÉES from *André Roux*. Drink most young.

Clair, Bruno C d'O r p w ★★★ –★★★★ Top class CÔTE DE NUITS estate for supple, subtle, savoury wines. Gd-value MARSANNAY, old-vine SAVIGNY La Dominode, GEVREY CHAMBERTIN (CLOS ST-JACQUES, Cazetiers) and standout CHAMBERTIN-CLOS DE BÈZE. Best whites from MOREY-ST-DENIS, CORTON-CHARLEMAGNE.

Clairet B'x Between rosé/red. B'x Clairet is AC. Try CHX Fontenille, Penin, Turcaud.

Clairette de Die N Rh w dr s/sw sp ★★★ NV Rh/low Alpine bubbles: flinty or (better) semi-sweet MUSCAT sparkling, beautiful setting. Underrated, muskily fruited, gd value or dry CLAIRETTE, can age 3–4 yrs. NB: Achard-Vincent, Carod, Jaillance (value), Poulet et Fils (terroir), J-C Raspail (organic, gd IGP SYRAH).

Clape, Auguste, Pierre, Olivier N Rh r (w) ★★★ –★★★★ 89′ 90′ 95′ 97 98′ 99′ 00 01′ 02 03′ 04′ 05′ 06′ 07′ 08 09′ 10′ 11′ 12′ 13′ 14′ 15′ 16′ The kings of CORNAS. Supreme SYRAH v'yds, many old vines, gd soil work. Profound, spiced reds, deep body, lingering tannins, need 6 yrs+, live 25+. Clear fruit in youngish-vines Renaissance. Gd CÔTES DU RH, VIN DE FRANCE (r), ST-PÉRAY (improved).

Clape, La L'doc r p w ★★–★★★★ Limestone massif twixt Narbonne and Mediterranean; once an island. High sunshine hours for warm, spicy reds, esp MOURVÈDRE. Sea air gives deliciously salty, herbal whites, based on BOURBOULENC with ageing potential. New appellation and also Cru du L'doc. CHX ANGLÈS, Camplazens, *l'Hospitalet*, La Négly, Mire l'Etang, Pech-Céleyran, Pech-Redon, *Rouquette-sur-Mer*, Ricardelle and Mas du Soleila, Sarrat de Goundy.

Climat Burg Individually named v'yd in Burg, eg. BEAUNE Grèves, MEURSAULT Tesson. System has UNESCO World Heritage status.

Clos A term carrying some prestige, reserved for distinct (walled) v'yds, often in one ownership (esp AL, Burg, CHAMP).

Clos de Gamot SW Fr r ★★★ 00 01' 02' 05' 08' 09' 10 11' 12 (14) (15) Textbook example of CAHORS before outsiders started messing about with it. ★★★★ low-yield CUVÉE Vignes Centenaires (best yrs only) miraculously survives recent Cahors fashions, deer and wild boar. Ageing required to show its best.

Clos de la Roche C d'O r ★★★★ 90' 93' 95 96' 98 99' 01 02' 03 05' 06 07 08 09' 10' 11 12' 13 14 15' Maybe finest GRAND CRU of MOREY-ST-DENIS, as much grace as power, more savoury than sumptuous, blueberries. Needs time. DUJAC, PONSOT references but try Amiot, ARLAUD, Castagnier, Coquard, H LIGNIER, LEROY, LIGNIER-Michelot, Remy, ROUSSEAU.

Clos des Lambrays C d'O r ★★★ 99' 02 03 05' 06 09' 10' 11 12' 13 14 15' (16) GRAND CRU v'yd at MOREY-ST-DENIS. A virtual monopoly of DOM du CLOS des Lambrays, invigorating wine in early-picked, spicy, stemmy style, total contrast to neighbour CLOS DE TART. New owner LVMH from 2014, rising prices, no style change yet.

Clos des Mouches C d'O r w ★★★ (w) 02 05' 09' 10' 11 14' 15' (16) Splendid PREMIER CRU BEAUNE v'yd, made famous by DROUHIN. *Whites* and reds spicy, memorable and consistent. BICHOT, CHANSON gd too. Little-known v'yds of the same name also found in SANTENAY (Clair, Moreau, Muzard), MEURSAULT (Germain).

Clos des Papes S Rh r w ★★★★ 89' 90' 95 98' 99' 00 01' 03' 04' 05' 06' 07' 08 09' 10' 11 12' 13' 14' 15' 16' Always classy CHÂTEAUNEUF DOM of Avril family, tiny yields. Rich, intricate, textured red, more succulent recently (mainly GRENACHE, MOURVÈDRE, drink at 2–3 yrs or from 8 yrs); *great white* (six varieties, complex, allow time, merits fine cuisine; 5–20 yrs).

Clos de Tart C d'O r ★★★★ 99' 00 01' 02' 03 05' 06 07 08' 09 10' 11 12 13' 14 15' Hugely expensive MOREY-ST-DENIS GRAND CRU. Sylvain Pitiot (director 1996–2014) made a powerful, late-picked style. Expect it to freshen up in new era.

Clos de Vougeot C d'O r ★★★→★★★★ 90' 93' 96' 99' 01 02' 03' 05' 06 07 08 09' 10' 11 12' 13' 14 15' (16) Celebrated CÔTE DE NUITS GRAND CRU with many owners. Occasionally sublime, needs 10 yrs+ to show real class. Style, quality depend on producer's philosophy, technique, position. Top: BOUCHARD, CH de la Tour (stems), DROUHIN, EUGÉNIE (intensity), *Faiveley*, Forey, GRIVOT, *Gros*, HUDELOT-Noëllat, JADOT, LEROY, LIGER-BELAIR, MÉO-CAMUZET, MONTILLE, MORTET, MUGNERET, *Vougeraie*.

Clos du Mesnil Champ ★★★★ KRUG's famous walled v'yd in GRAND CRU Le Mesnil. Esp long-lived, pure CHARD vintage, great yrs like 92 95 perfect now and to 2020+, 00, 03 a fresh miracle. 08 13 15 will be great classics.

Clos du Roi C d'O r ★★→★★★ Best v'yd in GRAND CRU CORTON, try Camille Giroud, DE MONTILLE, Pousse d'Or, VOUGERAIE; top PREMIER CRU v'yd in MERCUREY, less so in BEAUNE, special site in MARSANNAY (future Premier Cru?). The king or duke usually chose well.

Clos Rougeard Lo r w (sw) ★★★★ 03 05' 06 07 08 09' 10' 11 12 14 15 (16) Legendary/ICONIC small DOM of brothers Nady and late Charly Foucault. Great finesse, age brilliantly: SAUMUR Blanc, SAUMUR-CHAMPIGNY, Coteaux de Saumur. Antoine, Charly's son, made 2016. Up for sale?

Clos St-Denis C d'O r ★★★ 90' 93' 95 96' 99' 01 02' 03 05' 06 07 08 09' 10' 11 12' 13 14 15' (16) GRAND CRU at MOREY-ST-DENIS. Sumptuous wine in youth, growing silky with age. Try ARLAUD, Bertagna, Castagnier, DUJAC, JADOT, Jouan, Leroux, PONSOT.

Clos Ste-Hune Al w ★★★★ Top TRIMBACH bottling from GRAND CRU ROSACKER. Greatest RIES in ALSACE? Super 89 08 10 12 14 15'. Initially austere, needing 10–15 yrs+ ageing; complex mineral subtleties for great fish cuisine. House's new 1.9-ha GRAND CRU SCHLOSSBERG: 1st vintage 12; 13' even better esp for Ries in cool, classic vintage; a riveting contrast with Clos Ste-Hune.

Clos St-Jacques C d'O r ★★★ 90' 93 95 96' 98 99' 01 02' 03 05' 06 07 08 09' 10' 11

12' 13 14 15' Hillside PREMIER CRU in GEVREY-CHAMBERTIN with perfect se exposure. Excellent producers: CLAIR, ESMONIN, FOURRIER, JADOT, ROUSSEAU; powerful, velvety reds often ranked above many GRANDS CRUS.

Clovallon, Dom de L'doc r w ★★★ Haute Vallée de l'Orb. Catherine Roque created reputation for elegant PINOT N Pomarèdes and original white blend Aurièges. Now run by daughter Alix; mother at Mas d'Alezon, FAUGÈRES for ★★★Presbytère and Montfalette.

Coche-Dury C d'O r w ★★★★ Superb MEURSAULT DOM led by Jean-François Coche and son Raphaël. Exceptional whites from ALIGOTÉ to CORTON-CHARLEMAGNE; v. pretty reds too. Hard to find at sensible prices. Gd-value cousin Coche-Bizouard, sound but not same style.

Colin C d'O (r) w ★★★ →★★★★ Leading CHASSAGNE-MONTRACHET and ST-AUBIN family; new generation turning heads with brilliant whites, esp Pierre-Yves C-Morey and Philippe C. DOM Marc C remains classic source.

Collines Rhodaniennes N Rh r w ★★ Character and quality. N Rh IGP, incl Seyssuel, clear-fruited granite hillside reds v.gd value, often from top estates. Can contain young-vine CÔTE-RÔTIE. Mostly SYRAH (best), plus MERLOT, GAMAY, mini-CONDRIEU VIOGNIER (best), CHARD. Reds: A Perret, Bonnefond, E Barou, J-C Raspail, J-M Gérin, *Jamet* (v.gd), Jasmin, L Chèze, Monier-Pérreol, N Champagneux, S Ogier (v.gd), S Pichat. Whites: Alexandrins, A Perret (v.gd), Barou, F Merlin, *G Vernay (v.gd)*, P Marthouret, X Gérard, Y Cuilleron.

Collioure Rouss r p w ★★ →★★★ Table-wine twin of BANYULS from same dramatic coastal v'yds. Characterful reds, mainly GRENACHE, enjoy maritime influence. Rewarding whites based on GRENACHE BLANC and better Gris. Top: DOMS Bila-Haut, de la Rectorie, du Mas Blanc, La Tour Vieille, Madeloc, Vial-Magnères; Coume del Mas; Co-ops Cellier des Templiers, l'Etoile, Les clos de Paulilles.

Comté Tolosan SW Fr r p w ★→★★ Mostly DYA IGP covering most of sw and multitude of sins. ★★★CH de Cabidos (outstanding dry and sweet from PETIT MANSENG), ★★DOM de Moncaut (JURANÇON in all but name) and ★★Dom de Ribonnet (all colours and most CÉPAGES) stand out.

Condrieu N Rh w ★★★ →★★★★ 09 10' 11' 12' 13 14 15 16 Home of VIOGNIER; floral, musky aromas of apricot/pear from sandy granite slopes. Best: cool, pure, precise (esp 2014); but danger of excess oak, sweetness, alc, price. Rare white match for asparagus. 75 growers; quality varies. Best: A Perret (all three wines gd), Benetière (character), Boissonnet, CHAPOUTIER, C Pichon, DELAS, Faury (esp La Berne), F Merlin, F Villard (lighter recently), Gangloff (great style), GUIGAL (big), *G Vernay* (fine, classy), Niéro, ROSTAING, St Cosme, X Gérard (value), Y Cuilleron.

Corbières L'doc r (p) (w) ★★ →★★★ 08 09 10 11 12 13 14 15 16 Largest AC of L'DOC, with cru of Boutenac. Maybe others in pipeline, but not decided yet. Wines as varied as scenery: coastal lagoons, hot dry hills. Try: CHX Aiguilloux, Aussières, Borde-Rouge, de Cabriac, LA BARONNE, Lastours, la Voulte Gasparets, Les CLOS Perdus, Les Palais, Ollieux Romanis, Pech-Latt; DOMS de Fontsainte, de Villemajou, du Grand Crès, du Vieux Parc, Trillol, Villerouge; Clos de l'Anhel, Grand Arc, Serres-Mazard. Castelmaure an outstanding co-op.

Cornas N Rh r ★★★ 78' 83' 85' 88' 89' 90' 91' 94' 95' 96 97' 98' 99' 00' 01' 02 03' 04 05' 06' 07' 08 09' 10' 11' 12' 13' 14 15' 16' Top-quality N Rhô SYRAH, *très à la mode* (incl hunger for wines of departed growers). Deep, strongly fruited, mineral-tinted. Can drink some for vibrant early fruit, often need 5 yrs+. Stunning 2010, also 2015. Top: ALLEMAND (top 2), Balthazar (traditional), *Clape* (benchmark), Colombo (new oak), Courbis (modern), *Delas*, *Dom du Tunnel*, J&E Durand (racy fruit), G Gilles, JABOULET (St-Pierre CUVÉE), P&V Jaboulet, Lemenicier, M Barret (organic, improved), Tardieu-Laurent (deep, oak), Voge (oak), V Paris.

Corsica / Corse r p w ★→★★★ ACS Ajaccio, PATRIMONIO; better crus Calvi, Coteaux du Cap Corse, Sartène. IGP: Île de Beauté. Fragrant spicy reds from SCIACARELLO, more structured wines from NIELLUCCIO; gd rosés: *tangy, **herbal Vermentino whites***. Also sweet MUSCATS. Top: Abbatucci, Alzipratu, Canarelli, CLOS Capitoro, Clos d'Alzeto, Clos Poggiale, Fiumicicoli, *Peraldi*, Pieretti, *Nicrosi*, Saperale, *Torraccia*, Vaccelli. Original wines that rarely travel, but *vaut le voyage*.

Corton C d'O r (w) ★★★ →★★★★ 90' 95 96' 99' 01 02' 03' 05' 06 07 08 09' 10' 11 12' 13 14 15' (16) Over-large GRAND CRU. Most of hill should not be, but gives decent wines at price nonetheless. Don't expect all to be brooding monsters. CLOS du Roi v'yd can be both though. Bressandes is dense but suave, Renardes characterful, Rognet, Chaumes, Vigne au Saint more supple. Try d'Ardhuy, BONNEAU DU MARTRAY, BOUCHARD, Camille Giroud, CHANDON DE BRIAILLES, DOM des Croix, DRC, Dubreuil-Fontaine, FAIVELEY (CLOS DES CORTONS), MÉO-CAMUZET, Senard, TOLLOT-BEAUT. Occasional whites, eg. HOSPICES DE BEAUNE, CHANSON from Vergennes v'yd.

Corton-Charlemagne C d'O W ★★★ →★★★★ 99' 00' 02' 03 04 05' 06 07' 08 09' 10' 11 12' 13 15 (16) Potentially scintillating GRAND CRU, in style between MONTRACHET and CHAB Grand Cru. Sw- and w-facing limestone slopes, plus e band round top. Great tension, ageing potential often unused. Top: *Bonneau du Martray*, BOUCHARD, *Coche-Dury*, FAIVELEY, HOSPICES DE BEAUNE, JADOT, LATOUR, P Javillier, Rapet, Rollin, *Vougeraie*.

Costières de Nîmes S Rh r p w ★ →★★ 12' 13 15' 16' Region sw of CHÂTEAUNEUF, similar stony soils, gd quality. Red (GRENACHE, SYRAH) is robust, spicy fruit, ages well, gd value. Best: CHX de Grande Cassagne, de Valcombe, d'Or et des Gueules, Mas des Bressades (top fruit), Mas Carlot (gd fruit), Mas Neuf, Mourgues-du-Grès, Nages, Roubaud, Tour de Béraud; DOMS de la Patience, du Vieux Relais, Galus, M KREYDENWEISS, Petit Romain. Gd, *lively rosés*, *stylish whites* (ROUSSANNE).

Côte Chalonnaise Burg r w sp ★★ Region immediately s of C D'O; lighter wines, lower prices. BOUZERON for ALIGOTÉ, *Mercurey* and GIVRY for structured reds and interesting whites; *Rully* for accessible, juicy wines in both colours; MONTAGNY for leaner CHARD. Region needs a real locomotive, though.

Côte d'Or Burg *Département* name applied to central and principal Burg v'yd slopes: CÔTE DE BEAUNE and CÔTE DE NUITS. Not used on labels except for long-delayed BOURGOGNE C d'O AC, still expected imminently.

Côte de Beaune C d'O r w ★★ →★★★★ S half of C D'O. Also a little seen AC in its own right applying to top of hill above BEAUNE itself. Try from DROUHIN, which incl declassified Beaune PREMIER CRU.

Côte de Beaune-Villages C d'O r ★★ 09' 10' 11 12 14 15' (16) Reds from lesser villages of s half of C D'O. Nowadays usually NÉGOCIANT blends.

Côte de Brouilly Beauj r ★★ 09' 11' 13' 14 15' 16 Grown on flanks of volcanic hill overlooking BROUILLY, merits a premium and greater fame. Try CH Thivin, J-P Brun, L Martray, N Chanrion.

Côte de Nuits C d'O r (w) ★★ →★★★★ N half of C D'O. Nearly all red, from CHAMBOLLE-MUSIGNY, MARSANNAY, FIXIN, GEVREY-CHAMBERTIN, MOREY-ST DENIS, NUITS-ST GEORGES, VOSNE-ROMANÉE, VOUGEOT.

Côte de Nuits-Villages C d'O r (w) ★★ 05' 09' 10' 12' 13 14 15 (16) Junior AC for extreme n/s ends of CÔTE DE NUITS; well worth investigating for bargains. Chopin, Gachot-Monot, Jourdan are specialists, Ardhuy, D BACHELET, Loichet also v.gd. Single-v'yd versions beginning to appear.

Côte Roannaise Lo r p ★★ 12 13 14' 15' 16' Dynamic, exciting AC, lower slopes of granite hills w of Roanne. Excellent GAMAY. Esp: Désormière, Fontenay, Giraudon, Paroisse, Plasse, Pothiers, Sérol, Vial. White IGP Urfé from ALIGOTÉ, CHARD, ROUSSANNE, VIOGNIER. Gd 2016.

Côte-Rôtie N Rh r ★★★ →★★★★ 78' 85' 89' 90' 91' 95' 98' 99' 00 01' 03' 04 05' 06' 07' 08 09' 10' 11 12' 13' 14 15' 16' Finest Rh red, mainly SYRAH, touch of VIOGNIER,

FRANCE

style links to Burg. Violet airs, pure, complex, v. fine with age (5–10 yrs+). Exceptional, v. long-lived 2010, 2015. Top: *Barge* (traditional), Billon, Bonnefond (oak), Bonserine (esp La Garde), Burgaud, CHAPOUTIER, Clusel-Roch (organic), DELAS, DOM de Rosiers, Duclaux, Gaillard (oak), Garon, GUIGAL (long oaking), *Jamet* (wonderful), Jasmin, J-M Gérin (oak), J-M Stéphan (organic), Lafoy, Levet (traditional), *Rostaing* (fine), S Ogier (racy, oak), VIDAL-FLEURY (La Chatillonne).

Côtes Catalanes Rouss r p w ★★→★★★ IGP; quality belies humble status. Covers much of ROUSS. Numerous innovative, talented growers working with venerable old vines, esp GRENACHE, CARIGNAN. Best: DOMS GÉRARD GAUBY, *Casenove*, *Dom of the Bee*, *Jones*, L'Horizon, La Préceptorie Centernach, Le Soula, Matassa, Olivier Pithon, Padié, Roc des Anges, Soulanes, Treloar, Vaquer.

Côtes d'Auvergne Mass C 1 p (w) ★ ¹★★ AC (470 ha incl IGP) Clermont-Ferrand. GAMAY, some PINOT N, CHARD. Best reds improve 2–3 yrs. Villages: Boudes, Chanturgue, Châteaugay, Corent (p), Madargues (r). Producers: Bernard, CAVE St-Verny, Goigoux, Maupertuis, Montel, Pradier, Sauvat.

Côtes de Bordeaux B'x ★ AC launched in 2008 for reds. Embraces and permits cross-blending between CAS, FRANCS, BLAYE, CADILLAC and Ste-Foy from 2016. Growers who want to maintain *the identity of a single terroir* have stiffer controls (NB) but can put Cas, Cadillac, etc. before Côtes de B'x. BLAYE-CÔTES DE B'X, FRANCS-CÔTES DE B'X also produce a little dry white. With Ste-Foy-B'x, now 1000 growers in group. Try CHX Dudon, Malagar, Réaut.

Riedel now has a special glass for Prov rosé. Oh, for the cupboard space.

Côtes de Bourg B'x r w ★ ¹★★ 05' 08 09' 10' 12 14 15 16 Solid, savoury reds, a little white from e bank of Gironde. Mainly MERLOT but 10% MALBEC. On-site wine bar for tasting. Top CHX. Brûlesécaille, Bujan, Civrac, *Falfas*, Fougas-Maldoror, Grand-Maison, Grave (Nectar VIEILLES VIGNES), Haut-Guiraud, Haut-Macô, Haut Mondésir, Macay, Mercier, Nodoz, *Roc de Cambes*, Rousset, Sociondo.

Côtes de Duras SW Fr r p w ★→★★★ 14' 15' 16 Gd-value AOP s of BERGERAC searching for own identity. Nest of passionate organic growers like ★★★DOMS Mont Ramé, Mouthes-les-Bihan, Nadine Lusseau, Petit Malromé; ★★La Fon Longue, La Tuilerie la Brille, Les Cours, Les Hauts de Riquet, Mauro Guicheney. CH Condom's ★★★sweet still outstanding. Other gd growers: ★★Doms Chater, de Laulan, Grand Mayne.

Côtes de Gascogne SW Fr (r) (p) w ★★ DYA IGP. ★★Giants PRODUCTEURS PLAIMONT, and 900-ha+ DOM Tariquet dominate market for easy-quaffing wine-bar wines, mostly white. Fighting to survive the pressure ★★Doms Chiroulet, d'Arton, d'Espérance, de l'Herré de San Guilhem, Horgelus, Ménard, Millet, Miselle, Pellehaut and un des Cassagnoles. Or ★Chx de Jöy, de Laballe, de Lauroux, de Magnaut, Papolle, St Lannes. NB ★Sédouprat red CUVÉE Sanglier.

Côtes de Millau SW Fr r p w IGP ★ from upper Tarn Valley. DYA. Improving co-op with CUVÉE celebrating Lord Foster's viaduct work alongside worthy independents eg. ★DOM du Vieux Noyer.

Côtes de Montravel SW Fr w sw ★★ 12 14' 15' (16) Sub-AOP of BERGERAC; squeezed between dr and sw. Attractive, unfashionable and increasingly hard to find. Ideal with foie gras. Usually from SÉM.

Côtes de Provence Prov r p w ★→★★★ 10 11 12 13 14 15 16 (p w) DYA. Huge almost unavoidable AC. Mainly rosé, research improving quality; nowhere else takes rosé so seriously. Satisfying reds, mainly SYRAH, GRENACHE, CINSAULT, plus CAB. Fruity whites. Subzones: Fréjus, La Londe, Pierrefeu, STE-VICTOIRE. Try: Commanderie de Peyrassol, DOMS de la Courtade, des Planes, *Gavoty* (superb), La Bernarde, Rabiega, Roubine, *Richeaume*, Rimauresq, Ste Rosaline; CHX d'Esclans, de Selle, Léoube; CLOS Mireille. Sparkling to come. See COTEAUX D'AIX, BANDOL, COTEAUX VAROIS.

Côtes de Thongue L'doc r p w ★★ (p w) DYA. Best IGP of HÉRAULT, in Thongue Valley. Diverse blends and single varietals. Best reds age. DOMS ARJOLLE, Condamine l'Evèque, des Henrys, Filles de Septembre, l'Horte, LA CROIX BELLE.

Côtes de Toul Al r p w ★ DYA. V. light wines from Lorraine; mainly VIN GRIS.

Côtes du Brulhois SW Fr r p (w) ★→★★ 14' 15' (16) Lively AOP nr Agen; dark, brooding red best (some TANNAT obligatory). Gd co-op encourages handful of independents ★★DOM Bois de Simon, des Thermes, du Pountet; ★CH Coujétou-Peyret, la Bastide.

Côtes du Forez Lo r p (sp) ★→★★ DYA. Dynamic s-most Lo AC (200 ha), level with CÔTE-RÔTIE. GAMAY (r p). Bonnefoy, CLOS de Chozieux, Guillot, Mondon & Demeure, Real, Verdier/Logel. Excellent and expanding IGP: CHARD, CHENIN BL, PINOT GR, ROUSSANNE, VIOGNIER,

Côtes du Jura Jura r p w (sp) ★★→★★★ 99' 00 03' 05' 06 09 10 11 12 14 15 16 Revitalized region, trendy in sommelier community, so pricey, and for natural wines. Light bright reds from PINOT N, Poulsard, Trousseau. Try PIGNIER, Puffeney. Whites from fresh, fruity CHARD to deliberately oxidative SAVAGNIN or blends. NB: BERTHET-BONDEt, Bourdy, CH D'ARLAY, DOM DU PÉLICAN, DOM LABEt, Ganevat, LUCIEN AVIEt, STÉPHANE TISSOt. *See also* ARBOIS, CH CHALON, L'ETOILE ACS.

Côtes du Rhône S Rh r p w ★→★★ 13 15' 16' The broad base of S Rh, 170 communes. Incl gd lightish SYRAH of Brézème, St-Julien-en-St-Alban (N Rh). Split between enjoyable, handmade quality (numbers rising) and dull, mass-produced. Lively fruit more accentuated. 2015, 2016 v.gd. Mainly GRENACHE, also SYRAH, CARIGNAN. Best drunk young. Vaucluse top, then GARD (Syrah).

Côtes du Rhône-Villages S Rh r p w ★→★★ 10' 13 14 15' 16' Full-bodied, forthright reds from 7700 ha, incl 19 named S Rh villages. Best are generous, spicy, gd value. Red heart is GRENACHE, plus SYRAH, MOURVÈDRE. Improving *whites*, often incl VIOGNIER, ROUSSANNE added to rich base CLAIRETTE, GRENACHE BLANC – *gd with food. See* CHUSCLAN, LAUDUN, PLAN DE DIEU, ST-GERVAIS, SABLET, SÉGURET (QUALITY), VALRÉAS, VISAN (improving). New villages from 2016 vintage: Ste-Cécile (gd range DOMS), Suze-la-Rousse, Vaison la Romaine. NB: Gadagne, MASSIF D'UCHAUX (gd), PLAN DE DIEU (robust), PUYMÉRAS, SIGNARGUES. Try: CHX Fontségune, Signac; DOMS Aphillantes (character), Aure, Bastide St Dominique, *Biscarelle* (flair), Cabotte (bio), Coulange, Coste Chaude, Crève Coeur, Grand Veneur, Grands Bois, Gravennes, *Janasse*, Jérome, Mas de Libian, Montbayon, Montmartel, *Mourchon*, Pasquiers, Pique-Basse, Rabasse-Charavin, Réméjeanne, Renjarde, Romarins, Saladin, St-Siffrein, Ste-Anne, Valériane, Viret (cosmopolitan); CAVE de RASTEAU, Les Vignerons d'Estézargues.

Côtes du Roussillon-Villages Rouss r ★→★★★ 10 11 12 13 14 15 16 32 villages in n part of ROUSS with Caramany, Latour de France, Lesquerde, Tauravel, Les Aspres singled out on label. Co-ops inevitably important, but quality and character

---

Top Côtes du Rhône producers
CHX La Borie, La Courançonne, Fonsalette (beauty), Gigognan, Grand Moulas, Hugues, Montfaucon (w also), St Cosme, St-Estève, Trignon (incl VIOGNIER); DOMS André Brunel (stylish), Bastide St Dominique, Bramadou, Carabiniers (bio), Charvin (terroir, v.gd), Chaume-Arnaud (organic), CLOS des Cîmes (v. high v'yds), Combebelle, Coudoulet de BEAUCASTEL (classy r), Cros de la Mûre (great value), M Dumarcher (organic), Espigouette, Famille Perrin, Ferrand (full), Gramenon (bio), Grand Nicolet (genuine), Haut-Musiel, Janasse (old GRENACHE), Jaume, M-F Laurent (organic), Manarine, Réméjeanne (w also), Romarins, Soumade, Vieille Julienne (classy); CAVE Estézargues, DELAS, E GUIGAL (great value), GEORGES DUBOEUF, Maison Bouachon, Mas Poupéras; co-ops CAIRANNE, RASTEAU.

from independent estates: Boucabeille, **Cazes**, clos des Fées, Clot de l'Oum, des Chênes, **Gauby**, Les Vignes de Bila-Haut, Mas Becha, **Mas Crémat**, Modat, Piquemal, Rancy, Roc des Anges, Thunevin-Calvet. Côtes du Rouss to s is simpler: uncomplicated warming reds. *See also* CÔTES CATALANES.

Côtes du Tarn SW Fr r p w ★ DYA. IGP roughly co-extensive with GAILLAC. Off-dry SAUV BL from ★★DOM d'en Segur and Lou Bio range from DOM VIGNES de Garbasses outstanding. Some GAILLAC growers seeking escape from AOP rules.

Côtes du Vivarais S Rh r p w ★ 15' 16' Mostly DYA. Across hilly Ardèche country w of Montélimar. Definite improvement: quaffable, based on GRENACHE, SYRAH; some more sturdy, oak-aged reds. NB: Gallety (depth, lives well), Mas de Bagnols, **Vignerons de Ruoms** (value in different colours).

Coteaux Bourguignons Burg ★ DYA. New AC from 2011 replacing BOURGOGNE GRAND ORDINAIRE. Mostly reds, GAMAY, PINOT N. Main take-up is hard-to-sell basic BEAUJ reclassified under this sexier name. Main burg NÉGOCIANTS showing interest. Rare whites ALIGOTÉ, CHARD, MELON, PINOTS BL, GR.

Coteaux Champenois Champ r (p) w ★★★ (w) DYA. AC for still wines of CHAMP, eg. BOUZY. Vintages as for Champ. Better reds these days with climate change and better viticulture (esp 09 12').

Coteaux d'Aix-en-Provence Prov r p w ★★ Sprawling AC with Aix at centre, from Durance River to Mediterranean, from Rhône to STE-VICTOIRE mtn. Diversity of terroirs, grape varieties, both B'X, MIDI. Stylish wines. CHX Beaupré, Calissanne, La Realtière, Les Bastides, Les Béates, Revelette, **Vignelaure** and DOM du CH Bas. *See also* LES BAUX-DE-PROV.

Coteaux d'Ancenis Lo r p w (sw) ★→★★ 14 15 (16) Generally DYA. AOP (200-ha e of Nantais). Dry, DEMI-SEC, sweet CHENIN BL whites, age-worthy **Malvoisie** (PINOT GR); light reds, rosés mainly GAMAY, plus CABS FR, SAUV. Esp: Athimon et ses Enfants, Pierre Guindon, Pléiade, Quarteron. Less frost 2016.

Coteaux de Chalosse SW Fr r p w ★ DYA. Modest strictly local IGP from Les Landes, made from local grape varieties. Siimilar to Tursan, with which local co-op now merged. Gd with local cuisine.

Coteaux de Glanes SW Fr r p ★★ DYA IGP from Upper Dordogne. Locals can't get enough of these sunshiny wines from small democratic co-op. Ségalin grape gives extra pep to MERLOT, GAMAY.

Coteaux de l'Ardèche S Rh r p w ★→★★ 15' 16' Rocky hills w of Rh, wide selection, quality inching up, often gd value. New DOMS; fresh reds, some oaked (unnecessary); VIOGNIER (eg. CHAPOUTIER, Mas de Libian), MARSANNE. Best from SYRAH, also GAMAY (often old vines), CAB SAUV (Serret). Restrained, burg-style Ardèche CHARD by LOUIS LATOUR (Grand Ardèche v. oaky). DOMS du Colombier, Favette, Fluchier, Grangeon, Mazel, Vigier and CH de la Selve.

Coteaux de l'Aubance Lo w sw ★★→★★★ 89' 90' 95' 96' 97' 03 05' 07' 09 10' 11' 13 14' 15' (16) Small AC (160 ha) for long-ageing sweet CHENIN BL. Nervier, less rich than COTEAUX DU LAYON except SÉLECTION DES GRAINS NOBLES. S of LO nr Angers, less steep than Layon. Esp: Bablut, CH Princé, Haute Perche, Montgilet, Richou, Rochelles, Varière. Parts badly frosted 2016 but rest gd quality.

Coteaux de Saumur Lo w sw ★★→★★★ 05 07' 09 10' 11' 14' 15' (16) Sweet, late-harvest CHENIN BL. Like COTEAUX DU LAYON but less rich, more delicate, racy. Esp CHAMPS FLEURIS, Nerleux, St Just, Targé, Vatan. Gd 2014, 15, potential in 16.

Coteaux des Baronnies S Rh r p w ★ DYA. Rh IGP in high hills e of VINSOBRES. SYRAH (best), CAB SAUV, MERLOT, CHARD (for once gd, value), plus GRENACHE, CINSAULT, etc. Genuine, fresh country wines: improving simple reds, also clear VIOGNIER. NB: DOMS du Rieu-Frais, Le Mas Sylvia, Rosière.

Coteaux du Giennois Lo r p w ★→★★ DYA. Small AC (196 ha) widely scattered v'yds from Cosne to Gien. 2016 badly frosted. Racy, citrus SAUV BL (103 ha) a lighter style of SANCERRE or POUILLY-FUMÉ; can be v.gd. Light reds blend GAMAY/PINOT N. Best: BOURGEOIS, Charrier, Catherine & Michel Langlois, Emile Balland, Jean Marie Berthier (esp L'Inédit), Paulat, Treuillet, Villargeau.

Coteaux du Languedoc *See* LANGUEDOC.

Coteaux du Layon Lo w sw ★★→★★★★ 89 90 95 96 97 03 05' 07' 09 10' 11' 14' 15' (16) Heart of ANJOU: sweet CHENIN BL, varying sweetness with fine acidity, can be everlasting. Seven villages can add name to AC. Chaume now PREMIER CRU. Top ACs: BONNEZEAUX, QUARTS DE CHAUME. Growers: Baudouin, BAUMARD, Breuil, *Ch Pierre-Bise*, Chauvin, Delesvaux, des Forges, Guegniard, Juchepie, Ogereau, *Pithon-Paillé*, Soucherie. 2016 – crop cut by April frost.

Coteaux du Loir Lo r p w dr sw ★→★★★ 05' 08 09' 10' 11 14' 15' (16) N tributary of Loire, Le Loir, picturesque, dynamic region with Coteaux du Loir (80 ha), *Jasnières* (65 ha). Steely, fine, precise, long-lived CHENIN BL, GAMAY, peppery Pineau d'Aunis, some sparkling, plus Grolleau (rosé), CAB, CÔT. Top: Ange Vin, Breton, de Rycke, DOM DE BELLIVIÈRE, Fresneau, Gigou, Janvier, Le Briseau, Les Maisons Rouges. Gd 2014, 15; frost, hail 16.

Coteaux du Lyonnais Beauj r p (w) ★ DYA Junior BEAUJ. Best en PRIMEUR.

Coteaux du Quercy SW Fr r p ★ 12 14' 15 AOP S of CAHORS. CAB FR basis of everyday winter warmers gd with stews and game. Will keep. Worthy co-op challenged by ★★DOMS du Guillau, Merchien (IGP) and ★Doms d'Ariès, Mystère d'Éléna (Dom de Revel).

Coteaux du Vendômois Lo r p w ★→★★ 14 15 (16) AC, 28 communes, c.150 ha: Vendôme to Montoire in Le Loir Valley. Mostly VIN GRIS from Pineau d'Aunis (Chenin Noir) reds typically peppery, also blends of CAB FR, PINOT N, GAMAY. Whites: CHENIN BL, CHARD. Producers: Brazilier, Four à Chaux, J Martellière, Montrieux (Emile Heredia), Patrice Colin; CAVE du Vendôme-Villiers (gd).

Coteaux et Terrasses de Montauban SW Fr r p w ★→★★ DYA IGP created, dominated by ambitious DOM de Montels, which has spread to CAHORS (Dom Serre de Bovila). Huge range of gd-value wines. But don't forget ★Dom Biarnès, Mas des Anges.

Coteaux Varois-en-Provence Prov r p w ★→★★ 11 12 13 14 15 16 Overlooked AC sandwiched between bigger COTEAUX D'AIX and CÔTES DE PROV. Warming reds, fresh rosés from usual s varieties. Potential being realized, esp SYRAH. Try CHX la Calisse, Miraval (Brangelina's), Trians and DOMS des Alysses, *des Aspras*, des Chaberts, du Deffends, du Loou, *Routas*.

Coulée de Serrant Lo w dr sw ★★★★ 95 96 97 99 02 03 05 07 08 10' 11 12 13 14 15 (16) Historic, steep CHENIN BL monopole 7-ha bio v'yd overlooking Lo in heart of AC SAVENNIÈRES. Nicolas Joly's daughter Virginie now in charge. V. oxidative style – too often fascinating but faulty wines.

Courcel, Dom de C d'O r ★★★ Leading POMMARD estate, fine floral wines using ripe grapes and whole bunches. Top, age-worthy, PREMIERS CRUS Rugiens and Epenots, plus interesting Croix Noires.

Crémant In CHAMP, used to mean "creaming" (half-sparkling): now called *demi-mousse/perle*. Since 1975, AC for quality classic-method sparkling from AL, B'X, BOURGOGNE, Die, Jura, LIMOUX, Lo and Luxembourg.

Crépy Sav w ★★ DYA. Light, soft white from s shore of Lake Geneva. 80% min Chasselas. Largest producer: Grande CAVE de Crèpy Mercier (part bio).

Criots-Bâtard-Montrachet C d'O ★★★ 02' 04 05 06 07 08 09 10 11 12 13 14' 15 (16) Tiny MONTRACHET satellite, 1.57 ha. Less concentrated than BÂTARD, but chiselled sensuality at best. Fragmented holdings but try Belland, Blain-GAGNARD, Fontaine G, Lamy.

Crozes-Hermitage N Rh r w ★★→★★★ 09' 10' 12' 13' 14 15' 16' SYRAH from (mainly) flat v'yds nr River Isère: dark-berry fruit, liquorice, tar, mostly early-drinking (2–5 yrs). Often better from granite hills beside HERMITAGE: fine, red-fruited, can age; 2015 fun wines. Best (simple CUVÉES) ideal for grills, parties. Some oaked, older-vine wines cost more. Top: *A Graillot*, Aléofane (r w), Belle, *Chapoutier*, CH Curson, *Delas* (Le CLOS v.gd), DOM des Grands Chemins, E Darnaud; Doms Combier (organic), de *Thalabert* of JABOULET, des Entrefaux (oak), des Hauts-Chassis, des Lises (fine), *du Colombier*, Dumaine (organic), Fayolle Fils & Fille (stylish), Les Bruyères (organic, big fruit), Mucyn, Remizières (oak), Rousset, Y Chave. Drink white (MARSANNE) early, v.gd vintages recently. Value.

Cuve close Quicker method of making sparkling wine in a tank. Sparkle dies away in glass much quicker than with *méthode traditionnelle*.

Cuvée Wine contained in a *cuve* or vat. A word of many uses, incl synonym for "blend" and 1st-press wines (as in CHAMP). Often just refers to a "lot" of wine.

Dagueneau, Didier Lo w ★★★ →★★★★ 03 05' 07 08' 09' 10' 11 12' 13 14' 15' (16) Best producer of POUILLY-FUMÉ; remarkably precise SAUV BL. Now run by Didier's son Louis-Benjamin and daughter Charlotte. Louis-Benjamin on label. Indigenous yeasts. Top CUVÉES: Pur Sang, Silex. Also SANCERRE (Les Monts Damnés, CHAVIGNOL), JURANÇON. 2016: despite frost in Pur Sang v'yd, gd quality overall.

Dauvissat, Vincent Chab w ★★★★ Imperturbable bio producer of great classic CHAB from old barrels, incl local 132-litre *feuillettes*. Age-worthy wines similar to RAVENEAU cousins. Best: La Forest, Les CLOS, Preuses, Séchet. Try also Fabien D.

Deiss, Dom Marcel Al r w ★★★ Bio grower at Bergheim. Favours blended wines from individual v'yds, often different varieties co-planted, mixed success. Best wine RIES Schoenenbourg 10 11 12 13 15'.

Delamotte Champ BRUT; *Blanc de Blancs* 04 06 07 08'; CUVÉE Nicholas Delamotte. Fine small CHARD-dominated house at LE MESNIL. V.gd *saignée* rosé. Managed with SALON by LAURENT-PERRIER. Called "the poor man's Salon" but sometimes surpasses it, as in 85 02 04, delightful ready 07.

Delas Frères N Rh r p w ★→★★★ Consistent N Rh v'yd owner/merchant, with CONDRIEU, CROZES-HERMITAGE, CÔTE-RÔTIE, HERMITAGE v'yds. Best: Condrieu (CLOS Boucher), *Côte-Rôtie Landonne*, Hermitage DOM des Tourettes (r), M de la Tourette (w), Les Bessards (r, terroir, v, fine, smoky, long life). S Rh: esp CÔTES DU RH St-Esprit (r). Whites lighter recently. Owned by ROEDERER.

Demi-sec Half-dry: in practice more like half-sweet (eg. CHAMP typically 45g/l dosage).

Derenoncourt, Stéphane B'x Leading international consultant; self-taught, focused on terroir, fruit, balance. Own property, *Dom de l'A* in CAS.

Deutz Champ BRUT Classic and Rosé NV; Brut 04 06 08 09. Top-flight CHARD CUVÉE Amour de Deutz 04 06 08 09 12'; ★★★Amour de Deutz Rosé 06. One of top small CHAMP houses, ROEDERER-owned. V. dry, classic wines. *Superb Cuvée William Deutz* 02 88'. Careful buyer in top GRAND CRU sites.

Dirler-Cadé, Dom Al Excellent estate in Bergholtz. Exceptional old-vines MUSCAT GRAND CRU Saering, depth and sculpted elegance 09 12 13 14 in riper style of S AL. Fine RIES GC Saering 08 13 14 15'.

Domaine (Dom) Property. *See* under name, eg. TEMPIER, DOM.

Dom Pérignon Champ Luxury CUVÉE of MOËT & CHANDON. Ultra-*consistent quality*, creamy character, esp with 10–15 yrs bottle age; v. tight in youth. 96 superb at 20 yrs. Oenotèque (long bottle age, recent disgorgement, boosted price) renamed Plénitude; 7, 16, 30 yrs+ (P1, P2, P3); superb P2 98; unsung, excellent P2 93. Superb 02 on release now in transition to 2nd Plenitude, exotic 03, great 04, 06. More PINOT N focus in DP Rosé 04 05.

Dopff au Moulin Al w ★★★ Ancient, top-class family producer. Class act in GEWURZ GRANDS CRUS Brand, Sporen 09 10 12 13 14; lovely RIES SCHOFNENBOURG 10' 12, exceptional 13 come 2020; *Sylvaner de Riquewihr 14*. Pioneer of AL CRÉMANT; gd CUVÉES: Bartholdi, Julien, Bio. Specialist in classic dry wines.

Dourthe B'x Sizeable merchant/grower; wide range, quality emphasis. CHX: BELGRAVE, de Ricaud, LA GARDE, LE BOSCQ, Grand Barrail Lamarzelle Figeac, PEY LA TOUR, RAHOUL, REYSSON. *Dourthe No 1* (esp white) well-made generic B'X, reliable quality.

Drappier, André Champ Great family-run AUBE house. 15 ha of 56 ha v'yds now certified bio; *Pinot-led NV*, ★★BRUT ZÉRO, Brut *"sans souffre"* (no sulphur), Millésime d'Exception 06 08 09 10, ace Prestige CUVÉE Grande Sendrée 06 09' 10. Cuvée Quatuor (four *cépages*). Superb older vintages 95 85 82 (magnums).

DRC (Dom de la Romanée-Conti) C d'O r w ★★★★ Grandest estate in Burg. MONOPOLES ROMANÉE-CONTI and LA TÂCHE, major parts of ÉCHÉZEAUX, GRANDS-ÉCHÉZEAUX, RICHEBOURG, ROMANÉE-ST-VIVANT and a tiny part of MONTRACHET. Also CORTON from 2009. Crown-jewel prices. Keep top vintages for decades.

Drouhin, Joseph & Cie Burg r w ★★★→★★★★ Deservedly prestigious grower and merchant in BEAUNE; v'yds (all bio) incl (w) Beaune *Clos des Mouches*, LAGUICHE MONTRACHET. Notably fragrant reds from pretty CHOREY-LÈS-BEAUNE to majestic *Musigny*, GRANDS-ÉCHÉZEAUX, etc. Also DDO (Domaine Drouhin Oregon), *see* US.

Duboeuf, Georges Beauj r w ★★→★★★ Most famous name of BEAUJ, architect of worldwide Nouveau craze. Huge range of CUVÉES, many gd crus; MÁCON whites.

Dugat C d'O r ★★★ Cousins Claude and Bernard (Dugat-Py) make excellent, deep-coloured GEVREY-CHAMBERTIN, respective labels. Tiny volumes, esp GRANDS CRUS, huge prices, esp Dugat-Py. Try Claude D's NÉGOCIANT label, La Gibryotte.

Dujac, Dom C d'O r w ★★★→★★★★ MOREY-ST-DENIS grower; exceptional range of seven GRANDS CRUS, esp CLOS DE LA ROCHE, CLOS ST-DENIS, ÉCHÉZEAUX. Lighter colours but intense fruit, smoky, strawberry character from use of stems. Slightly deeper, denser wines in recent yrs. Also DOM Triennes in COTEAUX VAROIS.

Dureuil-Janthial Burg r w ★★ Top DOM in RULLY in capable hands of Vincent D-J, with *fresh, punchy whites* and cheerful, juicy reds. Try Maizières (r w) or PREMIER CRU Meix Cadot (w).

Durup, Jean Chab w ★★ Volume CHAB producer as DOM de l'Eglantière and CH de Maligny, now allied by marriage to Dom Colinot in IRANCY.

Duval-Leroy Champ Dynamic Vertus CHAMP house, family-owned. 200 ha of mainly fine CHARD crus. New shift to vegan-friendly Champ, ie. natural clarification and settling, avoiding milk-protein fining agents. V.gd Fleur de Champagne NV. Top Bl de Prestige *Femme* 96' 04 08 13 15'.

Échézeaux C d'O r ★★★ 90' 93 96' 99' 02' 03 05' 06 08 09' 10' 11 12' 13 14 15' (16) GRAND CRU next to CLOS DE VOUGEOT. Middling weight, but can have exceptionally intricate flavours and startling persistence. Best from Arnoux, DRC, DUJAC, EUGÉNIE, GRIVOT, GROS, Guyon, Lamarche, LIGER-BELAIR, Mongeard-MUGNERET, Mugneret-Gibourg, ROUGET, Tremblay.

Ecu, Dom de l' Lo (r) w dr (sp) ★★★ 10' 11 12 14' 15' Bio MUSCADET-SÈVRE-ET-MAINE (Granite, Taurus), GROS PLANT. Dynamic Frédéric Niger Van Herck has taken over from Guy Bossard. Gd CAB FR, PINOT N. Many different CUVÉES, growing park of amphorae. Badly frosted April 2016.

Edelzwicker Al w ★ DYA. Blended light white. CH d'Ittenwiller, HUGEL Gentil gd.

Yrs when Mistral blows have more concentration: longer-ageing Châteauneuf.

Eguisheim, Cave Vinicole d' Al r w ★★ Impeccable AL co-op. Excellent value: fine GRANDS CRUS Hatschbourg, HENGST, Ollwiller, Spiegel. Owns Willm. Top label: WOLFBERGER. Best: Grande Rés 09 10 11 12, Sigillé, Armorié. Gd CRÉMANT, PINOT N (esp 10' 11 12 15).

Entraygues et du Fel and Estaing SW Fr r p w ★→★★ DYA. Two tiny AOP neighbours in terraces above Lot Valley. Tingling CHENIN, from ★★DOM Méjanassère. Laurent Mousset for reds esp ★★La Pauca and excellent rosé. ★★Nicolas Carmarans now also making AOP reds from FER SERVADOU.

Entre-Deux-Mers B'X w ★→★★ DYA. Often gd-value dry white B'X from between the Rivers Garonne and Dordogne. Best: CHX BONNET, Fontenille, Haut Rion, Landereau, Les Arromans, Lestrille, Les Tuileries, Marjosse, Moulin de Launay, Nardique-la-Gravière, Sainte-Marie, *Tour de Mirambeau*, Turcaud.

Esmonin, Dom Sylvie C d'O r ★★★ Rich, dark wines from fully ripe grapes, esp since 2000. Lots of oak and lots of stems. Notable GEVREY-CHAMBERTIN VIEILLES VIGNES, CLOS ST-JACQUES. Cousin Frédéric has Estournelles St-Jacques.

AC Faugères named not for wine, but for brandy, Fine de Faugères, famous in C19.

Eugénie, Dom C d'O r (w) ★★★→★★★★ Formerly DOM Engel, bought by François Pinault of CH LATOUR in 2006. Now impressive wines at ditto prices. CLOS VOUGEOT, GRANDS-ÉCHÉZEAUX best.

Faiveley, J Burg r w ★★→★★★★ More grower than merchant, making succulent, richly fruity wines since sea-change in 2007. Gd-value from CÔTE CHALONNAISE, but save up for top wines from CHAMBERTIN-CLOS DE BÈZE, CHAMBOLLE-MUSIGNY, CORTON *Clos des Cortons*, NUITS. Ambitious recent acquisitions throughout C D'O and now DOM Billaud-Simon (CHAB).

Faller, Théo / Weinbach, Dom Al w ★★★→★★★★ Founded by Capuchin monks in 1612. Late Laurence Faller, taken before her time, made wines of great complexity: drier than most, esp GRANDS CRUS SCHLOSSBERG (RIES, esp 08 10' 13). Wines of great *character and elegance*. Esp CUVÉE Ste Catherine SÉLECTION DES GRAINS NOBLE GEWURZ 90 09 10 11 12 14 15. Older sister Catherine now at the helm.

Faugères L'doc r (p) (w) ★→★★★ 11 12 13 14 15 16 Early AC, 1982, and now Cru du L'doc. Compact, seven villages, defined by schist, for fresh spicy reds. Elegant whites; from MARSANNE, ROUSSANNE, VERMENTINO, GRENACHE BLANC. Est families as well as newcomers. Drink DOMS Cébène, Chaberts, Chenaie, des Trinités, JEAN-MICHEL ALQUIER, Léon Barral, Mas d'Alezon, OLLIER-TAILLEFER, St Antonin, *Sarabande* and many others.

Fèvre, William Chab w ★★★→★★★★ Biggest owner of CHAB GRANDS CRUS; Bougros and Les Clos outstanding. Small yields, no expense spared, priced accordingly, a top source for concentrated, age-worthy wines. Owned by HENRIOT.

Fiefs Vendéens Lo r p w ★→★★★ 09 10 14' 15' Mainly DYA AC. Wines from the Vendée nr Sables d'Olonne, from tourist wines to serious ageing examples. CHARD, CHENIN BL, MELON, SAUV BL (w), CAB FR, CAB SAUV, GAMAY, Grolleau Gris, Negrette, PINOT N (r p). Esp: Coirier, DOM St-Nicolas (bio – top producer), Mourat (122 ha), Prieure-la-Chaume (bio). Frosted 2016.

Fitou L'doc r ★★ 11 12 13 14 15 16 Characterful rugged red from hills s of Narbonne as well as tamer coastal v'yds. MIDI's oldest AC for table wine, created in 1948. 11 mths' ageing, benefits from bottle-age. Seek out CH de Nouvelles, Champs des Sœurs, DOM Bertrand-Bergé, Jones, Lérys, Rolland.

Fixin C d'O r (w) ★★★ 99' 02' 03 05' 06 07 08 09' 10' 11 12' 13 14 15 (16) Worthy and undervalued n neighbour of GEVREY-CHAMBERTIN. Sturdy, sometimes splendid reds but can be rustic. Best v'yds: CLOS de la Perrière, Clos du Chapitre, Clos Napoléon. Rising star is Amélie Berthaut, plus established DOMS Bart, CLAIR, FAIVELEY, Gelin, Guyard, Joliet, MORTET.

Fleurie Beauj r ★★★ 13 14 15' 16 Top BEAUJ cru for perfumed, strawberry fruit, silky texture. Racier from La Madone hillside, richer below. More and more single-v'yd wines. Classic names: Chignard, CLOS de la Roilette, Depardon, Métrat, Villa Ponciago, DUBOEUF, co-op. Naturalists: Balagny, Dutraive, Métras, Sunier. Newcomers: Graillot (DOM de Fa), Lafarge-Vial.

Fourrier, Jean-Claude C d'O r ★★★★ In hands of Jean-Marie F, this GEVREY-CHAMBERTIN DOM reached cult status, prices to match. Profound yet succulent reds, esp CLOS ST-JACQUES, Combe aux Moines, GRIOTTE-CHAMBERTIN.

Francs-Côtes de Bordeaux r w ★★ 09' 10' 12 14 15 16 Tiny B'X AC next to CAS. Fief of

Thienpont (PAVIE-MACQUIN) family. Mainly red from MERLOT but some gd white: can be tasty, attractive. Reds can age a little. Top CHX: Charmes-Godard, Francs, Laclaverie, La Prade, Le Puy, Marsau, *Puygueraud*.

Fronsac B'x r ★★→★★★ 05′ 06 08 09′ 10′ 11 12 14 15 16 Underrated hilly AC w of ST-ÉM; great-value MERLOT-dominated red, some ageing potential. Top CH: Arnauton, DALEM, Fontenil, *la Dauphine*, la Grave, la Rivière, la Rousselle, LA VIEILLE CURE, LES TROIS CROIX, Haut-Carles, Mayne-Vieil, *Moulin-Haut-Laroque*, Richelieu, Tour du Moulin, Villars. *See also* CANON-FRON.

Fronton SW Fr r p ★★ 14 15′16′ AOP n of Toulouse. Négrette grape (sometimes unblended here) hardly found elsewhere; suggests violets, cherries, liquorice. Best at 3 yrs. Try ★★CHX Baudare, best-known *Bellevue-la-Forêt*, *Bouissel*, Boujac, Caze, du Roc, Plaisance (esp Alabets), DOMS des Pradelles, Viguerie de Belaygues. AOP for whites coming shortly?

Fuissé, Ch Burg w ★★→★★★ A leader in POUILLY-FUISSÉ with some grand terroirs (Le CLOS, Combettes) and some more commercial bottlings.

Gagnard C d'O (r) w ★★★→★★★★ Well-known clan in CHASSAGNE-MONTRACHET. Long-lasting wines, esp Caillerets, BÂTARD from Jean-Noël G; while Blain-G, Fontaine G have full range incl rare CRIOTS-BÂTARD, MONTRACHET itself. Gd value offered by all Gagnards.

Gaillac SW Fr r p w dr sw sp ★→★★ (r) 14′ 15′ 16 (w sw) 12 14′ 15′ 16 (p w dr sp) DYA. Ever-improving AOP w of Albi. Eclectic grapes eg. Braucol, DURAS, Len de l'El, Mauzac lend unique character. ★★★Causse-Marines, de la Ramaye, Laurent Cazottes, Le Champ d'Orphée, Peyres-Roses, *Plageoles* (all bio); ★★L'Enclos des Braves, L'Enclos des Roses, La Ferme du Vert, DOMS Brin, d'Escausses, Cassagnoles, du Moullin, Mayragues (bio), Rotier, Sarrabelle, CHX Bourguet (w sw), Larroque, Palvié (r). Bargains from ★★Doms Duffau, Labarthe, La Chanade, Lamothe and Mas Pignou.

Ganevat Jura r w ★★★→★★★★★ CÔTES DU JURA superstar. Single-v'yd CHARD (eg. Chalasses, Grand Teppes), pricey but fabulous. Also innovative reds.

Gauby, Dom Gérard Rouss r w ★★★ Exemplary ROUSS producer, followed by several others in village of Calce. Bio. Both IGP CÔTES CATALANES, CÔTES DU ROUSS-VILLAGES Muntada; Les Calcinaires VIEILLES VIGNES. Associated with DOM Le Soula. Dessert wine Le Pain du Sucre, other novelties, with son Lionel an innovative winemaker.

Gers SW Fr r p w ★ DYA IGP usually sold as CÔTES DE GASCOGNE; indistinguishable.

Gevrey-Chambertin C d'O r ★★★→★★★★ 90′ 96′ 99′ 02′ 03 05′ 06 07 08 09′ 10′ 11 12′ 13 14 15′ 16 Village containing the great CHAMBERTIN, its GRAND CRU cousins and many other noble v'yds eg. PREMIERS CRUS Cazetiers, Combe aux Moines, Combottes, CLOS ST-JACQUES. Succulent fruit with savoury edge, value at village level, esp VIEILLES VIGNES bottlings. Top: BACHELET, BOILLOT, BURGUET, Damoy, DROUHIN, Drouhin-Laroze, DUGAT, Dugat-Py, Duroché, ESMONIN, FAIVELEY, FOURRIER, Géantet-Pansiot, Harmand-Geoffroy, JADOT, LEROY, MORTET, ROSSIGNOL-TRAPET, Roty, ROUSSEAU, Roy, SÉRAFIN, TRAPET.

Gigondas S Rh r p ★★→★★★ 78′ 89′ 90′ 95′ 98′ 99′ 00′ 01′ 03′ 04′ 05′ 06′ 07′ 08 09′ 10′ 11 12′ 13′ 14′ 15′ 16′ Top S Rh red. Handsome v'yds on stony clay-sand plain rise to Alpine limestone hills e of Avignon; GRENACHE, plus SYRAH, MOURVÈDRE. Robust, smoky, wines; best offer fine, clear, dark red fruit. Ace 2010, 15, 16. More oak recently, esp for US market, higher prices, but genuine local feel in many. Top: Boisson, Bosquets (gd modern), Bouïssière (punchy), Brusset, Cayron, CH de Montmirail, CLOS des Cazaux (value), Clos du Joncuas (organic, traditional), *Famille Perrin*, Goubert, Gour de Chaulé (fine), Grapillon d'Or, *les Pallières*, Moulin de la Gardette (stylish), Notre Dame des Pallières, P Amadieu, Pesquier, *Raspail-Ay*, Roubine, Santa Duc (now stylish), Semelles de Vent, St-Cosme (swish) St Gayan (long-lived), Teyssonières. Heady rosés.

FRANCE

Gimonnet, Pierre Champ ★★→★★★ 28 ha of GRAND and PREMIER CRUS on n Côte des Blancs. Enviably consistent CHARD. No wood. Ace CUVÉE Gastronome for seafood.

Girardin, Vincent C d'O r w ★★→★★★ White-specialist MEURSAULT-based grower/ NÉGOCIANT, now under BOISSET ownership.

Givry Burg r (w) ★★ 09' 10' 12 13 14 15' 16' Top tip in CÔTE CHALONNAISE for tasty reds that can age. Better value than MERCUREY. Rare whites nutty in style. Best (r): JOBLOT, CLOS Salomon, *Faiveley*, F Lumpp, Masse, Thénard.

Goisot Burg r w ★★★ Jean-Hugues G, outstanding producer in rural backwater of ST-BRIS. Single-v'yd versions of this SAUV AC, and Côtes d'Auxerre for CHARD, PINOT N. Hard to get nowadays, even from cellar door.

Gosset Champ Old AŸ house founded in C16, for complex CHAMP, traditional vinous style. Now moved to Épernay. V.gd CUVÉE Elegance NV more racy Traditional Grand Millésime 02 04, Prestige Celebris more precise, CHARD-driven in extra-BRUT style, fine 04, great 98; 15 Years cuvée v. variable.

Gouges, Henri C d'O r w ★★★ Grégory Gouges continues family success with rich, meaty, long-lasting NUITS-ST-GEORGES from several PREMIER CRU v'yds. Some find them too tannic in youth. Try Vaucrains, Les St-Georges or Chaignots. Interesting *white Nuits* incl PINOT BL.

Grand Cru Official term meaning different things in different areas. One of top Burg v'yds with its own AC. In AL, one of 51 top v'yds, each now with its own rules. In ST-ÉM, 60 per cent of production is St-Ém Grand Cru, often run-of-the-mill. In MÉD there are five tiers of Grands Crus Classés. In CHAMP top 17 villages are Grands Crus. Now new designation in Lo for QUARTS DE CHAUME, and emerging system in L'DOC. Take with pinch of salt in PROV.

Grande Rue, La C d'O r ★★★ 90' 95 96' 98 02' 03 05' 06 07 08 09' 10' 11 12' 13 14 15' (16) Starting to see best of this narrow strip of GRAND CRU between LA TÂCHE and ROMANÉE-CONTI. Not quite in same league, certainly not same price. MONOPOLE of DOM Lamarche.

Grands-Échézeaux C d'O r ★★★★ 90' 93 95 96' 99' 00 02' 03 05' 06 07 08 09' 10' 11 12' 13 14 15' (16) Superlative GRAND CRU next to CLOS DE VOUGEOT, but with a MUSIGNY silkiness. More weight than most ÉCHÉZEAUX. Top: BICHOT (CLOS Frantin), DRC, DROUHIN, EUGÉNIE, G Noellat, GROS, Lamarche, Mongeard-MUGNERET.

Grange des Pères, Dom de la L'doc r w ★★★ IGP Pays l'Hérault. Cult estate neighbouring MAS DE DAUMAS GASSAC, created by Laurent Vaillé for first vintage (1992). Red from SYRAH, MOURVÈDRE, CAB SAUV; white 80% ROUSSANNE, plus MARSANNE, CHARD. Stylish wines with ageing potential.

Gratien, Alfred and Gratien & Meyer Champ ★★★ BRUT 83' 96' 02 04 07 08' 09; Brut NV. CHARD-led Prestige CUVÉE Paradis Brut, Rosé (multi-vintage). Excellent quirky CHAMP and Lo house, now German-owned. Fine, v. dry, lasting, oak-fermented wines, incl *The Wine Society's house Champagne*. Careful buyer of top crus from favourite growers. Gratien & Meyer is counterpart at SAUMUR.

Graves B'x r w ★→★★ 05' 06 08 09' 10' 12 14 15 16 Name derived from gravel soils s of Bordeaux city. Juicy, appetizing reds, fresh SAUV/SÉM dry whites. One of best values in B'x today. Top CHX: ARCHAMBEAU, Brondelle, de Cérons, CHANTEGRIVE, CLOS Bourgelat, *Clos Floridène*, CRABITEY, Ferrande, Fougères, Grand Enclos du Ch de Cérons, Haura, Magneau, Pont de Brion, Rahoul, *Respide-Médeville*, Roquetaillade La Grange, St-Robert CUVÉE Poncet Deville, Vieux Ch Gaubert, Villa Bel Air.

Graves de Vayres B'x r w ★ DYA. Tiny AC within E-2-M zone. Red, white, *moelleux*.

Grignan-les-Adhémar S Rh r (p) w ★→★★ 15' 16' Mid-Rh AC; best reds hearty, tangy, herbal. Leaders: DOMS de Bonetto-Fabrol, de Montine (stylish red, gd white, rosé, also red CÔTES DU RH), Grangeneuve best (esp VIEILLES VIGNES), St-Luc and CHX Bizard, La Décelle (incl white CÔTES DU RH).

Griotte-Chambertin C d'O r ★★★★ 90′ 95 96′ 99′ 02′ 03 05′ 06 07 08 09′ 10′ 11 12′ 13 14 15′ (16) Small GRAND CRU next to CHAMBERTIN. Less weight but brisk red fruit and ageing potential, at least from DROUHIN, DUGAT, FOURRIER, *Ponsot*, R Leclerc.

Grivot, Jean C d'O r w ★★★ →★★★★ Huge improvements at this VOSNE-ROMANÉE DOM in past decade, reflected in higher prices. Superb range topped by GRANDS CRUS CLOS DE VOUGEOT, ÉCHÉZEAUX, RICHEBOURG.

Gros, Doms C d'O r w ★★★ →★★★★ Fine family of VIGNERONS in VOSNE-ROMANÉE with stylish wines from Anne (sumptuous RICHEBOURG), succulent reds from Michel (CLOS de Réas), much-improved Anne-Françoise (now in BEAUNE) and Gros Frère & Soeur (CLOS VOUGEOT En Musigni). Most offer value HAUTES-CÔTES DE NUITS. Anne has a stake in MINERVOIS.

Gros Plant du Pays Nantais Lo w (sp) ★→★★ DYA. Much-improved AC from GROS PLANT (FOLLE BLANCHE), best racy, saline, excellent with shellfish, esp oysters. Try: Basse Ville, Ecu, Haut-Bourg, Luneau-Papin, Preuille, Poiron-Dabin. Sparkling: either pure or blended.

Guigal, Ets E N Rh r w ★★→★★★★ Famous grower-merchant: CÔTE-RÔTIE mainly, plus CONDRIEU, CROZES-HERMITAGE, HERMITAGE, ST-JOSEPH v'yds. Merchant: Condrieu, Côte-Rôtie, Crozes-Hermitage, Hermitage, S Rh. Owns DOM de Bonserine (deep Côte-Rôtie), VIDAL-FLEURY (fruit, quality rising). Top, v. expensive Côte-Rôties La Mouline, La Landonne, La Turque (dark, ultra rich, new oak for 42 mths, so atypical), also v.gd Hermitage, St-Joseph Vignes de l'Hospice; all reds dense. Standard wines: gd, esp top-value CÔTES DU RH (r p w). Best whites: Condrieu, Condrieu La Doriane (oaky), Hermitage.

Hautes-Côtes de Beaune / Nuits C d'O r w ★★ (r) 09′ 10′ 12 13 14 15′ (16) (w) 12′ 13 14′ 15′ (16) ACS for villages in hills behind CÔTE DE BEAUNE/NUITS. Attractive lighter reds, whites for early drinking. Best whites: Devevey, MÉO-CAMUZET, Montchovet, Thevenot-le-Brun. Top reds: Carré, Cornu, Duband, Féry, GROS, Jacob, Jouan, Magnien, Mazilly, Naudin-Ferrand, Verdet. Also useful large co-op nr BEAUNE.

Haut-Médoc B'x r ★★→★★★ 04 05′ 06 08 09′ 10′ 11 12 14 15 16 Prime source of dry, digestible CAB/MERLOT reds. Usually gd value. Some variation in soils and wines: sand and gravel in s; heavier clay and gravel in n; sturdier wines. Five Classed Growths (BELGRAVE, CAMENSAC, CANTEMERLE, LA LAGUNE, LA TOUR-CARNET). Other top CHX: D'AGASSAC, BELLE-VUE, CAMBON LA PELOUSE, Charmail, CISSAC, CITRAN, Clément-Pichon, COUFRAN, de Lamarque, Gironville, LANESSAN, Larose Perganson, Paloumey, SÉNÉJAC, SOCIANDO-MALLET.

Haut-Montravel SW Fr w sw ★★ 11′ 12 14′ 15 (16) Sweetest of MONTRAVEL white AOPS, worthy rivals to better-known MONBAZILLAC, SAUSSIGNAC. ★★★CH Puy-Servain-Terrement outstanding. ★★DOMS Moulin Caresse, bargain Libarde not far behind.

Haut-Poitou Lo r p w sp ★→★★ 14 15 (16) Best age at least 5–6 yrs. AC (around 750 ha) n of Poitiers from CAB SAUV, CAB FR, GAMAY, CHARD, PINOT N, SAUV BL. Dynamic organic *Ampelidae* (Frédéric Brochet) dominates. IGP wines from 120 ha. Also La Tour Beaumont.

Heidsieck, Charles Champ Legendary house, smaller than before, but wines as brilliant as ever, under new perfectionist winemaker; BRUT Rés all toasty elegance, peerless *Blanc des Millénaires* 95 rumoured soon to have new vintage (04). Great mature Brut Res Vintage in prime form esp 83; CHAMP Charlie 82.

Heidsieck Monopole Champ Once-great CHAMP house. Fair quality, gd price. Gold Top 07 09. Part of VRANKEN group.

Hengst Al GRAND CRU. Gives powerful wines. Excels with top GEWURZ from JOSMEYER, ZIND-HUMBRECHT; also AUXERROIS, CHASSELAS, PINOT N.

Henri Abelé Champ New name for Abel Lepitre, old est house, now focusing on exports. Best CUVÉE Sourire de Reims 07, new Sourire Rosé 06 (pure PINOT N Les Riceys, sunny yr). Owned by Freixenet.

Henriot Champ BRUT Souverain NV much improved; ace BLANC DE BLANCS de CHARD NV; Brut 96' 02' 08'; Brut Rosé 06 09. Fine family CHAMP house. New long-aged *Cuve 38*, a solera of GRAND CRU Chard since 1990. Outstanding long-lived Prestige CUVÉE Les Enchanteleurs 88' 96 02 04 08'. Also owns BOUCHARD PÈRE & FILS, FÈVRE.

Hermitage N Rh r w ★★★→★★★★ 61' 66' 78' 83' 85' 88 89' 90' 91' 95' 96' 97' 98' 99' 00 01' 03' 04 05' 06' 07' 09' 10' 11' 12' 13' 14' 15' 16' (2010, 15 both brilliant) Hill on e Rhône bank with grandest, deepest, most elegant SYRAH and complex, nutty/white-fruited, fascinating white (MARSANNE, some ROUSSANNE) best left for 6–7 yrs+. Best: Belle, *Chapoutier*, Colombier, DELAS, Faurie (pure), GUIGAL, Habrard (w), *J-L Chave* (rich, elegant), M Sorrel (mighty Le Gréal r), Nicolas Perrin, *Paul Jaboulet*, Philippe & Vincent Jaboulet (r w), Tardieu Laurent (oak), TAIN co-op gd (esp Epsilon, Gambert de Loche).

Hortus, Dom de l' L'doc r w ★★★ An early PIC ST-LOUP producer. Deliciously intriguing white Bergerie IGP Val de Montferrand with seven grape varieties; elegant red Bergerie and oak-aged Grande CUVÉE. Also red CLOS du Prieur in cooler TERRASSES DU LARZAC.

Hospices de Beaune C d'O Spectacular medieval foundation with grand charity auction of CUVÉES from its 61 ha for Beaune's hospital, 3rd Sunday in Nov, run since 2005 by Christie's. Individuals can buy as well as trade. Standards more consistent under Roland Masse (retired 2015); another step forward with Ludivine Griveau taking over. Try BEAUNE cuvées, VOLNAYS or expensive GRANDS CRUS, (r) CORTON, ÉCHÉZEAUX, MAZIS-CHAMBERTIN, (w) BÂTARD-MONTRACHET.

Hudelot C d'O r w ★★★ VIGNERON family in CÔTE DE NUITS. New life breathed into H-Noëllat (VOUGEOT), while H-Baillet (CHAMBOLLE) challenging hard. Former more stylish, latter more punchy.

Huet Lo w ★★★★ 89' 90' 95' 96' 97' 02' 03' 05' 06 07 08' 09' 10' 11 13 14 15' (16) VOUVRAY bio estate. Anthony Hwang also owns Királyudvar in Tokaji (*see* Hungary). Now run by his children Sarah, Hugo. Single v'yds: CLOS du Bourg, Le Haut Lieu, Le Mont. Almost immortal esp sweet: 1919, 21, 24, 47, 59, 89, 90. Also *pétillant*. CHENIN BL benchmark. Lovely 2015 DEMI-SEC.

Hugel & Fils Al r w sw ★★→★★★ Top AL house (yellow labels) at Riquewihr famed for late-harvest wines, esp RIES, GEWURZ VENDANGE TARDIVE, SÉLECTION DE GRAINS NOBLES. Jubilee range discontinued; new release of superb Ries Schoelhammer 07 from GRAND CRU site.

IGP (Indication Géographique Protégée) The successor to VDQS. No difference in status, only in unhelpful name.

Irancy Burg r (p) ★★ 05' 09' 10 12 14' 15 (16) Light though structured red made nr CHAB from PINOT N and more rustic local César. Elbows on table stuff. Best v'yds: Palotte, Mazelots. Best growers: *Colinot*, *Dauvissat*, Renaud, Richoux, Goisot.

Irouléguy SW Fr r p (w) ★→★★★ 12' 14 15 (16) Basque AOP. Plenty of rosé for Atlantic beaches, but red (echoes of MADIRAN) from TANNAT/CAB FR more serious, eg. ★★★Ameztia, Arretxea, Mourguy; ★★Brana, Etchegaraya, Gutizia, Ilarria; ★Abotia, Bordathio, newcomers Bordaxuria and Xubialdea. Gd whites from Petit Courbu grape, esp excellent co-op (★★★Xuri d'Ansa).

Jaboulet Aîné, Paul N Rh r w Grower-merchant at Tain. Wines polished, sleek. Once-leading producer of HERMITAGE (esp ★★★★La Chapelle, quality varied since 90s, some revival since 2010 on reds), CORNAS St-Pierre, CROZES Thalabert (can be stylish), Roure (sound); owns DOM de Terre Ferme CHÂTEAUNEUF, merchant of other Rh, notably CÔTES DU RH *Parallèle 45*, CONDRIEU, VENTOUX (r, quality/value), VACQUEYRAS. Whites lack proper Rh body, drink most young, range incl new v. expensive La Chapelle white (not made every yr).

Jacquart Champ Simplified range from co-op-turned-brand, concentrating on what it does best: PREMIERS CRUS Côte des Blancs CHARD from member growers. Fine range of Vintage BLANC DE BLANCS 10 08 07 06 05 04 targeted at restaurants. V.gd Vintage Rosé 02 04 06. Globetrotting new winemaker.

Jacquesson Champ Bijou Dizy house for precise, v. dry wines. Outstanding single-v'yd Avize Champ Caïn 02 04 05 08'. Corne Bautray, all CHARD. Dizy 04 08 09, excellent *numbered NV cuvées* 730' 731 732 733 734 735 738 739' 740 741.

Jadot, Louis Burg r p w ★★→★★★★ High-performance merchant house across board with significant v'yd holdings in C D'O, MÂCON, BEAUJ; esp POUILLY-FUISSÉ (DOM Ferret), MOULIN-À-VENT (CH des Jacques, *Clos du Grand Carquelin*). Powerful whites now bottled with DIAM, structured long-lived reds.

Jasnières Lo w dr (sw) ★★→★★★ 03 05' 07 08' 09' 10' 11 14' 15' CHENIN BL, lively, sharp, dry to sweet, dynamic AC (65 ha), s-facing slopes Loir Valley. Esp: L'Ange Vin (also VIN DE FRANCE), Aubert la Chapelle, Breton, DE BELLIVIÈRE, Le Briseau, Gigou, Janvier, J-B Métais, Les Maisons Rouges, Ryke. Great ageing potential. 2016: frost, hail.

Jobard C d'O r w ★★★ VIGNERON family in MEURSAULT. Top DOMS are Antoine J, esp long-lived Poruzots, Genevrières, CHARMES; and Rémi Jobard for immediately classy Meursaults plus reds from MONTHÉLIE, VOLNAY.

Joblot Burg r w ★★ Outstanding GIVRY DOM; v. high viticultural standards, racy wines with complexity, ageing potential. Try PREMIER CRU La Servoisine in both colours.

Joseph Perrier Champ Fine family-run CHAMP house with v.gd PINOTS N, MEUNIER v'yds, esp in own Cumières DOM. Ace Prestige CUVÉE Joséphine 02 04 08' 09 12'. Excellent BRUT Royale NV, as generous as ever but more precise with less dosage. Tangy BLANC DE BLANCS, fine food wine. 15'; now drier, finer Cuvée Royale Brut NV; distinctive tangy Blanc de Blancs 02 04 06 08 13' 15'.

Josmeyer Al w ★★→★★★ Fine, elegant, long-lived wines. Superb RIES *grand cru Hengst* 10 12 13' 14' 15'. Also v.gd lesser varieties, esp 13 14 15 AUXERROIS. Smart bio, rigorous but realistic.

Juliénas Beauj r ★★★ 09' 13 14 15' 16 Rich, hearty; juicy, structured from surprisingly unfashionable cru. Discover: Aufranc, Burrier, Michel Tête, Santé, Trenel.

Jurançon SW Fr w dr sw ★→★★★ (sw) 05' 07' 11' 12 13 14 15 16 (dr) 12 14' 15' 16 Separate AOPS (sw and dr w), both styles balancing richness and acidity. DAGUENEAU's tiny, trendy ★★★★Jardins de Babylon does not overshadow ★★★DOMS *Cauhapé*, de Sarros, de Souch, Lapeyre, Larrédya, Thou; ★★CHX Jolys, Lapuyade and Doms Bellauc, Bellegarde, Bordenave, Capdevielle, Castéra, Guirardel, Haugarot, Nigri, Uroulat and CLOS Benguères; ★Gan co-op gd value.

Kaefferkopf Al w dr (sw) ★★★ The 51st GRAND CRU of AL at Ammerschwihr. Permitted to make blends as well as varietal wines, possibly not top-drawer.

Jura jewels

What other region has so many wine styles? They seem to like confusing customers. **Dry whites** from CHARD, many single-v'yd versions now. Also tangy blends with SAVAGNIN. Fresh or deliberately **oxidative** pure Savagnin may, many made in natural style can be pretty gamey. *See* CÔTES DU JURA, ARBOIS, L'ETOILE. Vin *typé* on labels means heading towards Sherry. *Vin ouillé* means "ullaged": the barrel has been topped-up to avoid oxidation. **Light reds** from Poulsard, Trousseau, PINOT N or blends. Some more rosé than red. Côtes du Jura, Arbois. Aged **sherrified whites** known as VIN JAUNE. *See* CH-CHALON. Intensely sweet *vin de paille* made fom red and white grapes. Fortified **Macvin**, local version of ratafia. Classic producers: Bourdy, MACLE, Overnoy, Puffeney. Avant garde: A&M TISSOT, GANEVAT, PIGNIER. Volume/value: co-ops (known here as CAVES Fruitières), Boilley, HENRI MAIRE, J TISSOT, LABET.

Kientzler, Andre Al w sw ★★→★★★ Small, v. fine grower at Ribeauvillé. V.gd RIES from GRANDS CRUS Osterberg, Geisberg **09 10 11 12 13' 14 15'**, lush GEWURZ from Grand Cru Kirchberg **05 10 12**. Rich, classic sweet wines. Model v'yd care, without faith in isms or fads.

Kreydenweiss, Marc Al w sw ★★→★★★ Thoughtful bio grower, esp for PINOT GR (v.gd GRAND CRU Moenchberg), PINOT BL, RIES. Top wine: Grand Cru Kastelberg, ages 20 yrs+ **08 09 10 13' 14 15'**; gd VENDANGE TARDIVE. Use of oak now more subtle. Gd Ries/Pinot Gr blend CLOS du Val d'Eléon. Also in COSTIÈRES DE NÎMES, S Rh (bio GRENACHE, SYRAH, MOURVÈDRE).

Krug Champ Grande CUVÉE ★★★★ Vintage **95' 98 00 02' 03**; Rosé; CLOS DU MESNIL **00' 03**; CLOS D'AMBONNAY **95' 98' 00**; Krug Collection **69' 76' 81 85**. Supremely prestigious house. Rich, nutty wines, oak-fermented; highest quality, ditto price. Vintage **03** a fine surprise, **02** magnificent. No vintage in **12**, a shame as great PINOT N yr.

Kuentz-Bas Al w sw ★→★★★ Largely bio grower-merchant at Husseren-les-CHX, esp PINOT GR, GEWURZ. Gd VENDANGES TARDIVES, esp **09 10**. Fine classic drier RIES **10 11 12 13 14 15' 16**.

Labet, Dom Jura ★★★ Key CÔTES DU JURA estate in s part of region (Rotalier). Best-known for range of single-v'yd CHARD whites, eg. En Billat, En Chalasse, La Bardette etc, gd PINOT N, VIN JAUNE.

Ladoix C d'O r w ★★ **02' 03 05' 08 09' 10' 11 12 14 15'** (16) Scarcely known CÔTE DE BEAUNE village despite sharing GRANDS CRUS CORTON, CORTON-CHARLEMAGNE. For value, try juicy reds esp Les Joyeuses and exuberant whites eg. Gréchons. DOMS Chevalier, Loichet, Mallard, Ravaut leading revival.

Ladoucette, de Lo (r) (p) w ★★★ **09 10 12 13 14** (15) Largest individual producer of POUILLY-FUMÉ at CH du Nozet. Pricey prestige brand Baron de L. SANCERRE Comte Lafond, La Poussie (serious erosion on Bué's most famous site now under repair); also owns CHAB Albert Pic, VOUVRAY Marc Brédif.

Lafarge, Michel C d'O r ★★★★ Classic VOLNAY bio estate run by Frédéric L, son of ever-present Michel, over 100 vintages between them. Outstanding, long-lived PREMIERS CRUS **Clos des Chênes**, Caillerets, CLOS du CH des Ducs. Also fine BEAUNE, esp Grèves and some whites. New FLEURIE project, Lafarge-Vial.

Lafon, Dom des Comtes Burg r w ★★★→★★★★ Fabulous bio MEURSAULT, MONTRACHET DOM, with red VOLNAY (esp **Santenots**) equally outstanding. Mixed results ageing whites, reds impeccably long-lived. Heritiers L label for excellent Mâconnais range, while Dominique L makes his own CÔTE DE BEAUNE wines separately.

Laguiche, Marquis de C d'O w ★★★★ Largest owner of Le MONTRACHET and a fine PREMIER CRU CHASSAGNE, both excellently made by DROUHIN.

Lalande de Pomerol B'x r ★★ **04 05 06 08 09' 10' 11 12 14 15 16** Variable satellite neighbour of POM. Similar style but less density. Follow top growers. 100 CHX: Ame de Musset, Bertineau St-Vincent, Chambrun, La Chenade, LA FLEUR DE BOÜARD, La Sergue, Les Cruzelles, Garraud, Grand Ormeau, Haut-Chaigneau, Jean de Gué, Labordière-Mondésir, **Les Hauts Conseillants**, Pavillon Beauregard, Perron (La Fleur), Sabines, Siaurac, TOURNEFEUILLE.

Landron, Doms Lo w dr sp ★★→★★★ **09 10 13 14' 15 16** Mustachioed, v.gd producer (48 ha) of bio MUSCADET-SÈVRE-ET-MAINE: Amphibolite, Fief du Breil.

Langlois-Château Lo (r) (w) sp ★★→★★★ SAUMUR, BOLLINGER-owned. Gd CRÉMANT de Lo esp Quadrille. Range of still wines, esp v.gd age-worthy Saumur Blanc VIEILLES VIGNES **05 08 09 11 14**.

Languedoc r p w General term for the MIDI. AC incl CORBIÈRES, MINERVOIS, ROUSS; AC Coteaux du L'doc no longer exists. Rules the same. Bottom of pyramid of MIDI ACs. Hierarchy of superior crus is work in progress. Subregions incl Cabrières, Grès de Montpellier, Pézenas, Quatourze, St Saturnin: usual L'doc grapes. Tiny

Grenache in Languedoc-Roussillon

All the ACS of L'DOC-ROUSS, in theory, are blends, but have a min of 70% GRENACHE Noir – with one exception. Grenache may be at its best in Rouss, where it also makes the most wonderful VDN. Travelling from w to e: **Dom Jones**, CÔTES CATALANES, Grenache Gris: Grenache Gris is much more rewarding than Blanc for whites and comes into its own in Rouss. **Mas Amiel**, MAURY SEC, Vers le Nord: Maury's leading estate. Grenache at its best, with a touch of SYRAH. **Coume del Mas**, COLLIOURE, Schistes: Old vines; deliciously refreshing, ripe, succulent. **Mas de Mon Père**, PAYS D'OC, Cause Toujours: Newish estate in Malepère. Unoaked Grenache with some CINSAULT, delicious fresh cherry fruit. **Dom Borie de Maurel**, MINERVOIS la Livinière, Belle de Nuit: Leading estate of this aspiring AC. *Elevage* in vat rather than barrel. **Dom Jean-Michel Alquier**, FAUGÈRES, Maison Jaune: Made in gd Grenache yrs; usually incl Syrah, MOURVÈDRE; more structured than some. **Dom Turner Pageot**, L'doc, B815: Grenache/Mourvèdre, from just outside Faugères. Oak-aged but subtly so. **Dom la Croix Belle**, Côtes de Thongue, Cascaillou: Fine eg. of Grenache. **Dom Cal Demoura**, TERRASSES DU LARZAC, Feu Sacré: Forward-looking estate. Blended with CARIGNAN, Syrah. **Dom de Joncas**, MONTPEYROUX, Joia: incl Syrah, Cinsault; benchmark fresh fruit. Alba, IGP Mont Baudile is pure Grenache Gris rosé.

Cabardès and Malepère where B'X meets Midi. CLAIRETTE du L'doc tiny, once-fashionable white. Not all ACs have much specific identity: go by grower.

Lanson Champ Black Label NV; Rosé NV; Vintage BRUT on a roll esp 96 ★★★ 02 08 12' 15. Renewed house, part of LANSON-BCC group. Ace prestige NV Lanson Père et Fils Noble CUVÉE BLANC DE BLANCS, rosé and vintage; new Brut vintage single-vyd CLOS Lanson 06. Extra Age multi-vintage, Blanc de Blancs esp gd. Experienced new cellarmaster (ex-MAILLY GRAND CRU), starting to allow some malolactic fermentation for a rounder style.

Lapierre, Marcel Beauj r ★★★ Mathieu runs cult DOM making sulphur-free MORGON, as pioneered by the late Marcel L. Try also fresh, juicy Raisins Gaulois.

Laplace, Dom SW Fr Oldest est of all MADIRAN growers. Flagship ★★★Ch d'Aydie and Odie d'Aydie need time. Contrast with lighter all-TANNAT IGP ★★Les Deux Vaches; ★Aramis, both from beyond limits of Madiran. Excellent ★★★PACHERENCS (dr sw).

Laroche Chab w ★★ Major player in CHAB with range from special CUVÉE *Res de l'Obediencerie* to GRANDS CRUS. Moving away from screwcaps (pity) and bio. Also in MIDI, Chile, South Africa.

Latour, Louis Burg r w ★★ →★★★★ Famous traditional family merchant making full-bodied whites from C D'O v'yds (esp CORTON-CHARLEMAGNE), Mâconnais, Ardèche (all CHARD) while reds are looking classier – CORTON, ROMANÉE-ST-VIVANT. Also owns Henry Fessy in BEAUJ.

Latricières-Chambertin C d'O r ★★★★ 90' 93 95 96' 99' 02' 03 05' 06 07 08 09' 10' 11 12' 13 14 15' (16) GRAND CRU next to CHAMBERTIN, rich if not quite as intense. Does well in warm dry yrs. Best: Arnoux, BIZE, Drouhin-Laroze, Duband, FAIVELEY, LEROY, Remy, ROSSIGNOL-TRAPET, TRAPET.

Laudun S Rh r p w ★→★★ 12' 13 15' 16' Sound CÔTES DU RH-VILLAGE, w bank. Excellent, clear, dashing whites. Early, red fruit/peppery reds (lots of SYRAH), lively rosés. Immediate flavours from CHUSCLAN-Laudun co-op. **Dom Pelaquié** best, esp stylish white. Also CHX Courac, de Bord, Juliette, St-Maurice, Maravilhas (bio, r w), Olibrius and DOM B Duseigneur (organic), Prieuré St-Pierre.

Laurent-Perrier Champ Important house; family presence less obvious, ripe for a change of ownership? BRUT NV (CHARD-led) still perfect apéritif. Distinctive skin-contact Rosé. Fine vintages: **02 04 06 08 12**. Grand Siècle CUVÉE multi-vintage on form, peerless Grand Siècle Alexandra Rosé **06**. Ultra-Brut should be better.

Leflaive, Dom Burg w ★★★★ 1st Vincent, then sadly missed Anne-Claude L, brought this DOM to top. Reference bio PULIGNY-MONTRACHET with GRANDS CRUS, incl Le MONTRACHET, CHEVALIER. *Fabulous premiers crus*: Pucelles, Combettes, Folatières etc. MÂCON Verzé for value.

Leflaive, Olivier C d'O r w ★★→★★★ White specialist NÉGOCIANT at PULIGNY-MONTRACHET, plus own v'yds now incorporated as Récolte du DOM. Exciting wines in recent times, challenging his cousins (*see* above). Also La Maison d'Olivier, hotel, restaurant, tasting room.

Leroux, Benjamin C d'O r w ★★★ Former manager of COMTE ARMAND, now building reputation as BEAUNE-based NÉGOCIANT equally at home in red or white. Poised, honest wines. Try PREMIERS CRUS from CHASSAGNE, GEVREY, VOLNAY.

Leroy, Dom C d'O r w ★★★★ Lalou Bize Leroy, ex-DRC, bio pioneer, delivers extraordinary quality from tiny yields. Also separate DOM d'Auvenay. Amazing treasure house of mature wines from family NÉGOCIANT, Maison Leroy. But if you need to ask the price....

L'Etoile Jura w ★★ AC of JURA known for elegant CHARD grown on limestone and marl. Top tips: Cartaux-Bougaud, DOM de Monthourgeau, Philippe Vandelle. Producers also make gd CRÉMANT, VIN JAUNE.

Liger-Belair, Comte C d'O r ★★★★ Comte Louis-Michel L-B makes brilliantly ethereal wines in VOSNE-ROMANÉE, an ever-increasing stable headed by monumental LA ROMANÉE. Try also village La Colombière, CLOS du CH, and PREMIER CRU Reignots.

Liger-Belair, Thibault C d'O r ★★★ →★★★★ Cousin of above, making vigorous plump burg notably NUITS-ST GEORGES, Les St-Georges and GRAND CRU RICHEBOURG. Also range of stellar MOULIN-A-VENT, single v'yds, v. old vines.

Lignier C d'O r w ★★→★★★ Family in MOREY-ST-DENIS. Best is Hubert (eg. CLOS DE LA ROCHE), now managed by son Laurent. Class also from Virgile Lignier-Michelot, but still awaiting return to form at DOM Georges L.

Limoux L'doc r w ★★ Still wine AC to complement sparkling BLANQUETTE, CRÉMANT de Limoux. Obligatory oak-ageing for white, from CHARD, CHENIN, MAUZAC, as varietal or blend. Red AC based on MERLOT, plus SYRAH, GRENACHE, CABS, CARIGNAN PINOT N, illogically for a cool climate, only allowed in CRÉMANT and for IGP. Growers: DOMS de Baronarques, de Fourn, Mouscaillo, RIVES-BLANQUES and Cathare, *Jean-Louis Denois*.

Lirac S Rh r p w ★★ 09' 10' 12' 13 15' 16' Four villages nr TAVEL, stony, gd soils. Spicy red (can live 5 yrs+), recent momentum from new CHÂTEAUNEUF owners achieving clearer fruit, more flair. Reds best, esp DOMS *de la Mordorée* (best, r w), Beaumont, Duseigneur (bio), Famille Brechet, Giraud, Joncier (bio, character), Lafond Roc-Epine, La Lôyane, Lorentino (stylish), La Rocalière (gd fruit), Maby (Fermade, gd w); CHX de Bouchassy, de Manissy, de Montfaucon (gd w CÔTES DU RH), de Ségriès, Mont-Redon, St-Roch; André Méjan, Mas Isabelle (handmade), Rocca Maura, R Sabon. Whites project freshness, body, go 5 yrs.

Listrac-Médoc H-Méd r ★★→★★★ 05' 06 08 09' 10' 11 12 14 15 16 Highest point in

---

Languedoc rising stars

All founded since 2000, and looking gd: **Cabardès** Cazaban; **Corbières** CLOS Perdus; **Faugères** Trinités; Cebène; **La Clape** Mas Soleilla; **Limoux** J Laurens; **Montpeyroux** Mas d'Amile, Joncas; **Muscat de Mireval** La Rencontre; **Pézenas** Le Conte de Floris, Monplézy, Mas Gabriel, Turner-Pageot; **Terrasses du Larzac** Pas de l'Escalette, Clos du Serres, La Traversée, Les VIGNES Oubliées; **IGP** Mas des Dames (also COTEAUX DU L'DOC), Senti-Kreyden.

MÉD (43m)! Much improved AC for B'x-lovers with shallow(er) pockets; now more fruit, depth and MERLOT. Gd whites under AC B'x. Best CHX: Cap Léon Veyrin, CLARKE, Ducluzeau, FONRÉAUD, Fourcas-Borie, FOURCAS-DUPRÉ, FOURCAS-HOSTEN, l'Ermitage, Mayne-Lalande, Reverdi, SARANSOT-DUPRÉ.

Long-Depaquit Chab w ★★★ BICHOT-owned CHAB DOM, incl flagship GRAND CRU brand La Moutonne.

Lorentz, Gustave Al w ★★→★★★ Grower/merchant at Bergheim. RIES is strength in GRANDS CRUS Altenburg de Bergheim; Kanzlerberg, age-worthy, needing patience 08 10' 12 14 15. Young volume wines (esp GEWURZ) are well made. Careful organic viticulture.

Lot SW Fr ★→★★ DYA. IGP of Lot département useful largely to growers (eg. CLOS DE GAMOT, DU CÉDRE) who make rosé and whites but whose AOP is limited to red. Also ★★DOMS Belmont, Sully, Tour de Belfort, esp ★★CLOS d'Auxnuon (nr Montcuq).

Loupiac B'x w sw ★★ 05' 07 09' 10' 11 13 14 15 16 Neglected SÉM-dominant *liquoreux*. Lighter, fresher than SAUT across River Garonne. Top CHX: CLOS Jean, Dauphiné-Rondillon, de Ricaud, Les Roques, Loupiac-Gaudiet, Noble.

Lubéron S Rh r p w ★→★★ 15' 16' Modish hilly appendix to S Rh; terroir is okay, not more. Too many technical wines, low on soul. SYRAH lead role. Bright star: CH de la Canorgue. Also gd: DOM de la Citadelle, Le Novi (terroir); Chx Clapier, Edem, Fontvert (gd w), O Ravoire, St-Estève de Neri (improving), Tardieu-Laurent (rich, oak), Cellier de Marrenon, Val-Joanis and *La Vieille Ferme* (can be VIN DE FRANCE).

Lussac-St-Émilion B'x r ★★ 08 09' 09' 10' 12 14 15 16 Lightest of ST-ÉM satellites; co-op main producer. Top CHX: Barbe Blanche, Bel Air, Bellevue, Courlat, DE LUSSAC, la Grenière, La Rose-Perrière, Le Rival, LYONNAT, Mayne-Blanc.

Macération carbonique Traditional fermentation technique: whole bunches of unbroken grapes in a closed vat. Fermentation inside each grape eventually bursts it, giving vivid, fruity, mild wine, not for ageing. Esp in BEAUJ, though not for best wines; now much used in the MIDI and elsewhere, even CHÂTEAUNEUF.

Macle, Dom Jura Jean M was the doyen of Jura's CH-Chalon VIN JAUNE, beautifully age-worthy wines. Still gd with next generation, and fine CÔTES DU JURA.

Mâcon Burg r (p) w DYA. Simple, juicy GAMAY reds and most basic rendition of Mâconnais whites from CHARD.

Mâcon-Villages Burg w ★★→★★★ 14' 15 (16) Chief appellation for Mâconnais whites. Individual villages may also use their own names eg. Mâcon-Lugny. Look to Lugny, Terres Secretes, Viré co-ops for best prices, or growers for individual quality: Guffens-Heynen, Guillot, Guillot-Broux, LAFON, LEFLAIVE, Maillet, Merlin.

Macvin Jura From se France, not Scotland. Grape juice is fortified by local marc to make a sweet apéritif between 16–22% alc. Most Jura producers make one.

Madiran SW Fr r ★★→★★★ 05' 09' 10' 11 12 13 (14) (15) Gascon AOP. TANNAT's home. Traditional style is dark, macho, tannic, needs yrs. Easier, fruitier wines on the increase. ★★★DOMS Berthoumieu, Capmartin, CLOS Basté, Damiens, Dou Bernès, Labranche-Laffont, Laffitte-Teston, *Laplace*, Pichard (improving) and CH de Gayon are giving modish Chx BOUSCASSÉ, *Montus*, gd run for money. ★★Barréjat, ★★Crampilh, Maouries, not far behind.

Madura, Dom de L'doc rw ★★★ Ex-*régisseur* of B'x CH FIEUZAL created own estate in ST-CHINIAN. Stylish Classique and Grand Vin.

Mähler-Besse B'x NÉGOCIANT in Chartrons district of B'x. Now owned by BORIE-MANOUX. Loads of old vintages. Mâhler-Besse family retains a share in CH PALMER.

Mailly-Champagne Champ ★★★ Top co-op, all GRAND CRU grapes in multiple orientations. Prestige CUVÉE des *Echansons* 02' 04 08' 09 12' great wine for long ageing. V. refined L'Intemporelle 99 02' 04 08'. New talented winemaker should take standards even higher.

Maire, Henri Jura r w sw ★→★★ Former legend, creator of Vin Fou, still a huge producer, mostly from own v'yds, sometimes using DOM names eg. Sobief, Bregand, or supermarket brand Auguste Pirou. At best sound.

Mann, Albert Al r w ★→★★★ Top grower at Wettolsheim: rich, elegant. V.gd AUXERROIS, PINOT BL, PINOT N; gd range of GRAND CRUS from Furstentum, HENGST, SCHLOSSBERG, Steingrubler. Esp fine 08 10 13' 15. Immaculate bio v'yds.

Maranges C d'O r (w) ★★ 05' 09' 10' 12 13 14 15' (16) Most S AC of CÔTE DE BEAUNE with relatively tannic reds. Gd value from PREMIER CRU. Best: BACHELET-Monnot, Chevrot, Contat-Grangé, Moreau.

Marcillac SW Fr r p ★★ Violet-hued like-or-hate AOP. Light, sharpish nr-varietals (Mansois, aka FER SERVADOU) from Aveyron. Best at 3 yrs. As gd with strawberries as with charcuterie or bangers and mash. ★★co-op (eg. single DOM de Ladrecht) works alongside ★★DOMS Costes, du Cros, largest independent grower (gd w IGPS too), Vieux Porche; ★de l'Albinie (adds CAB SAUV).

Margaux H-Méd r ★★→★★★★ 01 02 04 05' 06 08 09' 10' 11 12 14 15 16 Largest communal AC in MÉD famous for elegant, fragrant wines. Reality is diversity of style. Top CHX: BOYD-CANTENAC, BRANE-CANTENAC, DAUZAC, DU TERTRE, FERRIÈRE, GISCOURS, ISSAN, KIRWAN, LASCOMBES, MALESCOT-ST-EXUPÉRY, MARGAUX, PALMER, RAUZAN-SÉGLA, SIRAN. Gd-value CHX: ANGLUDET, LABÉGORCE, Paveil de Luze.

Marionnet, Henry Lo r w ★★→★★★ 14' 15' 16 Pioneer, conservative/innovative e-TOURAINE 60-ha DOM. Some ungrafted v'yds. SAUV BL (top CUVÉE Touraine Sauv L'Origine), GAMAY, Provignage (Romorantin planted 1850); also La Pucelle de Romorantin. Replanting, managing historic v'yd at CH de Chambord (1st vintage 2018).

Marmande SW Fr r p (w) ★→★★★ (r) 14' 15 (16) ★★★ Cult grower Elian da Ros leads way at improving Gascon AOP, where rare Abouriou grape a virtual exclusivity. ★★CH de Beaulieu SYRAH-based. ★★DOMS Beyssac, Bonnet, Cavenac and Ch Lassolle stick to B'x grapes. Merged co-ops still dull.

Marsannay C d'O r p (w) ★★→★★★ (r) 09' 10' 12' 13 14 15' (16) Most N AOC of CÔTE DE NUITS, hoping for PREMIERS CRUS (eg. CLOS du Roy, Longeroies, Champ Salomon) to be classified. Accessible, crunchy, fruit-laden reds, eg. Audoin, Bart, Bouvier, Charlopin, CLAIR, Fournier, Pataille, TRAPET. V.gd rosé needs 1–2 yrs age; whites less exciting.

Mas, Doms Paul L'doc r p w ★★★ Highly ambitious big player; 650 ha of own estates, controls 1312 ha from Grès de Montpellier to ROUSS. Based nr Pézenas. Mainly IGP. Innovative marketing. Esp known for Arrogant Frog range; also La Forge, Les Tannes, Les Vignes de Nicole and DOMS Ferrandière, Crès Ricards in TERRASSES DU LARZAC, Martinolles in LIMOUX and CH Lauriga in ROUSS, Côté Mas brand from Pézenas.

Mas Bruguière L'doc ★★★ Successful family estate in PIC ST-LOUP; Xavier talented 7th generation. L'Arbouse, La Grenadière and Le Septième.

Mas de Daumas Gassac L'doc r p w ★★(★) 05 06 07 08 09 10 11 12 13 14 15 16 Set new standards in MIDI with CAB-based reds from apparently unique soil. Quality now surpassed by others. Also *perfumed white* from CHENIN and several others; super-*cuvée Émile Peynaud* (r); rosé Frizant. Delicious sweet Vin de Laurence (MUSCAT/SERCIAL). Now 2nd generation.

Mas Jullien L'doc ★★★ Early TERRASSES DU LARZAC leader. Carignan Blanc, CHENIN BL for white. Red: Autour de Jonquières, Carlan, Les Derniers Etats d'Ame, Lous Rougeos from L'DOC varieties.

Massif d'Uchaux S Rh r ★★ 12' 13 15' 16' Gd Rh village, brightly fruited reds, not easy to sell, but best have style. NB: CH St Estève (incl gd VIOGNIER), DOMS Chapoton, *Cros de la Mûre* (character, gd value), de la Guicharde, La Cabotte (bio, on top form), Renjarde (polished fruit).

Maury Rouss r sw ★★→★★★ Reputation est on VDN GRENACHES BLANC, Noir, Gris, grown on island of schist. Now characterful dry red, AC Maury SEC prompted by recent improvements, led by *Mas Amiel*. New estates incl **Dom of the Bee**; Jones. Sound co-op. *Venerable old Rancios* esp rewarding.

Mazis- (or Mazy-) Chambertin C d'O r ★★★★ 90' 93 96' 99' 02' 03 05' 06 07 08 09' 10' 11 12' 13 14 15' (16) Most n GRAND CRU of GEVREY-CHAMBERTIN, top-class in upper part; *heavenly wines*. Best: Bernstein, DUGAT-PY, FAIVELEY, HOSPICES DE BEAUNE, LEROY, Maume (now Tawse), ROUSSEAU.

Mazoyères-Chambertin C d'O *See* CHARMES-CHAMBERTIN.

Médoc B'x r ★★→★★★ 05' 06 08 09' 10' 11 14 15 16 AC for reds in nr-flat n part of MÉD peninsula. Often more guts than grace. Many growers, so be selective. Top CHX: Castera, CLOS Manou, d'Escurac, Fontis, *Goulée*, GREYSAC, *La Tour-de-By*, LOUDENNE, Lousteauneuf, LES ORMES-SORBET, PATACHE D'AUX, POITEVIN, *Potensac*, PREUILLAC, Ramafort, Rollan-de-By (HAUT-CONDISSAS), TOUR HAUT-CAUSSAN, TOUR ST-BONNET, Vieux Robin.

Meffre, Gabriel S Rh r w ★★ Consistent large S Rh merchant, owns gd GIGONDAS DOM Longue-Toque. Recently improved fruit, less oak. Also bottles, sells CHÂTEAUNEUF (gd St-Théodoric, also small doms), VACQUEYRAS St Barthélemy. Reliable S/N Rh Laurus (new oak, gd 2015s) range, esp CONDRIEU, ST-JOSEPH.

Mellot, Alphonse Lo r p w ★★→★★★★ 05 06 08' 09' 10' 11 12' 13 14' 15' 16' Impeccable SANCERRE (r w), bio, La Moussière (r w), CUVÉE Edmond, Génération XIX (r w); several gd single v'yds: incl **Satellite**, En Champs (r). Les Pénitents (Côtes de La Charité IGP) CHARD, PINOT N. Alphonse Jnr now fully in charge.

Menetou-Salon Lo r p w ★★→★★★ 10' 11 12 13 14' 15' AOP 535 ha (349 w, 186 r) Nr-SANCERRE; similar SAUV BL from e/w v'yds. Devastating April 2016 frost. Some v.gd reds (PINOT N), esp Gilbert, Pellé. Best: BOURGEOIS, *Clement* (Chatenoy), Gilbert (bio), *Henry Pellé*, Jacolin, Jean-Max Roger, Teiller, Tour St-Martin.

Méo-Camuzet C d'O r w ★★★★ V. fine DOM in VOSNE-ROMANÉE (NB: Brûlées, Cros Parantoux), plus GRANDS CRUS CLOS DE VOUGEOT, CORTON, RICHEBOURG. Rich oaky style in youth, develops class with age. Also less expensive NÉGOCIANT CUVÉES from M-C Frère et Soeur.

Merande, Ch de Sav r ★★ Top producer delivers lasting MONDEUSE red (12): violets, spices, black fruits, saline finish of a great v'yd. Value.

Mercurey Burg r (w) ★★→★★★ 09' 10' 12 13 14 15' (16) Leading village of CÔTE CHALONNAISE, mostly muscular reds, improving whites, value. Try CH de Chamirey, de Suremain, FAIVELEY, Juillot-Theulot, Lorenzon, M Juillot, Raquillet.

Mesnil-sur-Oger, Le Champ ★★★★ Top Côte des Blancs village – long-lived CHARD. CORTON-CHARLEMAGNE of CHAMP.

Méthode Champenoise Champ Traditional method of putting bubbles into CHAMP by refermenting wine in its bottle. Outside Champ region, makers must use terms "classic method" or "*méthode traditionnelle*".

Meursault C d'O (r) w ★★★→★★★★ 02' 04 05' 07' 08 09' 10' 11 12 13 14' 15 (16) Source of some of Burg's best whites, rounded and rich from PREMIERS CRUS: Charmes, Genevrières, Perrières, more nervy from hillside v'yds *Narvaux*,

---

Grenache: better with Mourvèdre

GRENACHE in a blend with MOURVÈDRE often beats Grenache with SYRAH. The full-blown 2007 vintage at CHÂTEAUNEUF was saved by Mourvèdre in various blends, with 20% or more giving the wines much-improved structure and balance. Eg. CH de BEAUCASTEL (30%), Ch de Beaucastel Hommage à Jacques Perrin (60%), Ch de la Gardine CUVÉE des Générations (20%), CLOS du Caillou La Rés (25%), CLOS DES PAPES (20%), DOM Bois de Boursan Cuvée des Félix (25%). Same applied in 2015, with Mourvèdre often 1–2% alc below Grenache.

FRANCE

Tesson, *Tillets*. Producers: Ampeau, Boisson-Vadot, Boyer-Martenot, CH DE MEURSAULT, COCHE-DURY, Ente, Fichet, GIRARDIN, *Javillier*, JOBARD, *Lafon*, Latour-Labille, M BOUZEREAU, Martelet de Cherisey, Matrot, Mikulski, *P Morey*, PRIEUR, *Roulot*, V *Bouzereau*. See also BLAGNY.

Meursault, Ch de C d'O r w ★★ →★★★★ Huge strides lately at this 61-ha estate of big-biz Halley family: decent red from BEAUNE, POMMARD, VOLNAY. Now world-class white, mostly MEURSAULT, also v.gd BOURGOGNE BLANC, PULIGNY PREMIER CRU.

Midi The s of France. Broad term covering L'DOC, ROUSS. PROV. Extremes of quality, improvements with every vintage. Great promise, but no guarantee.

Minervois L'doc r (p) (w) ★★ 10 11 12 13 14 15 16 Hilly AC region, one of L'DOC's best. CRU La Livinière (potential AC) has stricter selection, lower yield, longer ageing. Characterful, savoury reds, esp CHX Bonhomme, Coupe-Roses, La Grave, La Tour Boisée, Oupia, St-Jacques d'Albas, Villerembert-Julien; Abbaye de Tholomiès, Borie-de-Maurel, Combe Blanche, *Ch de Gourgazaud*, CLOS Centeilles, DOM l'Ostal Cazes, Laville-Bertrou, *Ste Eulalie*. *Gros and Tollot* (from Burg) raising bar. Potential new crus Cazelles, Laure.

Miquel, Laurent L'doc ★★★ 200 ha v'yds in CORBIÈRES (Les Auzines) and ST-CHINIAN (Cazal Viel). Aromatic white specialists, IGP VIOGNIER, now adventurous ALBARIÑO too. Own v'yds plus NÉGOCIANT activity, with Vendanges Nocturnes, Nord Sud and Grands Blancs.

Mis en bouteille au château / domaine Bottled at CH, property, or estate. NB: *dans nos* CAVES (in our cellars) or *dans la région de production* (in the area of production) often used but mean little.

Moët & Chandon Champ By far largest CHAMP house – impressive quality for such a giant. New mega-winery at Gyé-sur-Seine devoted to rosé in volume to meet world demand (*see* AUBE). Fresher, less sweet BRUT Impérial NV continues to improve. New rare prestige CUVÉE MCIII "solera" concept aimed at wealthy technophiles, addicts of exclusiveness. Better value in run of Grand Vintages 76 92 95 02 04 12 ★★. Esp elegant 06, great 08. Branches across Europe and New World. *See also* DOM PÉRIGNON.

Monbazillac SW Fr w sw ★★ →★★★ 09 10 11' 12 14' (15) BERGERAC sub-AOP; ★★★★ *Tirecul-la-Gravière* worthy challenge to best SAUTERNES. Well up there too ★★★CLOS des Verdots, l'Ancienne Cure, Les Hauts de Caillavel and co-op's *Ch de Monbazillac*. ★★CHX de Belingard-Chayne, Grande Maison, Haut-Theulet, Péroula, de Rayre, Theulet will not disappoint.

Mondeuse Sav r w ★★ SAVOIE grape and wine. Both white and red varieties. Red in Arbin, BUGEY, Chignin etc.

Monopole A v'yd that is under single ownership.

Montagne-St-Émilion BX r ★★ 08 09' 10' 12 14 **15** 16 Largest satellite of ST-ÉM. Usually gd value. Top CHX: Beauséjour, Calon, Croix Beauséjour, La Couronne, Faizeau, Haut Bonneau, Maison Blanche, Montaiguillon, Rocher Calon, Roudier, Teyssier, *Vieux Ch St-André*.

Montagny Burg w ★★ 12 14' 15 (16) CÔTE CHALONNAISE village with crisp whites, mostly in hands of CAVE de BUXY while many NÉGOCIANTS make creditable examples. More growers needed; Aladame best but try Bernollin, Denizot, CH de la Saule.

Montcalmès, Dom L'doc ★★★ Brother and sister team in TERRASSES DU LARZAC. White AC from MARSANNE/ROUSSANNE, IGP CHARD, VIOGNIER; stylish blends of SYRAH/GRENACHE/MOURVÈDRE.

Monthélie C d'O r (w) ★★ →★★★ 02' 03' 05' 09' 10' 11 12 14 15' (16) Pretty reds, grown uphill from VOLNAY, but a touch more rustic. Best v'yds: Champs Fulliot, Duresses. Best: BOUCHARD PÈRE & FILS, *Ch de Monthélie* (Suremain), *Coche-Dury*, Darviot-Perrin, Florent Garaudet, LAFON.

Montille, de C d'O r w ★★★ Etienne de M has expanded classic VOLNAY DOM with v'yds in BEAUNE, NUITS-ST-GEORGES and outstanding VOSNE-ROMANÉE Malconsorts. Spicy whole-bunch style. Top whites incl PULIGNY-MONTRACHET Caillerets. Also runs mini-NEGOCIANT Deux Montille (w) and improving CH de Puligny.

Montlouis sur Loire Lo w dr sw sp ★★→★★★ 89′ 02 05′ 08′ 09 10′ 11 13 14′ 15 Dynamic sister AC (450 ha) to VOUVRAY, S side of Lo, CHENIN BL; 55 per cent sparkling, incl Pétillant Originel. Small vintages in 2012, 13, 14, 16 (frost). Top: Berger, CHANSON, CHIDAINE, Delecheneau, Jousset, Merias, Moyer, Saumon, *Taille-aux-Loups*, Vallée Moray, Weisskopf.

Cab Sauv most planted wine grape in world. Merlot no.2.

Montpeyroux L'doc ★★→★★★ Lively village within TERRASSES DU LARZAC with growing number of talented growers. Aspiring to cru status. Try: CHABANON, DOM D'AUPILHAC, Villa Dondona. Newcomers: Joncas, Mas d'Amile. Serious co-op.

Montrachet (or Le Montrachet) C d'O w ★★★★ 92′ 93 96′ 99 00′ 01 02′ 04 05′ 06 07 08 09′ 10 11 12 13 14′ 15 (16) GRAND CRU v'yd in both PULIGNY- and CHASSAGNE-MONTRACHET. Potentially much the greatest white burg: monumental, perfumed, intense, dry yet luscious. Top: BOUCHARD, DRC, LAFON, LAGUICHE (DROUHIN), LEFLAIVE, Ramonet. DOM THÉNARD improving?

Montravel SW Fr p w dr ★★★ (r) 12′ 14 (15′) (16) (p w) DYA. Sub-AOP of BERGERAC. Oaked MERLOT obligatory. Modern reds from ★★DOMS de Bloy, de Krevel; CHX Jonc Blanc, Laulerie, Masburel, Masmontet, Moulin-Caresse. ★★ dry white and rosé from same and other growers. *See also* CÔTES DE MONTRAVEL for medium-sweet, HAUT-MONTRAVEL for stickies.

Montus, Ch SW Fr r w ★★★ 00 01′ 05′ 09′ 10′ 11 12′ (14) (15) Traditional MADIRAN-lovers remain loyal to ALAIN BRUMONT's all-TANNAT well-oaked red (7 yrs min). Others will rate classy sweet and dry white PACHERENCS DU VIC-BILH (drink at 4 yrs+) on same level.

Moreau Burg r w ★★→★★★ Widespread family in CHAB esp *Dom Christian M* (try CLOS des Hospices) and DOM M-Naudet. Other Moreau families in CÔTE DE BEAUNE, esp Bernard M for vigorous CHASSAGNE and David M in SANTENAY.

Morey, Doms C d'O r w ★★★ VIGNERON family in CHASSAGNE-MONTRACHET, esp Jean-Marc (Chenevottes), Marc (Virondot), Thomas (fine, stony Baudines), Vincent (Embrazées, plumper style), Michel M-Coffinet (LA ROMANÉE). Also Pierre M in MEURSAULT for M Perrières and BÂTARD-MONTRACHET.

Morey-St-Denis C d'O r (w) ★★★→★★★★ 90′ 93 96′ 99′ 02′ 03 05′ 06 07 08 09′ 10′ 11 12′ 13 14 15′ (16) Terrific source of quality red burg, better value than neighbours GEVREY-CHAMBERTIN, CHAMBOLLE-MUSIGNY. GRANDS CRUS CLOS DE LA ROCHE, CLOS DE LAMBRAYS, CLOS DE TART, CLOS ST DENIS. And so many gd producers: Amiot, ARLAUD, Castagnier, CLOS DE TART, *Clos des Lambrays*, *Dujac*, Jeanniard, H LIGNIER, LIGNIER-Michelot, Perrot-Minot, PONSOT, Remy, *Roumier*, Taupenot-Merme.

Morgon Beauj r ★★★ 09′ 11′ 12 13 14 15′ 16 Powerful BEAUJ cru, volcanic slate of Côte du Py makes meaty, age-worthy wine, clay of Les Charmes for earlier, smoother drinking. Javernières v'yd combines both. Try Burgaud, CH de Pizay, *Ch des Lumières* (JADOT), Desvignes, Foillard, Gaget, Goddard, Lafont, LAPIERRE, Piron.

Mortet, Denis C d'O r ★★★→★★★★ Arnaud Mortet has refined late father's dark, powerful wines, from BOURGOGNE Rouge to CHAMBERTIN. Key wines GEVREY-CHAMBERTIN Mes Cinq Terroirs, PREMIERS CRUS Lavaut St-Jacques, Champeaux. More GRAND CRU from 2014, NÉGOCIANT wines from 2016.

Moueix, J-P et Cie B'x Libourne-based NÉGOCIANT and proprietor named after legendary founder. Son Christian runs company, his son Edouard increasingly prominent. CHX: BELAIR-MONANGE (since 2012 incorporating MAGDELAINE) HOSANNA, LA FLEUR-PÉTRUS, LATOUR-À-POMEROL, TROTANOY. Distributes PETRUS. Also in California (*see* DOMINUS ESTATE).

FRANCE

Moulin-à-Vent Beauj r ★★★ 03 05' 09' 10' 11' 12 14 15' 16 Grandest BEAUJ cru, transcending the GAMAY grape. Weight, spiciness of Rh but matures towards rich, gamey PINOT flavours. Increasing interest in single-v'yd bottlings from eg. DOM La Bruyère, CH du Moulin-à-Vent, JADOT's Ch *des Jacques*, Janin (CLOS Tremblay), Janodet, LIGER-BELAIR (Les Rouchaux), Merlin (La Rochelle).

Moulis H-Méd r ★★→★★★ 04 05' 06 08 09' 10' 11 12 14 15 16 Tiny inland AC w of MARGAUX, with some honest, gd-value wines. Top CHX: Anthonic, Biston-Brillette, BRANAS GRAND POUJEAUX, BRILLETTE, *Chasse-Spleen*, Duplessis, Dutruch Grand Poujeaux, *Gressier Grand Poujeaux*, MAUCAILLOU, Mauvesin Barton, *Poujeaux*.

Moutard Champ Quirky Aubois CHAMP house attached to old local grapes, incl PINOT BL and esp boudoirish Arban(n)e. Quality greatly improved by current Moutard, François. Fine CUVÉE des Six Cépages 02 04 06 09 10 12 14' 15.

Mugneret C d'O r w ★★★ VIGNERON family in VOSNE-ROMANÉE. Sublime, stylish wines from Dr. Georges M-Gibourg (esp ÉCHÉZEAUX), also Gérard M, Dominique M and Mongeard-M.

Mugnier, J-F C d'O r w ★★★→★★★★ Outstanding grower of CHAMBOLLE-MUSIGNY *Les Amoureuses* and *Musigny* at CH de Chambolle. Expect finesse not blockbusters. Style works well (and price more modest) with NUITS-ST-GEORGES CLOS de la Maréchale (reclaimed 2004).

Mumm, GH & Cie Champ Cordon Rouge NV; fine ★★Brut Sélection; Mumm de Cramant reborn as BLANC DE BLANCS NV (just as gd); Cordon Rouge 02 04 06' 08; Rosé NV. Major house of Pernod-Ricard. Ongoing rise in quality, esp CUVÉE R Lalou 02. Limited release of special terroir cuvées called Mumm RSVR: Mumm de Verzenay BLANC DE NOIRS 08, RSVR Blanc de Blancs 12.

Muré, Clos St-Landelin Al r w ★★ →★★★ One of AL's great names; esp fine, full-bodied GRAND CRU *Vorbourg Ries* and PINOT GR. *Pinot N Cuvée "V"* 10 11 12 13', ripe, vinous, is region's best. Exceptional PINOT N in 15 ★★.

Muscadet Lo w ★→★★ 89 10 12 13 14' 15' (16) Popular, bone-dry wine from nr Nantes. 8150 ha in total. Ideal with fish, seafood. Reviving reputation. Best SUR LIE. Choose zonal ACS: *see* following entries. Growers' woes continue in 2016: frost, mildew, sunburn, following small crops in 2012, 13, 14. Misguided push by NÉGOCIANTS to add extra varieties eg. COLOMBARD.

Muscadet-Coteaux de la Loire Lo w ★→★★★ 12 14' 15 (16) Small (140 ha), MUSCADET zone e of Nantes on both sides Loire. Esp Guindon, Landron-Chartier, La Pléiade, Les VIGNERONS de la Noëlle, Ponceau, Quarteron.

Muscadet Côtes de Grand Lieu Lo w ★→★★★ 12 14' 15 (16) A MUSCADET zonal AOP (200 ha) by Atlantic. Best SUR LIE: Eric Chevalier, Herbauges (largest), Malidain. Three small crops 2012–14, and frost in 2016.

Muscadet Sèvre et Maine Lo ★→★★★ 05' 06 09' 10 12 14' 15 (16) Largest (5890 ha) and best MUSCADET zone. Increasingly gd and great value. Top: Bonnet-Huteau, Caillé, *Chereau Carré*, Cormerais, Delhommeau, Douillard, DOM DE L'ECU, Dom de

---

Muscadet – the joy of age

Everyone looks for the latest vintage of MUSCADET, but top Muscadets (top producers, gd vintages, esp with long lees-ageing) can last and improve for 20 yrs+, ending up not unlike old CHAB. Look for newly coined Cru Communaux: Clisson, Gorges, Le Pallet, with Goulaine, CH-Thébaud, Monnières-St-Fiacre, Mouzillon-Tillières waiting in wings (long lees ageing and greater complexity). Look for: Bonnet-Huteau, Bruno Cormerais, CH de la Gravelle (Gunther Chereau), Daniel Rineau, DOM DE L'ECU (Frédéric Niger van Herck/Guy Bossard), DOM Michel Brégeon, Jérémie Huchet, Jérémie Mourat, Jo Landron, Les VIGNERONS du Pallet, Luneau-Papin, Marc Ollivier (Dom de la Pépière), Vincent Caillé (Le Faye d'Homme).

la Haute Fevrie, *Gadais*, Gunther-Chereau, Huchet, Landron, Lieubeau, Luneau-Papin, Métaireau, Olivier, *Sauvion*. Can age decades. Try Crus Communaux (Clisson, Gorges, Le Pallet: 60 ha), long lees ageing for extra complexity.

Muscat de Frontignan L'doc sw ★★ NV Small AC outside Sète for MUSCAT VDN. Also late-harvest, unfortified, oak-aged IGP wines. Quality improving. Leaders: CHX la Peyrade, de Stony; DOM du Mas Rouge. Delicious with blue cheese. Nearby Muscat de Lunel and Muscat de Mireval (Dom de la Rencontre) v. similar.

Muscat de Rivesaltes Rouss w sw ★★ Sweet grapey fortified MUSCAT VDN AC from large area centred on town of Rivesaltes. Muscat SEC IGP increasing as demand for sweet VDN declines. Look for DOM CAZES, Corneilla, Treloar; Baixas co-op.

Muscat de St-Jean de Minervois L'doc w sw ★★ Tiny AC for fresh, honeyed VDN MUSCAT. Try DOM de Barroubio, CLOS du Gravillas, Clos Bagatelle. Village co-op sticks to dry Muscat.

Musigny C d'O r (w) ★★★★ 85′ 89′ 90′ 91 93 95 96′ 98 99′ 01 02′ 03 05′ 06 08 09′ 10′ 11 12′ 13 14 15′ (16) GRAND CRU in CHAMBOLLE-MUSIGNY. Can be most beautiful, if not most powerful, of all red burgs. Best: DE VOGÜÉ, Drouhin, JADOT, LEROY, MUGNIER, PRIEUR, ROUMIER, VOUGERAIE.

Nature Unsweetened, esp for CHAMP: no dosage. Fine if v. ripe grapes, raw otherwise.

Négociant-éleveur Merchant who "brings up" (ie. matures) the wine.

Nerthe, Ch la S Rh r w ★★★ 89′ 90′ 95′ 96′ 98′ 99′ 00 01 03 04′ 05′ 06′ 07′ 09′ 10′ 11 12′ 13 15 16 CHÂTEAUNEUF estate. Oaked, polished, sadly more mainstream recently. Special CUVÉES delicious, deeply fruited, stylish Cadettes (r, allow time), oaked, rich, food-friendly Beauvenir (w, from 4 yrs). Runs v. fine TAVEL Prieuré Montézargues, gd-value *Dom de la Renjarde* CÔTES DU RH, gd ch Signac CHUSCLAN.

Noëllat C d'O r ★★★ Noted VOSNE-ROMANÉE family. Michel N improving while Georges N completely revitalized from 2010 under new generation. Try Beaux Monts, GRANDS-ÉCHÉZEAUX. Also v. stylish HUDELOT-N in VOUGEOT.

Nuits-St-Georges C d'O r ★★→★★★★ 90′ 93 96′ 99′ 02′ 03 05′ 06′ 07 08 09′ 10′ 11 12′ 13 14 15′ (16) Important wine town: underrated wines, typically sturdy, tannic, need time. Best v'yds: Cailles, Les St-Georges, Vaucrains in centre; Boudots, Cras, Murgers nearer VOSNE; various CLOS – de la Maréchale, des Corvées, des Forêts, St-Marc in Prémeaux. Many merchants, growers: Ambroise, CATHIARD, J Chauvenet, Confuron, *Faiveley*, Gavignet, GOUGES, GRIVOT, L'ARLOT, Lechéneaut, LEROY, *Liger-Belair*, Machard de Gramont, Michelot, *Mugnier*, R CHEVILLON, *Rion*.

Ollier-Taillefer, Dom L'doc ★★★ Dynamic FAUGÈRES family estate. Allegro (w); Collines (r p); Grand Rés (r) from old vines and oak-aged Castel Fossibus (r). New cuvée (r) Le Rève de Noé, SYRAH/MOURVÈDRE blend.

Orléans Lo r p w ★ DYA. AC for white (chiefly CHARD – local name Auvernat Blanc), VIN GRIS, rosé, reds (PINOT N, esp PINOT M, locally Gris Meunier) around Orléans (13 communes). Top: Deneufbourg, CLOS St Fiacre. April frost forces co-op to close.

Orléans-Clery Lo r ★ DYA. Separate micro AOP (28 ha); five communes sw of Orléans for CAB FR, within same zone as AC ORLÉANS. Producers: CLOS St Fiacre, Deneufbourg. Severe frost April 16.

Ostertag, Dom Al Bio DOM run with originality in prime RIES country. Ries Muenchberg 13 exquisite, fine PINOT N Fronholtz. André keen on 14, "young colts full of energy". True in Bas Rhin!

Pacherenc du Vic-Bilh SW Fr w dr sw ★★→★★★ AOP for MADIRAN's white cousins, based on GROS, PETIT MANSENG and sometimes local Aruffiac. Mostly same growers as Madiran but note too ★★CH Mascaaras. Dry DYA, but sweet, esp if oaked, will age well.

Paillard, Bruno Champ ★★BRUT Première CUVÉE NV; Rosé Première Cuvée; CHARD Rés Privée, Brut 02 04 06 08. New vintage BLANC DE BLANCS 95 02 08. Superb Prestige Cuvée Nec-Plus-Ultra 95′ 03. Youngest major CHAMP house. Refined, v.

dry style esp in long-aged Blanc de Blancs *Rés Privée*, Nec-Plus-Ultra. Bruno P heads LANSON-BCC and owns CH de Sarrin, Prov.

Palette Prov r p w ★★★ Tiny AC nr Aix-en-Prov. Characterful reds, fragrant rosés, intriguing forest-scented whites. Traditional, serious *Ch Simone*; more innovative CH Henri Bonnaud.

Patrimonio Cors r p w ★★→★★★ AC. Some of island's finest, from dramatic limestone hills in n CORS. Individual reds from NIELLUCCIO, intriguing whites, even *late-harvest*, from *Vermentino*. Top: Antoine Arena, CLOS de Bernardi, Gentile, Montemagni, Pastricciola, Yves Leccia at E Croce.

Pauillac H-Méd r ★★★→★★★★ 95′ 96′ 98 00′ 01 02 03′ 04′ 05′ 06 08′ 09′ 10′ 11 12 14 15 16 Communal AC in MÉD with 18 Classed Growths, incl LAFITE, LATOUR, MOUTON. Famous for pungent, long-lived wines, the acme of CAB SAUV. Other top CHX: BATAILLEY, CLERC MILON, D'ARMAILHAC, DUHART-MILON, GRAND-PUY-LACOSTE, LYNCH-BAGES, PICHON-BARON, PICHON-LALANDE, PONTET-CANET.

Pays d'Oc, IGP L'doc r p w ★→★★★ Largest IGP, covering whole of L'DOC-ROUSS. Focus on varietal wines; 58 different grapes allowed. Technical advances continue apace. Main producers: Jeanjean, DOMS PAUL MAS, GÉRARD BERTRAND, village co-ops. Extremes of quality; best are innovative, exciting.

Pécharmant SW Fr r ★★ 10 11′ 12′ (14) (15′) Biggest wines (keepers) from BERGERAC (inner AOP). ★★★*Ch de Tiregand*, CLOS des Côtes, DOM du Haut-Pécharmant, Les Chemins d'Orient; ★★La Métairie, CHX Beauportail, Champarel, Corbiac, de Biran, Dom des Bertranoux, du Rooy, Hugon, Terre Vieille benefit from iron- and manganese-based terroir.

Pélican, Dom du Jura Burg's MARQUIS D'ANGERVILLE tries his hand in Jura. fresh styles at 1st, more to come later.

Pernand-Vergelesses C d'O r w ★★★ (r) 99′ 02′ 03′ 05′ 06 08 09′ 10′ 11 12 13 14 15 (16) Village next to ALOXE-CORTON, incl part of CORTON-CHARLEMAGNE, CORTON. Île des Vergelesses v'yd 1st-rate for reds, elsewhere chiselled, precise whites. Growers: CHANDON DE BRIAILLES, CHANSON, Delarche, Dubreuil-Fontaine, JADOT, LATOUR, Rapet, Rollin.

Perrier Jouët Champ BRUT NV; Blason de France NV; Blason de France Rosé NV; Brut 02 04 06 08. Fine new BLANC DE BLANCS. 1st (C19) to make dry CHAMP for English market; strong in GRAND CRU CHARD, best for gd vintage and de luxe Belle Epoque 95 02′ 04 06 08′ 12 15, rosé 04 06, in painted bottle.

Pessac-Léognan B'x r w ★★★→★★★★ 00′ 01 02 04 05′ 06 08 09′ 10′ 11 12 14 15 16 AC created in 1987 for best part of n GRAV, incl all GRANDS CRUS: HAUT-BAILLY, HAUT-BRION, LA MISSION-HAUT-BRION, PAPE-CLÉMENT, etc. Firm, full-bodied, earthy, honeyed reds; B'X's finest dry whites. Value from Brown, Cantelys, DE ROCHEMORIN, Haut-Vigneau, Lafont Menaut, Loupuault Martillac.

Petit Chablis Chab w ★ DYA. Fresh, easy would be CHAB from outlying v'yds not on kimmeridgian clay. LA CHABLISIENNE co-op is gd, but prices too close to real thing.

Pfaffenheim Al ★→★★ Respectable AL co-op. Ripe, balanced wines from warm sites. Dopff & Irion, a once-famous house, now a brand of Pfaffenheim.

Pfersigberg Al GRAND CRU in two parcels; v. aromatic wines. GEWURZ does v. well 09 14. RIES esp 08 10 12 from BRUNO SORG, LÉON BEYER Comtes d'Eguisheim, Paul Ginglinger.

Philipponnat Champ Small house, intense, winey CUVÉES, now owned by LANSON-BCC group. NV, Rosé NV, BRUT 99 02, Cuvée 1522 02, remarkable single-v'yd *Clos des Goisses* 85′ 92 95 96 02 04 08 12′, late-disgorged vintage 90.

Picpoul de Pinet L'doc w ★→★★ DYA. MUSCADET of MIDI. AC (2013), Grand Vin du L'DOC, from PICPOUL grown around Pinet. Best: Félines-Jourdan, La Croix Gratiot, St Martin de la Garrigue; co-ops Pinet, Pomérols. Fresh, salty: perfect *with an oyster*, but sadly can be victim of fashion, too fruity, losing typical tang.

Pic St-Loup L'doc r (p) ★★→★★★ 10 11 12 13 14 15 16 Coolest, wettest part of L'DOC, v. pretty. AC demands high proportion of SYRAH, plus GRENACHE, MOURVÈDRE. Reds for ageing; white potential considerable but still AC L'doc or IGP. Growers: Bergerie du Capucin, Cazeneuve, CLOS de la Matane, Clos Marie, de Lancyre, *Dom de l'Hortus*, Gourdou, Lascaux, MAS BRUGUIÈRE, Mas Peyrolle, Valflaunès.

Pierre-Bise, Ch Lo r p w ★★→★★★★ 02 03 04 05' 06 07'(sw) 08 09 10' 11(sw) 14' 15 (16) V.gd DOM in COTEAUX DU LAYON, incl Chaume, QUARTS DE CHAUME, SAVENNIÈRES (CLOS de Grand Beaupréau, ROCHE-AUX-MOINES). Excellent ANJOU-GAMAY, ANJOU-VILLAGES (both CUVÉE Schist, Spilite), Anjou Blanc Haut de la Garde. Claude's sons now in charge. Gd reports from 2016.

Pignier Jura r w sw sp ★★★ Bio producer in s Jura. Great range of fresher styles, eg. Sauvageon and lively reds, plus classics incl quality VIN JAUNE.

Pinon, François Lo w sw sp ★★★ 89 90 95 96 97 02 03 05 08 09 10' 11 14' 15' (16) Excellent organic wines from Vernou, VOUVRAY. New single v'yd: Déronnières.

Piper-Heidsieck Champ Historic house on surging wave of quality. Model BRUT NV and new Brut Essentiel with more age, less sugar, ideal for sushi, sashimi. New Vintage 08 a classic (06 04). Exemplary Rare 02 06; 1st release of classy Rare Rosé 07.

Plageoles, Dom SW Fr r w sp GAILLAC Bernard Plageoles, rebel and purist, mentors many growers, reviving rare grapes such as Ondenc (base of famous sweet ★★★★Vin d'Autan), ★★Prunelard (deep fruity red), Verdanel (dr w, oak-aged). Try big spicy red from DURAS, lighter from FER SERVADOU (aka Braucol). *Brilliant dry sparkler* Mauzac Natur just as original.

Plan de Dieu S Rh r ★→★★★ 10' 12' 13 15' 16' Rh village nr CAIRANNE with stony, windswept plain. Heady, robust, GRENACHE-inspired, authentic wines; drink with game, stews. Gd choice. Best: CH la Courançonne, DOMS Aphillantes (character), Arnesque, Bastide St Vincent, Durieu (full), Espigouette, Longue Toque, Martin, Pasquiers, St-Pierre (gd traditional).

Pol Roger Champ Family-owned Épernay house. BRUT Rés NV excels, with slightly lower dosage; ★★★ Brut 98' 02' 04 06 08' 12; Rosé 04 06; Blanc de CHARD (renamed BLANC DE BLANCS) 06 08'. Fine *Pure Brut* (no dosage) great with seafood. Sumptuous CUVÉE Sir Winston Churchill 96' (esp in magnums) 02' 08'. Always a blue-chip choice. Particularly gd in dry, challenging 15 (from 2024).

Pomerol B'x r ★★★→★★★★ 98' 00' 01 04 05' 06' 08 09' 10' 11 12 14 15 16 Tiny AC bordering ST-ÉM; clay, gravel sandy soils. MERLOT-led, rich, supple style but long life. Top: CLINET, HOSANNA, L'ÉGLISE-CLINET, L'ÉVANGILE, LA CONSEILLANTE, LAFLEUR, LA FLEUR-PÉTRUS, LE PIN, PETRUS, TROTANOY, VIEUX-CH-CERTAN. Prices generally high; some value (Bellegrave, BOURGNEUF, CLOS du Clocher, LA POINTE).

Pommard C d'Or r ★★★(★) 90' 96' 98 99' 02' 03 05' 06 07 08 09' 10' 11 12 14 15' (16) Antithesis of neighbour VOLNAY; potent, tannic wines to age 10 yrs+. Best v'yds: Rugiens for power, Epenots for grace. Talk of promotion to GRAND CRU for these two; don't hold your breath. Growers: CH de Pommard, COMTE ARMAND, COURCEL, DE MONTILLE, Hospices de Beaune, Huber-Vedereau, J-M BOILLOT, Lejeune, Parent, Pothier-Rieusset, Rebourgeon.

Pommery Champ Historic house; brand now owned by VRANKEN. BRUT NV sure bet; Rosé NV; Brut 04 08 09 12'. Outstanding *Cuvée Louise* 02 04 08' 12 13, supple Wintertime BLANC DE NOIRS.

Ponsot C d'Or r w ★★→★★★★ Idiosyncratic, top-quality MOREY-ST-DENIS DOM now with 12 GRANDS CRUS, from CORTON to CHAMBERTIN, but esp *Clos de la Roche*, CLOS ST-DENIS. Unique white PREMIER CRU Monts Luisants from ALIGOTÉ.

Potel, Nicolas C d'Or r w ★★→★★★ Brand owned by Cottin Frères but since 2009 without its founder Nicolas, who now owns DOM de Bellene and NÉGOCIANT Maison Roche de Bellene in BEAUNE.

Pouilly-Fuissé Burg w ★★ →★★★ 09' 10' 11 12 13 14' 15 (16) Top AC of MÂCON; potent, rounded but intense whites; classification of terroirs pending. Wines from Fuissé most powerful, Vergisson for minerality. Enjoy young or with age. Top: Barraud, Bret, CH de Beauregard, CH DE FUISSÉ, Ch des Rontets, Cordier, Cornin, Drouin, Ferret, Forest, Merlin, Paquet, Robert-Denogent, Rollet, Saumaize, Saumaize-Michelin, VERGET.

Pouilly-Fumé Lo w ★★★★★ 05' 08 09' 10 12 13 14' 15' (16) E-bank neighbour of SANCERRE. 1287 ha SAUV BL. Some frost in 2016. Best can improve at least 7–8 yrs+. Growers: Bain, BOURGEOIS, Cailbourdin, Champeau, Chatelain, Ch de Favray, Ch de Tracy, DIDIER DAGUENEAU, Edmond and André Figeat, Jean Pabiot, Jonathan Pabiot, LADOUCETTE, Masson-Blondelet, Redde, Saget, Serge Dagueneau & Filles, Tabordet, Treuillet.

Pouilly-Loché Burg w ★★ 12 14 15 (16) Less-known neighbour of POUILLY-VINZELLES. CLOS des Rocs, Tripoz, Bret Bros gd, co-op dominant for volume.

Pouilly-sur-Loire Lo w ★→★★ DYA. In C19, Pouilly supplied Paris with CHASSELAS table grapes. Now only 30 ha remain; same zone as POUILLY-FUMÉ, milder wine. Upholding tradition: Gitton, Jonathan Pabiot, Landrat-Guyollot, Masson-Blondelet, Redde, Serge Dagueneau & Filles.

Pouilly-Vinzelles Burg w ★★ 12 13 14' 15 (16) Between POUILLY-LOCHÉ and POUILLY-FUISSÉ geographically and in quality. Best v'yd: Les Quarts. Best: Bret Bros, DROUHIN, Valette. Volume from CAVE des GRANDS CRUS Blancs.

Premier Cru First growth in B'x; 2nd rank of v'yds (after GRAND CRU) in Burg; 2nd rank in Lo: one so far, COTEAUX DU LAYON Chaume.

Only drink that tastes better in an aeroplane is tomato juice.

Premières Côtes de Bordeaux B'x w sw ★→★★ 10' 11 12 13 14 15 16 Same zone as CADILLAC-CÔTES DE B'X but for sweet whites only. Gently sweet, SÉM-dominated *moelleux*. Quality varies. Best CHX: Crabitan-Bellevue, du Juge, Fayau, Suau.

Prieur, Dom Jacques C d'O ★★★ Major MEURSAULT estate with extraordinary range of GRANDS CRUS from MONTRACHET to MUSIGNY. Style aims at weight from late-picking and oak more than finesse, but now signs of livelier approach. Labruyère MOULIN-À-VENT and CH ROUGET POM under same ownership.

Prieuré St Jean de Bébian L'doc ★★★ Pézenas estate with all 13 grape varieties of CHÂTEAUNEUF-DU-PAPE. Now owned by Russians with talented Aussie winemaker. La Chapelle, La Croix, Prieuré; old-vines red 1152.

Primeur "Early" wine for refreshment and uplift; esp from BEAUJ, VDP too. Wine sold en primeur is still in barrel, for delivery when bottled. Caution: fingers can get burned.

Producteurs Plaimont SW Fr SW France's ever growing co-op dominates Gascony, goes hunting for unknown Gascon grapes. Big in MADIRAN (acquiring independent DOMS), ST MONT (opening hotel in old abbey), CÔTES DE GASCOGNE. All colours, styles, mostly ★★, all tastes, purses.

Propriétaire récoltant Champ Owner-operator, literally owner harvester.

Puisseguin St-Émilion B'x r ★★ 08 09' 10' 12 14 15 16 Most e of four ST-ÉM satellites; wines firm, solid. Top CHX: Beauséjour, Branda, Clarisse, DES LAURETS, Durand-Laplagne, Fongaban, Guibot la Fourvieille, Haut-Bernat, La Mauriane, Le Bernat, Soleil. Also Roc de Puisseguin from co-op.

Puligny-Montrachet C d'O (r) w ★★★ →★★★★ 02' 04 05' 07 08 09' 10' 11 12 13 14' 15 (16) Should be most floral, fine-boned white burg. V'yds up hill fresh and mineral, richer and softer lower down. Band in middle best: Caillerets, Champ Canet, Combettes, Folatières, Pucelles alongside the MONTRACHET GRANDS CRUS. Producers: *J-M Boillot, Bouchard Père & Fils*, CARILLON, Chartron, CH de Puligny, *Dom Leflaive, Drouhin*, JADOT, *O Leflaive*, Pernot, *Sauzet*.

Puyméras S Rh r w ★ 15' 16' Respectable, hidden S Rh village, high, breezy v'yds, straightforward, supple plum-fruited reds based on GRENACHE, fair whites, decent co-op. Try CAVE la Comtadine, DOM du Faucon Doré (bio), Puy du Maupas.

Pyrénées-Atlantiques SW Fr DYA. IGP in Gascony and Béarn for wines not qualifying for local AOPS in far sw. Overlaps COMTÉ TOLOSAN. Thus ★★★CH Cabidos (superb PETIT MANSENG W SW), ★★DOM Moncaut (nr Pau), ★BRUMONT varietals can appear under either. Otherwise pot luck.

"Wine makes weekdays prosperous; wine makes Sundays happy." – Baudelaire

Quarts de Chaume Lo w SW ★★★→★★★★ 89' 90' 95' 96' 97' 02 03 05' 07' 10' 11' 14' 15' (16) 40 ha, slopes close to Layon, CHENIN BL. Strict rules need to be further tightened to justify GRAND CRU and price. Best richly textured. Esp: Baudouin, Bellerive, Branchereau, CH PIERRE-BISE, FL, Guegniard, Ogereau, Pithon-Paillé, Suronde (bought by Minière, BOURGUEIL). Avoid 2012.

Quincy Lo w ★→★★ 14' 15' 16 Revived AOP (277 ha; 60 ha: 1990) SAUV BL from sand/ gravel banks se of Vierzon. Celebrated 80 yrs AC: 2016. Growers: Mardon, Portier, Rouzé, Siret-Courtaud, Tatin-Wilk (DOMS Ballandors, Tremblay), Villalin.

Rancio Rouss Most original, lingering, delicious style of VDN, reminiscent of Tawny Port, or old Oloroso Sherry in BANYULS, MAURY, RASTEAU, RIVESALTES, wood-aged and exposed to oxygen, heat. Same flavour (pungent, tangy) a fault in table wine.

Rangen Al Most S GRAND CRU of AL at Thann. Extremely steep (average 90%) slopes, volcanic soils. Top: majestic RIES ZIND-HUMBRECHT (CLOS St Urbain 05' 08' 10'), SCHOFFIT (St Theobald 08' 10). Extra finesse in 2015.

Rasteau S Rh r (p) (w) br (dr) sw ★★ 09' 10' 11 12' 13 14' 15' 16' Full-throttle reds from clay soils, mainly GRENACHE. Best in hot yrs (09 10 15, 16). NB: Beaurenard (serious, age well), *Cave Ortas* (gd), CH La Gardine, *Ch du Trignon*, Famille Perrin; DOMS Beau Mistral, Collière, Combe Julière, Coteaux des Travers, Didier Charavin, Escaravailles, Girasols, Gourt de Mautens (talented, IGP wines from 2010), Grand Nicolet (character), Grange Blanche, Rabasse-Charavin, Soumade (polished), St Gayan, Trapadis. Grenache dessert VDN quality on the up (Doms Banquettes, Coteaux des Travers, Escaravailles, Trapadis).

Ravanès, Dom de L'doc IGP Coteaux de Murviel ★★ Marc Benin grows B'X varieties in L'DOC. Le Prime Verd is PETIT VERDOT; also original white Le Renard Blanc (Grenache Gris/MACABEO).

Raveneau Chab w ★★★★ Along with DAUVISSAT cousins, greatest CHAB producers, using old methods for *extraordinary long-lived wines*. Excellent value except in secondary market. Look for Blanchots, Les CLOS, Vaillons.

Rayas, Ch S Rh r w ★★★★ 78' 79 81' 85 86 88' 89 90' 93 94 95' 96' 98' 99 00 01 03 04' 05' 06' 07' 08 09' 10' 11' 12' 13' 14' 15' 16' Wonderful, time-warp 13-ha CHÂTEAUNEUF estate. Pale, subtle, aromatic, intricate reds (100% GRENACHE) whisper quality, offer delight, age superbly. White Rayas (GRENACHE BL, CLAIRETTE) v.gd over 18 yrs+. Gd-value, elegant second wine: *Pignan*. Supreme CH Fonsalette CÔTES DU RH, incl marvellous SYRAH. Decant them all; each is an occasion. Also gd CH des Tours VACQUEYRAS (peppery), VDP.

Regnié Beauj r ★★ 14 15' 16 Lightest of BEAUJ. Sandy soil gives easy, fruity wines, more body close to MORGON. Try Burgaud, de la Plaigne, Dupré, Rochette, Sunier.

Reuilly Lo r p w ★→★★★ 09' 10 14' 15' (16) Revived AC (225 ha; 30 ha: 1990) neighbour of QUINCY w of Bourges. SAUV BL (112 ha), rosés and *Vin Gris* from PINOT N (66 ha) and/or PINOT GR (47 ha). Improving Pinot N reds. Best: Claude Lafond, Jamain, Mardon, Renaudat, Rouze, Sorbe. 2016 gd but drink early.

Riceys, Les Champ p ★★★ DYA. Key AC in AUBE for a notable PINOT N rosé. Producers: *A Bonnet*, Jacques Defrance, Morize. Great 09; v. promising 14 after lean period 2011–13; 15' excels.

FRANCE

Richebourg C d'O r ★★★★ 90′ 93′ 95 96′ 98 99′ 00 02′ 03 05′ 06 07 08 09′ 10′ 11 12′ 13 14 15′ (16) VOSNE-ROMANÉE GRAND CRU. Magical burg with great depth of flavour, vastly expensive. Growers: DRC, GRIVOT, GROS, HUDELOT-Noëllat, LEROY, LIGER-BELAIR, MÉO-CAMUZET.

Rimage Rouss A growing mode: vintage VDN, super-fruity for drinking young. Think gd Ruby Port. Grenat is MAURY version.

Rion C d'O r (w) ★★→★★★ Related DOMS in NUITS-ST-GEORGES, VOSNE-ROMANÉE. Patrice R for excellent Nuits CLOS St Marc, Clos des Argillières and CHAMBOLLE-MUSIGNY. Daniel R for Nuits and Vosne PREMIERS CRUS; Bernard R more Vosne-based. All fairly priced.

Rivesaltes Rouss r w br dr sw ★★ NV or solera, occasionally vintage VDN from large area in n ROUSS. Grossly underappreciated; deserves revival. Long-lasting wines, esp RANCIOS. Look for: Boucabeille, des Chênes, des Schistes, DOM CAZES, Rancy, Roc des Anges, Sarda-Malet, Vaquer. You will not be disappointed.

Rives-Blanques, Ch L'doc sp w ★★★ LIMOUX. Irish-Dutch couple make BLANQUETTE and more recently CRÉMANT. Still wines, incl blend Trilogie and age-worthy CHENIN BL Dédicace. Dessert Lagremas d'Aur.

Roche-aux-Moines, La w sw ★★→★★★ 89′ 90′ 96′ 02 03 05′ 07 08′ 09 10′ 11 12 14′ 15′ (16) 33 ha cru of SAVENNIÈRES, ANJOU. Low yields (30hl/ha), big potential to age CHENIN BL. Growers: aux Moines, *Ch Pierre-Bise*, CLOS de la Bergerie (Joly), FL, Forges, Laureau.

Roederer, Louis Champ Top-drawer family-owned house with enviable v'yds: 40 per cent bio. Flavour, finesse ★★★BRUT Premier NV; Brut 04 06 07, BLANC DE BLANCS 08′ 09 13, Brut Saignée Rosé 09. Magnificent *Cristal* (can be greatest of all prestige CUVÉES, viz 88′ 04 06 07) and Cristal Rosé 96′ 02′ 09′. Superb late-release Cristal 95. V.gd new Brut Nature (pure Cumières 2006). Also owns DEUTZ, DELAS; CHX DE PEZ, PICHON-LALANDE. *See also* California.

Rolland, Michel B'x Fashionable French consultant winemaker and MERLOT specialist working in B'x and worldwide. Owner of FONTENIL in FRON. Interests in Argentina (CLOS de los Siete).

Rolly Gassmann Al w sw ★★★ Revered grower at Rorschwihr, esp Moenchreben. Off-dry style culminates in great rich GEWURZ CUVÉE Yves 05 07 08 09 11 12 14 15. New generation and bio methods bring more finesse.

Romanée, La C d'O r ★★★★ 02′ 03 05′ 06 07 08 09′ 10′ 11 12′ 13 14 15′ (16) Tiniest GRAND CRU in VOSNE-ROMANÉE, MONOPOLE of Comte LIGER-BELAIR. Exceptionally fine, perfumed, intense and understandably expensive.

Romanée-Conti, La C d'O r ★★★★ 78′ 85′ 88′ 89′ 90′ 93′ 95 96′ 97 98 99′ 00 01 02′ 03 05′ 06 07 09′ 10′ 11 12′ 13 14′ 15′ (16) GRAND CRU in VOSNE-ROMANÉE, MONOPOLE of DRC. 450 cases/yr. Most celebrated and expensive red wine in world, these days again deserving reputation. Cellar 15 yrs+. Beware fakes.

Romanée-St-Vivant C d'O r ★★★★ 90′ 93 95 96′ 99′ 02′ 03 05′ 06 07 08 09′ 10′ 11 12′ 13 14 15′ (16) GRAND CRU in VOSNE-ROMANÉE. Downslope from LA ROMANÉE-CONTI, haunting perfume, delicate but intense. Ready a little earlier than famous neighbours. Growers: if you can't afford DRC or LEROY, or CATHIARD now, try ARLOT, Follin-Arbelet, HUDELOT-Nöellat, JJ Confuron, LATOUR, Poiset.

Sancerre's Monts Damnes v'yd – Damned Hills – is hot, steep. Canada v'yd cold.

Rosacker Al GRAND CRU at Hunawihr. Limestone/clay makes some of longest-lived RIES in AL (CLOS STE-HUNE).

Rosé d'Anjou Lo p ★→★★ DYA. Rosé – off-dry to sweet (mainly Grolleau). Big AOP, 2100 ha. V. popular, usually well made. Look for: Clau de Nell, DOMS de la Bergerie, Grandes Vignes, Mark Angeli, Sablonnettes.

Rosé de Loire Lo p ★→★★ DYA. Driest of ANJOU's rosés: six grapes, esp GAMAY,

Grolleau. Big AC (1100 ha) chiefly from Anjou. Look for: Bablut, Bois Brinçon, Branchereau, Cady, CAVE de SAUMUR, CH PIERRE-BISE, Ogereau, Passavant, Richou, Soucherie.

Rosette SW Fr w s/sw ★★ AOP DYA. BERGERAC's best-kept secret for off-dry apéritif wines now out of the bag. Avoid oaked versions. Try ★★CLOS Romain, CHX Combrillac, de Peyrel, Monplaisir, Puypezat-Rosette, Spingulèbre; DOMS de Coutancie, de la Cardinolle, du Grand-Jaure; with foie gras or mushrooms.

Rossignol-Trapet Burg r ★★★ Equally bio cousins of DOM TRAPET, with healthy holdings of GRAND CRU v'yds esp CHAMBERTIN. Gd value across range from GEVREY VIEILLES VIGNES up. Also some BEAUNE v'yds from Rossignol side.

Rostaing, René N Rh r w ★★★ 95' 99' 01' 05' 06' 07' 09' 10' 11 12' 13' 14 15' 16' High-quality CÔTE-RÔTIE DOM: three tightly woven wines, all v. fine, pure, precise, careful oak, wait 6 yrs, then decant. Son Pierre started 2015. Complex, enticing, top-class Côte Blonde (5% VIOGNIER), also La Landonne (dark fruits, 15–20 yrs). Intricate, firm *Condrieu*, also L'DOC Puech Noble (r w).

Rouget, Emmanuel C d'O r ★★★★ Inheritor of legendary Henri Jayer estate in ÉCHÉZEAUX, NUITS-ST-GEORGES, VOSNE-ROMANÉE. Top wine Cros Parantoux (alarming price). New generation becoming usefully involved.

Roulot, Dom C d'O w ★★★→★★★★ Outstanding MEURSAULT DOM, now cult status so beware secondary market prices. Great PREMIERS CRUS eg. Charmes, CLOS des Bouchères, Perrières, value from top village sites Luchets, Meix Chavaux, Tesson Clos de Mon Plaisir.

Roumier, Georges C d'O r ★★★★ Reference DOM for BONNES-MARES and other *brilliant Chambolle* wines in capable hands of Christophe R. Long-lived wines but still attractive early. Cult status means hard to find now at sensible prices.

Rousseau, Dom Armand C d'O r ★★★★ Unmatchable GEVREY-CHAMBERTIN DOM with thrilling CLOS ST-JACQUES and GRANDS CRUS. Fragrance, balance, persistence throughout range, rarely missing a beat.

Roussette de Savoie Sav w ★★ S of Lake Geneva. 100% Roussette. Can age. From: de la Mar, Maillet, Quenard.

Roussillon Individual MIDI region, but often linked with L'DOC, and incl in AC L'doc. Original, traditional VDN (eg. BANYULS, MAURY, RIVESALTES). Younger vintage RIMAGE/Grenat now competing with aged RANCIO. Also appealing table wines. *See* CÔTES DU ROUSS-VILLAGES, COLLIOURE, new AC MAURY SEC and IGP CÔTES CATALANES.

Ruchottes-Chambertin C d'O r ★★★★ 90' 93' 95 96' 99' 00 02' 03 05' 06 07 08 09' 10' 11 12' 13 14 15' (16) Tiny GRAND CRU neighbour of CHAMBERTIN. Less weighty but ethereal, intricate, lasting wine of great finesse. Top growers: MUGNERET-Gibourg, ROUMIER, ROUSSEAU.

Ruinart Champ Oldest house (1729). High standards going higher still. Rich, elegant wines. "R" de Ruinart BRUT NV; Ruinart Rosé NV; "R" de Ruinart Brut 02' 04 06 08. Prestige CUVÉE *Dom Ruinart* is one of two best vintage BLANC DE BLANCS in CHAMP (viz 02' 04 08). DR Rosé also v. special 98 02'. NV Blanc de Blancs much improved esp in magnum, jeroboam. High hopes for 13, classic cool lateish vintage.

Rully Burg r w ★★ (r) 12 14' 15' (16) (w) 14' 15 (16) CÔTE CHALONNAISE village. *Light, fresh, tasty, gd-value whites*. Reds all about the fruit, not structure. Try C Jobard, Devevey, DROUHIN, DUREUIL-JANTHIAL, FAIVELEY, Jacqueson, Ninot, Rodet.

Sablet S Rh r (p) w ★★ 13 15' 16' Fun but also serious wines from improving CÔTES DU RH-VILLAGE. Sandy soils, neat red-berry reds, esp CAVE co-op Gravillas, CH du Trignon; DOMS de Boissan (full), Les Goubert, Pasquiers (full), Piaugier. *Gd full whites* for apéritifs, food, NB: Boissan, Piaugier, St Gayan.

Saint Mont SW Fr r p w ★★ (r) 14 (15') (16) (p w) DYA AOP from Gascon heartlands. Saxophonist J-L Garoussia (★DOM de Turet), CH de Bergalasse and ★★Dom des

Maouries ensure that co-op PRODUCTEURS PLAIMONT does not take over appellation as a brand.

Salon Champ ★★★★ Original BLANC DE BLANCS, from LE MESNIL in Côte des Blancs. Tiny quantities. Awesome reputation for long-lived luxury-priced wines: in truth, sometimes inconsistent. On song recently, viz 83' 90 97', but 99 disappoints, where is 02 going? Experts differ. *See also* DELAMOTTE.

Sancerre Lo (p) w ★→★★★★ 05' 08' 10 12 13 14' 15' 16' Luck of devil: untouched by 2016 frost. Exciting new generation. Touchstone SAUV BL (2291 ha), many fine reds (PINOT N 612 ha) Best: ALPHONSE MELLOT, Boulay, BOURGEOIS, Claude Riffault, Cotat (variable), Dezat, Dionysia, Fouassier, François Crochet, Jean-Max Roger, Joseph Mellot, Lucien Crochet, Mollet, Natter, Paul Prieur, Pierre Martin, Pinard, P & N Reverdy, Raimbault, Roblin, Thomas, Thomas Laballe, Vacheron, Vatan, Vattan, Vincent Delaporte.

Santenay C d'O r (w) ★★(★) 99' 02' 03 05' 09' 11 12 13 14 15' (16) S end of COTE DE BEAUNE, potential for fine reds not always realized. Some gd whites too. Best v'yds: CLOS de Tavannes, Clos Rousseau, Gravières (r w). Producers: Belland, Camille Giroud, Jessiaume, Lequin-Colin, MOREAU, Muzard, Vincent, V MOREY.

Saumur Lo r p w sp ★→★★★ 05' 09' 10' 12 14' 15' (16) Large AC. Whites: light to v. serious, age brilliantly; mainly easy reds except SAUMUR-CHAMPIGNY; pleasant rosés. Centre of Lo fizz production: CRÉMANT now most important, Saumur Mousseux. Saumur-Le-Puy-Notre-Dame AOP for CAB FR reds over 17 communes: misleadingly wide. Producers: Antoine Foucault, BOUVET-LADUBAY, CH de Brézé, CHAMPS FLEURIS, CLOS Mélaric, CLOS ROUGEARD, Guiberteau, Nerleux, Paleine, Parnay, René-Hugues Gay, Rocheville, St-Just, Targé, VIGNERONS de Saumur, VILLENEUVE, Yvonne.

Why does Sancerre grow Pinot N? Used to be owned by Counts of Champ.

Saumur-Champigny Lo r ★★→★★★ 96' 05' 09' 10 12 13 14' 15' (16) Nine-commune AC, one of best for CAB FR, aromatic, ages 15–20 yrs+ in gd vintages. Best: Bonnelière, Bruno Dubois, CH de VILLENEUVE, CH Yvonne, P Vadé; DOMS Antoine Sanzay, CHAMPS FLEURIS, CLOS Cristal, CLOS ROUGEARD, de la Cune, de Rocheville, de Targé, des Roches Neuves, du Val Brun, Filliatreau, Hureau, La Seigneurie, Nerleux, Petit St-Vincent, Saint Just and SAUMUR Co-op.

Saussignac SW Fr w sw ★★ 11 12' (14) (15') BERGERAC sub-AOP, wines slightly less sticky than those from adjoining MONBAZILLAC. Best: ★★★DOMS de Richard, La Maurigne, Les Miaudoux, Lestevénie; ★★CHX Le Chabrier, Le Payral, Le Tap.

Sauternes B'x w sw ★★→★★★★ 90' 95 96 97' 98 99' 01' 02 03' 05' 07' 09' 10' 11' 13 14 15 16 AC of five villages making France's best *liquoreux* from "noble rotted" grapes. Strong, luscious, golden and age-worthy. Some great yrs recently. Surprisingly food friendly. Classified (1855) CHX: CLOS HAUT-PEYRAGUEY, D'YQUEM, GUIRAUD, LAFAURIE-PEYRAGUEY, LA TOUR BLANCHE, RIEUSSEC, SIGALAS RABAUD, SUDUIRAUT. Dry wines labelled AC B'X Blanc.

Sauzet, Étienne C d'O w ★★★ Leading PULIGNY DOM with superb PREMIERS CRUS (Combettes, Champ Canet best) and GRANDS CRUS. V'yds now bio, fresh, lively wines, once again capable of ageing.

Savennières Lo w dr (sw) ★★→★★★★ 89' 96' 03 05' 07 08' 09 10' 11 12 14' 15' (16) Small ANJOU AC, high reputation; big variations in style, quality; v. long-lived whites (CHENIN BL) with marked acidity. Baudouin, *Baumard*, Bergerie, Boudignon, *Ch d'Epiré*, *Ch Pierre-Bise*, CH Soucherie, Closel, DOM FL, Laureau, Mahé, Mathieu-Tijou, Morgat, Ogereau, Pithon-Paillé. Top sites: CLOS du Papillon, COULÉE DE SERRANT, ROCHE-AUX-MOINES.

Savigny-lès-Beaune C d'O r (w) ★★★ 99' 02' 03 05' 09' 10' 11 12 14 15' (16) Important village next to BEAUNE; similar mid-weight wines, savoury touch (but can be rustic). Top v'yds: Dominode, Guettes, Lavières, Marconnets,

Vergelesses. Growers: *Bize*, Camus, ***Chandon de Briailles***, Chenu, CLAIR, DROUHIN, Girard, Guyon, LEROY, Pavelot, *Tollot-Beaut*.

Savoie r w sp ★★ →★★★ Alps. Vin de Sav AC (1980 ha) has 16 crus incl APRÉMONT, Chignin, CRÉPY, Jongieux, Ripaille. Separate ACs: Roussette de Sav (Altesse), SEYSSEL. Reds mainly GAMAY, MONDEUSE; whites: Altesse, Jacqùere, Mondeuse Blanc.

Schlossberg Al GRAND CRU at Kientzheim famed since C15. Glorious compelling RIES from FALLER (10) and new TRIMBACH; 15 should be great Ries yr here.

Schlumberger, Doms Al w sw ★ →★★★ Vast, top-quality AL DOM at Guebwiller owning approx one per cent of all Al v'yds. Holdings in GRANDS CRUS Kitterlé, Kessler and racy Saering 09 10' 12 13 15, Spiegel. Rich wines. Rare RIES, signature CUVÉE Ernest and now PINOT GR Grand Cru Kessler 09' 10' 12 13 14 15.

Schoenenbourg Al V. rich, successful Riquewihr GRAND CRU: PINOT GR, RIES, v. fine VENDANGE TARDIVE, SÉLECTION DES GRAINS NOBLES, esp DOPFF AU MOULIN. Also v.gd MUSCAT. HUGEL Schoelhammer from here.

Schoenheitz Al Rising estate in Munster Valley. Esp gd dry entry-level RIES 10' 11 12 13' 14. Lovely floral Ries Linnenberg 10 14 15.

Schoffit, Dom Al w ★★★ Exceptional Colmar grower Bernard S makes superb late-harvest GEWURZ, PINOT GR VENDANGE TARDIVE GRAND CRU RANGEN CLOS St Theobald 09 10' 12' 14 15 on volcanic soil. Contrast with RIES Grand Cru Sonnenberg 08 10' 13 on limestone. Delicious CHASSELAS.

Sec Literally means dry, though CHAMP SO called is medium-sweet (and better at breakfast, teatime, weddings than BRUT).

Séguret S Rh r p w ★★ 10' 12' 13 14 15' 16' Picturesque Prov hillside village nr GIGONDAS. V'yds mix plain and heights. One of top Rh villages. Mainly GRENACHE, peppery, quite deep reds, some full-on; clear-fruited whites. Esp CH la Courançonne (gd w), DOMS Amandine, de Cabasse (elegant), *de l'Amauve* (fine), Fontaine des Fées, Garancière, J David (bold, organic), Maison Plantevin, Malmont (stylish), *Mourchon* (robust), Pourra (intense, time), Soleil Romain.

Sélection des Grains Nobles Al Term coined by HUGEL for AL equivalent to German Beerenauslese, subject to ever-stricter rules. *Grains nobles* are grapes with "noble rot" for v. sweet wines.

Sérafin C d'O r ★★★ Deep colour, intense flavours, plenty of new wood: Serafin recipe for eg. GEVREY-CHAMBERTIN VIEILLES VIGNES, Cazetiers, CHARMES-CHAMBERTIN.

Seyssel Sav w sp ★★ AC since 1942. White (from Altesse, Molette), sparkling and CHASSELAS. Gd: Lambert de Seyssel.

Sichel & Co B'x r w ★★ One of B'x's most respected merchants (Sirius a top brand). Family-run; interests in CHX ANGLUDET, Argadens, PALMER and in CORBIÈRES (Ch Trillol). State-of-art storage facility.

Signargues S Rh ★ →★★ 15' 16' Modest CÔTES DU RH village between Avignon and Nîmes (w bank). Spicy, rather robust reds to drink inside 4 yrs. NB: CAVE Estézargues (punchy), CH Terre Forte (bio), DOMS des Romarins, Valériane, Haut-Musiel, La Font du Vent (best, deepest).

Simone, Ch Prov r p w ★★ →★★★ Historic estate outside Aix-en-Prov, where Winston Churchill painted Mont STE-VICTOIRE. Rougier family for nearly two centuries. Virtually synonymous with AC PALETTE. Age-worthy whites worth seeking out; characterful rosé, warming reds. Some rare grape varieties: (r) Castet, Manosquin.

Sipp, Louis Al w sw ★★ →★★★ Grower/NÉGOCIANT in Ribeauvillé. V.gd RIES GRAND CRU Kirchberg, superb grand cru Osterberg GEWURZ VENDANGE TARDIVE, esp 07 09'. Fine in classic drier yrs 08 10 12 13 14.

Sipp-Mack Al w sw ★★ →★★★ Excellent DOM at Hunawihr. Great RIES from GRANDS CRUS ROSACKER 10 12 13' 14 15'; v.gd PINOT GR.

Sorg, Bruno Al w ★★ →★★★ 1st-class small grower at Eguisheim; GRANDS CRUS Florimont (RIES 10 12 13' 14 15'), PFERSIGBERG (MUSCAT). Immaculate eco-friendly v'yds.

St-Amour Beauj r ★★ 14 15' 16 The most n BEAUJ cru: light, fruity, somewhat anonymous. Tediously recommended on 14 Feb. Try: DOM de Fa (Graillot), Janin, *Patissier*, Revillon.

St-Aubin C d'O r w ★★★ (r) 10' 11 12 13 14 15' (16) (w) 08 09' 10' 11 12 13 14' 15 (16) Fine source for *lively, refreshing whites*, adjacent to PULIGNY and CHASSAGNE, but usefully less expensive. Also pretty reds mostly for early drinking. Best v'yds: Chatenière, En Remilly, Murgers Dents de Chien. Best growers: COLIN, COLIN-MOREY, JC Bachelet, Lamy, Prudhon.

St-Bris Burg w ★ DYA. Neighbour to CHAB. AC for only SAUV BL in Burg. Fresh, lively, worth keeping from J-H GOISOT. Try also Bersan, de Moor, Simonnet-Febvre.

St-Chinian L'doc r p ★→★★★ 10 11 12 13 14 15 16 Large hilly area nr Béziers. Sound reputation. Incl CRUS of Berlou, Roquebrun on schist. Warm, spicy reds, based on SYRAH, GRENACHE, CARIGNAN, MOURVÈDRE. Whites from ROUSSANNE, MARSANNE, VERMENTINO, GRENACHE. Gd co-op Roquebrun; CHX de Viranel, Coujan; DOMS Borie la Vitarèle, des Jougla, la Dournie, MADURA, Navarre, Rimbert; CLOS Bagatelle, Mas Champart. Well worth detour.

St-Émilion B'x r ★★→★★★★ 00' 01 03 04 05' 08 09' 10' 11 12 14 15 16 Large MERLOT-led district on B'X's Right Bank. CAB FR also strong. ACS St-Ém and St-Ém GRAND CRU (lots of these). Top designation St-Ém PREMIER GRAND CRU CLASSÉ. Warm, full, rounded style; best firm, v. long-lived. Also modern and traditional styles. Top CHX: ANGÉLUS, AUSONE, CHEVAL BLANC, FIGEAC, PAVIE. Value: CARTEAU CÔTES-DAUGAY, DE FONBEL, Teyssier. Many attractive value wines.

St-Estèphe H-Méd r ★★→★★★★ 98 00' 01 02 03 04 05' 06 08 09' 10' 11 12 14 15 16 Most n communal AC in the MÉD. Solid, structured wines for ageing; consistent quality; value varies. Five Classed Growths: CALON-SÉGUR, COS D'ESTOURNEL, COS-LABORY, LAFON-ROCHET, MONTROSE. Also many top unclassified estates: CLAUZET, DE PEZ, HAUT-MARBUZET, LE CROCK, MEYNEY, ORMES-DE-PEZ, PHÉLAN-SÉGUR.

St-Gall Champ Brand of Union-CHAMP, top growers' co-op at AVIZE. BRUT NV; Extra Brut NV; Brut BLANC DE BLANCS NV; Brut Rosé NV; Brut Bl de Blancs 04 06 08'; CUVÉE Orpale Blanc de Blancs 02' 04 08' 09. Fine-value PINOT-led *Pierre Vaudon* NV. Makes top *vins clairs* for some great houses.

St-Georges d'Orques L'doc r p ★★→★★★ Most individual part of sprawling Grès de Montpellier, aspiring to individual cru status. Try CH l'Engarran, DOMS Henry, La Prose.

St-Georges-St-Émilion B'x r ★★ 08 09' 10' 12 14 15 16 Smallest of ST-ÉM satellites. Sturdy, structured. Best CHX: Calon, Macquin-St-Georges, St-André Corbin, ST-GEORGES, TOUR DU PAS-ST-GEORGES.

St-Gervais S Rh r (p) (w) ★ 15' 16' W-bank Rh village; gd soils but v. limited choice. Co-op low-key; best is long-lived (10 yrs+) DOM Ste Anne red (fresh, firm, strong MOURVÈDRE liquorice flavours); gd VIOGNIER. Also Dom Clavel (Syrius red).

St-Jacques d'Albas, Ch L'doc r p w ★★ Dynamic MINERVOIS estate since 2001: Le Petit St-Jacques, Le DOM, Le CH and SYRAH-dominant La Chapelle (all r).

St-Joseph N Rh r w ★★→★★★ 99' 05' 06' 07' 09' 10' 11' 12' 13' 14 15' 16' 40 miles of mainly granite v'yds along w bank of N Rh. SYRAH reds. Best, oldest v'yds nr Tournon: stylish, soft, red-fruited wines; further n darker, direct, peppery, more obvious oak. More complete, intricate than CROZES-HERMITAGE, esp CHAPOUTIER (Les Granits), Gonon (top class), *Gripa*, GUIGAL (Vignes de l'Hospice), *J-L Chave* (gd style); also A Perret, Chèze, Courbis (modern), Coursodon (racy, modern), Cuilleron, *Delas*, E Darnaud, Faury, F Villard, Gaillard, J&E Durand (fruit), Monier-Perréol (organic), Nicolas Perrin, P-J Villa, P Marthouret (traditional), Vallet, Vins de Vienne. Gd food-friendly *white (mainly Marsanne)*, esp A Perret, Barge, B Gripa, CHAPOUTIER (Les Granits), Cuilleron, Faury, Gonon (fab), Gouye (traditional), J Pilon.

> **New stars in the Southwest**
> **Ch de Peyrel, Rosette** renaissance from 2013 on. Delicious apéritif off-dry mostly from SÉM, MUSCADELLE. **Ch Trotteligotte, Cahors** one of CAHORS' most serious bio growers. Causse-style wines with real finesse. **Dom Courège-Longe, Buzet** David Sazi animates group "Buzet d'Auteurs" to stand up to powerful co-op. **Dom de Beyssac, Marmande** a Right-Bank bio estate with some Abouriou grapes. **Dom des Pradelles, Fronton** now under dynamic management of Noëlle Sanchez. **Dom La Fon Longue, Côtes de Duras** characterful red from higher ground in Loubès-Bernac area. **Dom Llaroude, Jurançon** Jeremy Estoigt has 7 ha at w end of appellation. Bio. **Dom Peyres-Roses, Gaillac** young grower Charles Bonnafont-Serre experiments with fashionable egg-shaped *cuves*. Passionately bio. **Dom Sédouprat, Côtes de Gascogne** unusually gd reds for area (CUVÉE Sanglier). **Dom Xubialdea, Irouléguy** Battit Ibagaray, with 7 ha, plants GROS MANSENG to density of 10,000/ha. Bio. **Sandrine Annibal, Thézac-Perricard** (IGP) best is off-dry Manseng, v. more-ish. Don't, whatever you do, forget Armagnac (GERS); France's best brandy.

St-Julien H-Méd r ★★★→★★★★ 00' 01 02 03 04 05' 06 08 09' 10' 11 12 14 15 16 Small mid-MÉD communal AC. 11 classified (1855) estates own 95 per cent of v'yds. Incl three LÉOVILLES, DUCRU-BEAUCAILLOU, GRUAUD-LAROSE. Few unclassified incl DU GLANA, GLORIA. Epitome of harmonious, fragrant, savoury red.

St-Nicolas-de-Bourgueil Lo r p ★★→★★★ 05' 06 08 09' 10' 11 12 14' 15' 16 Similar to BOURGUEIL: CAB FR but more expensive. Largely sand/gravel, light wines; more structured from limestone slopes. Some badly hit by 2016 frost. Try: CLOS des Quarterons, David, Delanoue, Frédéric Mabileau, Laurent Mabileau, Lorieux, Mabileau-Rezé, Mortier, Taluau-Foltzenlogel, Vallée, *Yannick Amirault*.

St-Péray N Rh w sp ★★ 12' 13' 14' 15' 16' Progressive white Rh (MARSANNE/ROUSSANNE) from hilly granite and lime v'yds opposite Valence. *Méthode Champenoise esp worth trying* (A Voge, J-L Thiers, R Nodin). Still white should have grip, be smoky, flinty. Best: CHAPOUTIER, *Clape* (pure), *Colombo* (stylish), Cuilleron, *du Tunnel*, Gripa (v.gd), J-L Thiers, R Nodin, Vins de Vienne, Voge (oak) and TAIN co-op.

St-Pierre de Soucy Sav From steep schist hillsides, this cru makes assertive fresh-tasting mix of Jacquère, CHARD, Mondeuse Blanche. Top: DOM des Ardoisière.

St-Pourçain Mass C r p w ★→★★ DYA. AC (640 ha in upper Loire [Allier].) Light red, rosé from GAMAY, PINOT N (AOP stupidly bans pure PINOT N), white from local Tressalier and/or CHARD, SAUV BL. Growers: Berioles, DOM de Bellevue, Grosbot-Barbara, Laurent, Nebout, Pétillat, Ray; gd co-op (VIGNERONS de St-Pourçain).

St-Romain C d'O r w ★★ (w) 12 14' 15 (16) *Crisp whites*, clean-cut reds from vines in side valley of CÔTE DE BEAUNE. Try Bellene, Buisson, de Chassorney, Gras, HOSPICES.

St-Véran Burg w ★★ 14' 15 (16) AC outside POUILLY-FUISSÉ with variable soils and results. Best offer quality (Chagnoleau, Corsin, Litaud, Merlin) and value (DUBOEUF, Deux Roches, Poncetys).

Ste-Croix-du-Mont B'x w sw ★★ 05' 07 09' 10' 11 13 14 15 16 Sweet white AC facing SAUTERNES across River Garonne. Best: rich, creamy, can age. Top CHX: Crabitan-Bellevue, du Mont, la Rame, *Loubens*, Pavillon.

Ste-Victoire Prov r p ★★ Subzone of CÔTES DE PROV from s slopes of Montagne Ste-Victoire. Dramatic scenery goes with gd wine. Try Mas de Cadenet, Mauvan.

Sur lie "On the lees". MUSCADET is often bottled straight from the vat, for max zest, body, character.

Tâche, La C d'O r ★★★★ 90' 93' 95 96' 98 99' 00 01 02' 03 05' 06 07 09' 10' 11 12' 13 14 15' (16) GRAND CRU of VOSNE-ROMANÉE, MONOPOLE of DRC. One of best v'yds on earth: full, perfumed, luxurious wine, tight in youth.

Taille-aux-Loups, Dom de la Lo w sw sp ★★★ 05' 07' 08' 09 10' 11 12 14' 15' (16r) Jacky Blot, one of Lo's most dynamic, impeccable producers: barrel-fermented MONTLOUIS, VIN DE FRANCE (aka VOUVRAY) majority dry, esp single v'yds – CLOS Mosny, Michet (Montlouis), Venise (Vouvray); Triple Zéro Montlouis *pétillant* (p w); v.gd reds from BOURGUEIL, DOM de la Butte. Badly frosted 2016 (Montlouis).

Tain, Cave de N Rh ★★→★★★ Top N Rh co-op, often mature v'yds, incl 25 per cent of HERMITAGE. Sound to v.gd red Hermitage, esp Epsilon, Gambert de Loche, abundant white Hermitage Au Coeur des Siècles. Gd ST-JOSEPH (r w), interesting Bio (organic) range (CROZES, St-Joseph), other wines modern, mainstream. Gd recent CROZES reds from hill and plain v'yds "GN", "BM", "LA". Whites light in 2015. Distinguished VIN DE PAILLE.

Taittinger Champ BRUT NV, Rosé NV, Brut 04 06 08, Collection Brut 89 90 95' jewels of this again-family-run Reims house. Epitome of apéritif style, exquisite weightlessness. Ace luxury *Comtes de Champagne* 95' 99 02' 04 06 08'; Comtes Rosé also shines in 06. Excellent single v'yd La Marquetterie. New English sparkling project in Kent, DOM Evremond. (*See also* Dom Carneros, California.)

Tavel S Rh p ★★ DYA. GRENACHE rosé, once robust, for vivid Mediterranean dishes. Now many slighter Prov-styles, often for apéritif; a pity. Top: DOM de l'Anglore (no SO2), Dom de la Mordorée (full), Corne-Loup, GUIGAL (gd), Lafond Roc-Epine, Maby, Moulin-la-Viguerie (organic, traditional), Prieuré de Montézargues (fine), Rocalière (v. fine); CHX Aquéria, Correnson (stylish), de Manissy, Ségriès, *Trinquevedel* (fine), VIDAL-FLEURY.

Tempier, Dom Prov r p w ★★★★ Estate that est MOURVÈDRE in AC BANDOL. Wines combine elegance, concentration and longevity. Maintains excellent quality; now rivalled by several others.

Terrasses du Larzac L'doc r p w ★★→★★★ Most n part of AC L'DOC. Wild, hilly region from Lac du Salagou to Aniane, incl MONTPEYROUX, St-Saturnin. AC since 2014; also gd Vin du L'doc. Cooler temperatures make for fresh wines. Several est and many rising stars, incl: CAL DEMOURA, CLOS des Serres, Jonquières, Mas de L'Ecriture, *Mas Jullien*, MONTCALMÈS, Pas de l'Escalette, Plan de l'Homme. *Definitely to watch.*

Thénard, Dom Burg r w ★★→★★★★ Historic producer with large holding of MONTRACHET, mostly sold on to NÉGOCIANTS, some v.gd reds from home base in GIVRY.

Thévenet, Jean Burg r w sw ★★★ Top MÂCONNAIS purveyor of rich and some semi-botrytized CHARD, eg CUVÉE Levroutée at DOM de la Bongran.

Thézac-Perricard SW Fr r p w ★★ 15' (16) IGP adjoining CAHORS (reds from MALBEC, MERLOT). Sandrine Annibal's ★★DOM de Lancement notable for exciting off-dry white from both MANSENG grapes. Reds keep her well ahead of a worthy ★co-op.

Thiénot, Alain Champ New generation now firmly at helm. Ever-improving quality: impressive, fairly priced ★★★BRUT NV; Rosé NV Brut; vintage Stanislas 02 04 06 08' 09 12 13; voluminous VIGNE aux Gamins (single v'yd AVIZE 02 04 06). CUVÉE Garance CHARD 07 sings, classic 08 for long haul. Also owns CHAMP CANARD-DUCHÊNE, CH Ricaud in LOUPIAC.

Thomas, André & fils Al w ★★★ V. fine grower at Ammerschwihr, rigorously organic, artist-craftsman in the cellar. V.gd RIES Kaefferkopf 08 10' 12, magnificent GEWURZ VIEILLES VIGNES 05 09' 10' 12 14.

Tissot Jura Plentiful family around ARBOIS. ★★★Stephane T (still uses parents' label Andre & Mireille Tissot), pioneer of single-v'yd CHARD, VIN JAUNE using bio/natural methods; outstanding CRÉMANT du Jura. ★★Jacques T for volume, value.

Tollot-Beaut C d'O r ★★★ Consistent CÔTE DE BEAUNE grower with 20 ha in BEAUNE (Grèves, CLOS du Roi), CORTON (Bressandes), SAVIGNY and at CHOREY-LÈS-BEAUNE base (NB: Pièce du Chapitre). Oaky style but it works.

Touraine Lo r p w dr sw sp ★→★★★★ 10 14' 15' 16 Huge region with many ACS (eg. VOUVRAY, CHINON, BOURGUEIL) also umbrella AC of variable quality: fruity reds (CAB FR, CÔT, GAMAY, PINOT N), whites (SAUV BL), rosés, sparkling. Producers: Bois-Vaudons, Corbillières, Joël Delaunay, Garrelière, Gosseaume, Jacky Marteau, La Chapinière, Lacour, Mandard, **Marionnet**, Morantin, Petit Thouars, **Presle**, Puzelat, Ricard, Roussely, Tue-Boeuf, Villebois. Touraine Village ACs Azay-le-Rideau, Chenonceaux, Mesland, Noble-Joué, Oisly. Too many bets on Sauv Bl and weedkillers. Parts badly frosted 2016.

Touraine-Amboise Lo r p (w) ★→★★ TOURAINE village-AC, 50/40 per cent red/rosé. François 1er pop blend (GAMAY/CÔT/CAB FR), top reds: Côt/Cab Fr, white: CHENIN BL. Best: Bessons, Closerie de Chanteloup, Dutertre, Frissant, Gabillière, Grange Tiphaine, Mesliard, Truet. Moving to cru for Chenin, Côt.

Touraine-Azay-le-Rideau Lo p w (sw) ★→★★ Tiny TOURAINE sub-AC. Rosé (60 per cent of AC; Grolleau 60% min), CHENIN BL-dry, off-dry white. Best: Aulée, Bourse, de la Roche, Grosbois, Nicolas Paget. Frosted 2016.

Touraine-Mesland Lo r p w ★★→★★ 10 14 15 (16) Small TOURAINE villages AC w of Blois, on n bank of Loire. No better than straight Touraine. Best: Girault (bio), Grandes Espérances.

Touraine-Noble Joué Lo p ★→★★ DYA. Delicious rosé from three PINOTS (N, M, GR). AOP mainly Indre Valley s of Tours. Best: Astraly, Cosson, Rousseau, Sard-Pierru. V. badly hit by 2016 frost.

Trapet C d'O r ★★★ Long-est GEVREY-CHAMBERTIN DOM making sensual bio wines from village up to GRAND CRU CHAMBERTIN plus AL whites by marriage. *See also* cousins ROSSIGNOL-TRAPET.

Trévallon, Dom de Prov r w ★★★ 00' 01 03 04 05 06 07 08 09 10 11 12 13 14 15 16 Once pioneering estate in LES BAUX, but IGP BOUCHES-DU-RH as no GRENACHE. Huge reputation fully justified. Intense, age-worthy CAB SAUV/SYRAH. *Barrique-aged white* from MARSANNE/ROUSSANNE, drop of CHARD and now GRENACHE BL.

Trimbach, FE Al w ★★★→★★★★ Matchless grower of AL RIES on limestone soils at Ribeauvillé, esp CLOS STE-HUNE **89** still great. 10' 13 classically cool; almost-as-gd (and much cheaper) *Frédéric Emile 10* 12 13. Dry, elegant wines for great cuisine. Look out for 1ST GRAND CRU label: from v'yds of Couvent de Ribeauville, cultivated by Trimbach.

Tursan SW Fr r r p w ★★ Mostly DYA. AOP in Landes. DOM de Perchade more authentic than delicious wines (CH de Bachen) that superstar chef Michel Guérard ★★ makes for his restaurants at Eugénie-les-Bains. Worthy co-op (now twinned with CHALOSSE) floundering a bit.

Vacqueyras S Rh (p) w ★★ 07' 09' 10' 11 12' 13 14 15' 16' Hearty, sun-filled, peppery, GRENACHE-centred neighbour of GIGONDAS; for game, big flavours. Lives 10 yrs+. Try: Arnoux Vieux Clocher, JABOULET; CHX de Montmirail, *des Tours* (v. fine); CLOS des Cazaux (racy, gd value); DOMS Amouriers, Archimbaud-Vache, Charbonnière, Couroulu (v.gd, traditional), Famille Perrin, Font de Papier (organic), Fourmone (gd form), Garrigue (traditional), Grapillon d'Or, Monardière (v.gd), Montirius (bio), Montvac (elegant), Roucas Toumba (organic), Sang des Cailloux (v.gd, esp Lopy), Semelles de Vent (clear fruit), Verde. *Full whites* (Clos des Cazaux, Sang des Cailloux).

358 vine varieties officially approved for growing in France, incl table grapes.

Val de Loire Lo r p w DYA. One of France's four regional IGPs, formerly Jardin de la France.

Valençay Lo r p w ★→★★ AOP (165 ha), e TOURAINE; esp SAUV BL, (CHARD); reds (mainly) CÔT, GAMAY, PINOT N. CLOS Delorme, Lafond, Preys, Sébastien Vaillant, Sinson, VIGNERONS de Valençay.

Valréas S Rh r (p) (w) ★★ 10' 12' 13 15' 16' CÔTES DU RH-VILLAGE in n Vaucluse truffle country, quality rising; large co-op. Grainy, peppery, direct, sometimes heady, red-fuited red (mainly GRENACHE), improving white. Esp: CH la Décelle, CLOS Bellane (gd white), des Grands Devers, DOM Gramenon (bio), du Mas de Ste-Croix, du Séminaire (organic), Emmanuel Bouchard (best, organic, character), Prévosse (organic).

VDN (Vin Doux Naturel) ROUSS Sweet wine fortified with wine alc, so sweetness natural, not strength. Speciality of ROUSS based on GRENACHE, Noir, Blanc or Gris, or MUSCAT. Top wines, esp aged RANCIOS, can provide fabulous drinking.

World's biggest barrel, 300,000 litres, made for Ch Puech-Haut, L'doc.

VDP (Vin de Pays) Potentially most dynamic category in France (with over 150 regions), allowing scope for experimentation. Renamed ICP (*Indication Géographique Protegée*) from 2009 vintage, but position unchanged and new terminology still not accepted by every area. Zonal names most individual: eg. CÔTES DE GASCOGNE, CÔTES DE THONGUE, Duché d'Uzès, Haute Vallée de l'Orb, among others. Enormous variety in taste and quality but never ceases to surprise.

VDQS (Vins Délimite de Qualité Supérieure) Now phased out.

VDT (Vin de Table) Category of standard everyday table wine now replaced by VIN DE FRANCE.

Vendange Harvest. **Vendange Tardive:** late-harvest; AL equivalent to German Auslese but usually higher alc.

Venoge, de Champ Venerable house revitalized under LANSON-BCC ownership. Gd niche blends: Cordon Bleu Extra-BRUT, vintage BLANC DE BLANCS 00 04 06 08 12 13 14 15'. Excellent vintage Rosé 06 09 CUVÉE 20 Ans, Prestige Cuvée Louis XV 10-yr-old BLANC DE NOIRS.

Ventoux S Rh r p w ★★ 15' 16' Rambling AC all around Mont Ventoux between Rh and Prov. A few front-running DOMS gd value. Juicy, tangy red (GRENACHE/SYRAH), café-style to deeper, improving quality), rosé, gd white (more oak). Best: CH Unang (gd w), Ch Valcombe, CLOS des Patris, Ferme St-Pierre (p w), Gonnet, *La Vieille Ferme* (r, can be VIN DE FRANCE) owned by BEAUCASTEL, Goult, St-Didier, St Marc; Doms Anges, Berane, Brusset, Cascavel, Champ-Long, Croix de Pins (gd w), Fondrèche (v.gd), Grand Jacquet, Martinelle (great fruit), Murmurium, Olivier B, PAUL JABOULET (v.gd), *Pesquié* (excellent), Pigeade (genuine), St-Jean du Barroux (organic), Terres de Solence, Verrière, VIDAL-FLEURY; co-op Bédoin.

Verget Burg w ★★ →★★★ Jean-Marie Guffens' MÂCONNAIS-based white wine merchant venture, nearly as idiosyncratic as his own DOM. Also varietal wines from S now

Vernay, Dom Georges N Rh r w ★★→★★★ 12' 13' 14' 15' 16' Top CONDRIEU name; three wines, all with flair, elegance; Terrasses de l'Empire *apéritif de luxe*; Chaillées d'Enfer, richness; Coteau de Vernon, mysterious, supreme style, lives 15 yrs+. CÔTE-RÔTIE and ST-JOSEPH (r) emphasize elegance and purity of fruit. V.gd VIN DE PAYS (r w).

Veuve Clicquot Champ Historic house of highest standing. Full-bodied, rich, fine: one of CHAMP's sure things. Yellow Label NV, ★★★White Label DEMI-SEC NV, new CUVÉE Rich (*doux*, dosage 60g/l+) Vintage Rés 02 04 06 08 12', Rosé Rés 08 12'. Luxury La Grande Dame 98 04, fine 06, ★★★★La Grande Dame Rosé 95 06. Part-oak-fermented vintages from 08. CAVE Privée re-release of older vintages esp 89 95 (magnums). Exemplary red winemaking unit for subtlest CHAMP rosés.

Veuve Devaux Champ Premium brand of powerful Union Auboise co-op. Excellent aged Grande Rés NV, Œil de Perdrix Rosé, Prestige CUVÉE D 02' 09, BRUT Vintage 09' 10 14 15.

Vézelay Burg r w ★→★★ Age 1–2 yrs. Magical location for tasty CHARD (BOURGOGNE Vézelay), light PINOT (generic Bourgogne), revived MELON (CÔTEAUX BOURGUIGNON). Try: DOM de la Cadette, des Faverelles, Elise Villiers, La Croix Montjoie.

Vidal-Fleury, J N Rh r w sw ★★→★★★ GUIGAL-owned Rh merchant/grower of CÔTE-RÔTIE. Top notch, tight, v. elegant *La Chatillonne* (12% VIOGNIER; much oak, wait min 6 yrs). Range wide, improving. Gd CAIRANNE, CHÂTEAUNEUF (r), CÔTES DU RH (r p w), MUSCAT DE BEAUMES-DE-VENISE, ST-JOSEPH (r w), TAVEL, VENTOUX.

Vieille Ferme, La S Rh r w ★→★★ Reliable gd-value brand; much has become VIN DE FRANCE, with VENTOUX (r), LUBÉRON (w) in some countries (France, Japan) from Famille Perrin of CH DE BEAUCASTEL. Back on form 2015, incl rosé.

Vieilles Vignes Old vines, which should make the best wine. Eg. DE VOGÜÉ, MUSIGNY, Vieilles Vignes. But no rules about age and can be a tourist trap.

Vieux Télégraphe, Dom du S Rh r w ★★★ 78' 81' 85 89' 90 94' 95' 96' 97 98' 99' 00 01' 03' 04' 05' 06' 07' 09' 10' 12' 13 14 15' 16' Big, high-quality estate; classic stony soils, intricate, take-your-time red CHÂTEAUNEUF; top two wines La Crau (crunchy, robust) and since 2011 Pied Long et Pignan (stylish). Also rich whites La Crau (v.gd 15), CLOS La Roquète (great with food, gd in lesser yrs eg. 02 08 11 14). Owns fine, slow-to-evolve, complex *Gigondas Dom Les Pallières* with US importer Kermit Lynch.

Vigne or vignoble Vineyard (v'yd), vineyards (v'yds).

Vigneron Vine-grower.

Villeneuve, Ch de Lo r w ★★★(★) 96 05 06 07 08' 09' 10' 11 12 14' 15 (16) Impeccable estate. Great SAUMUR Blanc (esp Les Cormiers – potential to age) and SAUMUR-CHAMPIGNY (esp VIEILLES VIGNES, Grand CLOS but only in gd vintages). Organic. New chai in old cellar.

Vin de France Replaces VIN DE TABLE. At last allows mention of grape variety and vintage. Often blends of regions with brand name. Can be source of unexpected delights if talented winemaker uses this category to avoid bureaucractic hassle. Eg. Yves Cuilleron VIOGNIER (N Rh).

Vin de paille Wine from grapes dried on straw mats, so v. sweet, like Italian passito. Esp in the Jura. *See also* CHAVE, VIN PAILLÉ DE CORRÈZE.

Vin gris "Grey" wine is v. pale pink, made of red grapes pressed before fermentation begins; unlike rosé (ferments briefly before pressing). Or from eg. PINOT GR, not-quite-white grapes. "Œil de Perdrix" means much the same; so does "blush".

Vin jaune Jura w ★★★ Speciality of Jura; inimitable yellow wine. SAVAGNIN, 6 yrs+ in barrel without topping up, develops flor: like Sherry but no added alc. Expensive to make. Separate AC for top spot, CH-CHALON. Sold in unique 62cl Clavelin bottles.

Vin paillé de Corrèze SW Fr r w 25 small growers and tiny co-op once more laying out grapes on straw in old way to make pungent wine once recommended to breast-feeding mothers. Wines will keep as long as you. If you're brave try ★Christian Tronche.

Vinsobres S Rh r (p) (w) ★★ 10' 12' 13 14 15' 16' AC notable for SYRAH. Best reds show decisive red fruit, punch, to drink with red meat. Leaders: CAVE la Vinsobraise; CH Rouanne; DOMS Bicarelle, Chaume-Arnaud (organic), Constant-Duquesnoy, Coriançon, Deurre (traditional), Famille Perrin (Hauts de Julien top class, others value), Jaume (modern, consistent), Moulin (traditional, gd r w), Péquélette (bio), Peysson.

Cool Syrah from the south

SYRAH can struggle outside N Rh, its clarity clouded by excess heat, leading to jammy flavours. The low Drôme area in S Rh has sufficient coolness to allow stylish ripening. Hence wines such as J-L CHAVE CÔTES DU RH Sélection Mon Coeur (Syrah from VINSOBRES), DOMS de l'Echevin St-Maurice Guillaume de Rouville (organic), Gramenon Sierra du Sud (bio), Peysson Côtes du Rh Bio & Élégant (organic).

Viré-Clessé Burg w ★★ 10' 12 13 14' 15 (16) AC based around two of best white villages of MÂCON. Known for exuberant rich style, sometimes late-harvest. Try Bonhomme, Bret Bros, Chaland, DOM de la Verpaille, Gondard-Perrin, J-P Michel, LAFON, *Thévenet*.

Visan S Rh r (p) (w) ★★ 12' 13 15' 16' Improving: reds have decent depth, with clear fruit, pepper, some more suave. Whites okay. Best: DOMS Art Mas (organic), Coste Chaude (gd fruit), des Grands Devers, Montmartel (organic), Dieulefit (bio), Florane, Fourmente (bio, esp Nature), Philippe Plantevin, Roche-Audran (organic, dashing), VIGNOBLE Art Mas.

Carignan, the bad boy of L'doc, is making gd. Look for varietal in Pays d'Oc.

Vogüé, Comte Georges de C d'O r w ★★★★ Iconic CHAMBOLLE estate, with lion's share of MUSIGNY. Heralded vintages from 90s taking time to come round, but getting there.

Volnay C d'O r ★★★→★★★★ 90' 95 96' 98 99' 02' 03 05' 06 07 09' 10' 11 14 15' (16) Best source for CÔTE DE BEAUNE reds except when it hails. Can be structured, should be silky. Best v'yds: Caillerets, Champans, CLOS des Chênes, Clos des Ducs, Santenots, Taillepieds, etc. Best growers: Bouley, D'ANGERVILLE, DE MONTILLE, H BOILLOT, HOSPICES DE BEAUNE→LAFARGE, LAFON, N Rossignol, Pousse d'Or.

Vosne-Romanée C d'O r ★★★→★★★★ 90' 93' 95 96' 99' 02' 03 05' 06 07 08 09' 10' 11 12 13 14 15' (16) Village with Burg's grandest crus (eg. ROMANÉE-CONTI, LA TÂCHE) and outstanding PREMIERS CRUS Malconsorts, Suchots, Brûlées, etc. There are (or should be) no common wines in Vosne. Many gd if increasingly pricey growers. Top: Arnoux-Lachaux, CATHIARD, Clavelier, DRC, EUGÉNIE, Forey, GRIVOT, GROS, Guyon, Lamarche, LEROY, LIGER-BELAIR, MÉO-CAMUZET, MUGNERET, NOËLLAT, ROUGET, Tardy.

Vougeot C d'O r w ★★★ 90' 96' 99' 02' 03 05' 06 07 08 09' 10' 11 12' 13 14 15' (16) Mostly GRAND CRU as CLOS DE VOUGEOT but also village and PREMIER CRU, incl outstanding white MONOPOLE, **Clos Blanc de V.** Clerget, HUDELOT-Noëllat, VOUGERAIE best.

Vougeraie, Dom de la C d'O r w ★★★→★★★★ Bio DOM uniting all BOISSET's v'yd holdings (since 1999). BOURGOGNE Rouge up to fine GRANDS CRUS eg. BONNES-MARES, Charmes-Chambertin, MUSIGNY. Whites now also strong suit, with unique **Clos Blanc de Vougeot** and four GRANDS CRUS incl BÂTARD-MONTRACHET, Charlemagne.

Vouvray Lo w dr sw sp ★★ →★★★★ (dr) 89 90 96' 02' 03 05' 07 08' 09 10 11 12 14 15' (16) (sw) 89' 90' 95' 96' 97' 03' 05' 08 09' 10 11 15' (16) AC e of Tours, on n bank of Loire. Best v'yds on *premier côte* above Loire. Variable quality but top producers reliably gd. DEMI-SEC is classic style, but in gd yrs *moelleux* can be lusciously sweet, almost immortal. Fizz variable (60 per cent of production): look for *pétillant* – a speciality. Try: Aubuisières, Autran, Bonneau, Brunet, Carême, *Champalou*, CLOS Baudoin, Florent Cosme, Fontainerie, Foreau, F PINON, Gaudrelle, *Huet*, Mathieu Cosme, Meslerie (Hahn), Perrault-Jadaud, *Taille-aux-Loups*, Vigneau-Chevreau. Old vintages: 21 24 37 47 59 70 71 must-try. Parts frosted 2016.

Vranken Champ Powerful CHAMP group. Sound quality. Leading brand: Demoiselle. Owns HEIDSIECK MONOPOLE, POMMERY. Extensive vyds in Prov, Camargue.

Wolfberger Al ★★ Principal label of EGUISHEIM co-op. V.gd quality for such a large-scale producer. Leading sparkling CRÉMANT producer; high tech for high quality.

Zind Humbrecht, Dom Al w sw ★★★★ Leading bio DOM sensitively run by Olivier H, great winemaker and president of GRAND CRU AL consortium: rich, balanced wines, drier, elegant, v. low yields. Top wines from single v'yds **Clos St-Urbain Grand Cru Rangen**: RIES 07 10' 15' a future great; Jebsal; superb PINOT GR 08 09 10 12 14, plus Grands Crus Hengst and Brand (Ries 10' 12 14 15), Goldert (MUSCAT 12). Real success in more subtle GC Ries like Brand, already delicious in 14.

Châteaux of Bordeaux

Abbreviations used in the text:

B'x	Bordeaux
Bar	Barsac
Cas	Castillon-Côtes de Bordeaux
E-2-M	Entre-Deux-Mers
Fron	Fronsac
Grav	Graves
H-Méd	Haut-Médoc
L de P	Lalande de Pomerol
List	Listrac
Mar	Margaux
Méd	Médoc
Mou	Moulis
Pau	Pauillac
Pe-Lé	Pessac-Léognan
Pom	Pomerol
Saut	Sauternes
St-Ém	St-Émilion
St-Est	St-Estèphe
St-Jul	St-Julien

AC	appellation contrôlée
ch(x)	château(x)
dom(s)	domaine(s)

It wasn't looking good in June 2016, with the eqivalent of nearly a year's worth of rain (750mm) having fallen in the first six months of the year. Then a hot, dry summer ensued (with a couple of bouts of rain in September to freshen things up), rot was kept at bay and the harvest delivered on a plate as and when growers desired. No wonder they are smiling, as both quality and quantity are present in 2016. The parallels are with 2009 and 2010 right across the board. Let's not forget, though, that 2015 was also a standout year and although 2014 didn't quite achieve greatness, its classic lines should provide good-value drinking in time.

Châteaux of Bordeaux entries also cross-reference to France.

In the meantime there is a reserve of good red vintages for drinking. The luscious 2009s are tempting at whatever level and in appellations like Castillon, Fronsac, Haut-Médoc and Graves the 2008s are drinking well. At *petit château* level the 2010s are opening up and the lighter but fruit-driven 2012s and 2013s also offer early drinking charm.

For all sorts of reasons St-Émilion is on a roll just now as the place to look for substantial, satisfying, modern-tasting wines at fair prices that are drinkable within two or three years. They may not be classic claret, with the freshness and "cut" of the Médoc, but they suit our crossover cooking, and people who drink red wine without food.

Among the Grands Crus the mature vintages to look for are 2000, 2001 (particularly Right Bank), 2002 (top-end Médoc) and 2004, with the very best 2007s also worthy of consideration. The 2006s are just beginning to open but hang on to the 2005s. Dry white Bordeaux remains consistent in quality and value, with another fine vintage in 2016, so don't hesitate here. And Sauternes continues its winning run (apart from 2012) with a richly botrytized 2016. The problem is one of being spoilt for choice: 2015, 2011, 2010, 2009, 2007, 2005 and 2001 are as good as it gets in this sweet-wine appellation. And 2014 and 2013 are not far behind.

A, Dom de L' Cas r ★★ 04 05' 06 07 08 09' 10' 11 12 14 15 MERLOT-led CAS property owned by consultant STÉPHANE DERENONCOURT and his wife. Bio. Punches above its weight.

Agassac, D' H-Méd r ★★ 06 07 08 09' 10' 11 12 14 15 Renaissance CH in S H-MÉD. Modern, accessible wine. CAB SAUV-led. Tourist-friendly.

Aiguilhe, D' Cas r ★★ 05 06 07 08 09 10 11 12 14 15 16 Large estate in CAS on high plateau. Same German aristo owner as CANON LA GAFFELIÈRE and LA MONDOTTE since 1998. MERLOT-led wine with *power and finesse*.

Andron-Blanquet St-Est r ★★ 01 03 04 05' 06 08 09' 10' 11 14 15 Sister CH to COS-LABORY. Solid in style.

Angélus St Ém r ★★★★ 96 98' 99 00' 01 02 03 04 05 06 07 08 09' 10' 11 12 13 14 15' 16 Promoted to PREMIER GRAND CRU CLASSÉ (A) in 2012 so prices up. Stéphanie de Boüard-Rivoal at helm. Cellars completely renovated (2013) incl new wrought-iron bell tower. Pioneer of modern ST-ÉM; dark, rich, sumptuous. Second label: Le Carillon de L'Angélus. Now a 3rd wine, No 3.

Angludet Marg r (w) ★★ 02 04 05 06 08 09' 10' 11 12 14 15 16 Owned and run by NÉGOCIANT SICHEL. CAB SAUV, MERLOT, 13% PETIT VERDOT. Fragrant, stylish, consistent wines. Second label: La Res d'Angludet.

Archambeau Grav r w dr (sw) ★★ (r) 06 08 09 10 11 14 15 (w) 10 11 12 13 14 15 Consistent property with v'yd in single block on hill at Illats. Gd *fruity dry white*; fragrant barrel-aged reds. Improving BAR classed-growth CH Suau in same stable.

Arche, D' Saut w sw ★★ 99 00 01' 02 03' 05 07 09' 10' 11' 13 14 15 Consistent, gd-value Second Growth on the edge of SAUT. Also has a hotel. Arche Lafaurie is special selection.

Armailhac, D' Pau r ★★★ 00 01 02 04 05' 06 07 08 09' 10' 11 12 13 14 15 16 Substantial Fifth Growth. (MOUTON) ROTHSCHILD owned since 1934. On top form, well priced. Usually little more forward than some PAUILLACS.

Arrosée, L' St-Ém r ★★★ 00 01 02 03 04 05' 06' 07 08 09' 10' 11 12 RIP from 2013, bought by Dillons of HAUT-BRION, integrated into neighbouring QUINTUS. Until then on top form since 2003. Mellow, harmonious wines with plenty of CAB FR, CAB SAUV (40%).

Aurelius St-Ém r ★★ 06 08 09 10 11 12 14 15 Top CUVÉE from the go-ahead ST-ÉM co-op – 50,000 bottles/yr. Modern, concentrated; 14 mths in new oak barrels.

The 1961 classification
A new classification to replace that of 1855 all but made it onto the books in 1961. Driven initially by producers and within a hair's breadth of being signed off by governing body, INAO, the new classification would have seen the number of MÉD CHX reduced from 60 to 55 and the number of levels from five to three. 17 of the original chx would have been dropped and 12 CRUS BOURGEOIS promoted. HAUT-BRION would have kept its 1855 status. Infighting among producers eventually led to project being shelved. So what's new?

Ausone St-Ém r ★★★★ 89' 90 95 96' 97 98' 99 00' 01' 02 03' 04 05' 06' 07 08 09' 10' 11 12 13 14 15' 16 Tiny but illustrious ST-ÉM First Growth (c.1500 cases) named after Roman poet; best position on CÔTES. Lots of CAB FR (55%). Long-lived wines with volume, texture, finesse. Pricey. Second label: Chapelle d'Ausone (500 cases). LA CLOTTE, FONBEL, MOULIN-ST-GEORGES, Simard in same Vauthier family stable.

Balestard la Tonnelle St-Ém r ★★ 01 03 04 05 06 08 09 10 11 12 14 15 16 Historic DOM owned by Capdemourlin family. Now rich, modern style but limestone terroir evident.

Barde-Haut St-Ém r ★★ 00 01 02 03 05' 06 07 08 09 10 11 12 14 15 16 Environmentally friendly GRAND CRU CLASSÉ. Sister property of CLOS L'ÉGLISE, HAUT-BERGEY and ST-ÉM GRAND CRU Poesia. Rich, modern, opulent.

Bastor-Lamontagne Saut w sw ★★ 99 01' 02 03' 05 07 09' 10 11 13 14 15 Large unclassified Preignac sister to BEAUREGARD and St-Robert in GRAVES. Part-owned and managed by SMITH-HAUT-LAFITTE team. Gd value; pure, harmonious. Second label: Les Remparts de Bastor.

Batailley Pau r ★★★ 02 03 04 05' 06 08 09' 10' 11 12 13 14 15 16 Much-followed Fifth Growth, owned by BORIE-MANOUX connections. Second label: Lions de Batailley.

Beaumont H-Méd r ★★ 05' 06 08 09 10' 14 15 16 Large sustainably cultivated estate (around 42,000 cases) owned by Castel and Suntory; early maturing, *easily enjoyable wines*.

Beauregard Pom r ★★★ 01 02 03 04 05' 08 09' 10' 12 14 15 16 Consistent mid-weight POM, converting to organics. Now more depth. Managed by SMITH-HAUT-LAFITTE. New high-tech winery from 2015. MICHEL ROLLAND consultant. Second label: Benjamin de Beauregard.

Beau-Séjour-Bécot St-Ém r ★★★ 95' 96 98' 99 00' 01 02 03 04 05' 06 08 09' 10' 11 12 14 15 Distinguished PREMIER GRAND CRU CLASSÉ (B) on limestone plateau. Family owned. CH Joanin Bécot in CAS same stable. Gd ageing potential.

Beauséjour-Duffau St-Ém r ★★★ 99 00 01 02 03 04 05' 06 08 09' 10' 11 12 14 15 16 Tiny PREMIER GRAND CRU CLASSÉ estate on côtes. Had critics purring since 2009. Managed by Thienpont-DERENONCOURT team. Second label: Croix de Beauséjour.

Beau-Site St-Est r ★★ 03 04 05 06 08 09 10 11 15 Gd-value CRU BOURGEOIS property. Sister to BATAILLEY and TROTTEVIEILLE. 70% CAB SAUV. Supple, fresh, accessible.

Belair-Monange St-Ém r ★★★ 96 98 99 00' 01 02 03 04 05' 06 08 09' 10' 11 12 13 14 15 16 PREMIER GRAND CRU CLASSÉ on limestone plateau named after mother of J-P MOUEIX. Absorbed Magdelaine in 2012. Loads of investment in v'yd. Fine, fragrant, elegant style; riper, fuller since 2008.

Belgrave H-Méd r ★★ 02' 03 04' 05' 06 08 09' 10' 11 12 13 14 15 16 Sizeable Fifth Growth managed by DOURTHE. CAB SAUV dominant. Modern-classic in style. Now consistent quality. Second label: Diane de Belgrave.

Bellefont-Belcier St-Ém r ★★ 02 03 04 05' 06 07 08' 09' 10' 14 15 ST-ÉM GRAND CRU CLASSÉ in St-Laurent-des-Combes. Chinese-owned. MICHEL ROLLAND consultant. C19 circular cellar. Suave, fresh but oaky.

Belle-Vue H-Méd r ★★ 05 06 07 08 09 10 11 12 14 15 Consistent, gd-value southern H-MÉD. Lots of PETIT VERDOT (20%). Dark, dense but firm, fresh and aromatic. CH Bolaire same stable.

Berliquet St-Ém r ★★ 01 02 04 05' 06 08 09 10 12 14 15 16 Tiny GRAND CRU CLASSÉ on côtes next to CANON and BÉLAIR-MONANGE. Fresh, elegant, ages well. Second label: Les Ailes de Berliquet.

Bernadotte H-Méd r ★★★ 00' 01 02 03 04 05' 06 07 08 09' 10' 11 14 Northern H-MÉD CH in St-Sauveur. Owned by a Hong Kong-based group: ROEDERER former owner. Savoury style. Recent vintages more finesse.

Beychevelle St-Jul r ★★★ 00' 01 02 03 04 05' 06 07 08 09' 10' 11 12 13 14 15 16 Fourth Growth with "dragon-boat" label – it's really a griffin's head. Wines of consistent elegance rather than power. New glass-fronted winery inaugurated in 2016. Second label: Amiral de Beychevelle.

Biston-Brillette Mou r ★★ 04 05' 06 08 09 10' 11 12 14 15 Family-owned CRU BOURGEOIS. Eric Boissenot consults. Gd-value, attractive, fruit-bound wines.

Bonalgue Pom r ★★ 04 05 06 08 09 10 11 12 14 15 Dark, rich, meaty. Appealing young but will age. As gd value as it gets. Owned by Bourotte family since 1926. Sister estates CLOS du Clocher, CH du Courlat in LUSSAC-ST-ÉMILION.

Bonnet r w ★★ (r) 10 11 12 14 15 (w) DYA. Owned by 92-yr-old veteran André Lurton. Big producer of some of the best E-2-M and red (Rés) B'X. LA LOUVIÈRE, COUHINS-LURTON, ROCHEMORIN and Cruzeau in PE-LÉ same stable.

Bon Pasteur, Le Pom r ★★★ 00 01 02 03 04 05' 06 08 09' 10' 11 12 13 14 15 16 Tiny property on ST-ÉM border owned by Chinese businessman. Former owner, MICHEL ROLLAND, makes the wine. Ripe, opulent, seductive wines guaranteed.

Boscq, Le St-Est r ★★ 04 05' 06 08 09' 10 11 12 14 15 Quality-driven ST-EST owned by DOURTHE. Consistently gd value.

Bourgneuf Pom r ★★ 03 04 05' 06 08 09 10 11 12 14 15 16 V'yd situated to w of POM plateau. Subtle, savoury wines. Frédérique Vayron adding more depth, purity since 2009. Gd value for POM.

Bouscaut Pe Lé r w ★★ (r) 01 04 05' 06 08 09 10' 11 12 14 15 16 (w) 05' 06 07 08 09 10' 11 12 13 14 15 16 GRAVES Classed Growth. MERLOT-based reds with 10% MALBEC. Sappy, age-worthy whites. Second label: Les Chênes de Bouscaut.

Boyd-Cantenac Marg r ★★★ 02 03 04 05' 06 08 09' 10' 11 12 14 15 Tiny Cantenac-based Third Growth. Same family ownership since 1932. CAB SAUV-dominated with a little peppery PETIT VERDOT. Gd value. Second label: Jacques Boyd.

Branaire-Ducru St-Jul r ★★★ 01 02 03 04 05' 06 08 09' 10' 11 12 13 14 15 16 Underestimated Fourth Growth across road from BEYCHEVELLE. Same ownership since 1993. V'yd scattered around AC. Consistent and gd value with ageing potential. Second label: *Duluc*.

Branas Grand Poujeaux Mou r ★★ 06 08 09 10 11 12 14 15 Tiny neighbour of CHASSE-SPLEEN and POUJEAUX. Ripe, fine, supple tannins. ANGÉLUS owner consults. Sister to Villemaurine (GRAND CRU CLASSÉ) in ST-ÉM. Second label: Les Eclats de Branas.

Brane-Cantenac Marg r ★★★ ★★★★ 99 00' 01 02 03 04 05' 06 08 09' 10' 11 12 13 14 15 16 CAB SAUV-led Second Growth on Cantenac plateau. 0.5% CARMENÈRE.

1855 gets legal

CHX listed in famous 1855 Classification have copyrighted term "1855" under European law. The idea is to provide protection against any misuse of the designation in a wine context. Action was taken following adverse publicity from dubious business practices of a company trading under the name. With the copyright achieved, only the 60 MÉD chx (plus HAUT-BRION) and 26 SAUT chx that comprise the classification can use 1855 on their labels.

Henri Lurton has taken it to new heights since 1992. Classic, fragrant MARG. Second label: Baron de Brane.

Brillette Mou r ★★ 04 05 06 08 09 10 11 12 14 15 Extensive CRU BOURGEOIS; v'yd on gravelly soils. Wines of gd depth, fruit. Wine shop. Second label: Haut Brillette.

Cabanne, La Pom r ★★ 04 05 06' 09 10 11 12 14 15 V'yd w of POM plateau. Modern cellars (2011). Firm when young; needs bottle age. Second label: DOM de Compostelle.

Caillou Saut w sw ★★ 97 98 99 01' 02 03' 05' 07 09' 10 11' 13 14 15 Discreet but well-run Second Growth BAR for pure, fruity *liquoreux*. 100% SÉM. Second label: Les Erables. Third wine: Les Tourelles.

Calon-Ségur St-Est r ★★★★ 95 96' 98 99 00' 01 02 03' 04 05' 06 07 08' 09' 10' 11 12 13 14 15' 16 Third Growth with great historic reputation. More CAB SAUV now (90% in great yrs). Eric Boissenot consults. Estate really flying since 2008. Second label: Le Marquis de Calon (60%+ MERLOT).

Cambon la Pelouse H-Méd r ★★ 05' 06 08 09 10' 11 12 14 15 Big, supple, s H-MÉD CRU BOURGEOIS. Special CUVÉE L'Aura.

Camensac H-Méd r ★★ 02 03 05 06 08 09 10' 11 12 14 15 Fifth Growth in n H-MÉD. Owned by Merlaut family. CHASSE-SPLEEN team handle winemaking; steady improvement from 2006. Eric Boissenot consults. Second label: Second de Camensac.

Canon St-Ém r ★★★ 00 01 02 03 04 05' 06 07 08' 09' 10' 11 12 13 14 15' 16 Esteemed PREMIER GRAND CRU CLASSÉ with walled v'yd on plateau. Wertheimer-owned, like RAUZAN-SÉGLA, ST-SUPÉRY. Now flying; elegant, long-lived wines. One of top wines of 2015. Former Cheval des Andes (Argentina) winemaker is new MD (2015). Second label: Croix Canon (until 2011 CLOS Canon).

Canon la Gaffelière St-Ém r ★★★ 98' 00' 01 02 03 04 05' 06 08 09' 10' 11 12 13 14 15 16 PREMIER GRAND CRU CLASSÉ on s slope. Same ownership as AIGUILHE, CLOS DE L'ORATOIRE, LA MONDOTTE in CAS. Stylish, upfront, impressive wines. Average age of v'yd 45 yrs. Organic certification.

Cantemerle H-Méd r ★★★ 04 05' 06 08 09' 10' 11 12 13 14 15 16 Large Fifth Growth in s H-MÉD with beautiful wooded park. On gd form these days – usually gd value too. Second label: Les Allées de Cantemerle.

Cantenac-Brown Marg r ★★→★★★ 00 01 02 03 04 05' 06 08 09' 10' 11 12 14 15 16 Third Growth with C19 mock-Tudor CH built by John Lewis Brown. Previously robust style; now more voluptous, refined. Dry white Alto (90% SAUV BL). Second label: BriO de Cantenac-Brown.

Capbern St-Est r ★★ 04 05 06 08' 09' 10' 11 12 13 14 15 Capbern-Gasqueton until 2013. Same management as sister CALON-SÉGUR. CAB SAUV-led (70%). Raised its game since 2008 – solid but polished wines.

Cap de Mourlin St-Ém r ★★→★★★ 01 03 04 05 06 08 09 10 11 12 14 15 GRAND CRU CLASSÉ on n slopes. MERLOT with 25% CAB FR, 10% CAB SAUV. MICHEL ROLLAND consults. More power, concentration than in past.

Carbonnieux Pe-Lé r w ★★★ 00 02 04 05' 06 08 09' 10 11 12 15 16 Léognan estate making sterling red and white; large volumes of both. C13 origins. Present owners since 1956. *The whites*, 65% SAUV BL, eg. 05 06 07 08 09 10 11 12 13 14 15, have ageing potential. Red can age as well. Second label: Tour Léognan.

Second labels: best buys

Reliable second labels from Classed Growth CH'x incl: Allées de CANTEMERLE, Alter Ego (PALMER), Dame de MONTROSE, Fiefs de LAGRANGE, Rés de LÉOVILLE (-BARTON), SEGLA (RAUZAN-), Tourelles de Longueville (PICHON BARON). But bear in mind you're paying premium for pedigree, and that a CRU BOURGEOIS of same price and same yr may well be better wine.

Carles, De r ★★★ 04 05' 06' 07 08 09 10 11 12 13 14 15 FRON property with C15 CH. Haut Carles: prestige CUVÉE with gravity-fed cellars. Opulent, rich, modern style.

Carmes Haut-Brion, Les Pe-Lé r ★★★ 03 04 05' 06 07 08 09' 10' 11 12' 13 14 15 16 Tiny walled-in neighbour of HAUT-BRION. 42% MERLOT, 40% CAB FR, structured but suave. New Philippe Starck designed winery inaugurated 2015. Second label: Le CLOS des Carmes.

Caronne-Ste-Gemme H-Méd r ★★ 05 06 08 09' 10' 11 12 14 15 Sizeable n H-MÉD estate nr ST-JUL. CAB SAUV led (60%). Wines fresh, structured; more depth recently.

Carruades de Lafite Pau ★★★ Second label of CH LAFITE. 20,000 cases/yr. Refined, smooth, savoury. Accessible earlier (30–50% MERLOT) but can age.

Carteau Côtes-Daugay St-Ém r ★★ 04 05 08 09 10 11 14 15 16 Gd-value ST-ÉM GRAND CRU; full-flavoured, supple wines. MERLOT-led (70%); 5th generation at helm.

Certan-de-May Pom r ★★★ 00' 01' 04 05' 06 08 09' 10' 11 12 14 15' 16 Neighbour of VIEUX-CH-CERTAN. Name has Scottish origins. Classic POM to age.

Chantegrive Grav r w ★★→★★★ 04 05' 06 08 09' 10' 11 12 14 15 16 Leading GRAV estate created in 1966; v.gd quality and value. Rich, finely oaked reds. CUVÉE Caroline is top, *fragrant white* 08 09 10 11 12 13 14 15 16.

Chasse-Spleen Mou r (w) ★★★ 03 04 05' 06 07 08 09' 10' 12 14 15 16 Big (100 ha), well-known MOU estate run by Céline Villars. Produces gd, often outstanding, long-maturing wine; classical structure, fragrance. Second label: L'Oratoire de Chasse-Spleen. Makes a little white.

Chauvin St-Ém r ★★ 05 06 08 09 10' 11 12 14 15 GRAND CRU CLASSÉ owned by Sylvie Cazes of LYNCH-BAGES. Fine tuning since 2014. New Cupid label.

Cheval Blanc St-Ém r ★★★★ 89 90' 94 95 96' 97 98' 99 00' 01' 02 03 04 05' 06 07 08 09' 10' 11 12 13 14 15' 16 PREMIER GRAND CRU CLASSÉ (A) superstar of ST-ÉM, easy to love. High percentage of CAB FR (60%). Firm, fragrant wines verging on POM. Delicious young; lasts a generation, or two. Same owners, management as YQUEM. Second label: Le Petit Cheval (none made 2015). New Le Petit Cheval Blanc from 2014 (100% SAUV BL).

Chevalier, Dom de Pe-Lé r w ★★★★ 98' 00' 01' 02 03 04' 05' 06 07 08 09' 10' 11 12 13 14 15' 16 V. special estate in Léognan pine woods owned by Bernard family since 1983. Pure, dense, finely textured red. Impressive, complex, long-ageing white has remarkable consistency; wait for rich flavours 98' 99 00 01 02 03 04 05' 06 07' 08' 09' 10 11 12 13 14 15' 16. Second label: Esprit de Chevalier. CLOS des Lunes, DOM de la Solitude, Lespault-Martillac same stable.

Cissac H-Méd r ★★ 00 03 04 05 08 09 10 12 14 Family-owned (5th generation) CRU BOURGEOIS. Firm, CAB SAUV-dominated wines that used to need time, recent vintages less austere. Second label: Reflets du CH Cissac.

Citran H-Méd r ★★ 00 04 05 06 08 09 10' 14 15 16 Sizeable s H-MÉD estate with historical monument CH. In Merlaut family hands since 1996. Medium-weight, ageing up to 10 yrs. Second label: Moulins de Citran.

Clarence de Haut-Brion, Le Pe-Lé r ★★★ 90 95 96' 98 00 01 02 03 04 05' 06 07 08 09' 10' 11 12 14 15 16 Second label of CH HAUT-BRION, until 2007 known as Bahans Haut-Brion. Blend changes considerably with each vintage (anything from 40–80% MERLOT) but same suave texture and elegance as *grand vin*.

Clarke List r (p) (w) ★★ 05' 06 08 09' 10' 11 12 14 15 16. Leading LIST owned by Benjamin de Rothschild. V.gd MERLOT-based red. Dark fruit, fine tannins. Also a dry white: Le Merle Blanc du CH Clarke. Ch Malmaison in MOU same stable. Foreign ventures too, incl Rimapere (NZ), Rupert & Rothschild Vignerons (South Africa).

Clauzet St-Est r ★★ 06 08 09 10 11 12 14 15 16 Gd-value CRU BOURGEOIS owned by Baron Velge since 1997. Steady investment and improvement. Now consistent quality; mid-term ageing potential. Also sister CH de Côme.

Clerc Milon Pau r ★★★ 98' 00 01 02 04 05' 06 07 08 09' 10' 11 12 13 14 15 16 V'yd tripled in size since (MOUTON) Rothschilds purchased in 1970 (now 40 ha). Broader and weightier than sister D'ARMAILHAC; consistent quality. Second label (since 2009): Pastourelle de Clerc Milon.

Climens Saut w sw ★★★★ 95 96 97' 98 99' 00 01' 02 03' 04 05' 06 07 08 09' 10' 11' 12' 13' 14 15 BAR Classed Growth managed with aplomb by Bérénice Lurton. Concentrated wines with vibrant acidity giving balance; ageing potential guaranteed. 100% SÉM. Certified bio (2014). Second label: Les Cyprès (gd value).

Ch Climens (bio, brilliant wines) now open to visitors. Well worth the detour.

Clinet Pom r ★★★★ 00 01 02 03 05' 06 07 08' 09' 10 11 12 14 15 16 Family-owned and -run (Ronan Laborde) estate on POM plateau. MERLOT-dominant. Sumptuous and modern in style; back on same form, consistency as 80s. Second label: Fleur de Clinet.

Clos de l'Oratoire St-Ém r ★★ 03 04 05' 06 08 09 10' 11 12 14 15 16 GRAND CRU CLASSÉ on n slopes of ST-ÉM. Same stable as CANON-LA-GAFFELIÈRE, LA MONDOTTE, polished and fair value.

Clos des Jacobins St-Ém r ★★→★★★ 00 01 02 03 04 05' 06 07 08 09' 10' 11 12 14 15 16 Côtes Classed Growth at top of game. Renovated, modernized and now showing great consistency; powerful, modern style. Same family owns GRAND CRU CLASSÉ CH La Commanderie.

Clos du Marquis St-Jul r ★★ 03 04 05' 06 07 08 09' 10' 11 12 13 14 15 16 More typically ST-JUL than stablemate LÉOVILLE-LAS-CASES; CAB SAUV dominates. Matures faster. Second label: La Petite Marquise.

Clos Floridène Grav r w ★★ (r) 09' 10' 11 12 14 15 (w) 05' 07 08' 09 10 11' 12 13 14 15 RIP Denis Dubourdieu 2016. Dubourdieu's creation now great legacy. SAUV BL/ SÉM from limestone provides fine, fresh white; much improved red. CHX DOISY-DAÈNE, Haura, REYNON same stable.

Clos Fourtet St-Ém r ★★★ 00 01 02 03 04 05' 06 07 08 09' 10' 11 12 14 15 16 PREMIER GRAND CRU CLASSÉ with C18 CH on limestone plateau on edge of town. Classic, stylish ST-ÉM. Consistently gd form. Trials with bio. St-Ém's Côte de Baleau and Les Grandes Murailles same stable. Second label: La Closerie de Fourtet.

Clos Haut-Peyraguey Saut w sw ★★★ 90' 95' 96 97' 98 99 00 01' 02 03' 04 05' 06 07 09' 10' 11' 12 13 14 15 16 Classed Growth SAUT owned by magnate Bernard Magrez; as are FOMBRAUGE, LA TOUR-CARNET, PAPE-CLÉMENT. Once part of LAFAURIE-PEYRAUGUEY. Elegant, harmonious, ageing potential. Second label: Symphonie.

Clos l'Église Pom r ★★★ 00' 01 02 03 04 05' 06 07 08 09' 10 11 12 13 14 15 Neighbour of L'ÉGLISE-CLINET. Opulent, elegant wine that will age. Same family owns BARDE-HAUT, Branon, HAUT-BERGEY, Poesia. Second label: Esprit de l'Église.

Clos Puy Arnaud Cas r ★★ 04 05' 06 08 09' 10 11 12 14 15 16 Bio estate owned by Thierry Valette. Leading light in CAS. Wines of depth with bright acidity. Earlier-drinking CUVÉE Pervenche.

Clos René Pom r ★★ 00' 01 04 05' 06 08 09 10 11 12 14 15 Substantial (for POM) estate; MERLOT-led with a little spicy MALBEC. Less sensuous, celebrated than top Pom but gd value, can age.

Clotte, La St-Ém r ★★ 01 03 04 05 06 08 09' 10' 11 12 15 16 Tiny côtes GRAND CRU CLASSÉ. Improving under AUSONE ownership (2014). Second label: L de La Clotte.

Conseillante, La Pom r ★★★★ 95' 96' 98 99 00' 01 02 03 04 05' 06' 07 08 09' 10' 11 12 13 14 15 16 Owned by Nicolas family since 1871. New *cuvier* (2012) and winemaker (2015). Some of noblest, most fragrant POM; almost Médocain in style. 80% MERLOT on clay, gravel soils. Second label: Duo de Conseillante.

Corbin St-Ém r ★★ 01 04 05 07 08 09' 10' 11 12 14 15' 16 Consistent, gd-value GRAND CRU CLASSÉ nr POM. Power and finesse. 2015 could be best yet.

Cos d'Estournel St-Est r ★★★★ 90' 95 96' 98' 00 01 02 03 04 05' 06 07 08 09' 10' 11 12 13 14 15' 16 Big Second Growth created by Louis d'Estournel in 1811. Eccentric pagoda chai. Refined, suave ST-EST. Cutting-edge cellars with lift system for gravity-feed. Pricey SAUV BL-dominated white; now more refined. Second label: Les Pagodes de Cos. Super-modern Goulée (MÉD) same stable (Goulée Blanc as well). Also CHAMPAGNE producer Pressoirs de France and Tokaji Hetszolo.

Cos-Labory St-Est r ★★ 98' 99 00 02 03 04 05' 06 07 08 09' 10' 11 12 14 15 16 Small family-owned Fifth Growth neighbour of COS D'ESTOURNEL. More depth, structure recently. One of best-value Classed Growths.

Coufran H-Méd r ★★ 03 04 05 06 08 09 10' 11 12 14 15 16 Sizeable estate in extreme n of H-MÉD owned by Miailhe family since 1924. Mainly MERLOT (85%) for supple wine; but can age. Verdignan sister property.

Couhins-Lurton Pe-Lé r w ★★ →★★★ (r) 04 05 06 08' 09 10' 11 12 14 15 (w) 04 05 06 07 08' 09 10' 11 12 13 14 15 *Fine*, tense, long-lived, Classed Growth *white* from SAUV BL (100%). Much-improved, MERLOT-based red. André Lurton-owned (BONNET).

Couspaude, La St-Ém r ★★★ 03 04 05 06 07 08 09' 10' 11 12 14 15 16 GRAND CRU CLASSÉ on limestone plateau. Modern style; rich, creamy with lashings of spicy oak. MICHEL ROLLAND consults.

Coutet Saut w sw ★★★ 90' 95 96 97' 98' 99 01' 02 03' 04 05 07 09' 10' 11' 12 13 14 15' 16 Sizeable BAR property. Consistently v. fine. CUVÉE Madame is a v. rich, old-vine, berry-by-berry selection 89 90 95 97 01 03. Second label: La Chartreuse de Coutet. V.gd dry white, barrel-fermented Opalie.

Couvent des Jacobins St-Ém r ★★ 00' 01 03 04 05 06 08 09' 10' 11 12 14 15 GRAND CRU CLASSÉ vinified within walls of town. MERLOT-led with CAB FR. Lighter style but can age. Second label: Le Menut des Jacobins.

Crabitey Grav r w ★★ (r) 06 08 09 10 11 12 14 15 (w) 10 11 12 13 14 15 Former orphanage at Portets. V'yd replanted in 80s, 90s. Owner Arnaud de Butler now making harmonious, CAB SAUV-led red and a little lively SÉM/SAUV BL white.

Crock, Le St-Est r ★★ 03 04 05 06 08 09' 10 11 12 14 15 Gd-value CRU BOURGEOIS in same family as LÉOVILLE-POYFERRÉ. Petit Verdot in blend. Solid, fruit-packed.

Croix, La Pom r ★★ 04 05 06 08 09 10 11 12 14 15 Owned by NÉGOCIANT Janoueix Organically run. MERLOT-led (60%). La Croix-St-Georges, HAUT-SARPE same stable.

Croix-de-Gay, La Pom r ★★★ 01' 02 04 05 06 09' 10' 11 12 14 15 16 Tiny MERLOT-dominant (95%) v'yd on POM plateau. Round, elegant style; consistent over yrs. New *cuvier* in 2014, SPECIAL CUVÉE La Fleur-de-Gay.

Croix du Casse, La Pom r ★★ 04 05 06 08 09 10 11 12 14 15 BORIE-MANOUX property since 2005. On sandy/gravel soils in s of POM. Steady progress. Medium-bodied; value for AC.

Croizet-Bages Pau r ★★ →★★★ 00' 02 03 04 05 06 08 09 10' 11 12 15 Striving Fifth Growth; still work to be done. Lately, more consistency but fails to excite. Same owner as RAUZAN-GASSIES.

Cru Bourgeois Now a certificate awarded annually. 278 CH'X (2014). Quality variable.

Cruzelles, Les L de P r ★★ 06 08 09 10 11 12 14 15 16 Consistent, gd-value wine. Ageing potential in top yrs. Same stable as L'ÉGLISE-CLINET and La Chenade (L DE P).

Picking on Castillon

Producers in POM and ST-ÉM have clearly earmarked CAS as gd-value area for investment. The following CHX all have ties to prestige Right Bank properties: Ampélia (GRAND-CORBIN-DESPAGNE), CLOS Les Lunelles (PAVIE), D'AIGUILHE (CANON LA GAFFELIÈRE), Goubau (LE PIN), Joanin Bécot (BEAU-SÉJOUR-BÉCOT), l'Aurage (TERTRE-RÔTEBOEUF), Montlandrie (L'ÉGLISE-CLINET). Consultant STÉPHANE DERENONCOURT owns DOM DE L'A. Tony Laithwaite (La Clarière) got there in 1965.

Dalem Fron r ★★ 04 05' 06 08 09' 10' 11 12 14 15 16 Leading FRON estate. MERLOT-dominated (90%). Smooth, ripe, fresh.

Dassault St-Ém r ★★ 01 02 03 04 05' 06 08 09' 10 11 12 14 15 16 Consistent, modern, juicy GRAND CRU CLASSÉ in n of AC. Second label: D de Dassault. La Fleur and Grand Cru Classé Faurie-de-Souchard same stable.

Dauphine, De la Fron r ★★ →★★★ 01 03 04 05 06' 08 09' 10' 11 12' 14 15 Substantial FRON estate. Change of ownership in 2015 but sweeping change under previous owners. Renovation of CH, v'yds plus new winery, additional land acquired, organic certification. Now more substance, finesse. Former CH Haut-Ballet absorbed in 2016. Second label: Delphis.

Merlot accounts for 66 per cent of red grapes planted in B'x.

Dauzac Marg r ★★ →★★★ 98' 99 00' 01 02 04 05 08' 09' 10' 11 12 14 15 16 Fifth Growth neighbour of SIRAN at Labarde; now dense, rich, dark wines. Bio trials. Owned by MAIF insurance company. Second label: La Bastide Dauzac. Also fruity Aurore de Dauzac and CH Labarde (H-MÉD).

Desmirail Marg r ★★ →★★★ 03 04 05 06 07 09' 10' 11 12 14 15 16 Third Growth at Cantenac owned by Denis Lurton. Fine, delicate style. Second label: Initial de Desmirail. Visitor-friendly.

Destieux St-Ém r ★★ 00' 01 03' 04 05' 06 07 08 09' 10' 11 12 14 15 Compact GRAND CRU CLASSÉ located at St-Hippolyte. Bold, powerful style; consistent. Late-harvest school. MICHEL ROLLAND consults.

Doisy-Daëne Bar (r) w dr sw ★★★ 90' 95 96 97' 98' 99 01' 02 03 04 05' 06 07 09 10' 11' 12 13 14 15' 16 Family-owned Second Growth; *fine, sweet Barsac.* Now incorporates former Doisy-Dubroca v'yd. L'Extravagant 01 02 03 04 05 06 07 09 10 11 12 13 14 15 an intensely rich, expensive CUVÉE. Also dry white Doisy-Daëne Sec.

Doisy-Védrines Saut w sw ★★★ 90 95 96 97' 98 99 01' 03' 04 05 07 09 10' 11' 12 13 14 15' 16 BAR estate owned by Castéja family (Joanne NÉGOCIANT). Richer style than DOISY-DAËNE. *Long-term fave;* delicious, gd value.

Dôme, Le St-Ém r ★★★ 05 06 08 09 10' 11 12 13 14 15 16 Microwine; rich, modern, more freshness than past. Two-thirds old-vine CAB FR, nr ANGÉLUS. Owner Jonathan Maltus has string of other gd ST-ÉMs: CH Teyssier (value), Laforge, Le Carré, Le Pontet, Les Astéries, Vieux-Ch-Mazerat.

Dominique, La St-Ém r ★★★ 98 00' 01 04 05' 06 08 09' 10' 11 12 14 15 16 GRAND CRU CLASSÉ next to CHEVAL BLANC. Went off boil in period 1996–2006 but now rich, powerful, juicy. Jean Nouvel-designed winery with rooftop restaurant (La Terrasse Rouge). Second label: Relais de la Dominique.

Ducru-Beaucaillou St-Jul r ★★★★ 96' 98 99 00' 01 02 03 04 05' 06 07 08 09' 10' 11 12 13 14 15' Outstanding Second Growth in astute hands of Bruno Borie. Excellent form except for patch in late 80s. Classic cedar-scented claret, suited to long ageing. Croix de Beaucaillou and Lalande-Borie sister estates. Also Fourcas-Borie in LIST.

Duhart-Milon Rothschild Pau r ★★★ 96' 98 00' 01 02 03 04' 05' 06 07 08 09' 10' 11 12 13 14 15 16 Fourth Growth stablemate of LAFITE. Winery in town of Pauillac. CAB SAUV-dominated (65–80%). V. fine quality, esp in last 10 yrs. Relatively gd value. Second label: Moulin de Duhart.

Durfort-Vivens Marg r ★★★ 98 00 02 03 04 05' 06 08 09' 10' 11 12 13 14 15 16 Much improved MARG Second Growth owned by Gonzague Lurton. CAB SAUV-dominated. Change to bio has made a difference. Second labels: Vivens and Relais de Durfort-Vivens.

Eglise, Dom de l' Pom r ★★ 00 01 02 03 04 05' 06 08 09 10' 11 12 14 15 Small BORIE-MANOUX property on clay/gravel plateau. V'yd averages 40 yrs. Consistent, fleshy wines of late.

Église-Clinet, L' Pom r ★★★→★★★★ 90' 94 95 96 98' 99 00' 01' 02 03 04 05' 06 07 08 09' 10' 11' 12 13 14 15 16 Tiny but high-flying POM estate. Denis Durantou owner. Great consistency; full, concentrated, fleshy wine but expensive. Second label: La Petite Église.

Evangile, L' Pom r ★★★★ 89' 90 95 96 98' 99 00' 01 02 03 04 05' 06 07 08 09' 10' 11 12 13 14 15 16 Rothschild (LAFITE)-owned property on POM plateau. Neighbour of CH LA CONSEILLANTE. MERLOT-dominated (80%) with CAB FR. Consistently rich, opulent in style. Second label: Blason de L'Evangile.

Fargues, De Saut w sw ★★★ 96 97 98 99' 01 02 03' 04 05' 06 07 09' 10' 11' 13 14 15' 16 Unclassified but top-quality SAUT owned by Lur-Saluces, ex-owners of YQUEM. Classic SAUT: rich, unctuous wines, but balanced.

Faugères St-Ém r ★★→★★★ 00' 03 04 05 06 07 08 09' 10' 11 12 14 15 Powerful, rich, modern GRAND CRU CLASSÉ in e of ST-ÉM. Sister CH Péby Faugères (100% MERLOT) also classified. Swiss-owned, Mario Botta-designed winery. Rocheyron, Cap de Faugères (CAS), LAFAURIE-PEYRAGUEY in same stable.

Ferrand, De St-Ém r ★★→★★★ 00 01 04 05 06 08 09' 10' 12 14 15 16 Big St-Hippolyte GRAND CRU CLASSÉ owned by Pauline Bich Chandon-Moët. ANGÉLUS owner consults. Fresh, firm, expressive.

Ferrande Grav r (w) ★★ 08 09 10 11 12 14 15 Substantial GRAVES property owned by NÉGOCIANT Castel. Investment and improvement; easy, enjoyable red; clean, fresh white.

Ferrière Marg r ★★★ 98 99 00' 02 03 04 05 06 08 09' 10' 12 14 15 Tiny Third Growth in MARG village. Organically certified. Converting to bio. Dark, firm, perfumed wines need time.

Feytit-Clinet Pom r ★★→★★★ 98 00 01 03 04 05' 06 08 09' 10' 11 12 13 14 15 16 Tiny Chasseuil family-owned and -run property. 90% MERLOT on clay-gravel soils. Top, consistent form. Rich, smooth, seductive. Highly prized at fair (for POM) price.

Fieuzal Pe-Lé r (w) ★★★ (r) 01 06 07 08 09' 10' 11 12 14 15 (w) 06 07 08 09' 10' 11 12 13 14 15 16 Classified PE-LÉ estate with Irish owner. Rich, ageable white; generous red. New gravity-fed winery. Converting to organics. Trials with bio. Second label: L'Abeille de Fieuzal (r w).

Figeac St-Ém r ★★★★ 96 98' 00' 01' 02 03 04 05' 06 07 08 09' 10' 11 12 13 14 15' 16 Large PREMIER GRAND CRU CLASSÉ owned by Manoncourt family; gravelly v'yd with unusual 70% CAB FR, CAB SAUV. Rich but always elegant wines; need long ageing like MÉD. Managed by co-owner of LA CONSEILLANTE. MICHEL ROLLAND consults. Second label: Petit-Figeac (from 2012), previously Grange Neuve de Figeac.

Filhot Saut w dr sw ★★ 97' 98 99 01 02 03' 04 05 07 09' 10' 11' 13 14 15 Extensive (350 ha) Second Growth with splendid C19 CH; v'yd just a part. Difficult young, more complex with age. Richer, purer from 2009.

Fleur Cardinale St-Ém r ★★ 04 05' 06 07 08 09' 10' 11 12 14 15 16 GRAND CRU CLASSÉ at St-Étienne-de-Lisse. In overdrive for last 15 yrs. Late harvesting. Consistent, ripe, unctuous, modern style.

Average size of estate in B'x is 17.2 ha (2015), double that of 20 yrs ago.

Fleur de Boüard, La r ★★→★★★ 05 06 07 08 09 10 11 12 13 14 15 16 Leading estate in L DE P. Unique winery with inverted, cone shaped vats. Rich, dark, dense, modern. Same stable as ANGÉLUS. Special CUVÉE, Le Plus, more extreme: 100% MERLOT aged 3 yrs in new oak barrels. Second label: Le Lion.

Fleur-Pétrus, La Pom r ★★★★ 95 96 98' 99 00' 01 02 03 04 05' 06 08 09' 10' 11 12 13 14 15 16 J-P MOUEIX property; much expanded v'yd since 80s. 8 ha to 18.7 ha today. 92% MERLOT with CAB FR and 0.5% PETIT VERDOT. Finer style than PETRUS or TROTANOY. Needs time.

Fombrauge St-Ém r ★★→★★★ 00' 01 02 03 04 05 06 08 09' 10' 11 12 14 15 16

Sizeable GRAND CRU CLASSÉ owned by Bernard Magrez (*see* PAPE-CLÉMENT). Rich, dark, chocolatey, modern. Magrez-Fombrauge is special red CUVÉE; also name for a little dry white B'X. Second label: Prélude de Fombrauge.

Fonbadet Pau r ★★ 02 03 04 05' 06 08 09' 10' 12 14 15 Small non-classified estate in PAU owned by Peyronie family. Undergoing change. Reliable, gd value.

Fonbel, De St-Ém r ★★ 07 08 09 10 11 12 14 15 16 Consistent source of juicy, fresh, gd-value ST-ÉM. Same owner as AUSONE, MOULIN-ST-GEORGES.

Approximately 300 négociants sell 70 per cent of wine produced in B'x.

Fonplégade St-Ém r ★★ 01 03 04 05 06 08 09' 10 12 14 15 16 American-owned GRAND CRU CLASSÉ. Investment, progression; concentrated, modern style. STÉPHANE DERENONCOURT consults from 2015. Second label: Fleur de Fonplégade.

Fonréaud List r ★★ 00' 03 04 05 06 08 09' 10' 11 12 14 15 16 One of bigger, better LIST for satisfying, savoury wines. Owned by Chanfreau family. Small volume of v.gd dry white: Le Cygne. *See* LESTAGE. Gd value.

Fonroque St-Ém r ★★★ 01 03 04 05 06 08 09' 10' 11 12 14 15 Classed Growth on côtes. Owned by MOUEIX family since 1931; Alain manages (*see* MAZEYRES). Bio paying off; more character, elegance.

Fontenil Fron r ★★ 04 05 06 08 09' 10' 11 12 14 15 16 Leading FRON, owned by MICHEL ROLLAND. Ripe, opulent, balanced. 2015 v.gd.

Forts de Latour, Les Pau r ★★★★ 95' 96' 98 00' 01 02 03 04' 05' 06 07 08 09' 10' 11 12 13 14 15 The (worthy) second label of CH LATOUR; authentic flavour in slightly lighter format at Second Growth price. No more en PRIMEUR sales; only released when deemed ready to drink – 2009 in 2016 (barely ready in fact).

Fourcas-Dupré List r ★★ 01 02 03 04 05 06 08 09 10' 11 12 14 15 16 Well-run property making fairly consistent wine in tight LIST style. Hautes Terres is atypical special CUVÉE (lots of MERLOT). Also a little SAUV BL-led white.

Fourcas-Hosten List r ★★ →★★★ 02 03 05 06 08 09 10' 11 12 14 15 16 Large LIST estate. Considerable investment and steady improvement; more precision, finesse. Eric Boissenot consults. Also a SAUV BL-led dry white.

France, De Pe-Lé r w ★★ (r) 00 03 04 05 06 08 09 10' 11 12 14 15 16 (w) 05 06 07 08 09 10 11 12 13 14 15 16 Neighbour of FIEUZAL; consistent wines in a ripe, modern style. White fresh and balanced. Second label: CH Coquillas.

Franc-Mayne St-Ém r ★★ 01 03 04 05 08 09 10' 12 14 15 16 GRAND CRU CLASSÉ on côtes. Same owners as CH DE LUSSAC. Luxury hotel too. Fresh, fruity, round but structured style. Second label: Les Cèdres de Franc-Mayne.

Gaby, Du Fron r ★★ 03 04 05 06 08 09 10 12 14 15 Splendid s-facing slopes in CANON-FRON. MERLOT-dominated wines that age well. Organic tendency. Also special Gaby CUVÉE.

Gaffelière, La St-Ém r ★★★ 96 98' 99 00' 01 02 03 04 05' 06 07 08 09' 10' 11 12 13 14 15 First Growth at foot of côtes. Investment, improvement; part of v'yd replanted; modern *cuvier*. Elegant, long-ageing wines. Owned by Malet Roquefort family since C16. Second label: CLOS la Gaffelière.

Garde, La Pe-Lé r w ★★ (r) 04 05 06 08 09' 10' 11 12 14 15 (w) 07 08 09 10' 11 12 13 14 15 Martillac property owned by NÉGOCIANT DOURTHE since 1990; supple, CAB SAUV/MERLOT reds. Tiny production of SAUV BL/Sauvignon Gris white.

Gay, Le Pom r ★★★ 01 03 04 05' 06 07 08 09' 10' 11 12 14 15 Fine v'yd on n edge of POM. Major investment, MICHEL ROLLAND consults. Now v. ripe, plummy in style. Barrel fermentation since 2014. CH Montviel, La Violette same stable. Second label: Manoir de Gay.

Gazin Pom r ★★★ 96 98' 99 00' 01 02 03 04 05' 06 08 09' 10' 11 12 13 14 15 16 Large POM estate owned by de Bailliencourt family. On v.gd form since mid-90s; generous, long ageing. Second label: L'Hospitalet de Gazin.

Gilette Saut w sw ★★★ 53 55 59 61 67 70 71 75 76 78 79 81 82 83 85 86 88 89 90 96 Extraordinary small Preignac CH stores its sumptuous wines in concrete vats for 16–20 yrs. Only around 5000 bottles of each. Can age further in bottle. Ch Les Justices is sister 03' 05 07 09 10' 11 13 14 15.

Giscours Marg r ★★★ 98 99 00' 01 02 03 04 05' 06 08' 09' 10' 11 12 14 15 16 Substantial Third Growth at Labarde. Full-bodied, long-ageing MARG capable of greatness (eg. 1970). The 80s were wobbly; steady improvement over last 20 yrs with new owner. Second label: La Sirène de Giscours. Little B'x rosé. Also CH Duthil H-MÉD and Le H-Méd de Giscours.

Glana, Du St-Jul r ★★ 00 04 05 06 08 09 10' 12 14 15 Big, unclassified CAB SAUV-led (65%) estate. Undemanding; robust; value. New barrel cellar and *vinothèque*. Second label: Pavillon du Glana.

Gloria St-Jul r ★★→★★★ 00' 01 02 03 04 05' 06 07 08 09' 10' 11 12 14 15 16 A widely dispersed estate with v'yds among the Classed Growths. CAB SAUV-dominant (65%). Same ownership as ST-PIERRE. Superb form recently.

Grand-Corbin-Despagne St-Ém r ★★→★★★ 96 98 99 00' 01 03 04 05 06 08 09' 10' 11 12 13 14 15 16 Gd-value GRAND CRU CLASSÉ on POM border; 7th-generation Despagne at helm. Aromatic wines now with riper, fuller edge. Can age. Organic cultivation. Also CHX Le Chemin (Pom), Ampélia (CAST). Second label: Petit Corbin-Despagne.

Grand Cru Classé St-Ém 2012: 64 classified; reviewed every 10 yrs.

Grand-Mayne St-Ém r ★★★ 90' 95 96 98 99 00' 01' 02 03 04 05' 06 07 08 09' 10' 11 12 14 15 16 Impressive GRAND CRU CLASSÉ owned by Nony family. Consistent, full-bodied, structured wines. Second label: Les Plantes du Mayne.

Grand-Puy-Ducasse Pau r ★★★ 96' 98' 00 01 02 03 04 05' 06 07 08 09' 10' 11 12 14 15 16 Fifth Growth owned by a bank (MEYNEY, TOUR DE MONS same stable). Steady improvement; more modern in 2015. Reasonable value. ANGÉLUS owner consults. Second label: Prélude à Grand-Puy-Ducasse.

Grand-Puy-Lacoste Pau r ★★★ 90' 95' 96' 98 00' 01 02 03 04 05' 06 07 08' 09' 10' 11 12 13 14 15 Fifth Growth famous for gd-value CAB SAUV-driven (75%) PAU to lay down. A London favourite. Owned by Borie family since 1978. Eric Boissenot consults. Second label: Lacoste-Borie.

Grave à Pomerol, La Pom r ★★★ 01 02 04 05 06 08 09' 10 11 12 14 15 16 Small property on w slope of POM plateau owned by J-P MOUEIX. MERLOT-dominant (85%). Reasonable value. Can age.

Greysac Méd r ★★ 04 05' 06 08 09 10' 11 12 14 15 Same stable as CH Rollan-de-Dy and HAUT-CONDISSAS. MERLOT-led, fine, fresh, consistent quality.

Gruaud-Larose St-Jul r ★★★★ 90' 95' 96' 98 99 00' 01 02 03 04 05' 06 07 08 09' 10' 11 12 14 15 16 One of biggest, best-loved Second Growths. Smooth, rich, vigorous claret. Visitor-friendly with 18m panoramic tower, shop, tasting room. Second label: *Sarget de Gruaud-Larose*.

Chinese own 3000 ha in B'x, or just under three per cent of surface area.

Guadet St-Ém ★★ 04 05 06 08 09 10 11 12 15 Tiny GRAND CRU CLASSÉ owned by Lignac family since 1844. Better form last 10 yrs. DERENONCOURT consults. Organic/bio.

Guiraud Saut (r) w (dr) sw ★★★ 96' 97' 98 99 00 01' 02 03 04 05' 06 07 08 09' 10' 11' 13 14 15 16 Substantial organically certified neighbour of YQUEM. Owners incl long-time manager, Xavier Planty, Peugeot (cars) family and DOM DE CHEVALIER, LA MONDOTTE connections. Top quality – more SAUV BL than most. Dry white G de Guiraud. Second label: Petit Guiraud.

Gurgue, La Marg r ★★ 04 05' 06 08 09' 10 11 12 14 15 CH MARGAUX neighbour. FERRIÈRE, HAUT-BAGES-LIBÉRAL same management. CAB SAUV-dominant. Fine, gd value.

Hanteillan H-Méd r ★★ 00' 03 04 05' 06 09' 10 12 14 15 Large CRU BOURGEOIS.

Round, balanced, early-drinking. Recent improvement. DERENONCOURT consults. Second label: CH Laborde.

Haut-Bages-Libéral Pau r ★★★ 98 00 01 02 03 04 05' 06 08 09' 10' 11 12 14 15 16 Lesser-known Fifth Growth (next to LATOUR) run by Claire Villars Lurton. CAB SAUV-led (70%). Conversion to bio. Results are excellent. Usually gd value.

Haut-Bailly Pe-Lé r ★★★★ 90' 95 96' 98' 99 00' 01 02 03 04 05' 06 07 08' 09' 10' 11' 12 14 15' 16 Superieur PE-LÉ Classed Growth owned by American banker. Run by Véronique Sanders, granddaughter of former owner. Red wine: refined, elegant style (parcel of v. old, 100-yr+ vines); also a little rosé. CH Le Pape (Pe-Lé) same ownership. Second label: La Parde de Haut-Bailly.

Haut-Batailley Pau r ★★★ 99 00 02 03 04 05' 06 07 08 09' 10' 11 12 13 14 15 Small Fifth Growth owned by François-Xavier Borie. Gentler than sister GRAND-PUY-LACOSTE. Cellars renovated; steady progression. Second label: La Tour-l'Aspic.

Haut-Beauséjour St-Est r ★★ 04 05 08 09 10 11 14 15 Property created and enhanced by owner Champagne ROEDERER. Juicy but structured. Sister of DE PEZ.

Haut-Bergeron Saut w sw ★★ 02 03 04 05 06 07 09 10 11 13 14 15 Preignac estate owned by Lamothe family. One of most consistent non-classified SAUT. 60 parcels of old vines. Mainly SÉM (90%). Rich, opulent, gd value.

Haut-Bergey Pe-Lé r (w) ★★→★★★ (r) 04 05 06 07 08 09 10 11 12 14 15 (w) 09 10 11 12 13 14 15 Non-classified property with Classed Growth pretentions. Completely renovated in 90s. Rich, bold red. Fresh, concentrated dry white. Also CUVÉE Paul red, rosé. CH Branon (PE-LÉ) same stable.

Haut-Brion Pe-Lé r ★★★★ (r) 86' 88' 89' 90' 93 94 95' 96' 97 98' 99 00' 01 02 03 04 05' 06 08 09' 10' 11' 12 13 14 15' 16 Only non-MÉD First Growth in list of 1855, owned by American Dillon family since 1935. Deeply harmonious, wonderful texture, for many no.1 or 2 choice of all clarets – and a (relative) steal. Constant renovation: next target the *cuvier*. Can be tasted at luxurious new restaurant Le Clarence in Paris. A little ***sumptuous dry white*** for tycoons: 01 02 03 04' 05' 06 07 08' 09 10' 11' 12 13 14 15' 16. *See* LA MISSION HAUT-BRION, LAVILLE-HAUT-BRION, LE CLARENCE DE HAUT-BRION, QUINTUS.

Haut Condissas Méd r ★★★ 05 06 07 08 09' 10' 11 12 14 15 Garage-style MÉD. Annual production 5000 cases. Sister to CH Rollan-de-By, GREYSAC. Rich, concentrated, consistent. MERLOT-LED plus PETIT VERDOT.

Haut-Marbuzet St-Est r ★★→★★★ 00' 01 02 03 04 05' 06 07 08 09' 10' 11 12 14 15 Started in 1952 with 7 ha; now 70; owned by Duboscq family. Fourth Growth quality, opulent, easy to love, but unclassified. Two-thirds of production sold directly by CH. Rich, unctuous wines matured in new oak BARRIQUES in cellars nr COS D'ESTOURNEL. Second label: MacCarthy.

Haut-Sarpe St-Ém r ★★ 01 04 05 06 08 09 10 11 12 14 15 GRAND CRU CLASSÉ owned by Janoueix family; 70% MERLOT. ANGÉLUS owner consults. Modern, lashings of oak.

Hosanna Pom r ★★★★ 99 00 01 03 04 05' 06 07 08 09' 10' 11 12 14 15 16 Tiny 4 ha v'yd in heart of POM plateau. Formerly Certan-Guiraud until bought and renamed by J-P MOUEIX in 1999. Wines have power, complexity, class and need time. Stablemate of FLEUR-PÉTRUS, TROTANOY.

Issan, D' Marg r ★★★ 01 02 03 04' 05' 06 07 08 09' 10' 11 12 13 14 15 16 Third Growth with moated CH. Fragrant wines; at top of game. Emmanuel Cruse (2015: 70th vintage for Cruse family) and Jacky Lorenzetti owners (see PEDESCLAUX).

Jean Faure St-Ém r ★★ 06 08 09 10 11 12 14 15 16 GRAND CRU CLASSÉ on clay, sand, gravel soils. Organic cultivation. 50% CAB FR gives fresh, elegant style. ANGÉLUS owner consults. Mas Amiel (MAURY) same stable.

Kirwan Marg r ★★★ 95 96 98 99 00' 01 02 03 04 05' 06 07 08 09 10' 11 12 14 15' 16 Third Growth on Cantenac plateau. CAB SAUV-dominant (60%). Dense, fleshy in 90s; now more finesse. Former PALMER winemaker at the helm. Second label: Charmes de Kirwan.

Labégorce Marg r ★★→★★★ 03 04 05' 07 08 09 10' 11 12 14 15 16 Substantial unclassified MARG owned by Nathalie Perrodo-Samani. Considerable investment and progression. Next-door Labégorce-Zédé absorbed in 2009. Fine, modern style. CH MARQUIS-D'ALESME same stable.

Lafaurie-Peyraguey Saut w SW ★★★ 85 86' 88' 89' 90' 95 96' 97 98 99 01' 02 03' 04 05' 06 07 09' 10' 11' 13 14 15 16 Leading Classed Growth at Bommes belongs to Lalique crystal-owner Silvio Denz (CH FAUGÈRES). Lalique design *Femme et Raisins* embossed on bottle. Rich, harmonious, sweet 90% SÉM. Second label: La Chapelle de Lafaurie-Peyraguey. Also a SÉM-led dry white B'X from 2015.

Lafite-Rothschild Pau r ★★★★ 88' 89' 90' 93 94 95 96' 97 98' 99 00' 01' 02 03' 04' 05' 06 07 08' 09' 10' 11' 12 13 14 15' 16 Big (112 ha) First Growth of famous elusive perfume and style, but never great weight, although more dense and sleek these days. Great vintages need keeping for decades. Winemaking team comprises Eric Kohler, Christophe Congé and Régis Porfilet. Joint ventures in Argentina, California, Chile, China, Italy, Portugal and the MIDI. Second label: CARRUADES DE LAFITE. Also owns CHX DUHART-MILON, L'ÉVANGILE, RIEUSSEC.

Lafleur Pom r ★★★★ 88' 89' 90' 93 94 95 96 98' 99' 00' 01' 02 03 04' 05' 06' 07 08 09' 10' 11' 12 13 14 15' 16 Superb but tiny family-owned and -managed property cultivated like a garden. Elegant, intense wine for maturing. Expensive. Dry white B'X Les Champs Libres same stable. Second label: *Pensées de Lafleur.*

Lafleur-Gazin Pom r ★★ 01 04 05 06 08 09 10 11 12 14 15 Small J-P MOUEIX estate located on n slope of POM plateau. Lighter, supple style.

Lafon-Rochet St-Est r ★★★ 95 96' 98 99 00' 01 02 03' 04 05' 06 08 09' 10' 11 12 13 14 15 16 Fourth Growth neighbour of COS D'ESTOURNEL run by Michel and Basile Tesseron. Eye-catching canary yellow buildings and label. High percentage of MERLOT (37%) adds opulence, texture but CAB SAUV provides structure to age. Conversion to bio. Second label: Les Pèlerins de Lafon-Rochet.

Lagrange St-Jul r ★★★ 90' 94 95 96 98 99 00' 01 02 03 04 05' 06 08 09' 10' 11 12 13 14 15 16 Substantial (118 ha) Third Growth owned since 1983 by Suntory. Tip-top condition. Much investment in v'yd and cellars. CAB SAUV-dominant (67%). Dry white Les Arums de Lagrange. Second label: Les Fiefs de Lagrange (gd value).

Lagrange Pom r ★★ 00 01 04 05 06 09 10 15 Tiny POM v'yd located on n border of plateau. Owned by Libourne NEGOCIANT J-P MOUEIX since 1953. 96% MERLOT. Lighter style but gd value.

Lagune, La H-Méd r ★★★ 96' 98 00' 02 03 04 05' 07 08 09' 10' 11 12 14 15 16 Third Growth in v. s of MÉD. Dipped in 90s; now on form. Fine-edged with more structure, depth. Organic certification from 2016. Oenologist Caroline Frey is owner/winemaker. Second label: Moulin de La Lagune. Also CUVÉE Mademoiselle L from v'yd in Cussac-Fort-Méd.

Lamarque, De H-Méd r ★★ 00' 03 04 05' 06 08 09' 10' 11 12 14 15 H-MÉD estate with splendid medieval fortress. V'yd borders MOU. Laser-optical sorting. Competent, mid-term wines, charm, value. Second label: D de Lamarque.

Lanessan H-Méd r ★★ 03 04 05 08 09 10' 11 12 14 15 Distinguished property just s of ST-JUL. Owned by Bouteiller family since C18. Improvement under wine-maker Paz Espejo. Second label: Les Calèches de Lanessan. Visitor friendly.

Langoa-Barton St-Jul r ★★★ 96' 98 99 00' 01 02 03 04' 05' 06 07 08 09' 10' 11 12 13 14 15 16 Third Growth sister CH to LÉOVILLE-BARTON, sometimes even more charm. In Barton hands since 1821. Consistent value. Second label: Rés de Léoville-Barton.

Larcis Ducasse St-Ém r ★★★ 90' 95 96 98 00 02 03 04 05' 06 07 08 09' 10' 11 12 13 14 15 16 Family-owned PREMIER GRAND CRU CLASSÉ run by Thienpont-DERENONCOURT duo. MERLOT-led (78%). Great in 50s, 60s. Spectacular form today. Second label: Murmure de Larcis Ducasse.

Cérons is B'x's smallest appellation with 27 ha (2015).

Larmande St-Ém r ★★ 01 03 04 05 06 07 08 09' 10 12 14 15 16 GRAND CRU CLASSÉ owned by La Mondiale insurance (as is SOUTARD). Sound but lighter weight. Second label: Le Cadet de Larmande.

Laroque St-Ém r ★★→★★★ 03 04 05 06 08 09' 10' 11 12 14 15 16 Large GRAND CRU CLASSÉ at St Christophe-des-Bardes. MERLOT-led (87%). Fresh, terroir-driven wines.

Larose-Trintaudon H-Méd r ★★ 05 06 07 08 09' 10 11 12 14 15 Largest v'yd in MÉD (190 ha). Sustainable viticulture. Smooth, balanced, generally for early drinking. Second label: Les Hauts de Trintaudon. Special CUVÉE, Larose Perganson, from separate parcels. Also CH Arnauld.

Laroze St-Ém r ★★ 98' 00 01 05 06 07 08 09' 10' 12 14 15 16 Family-owned GRAND CRU CLASSÉ. Lighter-framed wines from sandy soils; lately more depth. ANGÉLUS owner consults. Second label: La Fleur Laroze. Also Lady Laroze.

Larrivet-Haut-Brion Pe-Lé r w ★★★ (r) 01 02 03 04 05' 06 08 09 10' 11 12 14 15 16 Unclassified PE-LÉ property owned by Bonne Maman jam. Rich, modern red. Voluptuous, aromatic, SAUV BL/SÉM barrel-fermented white 06 07 08 09 10' 11 12 13 14 15 16. Ex-MONTROSE winemaker. Second label: Les Demoiselles de Larrivet-Haut-Brion.

Lascombes Marg r (p) ★★★ 99 00 01 02 03 04 05' 06 07 08 09' 10' 11 12 14 15 16 Second Growth owned by insurance group. Wines were wobbly; now rich, dark, concentrated, modern, but MARG perfume can be found. Lots of MERLOT (50%+). Ex-LAFITE winemaker. Second label: Chevalier de Lascombes.

Latour Pau r ★★★★ 86 88' 89 90' 91 94 95' 96' 97 98 99 00' 01 02 03' 04' 05' 06 07 08 09' 10' 11' 12 13 14 15' 16 First Growth considered the grandest statement of B'X. Profound, intense, almost immortal wines in great yrs; even weaker vintages have the unique taste and run for many yrs. *Grand vin* from historical "Enclos" v'yd; 100% organic. Winemaker Hélène Génin. Ceased en primeur sales in 2012; wines now only released when considered ready to drink (2000, 2007 in 2016). New cellars for greater storage capacity. Second label: LES FORTS DE LATOUR; *third label: Pauillac;* even this can age 12 yrs.

Latour-à-Pomerol Pom r ★★★ 90' 95 96 98' 99 00' 01 02 04 05' 06 07 08 09' 10' 11 12 14 15 16 Managed by J-P MOUEIX. V'yd surrounds POM church. 90% MERLOT. Extremely consistent, well-structured wines that age.

Latour-Martillac Pe-Lé r w ★★ (r) 00 01 02 03 04 05' 06 08 09' 10' 11 12 14 15 16 GRAV Cru Classé owned by Kressmann family since 1930. Regular quality; gd value at this level (w) 04 05 06 07 08 09 10' 11 12 13 14 15. Second label: Lagrave-Martillac (r w).

Laurets, Des St-Ém r ★★ 06 08 09 10 12 14 15 Substantial property, sits astride PUISSEGUIN-ST-ÉM and MONTAGNE-ST-ÉM. Les Laurets is a 100% MERLOT special CUVÉE. Owned by Benjamin de Rothschild of CH CLARKE.

Laville Saut w sw ★★ 03 04 06 07 09 10 11 13 14 15 Family-owned Preignac estate. Winemaker lectures at B'X's Faculty of Oenology. SÉM-dominated (85%) with a little SAUV BL, MUSCADELLE. Rich, lush, botrytized. Gd-value, non-classified SAUT.

Léoville-Barton St-Jul r ★★★★ 89' 90' 94' 95' 96' 98 99 00' 01 02 03' 04 05' 06 07 08' 09' 10' 11 12 13 14 15 16 Second Growth with longest-standing family ownership; in Anglo-Irish hands of Bartons since 1826 (Anthony Barton is present incumbent, assisted by daughter Lilian and granddaughter Mélanie). François Bréhant winemaker. Harmonious, classic claret; CAB SAUV-dominant (74%). Shares cellars with LANGOA-BARTON.

Léoville Las Cases St-Jul r ★★★★ 90' 93 94 95' 96' 97 98 99 00' 01 02 03' 04' 05' 06 07 08 09' 10' 11' 12 13 14 15' 16 Largest Léoville and original "Super Second"; *grand vin* from Grand Enclos v'yd. Up to 85% CAB SAUV. Elegant, complex, powerful wines. Sometimes more PAU than ST-JUL. Second label: Le Petit Lion; CLOS DU MARQUIS a separate wine. NÉNIN, POTENSAC same ownership.

Léoville-Poyferré St-Jul r ★★★★ 88 89' 90' 94 95 96' 98 99 00' 01 02 03 04 05' 06 07 08 09' 10' 11' 12 13 14 15 Run by Didier Cuvelier since 1979. Now at "Super Second" level with dark, rich, spicy, long-ageing wines. *Ch Moulin-Riche* is a separate 21-ha parcel. Second label: Pavillon de Léoville-Poyferré. CH LE CROCK same ownership.

Lestage List r ★★ 00 03 04 05 06 08 09 10 11 12 14 15 Same Chanfreau-family ownership as FONREAUD; more MERLOT (56%). Firm, slightly austere claret. New cuvier in 2016.

Lilian Ladouys St-Est r ★★ 03 04 05 06 07 08 09' 10' 11 12 14 15 Created in 80s; now 100 separate parcels of vines. More finesse in recent vintages. Same stable as PÉDESCLAUX. Second label: La Devise de Lilian.

Liversan H-Méd r ★★ 00 03 04 05 07 08 09 10 12 14 15 CRU BOURGEOIS in n H-MÉD. Same owner as PATACHE D'AUX. Round, savoury, approachable. Second label: Les Charmes de Liversan.

Loudenne Méd r ★★ 03 04 05 06 09' 10' 11 12 14 15 Large CRU BOURGEOIS, once Gilbeys, then Lafragette family, now Chinese-owned. Landmark C18 pink-washed *chartreuse* by river. Visitor-friendly. Ripe, round reds. Oak-scented SAUV BL 09 10 11 12 13 14 15. And, of course, a rosé.

Louvière, La Pe-Lé r w ★★★ (r) 01 02 04 05' 06 07 08 09' 10' 11 12 13 14 15 (w) 02 03 04' 05' 06 07 08 09' 10' 11 12 13 14 15 André Lurton's pride and joy. Excellent *white* (can be 100% SAUV BL), red of Classed Growth standard. *See also* BONNET, COUHINS-LURTON, DE ROCHEMORIN.

Lussac, De St-Ém r ★★ 05 06 07 08 09 10 11 12 14 15 Top estate in LUSSAC-ST-ÉM. Plenty of investment. MERLOT-led (80%) red. Same stable as FRANC-MAYNE. Second label: Le Libertin de Lussac.

Lynch-Bages Pau r (w) ★★★★ 89' 90' 94 95' 96' 98 99 00' 01 02 03 04' 05' 06 07 08 09' 10' 11 12 13 14 15 16 Always popular, now a star, far higher than its Fifth Growth rank. Rich CAB SAUV-led wine. Second label: Echo du Lynch-Bages Gd *Blanc de Lynch-Bages*, now fresher. New winery (2019) designed by Chinese architect Chien Cheng Pei. LES ORMES-DE-PEZ. Villa Bel Air (GRAV) same ownership.

Lynch-Moussas Pau r ★★ 01 02 03 04 05' 07 08 09 10' 11 12 14 15 Fifth Growth owned by BORIE-MANOUX. Improving CAB SAUV-dominated (75%) wines. Second label: Les Hautes de Lynch-Moussas.

Tea and wine meet
Tea and wine have much in common, from an ancient history to notions of terroir and gastronomy – not to mention tannins. Now they have been brought together through a cultural partnership between the wines of POM, ST-ÉM and FRON and the teas of Pu'er in South Yunnan Province, China. Towns Libourne and Pu'er have been twinned and the Right Bank wines are part of permanent exhibition at National Pu'er Tea Museum. All v. civilized.

Lyonnat St-Ém r ★★ 04 05 06 08 09 10 12 14 15 Leading LUSSAC-ST-ÉM. More precision of late. Also special CUVÉE Emotion.

Malartic-Lagravière Pe-Lé r (w) ★★★ (r) 99 00' 01 02 03 04' 05' 06 08 09' 10' 11 12 14 15 16 (w) 01' 02 03 04' 05' 06 07 08 09' 10' 11 12 13 14 15 16 Classed growth. Rich, modern red; a little lush white (majority SAUV BL). Belgian owner revolutionized, tripled size. CH Gazin Rocquencourt (Pe-Lé) same stable. Interests in Argentina.

Malescasse H-Méd r ★★ 02 03 04 05 06 08 09 10 11 12 14 15 CRU BOURGEOIS nr MOULIS. Supple, value wines. DERENONCOURT consults. Second label: La Closerie de Malescasse.

Malescot-St-Exupéry Marg r ★★★ 98 99 00' 01 02 03 04 05' 06 07 08' 09' 10' 11 12 14 15 16 On-form MARG Third Growth. Wines ripe, fragrant, finely structured. Owned by Zuger family since 1955.

Malle, De Saut r w dr sw ★★★ (w sw) 95 96' 97' 98 99 01' 02 03' 05 06 07 09 10' 11' 13 14 15 Preignac Second Growth making v. fine, medium-bodied SAUT; also M de Malle dry white GRAV. C18 CH an historical monument.

Margaux, Ch Marg (w) ★★★★ 88' 89' 90' 93 94 95' 96' 97 98' 99 00' 01' 02 03' 04' 05' 06' 07 08 09' 10' 11' 12 13 14 15' 16 First Growth; most seductive, fabulously perfumed and consistent wines. RIP (2016) long-term MD Paul Pontallier; Philippe Bascaules is replacement. Norman Foster-designed cellar extension 2015. Pavillon Rouge 03 04' 05' 06 08 09' 10' 11 12 14 15 is second label. *Pavillon Blanc* (100% SAUV BL) is best white of MÉD, recent vintages fresher 07 08 09' 10 11' 12' 13' 14 15.

Marojallia Marg r ★★★ 01 02 03 04 05' 06 07 08 09' 10 11 12 15 Micro-CH looking for big prices for big, rich, un-MARG-like wines. 70% CAB SAUV. 100 per cent new oak. Second label: CLOS Margalaine.

Marquis-d'Alesme Marg r ★★ →★★★ 01 04 05 08 09' 10' 11 12 14 15 Third Growth in MARG village. Investment and steady progress; 2015 best yet. New Chinese-inspired, high-tech cellars. Same stable as LABÉGORCE.

Marquis-de-Terme Marg r ★★ →★★★ 95 96 98 99 00' 01 02 03 04 05' 06 08 09' 10' 11 12 14 15 16 Fourth Growth with v'yd dispersed around MARG. Recent investment, renovation; previously solid wine, now more seductive. International Best of Wine Tourism Award 2017.

Maucaillou Mou r ★★ 04 05 06 08 09 10 11 12 14 15 16 Fairly consistent MOU estate. Family-owned (DOURTHE), visitor friendly. Clean, fresh, value wines.

Mayne Lalande List r ★★ 08 09 10 11 12 14 15 Leading LIST estate. CAB SAUV-led (60%). Full, finely textured. ANGÉLUS owner consults.

Mazeyres Pom r ★★ 01 04 05' 06 08 09 10 12 14 15 Lighter but consistent POM. Supple, earlier drinking style. Unusual 2–3% PETIT VERDOT. Organic certification. FONROQUE owner manages.

Meyney St-Est r ★★ →★★★ 01 02 03 04 05' 06 08 09' 10' 11' 12 14 15 Big river slope v'yd, superb site next to MONTROSE. Always robust, structured, age-worthy; up to 18% Petit Verdot. Recent investment. Same stable as GRAND-PUY-DUCASSE, LA TOUR DE MONS (owned by CA Grands Crus). ANGÉLUS owner consults. Second label: Prieur de Meyney.

Mission Haut-Brion, La Pe-Lé r ★★★★ 88 89' 90' 94 95 96' 98' 99 00' 01 02 03 04 05' 06 07 08 09' 10' 11' 12 13 14 15' 16 Owned by Dillon family of HAUT-BRION since 1983. Consistently grand-scale, full-blooded, long-maturing wine. Ex-cellar sale

---

Vintage bluster

A group of Britain's finest wine merchants have placed recent B'X vintages in the following qualitative order: 2005 (best), 2009, 2010, 2000, 2001, 2008, 2006, 2012, 2003, 2004, 2007, 2002, 2011. I'm not sure I entirely agree. What do you think?

at Sotheby's, New York raised $1.4 million in 2016. Second label: La Chapelle de la Mission. Magnificent sém-dominated white: previously Laville-Haut-Brion; renamed La Mission-Haut-Brion Blanc (2009) 10' 11' 12' 13 14 15.

Monbousquet St-Ém r (w) ★★★ 01 02 03 04 05' 06 07 08 09' 10' 11 12 14 15 16 GRAND CRU CLASSÉ on sand/gravel plain revolutionized by Gerard Pérse (PAVIE same stable). Concentrated, oaky, voluptuous wines. Rare *v.gd Sauv Bl/Sauvignon Gris* (AC B'X). Second label: Angélique de Monbousquet.

Monbrison Marg r ★★→★★★ 98 00 01 02 04 05' 06 08 09' 10' 11 12 14 15 16 Small, family-owned property at Arsac. 65% CAB SAUV. Delicate, fragrant MARG.

4 chx have in-house cooperages: Haut-Brion, Lafite, Margaux, Smith-Haut-Lafitte.

Mondotte, La St-Ém r ★★★★ 97 98' 99 00' 01 02 03 04' 05' 06 07 08 09' 10' 11 12 13 14 15 16 Tiny PREMIER GRAND CRU CLASSÉ on the limestone-clay plateau. Intense, firm, virile wines at a price. Organic certification. Same von Neipperg stable as CANON-LA-GAFFELIÈRE, CLOS DE L'ORATOIRE.

Montrose St-Est r ★★★★ 89' 90 93 94 95 96' 98 00' 01 02 03' 04 05' 06 07 08 09' 10' 11 12 13 14 15' 16 Second Growth with riverside v'yd. Famed for forceful, long-ageing claret. Vintages 1979–85 were lighter. Bouyges brothers owners; huge investment paying off. Environmentally friendly buildings. Second label: La Dame de Montrose. Third label: Le Saint-Estèphe de Montrose.

Moulin du Cadet St-Ém r p ★★ 00 01 03 05 08 09 10' 11 12 14 15 16 Tiny GRAND CRU CLASSÉ; same owner as SANSONNET. Gradual change; formerly robust, now more finesse, fragrance.

Moulinet Pom r ★★ 04 05 06 08 09 10 11 12 15 Large CH for POM. Chinese ownership (2016). DERENONCOURT consults. Lighter style.

Moulin-Haut-Laroque Fron r ★★ 05' 06 08 09' 10' 11 12 14 15 16 Leading FRON property run by Thomas Hervé. Consistent quality. Structured wines, can age. Value. Second label: CH Hervé Laroque.

Moulin Pey-Labrie Fron r ★★ 02 03 04 05' 08 09' 10' 11 12 14 15 16 Leading CH in CANON-FRON. Sturdy, well-structured wines that can age.

Moulin-St-Georges St-Ém r ★★★ 01 02 03 04 05' 06 08 09' 10' 11 12 13 14 15 16 Same stable as AUSONE, LA CLOTTE. Dense, stylish wines. Merits classification.

Mouton Rothschild Pau r (w) ★★★★ 82' 83' 85' 86' 88' 89' 90' 94 95' 96 97 98' 99 00' 01' 02 03 04' 05' 06' 07 08' 09' 10' 11' 12 13 14 15' 16 Philippine de Rothschild's three children now co-owners. Philippe Dhalluin the chief winemaker. Most exotic, voluptuous of PAU First Growths, now at top of game. English artist David Hockney illustrated 2014 label. White Aile d'Argent (SAUV BL/SÉM). Second label: Le Petit Mouton. *See also* D'ARMAILHAC, CLERC MILON.

Nairac Saut w sw ★★ 96 97' 98 99 01' 02 03 04 05' 06 07 09' 10 11 13 14 15 BAR Second Growth owned by Tari family. Rich but fresh; decent form. Second label: Esquisse de Nairac.

Nénin Pom r ★★★ 96 98 99 00' 01 02 03 04 05 06 07 08 09' 10' 11 12 13 14 15' 16 Same owners as LÉOVILLE-LAS-CASES; 20 yrs of investment, evolution. V'yd expanded. Restrained in style but generous, precise, built to age. 2015 the most precise vintage yet. Gd-value second label: Fugue de Nénin.

Olivier Pe-Lé r w ★★★ (r) 01 02 04' 05' 06 08 09' 10' 11 12 13 14 15 16 (w) 05' 06 07' 08 09 10' 11 12 13 14 15 16 Beautiful classified property with moated castle. Investment, application brought change. Now structured red, juicy SAUV BL-led (75%) white.

Ormes-de-Pez, Les St-Est r ★★ 01 02 03 04 05 06 07 08 09' 10' 11 12 14 15 16 Quality guaranteed. CAZES family of LYNCH-BAGES owners. Dense, fleshy wines to age.

Ormes-Sorbet, Les Méd r ★★ 01 02 03' 04 05 06 08 09' 10' 11 12 14 15 Reliably consistent, family-owned, CRU BOURGEOIS. CAB SAUV dominant (65%). Elegant, gently oaked wines that age. CH Fontis same stable.

BORDEAUX

Palmer Marg r ★★★★ 83' 85 86' 88' 89 90 94 95 96' 98' 99 00 01' 02 03 04 05' 06' 07 08' 09' 10' 11' 12 13 14 15' 16 Third Growth on a par with "Super Seconds" (occasionally Firsts). Voluptuous wine of power, delicacy and much MERLOT (40%). Dutch (MÄHLER-BESSE) and British (SICHEL) owners. 100% bio. Second label: *Alter Ego de Palmer*. Also original Vin Blanc de Palmer (Loset/ MUSCADELLE/ Sauvignon Gris). Has experimented with adding HERMITAGE as in C18.

Pape-Clément Pe-Lé r (w) ★★★★ (r) 94 95 96 98' 99 00' 01 02 03 04 05 06 07 08 09' 10' 11 12 13 14 15' 16 (w) 03 04 05' 07 08 09 10 11 12 13 14 15 16 Historic estate in B'x suburbs (wine shop and tastings as well). Owned by Bernard Magrez (*see* CLOS HAUT-PEYRAGUEY, FOMBRAUGE, LA TOUR-CARNET); dense, long-ageing reds. Tiny production of rich, oaky white.

Patache d'Aux Méd r ★★ 05' 06 07 09 10 11 12 14 15 16 Popular CRU BOURGEOIS located at Bégadan. Reliable largely CAB SAUV (60%) wine. DERENONCOURT consults. New ownership: Advini, via Antoine Moueix Properties.

Pavie St-Ém r ★★★★ 94 95 96 98 99 00 01' 02 04 05' 06 07 08 09' 10' 11 12 13 14 15' 16 PREMIER GRAND CRU CLASSÉ (A) splendidly sited on plateau and s côtes. Perse family owners. New-wave ST-ÉM: intense, oaky, strong. Impressive, state-of-the-art winery. Second label: Arômes de Pavie. Esprit de Pavie a simple AC B'X.

Pavie-Decesse St-Ém r ★★ 00' 01' 02 03 04 05' 06 07 08 09' 10' 11 12 14 15 16 Tiny Classed Growth. V. old vines. As powerful, muscular as sister PAVIE.

Pavie-Macquin St-Ém r ★★★ 90' 94 95 96' 98' 99 00' 01 02 03 04 05' 06 07 08 09' 10' 11 12 13 14 15 16 PREMIER GRAND CRU CLASSÉ with v'yd on limestone plateau; neighbour to TROPLONG-MONDOT. 80%+ MERLOT. Winemaker Nicolas Thienpont; DERENONCOURT consults. Sturdy, full-bodied wines need time. Second label: Les Chênes de Macquin.

Pédesclaux Pau r ★★ 02 03 04 05 06 09 10' 11 12 13 14 15 16 Underachieving Fifth Growth being revived and reorganized. Extensive investment in cellars and v'yd. Hits stride from 2014. Second label: Fleur de Pédesclaux.

Petit-Village Pom r ★★★ 98' 00' 01 03 04 05 06 07 08 09' 10' 11 12 13 14 15' 16 Much-improved POM opposite VIEUX-CH-CERTAN. MERLOT (75%) with CABS FR, SAUV. Owned by AXA Insurance. Suave, dense, increasingly finer tannins. Second label: Le Jardin de Petit-Village.

Petrus Pom r ★★★★ 79' 81 82' 83 85' 86 88' 89' 90 93' 94 95' 96 97 98' 99 00' 01 02 03 04' 05' 06 07 08 09' 10' 11' 12 13 14 15' 16 The (unofficial) First Growth of POM: MERLOT solo *in excelsis*. V'yd on blue clay gives 2500 cases of massively rich, concentrated wine for ageing. Modern cellar with concrete vats. Father, Jean-Claude Berrouet (45 vintages), to son (Olivier since 2007) winemakers. Jean-François MOUEIX owner. No second label.

Pey La Tour r ★★ 09 09 10 11 12 14 15 Large DOURTHE-owned estate. Quality-driven B'X SUPÉRIEUR. Three red CUVÉES: Rés du CH top selection. Also a rosé.

Peyrabon H-Méd r ★★ 04 05 06 09' 10 11 12 15 Consistent CRU BOURGEOIS owned by NÉGOCIANT (Millésima). Also La Fleur-Peyrabon in PAU.

Pez, De St-Est r ★★★ 01 02 03 04 05' 06 07 08 09' 10' 11 12 13 14 15 16 Ancient estate revamped by owner ROEDERER since 1995. Mainly MERLOT and CAB SAUV. Dense, reliable style.

Phélan-Ségur St-Est r ★★★ 98 00' 01 02 03 04 05' 06 07 08 09' 10' 11 12 14 15 16 Irish family origins. Today, the Gardinier family. Reliable, top-notch, unclassified CH; long, supple style. Second label: Frank Phélan.

Pibran Pau r ★★ 00' 01 03 04 05' 06 08 09' 10' 11 12 13 14 15 16 Small property allied to PICHON-BARON. Classy, MERLOT-led wine.

Pichon-Baron Pau r ★★★★ 89' 90' 93 94' 95 96 98 99 00' 01 02 03' 04 05' 06 07 08 09' 10' 11' 12 13 14 15 16 Owned by AXA Insurance; formerly CH Pichon-Longueville. Revitalized Second Growth with powerful, consistent PAU at a price. Potential for long ageing. Second labels: Les Tourelles de Longueville (approachable: more MERLOT); Les Griffons de Pichon Baron (CAB SAUV dominant).

Pichon-Longueville Comtesse de Lalande (Pichon Lalande) Pau r ★★★★ 86' 88' 89' 90' 94 95 96 98 99 00 01 02 03' 04 05' 06' 07 08 09' 10' 11 12 13 14 15 16 ROEDERER-owned Second Growth, overlooking LATOUR. Always among top performers; long-lived, wine of fabulous breed. MERLOT-marked in 80s, 90s; more CAB SAUV in recent yrs. New high-tech, gravity-fed winery and buildings. Organic trials. Second label: Rés de la Comtesse. DE PEZ, HAUT-BEAUSÉJOUR in same stable.

Pin, Le Pom r ★★★★ 85 86' 88 89 90' 94 95 96 97 98' 99 00 01' 02 04 05' 06' 07 08 09' 10' 11 12 14 16 The original of B'X cult mini-crus (1st vintage: 1979). Only 2.8 ha. Tiny cellar has now given way to modern winery. 100% MERLOT; almost as rich as its drinkers, but prices are scary. No second label. L'If in ST-ÉM and a v'yd in CAS new stablemates.

Plince Pom r ★★ 04 05 06 08 09 10 11 12 15 V'yd nr NÉNIN and LA POINTE. Machine harvested. Supple, fruity style.

Pointe, La Pom r ★★ 01 04 05 06 07 08 09' 10' 11 12 14 15 16 Large (for POM), well-managed estate. Investment, progress in last 10 yrs. One of best values in Pom.

Poitevin Méd r ★★ 08 09 10 11 12 14 15 Supple, elegant CRU BOURGEOIS. 50%+ MERLOT. Consistent quality. Also a dry white B'X.

Pontet-Canet Pau r ★★★★ 89' 90 94' 95 96' 98 99 00' 01 02' 03 04' 05' 06' 07 08 09' 10' 11 12 13 14 15 16 Fashionable, bio certified, Tesseron-family-owned Fifth Growth. Radical improvement has seen prices soar. 35 per cent aged in amphorae; rest in BARRIQUES. Second label: Les Hauts de Pontet-Canet.

Potensac Méd r ★★ 01 02 03 04 05' 07 08 09' 10' 11 12 13 14 15 16 Same stable as LÉOVILLE-LAS-CASES. Firm, vigorous wines for long ageing. Lots of old vine CAB FR (20%). Second label: Chapelle de Potensac.

Pouget Marg r ★★ 01 02 03 04 05' 06 08 09' 10' 11 12 14 15 Obscure Fourth Growth attached to BOYD-CANTENAC. 75%+ CAB SAUV. Sturdy; needs time.

Poujeaux Mou r ★★ 00' 01 03 04 05 08 09' 10' 11 12 14 15 16 Same owner as CLOS FOURTET. 50% CAB SAUV. DERENONCOURT consults. Full, robust wines that age. Second label: La Salle de Poujeaux. Also Haut de Poujeaux (H MÉD).

Premier Grand Cru Classé St-Ém 2012: 18 classified; ranked into A (4) and B (14).

Pressac, De St-Ém r ★★ 06 08 09 10 11 12 14 15 16 GRAND CRU CLASSÉ in e ST-ÉM. MERLOT (69%), CABS FR, SAUV, MALBEC, CARMENÈRE. Quality assured. Gd value.

Preuillac Méd r ★★ 06 08 09 10 11 12 15 Savoury, structured CRU BOURGEOIS. Chinese-owned. DERENONCOURT consults. Second label: Esprit de Preuillac.

Prieuré-Lichine Marg r ★★★ 90' 95 96 98' 99 00' 01 02 03 04 05 06 07 08 09' 10' 11 12 14 15 16 Fourth Growth owned by a NÉGOCIANT; put on map by Alexis Lichine. Fragrant MARG currently on gd form. V'yd expanded and new cuvier with "green" wall. Wine shop and tours. Second label: Confidences du Prieuré-Lichine. Gd SAUV BL/SÉM white B'X too.

Puygueraud r ★★ 02 03' 05' 06 08 09 10 11 12 14 15 16 Leading CH of this tiny FRANCS-CÔTES de B'X AC. Nicolas Thienpont the winemaker (see PAVIE-MACQUIN). MERLOT-led (70%). Oak-aged wines of surprising class. Special CUVÉE George with MALBEC (35%+) in blend. Also a little white (SAUV BL/Sauvignon Gris).

Quinault L'Enclos St-Ém r ★★→★★★ 09 10 11 12 14 15 16 GRAND CRU CLASSÉ located in

---

Sparkling Bordeaux

It's a lesser-known fact that B'X also makes sparkling wine, CRÉMANT de B'x. And judging by figures it's gaining traction. Six million bottles were produced in 2015, a figure that has quadrupled in 4 yrs. Grapes used are classic B'X varieties (SAUV BL, SÉM, CAB FR, MERLOT, etc.) which have to be picked by hand; production is *méthode traditionnelle*. Watch out, CHAMPAGNE.

Libourne. Same team and owners as CHEVAL BLANC. Now more freshness, finesse (and CAB SAUV). Aged in 500-litre casks.

Quintus St-Ém r ★★★ 11 12 13 14 15 16 Created by the Dillons of HAUT-BRION from former Tertre Daugay and L'ARROSÉE (added in 2013) v'yds. Now a 28-ha estate. Gaining in stature, finesse but price soared. Second label: Le Dragon de Quintus (bronze statue at property).

Rabaud-Promis Saut w sw ★★ →★★★ 97 98 99 01' 02 03' 04 05' 06 07 09' 10 11 12 13 14 15 16 First Growth located in Bommes. Organic tendencies. Quality, gd value.

Rahoul Grav r w ★★ (r) 05 08 09' 10 11 12 14 15 16 Owned by DOURTHE; improvement. Balanced red. SÉM-dominated white 10 11 12 13 14 15. Gd value.

Ramage-la-Batisse H-Méd r ★★ 05' 07 08 09 10 11 12 14 Reasonably consistent, widely distributed, CRU BOURGEOIS. CAB SAUV-led. Second label: L'Enclos de Ramage.

Rauzan-Gassies Marg r ★★★ 00 01' 02 03 04 05' 06 07 08 09' 10' 11 12 15 Family-owned, Second Growth; v'yds in MAR, Cantenac. Lags behind RAUZAN-SÉGLA but making strides to improve. Second label: Gassies.

Rauzan-Ségla Marg r ★★★★ 89' 90' 94' 95 96 98 99 00' 01 02 03 04' 05 06 07 08 09' 10' 11 12 13 14 15' 16 MARG Second Growth long famous for its fragrance; owned by Wertheimers of Chanel (*see* CANON). Improved cellars. Organic trials. New winemaker/manager from 2015. Second label: Ségla (value).

Raymond-Lafon Saut w sw ★★★ 90' 95 96' 97 98 99' 01' 02 03' 04 05' 06 07' 09' 10' 11' 13 14 15 16 Unclassified SAUT producing First Growth quality wine. Owned by Meslier family. Rich, complex SÉM-led wines that age.

Rayne Vigneau Saut w sw ★★★ 95 96 97 98 99 01' 03 05' 07 09' 10' 11' 13 14 15 16 Substantial First Growth at Bommes. Wines now rich, suave, age-worthy. Second label: Madame de Rayne. Dry, white B'X Le Sec de Rayne Vigneau.

Respide Médeville Grav r w ★★ (r) 05' 06 08 09 10 11 12 14 15 (w) 10 11 12 13 14 15 Top property for elegant red and complex *white*. Second label (r): Dame de Respide.

Reynon r w ★★ Leading CADILLAC-CÔTES DE B'X estate. Serious MERLOT-led red 05' 06 09' 10 11 12 14 15. Fragrant B'X white from SAUV BL 10' 11' 12 13 14 15. Owned by Dubourdieu family.

Reysson H-Méd r ★★ 05 06 08 09' 10' 11 12 14 15 MERLOT-led (90%) CRU BOURGEOIS owned by NÉGOCIANT DOURTHE. Modern style. Second label: Moulin de Reysson.

Rieussec Saut w sw ★★★★ 85 86' 88' 89' 90' 95 96' 97' 98 99 01' 02 03' 04 05' 06 07 09' 10' 11' 13 14 15 Worthy neighbour of YQUEM with v'yd in Fargues, owned by (LAFITE) Rothschilds. Fabulously powerful, opulent; SÉM-dominant (90%). Average 6000 cases/yr. Second label: Carmes de Rieussec. Dry "R" de Rieussec.

Rivière, De la Fron r ★★ 01 02 03 04 05' 06 08 09' 10 12 14 15 Largest (65 ha), most impressive FRON property with Wagnerian castle, cellars. Chinese-owned. Formerly big, tannic wines; now more refined. Second label: Les Sources. Also a little white and rosé.

Roc de Cambes r ★★★ 04 05 06 08 09 10 11 12 13 14 15 Undisputed leader in CÔTES DE BOURG; wines as gd as top ST-ÉM. Savoury, opulent but pricey. Same stable as TERTRE-ROTÉBOEUF.

Rochemorin, De Pe-Lé r w ★★ →★★★ (r) 05 06 08 09' 10' 11 12 14 15 (w) 07 08 09 10 11 12 13 14 15 Sizeable property at Martillac owned by André Lurton of LA LOUVIÈRE. Fleshy red; aromatic white (100% SAUV BL). Modern winery. Fairly consistent quality. CH Coucheroy (r w) also produced.

Rol Valentin St-Ém r ★★★ 01' 02 03 04 05' 06 07 08 09' 10' 11 12 13 14 15 Once garage-sized; now bigger v'yd with clay-limestone soils. 90% MERLOT. Rich, modern wines but balanced.

Rouget Pom r ★★ 98' 00' 01' 03 04 05' 06 07 08 09' 10' 11 12 13 14 15 Go-ahead estate on n edge of POM. Rich, unctuous wines. MICHEL ROLLAND consults. Second label: Le Carillon de Rouget. DOM JACQUES PRIEUR same owner.

Sales, De Pom r ★★ 01' 04 05 06 08 09 10 12 15 Biggest v'yd of POM (10,000 cases). 70% MERLOT with CABS FR, SAUV. Lightish wine; never quite poetry. Second label: CH Chantalouette (5000 cases).

Sansonnet St-Ém r ★★ 01 02 03 04 05' 06 08 09' 10' 11 12 13 14 15 16 Ambitious GRAND CRU CLASSÉ on limestone-clay plateau. Modern but refreshing. MOULIN DU CADET same stable.

Saransot-Dupré List r (w) ★★ 01 02 03 04 05 06 09' 10' 11 12 15 Small property with firm, fleshy wines. MERLOT-led but 1% CARMENÈRE. Also one of LIST's growing band of whites (SÉM 60%).

Sénéjac H-Méd r (w) ★★ 04 05' 06 08 09' 10' 11 12 14 15 S H-MÉD (Pian). Consistent, well-balanced wines that can be drunk young or age. Gd value.

Serre, La St-Ém r ★★ 02 03 04 05 06 08 09' 10 11 12 14 15 16 Small GRAND CRU CLASSÉ on the limestone plateau. 70% MERLOT. Fresh, stylish wines with fruit.

Sigalas-Rabaud Saut w sw ★★★ 90' 95' 96' 97' 98 99 01' 02 03 04 05' 07' 09' 10' 11 12 13 14 15 16 Tiny First Growth run by Laure de Lambert Compeyrot. *V. fragrant and lovely.* Second label: Le Lieutenant de Sigalas.

Siran Marg r ★★ →★★★ 01 02 03 04 05 06 07 08 09' 10' 11 12 14 15 16 Unclassified MARG estate run by Édouard Miailhe. Recent investment and change. Visitor friendly. Wines have substance, classic MARG fragrance. Second label: S de Siran.

Smith-Haut-Lafitte Pe-Lé r (p) (w) ★★★★ (r) 98 99 00' 01 02 03 04 05' 06 07 08 09' 10' 11 12 13 14 15' 16 (w) 06 07' 08' 09 10' 11 12 13 14 15 16 Celebrated Classed Growth with spa hotel (Caudalie), regularly one of PE-LÉ stars. White is full, ripe, sappy; red precise/generous. 2015 (r w) bottled with atypical black label to mark 25th anniversary of Cathiard ownership. Second label: Les Hauts de Smith. Also CAB SAUV-based Le Petit Haut Lafitte.

Sociando-Mallet H-Méd r ★★★ 90' 94 95 96' 98' 99 00' 01' 02 03 04 05' 06 07 08 09' 10' 11 12 14 15 Substantial estate just n of ST-EST built from scratch by former NÉGOCIANT; now managed by daughter Sylvie. Classed Growth quality. Conservative, big-boned wines to lay down for yrs. Second label: La Demoiselle de Sociando-Mallet. Also special CUVÉE Jean Gautreau.

Sours, De r p w ★★ Valid reputation for B'X rosé (DYA). 300,000 bottles/yr. Gd white; improving B'X red. Now owned by Jack Ma of Alibaba fame.

Soutard St-Ém r ★★★ 98' 00' 01' 05 06 07 08 08 09 10 11 12 14 15 16 *Potentially excellent* GRAND CRU CLASSÉ on limestone plateau. 65% MERLOT. Massive investment, still room for improvement; 2014 and 2015 more like it. Visitor friendly. Second label: Les Jardins de Soutard.

St-Émilion classification – current version

The latest classification (2012) incl a total of 82 CHX: 18 PREMIERS GRANDS CRUS CLASSÉS and 64 GRANDS CRUS CLASSÉS. The new classification, now legally considered an exam rather than a competition, was conducted by a commission of seven, nominated by INAO, none from B'X. CHX ANGÉLUS and PAVIE were upgraded to *Premier Grand Cru Classé* (A) while added to the rank of *Premier Grand Cru Classé* (B) were CANON LA GAFFELIÈRE, LA MONDOTTE, LARCIS DUCASSE and VALANDRAUD. New to status of *Grand Cru Classé* were Chx BARDE-HAUT, CLOS de Sarpe, Clos la Madeleine, Côte de Baleau, DE FERRAND, DE PRESSAC, FAUGÈRES, FOMBRAUGE, JEAN FAURE, La Commanderie, La Fleur Morange, Le Chatelet, Péby Faugères, QUINAULT L'ENCLOS, Rochebelle and SANSONNET. Although a motivating force for producers, classification (which is reviewed every 10 yrs) remains an unwieldy guide for consumers. Three disappointed candidates are challenging the classification in court; if successful it could be end of ranking system originally introduced in 1955.

> **Workload**
> An increasing number of B'X CHX are turning to specialist contractors to
> handle work in their v'yds. Reasons given: difficulty finding personnel,
> French administration and cost of buying equipment. Largest of
> contractors, Banton et Lauret, boasts 600 clients covering 6000 ha
> (or production equivalent of 33 million bottles) and an annual turnover
> of €17 million. Sounds gd, but B and L still have to find hands.

St-Georges St-Ém r ★★ 01 03 04 05' 06 08 09 10 11 14 V'yd represents 25 per cent of ST-GEORGES AC. Jean-Philippe Janoueix co-owner and manager. MERLOT-led with CABS FR, SAUV. Gd wine sold direct to public. Second label: Puy St-Georges.

St-Pierre St-Jul r ★★★90' 95' 96' 98 99 00' 01' 02 03 04 05' 06 07 08 09' 10' 11 12 13 14 15 16 Tiny go-ahead Fourth Growth. 75% CAB SAUV. Stylish, consistent, classic ST-JUL. *See* GLORIA.

Suduiraut Saut w sw ★★★★ 88' 89' 90' 95 96 97' 98 99' 01' 02 03' 04 05' 06 07' 09' 10' 11' 13 14 15' 16 One of v. best SAUT. Owner AXA achieved greater consistency, luscious quality. Second labels: Castelnau de Suduiraut; Les Lions de Suduiraut (fresher, fruitier). Dry wines "S" and entry level Le Blanc Sec.

Taillefer Pom r ★★ 00' 01' 02 03 04 05' 06 08 09' 10 11 12 14 15 Family property managed by Claire Moueix. Sandier soils. Lighter weight but polished and refined. Can age.

Talbot St-Jul r (w) ★★★ 90 94 95 96' 98' 99 00' 00' 01 02 03 04 05' 08' 09' 10' 11 12 14 15 16 Huge (107 ha) Fourth Growth in heart of AC ST-JUL owned by Cordier family since 1917. Wine rich, *consummately charming, reliable* (though wobbly in 2006–7). 66% CAB SAUV. Second label: Connétable de Talbot. Early-drinking SAUV BL-based white: Caillou Blanc.

Tertre, Du Marg r ★★★ 99 00' 01 03 04' 05' 06 08 09' 10' 11 12 14 15 16 Fifth Growth isolated s of MARG. Fragrant (20% CAB FR) fresh, fruity but structured wines. On top form. Same Dutch owner/manager as CH GISCOURS. Second label: Les Hauts du Tertre. Also VIN DE FRANCE dry white CHARD/VIOGNIER/GROS MANSENG/SAUV BL.

Tertre-Rôteboeuf St-Ém r ★★★★ 90' 93 94 95 96 97 98' 99 00' 01 02 03' 04 05' 06' 07 08 09' 10' 11 12 13 14 15 Tiny cult star making concentrated, exotic, MERLOT-based wine since 1979. Hugely consistent; can age. Frightening prices. Also v.gd ROC DE CAMBES (CÔTES DE BOURG).

Thieuley r p w ★★ E-2-M supplier of consistent quality AC B'X (r w); fruity CLAIRET; oak-aged CUVÉE Francis Courselle (r w). Run by sisters Marie and Sylvie (Courselle).

Tour-Blanche, La Saut (r) w sw ★★★ 88' 89' 90' 95 96 97' 98 99 01' 02 03' 04 05' 06 07 09' 10' 11' 13 14 15 16 Excellent First Growth SAUT; consistent quality. Mainly SÉM. Rich, bold, powerful wines on sweeter end of scale. Second label: Les Charmilles de Tour-Blanche.

Tour-Carnet, La H-Méd r ★★★ 00' 01 02 03 04 05' 06 08 09' 10' 11 12 14 15 16 N H-MÉD Classed Growth restored and modernized by Bernard Magrez (*see* FOMBRAUGE, PAPE-CLÉMENT). Rich, concentrated, opulent wines. Second label: Les Douves de CH La Tour Carnet. Also dry white B'X Blanc de La Tour Carnet.

Tour-de-By, La Méd r ★★ 01 02 03 04 05' 06 08 09 10 11 12 14 16 Substantial, family-run estate in n MÉD. Sturdy, reliable, CAB SAUV-led (60%) wines with fruity note. Also rosé and special CUVÉE Héritage Marc Pagès.

Tour de Mons, La Marg r ★★ 00 01 02 04 05' 06 08 09' 10 11 12 14 MARG CRU BOURGEOIS. Owned by CA GRANDS CRUS (*see* GRAND-PUY-DUCASSE). MERLOT-led (56%). Steady improvement.

Tour-du-Haut-Moulin H-Méd r ★★ 00' 02 03 04 05' 06 08 09 10 11 12 14 15 N H-MÉD CRU BOURGEOIS. CAB SAUV/MERLOT. Intense, structured wines to age.

Tour-du-Pas-St-Georges St-Ém r ★★ 03 04 05' 06 08 09' 10 11 12 14 15 ST-GEORGES-

ST-ÉM estate run by Pascal Delbeck and daughter, Marie-Amandine. Classic style.

Tour Figeac, La St-Ém r ★★ 00' 01' 02 04 05' 06 07 08 09' 10' 11 12 14 15 16 GRAND CRU CLASSÉ in FIGEAC, CHEVAL BLANC sector. DERENONCOURT consults. Gd proportion of CAB FR (40%). Full, fleshy, harmonious.

Tour Haut-Caussan Méd r ★★ 05' 06 08 09' 10' 11 12 14 15 Consistent CRU BOURGEOIS at Blaignan. 50/50 CAB SAUV/MERLOT. Value.

Tournefeuille L de P r ★★ 01' 03 04 05' 06 07 08 09 10' 11 12 14 15 Reliable L de P on clay and gravel soils. 30% CAB FR adds spice. CH Lécouyer (POM) same stable.

Tour-St-Bonnet Méd r ★★ 05 06 08 09' 10 11 12 14 15 CRU BOURGEOIS in n MÉD. Gravel soils. Reliable. Value.

Trois Croix, Les Fron r ★★ 06 07 08 09 10 11 12 13 14 15 16 Fine, balanced wines from consistent producer. 80% MERLOT. Gd value. Owned, managed by family of former MOUTON ROTHSCHILD winemaker.

Tronquoy-Lalande St-Est r ★★★ 04 05 06 07 08 09' 10' 11 12 14 15 16 Same owners as MONTROSE; plenty of investment. MERLOT-led wines now consistent, dark, satisfying. Second label: Tronquoy de Ste-Anne. Also a little SÉM-led white.

Troplong-Mondot St-Ém r ★★★ 90' 95 96' 98' 99 00' 01' 02 03 04 05' 06 07 08 09' 10 11 12 13 14 15 16 First Growth on the limestone plateau. Organic tendency. *Wines of power, depth* with increasing elegance these days. Second label: Mondot. Also one-star Michelin restaurant (Les Belles Perdrix).

Trotanoy Pom r ★★★★ 90' 93 94 95 96 98' 00' 01 02 03 04' 05' 06 07 08 09' 10' 11 12 13 14 15' 16 One of jewels in J-P MOUEIX crown. 90% MERLOT/10% CAB FR. On flying form; power, elegance. Long ageing. Second label: L'Espérance de Trotanoy.

Trottevieille St-Ém r ★★★ 90 94 95 96 98 99 00' 01 03' 04 05' 06 07 08' 09' 10' 11 12 14 15' 16 First Growth on limestone plateau. BORIE-MANOUX-owned. Much improved in new millennium; wines long, fresh, structured. Lots of CAB FR (40–50%) incl some pre-phylloxera vines. Second label: La Vieille Dame de Trottevieille (v.gd 15).

Valandraud St-Ém r ★★★★ 94 95' 96 98 99 00' 01' 02 03 04 05' 06 07 08 09' 10' 11 12 13 14 15 16 PREMIER GRAND CRU CLASSÉ in e ST-ÉM. Initially a garage wonder: brainchild of Jean-Luc and Murielle Thunevin. Formerly super-concentrated; now rich, dense but balanced. Also Valandraud Blanc (SAUV BL/Sauvignon Gris).

Vieille Cure, La Fron r ★★ 04 05 06 08 09' 10' 11 12 13 14 15 16 Leading FRON estate; US-owned. MERLOT-led (74%). ROLLAND associate consults. Value.

Vieux-Ch-Certan Pom r ★★★★ 85 86' 88' 89 90' 94 95' 96' 98' 99 00' 01' 02 04 05' 06 07 08 09' 10' 11' 12 13 14 15' 16 Rated close to PETRUS in quality; different in style (30% CAB FR, 10% CAB SAUV according to vintage); *elegance, harmony, fragrance.* Alexandre Thienpont and son Guillaume at helm.

Vieux Ch St-André St-Ém r ★★ 06 08 09' 10 11 12 14 15 Small MERLOT-based v'yd in MONTAGNE-ST-ÉM owned by former PETRUS winemaker. Gd value.

Villegeorge, De H-Méd r ★★ 05 06 08 09' 10 12 14 15 16 Tiny s H-MÉD. CAB SAUV-based wine. Lighter weight but fresh, elegant style. CHX Duplessis (MOU) and La Tour de Bessan (MARG) same stable.

Vray Croix de Gay Pom r ★★ 04 05' 06 08 09' 10' 11 12 14 15 16 Tiny v'yd in best part of POM. More finesse of late. Conversion to bio. CH LATOUR owner a shareholder. CHX Siaurac (L DE P), Le Prieuré (ST-ÉM) same stable.

Yquem Saut w sw (dr) ★★★★ 85 86' 88' 89' 90' 93 94 95' 96 97' 98 99' 00 01' 02 03' 04 05' 06' 07' 08 09' 10' 11' 13' 14 15' King of sweet wines. Strong, intense, luscious; kept 3 yrs in barrel. Most vintages improve for 15 yrs+, some live 100 yrs+ in transcendent splendour. 100 ha in production (75% SÉM/25% SAUV BL). Recent investment in cellars. No Yquem made 51, 52, 64, 72, 74, 92, 2012. Same owner/manager as CHEVAL BLANC. Makes small amount (800 cases/yr) of dry "Y" (pronounced "ygrec").

Italy

More heavily shaded areas are the wine-growing regions.

Abbreviations used in the text:

Ab	Abruzzo	**Mol**	Molise
Bas	Basilicata	**Pie**	Piedmont
Cal	Calabria	**Pu**	Puglia
Cam	Campania	**Sar**	Sardinia
E-R	Emilia-Romagna	**Si**	Sicily
F-VG	Friuli-Venezia Giulia	**T-AA**	Trentino-Alto Adige
Lat	Latium	**Tus**	Tuscany
Lig	Liguria	**Umb**	Umbria
Lom	Lombardy	**VdA**	Valle d'Aosta
Mar	Marches	**Ven**	Veneto

Of all the thousands of grape varieties a winemaker could choose, almost one-third are found in, or are native to, Italy. The country's old name of The Land of Vines is true. They grow on hills, in valleys and on plains in a diversity no other country matches. That's Italy, a nation only 150 years old and often still reluctant to admit its many constituents have ever really been united. So the one thing you won't find in Italy is consensus – or consistency. What you will is variety, originality, imagination and creativity. Quality, yes. And, of course, style. Italian wine is a roller coaster. But you knew that.

The question is how to enjoy it to the full. Officialdom is not the greatest help. There are rafts of DOCs that no consumer really needs to know about; some DOCs have a grape in their name (like Barbera d'Asti, for example); others just stick to a place name, famous or not. Little is straightforward: there are at least seven different vines called Trebbiano and 17 different vines called Malvasia in Italy, and they all give different wines. The only solution, in the end, is to revel in the variety.

Some of the greatest reds and whites in the world come from Italy, and it has some of the oldest estates and some of the most innovative. It's a country that believes in having lots of rules but doesn't really believe in keeping to them. Some things are constant: Tuscan red gets its character from Sangiovese; it's grown elsewhere but Tuscany is its heart. Piedmont is the land of Barolo, Barbera and Dolcetto. Grape varieties are at the heart of it all; some famous, others just being rescued from near extinction. You will find notes on some of the higher-profile ones in the kaleidoscope of places and personalities that follows.

TRENTINO–
ALTO ADIGE
○ Bolzano
○ Trento
FRIULI–
VENEZIA
GIULIA
VENETO
L. Garda
Verona   Trieste
○ Venice
Po
EMILIA–
ROMAGNA
Bologna

Florence
TUSCANY   MARCHES
Siena
L. Trasimeno
UMBRIA
L. Bolsena
LATIUM   ABRUZZO
L'Bracciano
Rome
MOLISE
CAMPANIA   Bari
○ Naples   PUGLIA
BASILICATA   Táranto

Adriatic Sea

SARDINIA

Cagliari

Tyrrhenian Sea

CALABRIA

○ Palermo   ○ Réggio

SICILY

Recent vintages

Amarone, Veneto & Friuli

2016 Very hot summer; big reds, slightly chunky whites.
2015 Very hot June, early July. Quantity good, quality better.
2014 Cool, wet summer, good September (whites), October (reds).
    Not memorable for Amarone.
2013 Good whites. Reds, especially passito, suffered October/November
    rain/hail.
2012 Prolonged heat and drought hit quantity and quality. Amarone
    should be good.

2011 "Best year ever" for Amarone. Whites balanced, concentrated. Some
reds very tannic, high alcohol.
2010 Cool year, good for lighter wines, though Amarone will be fragrant
and elegant.
2009 Classic passito. Good for Prosecco, Pinot Gr, etc. Drink Amarone
from 2015.

Campania & Basilicata

2016 Cold spring delayed flowering, hot summer allowed catch-up.
Best for Greco di Tufo.
2015 Wet winter, patchy spring, hot, dry early summer, late autumn.
Great results.
2014 Production 25 per cent down on 2013. Spotty quality. Choose carefully.
2013 Whites balanced, perfumed; reds less so, especially late-picked Aglianico.
2012 September rains saved the whites. Indian summer made
outstanding Aglianicos.
2011 Wines concentrated, rich; high alcohol, tannin in reds. Whites
better balanced.
2010 Whites lightish with good aromas. Late-picked Aglianicos belatedly
judged excellent.
2009 Ripe, healthy, aromatic whites; reds with substance and concentration.
Drink Aglianico/Taurasi from 2014.

Marches & Abruzzo

2016 Rain, cold and lack of sun made for a very difficult year. Pecorino
probably best.
2015 Hot summer, timely autumn rains, healthy grapes; good whites,
better reds.
2014 Marches: good reds and whites. Abruzzo: interesting at higher levels,
mainly late-picked.
2013 Hailstorms and rot. Fine September saved whites; reds better
than feared.
2012 Warm days and cool nights at vintage. Later-picked varieties best.
2011 Some overconcentrated, alcoholic and tannic reds. Best should age well.
2010 A difficult year but some better-than-expected results. Drinking now.
2009 Good to very good, especially whites. Drink Montepulciano d'Abruzzo/
Conero now.

Piedmont

2016 Potentially top vintage; high quantity and quality, very promising
throughout region.
2015 Outstanding Barolo/Barbaresco. Should be long-lived. Barbera/Dolcetto
also good. Quantity also up, as no doubt will be price.
2014 Later-picked grapes thrived, early ones (eg. Dolcetto) didn't.
2013 Bright, crisp whites and reds improving with time.
2012 Quality good to very good, volume very low.
2011 Forward, early-drinking, scented reds despite highish alcohol levels.
2010 Patient growers made very good wines. Now seen as potentially
top vintage.
2009 Good to very good, especially Nebbiolo. Drink Barolo/Barbaresco
from 2014 for 10 years+.
Fine vintages: 08 06 04 01 00 99 98 97 96 95 90 89 88. Vintages to keep:
01 99 96. Vintages to drink up: 03 00 97 90 88.

Tuscany

2016 Hot summer with a fresher September; promising from Chianti to Montalcino to Maremma. High quality but lower quantity.

2015 Grapes healthy but small: quantity slightly down, quality well up.

2014 Cool, wet summer, fine late season. Quantity up, quality patchy, buyer beware.

2013 Uneven ripening. Not a great year, but some peaks.

2012 Drought and protracted heat; classic wines saved by early September rain.

2011 Some charmingly fruity if alcoholic classic reds. Whites a bit unbalanced.

2010 By no means everywhere wonderful, as has been claimed for Brunello.

2009 Quality very good at least. Drink Chianti/Brunello now for 2–3 years.

Fine vintages: 08 07 06 04 01 99 97 95 90. Vintages to keep: 01 99.

Vintages to drink up: 03 00 97 95 90.

What do the initials mean?

DOC (*Denominazione di Origine Controllata*) Controlled Denomination of Origin, cf. AOC in France.

DOCG (*Denominazione di Origine Controllata e Garantita*) "G" = "Guaranteed". Italy's highest quality designation. Guarantee? It's still *caveat emptor*.

IGT (*Indicazione Geografica Tipica*) "Geographic Indication of Type". Broader and more vague than DOC, cf. Vin de Pays in France.

DOP/IGP (*Denominazione di Origine Protetta/IndicazioneGeografica Protetta*) "P" = "Protected". The EU's DOP/IGP trump Italy's DOC/IGT.

Accornero Pie ★★★ Italy's best GRIGNOLINO producer. V.gd: Bricco del Bosco (steel vat) and Vigne Vecchie (oak-aged). Also gd: BARBERA del Monferrato (Cima and Bricco Battista) and Brigantino sweet (MALVASIA di Casorzo).

Aglianico del Taburno Cam DOCG r dr ★→★★★ Around Benevento, to se. Spicier notes (leather, tobacco) and herbs, higher acidity than other Aglianicos. Gd: CANTINA del Taburno, La Rivolta.

Aglianico del Vulture Bas DOC(G) r dr ★→★★★ 06 07 08 10 11 12 13 (15) DOC after 1 yr, SUPERIORE after 2 yrs, RISERVA after 5. From slopes of extinct volcano Monte Vulture. More floral (violet), dark fruits (plum), smoke, spice than other Aglianicos. Gd: Basilisco, CANTINA di Venosa, CANTINE DEL NOTAIO, Elena Fucci, Eubea, Grifalco, Madonna delle Grazie, Mastrodomenico, Paternoster, Terre degli Svevi.

Alba Pie Major wine city of PIE, se of Turin in LANGHE hills; truffles, hazelnuts and Pie's, if not Italy's, most prestigious wines: BARBARESCO, BARBERA D'ALBA, BAROLO, DOGLIANI (DOLCETTO) Langhe, NEBBIOLO D'ALBA, ROERO.

Albana di Romagna E-R DOCG w dr sw s/sw (sp) ★→★★★ DYA. Italy's 1st white DOCG, justified only by sweet PASSITO; dry and sparkling unremarkable. FATTORIA ZERBINA (esp AR Passito RISERVA), Giovanna Madonia, PODERE Morini (Cuore Matto Riserva Passito), Raffaella Bissoni, Tre Monti.

Allegrini Ven ★★★ Grower world-famous for VALPOLICELLA, though top table wines *La Grola*, Palazzo della Torre, La Poja not DOC, while AMARONE is. Owner of Poggio al Tesoro in BOLGHERI, Poggio San Polo in MONTALCINO, TUS too.

Alta Langa Pie DOCG (p) w sp ★★→★★★ PIE's major zone for top-quality vintage METODO CLASSICO sparkling, produced only from PINOT N and CHARD. Best: Banfi, Cocchi, Fontanafredda, Gancia, Germano Ettore, Serafino Enrico.

Altare, Elio Pie ★★★ Past leader of modernist NEBBIOLO (BAROLO) and BARBERA: brief maceration, ageing in barriques. Try Barolo Cannubi and Barolo Arborina; also Arborina (Nebbiolo), Larigi (Barbera), LANGHE Rosso La Villa (Barbera/Nebbiolo).

Alto Adige T-AA DOC r p w dr sw sp ★★→★★★ Mountainous province of Bolzano (Austrian until 1919); today's best Italian whites? Germanic varieties dominate. Kerner, GEWURZ, SYLVANER, but PINOT GRIGIO too; probably world's best PINOT BIANCO. PINOT N can be excellent (but often overoaked) as can *Lagrein*.

Alto Piemonte Pie Microclimate and soils of ne PIE make it ideal for NEBBIOLO (locally called Spanna), but wines rarely 100%, with additions of other local grapes (Croatina, Uva Rara, Vespolina). Home of the DOC(G): BOCA, BRAMATERRA, Colline Novaresi, Coste della Sesia, Fara, GATTINARA, GHEMME, LESSONA, Sizzano, Valli Ossolane. Many outstanding wines.

Ama, Castello di Tus ★★★ Top CHIANTI CLASSICO estate of Gaiole. Plain *Chianti Classico is one of best*, and most expensive. Worth seeking: TUS/B'x blend Haiku and MERLOT L'Apparita, despite the high price. Outstanding Chianti Classico GRAN SELEZIONE San Lorenzo.

Amarone della Valpolicella Ven DOCG r ★★→★★★★ 06' 07 08 09 10 11' 12 13 15 Intense strong red from winery-raisined VALPOLICELLA grapes; relatively dry version of more ancient RECIOTO DELLA VALPOLICELLA; CLASSICO if from historic zone. (*See also* Valpolicella, and box p.155.) Older vintages rare, as 1st created in 50s.

Angelini, Paolo Pie ★★→★★★ Small family-run MONFERRATO estate: v.gd GRIGNOLINO del Monferrato Casalese.

Angelini, Tenimenti Tus *See* BERTANI DOMAINS (TOSCANA).

Antinori, Marchesi L&P Tus ★★→★★★★ Historic Florentine house of Antinori family, led by Piero and three daughters. Famous for CHIANTI CLASSICO (Tenute Marchese Antinori and *Badia a Passignano*, latter now elevated to Gran Selezione), also polished but oaky white Cervaro (Umb *Castello della Sala*), PIE (PRUNOTTO) wines. Pioneer TIGNANELLO and SOLAIA among few world-class SUPER TUSCANS. Also estates in TUS MAREMMA (Fattoria Aldobrandesca), MONTEPULCIANO (La Braccesca), MONTALCINO (Pian delle Vigne), BOLGHERI (Guado al Tasso), FRANCIACORTA (*Montenisa*), PUG (Tormaresca). RIES-based white from estate of Monteloro n of Florence. Interests in Calfornia, Romania etc.

Antoniolo Pie ★★★ Age-worthy benchmark GATTINARA. Outstanding Osso San Grato and San Francesco.

Argiano, Castello di Tus ★★★ Beautiful property, next to and distinct from estate called "Argiano", transformed by Sesti family into one of MONTALCINO's finest sources of BRUNELLO. Best is Brunello RISERVA Phenomena.

Argiolas, Antonio Sar ★★→★★★ Top producer using native island grapes. Outstanding crus *Turriga* (★★★), sweet Antonio Argiolas (named in honour of founder, died 2009 age 102), Iselis MONICA, VERMENTINO DI SARDEGNA, and top sweet Angialis (mainly local Nasco grape).

Asti Pie DOCG sw sp ★→★★★ NV PIE sparkler from MOSCATO Bianco grapes, inferior to MOSCATO D'ASTI, not really worth its DOCG. Sells like mad in Russia. Try BERA, Cascina Fonda, Caudrina, Vignaioli di Santo Stefano.

Avignonesi Tus ★★★ Large bio estate, Belgian-owned since 2007. 200 ha in MONTEPULCIANO and Cortona. *Italy's best Vin Santo*. VINO NOBILE has returned to 1st division after period in wilderness. Top is VN Grandi Annate but MERLOT Desiderio, CHARD Il Marzocco creditable internationals.

Azienda agricola / agraria An estate (large or small) making wine from own grapes.

Badia a Coltibuono Tus ★★→★★★ Historic CHIANTI CLASSICO. 100% SANGIOVESE barrique-aged Sangioveto is star wine, but entry-level Chianti Classico one of best too.

Banfi (Castello or Villa) Tus ★→★★★ Giant of MONTALCINO, 100s of ha, though not in ideal situations, at extreme s of zone; but top, limited production wine POGGIO all'Oro is a great BRUNELLO.

Barbaresco Pie DOCG r ★★→★★★★ 01 04 06' 07 08 09 10 11 12 13 14 Wrongly looked down upon as BAROLO's poor cousin: both 100% NEBBIOLO, similar complex

ITALY

Barbaresco subzones
There are substantial differences between BARBARESCO's four main
communes – **Barbaresco:** most complete, balanced. Asili (BRUNO GIACOSA,
CERETTO, Ca' del Baio, PRODUTTORI DEL BARBARESCO), Martinenga (Marchesi
di Gresy), Montefico (Produttori del Barbaresco, Roagna), Montestefano
(Produttori del Barbaresco, Rivella Serafino, Giordano Luigi), Ovello
(CANTINA del Pino, Rocca Albino), Pora (Ca' del Baio, Produttori del
Barbaresco), Rabaja (CASTELLO DI VERDUNO, Cortese Giuseppe, BRUNO
GIACOSA, Produttori del Barbaresco, Rocca Bruno), Rio Sordo (Cascina
Bruciata, Cascina delle Rose, Produttori del Barbaresco), Roncaglie
(Poderi Colla). **Neive:** most powerful, fleshiest. Albesani (Castello di
Neive, Cantina del Pino), Basarin (Adriano Marco e Vittorio, Giacosa
Fratelli, Negro Angelo), Bordini (La Spinetta), Currá (Rocca Bruno,
Sottimano), Gallina (Castello di Neive, ODDERO, Lequio Ugo), Serraboella
(Cigliutti). **San Rocco Seno d'Elvio:** readiest to drink, soft. Sanadaive
(Adriano Marco e Vittorio). **Treiso:** freshest, most refined. Bernardot
(CERETTO), Bricco di Treiso (PIO CESARE), Marcarini (Ca' del Baio),
Montersino (Abrigo Orlando), Nervo (RIZZI), Pajoré (Rizzi, Sottimano).

---

aromas and flavours, but plenty of differences. Barbaresco is influenced by
Tanaro River: warmer microclimate, more fertile soils and lower-lying, gentler
slopes, so earlier maturing, less austere, less "muscular" than Barolo, but
v. elegant Min 26 mths ageing, 9 mths in wood; at 4 yrs becomes RISERVA.
Like Barolo, most Barbaresco these days is sold under a cru name or *menzione
geografica*. (For top producers *see* box, above.)

Barbera d'Alba DOC r ★→★★★ Richest and most velvety of BARBERAS. Gd: GIACOMO
CONTERNO (Cascina Francia and Ceretta), RINALDI GIUSEPPE, VIETTI (Scarrone).

Barbera d'Asti DOCG r ★→★★★ Fruity, high-acid version of BARBERA grape. Higher
quality is Barbera d'Asti Superiore Nizza (or more simply, Nizza). Gd: Bersano
(Nizza La Generala), BRAIDA (Bricco dell'Uccellone, Bricco della Bigotta, Ai
Suma), Chiarlo Michele (Nizza La Court), Dacapo (Nizza), Marchesi Gresy
(Monte Colombo), VIETTI (La Crena).

Barbera del Monferrato Superiore Pie DOCG r ★→★★★ Relatively light and fruity
BARBERA with sharpish tannins. Gd: Accornero (Cima Riserva della Casa) and
Luli (Barabba).

Barberani ★★→★★★ Brothers Bernardo and Niccolò now in charge of organic
estate on slopes of Lago di Corbara turning out gd to excellent ORVIETO. Cru Luigi
e Giovanna is star, Orvieto Castagneto and (noble rot) Calcaia also excellent.
Reds gd too.

Bardolino Ven DOC(G) r p ★→★★ DYA Light summery red from Lake Garda.
Bardolino SUPERIORE DOCG has much lower yield than Bardolino DOC. Its pale-
pink CHIARETTO is one of Italy's best rosés. Gd producers: Albino Piona,
Cavalchina, Corte Gardoni, Costadoro, *Guerrieri Rizzardi*, Le Fraghe, Le VIGNE
di San Pietro, ZENATO, Zeni.

Barolo Pie DOCG r ★★★→★★★★ 96' 99' 01' 04' 06' 07 08 09 10' 11 (14) Italy's
greatest red? 100% NEBBIOLO, from any of 11 communes incl Barolo itself.
Traditionally a blend of v'yds or communes, but these days most is single v'yd
(like Burgundian crus), called M*enzione Geografica Aggiuntiva*. Best are age-
worthy wines of power, elegance, with alluring floral scent and sour red-cherry
flavour. Must age 38 mths before release (5 yrs for RISERVA), of which 18 mths
in wood. (For top producers *see* box, overleaf.) Division between traditionalists
(long maceration, large oak barrels) and modernists (shorter maceration, often
barriques) is less helpful these days as producers use techniques of both schools.

Top Barolos

Here are a few top crus and their best producers: **Bricco Boschis** (Castiglione Falletto) CAVALLOTTO (RISERVA VIGNA San Giuseppe; **Bricco delle Viole** (BAROLO) GD VAJRA; **Bricco Rocche** (Castiglione Falletto) CERETTO; **Brunate** (La Morra, Barolo) Ceretto, GIUSEPPE Rinaldi, ODDERO, Vietti; **Bussia** (Monforte) ALDO CONTERNO (Gran Bussia e Romirasco), Poderi Colla (Dardi Le Rose), Oddero (Bussia Vigna Mondoca); **Cannubi** (Barolo): BREZZA, LUCIANO SANDRONE (Cannubi Boschis), E. Pira e Figli – Chiara Boschis; **Cerequio** (La Morra, Barolo): Boroli, Chiarlo Michele, ROBERTO VOERZIO; **Falletto** (Serralunga): BRUNO Giacosa (Le Rocche del Falletto Riserva); **Francia** (Serralunga): GIACOMO CONTERNO (Barolo Cascina Francia and Monfortino); **Ginestra** (Monforte): CONTERNO FANTINO (Sorì Ginestra and Vigna del Gris), Domenico Clerico (Ciabot Mentin); **Lazzarito** (Serralunga): Germano Ettore (Riserva), VIETTI; **Monprivato** (Castiglione Falletto): Giuseppe MASCARELLO (Mauro); **Monvigliero** (VERDUNO): CASTELLO DI VERDUNO, COMM. GB BURLOTTO, PAOLO Scavino; **Ornato** (Serralunga): PIO CESARE; **Ravera** (Novello): Elvio Cogno (Bricco Pernice), GD VAJRA, VIETTI; **Rocche dell'Annunziata** (La Morra): Paolo Scavino (Riserva), Roberto Voerzio, Rocche Costamagna, Trediberri; **Rocche di Castiglione** (Castiglione Falletto): Brovia, Oddero, Vietti; **Vigna Rionda** (Serralunga): Massolino, Oddero; **Villero** (Castiglione Falletto): Boroli, Brovia, Giacomo Fenocchio. And the Barolo of Bartolo MASCARELLO blends together Cannubi San Lorenzo, Ruè and Rocche dell'Annunziata).

Bastianich ★★→★★★ American Joe Bastianich oversees 35 ha from his US base, with star consultant Maurizio Castelli. Knockout Vespa Bianco, typically Friulian blend of CHARD and SAUV BL with a *pizzico* of native Picolit and outstanding FRIULANO Plus.

Belisario Mar ★★→★★★ Largest producer of VERDICCHIO DI MATELICA. Many different bottlings; gd quality/price. Top: RISERVA Cambrugiano e Del Cero.

Benanti Si ★★★ Benanti family and Salvo Foti (until recently their winemaker) turned world on to ETNA. Bianco Superiore Pietramarina one of Italy's best whites. V.gd: mono-variety Nerello Cappuccio and NERELLO MASCALESE.

Berlucchi, Guido Lom ★★ Italy's largest producer of sparkling METODO CLASSICO with five million+ bottles from nearly 100 ha v'yd. FRANCIACORTA Brut Cuvée Imperiale is flagship.

Bersano Pie ★★★ Large-volume but gd-quality PIE producer. V.gd: BARBERA, Freisa and GRIGNOLINO.

Bertani Ven ★★→★★★ Long-est producer of VALPOLICELLA and SOAVE; v'yds in various parts of Verona province. Basic Veronese/Valpantena lines plus restoration of abandoned techniques, eg. white using skin maceration, red (Secco Bertani Original Vintage Edition). *See also* BERTANI DOMAINS (TOSCANA).

Bertani Domains (Toscana) Tus ★★→★★★ Previously Tenimenti Angelini. Angelini group has taken over Bertani name, using it for all operations incl TUS. Three major wineries: San Leonino, CHIANTI CLASSICO; Trerose, MONTEPULCIANO; Val di Suga, MONTALCINO (esp BRUNELLO Spuntali).

Biondi-Santi Tus ★★★★ Classic wines from traditional MONTALCINO estate that 1st created BRUNELLO, recently sold to Epi group (Piper-Heidsieck): Brunellos and esp RISERVAS high in acid, tannin requiring decades to develop fully. Recently tried for more user-friendly style.

Bisol Ven Top brand of PROSECCO; outstanding CARTIZZE and owner of beautiful Venissa island retreat in Venice lagoon; also rare, expensive Venissa white from rare Dorona grape.

Boca Pie DOC r ★→★★★ See ALTO PIEMONTE. NEBBIOLO (70–90%), incl up to 30% Uva Rara and/or Vespolina. Volcanic soil. Suitable for long ageing, potentially among greatest reds. Best: Le Piane. Gd: Carlone Davide, Castello Conti.

Bolgheri Tus DOC r p w (sw) ★★→★★★★ Arty walled village on w coast giving name to stylish, expensive SUPER TUSCANS, mainly French varieties. Big names: ALLEGRINI (Poggio al Tesoro), ANTINORI (Guado al Tasso), FRESCOBALDI (ORNELLAIA), FOLONARI (Campo al Mare), GAJA (CÀ MARCANDA), outstanding Le Macchiole and MICHELE SATTA, SASSICAIA (the original).

Bolla Ven ★★ Historic Verona firm for AMARONE, RECIOTO DELLA VALPOLICELLA, RECIOTO DI SOAVE, SOAVE, VALPOLICELLA. Today owned by powerful GRUPPO ITALIANO VINI.

Borgo del Tiglio F VG ★★★→★★★★ Nicola Manferrari is one of Italy's top white winemakers. COLLIO FRIULANO RONCO della Chiesa, Studio di Bianco esp impressive.

Boscarelli, Poderi Tus ★★★ Small estate of Genovese de Ferrari family with reliably high-standard VINO NOBILE DI MONTEPULCIANO, cru Nocio dei Boscarelli and RISERVA.

Botte Big barrel, anything from 6–250 hl, usually between 20–50, traditionally of Slavonian but increasingly of French oak. To traditionalists, the ideal vessel for ageing wines in which an excess of oak aromas is undesirable.

Brachetto d'Acqui / Acqui Pie DOCG r sw (sp) ★★ DYA. Pink version of ASTI, similarly undeserving for most part of its DOCG status, equally popular in Russia.

Braida Pie ★★★ Giacomo Bologna's children, Giuseppe and Raffaella, continue in his footsteps; BARBERA D'ASTI Bricco dell'Uccellone remains top, backed by Bricco della Bigotta and Ai Suma.

Bramaterra Pie DOC r See ALTO PIEMONTE. Gd: Antoniotti Odilio.

Breganze Ven DOC r w sp ★→★★★ (w) DYA (r) 08 09 10 11 13 15 Major production area for PINOT GR, also gd Vespaiolo (white, still and sparkling, sticky TORCOLATO); PINOT N, CAB. Main producers BEATO BARTOLOMEO, MACULAN.

Brezza Pie ★★→★★★ While the rest of the Brezza family run the Hotel BAROLO in the village of that name, Enzo B makes, from 17 ha+, some of Barolo's most authentic and best-value crus, incl Cannubi, Castellero, Sarmassa. Range incl BARBERA, DOLCETTO, Freisa, plus surprisingly gd CHARD.

Brigaldara Ven ★★★ Elegant but powerful benchmark AMARONE from estate of Stefano Cesari. Look for charming Dindarella Rosato.

Brolio, Castello di Tus ★★→★★★ Historic estate, CHIANTI CLASSICO's largest, and

---

Barolo subzones

The concept of "cru" is gaining acceptance although it is not allowed on the label. It is replaced (in BAROLO and BARBARESCO at least) by "geographic mentions" (*Menzioni Geografiche Aggiuntive*), known unofficially as subzones. Currently Barolo has 11 village mentions and 170 additional geographical mentions. Some of best incl (by commune): **Barolo:** Bricco delle Viole, Brunate, Bussia, Cannubi, Cannubi Boschis, Cannubi San Lorenzo, Cannubi Muscatel, Cerequio, Le Coste, Ravera, Sarmassa; **Castiglione Falletto:** Bricco Boschis, Bricco Rocche, Fiasco, Mariondino, Monprivato, Rocche di Castiglione, Vignolo, Villero; **Cherasco:** Mantoetto; **Diano d'Alba:** La VIGNA, Sorano (partly shared with Serralunga); **Grinzane Cavour:** Canova, Castello; **La Morra:** Annunziata, Arborina, Bricco Manzoni, Bricco San Biagio, Brunate, Cerequio, Fossati, La Serra, Rocche dell'Annunziata, Rocchettevino, Roggeri, Roncaglic; **Monforte d'Alba:** Bussia, Ginestra, Gramolere, Mosconi, Perno; **Novello:** Bergera, Ravera; **Roddi:** Bricco Ambrogio; **Serralunga d'Alba:** Baudana, Boscareto, Cerretta, Falletto, Francia, Gabutti, Lazzarito, Marenca, Ornato, Parafada, Prapò, Sorano, Vignarionda; **Verduno:** Massara, Monvigliero.

> **The best of Brunello**
> Any of the below provide a satisfying BRUNELLO DI MONTALCINO, but we
> have put a ★ next to the ones we think are best: Altesino, CASTELLO DI
> Argiano, Baricci★, BIONDI-SANTI★, GIANNI BRUNELLI★, Campogiovanni,
> Canalicchio di Sopra, Canalicchio di Sotto, Caparzo, CASE BASSE★,
> CASTELGIOCONDO, Castiglion del Bosco, Ciacci Piccolomini, COL D'ORCIA,
> Collemattoni, Colombini, Costanti, Cupano, Donatella Cinelli, Eredi
> FULIGNI, Fossacolle, Franco Pacenti, Il Colle, Il Marroneto★, Il Paradiso di
> Manfredi, La Gerla, La Magia, La Poderina, Le Potazzine, Le Ragnaie★,
> LISINI★, Mastrojanni★, PIAN DELL'ORINO★, Pieri Agostina, Pieve di Santa
> Restituta, POGGIO ANTICO, POGGIO DI SOTTO★, San Filippo, Salvioni★, Siro
> Pacenti, Stella di Campalto★, TENUTA IL POGGIONE★, TENUTA di Sesta,
> Uccelliera, Val di Suga.

supposedly oldest, now thriving again under Francesco RICASOLI after foreign-
managed decline. *V.gd* Chianti Classico and CC Colledilà Gran Selezione
(*see* Chianti Classico box, p.135).

Brunelli, Gianni Tus ★★★ Lovely refined user-friendly BRUNELLOS and ROSSOS from
two sites: Le Chiuse di Sotto n of MONTALCINO, and Podernovone to the s, with
spectacular views of Monte Amiata.

Brunello di Montalcino Tus DOCG r ★★★→★★★★ 90' 95 99' 01' 04' 06' 07 09
10' (13) (15') Top wine of TUS, dense but elegant with scent, structure; potentially
v. long-lived. Min 4 yrs ageing, 5 for RISERVA. Misguided moves to allow small
quantities of eg. MERLOT in this supposedly 100% varietal SANGIOVESE have been
fought off, but vigilance needed. (For top producers *see* box, above.)

Bucci Mar ★★★ Quasi-Burgundian VERDICCHIOS, slow to mature but complex with
age, esp RISERVA. Red Pongelli is user-friendly, fruity.

Burlotto, Commendatore GB Pie ★★★→★★★★ Commander GB Burlotto was one
of 1st to make/bottle top BAROLO in 1880. Descendant Fabio Alessandria's best:
crus Cannubi, Monvigliero.

Bussola, Tommaso Ven ★★★★ Self-taught Tommaso Bussola turns out some of
the great AMARONES, RECIOTOS and RIPASSOS of our time. The great Bepi QUINTARELLI
steered him; he steers his two sons.

Cà Bolani F-VG ★ Aquileia estate of 550 ha, n Italy's biggest v'yd, owned by ZONIN
family. High-tech winery. Best: SAUV BL Aquilis; also gd REFOSCO del PR.

Ca' dei Frati Lom ★★★ Foremost quality estate of revitalized DOC LUGANA, I Frati a
fine example at entry level; Brolettino a superior cru.

Ca' del Bosco Lom ★★★★ No 1 FRANCIACORTA estate owned by giant PINOT GR producer
Santa Margherita, still run by volcanic founder Maurizio Zanella. *Outstanding
classico-method fizz*, esp Annamaria Clementi (rosé too); both v. Krug-like. Great
Dosage Zero; excellent B'x-style Maurizio Zanella (r); burgundy-style PINOT N
Pinero; above average CHARD, for Italy that is.

Ca' del Prete Pie ★★→★★★ Small estate produces great Freisa d'ASTI, MALVASIA di
Castelnuovo Don Bosco.

Caiarossa Tus ★★★ Dutch-owned (Châteaux Giscours and du Tertre's Eric Jelgersma;
see B'x) estate, n of BOLGHERI. Excellent Caiarossa Rosso plus reds Pergolaia, Aria.

Caluso / Erbaluce di Caluso Pie DOCG w ★→★★★ Wines can be still, sparkling
(dry wines) and sweet (Caluso PASSITO). Gd producers: Cieck (Misobolo, Brut San
Giorgio); Favaro (Le Chiusure and Passito Sole d'Inverno); Ferrando; Orsolani
(La Rustia).

Ca' Marcanda Tus ★★★★ BOLGHERI estate of Angelo GAJA (founded 1996). Three
wines in order of price (high, higher, highest): Promis, Magari, Ca' Marcanda.
Grapes mainly international.

Campania We tend to think of Naples and Vesuvius, Capri and Ischia, Amalfi and Ravello when we think of Campania, so called because it was the "country" (*campania*) retreat of the Romans. Best wines come from mtns inland. Outstanding red grape AGLIANICO and at least three fascinating whites: FALANGHINA, GRECO, FIANO, all capable of freshness, complexity, character. Prices are not high. Classic DOCS incl Fiano d'Avellino, GRECO DI TUFO, TAURASI, with newer areas emerging, eg. Sannio, Benevento. Gd producers: Benito Ferrara, Caggiano, CANTINA del Taburno, Caputo, Colli di Lapio, D'Ambra, De Angelis, *Feudi di San Gregorio*, GALARDI, LA GUARDIENSE, Luigi Tecce, **Mastroberardino**, Molettieri, MONTEVETRANO, Mustilli, Terredora di Paolo, Trabucco, VILLA MATILDE.

Canalicchio di Sopra Tus ★★★ Dynamic Ripaccioli family make beautifully balanced, complex BRUNELLO (and RISERVA), ROSSO DI MONTALCINO.

Cantina A cellar, winery or even a wine bar.

Cantina del Notaio Bas ★★→★★★ Organic and bio estate specializing in AGLIANICO, incl white, rosé, sparkling and PASSITO. Star is La Firma, but super-ripe, AMARONE-like Il Sigillo almost as gd. Repertorio always bitingly tannic and overrated.

Capezzana, Tenuta di Tus ★★★ Noble TUS family estate of late wine legend Count Ugo Contini Bonacossi, now run by his children. Excellent CARMIGNANO (Villa di Capezzana, Villa di Trefiano) and exceptional VIN SANTO, one of Italy's five best.

Capichera Sar ★★★ Ragnedda family make some of SAR's best whites, noteworthy reds. Outstanding Isola dei Nuraghi Bianco Santigaìni, Vendemmia Tardiva and Vigna'ngena.

Cappellano Pie ★★★ The late Teobaldo Cappellano, a BAROLO hero, devoted part of his cru Gabutti to ungrafted NEBBIOLO (Pie Franco). Son Augusto keeps highly traditional style; also "tonic" Barolo Chinato, invented by an ancestor.

Caprai Umb ★★★→★★★★ Marco Caprai and consultant Attilio Pagli have turned large estate (nearly 200 ha) into MONTEFALCO leader. Many outstanding wines, eg. 25 Anni. Non-cru Collepiano is better for less oak, while ROSSO DI MONTEFALCO is smooth, elegant. GRECHETTO Grecante is reasonably priced.

Carema Pie DOC r ★★→★★★ 06' 07 08 09 10 11 (13) (15) Little known, light, intense, outstanding NEBBIOLO from steep lower Alpine slopes nr Aosta. Best: Luigi Ferrando (esp Etichetta Nera), Produttori Nebbiolo di Carema.

Carignano del Sulcis Sar DOC r p ★★→★★★ 08 09 10 12 13 (14) (15) Mellow but intense red from SAR's sw. Best: Rocca Rubia from CS di SANTADI, *Terre Brune*.

Carmignano Tus DOCG r ★★★ 02 04 06 07 08 09 10 11 12 (13) (15) Fine SANGIOVESE/B'x-grape blend invented in C20 by late Count Bonacossi of CAPEZZANA. Best: Ambra, Capezzana, Farnete, Piaggia, Le Poggiarelle, Pratesi.

Carnasciale, Il Tus ★★★ Exceptional B'x-style red from spontaneous CABERNET x MERLOT cross jealously guarded by Bettina Rogosky and family. "Caberlot" was discovered decades ago by their consultant agronomist Remigio Bordini. Carnasciale is second label.

Carpenè-Malvolti Ven ★★ Antonio Carpene and friends founded this winery in 1868, perhaps 1st to specialize in PROSECCO. Carpene range incl brut, dry and extra dry, though none is all that dry (probably gd thing).

Carpineti, Marco Lat w sw ★★ Phenomenal bio whites from little-known Bellone and Greco Moro, Greco Giallo varieties. Benchmark Caro and Ludum, one of Italy's best stickies.

Cartizze Ven ★★ DOCG PROSECCO from a hilly, difficult-to-work 106 ha in heart of CONEGLIANO VALDOBBIADENE. Often too sweet even though labelled dry. Best: Col Vetoraz; gd: BISOL.

Case Basse Tus ★★★★ Gianfranco Soldera makes mostly bio, long-oak-aged, definitive-quality BRUNELLO-style (if not DOCG) wines as before. Rare, precious.

Castel del Monte Pug DOC r p w ★→★★ (r) 08 09 10 11 (13) (15) (p w) DYA. Dry, fresh, increasingly serious wines of mid-PUG DOC. Gd Pietrabianca and excellent **Bocca di Lupo** from Tormaresca (ANTINORI). V.gd Le More from Santa Lucia. Interesting reds from Cocevola, Giancarlo Ceci. Il Falcone RISERVA is iconic.

Castellare Tus ★★★ Classy Castellina-in-CHIANTI producer of long standing. 1st-rate SANGIOVESE/MALVASIA Nera I Sodi di San Niccoló and updated CHIANTI CLASSICO, esp RISERVA Il Poggiale. Also POGGIO ai Merli (MERLOT), Coniale (CAB SAUV).

Castell' in Villa Tus ★★★ Individual, traditionalist CHIANTI CLASSICO estate in extreme sw of zone. Wines of class, excellence by self-taught Princess Coralia Pignatelli.

Castelluccio E-R ★★→★★★ Quality SANGIOVESE from E-R estate of famous oenologoist Vittorio Fiore, run by son Claudio. IGT RONCO dei Ciliegi and Ronco delle Ginestre are stars. Le More is tasty, relatively inexpensive Romagna DOC.

Castiglion del Bosco Tus ★★★ Ferragamo-owned up-and-coming BRUNELLO producer.

Wild boar in Chianti eat grapes: equivalent of 130,000 bottles of wine/yr.

Cavallotto Pie ★★★ Leading BAROLO traditionalist of Castiglione Falletto, v'yds in heart of zone. Outstanding RISERVA Bricco Boschis VIGNA San Giuseppe, Riserva Vignolo, v.gd LANGHE NEBBIOLO. Surprisingly gd GRIGNOLINO, Freisa too.

Cerasuolo d'Abruzzo Ab DOC p ★ DYA ROSATO version of MONTEPULCIANO D'ABRUZZO, not to be confused with red CERASUOLO DI VITTORIA from SI. Can be brilliant; best (by far) are: Emidio Pepe, Praesidium, Tiberio, VALENTINI.

Cerasuolo di Vittoria Si DOCG r ★★ 10 11 13 (15) Medium-bodied red from Frappato/NERO D'AVOLA in se of island. To date, absurdly, only SI DOCG. Try Arianna Occhipinti, COS, Gulfi, Paolo Calì, PLANETA, Valle dell'Acate.

Ceretto Pie ★★→★★★ Leading BARBARESCO (Asili, Bernradot) producer, BAROLO (Bricco Rocche, Brunate, Prapò), plus LANGHE Bianco Blange (ARNEIS). Older generation Bruno and Marcello handing over to Alessandro, Federico, Roberta, Lisa.

Cerro, Fattoria del Tus ★★★ Estate owned by insurance giant SAI, making v.gd DOCG VINO NOBILE DI MONTEPULCIANO (esp cru Antica Chiusina). SAI also owns Colpetrone (MONTEFALCO SAGRANTINO), La Poderina (BRUNELLO DI MONTALCINO) and 1000-ha n MAREMMA estate of Monterufoli.

Cesanese del Piglio or Piglio Lat DOCG r ★→★★ Medium-bodied red, gd for moderate ageing. Best: Petrucca e Vela, Terre del Cesanese. Cesanese di Olevano Romano, Cesanese di Affile are similar.

Chianti Tus DOCG r ★→★★★ Ancient region between Florence and Siena and its light red. Chianti has come a long way from the raffia-bottle-as-lamp days when it was laced with white grapes and beefed up with imports from the s. Typical TUS wine at a reasonable price.

Chianti Classico Tus DOCG r ★★→★★★ 04 06 07 08 09 10 11 12 13 (15) Historic CHIANTI zone became "CLASSICO" when the Chianti area was extended to most of central TUS in early C20. Covering all or part of nine communes, the land is hilly (altitude 250–500m) and rocky. The "Black Rooster" wine is traditionally blended: the debate continues over whether the support grapes should be French (eg. CAB SAUV) or native. Gran Selezione is new top level, above RISERVA. (*See also* box, right.)

Chiaretto Ven Pale, light-blush-hued rosé (the word means "claret"), produced esp around Lake Garda. *See* BARDOLINO.

Ciabot Berton Pie ★★★ Marco and Paola Oberto, following their father, have turned this La Morra estate into one of the best-value serious producers. Blended BAROLO is convincing, crus Roggeri, Rocchettevino have distinctive single-v'yd character.

Cinque Terre Lig DOC w dr sw ★★ Dry VERMENTINO-based whites from steepest Riviera coast of LIG. Sweet version is called SCIACCHETRÀ. Seek out Arrigoni, Bisson, Buranco and De Battè.

Cirò Cal DOC r (p) (w) ★→★★★ Brisk strong red from Cal's main grape, Gaglioppo, or light, fruity white from GRECO (DYA). Best: Caparra & Siciliani, IPPOLITO, **Librandi** (★★★Duca San Felice), San Francesco (Donna Madda, RONCO dei Quattroventi), SANTA VENERE.

Classico Term for wines from a restricted, usually historic and superior-quality area within limits of a commercially expanded DOC. *See* CHIANTI CLASSICO, VALPOLICELLA, VERDICCHIO, SOAVE, numerous others.

Clerico, Domenico Pie ★★★ Modernist BAROLO producer of Monforte d'ALBA, esp crus Ciabot Mentin Ginestra, Pajana, Percristina. Wines much less oaky than in a wrongly much-heralded past.

Coffele Ven ★★★ Sensitive winemaker in up-and-coming SOAVE-land, blessed with grapes on terraces on the higher slopes, v'yds created by father Bepino. Soave CLASSICO, cru Ca' Visco, RECIOTO Le Sponde all just as they should be.

Col d'Orcia Tus ★★★ Top-quality MONTALCINO estate (the 3rd-largest) owned by Francesco Marone Cinzano. Best wine: BRUNELLO RISERVA POGGIO al Vento.

Colla, Poderi Pie ★★★ Behind this winery is experience of Beppe Colla (soul and creator of PRUNOTTO 1956–90). Classic, traditional, age-worthy. Top: BARBARESCO Roncaglie, BAROLO Bussia Dardi Le Rose, LANGHE Bricco del Drago.

Colli = hills; singular: Colle. **Colline** (singular Collina) = smaller hills. *See also* COLLIO, POGGIO.

Colli di Catone Lat ★→★★★ Top producer of FRASCATI and IGT in the Roman hills of Monteporzio Catone. Outstanding aged whites from MALVASIA del Lazio (aka Malvasia Puntinata) and GRECHETTO. Look for Colle Gaio or Casal Pilozzo labels.

Colli di Lapio Cam ★★★ Clelia Romano's estate is Italy's *best Fiano* producer.

Colli di Luni Lig, Tus DOC r w ★★→★★★ VERMENTINO and Albarola whites; SANGIOVESE-based reds easy to drink, charming. Gd: Ottaviano Lambruschi (Costa Marina); Giacomelli (Boboli), La Baia del Sole (Oro d'Isèe); Bisson (Vigna Erta).

Collio F-VG DOC r w ★★→★★★★ Hilly zone on border with Slovenia. Esp known for complex, sometimes deliberately oxidized whites, some vinified on skins in earthenware vessels/amphorae in ground. Some excellent, some shocking blends from various French, German, Slavic grapes. Numerous gd-to-excellent producers: Aldo Polencic, BORGO DEL TIGLIO, Castello di Spessa, LA CASTELLADA, Fiegl, GRAVNER, Livon, MARCO FELLUGA, Podversic, Primosic, Princic, Radikon, Renato Keber, RUSSIZ SUPERIORE, *Schiopetto*, Tercic, Torpin, Venica & Venica, VILLA RUSSIZ

Colli Piacentini E-R DOC r p w ★→★★ DYA Light gulping wines, often fizzy, from eg. BARBERA, BONARDA (r), MALVASIA, Pignoletto (w), plus various PINOT varieties. Similar to OLTREPÒ PAVESE. Gd producers: Montesissa, Mossi, Romagnoli, Solenghi, La Stoppa, Torre Fornello, La Tosa. *See also* GUTTURNIO.

Colognole Tus ★★ Ex-Conti Spalletti estate making increasingly classy CHIANTI RÙFINA, RISERVA del Don from steep s-facing slopes of Monte Giovi.

Who makes really good Chianti Classico?

CHIANTI CLASSICO is a large zone with hundreds of producers, so picking out the best is tricky. The top get a ★: AMA★, ANTINORI, BADIA A COLTIBUONO★, Bibbiano, BROLIO, Cacchiano, CAFAGGIO, Capannelle, Casaloste, Casa Sola, CASTELLARE, CASTELL' IN VILLA, FELSINA★, FONTERUTOLI, FONTODI★, I Fabbri★, Il Molino di Grace, ISOLE E OLENA★, Le Boncie, Le Cinciole★, Le Corti, Le Filigare, Lilliano, Mannucci Droandi, MONSANTO★, Monte Bernardi, Monteraponi★, NITTARDI, NOZZOLE, Palazzino, Paneretta, Poggerino, Poggiopiano, QUERCIABELLA★, RAMPOLLA, Riecine, Rocca di Castagnoli, Rocca di Montegrossi★, RUFFINO, San Fabiano Calcinaia, SAN FELICE, SAN GIUSTO A RENTENNANO★, Savignola Paolina, Selvole, Vecchie Terre di Montefili, Verrazzano, Vicchiomaggio, VIGNAMAGGIO, Villa Calcinaia★, Villa La Rosa★, Viticcio, VOLPAIA★.

Colterenzio CS / Schreckbichl T-AA ★★ →★★★ Cornaiano-based main player among ALTO ADIGE co-ops. Whites (SAUV Lafoa, CHARD Altkirch, PINOT BIANCO Weisshaus Praedium) tend to be better than reds, despite renown of CAB SAUV Lafoa.

Conegliano Valdobbiadene Ven DOCG w sp ★→★★ DYA. Name for top PROSECCO, daunting to pronounce: may be used separately or together.

Conero DOCG r ★★→★★★ 09 11 12 13 (15) Aka ROSSO CONERO. Small zone making powerful, at times too oaky, MONTEPULCIANO. Try: GAROFOLI (Grosso Agontano), Le Terrazze (Praeludium), Marchetti (RISERVA Villa Bonomi), Moncaro, Monteschiavo (Adeodato), Moroder (Riserva Dorico), UMANI RONCHI (Riserva Campo San Giorgio).

Conterno, Aldo Pie ★★★→★★★★ Top estate of Monforte d'ALBA, was considered a traditionalist, esp concerning top BAROLOS Granbussia, Cicala, Colonello and esp Romirasco. Sons moving winery in more modernist direction.

Conterno, Giacomo Pie ★★★★ For many, estate's top wine, Monfortino, is best wine of Italy. V'yd (Cascina Francia) is in Serralunga while winery is in Monforte. Roberto C, son of late Giovanni (son of Giacomo), sticks religiously to formula of forebears, incl no temperature control in fermentation. Outstanding BARBERAS.

Conterno Fantino Pie ★★★ Two families joined to produce excellent modern-style BAROLO Sorì Ginestra, Mosconi, and VIGNA del Gris at Monforte d'ALBA. Also NEBBIOLO/BARBERA blend Monprà.

Conterno Paolo Pie ★★→★★★ A family of NEBBIOLO and BARBERA growers since 1886, current *titolare* Giorgio continues with textbook cru BAROLOS Ginestra and Riva del Bric, plus particularly fine LANGHE *Nebbiolo Bric Ginestra*.

Contini Sar ★★★ Benchmark producer of VERNACCIA di Oristano, oxidative-styled whites not unlike very gd Amontillado or Oloroso. Antico Gregori one of Italy's best whites.

Conti Zecca Pug ★★→★★★ SALENTO estate with 320 ha, producing almost two million bottles. Donna Marzia line of Salento IGT wines is gd value, as is SALICE SALENTINO Cantalupi. Many wines; best-known is NEGROAMARO/CAB SAUV blend Nero.

Contucci Tus ★★→★★★ Iconic Contucci family winery in centre of Montepulciano town. Going for centuries, style is a little old-fashioned, though classic. Various VINO NOBILES (incl RISERVA and crus Mulinvecchio, Pietra Rossa).

Copertino Pug DOC r (p) ★★★ 08 10 11 (12) (13) (15) Smooth, savoury red of NEGROAMARO from heel of Italy. Gd: CS Copertino, MONACI.

Correggia, Matteo Pie r ★★★ Leading producer of ROERO (RISERVA Rochè d'Ampsej, Val dei Preti), Roero ARNEIS, plus BARBERA D'ALBA (Marun).

CS (Cantina Sociale) Cooperative winery.

Cusumano Si ★★→★★★ Recent major player with 500 ha in various parts of SI. Reds from NERO D'AVOLA, CAB SAUV, SYRAH; whites from CHARD, INSOLIA. Gd quality, value.

Dal Forno, Romano Ven ★★★★ V. high-quality VALPOLICELLA, AMARONE, RECIOTO grower whose perfectionism is more remarkable for fact that his v'yds are outside CLASSICO zone.

De Bartoli, Marco Si ★★★ The late great Marco de Bartoli, scion of two MARSALA houses, fought all his life for "real" Marsala and against cooking or flavoured Marsala. His dry Vecchio Samperi couldn't be called "Marsala" because it wasn't fortified. His masterpiece is 20-yr-old Ventennale, a blend of old and recent wines. His children now in charge. Delicious table wines (eg. *Grillo*), outstanding sweet ZIBIBBO di PANTELLERIA Bukkuram.

Dei Pie ★★→★★★ Pianist Caterina Dei runs this aristocratic estate in MONTEPULCIANO, making VINO NOBILES with artistry and passion. Her *chef d'oeuvre* is Bossona.

Derthona Pie w ★→★★★ Timorasso grapes grown in COLLI Tortonesi. One of Italy's unique whites (like v. dry Ries from Rheinhessen). Gd: Boveri Luigi, Claudio Mariotto, La Colombera, VIGNETI MASSA, Mutti.

Di Majo Norante Mol ★★→★★★ Best known of Mol with decent Biferno Rosso Ramitello, Don Luigi Molise Rosso RISERVA, Mol AGLIANICO Contado. Whites uninteresting; MOSCATO PASSITO Apianae quite gd.

DOC / DOCG Quality wine designation: *see box, p.127.*

Dogliani Pie DOCG r ★→★★★ 10 11 12 13 (15) DOCG from PIE, Dolcetto *in purezza* though they have forbidden mention of grape on label to confuse you. Some to drink young, some for moderate ageing. Gd: Bricco Rosso, Chionetti, Clavesana, EINAUDI, Francesco Boschis, Marziano Abbona, Osvaldo Barbaris, Pecchenino.

Donnafugata Si r w ★★→★★★ Classy range of SI wines incl reds Mille e Una Notte, Tancredi; whites Chiaranda and Ligheia. Also v. fine MOSCATO PASSITO di PANTELLERIA Ben Ryé.

Duca di Salaparuta Si ★★ Once on list of every Italian restaurant abroad with Corvo brand, now owned by Ilva of Saronno. More upscale wines incl Kados (w) from GRILLO grapes and NERO D'AVOLA wines Passo delle Mule, Triskele (Nero d'Avola/MERLOT). Plus old favourite Duca Enrico.

Einaudi, Luigi Pie ★★★ 52-ha estate founded late C19 by ex-president of Italy, in DOGLIANI but with land in BAROLO. Solid Barolos from Cannubi and Terlo Costa Grimaldi v'yds. Top Dogliani (DOLCETTO) from Vigna Tecc.

Elba Tus r w (sp) ★→★★ DYA. Island's white, TREBBIANO/ANSONICA, can be v. drinkable with fish. Dry reds are based on SANGIOVESE. Gd sweet white (MOSCATO) and red (**Aleatico Passito DOCG**). Gd: Acquabona, Sapereta.

Enoteca Wine library; also shop or restaurant with ambitious wine list. There is a national enoteca at the *fortezza* in Siena.

Erbaluce di Caluso (Caluso) DOCG w ★→★★★ Can be still, sparkling (dry wines) and also sweet (Caluso PASSITO). Gd: Cieck (Misobolo, Brut San Giorgio), Favaro (Le Chiusure and Passito Sole d'Inverno), Ferrando, Orsolani (La Rustia).

Esino Mar DOC r w ★→★★★ (r) 08 09 10 11 12 13 (15) Alternative DOC of VERDICCHIO country permits 50% other grapes with Verdicchio for Bianco; 40% with SANGIOVESE/MONTEPULCIANO for Rosso. Best reds from Belisario (Colferraio), Monte Schiavo (Adeodato).

Est! Est!! Est!!! Lat DOC w dr s/sw ★ DYA. Unextraordinary white from Montefiascone, n of Rome. Trades on improbable origin of its name. Best is FALESCO.

Etna Si DOC r p w ★★→★★★ (r) 08 09 10 11 12 13 14 (15) Wine from high-altitude volcanic slopes, currently Italy's hottest. New money brings flurry of planting and some excellent (and some overrated) wines. Burgundian-styled, but based on NERELLO MASCALESE (r) and CARRICANTE (w). For red try: Benanti (Rovittello, Serra della Contessa, I Monovitigni), Calcagno (Arcuria), Cottanera, Girolamo Russo (FEUDO), Graci (Quota 600), I VIGNERI (VINUPETRA), Passopisciaro (Porcaria, Rampante, Sciaranuova, TASCA D'ALMERITA (Tascante), Tenuta delle TERRE NERE (Calderara Sottana, La VIGNA di Don Peppino, Guardiola). For white try: BENANTI (EBS, Pietramarina), Barone di Villagrande (EBS); Fessina (EB, Bianco A' Puddara), I Vigneri (EB, Aurora), Girolamo Russo (EB, Nerina), TERRE NERE (Vigne Niche).

Falchini Tus ★★→★★★ Producer of gd DOCG VERNACCIA DI SAN GIMIGNANO (VIGNA a Solatio and oaked Ab Vinea Doni), top B'x blend **Campora**, SANGIOVESE-based Paretaio. Riccardo Falchini was champion of fine SAN GIMIGNANO, ably succeeded by his half-American children.

Falerno del Massico Cam ★★→★★★ DOC r w ★★ (r) 09 10 11 12 13 (15) Falernum was the Yquem of ancient Rome. Today elegant red from AGLIANICO, fruity dry white from FALANGHINA. Best: Amore Perrotta, Felicia, Moio, Trabucco, VILLA MATILDE.

Fara Pie *See* ALTO PIEMONTE.

Faro Si DOC r ★★★ 06' 08 09 10 11 12 13 14 (15) Intense, harmonious red from

NERELLO MASCALESE and Nerello Cappuccio in hills behind Messina. Salvatore Geraci of Palari most famous, but Bonavita and Cuppari just as gd.

Felluga, Livio F-VG ★★★ Consistently fine FRIULI COLLI ORIENTALI wines, esp blends Terre Alte; *Pinot Gr*, FRIULANO, RIBOLLA GIALLA, PICOLIT (Italy's best?), MERLOT/REFOSCO blend Sossó.

Felluga, Marco F-VG *See* RUSSIZ SUPERIORE.

Felsina Tus ★★★ CHIANTI CLASSICO estate of distinction in se corner of zone: classic RISERVA Rancia and IGT Fontalloro, both 100% SANGIOVESE. Also remarkably gd (for Italy) CHARD, I Sistri. Castello di Farnetella, gd CHIANTI Colli Senesí, in same family.

Fenocchio Giacomo Pie ★★★ Small but outstanding Monforte d'ALBA-based BAROLO cellar. Traditional style, min intervention, ageing in large Slavonian oak BOTTI. Crus: Bussia, Cannubi, Villero.

Ferrara, Benito Cam ★★★ Maybe Italy's best GRECO DI TUFO producer. Talent shows in excellent TAURASI too.

Ferrari T-AA sp ★★→★★★ Trento maker of best METODO CLASSICO wines outside FRANCIACORTA. Giulio Ferrari is top cru. Also gd: CHARD-based Brut RISERVA Lunelli, PINOT N-based Extra Brut Perle' Nero.

Feudi di San Gregorio Cam ★★→★★★ Much-hyped CAM producer, with DOCGS TAURASI Piano di Montevergine, FIANO DI AVELLINO Pietracalda, GRECO DI TUFO Cutizzi. Also IGT reds Serpico (AGLIANICO), Patrimo (MERLOT), whites FALANGHINA, *Campanaro* (Fiano/Greco). *See also* BASILISCO.

Fiano di Avellino Cam DOCG w ★★★ 06' 08 10 12 15 Can be either steely (most typical) or lush. Volcanic soils best. Gd: Cirò Picariello, COLLI di Lapio-Romana Clelio, Mastroberardino, Pietracupa, Vadiaperti, Quintodecimo, Villa Diamante.

Fino, Gianfranco Pug ★★★ Greatest PRIMITIVO, from old, low-yielding bush vines. Outstanding "Es" among Italy's top 20 reds.

Florio Si Historic quality maker of MARSALA. Specialist in Marsala Vergine Secco. For some reason Terre Arse (= burnt lands), its best wine, doesn't do well in the UK.

Folonari Tus ★★→★★★ Ambrogio Folonari and son Giovanni, ex-RUFFINO, have v'yds in TUS and elsewhere. Estates/wines incl *Cabreo* (CHARD and SANGIOVESE/CAB SAUV), NOZZOLE (incl top Cab Sauv Pareto), La Fuga (BRUNELLO DI MONTALCINO), Gracciano Svetoni (VINO NOBILE DI MONTEPULCIANO). Also wines from BOLGHERI, MONTECUCCO, FRIULI COLLI ORIENTALI.

Fongaro Ven Classic-method sparkling Lessini Durello (Durello = grape). High quality, even higher acidity, age-worthy.

Fontana Candida Lat ★★ Biggest producer of once-fashionable FRASCATI. Single-v'yd Santa Teresa much lauded, and that's Frascati's big problem in a nutshell. Part of huge GRUPPO ITALIANO VINI.

Fontanafredda Pie ★★→★★★ Large producer of PIE wines on former royal estates, incl BAROLO Serralunga and Barolo *crus* Lazzarito Mirafiore and La Rosa. Gd LANGHE NEBBIOLO *Mirafiore*. Plus ALBA DOCS, sparklers dry (Contessa Rosa Pas Dosè) and sweet (ASTI).

Fonterutoli Tus ★★★ Historic CHIANTI CLASSICO estate of Mazzei family at Castellina with castle and space-age CANTINA in wild heart of TUS hills. Notable: Castellodi Fonterutoli (once v. dark, oaky CHIANTI CLASSICO, now more drinkable), IGT Siepi (SANGIOVESE/MERLOT). TENUTA di Belguardo in MAREMMA (gd MORELLINO DI SCANSANO) and Zisola in SI under same ownership.

Fontodi Tus ★★★→★★★★ Outstanding estate at Panzano making one of v. best CHIANTI CLASSICOS, also VIGNA del Sorbo (was RISERVA, now Gran Selezione) and memorable all-SANGIOVESE Flacciatello. IGTS PINOT N, SYRAH Case Via among best of these varieties in TUS. Now experimenting with fermentation in ceramic containers, resultant wine called Dino (v. limited production).

Foradori T-AA ★★★ Elizabetta F has been a pioneer for 30 yrs, mainly via great red grape of TRENTINO, **Teroldego**. Now she ferments in *anfora* with reds like Morei, Sgarzon and whites like Nosiola Fontanabianca. Top wine remains TEROLDEGO-based Granato.

Franciacorta Lom DOCG w (p) sp ★★→★★★★ Italy's major zone for top-quality METODO CLASSICO sparkling. Best: Barone Pizzini, Bellavista, **Ca' del Bosco**, Cavalleri, Gatti, Uberti, Villa. V.gd: Contadi Castaldi, Monte Rossa, Ricci Curbastri.

Frascati Lat DOC w dr sw s/sw (sp) ★→★★ DYA. Best-known wine of Roman hills, under constant threat from urban expansion. From MALVASIA di Candia and/or TREBBIANO Toscano, most is disappointingly neutral. Gd stuff is Malvasia del Lazio (aka M Puntinata), low crop makes it uncompetitve. Look for Castel de Paolis, Conte Zandotti, Villa Simone, Santa Teresa from FONTANA CANDIDA or Colle Gaio from COLLI DI CATONE, 100% Malvasia del Lazio though IGT.

Frascole Tus ★★→★★★★ Most n winery of most n CHIANTI RUFINA zone, tucked in foothills of Apennines, small estate run organically by Enrico Lippi, with an eye for typicity. CHIANTI RUFINA is main driver but VIN SANTO simply to die for.

Frescobaldi Tus ★★→★★★★ Ancient noble family, leading CHIANTI RUFINA pioneer at NIPOZZANO estate (look for **Montesodi** ★★★), also BRUNELLO from Castelgiocondo estate in MONTALCINO. Sole owners of LUCE estate (MONTALCINO), ORNELLAIA (BOLGHERI). V'yds also in COLLIO, Maremma, Montespertoli.

Friulano F-VG ★→★★ EU-forced name of what used to be called Tocai Friulano. Fresh, pungent, subtly floral whites, best from COLLIO, COLLI ORIENTALI, ISONZO. Many gd producers: BORGO DEL TIGLIO (oak-aged Ronco della Chiesa), Cantarutti, Dario Raccaro, Doro Princic, Drius, Ermacora, LIVIO FELLUGA, Ronco del Gelso (Toc Bas), Scarbolo, Toros, Vie di Romans (Dole). New name for ex-Tocai from Ven is "Tai".

Friuli Colli Orientali F-VG DOC r w dr sw ★★→★★★★ (Was Colli Orientali del Friuli.) The e hills of F-VG, on Slovenian border. Zone similar to COLLIO but less experimental, making more reds and stickies. Top: Aquila del Torre, Ermacora, Gigante, Iole Grillo, La Busa dla Lofi, La Sclusa, LIVIO FELLUGA, Meroi, Miani, Moschioni, Petrussa, Rodaro, Ronchi di Cialla, Ronco del Gnemiz, VIGNA Petrussa. Sweet from VERDUZZO grapes (called Ramandolo if from specific DOCG zone: Anna Berra best) or Picolit grapes (Aquila del Torre, LIVIO FELLUGA, Marco Sara, Ronchi di Cialla, Vigna Petrussa) can be amazing.

Friuli Grave F-VG DOC r w ★→★★ (r) 10 11 12 13 (15) Previously Grave del Friuli. Largest DOC of F-VG, mostly on plains. Important volumes of underwhelming wines. Exceptions from Borgo Magredo, Di Lenardo, RONCO Cliona, San Simone, Villa Chiopris.

Friuli Isonzo F-VG DOC r w ★★★ Used to be just Isonzo. Gravelly, well aired river plain with many varietals and blends. Stars mostly white, scented, structured: JERMANN's Vintage Tunina; LIS NERIS' Gris, Tal Luc and Lis; Ronco del Gelso's MALVASIA, PINOT GRIGIO (Sot lis rivis) and FRIULANO (Toc Bas); VIE DI ROMANS' Flors di Uis and Dessimis. Gd: Borgo Conventi, Pierpaolo Pecorari.

Friuli-Venezia Giulia F-VG Ne region of Italy. Wine-wise best in the hills on Slovenian border rather than on alluvial plains to the w. DOCS like ISONZO, COLLI ORIENTALI, Latisana, Aquileia all now preceded on label by "Friuli", only COLLIO, theoretically the best, retaining its old name. Some gd reds, but home to Italy's best whites, along with ALTO ADIGE.

Frizzante Semi-sparkling, up to 2.5 atmospheres, eg. MOSCATO D'ASTI, much PROSECCO, LAMBRUSCO and the like; nw Italy home to large numbers of lightly fizzing wines that never seem to make it out into wide world. It's world's loss.

Fucci, Elena Bas ★★★ AGLIANICO DEL VULTURE Titolo made from 55–70-yr-old vines in Mt Vulture's one true "Grand Cru"; one of Italy's 20 best wines. Seek out 08 11 13.

Fuligni Tus ★★★→★★★★ Outstanding producer of BRUNELLO, ROSSO DI MONTALCINO.

Gaja Pie ★★★★ Old family firm at BARBARESCO led by Angelo Gaja, apostle of top-end Italian wine; daughter Gaia G following. High quality, higher prices. Barbaresco remains DOCG, other previously 100% NEBBIOLO wines Costa Russi, Sorì San Lorenzo, Sorì Tildin, plus BAROLO Sperss having been declassed to LANGHE DOC, but now going, not surprisingly, back to Barbaresco and Barolo. Splendid CHARD (Gaia e Rey). Also owns CA' MARCANDA in BOLGHERI, Pieve di Santa Restituta in MONTALCINO.

Galardi Cam ★★★ Producer of Terra di Lavoro, much-awarded AGLIANICO/Piedirosso blend, in n CAM. Makes only one wine.

Garda Ven DOC r p w ★→★★ (r) 10 11 12 13 15 (p w) DYA. Catch-all DOC for early-drinking wines of various colours from provinces of Verona in Ven, Brescia and Mantua in Lom. Gd: Cavalchina, Zeni.

Garofoli Mar ★★→★★★ Quality leader in the Mar, specialist in VERDICCHIO (Macrina, Podium, Serra Fiorese), CONERO (Grosso Agontano, Piancarda).

Gattinara Pie DOCG r ★★→★★★ 04' 06 07 08 09 10 11 12 (13) (15) Best-known of a cluster of ALTO PIE DOC(G)s based on NEBBIOLO. Volcanic soil. Suitable for long ageing. Best: Antoniolo (Osso San Grato, San Francesco), Bianchi, Larretti Paride, Nervi, Torraccia del Piantavigna, Travaglini (RISERVA and Tre Vigne). *See also* ALTO PIEMONTE.

Gavi / Cortese di Gavi Pie DOCG w ★→★★★ DYA. At best, subtle dry white of Cortese grapes, though much is dull, simple or sharp. Most comes from commune of Gavi, hence Gavi di Gavi, now prosaically known as Gavi del Comune di Gavi. Best: Bruno Broglia/La Meirana, Castellari Bergaglio (Rovereto Vignavecchia and Rolona, Fornaci v.gd Gavi di Tassarolo), Castello di Tassarolo, Chiarlo (Rovereto), Franco Martinetti, La Giustiniana, La Raia, La Toledana, Tenuta San Pietro, Villa Sparina.

Germano, Ettore Pie ★★★ Small family Serralunga estate run by Sergio and wife Elena. Top BAROLOS: RISERVA Lazzarito and Cerretta. V.gd: LANGHE RIES Herzù and ALTA LANGA.

Ghemme Pie DOCG r *See* ALTO PIEMONTE. NEBBIOLO (at least 85%), incl up to 15% Uva Rara and/or Vespolina. Gd: Antichi Vigneti di Cantalupo (Collis Braclemae), Ioppa (Balsina), Torraccia del Piantavigna (VIGNA Pelizzane).

Giacosa, Bruno Pie ★★★→★★★★ Arguably Italy's greatest winemaker, crafting splendid traditional-style BARBARESCOS (Asili), BAROLOS (Falletto, Rocche del Falletto). Top wines (ie. RISERVAS) get famous red label. Range of fine reds (BARBERA, Dolcetto, NEBBIOLO), whites (ARNEIS), amazing METODO CLASSICO Brut.

Grappa Pungent spirit made from grape pomace (skins, etc., after pressing), can be anything from disgusting to inspirational. What the French call "marc".

Grasso, Elio Pie ★★★→★★★★ Top BAROLO producer (crus Gavarini VIGNA Chiniera, Ginestra Casa Maté); v.gd BARBERA D'ALBA Vigna Martina, DOLCETTO d'Alba. Son Gianluca now effectively taken over from dad Elio.

Gravner, Josko F-VG ★★★→★★★★ Controversial but talented COLLIO producer (unlike some who copy him), vinifies on skins (r w) in buried amphorae without temperature control; long ageing, bottling without filtration. Wines either loved for complexity or loathed for oxidation and phenolic components. Look out for Breg (white blend) and RIBOLLA GIALLA 2006 for something different.

Greco di Tufo Cam DOCG w (sp) ★★→★★★ DYA is one of Italy's most famous wines; better versions are among Italy's best whites: citrus with hints of orange peel, at best age-worthy. V.gd examples from Benito Ferrara (VIGNA Cicogna), Di Prisco, FEUDI DI SAN GREGORIO (Cutizzi), Macchialupa, *Mastroberadino* (Nova Serra, Vignadangelo), Pietracupa, Quintodecimo (Giallo d'Arles), Vadiaperti (Tornante).

Grignolino Pie DOC r ★★→★★★ DYA Two DOCS: Grignolino d'ASTI, Grignolino del Monferrato Casalese. At best, light, perfumed, crisp, high in acidity, tannin. D'Asti: try Braida, Cascina Tavijin, Crivelli, Incisa della Rocchetta, Spertino. Monferrato C: try Accornero (Bricco del Bosco "fresh" version, Bricco del Bosco Vigne Vecchie "historical" version – vinified like BAROLO), Bricco Mondalino, Canato (Celio), Il Mongetto, Pio Cesare.

Gruppo Italiano Vini (GIV) Complex of co-ops and wineries, biggest v'yd holders in Italy. Estates incl: Bigi, BOLLA, Ca'Bianca, Conti Serristori, FONTANA CANDIDA, Lamberti, Macchiavelli, MELINI, Negri, Santi, Vignaioli di San Floriano. Also expanded into S: SI, Bas.

Guardiense, La Cam ★★→★★★ Dynamic co-op, 1,000+ grower-members, 2,000 ha, outstanding-value whites (FALANGHINA Senete, FIANO COLLI di Tilio, GRECO Pietralata) and reds (esp I Mille per l'AGLIANICO); technical direction by Riccardo Cotarella. World's largest producer of Falanghina.

Guerrieri Rizzardi ★★→★★★ Long-est aristocratic producers of wines of Verona, esp of Veronese GARDA. Gd BARDOLINO CLASSICO Tacchetto, elegant AMARONE Villa Rizzardi and cru Calcarole; ROSATO Rosa Rosae. V.gd SUAVE Classico Costeggiola.

Gulfi Si ★★★ SI's best producer of NERO D'AVOLA, 1st to bottle single-*contrada* (cru) wines. Outstanding: Nerobufaleffj and Nerosanlorè. Gd: Cerasuolo di Vittoria Classico, Nerobaronj.

Gutturnio dei Colli Piacentini E-R DOC r dr ★→★★ DYA. BARBERA/BONARDA blend from the COLLI PIACENTINI; sometimes frothing. Producers: Castelli del Duca, La Pergola, La Stoppa, La Tosa.

Haas, Franz T-AA ★★★ ALTO ADIGE producer of excellence and occasional inspiration; v.gd PINOT N, LAGREIN (Schweizer), IGT blends, esp Manna (w).

Hofstätter T-AA ★★★ Top-quality producer; gd PINOT N. Look for Barthenau VIGNA Sant'Urbano. Also South Tyrol whites, mainly GEWURZ (esp Kolbhof, one of Italy's two best).

Alba's white truffle market held every wkd in season, Oct/Nov. Take chequebook.

IGT (Indicazione Geografica Tipica) Increasingly known as *Indicazione Geografica Protetta* (IGP). *See* box, p.127.

Ippolito 1845 Cal ★→★★ Still going strong after over 1.5 centuries, this CIRÒ Marina-based winery claims to be oldest in Cal. Run quasi-organically, international and indigenous grapes. Top: Cirò RISERVA COLLI del Mancuso, Pecorello Bianco.

Ischia Cam DOC (r) w ★→★★ DYA. Island off Naples, own grape varieties (w: Biancolella, Forastera; r: Piedirosso, also found in CAM). Frassitelli v'yd best for Biancolella. Best: D'Ambra (Biancolella Frassitelli, Forastera). V.gd: Antonio Mazzella (VIGNA del Lume).

Isole e Olena Tus ★★★→★★★★ Top CHIANTI CLASSICO estate run by astute Paolo de Marchi, with superb red IGT Cepparello. Outstanding VIN SANTO; v.gd CAB SAUV, CHARD, SYRAH. Also owns Proprietà SPERINO in LESSONA.

Jermann, Silvio F-VG ★★→★★★ Famous estate with v'yds in COLLIO and ISONZO: top white blend Vintage Tunina, v.gd Vinnae (mainly RIBOLLA GIALLA), CHARD ex-Dreams.

Lacrima di Morro d'Alba Mar DYA. Curiously named rose-scented MUSCATty light red from small commune in the Mar, no connection with ALBA or La Morra (PIE). Gd: Luigi Giusti (Luigino Vecchie Vigne), Mario Lucchetti (SUPERIORE Guardengo), Marotti Campi (Superiore Orgiolo and Rubico), Stefano Mancinelli (Superiore, Sensazioni di Frutto). For PASSITO: Lucchetti, Stefano Mancinelli (Re Sole), Vicari (Amaranto del Pozzo Buono).

Lacryma (or Lacrima) Christi del Vesuvio Cam r p w dr (sw) (sp) ★→★★ DOC Vesuvio wines based on Coda di Volpe (w), Piedirosso (r). Despite romantic name

Vesuvius comes nowhere nr ETNA in quality stakes. Sorrentino and De Angelis best; Caputo, MASTROBERARDINO, Terredora less inspired.

Lageder, Alois T-AA ★★→★★★ Top ALTO ADIGE producer. Most exciting wines are single-v'yd varietals: *Sauv Bl Lehenhof*, PINOT GR Benefizium Porer, CHARD Löwengang, GEWURZ Am Sand, PINOT N Krafuss, LAGREIN Lindenberg, CAB SAUV Cor Römigberg. Also owns Cason Hirschprunn for v.gd IGT blends.

Lago di Corbara Umb r ★★ 10 11 12 13 (15) Relatively recent DOC for quality reds of the ORVIETO area. Best from Barberani (Villa Monticelli), Decugnano dei Barbi (Il).

Lagrein Alto Adige T-AA DOC r p ★★→★★★ 06 07 08 09 11 12 13 (15) Alpine red with deep colour, rich palate (plus a bitter hit at back); refreshing pink *Kretzer*, *rosé* made with Lagrein. Top Alto Adige: CS Andriano, CANTINA Santa Maddalena, Gojer, Ignaz Niedrist, Josephus Mayr, LAGEDER, MURI GRIES (cru Abtei), Niedermayr, Plattner. From TRENTINO try Francesco Moser's Deamater.

Lambrusco E-R DOC (or not) r p w dr s/sw ★→★★ DYA. Once v. popular fizzy red from nr Modena, mainly in industrial, semi-sweet, non-DOC version. The real thing is dry, acidic, fresh, lively and *combines magically with rich* E-R fare. DOCs: L Grasparossa di Castelvetro, L Salamino di Santa Croce, L di Sorbara. Best: [Sorbara] Cavicchioli (VIGNA del Cristo Secco and Vigna del Cristo Rose), Cleto Chiarli (Antica Modena Premium), Paltrinieri (FRIZZANTE Etichetta Bianca Fermentazione Naturale and Leclisse). Grasparossa: Cleto Chiarli (Vigneto Enrico Cialdini), Fattoria Moretto (Monovitigno and Vigna Canova), TENUTA Pederzana (Canto Libero Semi Secco), Vittorio Graziano (Fontana dei Boschi). Maestri: Cantine Ceci (Nero di Lambrusco Otello), Dall'Asta (Mefistofele). Salamino: Cavicchioli (Tre Medaglie Semi Secco), Luciano Saetti (Vigneto Saetti), Medici Ermete (Concerto Grancconcerto).

Langhe Pie The hills of central PIE, home of BAROLO, BARBARESCO, etc. DOC name for several Pie varietals plus blends Bianco and Rosso. Those wishing to blend other grapes with their NEBBIOLO (ie. GAJA), can at up to 15% as "Langhe Nebbiolo".

Le Piane Pie ★★★ BOCA DOC has resurfaced thanks to Christoph Kunzli. Gd: Piane (Croatina).

Les Cretes VdA ★★★ Costantino Charrère is father of modern VALLE D'AOSTA viticulture and saved many forgotten varieties. Outstanding Petite ARVINE, two of Italy's best CHARDS; v.gd Fumin.

Lessona Pie DOCG r *See* ALTO PIEMONTE. NEBBIOLO (at least 85%). Elegant, age-worthy, fine bouquet, long savoury taste. Best: Proprietà SPERINO (*see also* ISOLE E OLENA). Gd: Colombera & Garella, Tenute Sella, La Prevostura.

Librandi Cal ★★★ Top producer pioneering research into Cal varieties. V.gd red CIRÒ (*Riserva Duca San Felice* is ★★★), IGT Gravello (CAB SAUV/Gaglioppo blend), Magno Megonio (r) from Magliocco grape, IGT Efeso (w) from Mantonico.

Liguria Lig ★→★★ Steep, rocky Italian riviera: most wines sell to sun-struck tourists at fat profits, so don't travel much. Main grapes: VERMENTINO (w) – best producer is Lambruschi – and DOLCETTO (r), but don't miss CINQUE TERRE'S SCIACCHETRÀ or red Ormeasco di Pornassio.

Lisini Tus ★★★→★★★★ Historic estate for some of the finest and longest-lasting BRUNELLO, esp RISERVA Ugolaia.

Lis Neris F-VG ★★★ Top ISONZO estate for whites, esp PINOT GR (Gris), SAUV BL (Picol), FRIULANO (Fiore di Campo), plus outstanding blends Confini and Lis. V.gd Lis Neris Rosso (MERLOT/CAB SAUV), sweet white Tal Luc (VERDUZZO/RIES).

Locorotondo Pug DOC w (sp) ★ DYA Thirst-quencher dry white from Verdeca and Bianco d'Alessano grapes.

Luce Tus ★★★ FRESCOBALDI now sole owner (bought out original partner Mondavi). SANGIOVESE/MERLOT blend for oligarchs, but lovely Luce BRUNELLO DI MONTALCINO too.

Lugana DOC w (sp) ★★→★★★ DYA. Much-improved white of s Lake Garda, main grape TREBBIANO di Lugana. Best: CA DEI FRATI (I Frati, esp Brolettino), Ottella (Brut, Le Crete), ZENATO (oaked), Fratelli Zeni, Le Morette (owned by Valerio ZENATO). For Trebbiano di SOAVE, try: Suavia (Massi Fitti).

Lungarotti Umb ★★★ Leading producer of TORGIANO, with cellars, hotel and museum, nr Perugia. Star wines DOC Rubesco, DOCG RISERVA **Monticchio**. Gd IGT Sangiorgio (SANGIOVESE/CAB SAUV), Aurente (CHARD) and Giubilante. Gd MONTEFALCO SAGRANTINO.

Macchiole, Le Tus ★★★ One of few native-owned wineries of BOLGHERI; one of 1st to emerge after SASSICAIA. Cinzia Merli, with oenologist Luca d'Attoma, makes Italy's best CAB FR (Paleo Rosso), one of best MERLOTS (Messorio), SYRAHS (Scrio).

Maculan Ven ★★★ Quality pioneer of Ven, Fausto Maculan continues to make excellent CAB SAUV (Fratta, Palazzotto). Perhaps best-known for sweet TORCOLATO (esp RISERVA Acininobili).

Malvasia delle Lipari Si DOC w sw ★★★ Luscious sweet wine, made with one of the many MALVASIA varieties.

Mamete Prevostini Lom ★★ →★★★ Relatively new producer of VALTELLINA. Pure varietal (NEBBIOLO) DOCG wines of class mainly from Sassella SUPERIORE but also Inferno, Grumello Superiore. Two *fine Sforzatos*.

Manduria (Primitivo di) Pug DOC r s/sw ★★→★★★ Manduria is the spiritual home of PRIMITIVO, alias ZIN, so expect wines that are gutsy, alcoholic, sometimes porty to go with full-flavoured fare. Gd producers, located in Manduria or not: Cantele, CS Manduria, de Castris, Gianfranco Fino, Polvanera, Racemi.

Marcato Ven New owner Gianni Tessari likely to improve already v.gd Lessini Durello sparklers and Durella PASSITO stickie.

Marchesi di Barolo Pie ★★ Large, historic BAROLO producer, making crus Cannubi and Sarmassa, plus other ALBA wines. Favours enlargement of famous Cannubi cru to incl other Cannubi areas: C. Boschis, C. Muscatel, C. San Lorenzo, C. Valletta.

Maremma The fashionable coastal area of s TUS, largely recovered from malarial marshland in early C20. DOC(G)S: MONTEREGIO, MORELLINO DI SCANSANO, PARRINA, Pitigliano, SOVANA (Grosseto) Maremma Toscana IGT, more recently Maremma Toscana DOC.

Marrone, Agricola Pie ★★ →★★★ Small estate, low price but gd-quality BAROLO. Gd: ARNEIS, BARBERA D'ALBA, Pichemej.

Marsala Si DOC w sw si's once-famous fortified (★→★★★), created by Woodhouse Bros of Liverpool in 1773. Downgraded in C20 to cooking wine (no longer qualifies for DOC). Can be dry to v. sweet; best is bone-dry Marsala Vergine, potentially a useful, if hardly fashionable, apéritif. *See also* DE BARTOLI.

Marzemino Trentino T-AA DOC r ★→★★ 12 13 (15) Pleasant everyday red: sour red berries, violets, fresh herbs, high acid, mid-weight. Isera and Ziresi are subzones. Best: Riccardo Battistotti, Conti Bossi Fredrigotti, Bruno Grigoletti, Eugenio Rosi (Poiema). Gd: De Tarczal, Enrico Spagnolli, Letrari, Longariva, Vallarom, VallisAgri (VIGNA Fornas), Vilar.

Mascarello Pie The name of two top producers of BAROLO: the late Bartolo M, of Barolo, whose daughter Maria Teresa continues her father's highly traditional path; and Giuseppe M, of Monchiero, whose son Mauro makes v. fine, traditional-style Barolo from the great **Monprivato** v'yd in Castiglione Falletto. Both are deservedly iconic.

Masi Ven ★★→★★★ Archetypal yet innovative producer of the wines of Verona, led by inspirational Sandro Boscaini. VALPOLICELLA, AMARONE, RECIOTO, SOAVE, etc., incl fine Rosso Veronese **Campo Fiorin**. Also makes Amarone-style wines in F-VG and Argentina. V.gd barrel-aged red IGT Toar, from CORVINA and Oseleta grapes, also Osar (Oseleta). Top Amarones Costasera, Campolongo di Torbe. New F-VG Moxxé fizz from PINOT GRIGIO/partly dried VERDUZZO.

Massa, Vigneti Pie ★★★ Walter Massa brought Timorasso (w) grape back from nr-extinction. Coste del Vento, Montecitorio, Sterpi outstanding examples. Gd: BARBERA Bigolla.

Massolino Vigna Rionda Pie ★★★ One of finest BAROLO estates in Serralunga. Excellent Parafada, Margheria have firm structure, fruity drinkability; long-ageing VIGNA Rionda best.

Mastroberardino Cam ★★★ Historic producer of mountainous Avellino province in CAM, quality torch-bearer for Italy's s during dark yrs of mid-C20. Top *Taurasi* (look for Historia Naturalis, Radici), also FIANO DI AVELLINO More Maiorum, GRECO DI TUFO Nova Serra. Antonio M essentially saved Fiano (if not Greco too) from extinction.

Melini Tus ★★ Major producer of CHIANTI CLASSICO at Poggibonsi, part of GIV. Gd quality/price, esp Chianti Classico Selvanella and RISERVAS La Selvanella and Masovecchio.

Metodo classico or tradizionale Italian for "Champagne method".

Mezzacorona T-AA ★→★★ Massive TRENTINO co-op in commune of Mezzocorona (sic) with wide range of gd technical wines, esp TEROLDEGO ROTALIANO Nos and METODO CLASSICO Rotari.

Monaci Pug r p ★★→★★★ Estate owned by family of Severino Garofano, leading oenologist in SALENTO. Characterful NEGROAMARO red (Eloquenzia, I Censi, late-picked Le Braci) and ROSATO (Girofle), also Uva di Troia (Sine Pari) and AGLIANICO (Sine Die).

Monferrato Pie DOC r p w sw ★→★★ Hills between River Po and Apennines. Some of Italy's most delicious and fairly priced wines from typical local grapes BARBERA, Freisa, GRIGNOLINO, MALVASIA di Casorzo and Malvasia di Schierano, Ruché.

Monica di Sardegna Sar DOC r ★→★★ DYA. Lightish quaffing wine from SAR. Same grape also DOC in Cagliari. Best: Argiolas (Iselis), CANTINA SANTADI (Antigua), Contini, Dettori (Chimbanta), Ferruccio Deiana (Karel), Josto Puddu (Torremora).

Monsanto Tus ★★★ Esteemed CHIANTI CLASSICO estate, esp for Il Poggio RISERVA (1st single-v'yd Chianti Classico), Chianti Classico Riserva, IGTS Fabrizio Bianchi (CHARD), Nemo (CAB SAUV).

Montagnetta, La Pie ★★→★★★ Arguably Italy's best producer of many different Freisas. V.gd: Freisa D'ASTI SUPERIORE Bugianen.

Montalcino Tus Small, exquisite hilltop town in province of Siena, famous for concentrated, expensive BRUNELLO and more approachable, better-value ROSSO DI MONTALCINO, both still 100% SANGIOVESE despite occasional efforts by big boys to squeeze a bit of MERLOT into the Rosso.

Montecarlo Tus DOC r w ★★ (w) DYA. White, and increasingly red, wine area nr Lucca. Producers: Buonamico, Carmignani, Fattoria del Teso, La Torre, Montechiari.

Monte Carrubo Si r ★★★ Pioneer Peter Vinding-Diers planted SYRAH on a former volcano s of Etna. Exciting, complex results.

Montecucco Tus SANGIOVESE-based TUS DOC between Monte Amiata and Grosseto, increasingly trendy as MONTALCINO land prices ineluctably rise. As Montecucco Sangiovese it is DOCG. Look for CASTELLO DI POTENTINO (Sacromonte, Piropo), also Begnardi, Ciacci Piccolomini, Colli Massari, Fattoria di Montecucco, Villa Patrizia.

Montefalco Sagrantino Umb DOCG r dr (sw) ★★★→★★★★ Super-tannic, powerful, long-lasting wines, potentially great but difficult to tame the phenolics without denaturing the wine. Traditional bittersweet PASSITO version may be better suited to grape, though harder to sell. Gd: Adanti, Antano Milziade, Antonelli, Benincasa, CAPRAI, Colpetrone, LUNGAROTTI, Paolo Bea, Scacciadiavoli, Tabarrini, Terre de' Trinci.

Montepulciano d'Abruzzo Ab DOC r p ★★→★★★ (r) 10 11 12 13 (15) 1st all-region DOC of Italy. Subdenomination: Colline Teramane (now DOCG), wines often tough, charmless despite hype, and Controguerra (DOC), usually more balanced. Reds can be either light, easy-going or structured, rich. Look for Cataldi Madonna (Toni, lighter Malandrino), Emidio Pepe, Marina Cvetic (S. Martino Rosso), Tiberio, Torre dei Beati (Cocciapazza, Mazzamurello), VALENTINI (best, age-worthy), Zaccagnini. For Cerasuolo d'Abruzzo: Cataldi Madonna (Pie delle Vigne), Emidio Pepe, Tiberio, Praesidium, Valentini.

Monte Schiavo Mar ★★→★★★ Switched-on, medium-size producer of VERDICCHIO, MONTEPULCIANO-based wines of various qualities, gd to excellent. Owned by world's largest manufacturer of olive-oil processing equipment, Pieralisi.

Montevertine Tus ★★★★ Radda estate. Non-DOCG but classic CHIANTI-style wines. IGT *Le Pergole Torte* a fine, world-class example of pure, long-ageing SANGIOVESE. The great "Maestro Assaggiatore" (Master Taster), Giulio Gambelli, was consultant oenologist here for decades.

Montevetrano Cam ★★★ Iconic CAM *azienda*, owned by Silvia Imparato, consultant Riccardo Cotarella. Superb IGT Montevetrano (AGLIANICO, CAB SAUV, MERLOT).

Morella Pug ★★★ Gaetano Morella and wife Lisa Gilbee make outstanding PRIMITIVO (Old Vines and La Signora) from c.90-yr-old vines.

Morellino di Scansano Tus DOCG r ★→★★★ 10 11 13 (15) SANGIOVESE red from MAREMMA. Used to be relatively light, simple, now, sometimes regrettably, gaining weight, substance, perhaps to justify its lofty DOCG status. Best: Le Pupille, Mantellassi, MORIS FARMS, PODERE 414, POGGIO Argentiera, Terre di Talamo, *Vignaioli del Morellino di Scansano* (co-op).

Moris Farms Tus ★★★ One of 1st new-age producers of TUS'S MAREMMA, with MONTEREGIO and *Morellino di Scansano* DOCS, plus VERMENTINO IGT. Top cru is now iconic IGT Avvoltore, a rich SANGIOVESE/CAB SAUV/SYRAH blend. But do *try basic Morellino*.

Moscato d'Asti Pie DOCG w sw sp ★★→★★★ DYA Similar to DOCG ASTI, but usually better grapes; lower alc, lower pressure, sweeter, fruitier, often from small producers. Best DOCG MOSCATO: L'Armangia, Bera, *Braida*, Ca' d'Gal, Cascina Fonda, Caudrina, Elio Perrone, Forteto della Luja, Il Falchetto, Icardi, Isolabella, La Morandina, Marchesi di Grésy, Marino, Mauro Negri, Marino, Rivetti, Saracco, Scagliola, *Vajra*, VIETTI, Vignaioli di Sante Stefano.

Muri Gries T-AA ★★→★★★ This monastery, in Bolzano suburb of Gries, is a traditional and still top producer of LAGREIN ALTO ADIGE DOC. Esp cru Abtei-Muri.

Nals Margreid T-AA ★★→★★★ Small quality co-op making mtn-fresh whites (esp PINOT BIANCO Sirmian), from two separate communes of ALTO ADIGE. Harald Schrafft is an inspired winemaker, despite his apparent youth.

Nebbiolo d'Alba Pie DOC r dr ★★→★★★ 10 11 12 13 (14) (15) Sometimes a worthy replacement for BAROLO/BARBARESCO, though it comes from a distinct area between the two and may not be used as a declassification from top DOCGS. Gd: BRUNO GIACOSA (Valmaggiore), Fratelli Giacosa, BREZZA (VIGNA Santa Rosalia), PAITIN, SANDRONE LUCIANO (Valmaggiore).

Nebbiolo Langhe Pie ★★ Like the above but from a wider area: LANGHE hills. Unlike NEBBIOLO D'ALBA may be used as a downgrade from BAROLO or BARBARESCO. Gd: BURLOTTO, GIUSEPPE RINALDI, PIO CESARE, VAJRA. *See also* GAJA.

Negrar, Cantina Ven ★★→★★★ Aka CS VALPOLICELLA. Major producer of high-quality Valpolicella, RIPASSO, AMARONE; grapes from various parts of CLASSICO zone. Look for brand name Domini Veneti.

ITALY

Nino Franco Ven ★★★ →★★★★ Winery of Primo Franco, named after his grandfather. Among v. finest PROSECCOS: Primo Franco Dry, Rive di San Floriano Brut. Excellent CARTIZZE, *delicious basic Prosecco di Valdobbiadene Brut.*

Nipozzano, Castello di Tus ★★★ FRESCOBALDI estate in RÚFINA, e of Florence, making excellent CHIANTI Rúfina RISERVAS (esp Vecchie Viti) Nipozzano and **Montesodi**.

Nittardi Tus ★★→★★★ Reliable source of quality modern CHIANTI CLASSICO. German proprietor Peter Femfert; oenologist Carlo Ferrini.

Nozzole Tus ★★→★★★ Famous estate in heart of CHIANTI CLASSICO, n of Greve, owned by Ambrogio and Giovanni FOLONARI. V.gd Chianti Classico Nozzole, excellent CAB SAUV Pareto.

Nuragus di Cagliari Sar DOC w ★★ DYA. Lively, uncomplicated SAR wine from Nuragus grape, finally gaining visibility.

Occhio di Pernice Tus "Partridge's eye". A type of VIN SANTO made predominantly from black grapes, mainly SANGIOVESE. *Avignonesi's is definitive.* Also an obscure black variety found in RÚFINA and elsewhere.

Oddero Pie ★★★ Traditionalist La Morra estate for excellent BAROLO (Brunate, Villero, VIGNA Rionda RISERVA), BARBARESCO (Gallina) crus, plus other serious PIE wines.

Oltrepò Pavese Lom DOC r w dr sw sp ★ →★★★ Multi-DOC, incl numerous varietal and blended wines from Pavia province; best is SPUMANTE. Gd growers: Anteo, Barbacarlo, CS Casteggio, Frecciarossa, Le Fracce, Monsupello, Mazzolino, Ruizde Cardenas, Travaglino; La Versa co-op.

Ornellaia Tus ★★→★★★★★ 04 06' 08 10 11 12 13 (15) Fashionable estate nr BOLGHERI founded by Lodovico ANTINORI, now owned by FRESCOBALDI. Top wines of B'x grapes/method: Bolgheri DOC Ornellaia, IGT Masseto (MERLOT). Gd: Bolgheri DOC Le Serre Nuove, IGT Le Volte; new Bianco SAUV BL/VIOGNIER.

Orsi Vigneto San Vito E-R ★★ Property in COLLI Bolognesi run by dynamic young producer, Federico Orsi. Speciality is sparkling Pignoletto *sui lieviti* (on the yeasts): second fermentation in the bottle, no disgorgement. Also experimenting with Georgian *qvevri* (clay jars).

Orvieto Umb DOC w dr sw s/sw ★→★★★ DYA Classic Umb white, blend of mainly Procanico (TREBBIANO)/GRECHETTO. *Secco* most popular today. Top: BARBERANI Castagneto, Luigi e Giovanna; *amabile* more traditional. Sweet versions from noble-rot (*muffa nobile*) grapes can be superb, eg. Barberani Calcaia. Other gd: Bigi, Cardeto, **Castello della Sala**, Decugnano dei Barbi, La Carraia, Palazzone.

Pacenti, Siro Tus ★★★ Modern-style BRUNELLO, ROSSO DI MONTALCINO from small, caring producer.

Paitin Pie ★★→★★★ Pasquero-Elia family have been bottling BARBARESCO since C19. Used to be intensely authentic, had a flutter with modernism (new barriques); today back on track making "real" Barbaresco in large barrels. Sorì Paitin is star.

Paltrinieri ★★ Specialist in LAMBRUSCO di Sorbara, Alberto Paltrinieri runs this 15-ha family estate as if end product were Vintage Champagne. Various bottlings: pale in colour, lively acidity, sparkle, ripe fruit, *v. much the real thing*, million miles from sweet industrial gloop of yore.

Pantelleria Si Windswept, black-(volcanic) earth SI island off Tunisian coast, famous for superb MOSCATO d'Alessandria stickies. PASSITO versions particularly dense/ intense. Look for DE BARTOLI (Bukkuram), DONNAFUGATA (Ben Ryé), Ferrandes.

Parrina, La Tus ★★ Sizeable estate on TUS coast dominates DOC Parrina; French and indigenous grapes, solid rather than inspired wines.

Passito Tus, Ven One of Italy's most ancient and most characteristic wine styles, from grapes hung up, or spread on trays to dry, briefly under harvest sun (in s) or over a period of weeks or mths in airy attics of winery – a process called *appassimento*. Best-known versions: VIN SANTO (TUS); AMARONE/RECIOTO (Ven), VALPOLICELLA/SOAVE. *See also* MONTEFALCO, ORVIETO, TORCOLATO, VALLONE.

Pian dell'Orino ★★★ Caroline Pobitzer and Jan Erbach run this small MONTALCINO estate as committed biodynamicists. BRUNELLO seductive, technically perfect, Rosso nearly as gd. Many epic wines.

Piave Ven DOC r w ★→★★ (r) 11 12 13 (15) (w) DYA. Volume DOC on plains of e Ven for budget varietals. CAB SAUV, MERLOT, Raboso reds can all age moderately. Above average from Loredan Gasparini, Molon, Villa Sandi.

Picolit F-VG DOCG w sw s/sw ★★→★★★ 08 09 10 12 13 (15) Quasi-mythical sweet white from FRIULI COLLI ORIENTALI, might disappoint those who can a) find it and b) afford it. Most from air-dried grapes. Little consistency of style: light, delicately sweet (rare nowadays) to super-thick and sweet. Gd: Aquila del Torre, Ermacora, Girolamo Dorigo, I Comelli, LIVIO FELLUGA, Marco Sara, Paolo Rodaro, Ronchi di Cialla, VIGNA Petrussa.

Piedmont / Piemonte Pie Alpine foothill region; with TUS, Italy's most important for quality. TURIN is capital, MONFERRATO (ASTI) and LANGHE (ALBA) important centres. No IGTS allowed; Pie DOC is lowest denomination, for basic reds, whites, SPUMANTE, FRIZZANTE. Grapes incl: BARBERA, Brachetto, Cortese, DOLCETTO, Freisa, GRIGNOLINO, MALVASIA di Casorzo, Malvasia di Schierano, MOSCATO, NEBBIOLO, Ruché, Timorasso. *See also* ALTO PIEMONTE, BARBARESCO, BAROLO, ROERO.

Pieropan Ven ★★★ Nino Pieropan is veteran quality leader of SOAVE, the man who brought a noble wine back to credibility. Cru *La Rocca* is still ultimate oaked Soave; Calvarino best of all.

Pio Cesare Pie ★★→★★★ Veteran ALBA producer, offers BAROLO, BARBARESCO in modern (barrique) and traditional (large-cask-aged) versions. Also Alba range, incl whites (eg. GAVI). Particularly gd NEBBIOLO D'ALBA, *a little Barolo at half the price*.

Planeta Si ★★→★★★ Leading SI estate with six v'yd holdings in various parts of island, incl Vittoria (CERASUOLO), Noto (NERO D'AVOLA Santa Cecilia) and most recently on ETNA. Wines from native and imported varieties. La Segreta is brand of gd-value white (CHARD, FIANO, Grecanico, VIOGNIER), red (MERLOT, Nero d'Avola, SYRAH). NB Cometa Fiano.

C18 Picolit was exported all over Europe, in bottles specially made in Murano.

Podere Tus Small TUS farm, once part of a big estate.

Poggio Tus Means "hill" in TUS dialect. "Poggione" means "big hill".

Poggio Antico Tus ★★★ Paola Gloder looks after this 32 ha estate, one of highest in MONTALCINO at c 500m. Style is restrained, consistent, at times too herbal.

Poggio di Sotto ★★★ Small MONTALCINO estate with a big reputation recently. Has purchased adjacent v'yds. Top BRUNELLO and Rosso of traditional character with idiosyncratic twist.

Poggione, Tenuta Il Tus ★★★ MONTALCINO estate making consistently excellent BRUNELLO and Rosso despite huge production (c.500,000 bottles) from 125-ha v'yd in s of zone. Fabrizio Bindocci succeeded legendary Pierluigi Talenti, and is nurturing son Alessandro to take over eventually.

Poggiopiano Tus ★★→★★★ Smooth-drinking yet serious CHIANTI CLASSICO from Bartoli family of San Casciano. CHIANTIS are pure SANGIOVESE, but SUPER TUSCAN Rosso di Sera incl up to 15% Colorino.

Poggio Scalette Tus ★★★ Oenologist Vittorio Fiore's family estate. Above-average CHIANTI CLASSICO and B'x-blend Capogatto. Pride of place goes to 100% SANGIOVESE Il Carbonaione; needs several yrs bottle age.

Poliziano Tus ★★★ MONTEPULCIANO estate of Federico Carletti. Superior if often v. dark, herbal VINO NOBILE (esp cru Asinone); gd IGT Le Stanze (CAB SAUV/MERLOT).

Pomino Tus DOC r w ★★★ (r) 09 10 11 12 13 (15) Appendage of RÚFINA, with fine red and white blends (esp Il Benefizio). Virtually a FRESCOBALDI exclusivity.

Potazzine, Le Tus ★★★ Giuseppe and Gigliola Gorelli named their wine after their

> **The best of Prosecco**
> PROSECCO is the wine, GLERA the grape variety with which it is made
> (meant to ward off copycats). Quality is esp high in the Valdobbiadene.
> Look for: Adami, Biancavigna, BISOL, Bortolin, Canevel, CARPENÈ-MALVOLTI,
> Case Bianche, Col Salice, Col Vetoraz, Le Colture, Gregoletto, La Riva
> dei Frati, Mionetto, Nino Franco, Ruggeri, Silvano Follador, Zardetto.

two *"potazzine"* (little birds, ie. children). V'yd is quite high, just s of MONTALCINO. Outstanding BRUNELLOS and Rossos, serious and v. drinkable. Try them at family's restaurant in centre of town.

Prà Ven ★★★ Leading SOAVE CLASSICO producer, esp crus Monte Grande, Staforte – latter 6 mths in steel tanks on lees with mechanical *bâtonnage* – v. tasty. Excellent VALPOLICELLAS La Formica, Morandina.

Produttori del Barbaresco Pie ★★★→★★★★ One of Italy's earliest co-ops, perhaps best in world. Aldo Vacca and team make excellent traditional straight BARBARESCO plus crus Asili, Montefico, Montestefano, Ovello, Pora, Rio Sordo.

Prosecco Ven DOC(G) w sp ★→★★ DYA. World has gone mad for Italy's favourite fizz. For details plus selection of producers *see* box, above.

Prunotto, Alfredo Pie ★★★→★★★★ Traditional ALBA company modernized by ANTINORI in 90s, run by Piero A's daughter Albiera. V.gd BARBARESCO (Bric Turot), BAROLO (Bussia), NEBBIOLO (Occhetti), BARBERA D'ALBA (Pian Romualdo), BARBERA D'ASTI (Costamiole), MONFERRATO Rosso (Mompertone, Barbera/SYRAH blend).

Puglia The 360-km heel of the Italian boot. Generally gd-value, easy-drinking wines (mainly red) from various grapes like NEGROAMARO, PRIMITIVO and Uva di Troia, but dubious winemaking talent and old equipment a real problem. Most interesting wines from SALENTO peninsula incl DOCS BRINDISI, COPERTINO, SALICE SALENTINO.

Querciabella Tus ★★★→★★★★ Top CHIANTI CLASSICO estate with IGT crus Camartina (CAB SAUV/SANGIOVESE) and barrel-fermented CHARD/PINOT BL Batàr. Purchases in Radda and MAREMMA provide more grapes for Chianti Classico and recent, as yet unconvincing, Turpino (CAB FR, SYRAH, MERLOT) respectively.

Quintarelli, Giuseppe Ven ★★★★ Arch-traditionalist, artisanal producer of sublime VALPOLICELLA, RECIOTO, AMARONE; plus a fine Bianco Secco, a blend of various grapes. Daughter Fiorenza and sons now in charge, altering nothing, incl the old man's ban on spitting when tasting.

Quintodecimo Cam ★★★ Oenology professor/winemaker Luigi Moio's beautiful estate; great GRECO DI TUFO (Giallo d'Arles), TAURASI.

Ratti, Renato ★★→★★★ Iconic BAROLO estate. Son Pietro now in charge. Modern wines; short maceration but plenty of substance, esp Barolos Rocche dell'Annunziata and Conca.

Recioto della Valpolicella Ven DOCG r sw (sp) ★★★→★★★★ Historic, made from PASSITO grapes along lines est before C6; unique, potentially stunning, with sumptuous cherry-chocolate-sweet fruitiness.

Recioto di Soave Ven DOCG w sw (sp) ★★★→★★★★ SOAVE from half-dried grapes: sweet, fruity, slightly almondy; sweetness is cut by high acidity. Drink with cheese. Best: Anselmi, Coffele, Gini, PIEROPAN, Tamellini; often v.gd from Ca' Rugate, Pasqua, PRÀ, Suavia, Trabuchi.

Refosco (dal Peduncolo Rosso) F-VG ★★ 10 11 12 13 (15) Gutsy red of rustic style. Best: FRIULI COLLI ORIENTALI DOC, *Volpi Pasini*; gd: LIVIO FELLUGA, Miani and CA' BOLANI, Denis Montanara, Dorigo, Ronchi di Manzano, Venica in Aquileia DOC.

Ricasoli Tus Historic Tuscan family. First Italian Prime Minister Bettino R devised the classic CHIANTI blend. Main branch occupies medieval Castello di BROLIO. Related Ricasoli own Castello di Cacchiano, Rocca di Montegrossi.

Riecine Tus ★★★→★★★★ Once excellent estate owned by legendary founder John Dunkley at Gaiole-in-CHIANTI now trying to find its way back. SANGIOVESE specialist; La Gioia potentially outstanding.

Rinaldi, Giuseppe Pie ★★★ Beppe Rinaldi is an arch-traditionalist of BAROLO, v'yds in heart of zone. Outstanding: Brunate and Tre Tine. Don't miss v.gd Freisa.

Ripasso Ven *See* VALPOLICELLA RIPASSO.

Riserva Wine aged for a statutory period, usually in casks or barrels.

Rivetti, Giorgio (La Spinetta) Pie ★★★ Fine MOSCATO D'ASTI, excellent BARBERA, series of super-concentrated, oaky BARBARESCOS. Also owns v'yds in BAROLO, CHIANTI COLLI Pisane DOCGS, and traditional SPUMANTE house Contratto.

Rizzi Pie ★★→★★★ Sub-area of Treiso, commune of BARBARESCO, where Dellapiana family look after 35 ha v'yd. Top cru is Barbaresco Pajore. Fondetta and Boito also gd, seem light but go deep, though quite austere.

Rocca, Bruno Pie ★★★ Outstanding modern-style BARBARESCO (Rabajà, Coparossa, Maria Adelaide) and other ALBA wines, also v. fine BARBERA d'Asti.

Rocca Albino ★★★ A foremost producer of elegant, sophisticated BARBARESCO: top crus VIGNETO Loreto, Brich Ronchi.

Rocca delle Macie Tus ★★ Large estate in Castellina-in-Chianti run by Sergio Zingarelli, son of spaghetti-western film-maker Italo. Gd quaffing CHIANTI, plus top wines incl Gran Selezione Sergio Zingarelli and Fizzano. Also Campo Macione estate in Scansano zone.

Roero Pie DOCG r ★★→★★★ 06 07 08 09 10 11 13 (15) Serious, occasionally BAROLO-level NEBBIOLOS from LANGHE hills. Also gd ARNEIS (w ★★→★★★). Best: Agricola Marrone (Langhe Arneis – Tre Fie), Almondo, Ca' Rossa, Cascina Chicco, Correggia, GIACOSA BRUNO, Malvirà, Morra, Negro (Perdaudin), Pioiero, Taliano, Val di Prete.

Romagna Sangiovese Mar DOC r ★★→★★★ At times too herbal and oaky, but often well-made, even classy SANGIOVESE red. Gd: Cesari, Drei Donà, Nicolucci, Papiano, Paradiso, Tre Monti, Trere (E-R DOC), Villa Venti (Primo Segno), FATTORIA ZERBINA. Seek also ici ronco delle Ginestre, Ronco dei Ciliegi from CASTELLUCCIO.

Ronco Term for a hillside v'yd in ne Italy, esp F-VG.

Rosato General Italian name for rosé. Other rosé wine names incl CHIARETTO from Lake Garda; CERASUOLO from Ab; Kretzer from ALTO ADIGE.

Rosso Conero Mar *See* CONERO.

Rosso di Montalcino Tus DOC r ★★→★★★ 10 11 12 13 (15) DOC for earlier-maturing wines from BRUNELLO grapes, usually from younger or lesser v'yd sites.

Rosso di Montefalco Umb DOC r ★★→★★★ 10 11 12 13 (15) SANGIOVESE/SAGRANTINO blend, often with a splash of softening MERLOT. *See* MONTEFALCO SAGRANTINO.

Rosso di Montepulciano Tus DOC r ★ 12 13 (15) Junior version of VINO NOBILE DI MONTEPULCIANO, growers similar.

Rosso Piceno / Piceno Mar DOC r ★ 10 11 13 (15) Generally easy-drinking blend of MONTEPULCIANO/SANGIOVESE now often sold as plain Piceno to help distinguish it from all other Rossos of Italy. SUPERIORE means it come from far s of region. Gd: Boccadigabbia, BUCCI, Fonte della Luna, Montecappone, MONTE SCHIAVO, Saladini Pilastri, Terre Cortesi Moncaro, Velenosi Ercole, Villamagna.

Ruffino Tus ★→★★★ Venerable CHIANTI firm, in hands of FOLONARI family for 100 yrs, split apart a few yrs ago. This part, at Pontassieve nr Florence, then bought by US giant Constellation Brands, produces reliable wines such as CHIANTI CLASSICO RISERVA Ducale and Ducale Oro, Greppone Mazzi in MONTALCINO, Lodola Nuova in MONTEPULCIANO, not to mention Borgo Conventi in F-VG.

Rúfina Tus ★★→★★★ Most n sub-zone of CHIANTI, e of Florence in s-facing foothills of Apennines, known for refined wines capable of long ageing. Gd-to-outstanding: CASTELLO DI NIPOZZANO (FRESCOBALDI), Castello del Trebbio, Colognole, Frascole,

Grati/Villa di Vetrice, I Veroni, Lavacchio, *Selvapiana*, Tenuta Bossi, Travignoli. Don't confuse with Ruffino, which happens to have HQ in Pontassieve.

Russiz Superiore F-VG ★★ →★★★ LIVIO FELLUGA's brother, Marco, est v'yds in various parts of F-VG. Now run by Marco's son Roberto. Wide range; best is PINOT GRIGIO and COLLIO Bianco blend Col Disòre.

Salento Pug Flat s peninsula at tip of Italy's heel; seems unlikely for quality, but deep soils, old ALBERELLO vines and sea breezes combine to produce remarkable red and rosé from NEGROAMARO, PRIMITIVO, with a bit of help from MONTEPULCIANO, MALVASIA Nera, local Sussumaniello. *See also* PUG, SALICE SALENTINO.

Sar claims to have 150 indigenous grape varieties of its own. And 4 million sheep.

Salice Salentino Pug DOC r ★★ →★★★ 08 10 11 13 (15) Best-known of Salento's too many NEGROAMARO-based DOCS. RISERVA after 2 yrs. Gd: Agricole VALLONE (Vereto Riserva), Cantele, Due Palme, Leone de Castris (Riserva), Mocavero.

Salvioni Tus ★★★ →★★★★ Aka La Cerbaiola; small, high-quality MONTALCINO operation of irrepressible Giulio Salvioni. BRUNELLO, ROSSO DI MONTALCINO among v. best available, worth not inconsiderable price.

Sandrone, Luciano Pie ★★★ Exponent of modern-style ALBA wines with deep, concentrated BAROLO Cannubi Boschis and Le VIGNE. Also gd BARBERA D'ALBA, DOLCETTO, NEBBIOLO D'ALBA.

San Felice Tus ★★ →★★★ Important historic TUS grower, owned by Gruppo Allianz, run by Leonardo Bellaccini. Fine CHIANTI CLASSICO and RISERVA POGGIO Rosso from estate in Castelnuovo Berardenga. Vitiarium is an experimental v'yd for obscure varieties, the excellent Pugnitello (IGT from that grape) a 1st result. Gd too: IGT *Vigorello* (first SUPER TUSCAN, from 1968), BRUNELLO DI MONTALCINO Campogiovanni.

San Gimignano Tus Tourist-overrun TUS town famous for its towers and dry white VERNACCIA DI SAN GIMIGNANO DOCG. Forgettable reds. Producers: Cesani, FALCHINI, Guicciardini Strozza, Il Palagione, Montenidoli, Mormoraia, Panizzi, Pietrafitta, Pietrasereno, Podera del Paradiso.

San Giusto a Rentennano Tus ★★★ →★★★★ Top CHIANTI CLASSICO estate owned by cousins of RICASOLI. Outstanding SANGIOVESE IGT Percarlo, sublime VIN SANTO (Vin San Giusto), MERLOT (La Ricolma).

San Guido, Tenuta Tus *See* SASSICAIA.

San Leonardo T-AA ★★★ Top TRENTINO estate of Marchesi Guerrieri Gonzaga. Main wine is B'x blend, San Leonardo, Italy's most claret-like wine. Forgettable MERLOT Villa Gresti.

San Michele Appiano T-AA Historic co-op (c.400 ha) run hands-on by Hans Terzer. *Mtn-fresh whites*, brimming with varietal typicity, drinkability, are speciality. PINOT BIANCO Schulthauser, Sanct Valentin SAUV BL impressive, as are CHARD, GEWURZ, PINOT GR, PINOT N.

Santadi Sar ★★★ SAR's, and one of Italy's, best co-ops, esp for CARIGNANO-based reds Terre Brune, Grotta Rossa, Rocca Rubia RISERVA (all DOC CARIGNANO DEL SULCIS).

Santa Maddalena / St-Magdalener T-AA DOC r ★★ →★★★ DYA. Teutonic-style red from SCHIAVA grapes from v. steep slopes behind ALTO ADIGE capital Bolzano. Notable: CS St-Magdalena (Huck am Bach), Gojer, Hans Rottensteiner (Premstallerhof), Heinrich Rottensteiner, Josephus Mayr.

Sant'Antimo Tus DOC r w sw ★★ →★★★ Lovely little Romanesque abbey gives its name to this catch-all DOC for (almost) everything in MONTALCINO zone that isn't BRUNELLO DOCG or Rosso DOC.

Saracco, Paolo Pie ★★★ Top MOSCATO d'ASTI. V.gd: LANGHE RIES, PINOT N.

Sardinia / Sardegna Sar The Med's 2nd-largest island produces much decent and some outstanding wine. Top denominations incl *Vermentino di Gallura* DOCG, VERMENTINO DI SARDEGNA (little less alc, little less character), Sherry-like VERNACCIA DI

ORISTANO, and Nuragus among whites, late-harvest sweet Nasco wines; CANNONAU (GRENACHE) and CARIGNANO among reds (Sar was long occupied by Spanish). Outstanding wines: *Turriga* (r) from ARGIOLAS, VERMENTINO from Capichera, Terre Brune and Rocca Rubia from SANTADI.

Sassicaia Tus DOC r ★★★★ 85' 88' 90' 95' 97 98' 99 01' 04' 05 06 07' 08 09 10 11 12 (13) (15) Italy's sole single-v'yd DOC (BOLGHERI), a CAB (SAUV/FR) made on First Growth lines by Marchese Incisa della Rocchetta at TENUTA San Guido. More elegant than lush, made for age – and often bought for investment, but hugely influential in giving Italy a top-quality image. The 1985 is one of Italy's three greatest wines ever made.

Satta, Michele Tus ★★★ Virtually the only BOLGHERI grower to succeed with 100% SANGIOVESE (Cavaliere). Also Bolgheri DOC red blends Piastraia, SUPERIORE I Castagni.

Scacciadiavoli Umb ★★ From 35 ha in MONTEFALCO, some of most approachable wines of that sometimes redoubtable DOC. Rosso and Bianco Montefalco combine complexity with drinkability; SAGRANTINO goes into DOCG red, also into SPUMANTE Brut, Rosé Brut.

Scavino, Paolo Pie ★★★ Modernist BAROLO producer of Castiglione Falletto, esp crus Rocche dell'Annunziata, Bric del Fiasc, Cannubi, Monvigliero. Others often too oaky.

Schiava Alto Adige T-AA DOC r ★ DYA. Schiava (VERNATSCH in German) gives practically tannin-free, easy-glugging red from most s territory of German-speaking world. Today rapidly disappearing from Tyrolean v'yds.

Schiopetto, Mario F-VG ★★★→★★★★ Legendary late COLLIO pioneering estate now owned by Volpe Pasini's Rotolo family. V.gd DOC SAUV BL, *Pinot Bl*, RIBOLLA GIALLA, IGT blend Blanc des Rosis, etc.

Sella & Mosca Sar ★★ Major SAR grower and merchant with v. pleasant white Torbato (esp Terre Bianche) and light, fruity VERMENTINO Cala Viola (DYA). Gd Alghero DOC Marchese di Villamarina (CAB SAUV) and Tanca Farrà (CANNONAU/Cab Sauv). Also interesting Port-like Anghelu Ruju.

Selvapiana Tus ★★★ CHIANTI RUFINA estate among Italian greats. Best: RISERVA Bucerchiale, IGT Fornace; but even *basic Chianti Rúfina is a treat*. Also fine red POMINO, Petrognano.

Settesoli, CS Si ★→★★ Co-op with some 6000 ha, giving si gd name with reliable, gd-value native and international varietals.

Sforzato / Sfursat Lom ★★★ AMARONE-like dried-grape NEBBIOLO from VALTELLINA in extreme n of Lom on Swiss border. Ages beautifully.

Sicily Si The Med's largest island, modern source of *exciting original wines and value*. Native grapes (r. Frappato, NERO D'AVOLA, NERELLO MASCALESE, w. CATARRATTO, Grecanico, GRILLO, INZOLIA), plus internationals. V'yds on flatlands in w, hills in centre, volcanic altitudes on Mt Etna.

Soave Ven DOC w (sw) ★→★★★ Famous, hitherto underrated, Veronese white. GARGANEGA, TREBBIANO di Soave, CHARD. Wines from volcanic soils of CLASSICO zone can be intense, saline, v. fine, quite long-lived.

Soave's v'yds officially "rural landscape of historical interest": no more building? **Solaia** Tus r ★★★★ 85' 90' 95' 97' 99' 01 04 06 07 08 09 10 11 12 13 (15) Occasionally magnificent CAB SAUV/SANGIOVESE blend by ANTINORI, made to highest B'x specs; needs yrs of laying down.

Speri Ven ★★ VALPOLICELLA family estate with sites such as outstanding Monte Sant'Urbano. Unpretentious, traditional-style CLASSICO SUPERIORE, AMARONE, RECIOTO. No frills, *just gd wine*.

Spumante Sparkling. What used to be called ASTI Spumante is now just Asti.

Südtirol T-AA The local name of German-speaking South Tyrol ALTO ADIGE.

Superiore Wine with more ageing than normal DOC and 0.5–1% more alc. May indicate a restricted production zone, eg. ROSSO PICENO Superiore.

Super Tuscan Tus Wines of high quality and price developed in 70s/80s to get round silly laws then prevailing. Now, esp with Gran Selezione on up, increasingly irrelevant. Wines still generally considered in Super Tuscan category, strictly unofficially: CA' MARCANDA, Flaccianello, Guado al Tasso, Messorio, ORNELLAIA, REDIGAFFI, SASSICAIA, Solaia, TIGNANELLO.

Tasca d'Almerita Si ★★★ New generation of Tasca d'Almeritas runs historic, still prestigious estate, which kept the flag flying for SI in dark yrs. High-altitude v'yds; balanced IGTs under its old Regaleali label, CHARD and CAB SAUV gd, but star, as ever, is NERO D'AVOLA-based *Rosso del Conte*.

Taurasi Cam DOCG r ★★★ 04 06 07 08 09 10 11 12 13 (15) The s's answer to the n's BAROLO and the centre's BRUNELLO, needs careful handling and long ageing. There are friendlier versions of AGLIANICO but none so potentially *complex, demanding, ultimately rewarding.* Made famous by MASTROBERARDINO, other outstanding: Caggiano, Caputo, FEUDI DI SAN GREGORIO, Luigi Tecce, Molettieri, Quintodecimo (VIGNA Grande Cerzito), Terredora di Paulo.

Tedeschi Ven ★★★ Bevy of v. fine AMARONE, RECIOTO, VALPOLICELLA. Amarone Capitel Monte Olmi and Recioto Capitel Monte Fiontana best.

Tedeschi, Fratelli Ven ★★ →★★★ One of original quality growers of VALPOLICELLA when zone was still ruled by mediocrities.

Tenuta An agricultural holding (*see* under name – eg. SAN GUIDO, TENUTA).

Terlano T-AA w ★★ →★★★ DYA. ALTO ADIGE Terlano DOC applies to one white blend and eight white varietals, esp PINOT BL, SAUV BL. Can be v. fresh, zesty or serious and surprisingly long-lasting. Best: CS Terlano (esp Pinot Bl Vorberg), LAGEDER, Niedermayr, Niedrist.

Best Tus wine visits incl Antinori, Castello di Ama, Nipozzano, Cappezzana.

Teroldego Rotaliano T-AA DOC r p ★★ →★★★ TRENTINO's best local variety makes seriously tasty wine on flat Campo Rotaliano. *Foradori* is tops. Gd: Dorigati, Endrizzi, MEZZACORONA'S RISERVA Nos, Zeni.

Terre del Barolo Pie ★ →★★ Co-op in Castiglione Falletto; c.700 members; millions of bottles of BAROLO and other LANGHE wines; remarkably consistent quality.

Terre Nere, Tenuta delle Si ★★★ Italian-American distributor Marc de Grazia shows great wine can be made from NERELLO and CARRICANTE grapes, on coveted n side of Mt Etna. Top: Guardiola, Vigne Niche. One to watch.

Terriccio, Castello del Tus ★★★ Large estate s of Livorno: excellent, v. expensive B'x-style IGT Lupicaia, v.gd IGT Tassinaia. Impressive IGT Terriccio, unusual blend of mainly Rhône grapes.

Tiberio ★★★ Outstanding TREBBIANO D'ABRUZZO Fonte Canale (60-yr-old vines) one of Italy's best whites; much-awarded PECORINO also exceptional. V.gd: CERASUOLO D'ABRUZZO, MONTEPULCIANO D'ABRUZZO.

Tiefenbrunner T-AA ★★ →★★★ Grower-merchant in Teutonic castle (Turmhof) in s ALTO ADIGE. Christof T succeeds father Herbert (winemaker since 1943). Wide range of mtn-fresh white and well-defined red varietals: French, Germanic and local, esp 1000-m-high MÜLLER-T *Feldmarschall*, one of Italy's best whites

Tignanello Tus r ★★★★ 04' 06' 07' 08 09 10 11 12 (13) (15) SANGIOVESE/CAB SAUV blend, barrique-aged, wine that put SUPER TUSCANS on map, created by ANTINORI's great oenologist Giacomo Tachis in early 70s. Today one of greatest cash-cows of world wine.

Tommasi Ven ★★★ 4th generation now in charge. Top: AMARONE, RISERVA Ca' Florian, VALPOLICELLA Rafael. Other estates in Ven (Filodora), PU (Masseria Surani), OLTREPÒ PAVESE (TENUTA Caseo).

Torcolato Ven Sweet wine from BREGANZE in Ven; Vespaiolo grapes laid on mats or hung up to dry for mths, as nearby RECIOTO DI SOAVE. Best: CS Beato Bartolomeo da Breganze, MACULAN.

Torgiano Umb DOC r p w (sp) ★★ and **Torgiano, Rosso Riserva** DOCG r ★★→★★★ 01' 04 06 07 08 09 10 11 (12) (13) (15) Gd-to-excellent red from Umb, virtually an exclusivity of LUNGAROTTI. *Vigna Monticchio* Rubesco RISERVA is outstanding in vintages: 75 79 85 97; keeps many yrs.

Torrette VdA DOC r ★→★★★ Blend based on Petit Rouge and other local varieties. Gd: Anselmet, L'Atoueyo (Torrette Superieur), Didier Gerbelle, Elio Ottin (Torrette Superieur), Feudo di San Maurizio (Torrette Superieur), LES CRETES.

Travaglini Pie ★★★ Along with Antoniolo, solid producer of n PIE NEBBIOLO, with v.gd GATTINARA RISERVA, Gattinara Tre Vigne, and pretty gd Nebbiolo Coste della Sesia.

Trebbiano d'Abruzzo Ab DOC w ★→★★★★ DYA. Generally crisp, simple wine, but VALENTINI's and Tiberio's Fonte Canale are *two of Italy's greatest* whites.

Trediberri Pie ★★★ Dynamic estate, top BAROLO Rocche dell'Annunziata; v.gd BARBERA D'ALBA, LANGHE Rosato.

Trentino T-AA DOC r w dr sw ★→★★★ DOC for 20-odd wines, mostly varietally named. Best: CHIARD, PINOT BL, MARZEMINO, TEROLDEGO. Provincial capital is Trento, which is DOC name for potentially high-quality METODO CLASSICO wines.

Trinoro, Tenuta di Tus ★★★ Individualist TUS red wine estate, pioneer in DOC Val d'Orcia between MONTEPULCIANO and MONTALCINO. Heavy accent on B'x grapes in flagship TENUTA di Trinoro, also in Palazzi, Le Cupole and Magnacosta. Andrea Franchetti also has v'yds on Mt Etna.

Tua Rita Tus ★★→★★★★ 1st producer to est Suvereto, some 20-km down coast, as new BOLGHERI in 90s. Producer of possibly Italy's greatest MERLOT in Redigaffi, also outstanding B'x blend *Giusto di Notri*. *See* VAL DI CORNIA.

Tuscany / Toscana Focal point of Italian wine's late-C20 renaissance, 1st with experimental SUPER TUSCANS, then modernized classics, CHIANTI, VINO NOBILE, BRUNELLO. Development of coastal zones like BOLGHERI, MAREMMA, has been a major feature of Tus wine over last half-century.

Umani Ronchi Mar ★★→★★★ Leading Mar producer, esp for VERDICCHIO (Casal di Serra, Plenio), CONERO Cumaro, IGTS Le Busche (w), Pelago (r).

Vajra, GD Pie ★★★ Leading quality BAROLO producer in Vergne. Outstanding Barolo Bricco delle Viole and LANGHE Freisa Kyè. Gd: Langhe Ries Petracine, Serralunga's Luigi Baudana Barolos.

Valdadige T-AA DOC r w dr s/sw ★ Name (in German: *Etschtaler*) for simple wines of valley of Adige, from ALTO ADIGE through TRENTINO to n Ven.

Val di Cornia Tus DOC r p w ★★→★★★ 06'07 08 09 10 11 12 13 (15) Quality zone s of BOLGHERI. CAB SAUV, MERLOT, MONTEPULCIANO, SANGIOVESE, SYRAH. Look for: Ambrosini, Bulichella, Gualdo del Re, Incontri, Jacopo Banti, Montepeloso, Petra, Russo, San Michele, TENUTA Casa Dei, Terricciola, TUA RITA.

Valentini, Edoardo Ab ★★★→★★★★ Collectors seek out r MONTEPULCIANO D'ABRUZZO and w TREBBIANO D'ABRUZZO that are among Italy's v. best wines. Traditional, age-worthy; 70s wines esp memorable.

Valle d'Aosta VdA DOC r p w ★★ Regional DOC for some 25 Alpine wines, geographically or varietally named, incl Arnad Montjovet, Blanc de Morgex, Chambave, Donnas, Enfer d'Arvier, Fumin, Nus MALVOISIE, Premetta, Torrette. Tiny production, wines rarely seen abroad but potentially worth finding.

Valle Isarco T-AA DOC w ★★ DYA. ALTO ADIGE DOC for seven Germanic varietal whites made along the Isarco (Eisack) River ne of Bolzano. Gd GEWURZ, MÜLLER-T, RIES, SILVANER. Top: Abbazia di Novacella, Kofererhof, Kuenhof, Manni Nossing.

Valpolicella Ven DOC(G) r ★→★★★★ Complex denomination, runnng from light quaffers with a certain fruity warmth through stronger SUPERIORES (that may or may not be RIPASSO) to AMARONES and RECIOTOS. Today straight Valpol is getting hard to find, a shame, as all best grapes going into trendy, profitable Amarone, which often disappoints (*see* box, right).

Valpolicella Ripasso Ven DOC r ★★→★★★ 09 10 11 12 13 (15) Valpolicella that is re-fermented on RECIOTO or AMARONE grape-skins to make a more age-worthy wine. Best: BUSSOLA, Castellani, DAL FORNO, QUINTARELLI and ZENATO.

Valtellina Lom DOC/DOCG r ★→★★★ Long e to w valley (most Alpine valleys run n to s) on Swiss border. Steep terraces have for millennia grown NEBBIOLO (here called CHIAVENNASCA) and related grapes. DOCG Valtellina SUPERIORE has five zones: Grumello, Inferno, Sassella, Maroggia, Valgella. Wines and scenery both worth detour. Best today: Fay, MAMETE PREVOSTINI, Nera, Nino Negri, Plozza, Rainoldi, Triacca. DOC Valtellina has less stringent requirements. *Sforzato* is its AMARONE.

Vecchio Samperi Si *See* DE BARTOLI.

Verdicchio dei Castelli di Jesi Mar DOC w (sp) ★★→★★★ DYA. Versatile white from nr Ancona on Adriatic; light and quaffable or sparkling or structured, complex, long-lived (esp RISERVA DOCG, min 2 yrs old). Also CLASSICO. Best: Andrea Felici, *Bucci* (Riserva), Borgo delle Oche, Coroncino (Gaiospino e Straccacio), Fazi Battaglia (Riserva San Sisto), GAROFOLI (Podium), La Staffa, Marotti Campi (Salmariano), MONTE SCHIAVO (Le Giuncare), Montecappone (Federico II), Santa Barbara, Sartarelli (Balciana, a rare late harvest, and Tralivio), UMANI RONCHI (Plenio and Casal di Serra).

Verdicchio di Matelica Mar DOC w (sp) ★★→★★★ DYA. Similar to last, smaller, more inland, higher, so more acidic, so longer lasting though less easy-drinking young. RISERVA is likewise DOCG. Esp Barone Pizzini, Belisario, Bisci, Collestefano, La Monacesca (Mirum), Pagliano Tre, San Biagio.

Verduno Pie DOC r ★★ DYA. Berry and herbal flavours. Gd: Ascheri (Do ut Des), Bel Colle (Le Masche), CASTELLO DI VERDUNO (Basadone), Fratelli Alessandria, GB Burlotto.

Verduno, Castello di Pie ★★★ Husband/wife team, v.gd BARBARESCO Rabaja and BAROLO Monvigliero.

Verduzzo F-VG DOC (Friuli Colli Orientali) w dr sw s/sw ★★→★★★ Full-bodied white from local variety. Ramandolo (DOCG) is well-regarded subzone for sweet wine. Top: Anna Berra, Dorigo, Meroi.

Vermentino di Gallura Sar DOCG w ★★→★★★ DYA. VERMENTINO makes gd light wines in TUS, LIG and all over SAR, but best, most intense in ne corner of island, under this its DOCG name. Try Capichera, CS di Gallura, CS del Vermentino/ Monti, CS Giogantino, Depperu.

Vermentino di Sardegna Lig DOC w ★★ DYA. From anywhere on SAR; generally fails to measure up to VERMENTINO DI GALLURA for structure, intensity of flavour. Gd producers: ARGIOLAS, *Santadi, Sella & Mosca*.

Vernaccia di Oristano Sar DOC w dr ★→★★★ SAR flor-affected wine, similar to light Sherry, a touch bitter, full-bodied. SUPERIORE 15.5% alc, 3 yrs of age. Delicious with *bottarga* (compressed fish roe). Kill to try it. Top: CONTINI. Gd: Serra, Silvio Carta.

Vernaccia di San Gimignano Tus *See* SAN GIMIGNANO.

24/7 wine fountain in Caldari di Ortona, Ab, intended for pilgrims. Start walking.

Vie di Romans F-VG ★★★→★★★★ Gianfranco Gallo has built up his father's ISONZO estate to top FV-G status. Outstanding Isonzo PINOT GR Dessimis, SAUV BL Piere and Vieris (oaked), Flors di Uis blend and MALVASIA. Disappointing CHARD by world standards.

Vietti Pie ★★★ Veteran grower of characterful PIE wines at Castiglione Falletto, incl BARBARESCO Masseria, BARBERA D'ALBA Scarrone, BARBERA D'ASTI la Crena. *Textbook Barolos*: Lazzarito, Brunate, Ravera, Rocche, Villero.

> **Valpolicella: the best**
>
> VALPOLICELLA has never been better than today. AMARONE DELLA VALPOLICELLA and RECIOTO DELLA VALPOLICELLA have now been elevated to DOCG status, while Valpolicella RIPASSO has at last been recognized as a historic wine in its own right. The following producers make gd to great wine: Accordini Stefano★, ALLEGRINI★, Begali, BERTANI, BOLLA, Boscaini, Brigaldara★, BRUNELLI, BUSSOLA★, Ca' la Bianca, Ca' Rugate, Campagnola, CANTINA Valpolicella, Castellani, Corteforte, Corte Sant'Alda, CS Valpantena, DAL FORNO★, GUERRIERI-RIZZARDI★, Le Ragose, Le Salette, MASI★, Mazzi★, Nicolis, QUINTARELLI★, Roccoli Grassi★, Serego Alighieri★, Speri★, TEDESCHI★, Tommasi★, Valentina Cubi, Venturini, VIVIANI★, ZENATO, Zeni.

Vignamaggio Tus ★★→★★★ Historic, beautiful and v.gd CHIANTI CLASSICO estate, nr Greve. Leonardo da Vinci painted the Mona Lisa here. RISERVA is called – you guessed it.

Vigna (or vigneto) A single v'yd, generally indicating superior quality.

Vigna Petrussa F-VG ★★★ Small family estate: high-quality Schiopppettino, Picolit.

Villa Matilde Cam ★★★ Top CAM producer of FALERNO Rosso (VIGNA Camarato), Bianco (Caracci), PASSITO Eleusi.

Villa Russiz F-VG ★★★ Historic estate for DOC COLLIO. V.gd SAUV BL and MERLOT (esp "de la Tour" selections), PINOT BL, PINOT GR, FRIULANO, CHARD.

Vino Nobile di Montepulciano Tus DOCG r ★★→★★★ 04 06' 07 08 09 10 11 12 13 (15) Historic Prugnole Gentile aka SANGIOVESE-based wine from the TUS town (as distinct from grape) MONTEPULCIANO, often tough with drying tannins, but complex and long-lasting from best producers: AVIGNONESI, Bindella, Boscarelli, La Braccesca, La Calonica, Carmelo, Le Casalte, Contucci, Dei, Fattoria del Cerro, Gracciano della Seta, Icario, Nottola, POLIZIANO, Romeo, Salcheto, Trerose, Valdipiatta, Villa Sant'Anna. RISERVA after 3 yrs.

Vin Santo / Vinsanto / Vin(o) Santo T-AA, Tus DOC w sw s/sw ★★→★★★★ Sweet PASSITO wine, usually TREBBIANO, MALVASIA and/or SANGIOVESE in TUS (Vin Santo), Nosiola in TRENTINO (Vino Santo). Tus versions extremely variable, anything from off-dry and Sherry-like to sweet and v. rich. May spend 3-10 unracked yrs in small barrels called *caratelli*. *Avignonesi's is legendary*; plus CAPEZZANA, Fattoria del Cerro, FELSINA, FRASCOLE, ISOLE E OLENA, Rocca di Montegrossi, SAN GIUSTO A RENTENNANO, SELVAPIANA, Villa Sant'Anna, Villa di Vetrice. *See also* OCCHIO DI PERNICE.

Viviani Ven ★★★ Claudio V. shows how modern VALPOLICELLA, AMARONE can be. V.gd CLASSICO SUPERIORE Campo Morar, better RECIOTO La Mandrella, outstanding Amarone Casa dei Bepi, Tulipano Nero.

Voerzio, Roberto Pie ★★★ BAROLO modernist; concentrated, structured Barolos. More impressive/expensive than delicious, usually aged in small toasted French barriques. Range incl Brunate, Cerequio, Rocche dell'Annunziata-Torriglione, Sarmassa, Serra; excellent BARBERA D'ALBA.

Volpaia, Castello di Tus ★★→★★★ V.gd CHIANTI CLASSICO estate at Radda. SUPER TUSCANS Coltassala (SANGIOVESE/Mammolo), Balifico (Sangiovese/CAB SAUV).

Zenato Ven ★★ V. reliable, sometimes inspired for GARDA wines, also AMARONE, LUGANA, SOAVE, VALPOLICELLA.

Zerbina, Fattoria E-R ★★★ Leader in Romagna; best sweet ALBANA DOCG (Scacco Matto), v.gd SANGIOVESE (Pietramora); barrique-aged IGT Marzieno.

Zibibbo Si ★★ dr sw Alluring SI table wine from the MUSCAT d'Alessandria grape, most associated with PANTELLERIA and extreme w Si. Dry version exemplified by DE BARTOLI.

Zonin ★→★★ One of Italy's biggest estate owners, based at Gambellara in Ven, but also big in F-VG, TUS, PUG, SI and elsewhere in world (eg. Virginia, US).

Germany

Abbreviations used in the text:

Bad	Baden
Frank	Franken
M-M	Mittelmosel
M Rh	Mittelrhein
Mos	Mosel
Na	Nahe
Pfz	Pfalz
Rhg	Rheingau
Rhh	Rheinhessen
Sa-Un	Saale-Unstrut
Sachs	Sachsen
Würt	Württemberg

More heavily shaded areas are the wine-growing regions.

During the last decades German wines have made tremendous progress: we've seen 30 years of continous improvement. Now, if you talk to young growers, those aged 25–35, who will shape Germany's wine for the next 30 years, you become aware of a generation full of passion and of already astonishing experience. They've made wine in Burgundy, in New Zealand, in South Africa and elsewhere. It's part of a quest for ever-greater improvements at home; they want to see what can be adapted to their own conditions and grapes. And the wines that these young growers make are not imitations; they are really innovative. There need be no worries about Germany's next 30 or so vintages. Climate change so far has been on Germany's side. Riper and earlier vintages lend themselves to the way Germans now want their wine: dry, to drink with modern cooking.

Recent vintages

Mosel

Mosels (including Saar and Ruwer wines) are so attractive young that their capabilities for developing are not often enough explored. But fine Kabinetts can gain from at least 5 years in bottle and often much more: Spätlese from 5–20, and Auslese and BA anything from 10–30 years. Compared with the rest of Germany the Mosel is still tentative about making fully dry, Trocken wines, though climate change is helping encourage them. The Saar and Ruwer make leaner wines than the Mosel, but surpass the whole world for elegance and thrilling, steely "breeding".

2016 Wet spring, local hail in May (Wehlen, Graach), wet summer; despair until September when weather changed. Splendid October; quality much better than anticipated, but a Kabinett and Spätlese, not Auslese, year.

2015 Hot, dry summer, damp September, sunny October; Spätlesen, Auslesen to keep.

2014 September saved vintage, but careful selection necessary. Classical: Trocken to Auslese.

2013 Top wines have freshness, elegance (but rare). Mittelmosel better than Saar, Ruwer.

2012 Classic wines mostly from QbA to Auslese. Low quantity.

2011 Brilliant vintage, particularly in Saar, Ruwer, with sensational TBAs.

2010 High acidity identifying feature, some good Spätlesen, Auslesen.

2009 Magnificent Spätlesen, Auslesen, good balance. Keep.

2008 Kabinetts, Spätlesen can be fine, elegant. Now perfect to drink.

2007 Good quality, quantity. Now approaching maturity.

2005 Very ripe, better acidity than, say, 2003. Exceptional (Saar). Drink or keep.

2004 Fine year to drink.

Fine vintages: 03 01 99 97 95 94 93 90 89 88 76 71 69 64 59 53 49 45 37 34 21.

Rheinhessen, Nahe, Pfalz, Rheingau, Ahr

Apart from Mosels, Rheingau wines tend to be longest-lived of all German regions, improving for 15 years or more, but best wines from Rheinhessen, the Nahe and Pfalz can last as long. Modern-style dry wines such as *Grosses Gewächs* are generally intended for drinking within 2–4 years, but the best undoubtedly have the potential to age interestingly. The same holds for Ahr Valley reds: their fruit makes them attractive young, but best wines can develop for 10 years and longer.

2016 Rainy spring and summer caused downy mildew problems. September brought hot temperatures and sunburn. Quality, quantity very mixed.

2015 Hot, dry summer. Rheingau excellent, both dry and nobly sweet.

2014 Complicated, but Ries, Spätburgunder generally okay, even good if selection was careful.

2013 Much variation; best in south Rheinhessen, Franconia, Ahr Valley.

2012 Quantities below average, but very good, classical at every level.

2011 Fruity wines, with harmonious acidity.

2010 Uneven quality, some very good Spätburgunder; dry whites should be drunk now.

2009 Excellent wines, especially dry. Some acidification needed.

2008 Riesling of great raciness, ageing well.

2007 Dry wines now mature. Drink.
2005 High ripeness levels, excellent acidity, extract. Superb year.
Drink or keep.
2004 Ripe and healthy throughout the Rhine. Big crop; some dilution,
not at top estates.
Fine vintages: 03 02 01 99 98 97 96 93 90 83 76 71 69 67 64 59 53 49 45 37
34 21.

German vintage notation

The vintage notes after entries in the German section are mostly given
in a different form from those elsewhere in the book. If the vintages of
a single wine are rated, or are for red wine regions, the vintage notation
is identical with the one used elsewhere (*see* front jacket flap). But for
regions, villages or producers, two styles of vintage are indicated:
Bold type (eg. **14**) indicates classic, ripe vintages with a high proportion
of SPÄTLESEN and AUSLESEN; or, in the case of red wines, gd phenolic
ripeness and must weights.
Normal type (eg. 15) indicates a successful but not outstanding vintage.
Generally, German white wines, esp RIES, can be drunk young for their
intense fruitiness, or kept for a decade or two to develop more aromatic
subtlety and finesse.

Adams Rhh ★★→★★★ Family estate led since 2011 by oenologist Simone A,
proving why PINOT N from INGELHEIM was considered to be among Germany's
best in C19. Also delicate limestone-driven CHARD (discretely oaked, no malo)
and substantial PINOT GR.

Adelmann, Weingut Graf Würt ★★→★★★ Young count Felix Adelmann now in
charge at idyllic Schloss Schaubeck. New winemaker too: a lot of drive, but
no palace revolution. V.gd 2013 RIES (GROSSE LAGE Süssmund).

Ahr ★★→★★★★ 05 09 11 12 13' 14 15' 16 River valley s of Bonn. Crisp, fruity
SPÄTBURGUNDER from slate. Best: Adeneuer, Deutzerhof, Heiner-Kreuzberg,
Josten & Klein, KREUZBERG, MEYER-NÄKEL, Nelles, Paul Schumacher, STODDEN, co-op
Mayschoss-Altenahr.

Aldinger, Gerhard Würt ★★★ Gerd Aldinger is known for dense LEMBERGER,
SPÄTBURGUNDER, complex SAUV BL. Sons Hansjörg and Matthias try TROLLINGER
without added sulphur, GRÜNER V and SEKT with 5 yrs of lees ageing (Brut
Nature **09 10**).

Alte Reben Old vines. Increasingly common designation on German labels; an
obvious analogy to French term vieilles vignes. Analogy is perfect: no min age.

Alter Satz Frank Designation for wines from old co-planted (different varieties
all mixed up) v'yds, esp in FRANK, many of them being more than 100 yrs
old and ungrafted. Try Hartmut Scheuring, Nico Scholtens, Otmar Zang (w)
or Stritzinger (r).

Amtliche Prüfungsnummer (APNr) Official test number, on every label of a quality
wine. Useful for discerning different lots of AUSLESE a producer has made from
the same v'yd.

Assmannshausen Rhg ★★→★★★★ 97 99' 05' 08 09 10 11 12 13' 14 15 The only RHG
village with tradition for *Spätburgunder*. Wines from GROSSE Lage v'yd Höllenberg
(45 ha on slate) age extremely well. Growers: BISCHÖFLICHES WEINGUT RÜDESHEIM,
CHAT SAUVAGE, HESSISCHE STAATSWEINGÜTER, Kesseler, König, KRONE, Mumm.

Auslese Wines from selective harvest of super-ripe bunches affected by noble rot
(*Edelfäule*) and correspondingly unctuous in flavour.

Ayl Mos ★→★★★ All v'yds known since 1971 by name of historically best site: Kupp. Such are German wine laws. Growers: BISCHÖFLICHE WEINGÜTER TRIER, *Lauer*, Vols.

Bacharach M Rh ★→★★★ 01 05 08 09 11 12 13 14 15 Small, idyllic town; centre of M RH RIES. Classified GROSSE LAGE: Hahn, Posten, Wolfshöhle. Growers: Bastian, JOST, KAUER, Ratzenberger.

Baden Huge sw region and former Grand Duchy owing its existence to post-Napoleonic reshapings, 15,000 ha stretched over 230 km, best-known for PINOT N, GRAU- and WEISSBURGUNDER and pockets of RIES, usually dry. Many co-ops. Best areas KAISERSTUHL, ORTENAU.

Bassermann-Jordan Pfz ★★★ 49 ha at DEIDESHEIM, FORST, RUPPERTSBERG. *Majestic dry Ries,* lavish sweet wines and, recently, experiments with prolonged cask ageing (Res Probus) and terracotta vinification (Pithium).

Becker, Friedrich Pfz ★★→★★★★ Outstanding SPÄTBURGUNDER (Kammerberg, Sankt Paul, Res, Heydenreich) 07' 08 09 10 11 12 13' 14 from most s part of PFZ; some v'yds actually lie across border in Alsace. Gd whites (CHARD, RIES, PINOT GR) too.

Becker, J B Rhg ★★→★★★ 89 90 92 94 97 01 05 08 09 10 11 12 13 14 15 Hajo Becker and his sister Maria produce delightfully old-fashioned, cask-aged (and long-lived) dry RIES, SPÄTBURGUNDER at WALLUF and Martinsthal. Mature vintages are outstanding value.

Beerenauslese (BA) Luscious sweet wine from exceptionally ripe, individually selected berries concentrated by noble rot. Rare, expensive.

Bercher Bad ★★★ Cousins Arne and Martin B are experts on PINOT from volcanic soils at Burkheim, Jechtingen and Sasbach. Outstanding 15' GRAUBURGUNDER GG Feuerberg Haslen.

Bergdolt Pfz ★★★ Organic estate at Duttweiler, known for its WEISSBURGUNDER GG Mandelberg 98' 01' 02 04' 05 07 08 09' 10 11 12' 13 14 15. Gd RIES and SPÄTBURGUNDER too.

Bernkastel M-M ★→★★★★ Senior wine town of the M-M, known for timbered houses and flowery, perfectly round RIES. GROSSE LAGE: DOCTOR, Lay. Top growers: Kerpen, LOOSEN, JJ PRÜM, Studert Prüm, THANISCH (both estates), WEGELER "Kurfürstlay" GROSSLAGE name is a deception: avoid.

Bischöfliches Weingut Rüdesheim Rhg ★★★ 8 ha of best sites in RÜDESHEIM, ASSMANNSHAUSEN, JOHANNISBERG; vault cellar in Hildegard von Bingen's historic monastery. Peter Perabo (ex-KRÖNE) is *Pinot N specialist*, but RIES also v.gd: look for 15' Berg Rottland from vines planted in 1960.

Bischöfliche Weingüter Trier Mos ★★ 120 ha of mostly 1st-class v'yds uniting historical donations. Not v. reliable; do not buy without prior tasting.

Bodensee Bad Idyllic district of s BAD, on Lake Constance, at considerable altitude: 400–580m. Dry MÜLLER-T with elegance, light but delicate SPÄTBURGUNDER. Top villages: Hagnau, Meersburg, Reichenau. Lovely holiday wines.

Boppard M Rh ★→★★★ Wine town of M RH with GROSSE LAGE Hamm, an amphitheatre of vines. Growers: Lorenz, M Müller, Perll, WEINGART. Unbeatable *value.*

Brauneberg M-M ★★★→★★★★ 59 71 83 90 96 97 99 01 04 05 07 08 09 11 12 13 14 15 16 Top village nr BERNKASTEL; excellent full-flavoured RIES of great raciness. GROSSE LAGE v'yds Juffer, Juffer-SONNENUHR. Growers: *F Haag*, *W Haag*, KESSELSTATT, Paulinshof, RICHTER, SCHLOSS LIESER, THANISCH.

Bremer Ratskeller Town hall cellar in n Germany's commercial town of Bremen, founded in 1405, a UNESCO World Heritage Site. Oldest wine is a barrel of 1653 RÜDESHEIMER Apostelwein.

Breuer Rhg ★★★→★★★★ Exquisite RIES from RÜDESHEIM and RAUENTHAL, old-school and v. modern at same time. Berg Schlossberg has depth at 12% alc, Nonnenberg transforms austerity into age-worthiness, inexpensive Terra Montosa shows what RHG Ries is all about. Gd SEKT, SPÄTBURGUNDER too.

Buhl, Reichsrat von Pfz ★★★ Historic PFZ estate at DEIDESHEIM. Since ex-Bollinger (*see* France) cellarmaster Mathieu Kauffmann joined (in 2013), stunning SEKT, and textbook "French-style" GGs: bone-dry with remarkable minerality.

Bunn, Lisa Rhh ★★→★★★ Shooting star in NIERSTEIN, astonishingly serene at age of 30, refined Hipping RIES, stylish Res CHARD, remarkable ST-LAURENT (r).

Bürgerspital zum Heiligen Geist Frank ★★★ Ancient charitable estate with great continuity: only six directors in past 180 yrs. Traditionally made whites (*Silvaner*, RIES) from best sites in/around WÜRZBURG. At 700-yr-celebration in early 2016, old vintages showed top form: 1904 dry Schalksberg (from co-planted v'yd), 49 Stein dry Silvaner, 53 Hohburg Silvaner TBA.

Bürklin-Wolf, Dr. Pfz ★★→★★★★ Historic estate with one of best v'yd portfolios in MITTELHAARDT district, 30 ha GROSSE LAGE and ERSTE LAGE sites (estate-own classification since 1994) at FORST and DEISDESHEIM etc. Bio farming (incl use of horses).

Busch, Clemens Mos ★★★ Clemens Busch and son Johannes make powerful dry and elegant sweet RIES from parcels Fahrlay, Falkenlay, Rothenpfad, Raffes in steep Pündericher Marienburg. Bio.

Castell'sches Fürstliches Domänenamt Frank ★→★★★ Superb SILVANER, RIES from monopoly v'yd *Casteller Schlossberg*. New manager Björn Probst (since 2017) worked beside his predecessor Karl-Heinz Rebitzer, style unchanged.

Chat Sauvage Rhg ★★★→★★★★ 07 08 09 10 11 12 13' 14 Founded in 2000 by Hamburg entrepreneur Günter Schulz, now among the finest RHG PINOT N producers. V'yds at ASSMANNSHAUSEN, JOHANNISBERG, LORCH and RÜDESHEIM. Makes some CHARD too.

Christmann Pfz ★★★ VDP president Steffen Christmann is a MITTELHAARDT bio pioneer, best known for his RIES Königsbacher Idig 04 05' 08' 10' 11 12' 13 14 15'.

Clüsserath, Ansgar Mos ★★★ Tense RIES from TRITTENHEIMER Apotheke. KABINETTS are delicious, crystalline.

Corvers-Kauter Rhg ★★★ Textbook mineral RÜDESHEIM RIES: crystalline, pure.

Crusius, Dr. Na ★★→★★★ Family estate at TRAISEN, NA. Vivid, age-worthy RIES from sun-baked Bastei and Rotenfels of Traisen and SCHLOSSBÖCKELHEIM.

Deidesheim Pfz ★★→★★★★ 01 05 08 09 11 12 13 14 15 Central MITTELHAARDT village, long-lived RIES from GROSSE LAGE parcels in six v'yds: Grainhübel, Hohenmorgen, Kalkofen, Kieselberg, Langenmorgen, Paradiesgarten. Top growers: BASSERMANN-JORDAN, Biffar, BUHL, BÜRKLIN-WOLF, CHRISTMANN, DEINHARD, Fusser, MOSBACHER, VON WINNING. Gd co-op, 1st-class v'yds and young, ambitious team.

Deinhard, Dr. Pfz ★★★ Since 2008, a brand of the VON WINNING estate, continuing to produce PFZ RIES of classical style.

Diel, Schlossgut Na ★★★→★★★★ Caroline Diel follows her father: exquisite *GG Ries* (best usually Burgberg of Dorsheim). Magnificent SPÄTLESEN, serious *Sekt* (Cuvée Mo 6 yrs on lees).

Doctor M-M Emblematic steep v'yd at BERNKASTEL, the place where TBA was invented (1921, THANISCH). Only 3.2 ha, and four producers: KESSELSTATT, both Thanisch estates, WEGELER. RIES of extraordinary richness, but pricey – and, unfortunately, not available on prescription.

6766 ha of German v'yd certified organic (2015): 6.6 per cent of total.

Dönnhoff Na ★★★→★★★★ 90 97 01 05 07 08 09 11 12 13 14 15 16 Cornelius D now in charge, in style slightly drier than father Helmut. Gd value are RIES Tonschiefer and Roxheim *Höllenpfad* (fine, elegant). Outstanding GG from NIEDERHAUSEN (Hermannshöhle), *Norheim (Dellchen)*; SCHLOSSBÖCKELHEIM (Felsenberg). Dazzling EISWEIN from Oberhauser Brücke v'yd.

Durbach Bad ★★→★★★ ORTENAU village for full-bodied RIES, locally called

> **New EU terminology**
> Germany's part in the new EU classification involves, firstly, abolishing the term *Tafelwein* in favour of plain *Wein* and secondly changing LANDWEIN to *geschützte geographische Angabe* (ggA), or Protected Geographical Indication. QUALITÄTSWEIN and QUALITÄTSWEIN MIT PRÄDIKAT will be replaced by *geschützte Ursprungsbezeichnung* (gU), or Protected Designation of Origin. The existing terms – SPÄTLESE, AUSLESE and so on (*see* box, p.165) – will be tacked on to gU where appropriate; the rules for these styles won't change.

Klingelberger, from granite soils in steep Plauelrain v'yd. Top growers: Graf Metternich, H Männle, LAIBLE (both), MARKGRAF VON BADEN.

Egon Müller zu Scharzhof Mos ★★★★ 59 71 76 83 85 88 89 90 93 94 95 96 97 98 99 01 02 03 04 05 06 07 08 09 10 11 12 13 14 15 16 Legendary SAAR estate at WILTINGEN with a treasure of old vines. Its racy SCHARZHOFBERGER RIES is among world's greatest wines: sublime, vibrant, immortal. *Kabinett* featherlight, long-lived – and now v. pricey: 15 ALTE REBEN KABINETT fetched €200/bottle at auction. SPÄTLESEN miraculously rich and slender at same time, AUSLESEN ethereal, Goldkapsel the ultimate.

Einzellage Individual v'yd site. Never to be confused with GROSSLAGE.

Eiswein Made from frozen grapes with ice (ie. water content) discarded, thus v. concentrated; of BA ripeness or more. Outstanding Eiswein vintages: 98 02 04 08.

Ellwanger Würt ★★→★★★ Jürgen Ellwanger pioneered oak-aged reds in WÜRT; sons Jörg and Felix turn out sappy but structured LEMBERGER, SPÄTBURGUNDER and ZWEIGELT.

Emrich-Schönleber Na ★★★ Werner Schönleber and son Frank make precise RIES from Monzingen's classified Frühlingsplätzchen and Halenberg (usually better).

Erden M-M ★★★→★★★★ 90 97 01 03 05 08 09 11 12 13 14 15 16 Village on red slate soils; noble AUSLESEN and TROCKEN RIES with rare delicacy. GROSSE LAGE: Prälat, Treppchen. Growers: Bremer Ratskeller, JJ Christoffel, LOOSEN, MERKELBACH, MARKUS MOLITOR, Mönchhof, Schmitges.

Erste Lage Classified v'yd, 2nd-from-top level, according to VDP. (Not all growers belong to VDP, but best usually do.) Similar to Burgundy's Premier Cru: category between ORTSWEIN and GROSSE LAGE. However, not in use in AHR, M RH, MOS, NA, RHH.

Erstes Gewächs Rhg "First growth". Only for RHG v'yds, but VDP-members there changed to the GG designation after 2012. Pay attention.

Erzeugerabfüllung Bottled by producer. Incl the guarantee that only own grapes have been processed. May be used by co-ops also. GUTSABFÜLLUNG is stricter, applies only to estates.

Escherndorf Frank ★★★ 08 09 10 11 12 13 14 15 (16) Village with steep GROSSE LAGE Lump ("scrap" – as in tiny inherited parcels). Marvellous *Silvaner* and RIES, dry and sweet. Growers: Fröhlich, H SAUER, R SAUER, Schäffer.

Feinherb Imprecisely defined traditional term for wines with around 10–20g sugar/litre, not necessarily tasting sweet. More flexible than HALBTROCKEN. I often choose Feinherbs.

Forst Pfz ★★→★★★★ 90 97 01 05 08 09 11 12 13 14 15 16 Outstanding MITTELHAARDT village. Full-bodied and fine at the same time. GROSSE LAGE v'yds: Jesuitengarten, Kirchenstück, Freundstück, Pechstein, Ungeheuer. Top growers: Acham-Magin, BASSERMANN-JORDAN, VON BUHL, BÜRKLIN-WOLF, MOSBACHER, von Winning, WOLF.

Franken / Franconia Region of distinctive dry wines, esp *Silvaner*, mostly bottled in round-bellied flasks (BOCKSBEUTEL). Centre is WÜRZBURG. Top villages: Bürgstadt, ESCHERNDORF, IPHOFEN, Klingenberg, Randersacker.

> **Grosse Lage / Grosslage: spot the difference**
> *Bereich* means district within an *Anbaugebiet* (region). *Bereich* on a
> label should be treated as a flashing red light; the wine is a blend from
> arbitrary sites within that district. Do not buy. The same holds for wines
> with a GROSSLAGE name, though these are more difficult to identify. Who
> could guess if "Forster Mariengarten" is an EINZELLAGE or a *Grosslage*?
> (It's Gross.) But now, from the 2012 vintage, it's even more tricky. Don't
> confuse *Grosslage* with GROSSE LAGE: the latter refers to best single v'yds,
> Germany's Grands Crus according to the classification set up by wine-
> grower's association VDP. They weren't thinking about you.

Franzen Mos ★★ →★★★ From Europe's steepest v'yd, Bremmen Calmont, and nearby Neefer Frauenberg, young Kilian F makes dense, minerally RIES, mostly dry.

Fricke, Eva Rhg ★★ →★★★ Born nr viticultural background, now rising star in RHG: expressive, taut RIES (10 ha, organic) from KIEDRICH, LORCH.

Fuder Traditional German cask, sizes 600–1800 litres depending on region, traditionally used for fermentation and (formerly long) ageing.

Fürst, Weingut Frank ★★★ →★★★★ Successful father-son team at Bürgstadt with v'yds there and on steep terraces of Klingenberg. *Spätburgunders* 97' 99 01 05' 08 09 10 11 12 13 14 (15) of great finesse from red sandstone, dense FRÜHBURGUNDER, excellent whites too. Pur Mineral [*sic*] is a reliable mid-price label.

Gallais, Le Mos The 2nd estate of EGON MÜLLER ZU SCHARZHOF with 4-ha-monopoly Braune Kupp at WILTINGEN. Soil is schist with more clay than in SCHARZHOFBERG; AUSLESEN can be exceptional.

Geisenheim Rhg Town primarily known for Germany's top university of oenology and viticulture. One GROSSE LAGE too: Rothenberg.

GG (Grosses Gewächs) "Great/top growth". This is the top dry wine from a VDP-classified GROSSE LAGE (since 2012). *See also* ERSTES GEWÄCHS.

Goldkapsel / Gold Capsule Mos, Na, Rhg, Rhh Designation (and physical sealing) mainly for AUSLESE and higher. V. strict selection of grapes. Lange Goldkapsel (Long Gold Capsule) should be even better.

Graach M-M ★★★ →★★★★ Small village between BERNKASTEL and WEHLEN. GROSSE LAGE v'yds: Domprobst, Himmelreich, Josephshof. Top growers: Kees-Kieren, LOOSEN, MARKUS MOLITOR, *JJ Prüm*, SA PRÜM, SCHAEFER, *Selbach-Oster*, Studert-Prüm, VON KESSELSTATT, WEGELER. Threatened by planned new Autobahn.

Grans-Fassian Mos ★★★ Fine estate, known for steely, age-worthy RIES from v'yds in Drohn, Leiwen, TRITTENHEIM, PIESPORT. EISWEIN a speciality.

Grosse Lage The top level of the VDP's new classification, but only applies to VDP members. *NB* Not on any account to be confused with GROSSLAGE. The dry wine from a Grosse Lage site is called GG.

Grosser Ring Mos Group of top (VDP) MOS estates, whose annual Sept auction at TRIER sets world-record prices.

Grosslage Term destined, maybe even intended, to confuse. A collection of secondary v'yds with supposedly similar character – but no indication of quality. Not on any account to be confused with GROSSE LAGE.

Gunderloch Rhh ★★★ →★★★★ 90 97 01 05 07 08 09 11 12 13 14 15 16 The late Fritz Hasselbach made ROTER HANG area world-famous (again), son Johannes builds on this: classics will not change, eg. nobly sweet RIES from GROSSE LAGE Rothenberg or culinary *Kabinett Jean-Baptiste*. But TROCKEN wines now much drier than before.

Gut Hermannsberg Na ★★ →★★★ Former state domain at NIEDERHAUSEN, privatized and reborn in 2010. Powerful RIES from GROSSE LAGE v'yds in NIEDERHAUSEN, SCHLOSSBÖCKELHEIM, TRAISEN.

Gutsabfüllung Estate-bottled, and made from own grapes.

Gutswein Wine with no v'yd or village designation, but only the producer's name: entry level category. Ideally, Gutswein should be a ERZEUGERABFÜLLUNG (from own grapes), but is not always the case.

Haag, Fritz Mos ★★★★ 90 96 97 99 01 04 05 07 08 09 10 11 12 13 14 15 (16) BRAUNEBERG's top estate; Oliver Haag is following the footsteps of his father Wilhelm, but wines are more modern in style. *See also* SCHLOSS LIESER.

Haag, Willi Mos ★★→★★★ BRAUNEBERG family estate, led by Marcus Haag. Old-style RIES, mainly sweet, rich but balanced, and inexpensive.

Haart, Julian Mos ★★→★★★ Talented nephew of Theo Haart (*see* next entry). First vintage 2010. v'yds in Wintrich and PIESPORT. An estate to watch.

Haart, Reinhold M-M ★★★→★★★★ Best estate in PIESPORT. Aromatic, mild RIES, SPÄTLESEN, AUSLESEN and higher PRÄDIKAT wines are *racy, copybook, Mosel Ries* – with great ageing potential.

Halbtrocken Medium dry with 9–18g unfermented sugar/litre, inconsistently distinguished from FEINHERB (which sounds better).

Hattenheim Rhg ★★→★★★★ 01 05 08 09 11 12 13 14 15 16 Town famous for GROSSE LAGEN Nussbrunnen, Hassel, Mannberg, Schützenhaus, STEINBERG, Wisselbrunnen. Estates: Barth, HESSISCHE STAATSWEINGÜTER, Knyphausen, Lang, LANGWERTH, Ress, SPREITZER. Classic RHG RIES. The *Brunnen* ("well") v'yds lie on a rocky basin that collects water, protection against drought.

Heger, Dr. Bad ★★★ KAISERSTUHL estate known for dry parcel selections from volcanic soils in Achkarren and IHRINGEN, esp Häusleboden (SPÄTBURGUNDER) and Vorderer Berg for steepest Winklerberg terraces. Glorious MUSKATELLER BA.

Hessische Bergstrasse Hess ★→★★★ 09 11 12 13 14 15 (16) Germany's smallest wine region (only 440 ha), n of Heidelberg. Pleasant RIES from HESSISCHE STAATSWEINGÜTER, Simon-Bürkle, Stadt Bensheim.

Hessische Staatsweingüter Hess, Rhg State domain of big – and historical – dimensions, holding 220 ha in ASSMANNSHAUSEN, RÜDESHEIM, *Rauenthal*, HOCHHEIM and along HESSISCHE BERGSTRASSE. C12 Cistercian abbey KLOSTER EBERBACH has vinotheque, 12 historical presses. Quality is sound, but selective. SEKT can be exquisite.

Heyl zu Herrnsheim Rhh ★★→★★★ Historic NIERSTEIN estate, bio, part of the ST-ANTONY estate. GG from monopoly site Brudersberg can be excellent.

Heymann-Löwenstein Mos ★★★ Reinhard Löwenstein works 14 ha at WINNINGEN nr Koblenz, mostly RIES on steep terraces. Spontaneously fermented Blaufüsser Lay, Laubach, Rothlay have individuality, character.

Hochgewächs Designation for a MOS RIES that obeys stricter requirements than plain QbA, today rarely used. A worthy advocate is *Kallfelz* in Zell-Merl.

Hochheim Rhg ★★→★★★ 90 97 01 03 04 05 07 08 09 10 11 12 13 14 15 16 Town e of main RHG, on River Main. Rich RIES from GROSSE LAGE v'yds: Domdechaney, Hölle, Kirchenstück, Reichestal. Growers: Domdechant *Werner*, Flick/Königin Victoriaberg, Himmel, *Künstler*, HESSISCHE STAATSWEINGÜTER.

Kabinett

Many are afraid that climate change will make KABINETT an endangered species: a Kabinett worthy of its name needs to be light, fragrant – poised between greenish flavours and too much richness. The window for harvesting gets ever narrower. So now growers are rediscovering abandoned sites in cooler side valleys, or are climbing in altitude. Try MUSKATELLER Kabinett made by the local co-op on the island of Reichenau, BODENSEE (400m altitude). Delicacy at 10% alc – balance of sweetness and acidity like MOS of 20 yrs ago.

Hock Traditional English term for Rhine wine, derived from HOCHHEIM.

Hoensbroech, Weingut Reichsgraf zu Bad ★★→★★★ Top KRAICHGAU estate on v. calcareous loess soils. Dry WEISSBURGUNDER Michelfelder Himmelberg is a classic.

Hövel, Weingut von Mos ★★★ Fine SAAR estate with v'yds at Oberemmel (Hütte – filigree wines – is 4.8 ha monopoly), at KANZEM (Hörecker) and in SCHARZHOFBERG. Now bio.

Huber, Bernhard Bad ★★★ Julian H continues to produce supple SPÄTBURGUNDER (esp *Alte Reben*, Bombacher Sommerhalde) and burgundy-style CHARD (ALTE REBEN, Hecklinger Schlossberg, Malterdingen Bienenberg).

Ihringen Bad ★→★★★ Village in KAISERSTUHL known for fine SPÄTBURGUNDER, GRAUBURGUNDER on steep volcanic Winklerberg. Top growers: DR. HEGER, Konstanzer, Michel, Stigler.

Immich-Batterieberg M-M ★★ Comeback of an old name. New owners (since 2009) make piquant dry and off-dry RIES from Batterieberg, Ellergrub, Steffensberg v'yds in Enkirch, but no sweet wines.

Ingelheim Rhh ★★→★★★ A RHH town with limestone beds under v'yds; historic fame for SPÄTBURGUNDER being reinvigorated by Simone ADAMS, J Neus and Schloss Westerhaus.

Iphofen Frank ★★→★★★ 90 97 01 05 08 09 11 12 13 14 15 16 STEIGERWALD village with famous GROSSE LAGE Julius-Echter-Berg (named after C16 prince-bishop keen on witch trials). Rich, aromatic, well-ageing SILVANER from gypsum soils. Growers: Arnold, Emmerich, JULIUSSPITAL, RUCK, VETTER, WELTNER, *Wirsching*, Zehntkeller.

Jahrgang Year – as in "vintage".

Johannisberg Rhg ★★→★★★★ 01 05 07 08 09 11 12 13 14 15 (16) RHG village known for berry- and honey-scented RIES. GROSSE LAGE v'yds: Hölle, Klaus, SCHLOSS JOHANNISBERG. GROSSLAGE (avoid!): Erntebringer. Top growers: CHAT SAUVAGE, JOHANNISHOF (Eser), PRINZ VON HESSEN, SCHLOSS JOHANNISBERG.

Johannishof (Eser) Rhg ★★→★★★ Family estate with v'yds at JOHANNISBERG, RÜDESHEIM. Johannes Eser makes RIES with perfect balance of ripeness and steely acidity.

Josephshöfer Mos ★★→★★★ 83 90 03 05 08 09 11 12 13 14 15 16 GROSSE LAGE v'yd at GRAACH, the sole property of KESSELSTATT. Harmonious, berry-flavoured RIES.

Jost, Toni M Rh ★★★ Leading estate in BACHARACH with monopoly Hahn, now led by Cecilia J. Aromatic RIES with nerve, and recent trials with PINOT N. Family also run an estate at WALLUF (RHG).

Juliusspital Frank ★★★ Ancient WÜRZBURG charity with top v'yds all over FRANK known for *dry Silvaners* that age well. Recently less opulence and more structure – GGS now cellared 1 yr more before sale.

Kabinett *See* box, right. Germany's unique featherweight contribution, but with climate change ever more difficult to produce.

Kaiserstuhl Bad Outstanding district nr Rhine with notably warm climate and volcanic soil. Renowned above all for SPÄTBURGUNDER and GRAUBURGUNDER.

Kanzem Mos ★★★ 90 01 04 05 07 08 09 11 12 14 15 (16) SAAR village with steep GROSSE LAGE v'yd on slate and weathered Rotliegend (red rock): Altenberg. Growers: BISCHÖFLICHE WEINGÜTER TRIER, *Van Volxem*, VON OTHEGRAVEN.

Karlsmühle Mos ★★★ Estate with two Lorenzhöfer monopoly sites. Classic RUWER RIES.

The capital Berlin has seven small v'yds – all in all around 2000 vines.

Karthäuserhof Mos ★★★★ 90 01 05 07 08 09 10 11 12 13 14 15 16 Outstanding RUWER estate with monopoly v'yd Karthäuserhofberg. Characteristic neck-only label stands for refreshing dry and sublime sweet wines.

Kasel Mos ★★→★★★ Village for flowery and well-ageing RUWER Valley RIES. Top growers: Beulwitz, BISCHÖFLICHE WEINGÜTER TRIER, KARLSMÜHLE, *Kesselstatt*.

Germany's quality levels

The official range of qualities and styles in ascending order is (take a deep breath):

1 Wein: formerly known as *Tafelwein*. Light wine of no specified character, mostly sweetish.

2 ggA: *geschützte geographische Angabe*, or Protected Geographical Indication, formerly known as *Landwein*. Dryish *Wein* with some regional style. Mostly a label to avoid, but some thoughtful estates use the *Landwein*, or ggA designation to bypass official constraints.

3 gU: *geschützte Ursprungsbezeichnung*, or protected Designation of Origin. Replacing QUALITÄTSWEIN.

4 Qualitätswein: dry or sweetish wine with sugar added before fermentation to increase its strength, but tested for quality and with distinct local and grape character. Don't despair.

5 Kabinett: dry/dryish natural (unsugared) wine of distinct personality and distinguishing lightness. Can occasionally be sublime – esp with a few yrs' age.

6 Spätlese: stronger, often sweeter than KABINETT. Full-bodied. Today many top SPÄTLESEN are TROCKEN or completely dry.

7 Auslese: sweeter, sometimes stronger than Spätlese, often with honey-like flavours, intense and long-lived. Occasionally dry and weighty.

8 Beerenauslese (BA): v. sweet, sometimes strong and intense. Can be superb.

9 Eiswein: from naturally frozen grapes of BA/TBA quality: concentrated, sharpish and v. sweet. Some examples are extreme, unharmonious.

10 Trockenbeerenauslese (TBA): intensely sweet and aromatic; alcohol slight. Extraordinary and everlasting.

Kauer M Rh ★★→★★★ Family estate at BACHARACH. Fine, aromatic organic RIES. Randolf Kauer is professor of organic viticulture at GEISENHEIM.

Keller, Franz Bad *See* SCHWARZER ADLER.

Keller, Weingut Rhh ★★★→★★★★ Star of RHH known for powerful GG RIES from Dalsheimer Hubacker and pricey G-Max. Also Ries from NIERSTEIN (Hipping and Pettenthal).

Kesseler, August Rhg ★★★→★★★★ Passionate grower; elegant SPÄTBURGUNDER from ASSMANNSHAUSEN, RÜDESHEIM. Also outstanding RIES: quaffable dry Pfaffenwies from LORCH, complex Berg Schlossberg and Berg Roseneck GGS from Rüdesheim. Breathtaking 11 Berg Schlossberg BA GOLDKAPSEL.

Kesselstatt, Reichsgraf von Mos ★★→★★★★ In her 30 yrs+ of hard work, Annegret Reh-Gartner (died 2016) made this estate splendid: 35 ha top v'yds on MOS and both tributaries, incl remarkable stake in SCHARZHOFBERG. Selective buyers can find pearls.

Kiedrich Rhg w ★★→★★★★ Village linked inseparably to the WEIL estate; top v'yd Gräfenberg. Other growers (eg. FRICKE, PRINZ VON HESSEN, Knyphausen) own only small plots here.

Kloster Eberbach Rhg Glorious C12 Cistercian abbey in HATTENHEIM with iconic STEINBERG, domicile of HESSISCHE STAATSWEINGÜTER.

Klumpp, Weingut Bad ★★★ Rising star in Kraichgau. SPÄTBURGUNDER LEMBERGER of depth, elegance. Markus Klumpp is married to Meike Näkel of MEYER-NÄKEL.

Knewitz, Weingut Rhh ★★★ 20 ha family estate puts Appenheim village on map. Young brothers Tobias and Björn make focused, skillful whites. Hundertgulden RIES 15' is remarkable, as are Ries ORTSWEIN, WEISSBURGUNDER and CHARD.

Knipser, Weingut Pfz ★★★→★★★★ N PFZ family estate, barrique-aged SPÄTBURGUNDER, straightforward RIES (GG Steinbuckel), Cuvée X (B'x blend). Many specialities, incl historical bone-dry Gelber Orleans.

Koehler-Ruprecht, Weingut Pfz ★★ →★★★ 97 99 01 05 07 08 09 10 11 12 13 Kallstadt estate, formerly known for Bernd Philippi's traditional winemaking, esp RIES Saumagen R. Now in new hands: Philippi has left.

Kraichgau Bad Small district se of Heidelberg. Top growers: Burg Ravensburg/ Heitlinger, HOENSBROECH, Hummel, KLUMPP.

Kreuzberg Ahr ★★★ Ludwig Kreuzberg has made a name for brisk, not overalcoholic, distinctly cool-climate SPÄTBURGUNDER.

Krone, Weingut Rhg ★★→★★★ 99' 05 06 07 08 09 10 11 12 13 Estate in ASSMANNSHAUSEN, run by WEGELER; some of best and oldest SPÄTBURGUNDER v'yds in the GROSSE LAGE Höllenberg. Sublime reds; whites less exciting.

Kühling-Gillot Rhh ★★★ →★★★★ Top bio estate, run by Caroline Gillot and husband HO Spanier. Best in already outstanding range of ROTER HANG RIES: GG Rothenberg "wurzelecht" from ungrafted, 70 yrs+ vines.

Kühn, Peter Jakob Rhg ★★★ →★★★★ Excellent estate in OESTRICH led by P J Kühn and son. Obsessive bio v'yd management and long macerations shape *nonconformist but exciting* RIES. Lenchen TBA 15' is a miracle of freshness.

Kuhn, Philipp Pfz ★★★ Reliable producer in Laumersheim. Dry RIES rich and harmonious (now also SAUMAGEN) and barrel-aged SPÄTBURGUNDER succulent and complex.

Künstler Rhg ★★★ Superb dry RIES in GROSSE LAGE sites at HOCHHEIM, eg. Hölle 03 04 05 07' 08 09' 10 11 12 13 14 15, Kostheim, and now on other side of RHG at RÜDESHEIM (15' Berg Schlossberg).

Kuntz, Sybille ★★★ Progressive individual organic 12-ha estate at Lieser, esp Niederberg-Helden v'yd. Intense wines, one of each ripeness category, intended for gastronomy, listed in many top restaurants.

Laible, Alexander ★★ →★★★ New DURBACH estate of ANDREAS LAIBLE's (*see* next entry) younger son; aromatic dry RIES and WEISSBURGUNDER.

Laible, Andreas Bad ★★★ Crystalline dry RIES from DURBACH's Plauelrain v'yd and gd SCHEUREBE, GEWÜRZ. In 2014, outstanding PINOT GR *GG Stollenberg*: creamy and tight-knit at same time.

Landwein Now "ggA". *See* box, p.161.

Langwerth von Simmern Rhg ★★ →★★★ Famous Eltville estate, with traditional winemaking. Top v'yds: Baiken, Mannberg (monopoly), Marcobrunn. Now back on form.

Lauer Mos ★★★ Fine, precise RIES: tense, poised. Parcel selections from huge Ayler Kupp v'yd. Best: Kern, Schonfels, Stirn.

Leitz, Josef Rhg ★★★ RÜDESHEIM family estate for rich but elegant dry and sweet RIES, esp from classified v'yds. Outstanding 15' GG trio: Roseneck (backward, floral), Schlossberg (future), Rottland (salty).

Liebfrauenstift, Weingut Rhh Owner of best plots of historical LIEBFRAUENSTIFT-KIRCHENSTÜCK v'yd. Formerly linked to a merchant house, but now autonomous. Promising: Katharina Prüm (of JJ PRÜM) consults.

Liebfrauenstift-Kirchenstück Rhh A walled v'yd in city of Worms producing flowery RIES from gravelly soil. Producers: Gutzler, Schembs, Weingut LIEBFRAUENSTIFT. Not to be confused with Liebfraumilch, a cheap and tasteless imitation.

Loewen, Carl Mos ★★★ RIES of elegance, tension, complexity. Best sites at Leiwen (GROSSE LAGE Laurentiuslay), Thörnicher Ritsch and Longuicher Maximin Herrenberg (planted 1896, ungrafted). Entry-level Ries Varidor excellent *value*.

Loosen, Weingut Dr. M-M ★★→★★★★ 90 97 01 05 08 09 10 11 12 13 14 15 16 Charismatic Ernie Loosen produces traditional RIES from old vines in BERNKASTEL, ERDEN, GRAACH, ÜRZIG, WEHLEN. Erdener Prälat AUSLESE is cultish. Dr. L Ries, from bought-in grapes, is reliable. *See also* WOLF (PFZ), Chateau Ste Michelle (Washington State), J. Christopher (Oregon).

Lorch Rhg ★→★★★ Village in extreme w of RHG. Sharply crystalline wines, now rediscovered. Best: CHAT SAUVAGE, FRICKE, Johanninger, KESSELER, von Kanitz.

Löwenstein, Fürst Frank, Rhg ★★★ Princely estate with holdings in RHG, FRANK. Classic Rhg RIES from HALLGARTEN, unique *Silvaner, Ries from ultra-steep v'yd Homburger Kallmuth*.

Marcobrunn Rhg Historic v'yd in Erbach; potentially one of Germany's v. best. Contemporary wines scarcely match its past fame.

Markgräflerland Bad District s of Freiburg, cool climate due to breezes from Black Forest. Typical GUTEDEL a pleasant companion for local cuisine. Climate change makes PINOT varieties successful.

Markgraf von Baden Bad ★★→★★★ Important noble estate (135 ha) at Salem castle (BODENSEE) and Staufenberg castle (ORTENAU), young Prince Bernhard being more involved than his father was. Rising quality.

Maximin Grünhaus Mos ★★★★ 83 90 97 99 01 05 07 08 09 11 12 13 14 15 16 Supreme RUWER estate led by Carl von Schubert who also presides over GROSSER RING (VDP MOS). V. traditional winemaking shapes herb-scented, *delicate, long-lived Ries*. Astonishing WEISSBURGUNDER, PINOT N.

Merkelbach, Weingut M-M ★★→★★★ Tiny Estate at ÜRZIG, 2 ha. Brothers Alfred and Rolf (both c.80), inexpensive MOS made not to sip, but to drink. Superb list of old vintages.

Meyer-Näkel Ahr ★★★→★★★★ Werner Näkel and daughters make fine AHR Valley SPÄTBURGUNDER that exemplifies modern, oak-aged style. Also in South Africa (Zwalu, together with Neil Ellis) and Portugal (Quinta da Carvalhosa).

Mittelhaardt Pfz The n central and best part of PFZ, incl DEIDESHEIM, FORST, RUPPERTSBERG, WACHENHEIM; largely planted with RIES.

Mittelmosel M-M Central and best part of MOS, a RIES eldorado, incl BERNKASTEL, BRAUNEBERG, GRAACH, PIESPORT, WEHLEN, etc.

Mittelrhein M Rh ★★→★★★ Dramatically scenic Rhine area nr tourist-magnet Loreley. Best villages: BACHARACH, BOPPARD. Delicate yet *steely Ries, underrated* and underpriced.

Molitor, Markus M-M, Mos ★★★ Growing estate (now 100 ha in 170 parcels throughout M-M and SAAR) led by perfectionist Markus M. Offers styles, v'yds and vintages in amazing depth.

Mosbacher Pfz ★★★ Some of best GG RIES of FORST: rather refined than massive. Traditional ageing in big oak casks. Excellent SAUV BL too ("Fumé").

Mosel (Moselle in French) Wine-growing area formerly known as Mosel-Saar-Ruwer. Conditions on the RUWER and SAAR tributaries are v. different from those along the Mosel. 60% RIES.

Moselland, Winzergenossenschaft Mos Huge MOS co-op, at BERNKASTEL, after mergers with co-ops in NA, PFZ; 3290 members, 2400 ha. Little is above average.

Müller-Catoir, Weingut Pfz ★★→★★★ Aged AUSLESEN, BA, TBA 83 90 97 98 01 can be delicious; 2011 Schlössel RIESLANER TBA.

Nackenheim Rhh ★→★★★★ NIERSTEIN neighbour with GROSSE LAGE Rothenberg on

---

Call me honey

Urban beekeeping is so last yr. Now it's v'yds: growers are befriending apiculturists. Bees in vines are better proof of sustainability and a greener approach than eco certificates. The most prestigious grower's honey is from EGON MÜLLER Jr. (aged 17) from hives in the SCHARZHOFBERG. Other honey producers incl MAXIMIN GRÜNHAUS, WEINGUT ODINSTAL and FRANK estates Benedikt Braun and Dieter Wolfahrt.

red shale, famous for **Rhh's richest Ries**, superb TBA. Top growers: *Gunderloch*, KÜHLING-GILLOT.

Nahe Tributary of the Rhine and dynamic region with dozens of lesser-known producers, excellent value. Great variety of soils; best RIES from slate has almost MOS-like raciness.

Naturrein "Naturally pure": designation on old labels (pre-1971), indicating as little technical intervention as possible, esp no chaptalizing (sugar added at fermentation). Should be brought back.

Mos has highest number of single v'yd designations (507).

Neipperg, Graf von Würt ★★★ Noble estate in Schwaigern: reds (LEMBERGER, SPÄTBURGUNDER) of grace and purity. Count Karl-Eugen von Neipperg's younger brother Stephan makes wine at Château Canon la Gaffelière in St-Émilion and elsewhere.

Niederhausen Na ★★→★★★★ Village of the middle NA Valley. Complex RIES from famous GROSSE LAGE Hermannshöhle and neighbouring steep slopes. Growers: CRUSIUS, DÖNNHOFF, GUT HERMANNSBERG, J Schneider, Mathern, von Racknitz.

Nierstein Rhh ★→★★★★ 90 97 01 05 07 08 09 11 12 13 14 15 16 Important wine town (c.800 ha) with accordingly variable wines. Best are rich, tense, eg. GROSSE LAGE v'yds Brudersberg, Hipping, Oelberg, Orbel, Pettenthal. Growers: BUNN, FE Huff, Gehring, GUNDERLOCH, Guntrum, HEYL ZU HERRNSHEIM, KELLER, KÜHLING-GILLOT, Manz, Schätzel, ST-ANTONY, Strub. But *beware Grosslage Gutes Domtal*: a supermarket deception.

Ockfen Mos ★★→★★★ Village with almost atypical sturdy SAAR RIES from GROSSE LAGE v'yd Bockstein. Growers: OTHEGRAVEN, SANKT URBANS-HOF, WAGNER, *Zilliken*.

Odinstal, Weingut Pfz ★★→★★★ Highest v'yd of PFZ, 150m above WACHENHEIM. Bio farming and low-tech vinification bring pure RIES, SILVANER, GEWURZ. Harvest often extends into Nov.

Oechsle Scale for sugar content of grape juice.

Oestrich Rhg ★★→★★★ Exemplary steely RIES and fine AUSLESEN from GROSSE LAGE v'yds: Doosberg, Lenchen. Top growers: August Eser, KÜHN, Querbach, SPREITZER, WEGELER.

Oppenheim Rhh ★→★★★ Town S of NIERSTEIN, GROSSE LAGE Kreuz, Sackträger. Growers: Guntrum, Kissinger, KÜHLING-GILLOT, Manz. Spectacular C13 church.

Ortenau Bad (r) w ★★ District around and S of city of Baden-Baden. Mainly Klingelberger (RIES) and SPÄTBURGUNDER from granite soils. Top villages: DURBACH, Neuweier, Waldulm.

Ortswein Second rank up in VDP's pyramid of qualities: a village wine, rather than a single v'yd.

Othegraven, von Mos ★★★ Fine SAAR estate with superb GROSSE LAGE Altenberg of KANZEM, as well as parcels in OCKFEN (Bockstein) and Wawern (Herrenberg). Since 2010 owned by TV star Günther Jauch.

Palatinate English for PFZ.

Pfalz 2nd-largest German region, balmy climate, Lucullian lifestyle. MITTELHAARDT RIES best; S Pfalz (SÜDLICHE WEINSTRASSE) is better suited to PINOT varieties. ZELLERTAL now fashonable: cool climate.

Piesport M-M ★→★★★★ 01 03 05 07 08 09 11 12 13 14 15 16 M-M village for rich, aromatic RIES (typically SPÄTLESE and sweeter). GROSSE LAGE v'yds Domherr and Goldtröpfchen. Growers: GRANS-FASSIAN, Joh Haart, JULIAN HAART, K Hain, KESSELSTATT, *Reinhold Haart*, SANKT URBANS-HOF. Avoid GROSSLAGE Michelsberg.

Prädikat Legally defined special attributes or qualities. *See* QMP.

Prinz, Fred Rhg ★★→★★★ Organic RHG estate producing floral RIES from Hallgartener v'yds Jungfer 03 12 13, herbal Schönhell 13 14.

Prinz von Hessen Rhg ★★★ Glorious wines of vibrancy and precision from historic JOHANNISBERG estate, esp at SPÄTLESE and above, and mature vintages.

Prüm, JJ Mos ★★★★ 71 76 83 88 89 90 94 95 96 97 99 01 02 03 04 05 06 07 08 09 10 11 12 13 14 15 16 Legendary WEHLEN estate; also BERNKASTEL, GRAACH. Delicate but extremely long-lived wines with astonishing finesse and distinctive character.

Prüm, SA Mos ★★ Less traditional in style and less consistent than WEHLEN neighbour JJ PRÜM. Be v. selective.

QbA (Qualitätswein bestimmter Anbaugebiete) "Quality Wine", controlled as to area, grape(s), vintage. May add sugar before fermentation (as in French chaptalization). Intended as middle category, but now VDP obliges its members to label their best dry wines (GGS) as QbA. New EU name gU is scarcely found on labels (*see* box, p.161).

QmP (Qualitätswein mit Prädikat) Top category, for all wines ripe enough not to need sugaring (KABINETT to TBA).

Randersacker Frank ★★→★★★ Village s of WÜRZ with GROSSE LAGE: Pfülben. Top growers: BÜRGERSPITAL, JULIUSSPITAL, STAATLICHER HOFKELLER, SCHMITT'S KINDER, STORRLEIN & Krenig.

Ratzenberger M Rh ★★→★★★ Estate making racy, dry and off-dry RIES in BACHARACH; best from GROSSE LAGE v'yds: Posten and Steeger St-Jost. Gd SEKT too.

Rauenthal Rhg ★★→★★★★ Once RHG'S most expensive RIES. *Spicy, austere but complex* from inland slopes. GROSSE LAGE v'yds: Baiken and Rothenberg. Top growers: a ESER, Breuer (with monopoly Nonnenberg), HESSISCHE STAATSWEINGÜTER, LANGWERTH VON SIMMERN.

Raumland Rhh ★★★ SEKT expert with deep cellar and a full range of fine balanced cuvées. Superb 04 CHARD Brut, disgorged 2014.

Rebholz, Ökonomicrat Pfz ★★★ Top SÜDLICHE WEINSTRASSE estate; bone dry, zesty and reliable RIES (GG Im Sonnenschein, Ganz Horn). Kastanienbusch GG 04 05 07' 08' 09 11' 12 14 15 (no 2013) from red schist legendary. Gd CHARD, SPÄTBURGUNDER.

Restsüsse Unfermented grape sugar remaining in (or in cheap wines added to) wine to give it sweetness. Can range from 1g/l in a TROCKEN wine to 300g in a TBA.

Rheingau Birthplace of RIES. Historic s-facing slopes of Rhine between Wiesbaden and RUDESHEIM. Classic, substantial Ries, famous for steely backbone, and small amounts of delicate SPÄTBURGUNDER. Also centre of SEKT production.

Rheinhessen Germany's by far largest region (26,500 ha), between Mainz and Worms. Much dross, but also treasure trove of well-priced wines from gifted young growers.

Richter, Weingut Max Ferd M-M ★★→★★★ Reliable estate, at Mülheim. Esp gd RIES KABINETT, SPÄTLESEN: full and aromatic. Round, pretty Brut (EISWEIN dosage). Thoughtful winemaking.

Riffel Rhh ★★→★★★ Bingen's Scharlachberg – top site – lacked ambassador until Erik Riffel went organic, achieved spectacular improvement. Try RIES Turm or inexpensive ORTSWEIN.

Rings, Weingut Pfz ★★★→★★★★ Brothers Steffen and Andreas are shooting stars in PFZ: remarkable dry RIES esp from Kallstadt (Steinacker, SAUMAGEN), equally gd SPÄTBURGUNDER (Saumagen, Felsenberg im Berntal).

Newest trend: estate-made mulled wine. Schloss Wackerbarth uses 1834 recipe.

Roter Hang Rhh Leading RIES area of RHH (NACKENHEIM, NIERSTEIN, OPPENHEIM). Name ("red slope") refers to red shale soil, but now a 2nd meaning arises: climate change encourages red varieties (SPÄTBURGUNDER, LEMBERGER).

Ruck, Johann Frank ★★★ Spicy, age-worthy SILVANER, RIES, SCHEUREBE and TRAMINER from IPHOFEN.

Rüdesheim Rhg ★★→★★★★ 90 01 05 08 09 10 11 12 13 14 15 16 Most famous

> **Scheurebe: don't judge a grape by its breeder**
> A new grape for SAUV BL lovers: SCHEUREBE. If you want spiciness and a
> tight, RIES-like structure, Scheurebe is worth a look. Best (all TROCKEN)
> incl: SP, Pfeffingen; Weegmüller (PFZ); Kronsberg ALTE REBEN, WIRSCHING;
> Estheria, RUCK; Julius-Echter-Berg, Emmerich; Marsberg, Winzerhof
> Stahl; Zehnthof Weickert (FRANK); Kalkstein, Manz; Katharina Wechsler
> (RHH); Plauelrain, ANDREAS LAIBLE (BAD); SCHLOSS PROSCHWITZ (SACHS). HORST
> SAUER makes a brilliant sweet SPÄTLESE. Many occasionally make nobly
> sweet versions too, as do eg. WITTMANN, Seehof Fauth (Rhh). On the
> grape's 100th anniversary in 2016 it turned out that Georg Scheu, the
> breeder, was deemed "politically absolutely reliable" in the 30s by his
> boss Dr. Richard Wagner, a major Nazi official.

RHG RIES on slate, best GROSSE LAGE v'yds (Kaisersteinfels, Roseneck, Rottland, Schlossberg) called Rüdesheimer Berg. Full-bodied but never clumsy wines, floral, gd even in off-yrs. Best growers: *Breuer*, CHAT SAUVAGE, CORVERS-KAUTER, HESSISCHE STAATSWEINGÜTER, *Johannishof*, KESSELER, KÜNSTLER, LEITZ, Ress.

Ruppertsberg Pfz ★★→★★★ MITTELHAARDT village known for elegant RIES. Growers: BASSERMANN-JORDAN, Biffar, BUHL, BÜRKLIN-WOLF, CHRISTMANN, VON WINNING.

Ruwer Mos Tributary of MOS nr TRIER, higher in altitude than M-M, but not as cold as SAAR. Quaffable light dry and intense sweet RIES. Best growers: Beulwitz, Karlsmühle, KARTHÄUSERHOF, KESSELSTATT, MAXIMIN GRÜNHAUS.

Saale-Unstrut Sa-Un 09 11 12 15 N region around confluence of these two rivers nr Leipzig. Terraced v'yds have Cistercian origins. Quality leaders: Böhme, Born, Gussek, Kloster Pforta, Lützkendorf, Pawis.

Saar Mos Tributary of Mosel, bordered by steep slopes. Most austere, steely, *brilliant Ries* of all, consistency favoured by climate change. Villages incl: AYL, KANZEM, OCKFEN, SAARBURG, Serrig, WILTINGEN (SCHARZHOFBERG).

Saarburg Mos SAAR Valley small town. Growers: WAGNER, ZILLIKEN. GROSSE LAGE: Rausch.

Sachsen 03 05 09 11 12 15 Region in Elbe Valley around Meissen and Dresden. Characterful dry whites. Best growers: Aust, Richter, *Schloss Proschwitz*, Schloss Wackerbarth, Schuh, Schwarz, ZIMMERLING.

Salm, Prinz zu Na, Rhh Owner of Schloss Wallhausen ★★→★★★ in NA and Villa Sachsen ★→★★ in RHH; ex-president of VDP. RIES at Schloss Wallhausen (organic) has made gd progress recently.

Salwey Bad ★★★ Leading KAISERSTUHL estate. Konrad S picks early for freshness. Best: GGS Henkenberg and Eichberg GRAUBURGUNDER, Kirchberg SPÄTBURGUNDER and WEISSBURGUNDER.

Sankt Urbans-Hof Mos ★★★ Large family estate based in Leiwen, v'yds along M-M and SAAR. Limpid RIES, impeccably pure, racy. Brilliant range of AUSLESEN 15 (from Leiwen, OCKFEN, PIESPORT).

Sauer, Horst Frank ★★★ Finest exponent of ESCHERNDORF's top v'yd Lump. Racy, straightforward *dry Silvaner* and RIES, sensational TBA.

Sauer, Rainer Frank ★★★ Top family estate producing seven different dry SILVANERS from ESCHERNDORF's steep slope Lump. Best: GG am Lumpen, ALTE REBEN and "L" 99' 03' 04 07' 08 13 14 15.

Saumagen Popular local dish of PFZ: stuffed pig's stomach. Also one of best v'yds of region: a calcareous site at Kallstadt producing excellent RIES, PINOT N.

Schaefer, Willi Mos ★★★ Willi S and son Christoph finest in GRAACH (but only 4 ha). MOS RIES at its best: pure, crystalline, feather-light, rewarding at all levels.

Schäfer-Fröhlich Na ★★★ Ambitious NA family estate known for spontaneously fermented RIES of great intensity, *GG* incl Bockenau Felseneck and Stromberg.

Scharzhofberg Mos ★★→★★★★ Superlative SAAR v'yd: a rare coincidence of microclimate, soil and human intelligence to bring about perfection of RIES. Top estates: BISCHÖFLICHE WEINGÜTER TRIER, EGON MÜLLER, KESSELSTATT, VAN VOLXEM, VON HÖVEL.

Schlossböckelheim Na ★★→★★★★ Village with top NA v'yds, incl GROSSE LAGE Felsenberg, Kupfergrube. Firm, demanding RIES. Top growers: C Bamberger, CRUSIUS, DÖNNHOFF, GUT HERMANNSBERG, SCHÄFER-FRÖHLICH.

Schloss Johannisberg Rhg ★★→★★★ Historic RHG estate and Metternich mansion, 100% RIES, now owned by Henkell (Oetker group). Usually v.gd SPÄTLESE Grünlack ("green sealing-wax"), AUSLESE Rosalack.

Schloss Lieser M-M ★★★ Within the HAAG family, roles are clearly defined: Oliver (FRITZ HAAG) at his father's BRAUNEBERG estate is the modernist, elder brother Thomas at Lieser the traditionalist. Racy RIES from Niederberg Helden v'yd, as well as plots in BRAUNEBERG, WEHLEN.

Schloss Proschwitz Sachs ★★ Prince Lippe's resurrected estate at Meissen, leading former East Germany in quality; esp with *dry Weissburgunder*, GRAUBURGUNDER. A great success.

Schloss Reinhartshausen Rhg ★★ Famous estate in Erbach, formerly in Prussian royal family, now in the hands of the Lergenmüller family of PFZ. To watch.

Schloss Vollrads Rhg ★★→★★★★ One of greatest historic RHG estates, now owned by a bank. Obvious improvements in 2015 (eg. silky Edition FEINHERB and classical fruity KABINETT).

Schmitt's Kinder Frank ★★→★★★ Family estate in RANDERSACKER, s of WÜRZBURG, known for classical dry SILVANER, barrel-aged SPÄTBURGUNDER, sweet RIESLANER.

Schnaitmann Würt ★★→★★★★ Excellent barrel-aged reds from WÜRT: SPÄTBURGUNDER, LEMBERGER from GROSSE LAGE Lämmler v'yd. Wines from lesser grapes (SCHWARZRIESLING, TROLLINGER) tasty too.

Schneider, Cornelia and Reinhold Bad ★★★ Age-worthy SPÄTBURGUNDERS 05 07 08 09 10 11 12 13 14 15 from Endingen, KAISERSTUHL, denoted by letters – R for volcanic soil, C for loess – and old-fashioned RULÄNDER.

Schneider, Markus Pfz ★★ Shooting star in Ellerstadt, PFZ. A full range of soundly produced, trendily labelled wines.

Schoppenwein Café (or bar) wine, ie. wine by the glass.

Schwarzer Adler Bad ★★→★★★ Michelin-starred (French) restaurant (continuously since 1969) at Oberbergen, KAISERSTUHL, wine estate for Burgundy-influenced, distinctly culinary GRAU-, WEISS-, SPÄTBURGUNDER. Owner Fritz Keller was one of first in Germany to try barrique ageing (mid-80s).

Schwegler, Albrecht Würt ★★★→★★★★ Small estate; red blends Beryll, Saphir, Granat 90' 94' 99' 03 05' 06' 07 09 10' 11 12 13 vary according to yr. Worth looking for.

Sekt German sparkling wine, v. variable in quality. Bottle fermentation not mandatory. Sekt specialists incl Bardong, RAUMLAND, Schembs, Schloss Vaux, Solter, S Steinmetz, Wilhelmshof. Melsheimer is a delight.

Selbach-Oster M-M ★★★ Scrupulous ZELTINGEN estate with excellent v'yd portfolio, best-known for sweet PRÄDIKAT wines.

Sonnenuhr M-M Sundial. Name of GROSSE LAGE sites at BRAUNEBERG, WEHLEN, ZELTINGEN.

Müller-T is an underrated food match: try with freshwater fish or asparagus.

Sorentberg M-M ★★ V'yd in a side valley of M-M nr Reil, fallow for 50 yrs, now replanted by young Tobias Treis and partner from South Tyrol. Red slate, RIES and promising first results. To watch.

Spätlese Late-harvest. One level riper and potentially sweeter than KABINETT. Gd examples are at least 7 yrs. Spätlese TROCKEN designation is now about to be abandoned by VDP members: a shame.

Spreitzer Rhg ★★★ Brothers Andreas and Bernd S produce deliciously *racy*, *harmonious* RIES from v'yds in HATTENHEIM, OESTRICH, Mittelheim. Outstanding 15s, with a breathtaking Rosengarten TBA GOLDKAPSEL on top.

Staatlicher Hofkeller Frank ★★ Bavarian state domain; 120 ha of fine FRANK v'yds, spectacular cellars under the great baroque Residenz at WÜRZBURG.

Staatsweingut / Staatliche Weinbaudomäne State wine estates or domains exist in BAD (IHRINGEN, Meersburg), WÜRT (Weinsberg), RHG (HESSISCHE STAATSWEINGÜTER), RHH (OPPENHEIM), PFZ (Neustadt) MOS (TRIER). Some have been privatized in recent yrs, eg. at Marienthal (AHR), NIEDERHAUSEN (NA).

St-Antony Rhh ★★→★★★ NIERSTEIN estate with exceptional v'yds. Improvements through new owner (same as HEYL ZU HERRNSHEIM). Brilliant 15' Ölberg.

Steigerwald Frank District in e FRANK. V'yds at considerable altitude, but soils allow powerful SILVANER, RIES. Best: CASTELL, Roth, RUCK, WELTNER, *Wirsching*.

Steinberg Rhg ★★★ Partly walled v'yd at HATTENHEIM, est by Cistercian monks 700 yrs ago: a German Clos de Vougeot. Monopoly of HESSISCHE STAATSWEINGÜTER. Phyllite schist, berry-scented RIES.

Steinwein Frank Wine from WÜRZBURG's best v'yd, Stein. Goethe's favourite. BURGERSPITAL, JULIUSSPITAL, STAATLICHER HOFKELLER all make it.

Stodden Ahr ★★★→★★★★ AHR SPÄTBURGUNDER with a burgundian touch, delicately extracted and subtle. Best usually ALTE REBEN and Rech Herrenberg. Pricey – but production is tiny.

Südliche Weinstrasse Pfz District in s PFZ, famous esp for PINOT varieties. Best growers: BECKER, Leiner, Minges, Münzberg, REBHOLZ, Siegrist, WEHRHEIM.

Tauberfranken Bad (r) w Underrated cool-climate district of ne BAD: FRANK-style SILVANER, RIES from limestone soils. Frost a problem. Best grower: Schlör.

Thanisch, Weingut Dr. M-M ★★→★★★ BERNKASTEL estate, founded 1636, famous for its share of DOCTOR v'yd. After family split-up in 1988 two homonymous estates with similar qualities: Erben (heirs) Müller-Burggraef and Erben Thanisch.

Traisen Na ★★ Small NA village, incl GROSSE LAGE v'yds Bastei and Rotenfels.

Trier Mos The n capital of ancient Rome, on MOS, between RUWER and SAAR. Big charitable estates have cellars here among awesome Roman remains.

Trittenheim M-M ★★→★★★ 01 05 07 08 09 11 12 13 14 15 16 Racy, textbook M-M RIES if from gd plots within extended GROSSE LAGE v'yd Apotheke. Growers: A CLÜSSERATH, Clüsserath-Weiler, E Clüsserath, GRANS-FASSIAN, Milz.

Trocken Dry. Used to be defined as max 9g/l unfermented sugar. Generally the further s in Germany, the more Trocken wines.

Trockenbeerenauslese (TBA) Sweetest and most expensive category of German wine, extremely rare, viscous and concentrated with dried-fruit flavours. Made from selected dried-out grapes affected by noble rot (botrytis). Half bottles a gd idea.

Ürzig M-M ★★★→★★★★ 71 83 90 97 01 03 04 05 07 08 09 11 12 13 14 15 16 River village on red sandstone and red slate, famous for ungrafted old vines and *unique spicy Ries*. GROSSE LAGE v'yd: Würzgarten. Growers: Berres, Christoffel, Erbes, LOOSEN, MARKUS MOLITOR, Mönchhof, Rebenhof. Threatened by controversial (will it be safe?) Autobahn bridge 160m high.

Van Volxem Mos ★★★ Historical SAAR estate revived by obsessed Roman Niewodniczanski. Low yields from top sites (KANZEM Altenberg, SCHARZHOFBERG,

---

Wine prices, then and now

An old price list, typed on a typewriter, gives the 1986 prices of JJ PRÜM wines: WEHLENER Sonnenuhr AUSLESE GOLDKAPSEL 83 cost DM38 (c.\$20 or £13 then) but would easily fetch ten times that today. BEERENAUSLESE 71 sold at DM220 (an enormous price then), but KABINETTS were unexpensive (DM9–10).

Wawern Goldberg, WILTINGEN Gottesfuss), mainly dry or off-dry. Outstanding 15s: dense and focused, made for decades. New project with MARKUS MOLITOR in previously abandoned parts of OCKFENER Geisberg.

Verband Deutscher Prädikatsweingüter (VDP) Pace-making association of 200 premium growers. Look for its eagle insignia on wine labels, and for GROSSE LAGE logo on wines from classified v'yds. A VDP wine is usually a gd bet. President: Steffen CHRISTMANN.

Vetter, Stefan Frank ★★→★★★ Natural wine (*see* A Little Learning): SILVANER fermented on skins. To watch.

Nazi legislation of 1937 banned Spätburgunder from Mos – changed only in 1987.

Vollenwelder Mos ★★★ Daniel Vollenweider from Switzerland has revived the Wolfer Goldgrube v'yd nr Traben-Trarbach (since 2000). *Excellent Ries*, but v. small quantities.

Wachenheim Pfz ★★★ Celebrated village with, according to VDP, no GROSSE LAGE v'yds. See what you think. Top growers: Biffar, BÜRKLIN-WOLF, ODINSTAL, Karl Schäfer, WOLF.

Wageck Pfz ★★→★★★ MITTELHAARDT estate for unaffected, brisk CHARD (still and sparkling) and PINOT N of great finesse.

Wagner, Dr. Mos ★★→★★★ Estate with v'yds in OCKFEN and Saarstein led by young Christiane W. SAAR RIES with purity, freshness.

Wagner-Stempel Rhh ★★★ Seriously crafted RHH wines from Siefersheim nr NA border. Excellent RIES GGS Heerkretz and Höllenberg from porphyry soils need time to develop rich perfume.

Walluf Rhg ★★★ Underrated village, 1st with important v'yds as one leaves Wiesbaden, going w. GROSSE LAGE v'yd: Walkenberg. Growers: *JB Becker, Jost.*

Wegeler M-M, Rhg ★★→★★★★ Important family estates in OESTRICH and BERNKASTEL plus a stake in the famous KRONE estate of ASSMANNSHAUSEN. Geheimrat J blend maintains high standards, single-v'yd RIES usually outstanding value. Old vintages available. Sensational TBAS 15' from CHISENHEIM.

Wehlen M-M ★★★★→★★★★ 90 97 01 03 04 05 07 08 09 10 11 12 13 14 15 16 Wine village with legendary steep SONNENUHR v'yd expressing RIES from slate at v. best: rich, fine, everlasting. Top growers: JJ PRÜM, Kerpen, KESSELSTATT, LOOSEN, MARKUS MOLITOR, RICHTER, SA PRÜM, SELBACH-OSTER, Studert-Prüm, WEGELER. Concern that just-built Autobahn above v'yds will affect water balance in subsoil.

Wehrheim, Weingut Dr. Pfz ★★★ Top organic estate of SÜDLICHE WEINSTRASSE. V. dry, culinary style, esp white PINOT varieties.

Weil, Robert Rhg ★★★→★★★★ 17 37 49 59 75 90 97 01 04 05 07 08 09 10 11 12 13 14 15 16 Outstanding estate in KIEDRICH with classified v'yds Gräfenberg (steep slope on phyllite schist), Klosterberg, Turmberg. Superb sweet KABINETT to EISWEIN, gd GG; entry-level wines more variable.

Weingart M Rh ★★★ Outstanding estate at Spay, v'yds in BOPPARD (esp Hamm Feuerlay). Refined, taut RIES, low-tech in style, superb value.

Weingut Wine estate.

Weins-Prüm, Dr. M-M Small estate (4 ha) with important v'yd holdings in ERDEN, GRAACH, ÜRZIG, WEHLEN in 2016 bought by Katharina Prüm (of J J PRÜM) and Wilhelm Steifensand (WEINGUT LIEBFRAUENSTIFT). The label will cease to exist.

Weissherbst Pale-pink wine, made from a single variety, often SPÄTBURGUNDER. V. variable quality.

Weltner, Paul Frank ★★→★★★ STEIGERWALD family estate. Densely structured, age-worthy SILVANER from underrated Rödelseer Küchenmeister v'yd and neighbouring plots at IPHOFEN.

Wiltingen Mos ★★→★★★★ Heartland of the SAAR. SCHARZHOFBERG crowns a series of GROSSE LAGE v'yds (Braune Kupp, Braunfels, Gottesfuss, Kupp). Top growers: BISCHÖFLICHE WEINGÜTER TRIER, EGON MÜLLER, KESSELSTATT, LE GALLAIS, Sankt Urbans-Hof, VAN VOLXEM, Vols.

Winning, von Pfz ★★★→★★★★ DEIDESHEIM estate, incl former DR. DEINHARD. *Ries of great purity*, terroir expression, slightly influenced by fermentation in new FUDER casks. Also ambitious PINOT N and SAUV BL.

Geisenheim researchers test robot v'yd worker: does overtime without complaint.

Winningen Mos ★★→★★★ Lower MOS town nr Koblenz; powerful dry RIES. GROSSE LAGE v'yds: Röttgen, Uhlen. Top growers: HEYMANN-LÖWENSTEIN, Knebel, Kröber, Richard Richter.

Wirsching, Hans Frank ★★★ Renowned estate in IPHOFEN known for classically structured dry RIES and *Silvaner*. Andrea W extends range with spontaneously fermented Ries Sister Act and kosher SILVANER. Excellent SCHEUREBE too.

Wittmann Rhh ★★★ Philipp Wittmann has propelled this bio estate to the top ranks. Crystal-pure, zesty dry RIES GG (Morstein 04 05 06 07' 08 11 12' 13 14 15). Pricey, though.

Wöhrle Bad ★★★ Organic pioneer at Lahr (25 yrs+), son Markus a PINOT expert, excellent GGS 15' (Kirchgasse GRAUBURGUNDER, Herrentisch WEISSBURGUNDER, Gottsacker CHARD).

Wöhrwag Würt ★★→★★★ Source of elegant dry RIES – arguably best in all WÜRT. Now children Johanna, Philipp, Moritz involved too. Reds also gd.

Wolf JL Pfz ★★→★★★ WACHENHEIM estate, leased by Ernst LOOSEN of BERNKASTEL. Dry PFZ RIES (esp Forster Pechstein), sound and consistent rather than dazzling.

Württemberg Formerly known as "TROLLINGER republic", today with a full range of serious reds, esp LEMBERGER, SPÄTBURGUNDER. Only 30 per cent white varieties, gd SAUV BL, RIES needs altitude v'yds.

Würzburg Frank ★★→★★★★ Great baroque city on the Main, centre of FRANK wine. Classified v'yds: Innere Leiste, Stein, Stein-Harfe. Growers: BÜRGERSPITAL, JULIUSSPITAL, Reiss, STAATLICHER HOFKELLER, Weingut am Stein.

Zell Mos ★→★★★ Best-known lower MOS village, notorious for GROSSLAGE Schwarze Katz (Black Cat): avoid! Gd v'yd: Merler Königslay-Terrassen. Top grower: Kallfelz.

Zellertal Pfz N PFZ area, high, cool, recent gold-rush: Battenfeld-Spanier, KUHN have bought in Zellertal's best RIES v'yd Schwarzer Herrgott or neighbouring RHH plot Zellerweg am Schwarzen Herrgott. Gd local estates: Bremer, Janson Bernhard, Klosterhof Schwedthelm.

Zeltingen M-M ★★→★★★ Top but sometimes underrated MOS village nr WEHLEN. Rich though crisp RIES. GROSSE LAGE v'yd: SONNENUHR. Top growers: JJ PRÜM, MARCUS MOLITOR, SELBACH-OSTER.

Germany's 1st Chard planted 1952, by mistake – supposed to be Weissburgunder.

Ziereisen Bad ★★→★★★★ 03 04 05 07 08 09 10 11' 12 13 14 15 16 Outstanding estate in MARKGRÄFLERLAND, mainly PINOTS. Even entry-level wines show class. Best are SPÄTBURGUNDERS from small plots: Rhini, Schulen. Jaspis = old-vine selections. Newest sensation: GUTEDEL at €120 – and worth it.

Zilliken, Forstmeister Geltz Mos ★★★→★★★★ 93 94 95 96 97 99 01 04 05 07 08 09 10 11 12 13 14 15 SAAR family estate: intense racy/savoury *Ries from Saarburg Rausch* and OCKFEN Bockstein, incl superb long-lasting AUSLESE, EISWEIN. V.gd SEKT too.

Zimmerling, Klaus Sachs ★★★ Small, perfectionist estate, one of first to be est after the wall came down. Best v'yd is Königlicher Weinberg (King's v'yd) at Pillnitz nr Dresden. RIES, sometimes off-dry, can be exquisite.

Luxembourg

The figures say Luxembourgers drink more wine per head than anyone (except for the Vatican): 50.7 litres a year. Of course this includes visitors. So there is little incentive to export, and no great demand. These are Moselle wines that have little to do with the Mosel, even though it's the same river. There are no steep slate slopes; the soil is limestone, and has more in common with Chablis or Champagne than Piesport. Riesling is in a minority: 11%. The big ones are Müller-Thurgau (aka Rivaner), Auxerrois and Pinots Blanc and Gris. Crémant fizz can be good. Climate change has been kind: 2009 and 2011 were brilliant, as was 2015, and 2016 seems to be much better than fair, even if frost reduced the quantity.

Most whites have strong acidity and some sweetness – labels don't differentiate between dry and off-dry. A common term (but of little significance) is "Premier Grand Cru". More reliable are groups of winemakers who come together to promote their high standards: Domaine et Tradition (seven producers) has most credibility. Two more are Privatwenzer ("Private Wine-growers") and Charta Schengen Prestige (designed to include producers in neighbouring areas of Germany and France).

Alice Hartmann ★★★ →★★★★ 11 12 13 14 15' Star producer, in Wormeldange, with parcel selections from Luxembourg's best RIES v'yd, Koeppchen (peppermint-scented Les Terrasses 15; dense La Chapelle 14; skillfully botrytis-influenced Au Coeur 14). Top series Sélection du Château comprises a mineral Ries in a Spätlese Feinherb style (*see* Germany), slightly oak-influenced CHARD and delicate PINOT N. Excellent Crémant too (Grande Cuvée, Rosé Brut). Also owns v'yds in Burgundy (St Aubin) Mittelmosel (Trittenheim) and leases a plot in Scharzhofberg.

Aly Duhr ★★ →★★★ V.gd PINOT GR from Machtum, gd off-dry RIES from Ahn and elegant Ries Vendange Tardive.

Bernard-Massard ★→★★★ Big producer, esp Crémant. Top labels: Château de Schengen and Clos des Rocher. Makes Sekt in Germany too.

Château Pauqué ★★★ International in style. V.gd CHARD, silky RIES Sous la Roche, oak-influenced but still fresh Clos du Paradis AUXERROIS.

Gales ★★ →★★★ Comparatively big but reliable producer at Remich, celebrated 100 yrs in 2016. Best: Crémant (inexpensive Héritage Brut, Prestige Cuvée G Brut) and Domaine et Tradition labels (eg. mineral PINOT BL 15, finely nuanced PINOT N 15'). Also De Nos Rochers range and Charta Schengen. Old cellar labyrinth worth seeing.

Schumacher-Knepper ★★ →★★★ Some excellent wines under Ancien Propriété Constant Knepper label (Wintringer Felsberg RIES 15'). Floral PINOT BL and savoury Elbling.

Sunnen-Hoffmann ★★★ Perfectionist bio family estate at Remerschen: textbook AUXERROIS, serious Ries (Domaine et Tradition Vieilles Vignes 15'), tight, dry PINOT GR, delicate and pure GEWÜRZ 15', outstanding Crémant L et F Brut (Pinot N Rosé).

Other good estates: Mathis Bastian, Cep d'Or, Duhr Frères/Clos Mon Vieux Moulin, Frank Kayl, Paul Legill, Ruppert, Schmit-Fohl, Stronck-Pinnel. Domaines Vinsmoselle is a union of co-ops.

Spain

Abbreviations used in the text:

Alel	Alella	**Min**	Minho
Alen	Alentejo	**Mont-M**	Montilla-Moriles
Alg	Algarve	**Mont**	Montsant
Alic	Alicante	**Mur**	Murcia
Ara	Aragón	**Nav**	Navarra
Bair	Bairrada	**Pen**	Penedès
Bei Int	Beira Interior	**Pri**	Priorat
Bier	Bierzo	**P Vas**	País Vasco
Bul	Bullas	**Rib del D**	Ribera
Cád	Cádiz		del Duero
Can	Canary Islands	**Rio**	Rioja
C-La M	Castilla-	**R Ala**	Rioja Alavesa
	La Mancha	**R Alt**	Rioja Alta
C y L	Castilla y León	**RB**	Rioja Baja
Cat	Catalonia	**Rue**	Rueda
Cos del S	Costers del Segre	**Set**	Setúbal
Emp	Empordà		
Ext	Extremadura		
Gal	Galicia		
Jum	Jumilla		
La M	La Mancha	**Som**	Somontano
Lis	Lisboa	**Tej**	Tejo
Mad	Madrid, Vinos de	**U-R**	Utiel-Requena
Mad V	Madrid, Vinos de	**V'cia**	Valencia
Mall	Mallorca	**Vin**	Vinho Verde
Man	Manchuela		
Mén	Méntrida		

I admit I used to find Spanish wines rather heavy going. With brilliant exceptions in Rioja, Ribera del Duero, Catalonia and, of course, Sherry there were too many reds apparently doing their best to taste like Rioja. Now far fewer wines are overoaked and overextracted, and if you avoid those excessively heavy, broad-shouldered bottles you'll avoid most of them. With less tannin and oak to mask the fruit, the country's red grapes are allowed to express themselves; look for Garnachas of depth and subtlety and Tempranillos of rich juiciness; and whites of crisp, salty freshness. It's one of the most exciting developments of the past few years: this chapter now holds as much excitement as any. Everyone in Spain is in the vineyard. The talk is all about the soil, and whether to name the terroir and the particular vineyard parcel on the label. Some argue that the terms Reserva and Gran Reserva are long overdue for retirement. Much better to use the terroir, they say, to classify quality. You could say it's the wine world's direction of travel. The problem is that plenty of regions have not mapped their soils. Where they have, they have not done anything sensible with the analysis. In some cases it is just locked away in cupboards. Rome was not built in a day; nor Madrid either.

Recent Rioja vintages

2016 Difficult spring, very hot summer, rain at harvest. Time will tell.

2015 Smiles all round. Promising to be as good as 2010.

2014 After two small vintages, a return to form in quality and quantity.

2013 Cool, wet year, small harvest, with some good wines.

2012 Good. One of lowest yields for two decades.

2011 Officially "excelente"; some jammy fruit, more concentrated than 2010.

2010 "Excelente". A perfect year, proving itself as the wines mature.

2009 Can drink now, but will develop further. Some wines notably tannic.

2008 Cool year, wines fresh and aromatic, a little lower in alcohol.

2007 Difficult vintage, ready for drinking.

2006 Drinking well now. Light fragrant vintage.

2005 A standout vintage on heels of 2004. Enjoy now or keep.

Aalto Rib del D r ★★★→★★★★ Modern wines; long tradition: Javier Zaccagnini, ex-director RIB DEL D CONSEJO, Mariano Garcia, ex-VEGA SICILIA winemaker. Savoury Aalto; PS (200 small plots) super-rich, needs a decade. Garcia's family wineries: MAURO (C Y L), Maurodos (TORO). Zaccagnini makes elegant Sei Solo, Preludio at Aalto.

Abadal, Bodegas Cat Charming family business in Plà de Bages DO offering popular wines and CAT specialities under series of brands: Abadal, La Fou (in Terra Alta DO), Ramón Roqueta. Latest project: restoring and making wine in century-old stone fermentation tanks in v'yds. Result: crisp, unoaked, PINOT-like reds.

Abadía Retuerta C y L r ★★ →★★★ One of CYL stars, next door to RIB DEL D; grand hotel (Michelin star) in former monastery. V.gd white blend DYA Le Domaine. Single-v'yd international reds steadily improving. Selección Especial TEMPRANILLO/ SYRAH/CAB SAUV an original blend.

Abel Mendoza R Ala ★★ →★★★ Elegant RIO from thoughtful winemaker, working in small batches with careful barrel selections. Jarrarte is popular, accessible choice, Grano a Grano for long cellaring with its every-berry-hand-selected TEMPRANILLO.

Agustí Torelló Mata Cava ★★ →★★★ Small family CAVA specialist. Kripta and Bayanus 375 (in half bottles) stand out.

Alexander Jules Sherry ★★ →★★★ Négociant bottling selected BUTTS from eg. SÁNCHEZ ROMATE, ARGÜESO. Currently available in US, Japan, Spain.

Alicante r w sw ★ →★★★ Spiritual home of MONASTRELL, with spicy reds and fortified *Fondillón*. In dry interior, old bush vines thrive. Top: ARTADI, Bernabé Navarro (pioneer in natural wines, uses clay *tinajas*), Bruno Prats, ENRIQUE MENDOZA.

Almacenista Sherry, Man ★★ →★★★★ A Sherry stockholding cellar, often v. small, ageing fine wines to sell to BODEGAS. Few left; many preferred open market, eg. EL MAESTRO SIERRA. Often terrific quality. LUSTAU pioneered outstanding portfolio.

Álvaro Domecq Sherry, Man ★★ →★★★ Fine old BODEGA based on SOLERAS of Pilar Aranda, JEREZ's oldest bodega. Polished, elegant wines. Gd FINO La Janda. Excellent 1730 VORS series.

Alvear Mont-M ★★ →★★★ Impressive showcase of diversity of PX grape in MONT-M. Gd, dry FINO CB and Capataz, lovely sweet SOLERA 1927, unctuous DULCE Viejo. Also owns Palacio Quemado BODEGA in Ext.

Añada Vintage.

Argüeso, Herederos de Man ★★ →★★★ One of SANLÚCAR's top producers. V.gd San León, dense and salty *San León Res* and youthful Las Medallas; also impressively lively VORS AMONTILLADO Viejo.

Arrayán, Bodegas ★★ In just over a decade Arrayán highlighted qualities of MÉN. Revival of Albillo Real (w) grape promising. La Suerte de Arrayán shows juicy pleasure of GARNACHA.

Artadi Alic, Nav ★★ →★★★★ Juan Carlos López de Lacalle left RIO DO end 2015, because of its failure to recognize single v'yds and terroirs. Wines now "Álava": Basque subregion of Rio. Gd-value Viñas de Gain, luxuriant La Poza de Ballesteros and dark, stony El Carretil; outstanding single-v'yd El Pisón. Also in ALIC with v.gd El Sequé (r), NAV with Artazuri (r, DYA p).

Arzuaga Rib del D ★★ Generous, approachable. Classic GRAN RES. Hotel within v'yds.

Baigorri R Ala r w ★★ →★★★ Wines as glamorous as glassy architecture. Bold modern RIO. Fine white. Gd new varietal range: GARNACHA, Maturana. Polished Garage wins prizes. RES more approachable. Restaurant with v'yd views.

Barajuela, La Sherry Innovative project. Grapes briefly sun-dried, as in past, to raise alc closer to min required for Sherry. Result is unfortified wine from Sherry terroir, with a fresher, fruitier character. Tiny production.

Barbadillo Man ★ →★★★★ Dominates SANLÚCAR's upper town; based in former palace. Range runs from reliable to outstanding, from supermarket to v. finest. Pioneer of MANZANILLA EN RAMA. Reliquía range unbeatable, esp AMONTILLADO, PALO CORTADO. Outstanding century-old Versos Amontillado, just 100 bottles released 2016. Also DYA Castillo San Diego (w), local bestseller, from PALOMINO. Also owns Vega Real (RIB DEL D), BODEGA Pirineos (SOM).

Barón de Ley RB r p w ★ →★★★ Former Benedictine monastery now home to reliable

BODEGA; reputation for innovation, with blends and varieties, as well as classics.

Báscula, La Alic, Rio, Jum r w sw ★★ Gd-value quality brand with wines from upcoming regions, plus classics, eg. ALIC, JUM, RIB DEL D, RIO, Terra Alta, YECLA. Run by South African Bruce Jack and British MW Ed Adams.

Belondrade C y L, Rue r w ★★ ᐩ★★★ Didier Belondrade launched his RUE in 1994, showing Rueda can be not just DYA. Textured VERDEJO, lees-aged in oak. Quinta Apollonia (w) and light, summery, Quinta Clarisa TEMPRANILLO (r), both C y L.

Beronia Rio r p w ★→★★★ Award-winning, reliable RIO BODEGA. Gd VIURA (w); polished revived RES. Owned by GONZÁLEZ BYASS.

Bierzo Bier r w ★→★★★ Hottest spot in Spain, in fashion terms, with its crunchy *Pinot-like red* – Mencía grown on slate soils, and ethereal GODELLO (w). On wrong soils Mencía can be rustic, harsh, but best are DESCENDIENTES DE J PALACIOS, RAÚL PÉREZ, plus Dominio de Tares, Gancedo, Luna Berberide, Peique, Pittacum.

Binissalem Mall r p w sp ★→★★ Traditional island DO ne of Palma. Mainly red, mainly tannic Mantonegro, with Callet, Gorgollasa and CAB SAUV; whites mainly Prensal Blanc plus CHARD, MOSCATEL. BODEGAS Biniagual, Jaume de Puntiró, Macià Batle, Tianna Negre.

Bodega A cellar; a wine shop; a business making, blending and/or shipping wine.

Butt Sherry 600-litre barrel of long-matured American oak used for Sherry. Filled $^5/_6$ full, allows space for FLOR to grow. Popular in Scotland, post-Sherry use, for adding final polish to whisky.

Calatayud Ara r p w ★→★★★ Recognition of quality of old-vine GARNACHA grown at 700–900m finally putting Calatayud on map, though still best known for cheap co-op wines. Best: BODEGAS Ateca (*see* JUAN GIL), EL ESCOCÉS VOLANTE, Lobban El Gordito (by Pamela Geddes).

Callejuela Sherry, Man ★★ ᐩ★★★ Blanco brothers, working with influential winemaker Ramiro Ibañcz, have v'yds in some of Sherry's most famous PAGOS. New range, esp vintage MANZANILLA 2011, to be released annually, cask at a time.

Cava means "cellar". Can't call it "Champan/Champagne". "Cava": easy choice

Campo de Borja Ara r p w ★ ★★★ Self-proclaimed "Empire of GARNACHA". Heritage of old vines, plus young v'yds makes for spot-on source of gd-value Garnacha, now showing serious quality eg. BODEGAS Alto Moncayo, Aragonesas, Borsao.

Campo Viejo Rio r p w sp ★ ᐩ★★ RIO's biggest brand. In addition to value RES, GRAN RES, showing more diversity with varietal GARNACHA, and adding TEMPRANILLO Blanco to white Rio. Part of Pernod Ricard (also owns Calatrava-designed Ysios winery in Rio).

Canary Islands r p w ★→★★★ Highly rated producer of ISLAND WINES; seven main islands, nine DOS. TENERIFE alone has five DOS. Focus on rare varieties, and distinct microclimates. Fresh, elegant wines. Dry white LISTÁN (aka PALOMINO) and Marmajuelo, black Listán Negro, Negramoll (TINTA NEGRA), Vijariego offers *enjoyable original flavours*. Gd dessert MOSCATELS, MALVASÍAS esp fortified El Grifo from Lanzarote. SUERTES DEL MARQUÉS top producer.

Cañas, Luis R Ala r w ★→★★★ Often-gonged family business; ever-reliable. Classics eg. Selección de la Familia RES, youthful, enjoy now GRAN RES, as well as moderns eg. ultra-concentrated Hiru 3 Racimos, Amaren, styles that need cellaring.

Capçanes, Celler de Mont r p w sw ★→★★ One of Spain's top co-ops. Great-value, expressive wines from MONT. Also a kosher specialist esp Peraj Ha'abib.

Cariñena Ara r p w ★→★★ The one DO that is also name of a grape variety. Solid, not exciting, but gd value; top pick is 3 de Tres Mil from VINO DE PAGO FINCA Aylés.

Casa Castillo Jum r ★★→★★★ Proves JUM can be tiptop. Family business high up in Jum *altiplano*. Excellent El Molar GARNACHA, Valtosca SYRAH, v. fine Las Gravas single-v'yd blend, MONASTRELL esp PIE FRANCO (plot escaped recent phylloxera).

SPAIN

Castaño Mur r p w sw ★→★★ Castaño family is YECLA. Fine MONASTRELLS. Delicious sweet DULCE (r).

Castell del Remei Cat, Cos del S TOMÀS CUSINÉ back in charge of historic property, to create a group incl Cara Nord, Cérvoles, Vilosell wines. Try textured FINCA Macons MACABEO (w) from centenarian vines.

Castell d'Encús Cos del S r w ★★→★★★ CAT wineries are searching for climates. Raül Bobet (also of PRI FERRER-BOBET) there 1st. At 1000m, he has all the cool climate he wants for *superbly fresh, original wines*. Ancient meets modern: grapes fermented in stone *lagares*, winery is up to date. In less than a decade Ekam RIES, Thalarn SYRAH, Acusp PINOT have become classics.

Castilla y León r p w ★→★★★ Spain's largest wine region. Best are v.gd; plenty to enjoy, but v. variable. DOS: Arribes, BIERZO, CIGALES, Tierra de León, Tierra del Vino de Zamora; Valles de Benavente. Red grapes incl Juan Garcia, MENCÍA, TINTA DEL PAÍS; white Doña Blanca. Gd, deeply coloured ROSADO from Prieto Picudo grape.

Castillo de Cuzcurrita R Alt Walled v'yd, C14 castle, excellent consultant Ana Martín. Great basis for v. fine RIO.

Castillo Perelada Emp, Pri r p w sp ★→★★★ Glamorous estate. Vivacious CAVAS, esp Gran Claustro; modern reds, incl coastal FINCA Garbet SYRAH. Rare 12-yr-old, SOLERA-aged GARNATXA de l'EMPORDÀ. V. fine Casa Gran del Siurana, Gran Cruor, Syrah blend from PRI.

Catalonia r p w sp Vast DO, covers whole of Cat: seashore, mtn, in-between. Has own language and v. strong cultural identity. Top chefs and top BODEGAS (eg. TORRES), many v. creative. Yet actual DO is just umbrella, with little identity of its own.

Cava Spain's traditional-method sparkling. Zero dosage Brut Nature popular given ripeness of Mediterranean fruit. Majority made in PEN – in or around San Sadurní d'Anoia – also RIO (esp MUGA Conde de Haro), V'CIA. Local grapes back in favour: MACABEO (VIURA of RIO), PARELLADA, XAREL.LO (best for ageing). Best can age 10 yrs, though 9 mths is min for ageing. New highest category for single-v'yd wines with lower yields is *paraje calificado*. Still too much low-quality fizz, so some producers are leaving DO. *See* CONCA DEL RÍU ANOIA, CLÀSSIC PENEDÈS.

César Florido Sherry ★→★★★ Master of MOSCATEL, since 1887. Explore gloriously scented, succulent trio: Dorado, Especial, Pasas.

Chipiona Sherry Sherry's MOSCATEL grapes come from this sandy, coastal zone. Mainly co-ops. CÉSAR FLORIDO family leads the way.

Cigales C y L r p ★→★★ Squeezed between RIB DEL D and TORO, Cigales still fights for attention. Value reds, rosés.

Clàssic Penedès Pen Recent category of DO PEN for traditional-method sparkling, higher quality than CAVA. Min 15 mths ageing. Since 2017, organically grown grapes. Members incl Albet i Noya, Colet, LOXAREL, Mas Bertran.

Clos Mogador Pri r w ★★★→★★★★ One of PRI's founding quintet and mentor to many. Still commands respect. One of 1st to gain a VI DE FINCA designation. Spicy, honeyed Clos Nelin white, forerunner of trend for GARNACHA BLANCA blends.

Codorníu Raventós Cos del S, Pen, Pri, Rio r p w sp ★→★★★★ Spain's oldest family business; art nouveau winery worth a visit. Experimental BODEGA led by winemaker Bruno Colomer has seen improvements across range. Outstanding Ars Collecta CAVAS: Jaume Codorníu; three single-v'yd, single-variety Cavas, and 456, a blend of three v'yds and most expensive Cava ever produced. Elsewhere, Legaris in RIB DEL D and Raimat in COS DEL S continue to improve. Bodega Bilbaínas in RIO has bestseller VIÑA Pomal, top Altos de la Caseta, Vinos Singulares varietals incl Maturana Blanca, original Cava Blanc de Noirs (GARNACHA). *See also* SCALA DEI.

Conca de Barberà Cat r p w Small CAT DO once purely a feeder of quality fruit to large enterprises, now some excellent wineries, incl bio Escoda-Sanahuja. Top TORRES wines Grans Muralles, Milmanda both made in this DO.

Conca del Ríu Anoia Cat Small traditional-method sparkling DO created in 2013 by RAVENTÓS I BLANC to provide tighter quality controls than CAVA. Organic production, lower yields, min ageing 18 mths, only local grape varieties.

Consejo Regulador Organization that controls a DO – each DO has its own. Quality as inconsistent as wines they represent: some bureaucratic, others enterprising.

Contador Cat, R Alt r w ★★→★★★ Benjamín Romeo (ex-ARTADI) is a RIO scrupulously focused on his terroir and his c.20 small v'yds. Rich, *top white Que Bonito Cacareaba.* Flagship red Contador, "super-second" La Cueva del Contador. Dense but elegant single-v'yd La Viña de Andrés. Wines to lay down. Macizo is his powerful, silky GARNACHA BLANCA/XARELLO blend (w) in CAT.

Contino R Ala r p w ★★→★★★★ Estate incl one of RIO's great single v'yds. Jesús Madrazo's dedication produces outstanding RES, tiptop GRACIANO, lovely white Rio and pale ROSADO. Now CVNE-owned. Will there be changes?

Costers del Segre r p w sp ★→★★★ Geographically divided DO somehow manages to draw mountainous CASTELL D'ENCÚS and lower-lying CASTELL DEL REMEI, Raimat, within same boundary.

Crianza Guarantees ageing of wine, not quality. New or unaged wine is Sin Crianza (without oak) or JOVEN. In general Crianzas must be at least 2 yrs old (with 6 mths to 1 yr in oak) and must not be released before 3rd yr. *See* RES.

Cusiné, Tomás Cos del S r w ★★→★★★ One of Spain's most innovative winemakers, now returned to CASTELL DEL REMEI. Individual, modern, incl TEMPRANILLO blend Vilosell; creative ten-variety white blend Auzells, and Cérvoles.

CVNE R Ala, R Alt r p w ★→★★★★ One of RIO's great names. Pronounced *"coo-nee"*, Compañía Vinícola del Norte de España founded 1879. Most impressive at top end, ethereal, less oak than most in Rio. Real de Asúa winery makes gd Imperial RES; outstanding, elegant Imperial GRAN RES; modern Real de Asúa from R Alt. excellent R Ala winery VIÑA Real. Latest white is Monopole Classico aged in American oak then blended in Sherry barrels, following traditional recipe. Wines can be long ageing: seek out **62 64 70.** CONTINO is member

Delgado Zuleta Man ★→★★ Oldest (1744) SANLUCAR hrm Flagship is 6/7-yr-old *La Goya* MANZANILLA PASADA, served at wedding of King Felipe VI of Spain; also 10-yr-old Goya XL EN RAMA. Impressively aged 40-yr-old Quo Vadis? AMONTILLADO.

Díez-Mérito Sherry ★→★★★ Cellars now owned by Salvador Espinosa. Reliable Bertola range; plus fine aged VORS Sherries: AMONTILLADO *Fino Imperial*, Victoria Regina OLOROSO, Vieja SOLERA PX.

Garnacha

For so long Spain's ugly duckling variety, GARNACHA has in recent yrs turned into a swan. **Aragón:** home of Garnacha. It's easy to make a rich, juicy, rustic red here. What ARA has is old vines and altitude, offering freshness, balance and less alc. **Gredos:** these Garnachas nr Madrid have driven excitement in variety. Once used to make cheap wine for city, old bush vines offer v. low yields and concentration. **Navarra:** Viña Zorzal has popular, juicy Garnachas. DOMAINES LUPIER focuses on v. old bush vines. **Priorat:** where Spanish Garnacha 1st showed potential. Today most often used in blends, and shows beautifully with CARIÑENA's blue fruit. ALVARO PALACIOS' FINCA Dofí is as close to being 100% Garnacha as could be. Shows an entirely different vision of Garnacha from PRI's 1st yrs. Gone is robust, hearty, overheated fruit; here is all about elegance, refinement. **Rioja:** DO of TEMPRANILLO and blends discovering Garnachas from Tudelilla and RB. Try CONTINO; BODEGAS Bilbaínas (Garnacha Blanc de Noirs CAVA); Vintae, winemaking team with Garnachas de España project, even makes Icewine in RIO. GARNACHA BLANCA gaining ground too.

DO / DOP (Denominación de Origen / Protegida) Former *Denominación de Origen* (DO) and DO *Calificada* are now grouped as DOP along with the single-estate PAGO denomination. Lesser category VCPRD is becoming VCIG, *Vinos de Calidad de Indicación Geográfica*. Keep up at the back, there.

Domaines Lupier Nav r ★★★ Young couple rescuing scattered v'yds of old GARNACHA focus on making just two wines: floral La Dama; dense, bold El Terroir. Bio.

Dominio de Tares Bier r w ★★ →★★★ Outstanding MENCÍA: old-vine Cepas Viejas, Tares P3. Also gd GODELLO. In same group, Pazos de Lusco (RÍAS BAIXAS), Dominio dos Tares (C Y L) – its Cumal is fine example of local Prieto Picudo grape.

Dulce Sweet.

Emilio Hidalgo Sherry ★★★ →★★★★ Outstanding small family BODEGA. All wines (except PX) start by spending time under FLOR. Excellent 15-yr-old La Panesa FINO, intense 50-yr-old AMONTILLADO Tresillo 1874, rare Santa Ana PX 1861.

Empordà Cat r p w sw ★→★★ One of number of centres of creativity in CAT. Best: CASTILLO PERELADA, Celler Martí Fabra, Pere Guardiola, Vinyes dels Aspres. Quirky, young Espelt grows 17 varieties: try GARNACHA/CARIGNAN Sauló. Sumptuous natural sweet wine from Celler Espolla: SOLERA GRAN RES.

Enrique Mendoza Alic r w sw ★→★★ Hospitable, indefatigable Pepe Mendoza is godfather in resurgence of DO and of MONASTRELL grape. Top wines from dry inland *altiplano*: vibrant Tremenda, single v'yd Las Quebradas. Honeyed MOSCATEL.

Epicure Wines Cat, Pri r w sp ★★ Award-winning sommelier Franck Massard building portfolio of characterful wines from DOS across Spain, incl CAVA, MONT, RIBEIRA SACRA, Terra Alta, VALDEORRAS. Lively ROSADO Mas Amor.

Equipo Navazos Sherry ★★★ →★★★★ Jesús Barquín and Eduardo Ojeda are team (*equipo*) who transformed perception of Sherry with négociant approach, selecting individual BUTTS. Collaborations incl Dirk Niepoort, Colet-Navazos (sparkling; uses sherry in *liqueur d'expedition*), Navazos-Palazzi (brandy), Perez Barquero (MONT-M), RAFAEL PALACIOS. FLOR Power is unfortified, flor-aged wine: homage to traditional winemaking of JEREZ.

El Escocés Volante is known as La Multa ("traffic fine"): guess why?

Escocés Volante, El Gal, Ara r w ★★ Norrel Robertson, Scot, MW, lives in CALATAYUD, specializes in recuperating old-vine GARNACHA grown on slate at altitude. Newest release Manda Huevos is perfumed blend of old and v. old Garnacha with Bobal and Moristel. Also works with eg. Martín Códax co-op making ALBARIÑO, RÍAS BAIXAS; GODELLO, MONTERREI (w).

Espumoso Sparkling, but not made according to traditional method, unlike CAVA, so usually cheaper.

Ferrer-Bobet Pri r ★★★ Polished, complex wines by Sergi Ferrer-Salat (founder Barcelona's Monvínic wine bar/shop) and Raül Bobet (CASTELL D'ENCÚS). Slate soils, old vines culminate in Selecció Especial Vinyes Velles. Spectacular winery.

Finca Farm or estate (eg. FINCA ALLENDE).

Finca Allende R Alt r w ★★ →★★★★ Top (in all senses) RIO BODEGA at BRIONES in ancient merchant's house with tower looking over town to v'yds, run by irrepressible Miguel Ángel de Gregorio. Serious approach: single v'yd Calvario, pure, fine Aurus. Leader in white: powerful Allende Blanco, v. fine, aromatic Martíres. FINCA Nueva is pret-à-porter range. Also Finca Coronado in LA MANCHA.

Finca Sandoval Man r ★★ →★★★ In wine-writer Victor de la Serna, DO MAN and SYRAH, MONASTRELL, BOBAL have an articulate champion. FINCA Sandoval is top wine, Salia the second label.

Flor Sherry Spanish for "flower": refers to the layer of *Saccharomyces* yeasts that develop naturally and live on top of FINO/MANZANILLA Sherry in a BUTT $^5/_6$ full. Flor consumes oxygen and other compounds (process known as "biological ageing") and protects wine from browning (oxidation). Traditional AMONTILLADOS begin as Finos or Manzanillas before the flor dies naturally or with addition of fortifying spirit. Flor grows a thicker layer nearer the sea at EL PUERTO DE SANTA MARÍA and SANLÚCAR, hence finer character of Sherry there. Most abundant in spring, autumn.

Fondillón Alic sw ★→★★★ Fabled unfortified *rancio* semi-sweet wine from overripe MONASTRELL grapes, made to survive sea voyages. Now matured in oak for min 10 yrs; some SOLERAS of great age. Sadly shrinking production: GUTIÉRREZ DE LA VEGA, Primitivo Quiles.

Freixenet Pen, Cava r p w sp ★→★★★ Biggest CAVA producer. Best-known for black-bottled Cordón Negro, standard Carta Nevada. Elyssia is step up; refreshed by CHARD, PINOT N. Casa Sala is prestige top label, single-v'yd *paraje calificado* Cava. La Freixeneda (r) newly launched from family's C13 estate. Other Cava brands in Ferrer family: Castellblanch, Conde de Caralt, Segura Viudas. Plus: Morlanda (PRI), Solar Viejo (RIO), Valdubón (RIB DEL D), Vionta (RÍAS BAIXAS). Also B'x négociant Yvon Mau, Henri Abelé (Champagne), Gloria Ferrer (US), Wingara (Australia).

Fundador Pedro Domecq Sherry Former Domecq BODEGAS sliced up through multiple mergers. VORS wines now owned by OSBORNE; *La Ina, Botaina, Rio Viejo*, Viña 25 by LUSTAU. Andrew Tan of Emperador, world's largest brandy company, bought remainder, focus on Fundador brandy. Group also incl Harvey's, famed for Bristol Cream and v. fine VORS, and Garvey, known for *San Patricio* FINO.

Galicia r w (sp) Rainy nw corner of Spain; some of best whites (*see* RÍAS BAIXAS, MONTERREI, RIBEIRA SACRA, RIBEIRO, VALDEORRAS), bright crunchy reds (MENCIA. Plenty of interest, esp in re-emerging smaller DOS of Ribeiro, Ribeira Sacra, Monterrei.

Garvey Sherry ★→★★ One of last remnants of Ruiz-Mateos empire whose demise damaged much of Sherry business. Best known for San Patricio FINO.

Genéricos Rio Unappealing word in RIO to describe important, often appealing category: wines (usually prestige) that only declare vintage, make no statement about ageing (eg. RES or GRAN RES). Genéricos need not follow DO winemaking, ageing rules. Can enable them to express terroir better, but some overextracted.

González Byass Sherry ★★→★★★★ GB (founded 1845) remains a family business. Cellarmaster Antonio Flores is a debonair, poetic presence. From the most famous of FINOS, *Tío Pepe*, Flores has developed *a fascinating portfolio: en rama and the Palmas Finos*. Alongside remain consistently polished VIÑA AB AMONTILLADO, Matúsalem OLOROSO, Noë PX. Also gd brandies; table wines, incl BERONIA (RIO), Vilarnau (CAVA), Viñas del Vero (SOMONTANO); plus (not so gd, but popular) Croft Original Pale Cream. FINCA Moncloa, close by, produces still reds; also Tintilla de Rota.

Gramona Pen, Cava r w sw sp ★★→★★★★ A taste of what CAVA can achieve. Cousins make impressively long-aged Cavas, esp Imperial GRAN RES, III Lustros, Celler Battle Gran Res. Hive of research, investigation too, incl bio; sweet incl Icewines, experimental wines.

Gran Reserva In RIO Gran Res spends min 2 yrs in 225-litre barrique, 3 yrs in bottle. Seek out superb old Rio Gran Res, often great value. Many recent less exciting.

Guita, La Man ★→★★★ Reliable *Manzanilla*. Grupo Estévez-owned (also VALDESPINO).

Gutiérrez Colosía Sherry ★→★★★ Rare remaining riverside BODEGA in EL PUERTO DE SANTA MARÍA. Former ALMACENISTA. Excellent old PALO CORTADO.

Gutiérrez de la Vega Alic r w sw ★★→★★★ In ALIC, but no longer in DO, after disagreement over regulations. Lovely expression of MOSCATEL, esp Casta Diva. Also expert in FONDILLÓN. Cellar full of SOLERAS.

Hacienda Monasterio Rib del D r ★★★ On 160-ha property PETER SISSECK makes TINTO FINO/CAB blends. More accessible in price, palate than his PINGUS. Youthful subtly oaked Cosecha, complex RES; Res Especial is richly textured, dense.

Haro R Alt Picturesque city at heart of R Alt, reputation made when railway built enabling exports to n coast and B'x. Visit great names of RIO clustered in station district, incl BODEGAS BILBAÍNAS, CVNE, Gomez Cruzado, LA RIOJA ALTA, LÓPEZ DE HEREDÍA, MUGA, RODA.

Harvey's Sherry ★→★★★ Once-great Sherry name. Famed for Bristol Cream, recently bought by Emperador, along with Fundador brandy.

Hidalgo-La Gitana Man ★★→★★★★ Historic (1792) SANLÚCAR firm. Ultra-delicate MANZANILLA La Gitana a classic. EN RAMA has more character. Finest Manzanilla is single v'yd *Pastrana Pasada*, verging on AMONTILLADO maturity. Outstanding VORS, incl Napoleon Amontillado, Wellington *Palo Cortado*, Triana PX.

Island wines Latest topic of interest in Spain; esp CAN but also MALLORCA. Distinct viticultural, varietal, climatic differences make for distinctive wines.

J Chivite Family Estates Nav r p w sw ★★→★★★ Popular DYA range Gran Feudo, esp ROSADO Sobre Lías (*sur lie*). Pale Las Fincas Rosado; Colección 125, incl outstanding CHARD, *one of Spain's top Chards*. Gd late-harvest MOSCATEL.

Jerez de la Frontera Sherry Capital of Sherry region, between Cádiz and Seville. "Sherry" is corruption of C8 "Sherish", Moorish name of city. Pronounced "*hereth*". In French, Xérès. Hence DO is Jerez-Xérès-Sherry. MANZANILLA has own DO: Manzanilla-SANLÚCAR DE BARRAMEDA.

Joven Young, unoaked wine. *See also* CRIANZA.

Juan Gil Family Estates Jum r w ★→★★★ Old family business relaunched in 2002 to make the best in JUM. Gd young MONASTRELLS (eg. 4 Meses); powerful, long-lived top wines Clio and El Nido. Group also incl impressive modern wineries incl Ateca (CALATAYUD), Can Blau (MONT), Shaya (RUE).

Jumilla Mur r (p) (w) ★→★★★ Arid v'yds in mts n of Mur; old MONASTRELL vines revived by committed growers. TEMPRANILLO, MERLOT, CAB, SYRAH, PETIT VERDOT too. Top: CASA CASTILLO, JUAN GIL. Also: Agapito Rico, Carchelo, CASTAÑO, Luzón.

Juvé & Camps Pen, Cava w sp ★★→★★★ Consistently gd family firm for quality CAVA. RES de la Familia is stalwart, with top-end GRAN RES.

There are six twists on wire cage of a Cava bottle. Make your guests guess.

La Mancha Pen, Cava r p w ★→★★ Quixote country, but Spain's least impressive (except for its size) wine region, s of Madrid. Too much bulk wine, yet excellence possible: JUAN GIL Volver, MARTÍNEZ BUJANDA'S FINCA Antigua, PESQUERA'S El Vínculo.

León, Jean Pen r w ★★→★★★ Pioneer of CAB, CHARD in Spain; TORRES-owned since 1995, recovering quality under Mireia Torres. Gd, oaky Chards, expressive 3055 *Merlot*; elegant Vinya La Scala Cab.

López de Heredia R Alt r p w ★★→★★★★ One of R Alt's old guard (1877), with ethereal aged wines that have magically become fashionable again. Remarkable swiss "château" is HARO landmark. Place to see how RIO was made (as it is still is). Cubillo is younger range with GARNACHA; darker Bosconia; delicate, ripe *Tondonia*. Whites have seriously long barrel and bottle age: fascinating Gravonia, Tondonia GRAN RES. Parchment-like Gran Res ROSADO.

Loxarel Pen r p w sp ★★ Josep Mitjans is a man passionately committed to his terroir and to XAREL.LO variety. (Loxarel is re-working of letters of grape variety.) Range incl (r) Xarel.lo, skin contact and amphora wines. Cent Nou 109 Brut Nature RES is quirky treat: traditional method sparkling, but lees never disgorged. Complex, cloudy, unsulphured, v. youthful after 109 mths. Bio.

Lustau Sherry ★★★→★★★★ Launched original ALMACENISTA collection. Range incl Sherries from JEREZ, SANLÚCAR, EL PUERTO. Only BODEGA to produce EN RAMA Sherries from the three Sherry towns – fascinating contrasts. Emilín is superb MOSCATEL, VORS PX is outstanding, carrying age and sweetness lightly. One of few bodegas to release vintage Sherries.

Madrid, Vinos de r p w ★→★★ For many yrs GARNACHA provided workhorse wines.

Today old vines part of an exciting wave of quality. Go-ahead names: Bernabeleva, Comando G, El Regajal, Jeromín, Licinia, Marañones, Tagonius.

Maestro Sierra, El Sherry ★★★ Small, traditional BODEGA in JEREZ, *brilliant quality*, run by Mari-Carmen Borrego, following on from her mother Pilar Plá. Fine FINO, AMONTILLADO 1830 VORS, OLOROSO 1/14 VORS. Old cellar, worth visit.

Málaga r w sw ★→★★★ MOSCATEL-lovers should explore hills of Málaga. TELMO RODRIGUEZ revived ancient glories with subtle, sweet **Molino Real**. Barrel-aged No 3 Old Vines Moscatel from Jorge Ordóñez is gloriously succulent. Bentomiz has impressive portfolio of Moscatels. Sierras de Málaga DO for dry Moscatel table wines; Ordóñez' Botani is delicately aromatic.

Mallorca r w ★→★★★ Constantly improving, if high priced and hard to find off island. Incl 4 Kilos, Án Negra, Biniagual, Binigrau, Hereus de Ribas, Son Bordils. Reds blend traditional varieties (Callet, Fogoneu, Mantonegro) plus CAB, SYRAH, MERLOT. Whites (esp CHARD) improving fast. Two DOS: BINISSALEM, PLÁ I LLEVANT.

Manchuela C-La M r w sw ★→★★ Traditional region for bulk wine, now showing some promise, eg. Bobal, MALBEC, PETIT VERDOT. Pioneer FINCA SANDOVAL followed by Alto Landón and Ponce, producer of PIE FRANCO (rare, ungrafted vines) wine.

Marqués de Cáceres R Alt r p w ★→★★ Significant contribution to RIO in 70s, introducing French winemaking techniques. Fresh white, rosé. Gaudium is modern top wine; GRAN RES traditional classic. Owns Deusa Nai in RÍAS BAIXAS.

Marqués de Murrieta R Alt r p w ★★★ →★★★★ Glamorously refitted BODEGA, but underneath still one of RIO's traditional greats, famous for magnificent long-aged Castillo de Ygay GRAN RES. Latest release of Gran Res Blanco is 86, and Gran Res Tinto 75. Best-value is dense, flavoursome RES. Dalmau is contrastingly modern. **Capellunia** is fresh, taut, complex white, one of Rio's v. best. 1st ROSADO, v. pale Primer Rosé, launched 16. V.gd Pazo de Barrantes ALBARIÑO (RÍAS BAIXAS).

Marqués de Riscal R Ala, Rue r (p) w ★★→★★★★ Riscal is so much more than Frank Gehry's flashy titanium-roofed hotel. This is living history of RIO, BODEGA recently able to put on a tasting of every vintage going back to its 1st in 1862. Take your pick on styles today: reliable RES, modern, youthful FINCA Torrea, balanced GRAN RES. Powerful **Barón de Chirel Res**. Pioneer in RUE (since 72) making vibrant DYA SAUV BL, VERDEJO.

Martínez Bujanda, Familia C-La M, Rio r p w ★→★★ Commercially astute business with a number of wineries; also makes private-label wines. Most attractive are **Finca Valpiedra**, charming single estate in RIO; FINCA Antigua in LA M.

Mas Doix Pri r ★★→★★★ Fine family business in Poboleda, blessed with 70–100-yr-old GARNACHA and CARIÑENA grown on slate. Les Crestes is lively young Garnacha. Treasure is rare, superb Cariñena, all blueberry and velvet, astonishingly pure, named after yr v'yd was planted, *1902*.

Mas Martinet Pri r ★★→★★★ Wines of Sara Pérez have fine pedigree. Daughter of Josep Lluís Pérez, one of original PRI quintet, most passionate of Pri's 2nd generation, ever innovating, fermenting freshly picked grapes in vats in v'yds, and in *amphoras*. Venus La Universal is other project.

Mauro C y L r w ★★ →★★★ Founded by Mariano Garcia of AALTO and formerly VEGA SICILIA. Full-bodied, oak-aged signature of Garcia with Tereus and VS. Latest release is GODELLO. Now joined by sons, Eduardo and Alberto, also working at Maurodos (TORO), Paixar (BIERZO).

Méntrida C-La M r p ★→★★ Former co-op country s of Madrid, now being put on map by ARRAYÁN, Canopy and Jiménez-Landi with GARNACHA, Albillo grapes.

Monterrei Gal r w ★→★★★ Small DO on Portuguese border, where once Romans made wine. Discovering its potential, with impressive array of local varieties, blends. Best: Quinta da Muradella: fascinating parcels of unusual vines.

Montilla-Moriles ★→★★★ Andalucian DO nr Córdoba. Hidden treasure, too often regarded as JEREZ's poor relation, as a result can be great value. Best to shop nr top end for superbly rich PX, some with long ageing in SOLERA. Top: ALVEAR, PÉREZ BARQUERO, TORO ALBALÁ. Important source of PX for use in Jerez DO.

Montsant Cat r (p) w ★→★★★ Tucked in around PRI, MONTSANT can suffer in shadow of its famous neighbour. Varied soils, incl slate. Fine GARNACHA BLANCA, esp from Acústic. Dense, balsamic reds: Alfredo Arribas, Can Blau, CAPÇANES, Domenech, Espectacle, Joan d'Anguera, Mas Perinet, Masroig, Venus la Universal.

Muga R Alt r p w (sp) ★★→★★★★ Impressively tall and friendly family producing some of R Alt's most aromatic, balanced reds. Gd barrel-fermented DYA VIURA; textbook dry ROSADO; lively CAVA; reds finely crafted, delicate. Best: Selección Especial, wonderfully fragrant GRAN RES **Prado Enea**; modern, powerful *Torre Muga*; expressive, complex Aro.

Mustiguillo V'cia r w ★★→★★★ Pioneering BODEGA led renaissance of unloved local Bobal grape. Created a PAGO, El Terrerazo. Mestizaje is juicy young red, while FINCA Terrerazo shows refinement. Top wine is Quincha Corral. Reviving local Merseguera grape with Finca Calvestre white.

Navarra r p (w) sw ★→★★★ Next door to RIO and always in its shadow. Early focus on international varieties confused its identity. Best: old-vine GARNACHA. Up-and-coming incl Pago de Larrainzar, Tandem. Also ARTADI's Artazu, J CHIVITE FAMILY ESTATES, DOMAINES LUPIER, Nekeas, OCHOA, Otazu, Pago de Cirsus.

Ochoa Nav r p w sw sp ★→★★ Ochoa *padre* led modern growth of NAV, daughters now carry the torch. Winemaker Adriana O calls her range "8a", incl Mil Gracias Graciano and fun, sweet, Asti-like sparkling MdO".

Osborne Sherry ★★→★★★★ Osborne (1772) is all about fine old age. Outstanding v. old SOLERAS incl AOS AMONTILLADO, PDP PALO CORTADO, OLOROSO Seco BC 200, PX Solera Vieja. Owns former DOMECQ VORS incl 51–1a Amontillado. Based in EL PUERTO its FINO Quinta and mature Coquinero FINO typical of zone. Also makes table wines in RIO, RUE, RIB DEL D.

Pago, Vinos de Pago denotes (single) v'yd. Variable quality and lack of objective assessment of current VInos de Pago makes them much criticized. Obvious absentees incl ALVARO PALACIOS' L'Ermita, PINGUS, Calvario (FINCA ALLENDE), CONTINO's VIÑA del Olivo, TORRES properties. Pri Vi de Finca, CAVA *paraje calificado* go some way to find a different quality category.

Pago de los Capellanes Rib del D ★★→★★★ V. fine estate, once belonging to chaplains as name suggests, BODEGA founded 1996. All TEMPRANILLO, modern, expressive, matured in French oak. El Nogal has plenty of yrs ahead; top El Picon reveals best of RIB DEL D.

Pagos, Grandes Network of BODEGAS across Spain with commitment to quality, work together for collective marketing. Some are VINOS DE PAGO but not all, others family-owned estates.

Palacio de Fefiñanes Gal w ★★★→★★★★ Ethereal ALBARIÑOS. **Standard DYA wine** one of finest. Two superior styles: barrel-fermented 1583 (yr winery was founded, oldest winery of DO); super-fragrant, pricey, lees-aged, mandarin-scented "III". Historic palace/winery worth visit.

Palacios, Álvaro Bier, Pri, Rio r ★★★→★★★★ By personality and consistently gd quality, Álvaro Palacios helped build global reputation for Spanish wine. One of quintet who revived PRI. B'x-trained; has vision to recognize villages and terroirs in Burgundian fashion. Wines live up to hype. Old vines Les Terrasses; Finca Dofí mainly GARNACHA with dark undertone. Super-pricey L'Ermita is powerful, dense from low-yielding Garnacha. At PALACIOS REMONDO recuperating reputation of RIO Baja and its Garnachas. Also with nephew at DESCENDIENTES DE J. PALACIOS.

Palacios, Descendientes de J Bier r ★★★→★★★★ Superb wines, showing MENCÍA at its best. Ricardo Pérez Palacios, nephew of ÁLVARO PALACIOS, grows old vines on steep slate. Sadly not all BIER lives up to this promise. Gd-value, floral *Pétalos*. Las Lamas, Villa de Corullón both superb; exceptional single-v'yd La Faraona (but only one barrel). New winery, and more single-v'yd wine in store. Bio.

Palacios, Rafael Gal w ★★★ →★★★★ Rafael Palacios, ÁLVARO's younger brother, can't put a foot wrong in VALDEORRAS. Singular focus on GODELLO across many tiny v'yds over more than a decade. Textured Louro do Bolo; As Sortes, a step up; and most recently *O Soro*, surely Spain's best white.

Palacios Remondo RB r w ★★ →★★★ ÁLVARO PALACIOS returned to family winery to help turn RIO round, brings spotlight on forgotten potential of RB. Promotes concept of villages or crus, as in Burgundy. Complex, oaked Plácet (w) originally created by brother RAFAEL PALACIOS. Reds: organic, GARNACHA-led, red-fruited La Montesa; big, mulberry-flavoured, old-vine Propriedad. More Garnachas on way.

Pariente, José Rue w ★★ →★★★ Victoria Pariente makes VERDEJOS of shining clarity under her father's name. Cuvée Especial fermented in concrete eggs gains fascinating complexity. Silky late-harvest Apasionado. Daughter Martina now joins team, also runs Prieto Pariente with brother Ignacio, working in C Y L and with GARNACHA in Sierra de Gredos.

Pazo Señorans Gal w ★★★★ Exceptionally fragrant ALBARIÑOS from RÍAS BAIXAS benchmark. V. fine Selección de Añada, proof v. best Albariños age beautifully.

Pedro Romero Sherry ★ →★★ Leading MANZANILLA producer, esp Pasada-style Aurora. Owns v. old SOLERAS, incl from Gaspar Florido. Oldest is piercing, concentrated, from Ansar Real PALO CORTADO solera (1820). A supplier to EQUIPO NAVAZOS.

Penedès Cat r w sp ★ →★★★★ Demarcated region w of Barcelona, best-known for CAVA. Identity confused since arrival of all-embracing CAT DO. Best: Agusti Torelló Mata, Alemany i Corrio, Can Rafols dels Caus, GRAMONA, JEAN LEÓN, Parés Baltà, TORRES.

Torres has splendid winery restaurant, Mas Rabell. Allow plenty of time.

Pérez, Raúl Bier One of Spain's most creative winemakers. Family winery is Castro Ventosa, BIER. Works mainly in nw. Experimental, terroir-driven; many interesting wines. Magnet for visiting international winemakers keen to share ideas.

Pérez Barquero Mont-M ★ →★★★ Leader in revival of MONT-M PX. Fine Gran Barquero FINO, AMONTILLADO, OLOROSO; v.gd La Cañada PX. Supplier to EQUIPO NAVAZOS.

Pérez Pascuas Rib del D r ★★ →★★★ Family business making classic RIB DEL D wines from TINTO FINO. Gd-value RES.

Pesquera, Grupo Rib del D r ★★ Veteran farmer/tractor-dealer Alejandro Fernández was part of the making of RIB DEL D with his simply named Tinto Pesquera. Wines less exciting than once were. Daughters joined business; father still hands-on. Also at Condado de Haza, Dehesa La Granja (C Y L), El Vínculo (LA MANCHA).

Pie franco Ungrafted vine, on own roots. Usually old.

Pingus, Dominio de Rib del D r ★★★★ One of RIB DEL D's modern treasures. Tiny bio winery of Pingus (PETER SISSECK's childhood name), made with old vine TINTO FINO. Pingus reveals refinement of variety. *Flor de Pingus* from younger vines; Amelia is single barrel named after his wife. PSI uses grapes from growers, project to encourage estate to keep tending oldest vines.

Plá i Llevant Mall r w ★ →★★★ Thirteen wineries comprise this tiny, lively island DO. Aromatic whites from CHARD and Premsal; intense, spicy reds from CAB SAUV, MERLOT and Callet. Best: Jaime Mesquida, Miguel Oliver, Toni Gelabert, Vins Can Majoral. Exports small, so enjoy on the island.

Priorat r w ★★ →★★★★ Some of Spain's finest wines. Magical mtn, enclosed isolation, named after old monastery tucked under craggy cliffs. Rescued in 80s by quintet of René Barbier of CLOS MOGADOR, ÁLVARO PALACIOS, others. Experience, expense put paid to overoaking. In its place is remarkable purity, sense of place. Pri has pioneered introduction of "village" crus within Pri and Vi de FINCA.

Puerto de Santa María, El Sherry One of three towns forming the "Sherry Triangle". Production now in decline; remaining BODEGAS incl GUTIÉRREZ COLOSÍA, OSBORNE, TERRY. Puerto FINOS are prized as less weighty than JEREZ, not as "salty" as SANLÚCAR. Taste Lustau's three EN RAMAS to taste different characters of Sherries aged in the three towns.

Quinta Sardonia C y L r ★★★ Glossy non-DO project, TEMPRANILLO blends, based in Sardón de Duero, between ABADÍA RETUERTA and MAURO, launched by PETER SISSECK. Member of TERRAS GAUDA group. Bio.

Raventós i Blanc Pen p w ★★→★★★ One of stars of Spain's traditional method sparklings. Pepe R created higher specfication CONCA DEL RÍU ANOIA DO as his alternative to CAVA. V. fine ROSADO De Nit. Zero SO2 Extrem (no added sulphur) v. lively, textured. Textures de Pedra is ringingly pure Blanc de Noirs. Bio.

Recaredo Pen, Cava w sp ★★→★★★ Superb CAVA producer, hand-disgorges all bottles. Few wines, all outstanding. Tops is characterful, mineral *Turó d'en Mota*, from vines planted 1940, ages brilliantly. Bio.

Remelluri, La Granja Nuestra Señora R Ala r w ★★→★★★ Welcome return for TELMO RODRIGUEZ to his family property working with his sister. Campaigner for focus on terroir, varieties, esp GARNACHA, against corporate character of much RIO.

Reserva (Res) Rare in the wine world, Res has actual meaning in RIO, where Res means aged for min 3 yrs of which 1 yr is in oak. Increasingly producers prefer to ignore regulations, in order to choose oak larger than regulation 225 litres, and to age for different periods.

Rey Fernando de Castilla Sherry ★★→★★★★ Gloriously consistent quality. Classic series is reliable; instead, seek out terrific oxidatively aged Antique Sherries; all qualify as VOS or VORS, but label does not say so. Youngest of these, Antique FINO, is fascinating, complex, fortified to historically correct 17% alc. Also v. fine brandy, vinegar. Favoured suppplier to EQUIPO NAVAZOS.

Rías Baixas Gal (r) w ★★→★★★ Atlantic DO growing ALBARIÑO in five subzones, mostly DYA. Best incl Fillaboa, Forjas del Salnés (Cos Pes, FINCA Genoveva), Gerardo Méndez, Martín Códax, PALACIO DE FEFIÑANES, Pazo de Barrantes, PAZO SEÑORANS, Quinta do Couselo, TERRAS GAUDA, *Zárate*. Until recently Spain's premier DO for whites, now at risk of overproduction, becoming just another commercial white. Influential new generation of consultant winemakers incl Raúl Pérez (Sketch), Dominique Roujou de Boubée (As Bateas for Adega Pombal).

Ribeira Sacra Gal r w ★★→★★★ Source of excellent GAL whites, from steep terraces running dizzyingly down to River Sil. Increasingly fashionable. Top: Algueira, Dominio do Bibei (Lapola), Guímaro. MENCÍA v. promising, eg. perfumed Lalama from Dominio do Bibei, Adegas Moure.

Ribeiro Gal (r) w ★→★★★ Historic region, famed in medieval times for Tostado, sweet wine. Undergoing revival, with fresh, light whites made from GODELLO, LOUREIRO, Treixadura. Top: Casal de Armán, Coto de Gomariz, VIÑA Meín.

Ribera del Duero r p (w) ★→★★★★ Ambitious DO with great appeal in Spain, created 1982. Anything that incl AALTO, HACIENDA MONASTERIO, PESQUERA, PINGUS, VEGA SICILIA has to be serious, but with 280 BODEGAS consistency hard to find. Too many v'yds planted in wrong places. With time elegance breaking through. Other top names: ALIÓN, Cillar de Silos, *Pago de los Capellanes*. Also of interest: Alonso del Yerro, ARZUAGA, Bohórquez, Dominio de Atauta, Emilio Moro, FINCA Villacreces, La Horra, Matarromera, O Fournier, PÉREZ PASCUAS, Protos, Sastre, Valdubón, Tomás Postigo. *See also* C Y L neighbours ABADÍA RETUERTA, MAURO.

Rioja r p w sp ★→★★★★ *See* box, right.

Rioja Alta, La R Alt r ★★→★★★★ For lovers of classic RIO, a go-to BODEGA. Vanilla-

> **Rioja: site or no site?**
> RIO has been through a turbulent few yrs arguing about whether or
> how to recognize single v'yds and village wines. There are at least four
> sides: BODEGAS that choose to leave the DO, the campaign for single v'yds
> and village recognition, the cross-village blends that want to emphasize
> quality and the large brands that want high volume and low prices.
> Finally peace seems to have broken out. There will be a way of naming
> v'yds, and extra interest for Rio-lovers.

edged **Gran Res 904** and GRAN RES 890, aged 6 yrs in oak are stars. But rest of
range from **Ardanza**, down to Arana, Alberdi each carry classic house style. Also
owns R Ala Torre de Oña, RÍAS BAIXAS Lagar de Cervera, RIB DEL D Áster.

Rioja 'n' Roll Something new for RIO. New generation of winemakers formed a
network for fun and for marketing. All are linked by small production, and
serious focus on v'yds. Members: Alegre & Valgañón, Artuke, Barbarot, Exopto,
Laventura, Olivier Rivière, Sierra de Toloño.

Roda Rib del D, R Alt r ★★→★★★ Modern HARO BODEGA, though at 25+ yrs more
of a modern classic. Serious RES reds from low-yield TEMPRANILLO, backed by
continued research: Roda, Roda I, Cirsión and approachable Sela. More recently
repeated approach with RIB DEL D Bodegas La Horra, making Corimbo and
Corimbo I. Also outstanding olive oil, Aubocassa.

Rosado Rosé. NAV GARNACHA rosados finally lost out to Provence paleness. Recently
Spain is fighting back esp with: Las FINCAS from J. CHIVITE FAMILY ESTATES, SCALA
DEI's Pla des Àngels (PRI), Ramón Bilbao's Lalomba (RIO), MARQUÉS DE MURRIETA's
Primer Rosé (Rio), among others.

Rueda C y L w ★→★★★ Spain's response to SAUV BL: zesty VERDEJO. Mostly DYA
whites. "Rueda Verdejo" is 100% indigenous Verdejo. "Rueda" is blended with
eg. Sauv Bl, VIURA. Too much poor quality. Best: **Belondrade**, Javier Sanz, JOSÉ
PARIENTE, MARQUÉS DE RISCAL, Naia, Ossian, Palacio de Bornos, Shaya, Sitios de
BODEGA, Viñedos de Nieva, Vinos Sanz.

Saca A withdrawal of Sherry from the SOLERA (oldest stage of ageing) for bottling. For
EN RAMA wines most common *sacas* are in *primavera* (spring) and *otoño* (autumn),
when FLOR is richest, most protective.

Sánchez Romate Sherry ★★→★★★ Old (1781) BODEGA with extensive range,
also sourcing and bottling rare BUTTS for négociants and retailers. 8-yr-old
Fino Perdido, nutty AMONTILLADO NPU, PALO CORTADO Regente, excellent VORS
AMONTILLADO and OLOROSO La Sacristía de Romate, unctuous Sacristía PX.

Sandeman Sherry ★→★★ More famous for its Port than Sherry. Interesting VOS
wines: Royal Esmeralda AMONTILLADO, Royal Corregidor Rich Old OLOROSO.

Sanlúcar de Barrameda Sherry, Man Sherry-triangle town (with JEREZ, EL PUERTO
DE STA MARÍA) at mouth of River Guadalquivir. Humidity in low-lying cellars
encourages FLOR. Sea air said to give wines perfect microclimate. Wines aged
under flor in Sanlúcar BODEGAS qualify for DO MANZANILLA-Sanlúcar de Barrameda.

Scala Dei Pri r w ★★★→★★★★ Tiny v'yds of "stairway to heaven" cling to craggy
slopes that tower over old monastery. Managed by part-owner CODORNÍU.
Winemaker RICARD ROFES restoring traditional methods, fermenting in stone
lagares. Focus on local varieties, esp GARNACHA. Single-v'yds Sant'Antoni and Mas
Deu give clear v'yd expression. For contrast Pla de Àngels is refreshing ROSADO.

Sierra Cantabria R Ala, Toro r w ★★→★★★★ Persistent quiet excellence reflects
Eguren family themselves and their approach, specializing in single-v'yd,
minimal-intervention wines. Organza, white. Reds, all TEMPRANILLO. At Viñedos
de Paganos, superb El Puntido; powerful, structured La Nieta. Other properties
incl Señorio de San Vicente in RIO and Teso la Monja in TORO.

Sisseck, Peter Rib del D With his thoughtful and generous contibution to his adoptive region of RIB DEL D, Sisseck (a Dane by birth) has reinforced the DO's (and Spain's) global reputation. Through PINGUS, PSI and HACIENDA MONASTERIO he offers different expressions of region. His work with DO on its terroir classification should do much to raise overall quality in long term.

Solera Sherry System for blending Sherry and, less commonly, Madeira (*see* Portugal). Consists of topping up progressively more mature BUTTS with younger wines of same sort from previous stage, or *criadera*. Maintains vigour of FLOR, gives consistency, refreshes mature wines.

Somontano r p w ★→★★ DO in Pyrénéan foothills still searching for an identity, given many international varieties in v'yd. Opt for GEWURZ – rare for Spain. Try Enate, Viñas del Vero (owned by GONZÁLEZ BYASS) – its high-altitude property Secastilla has old-vine GARNACHA, GARNACHA BLANCA; may prove to be best variety.

Suertes del Marqués Can r w ★★→★★ Rising star in Tenerife. Founded 2006, works with 21 plots of LISTÁN Blanco and Listán Negro. Exceptional v'yds, with unique *trenzado* – plaited vines.

Telmo Rodríguez, Compañía de Vinos Rio, Mál, Toro r w sw ★★→★★★ Telmo Rodríguez has returned to RIO family BODEGA REMELLURI. His pioneering business, rediscovering old vines across Spain, still continues. MÁLAGA (*Molino Real* MOSCATEL), ALIC (Al-Murvedre), Rio (Lanzaga), RUEDA (Basa), TORO (Dehesa Gago), Cigales (Pegaso), *Valdeorras* (DYA Gaba do Xil GODELLO). Return to Rio has led to launch of exceptionally pure Las Beatas, tiny single v'yd of old-vine GARNACHA.

Terras Gauda Gal w ★★→★★★ Textured, complex ALBARIÑO blends. Also zesty, grapefruit-like La Mar, mainly from rare grape Caiño Blanco. Same group as Pittacum (BIE) and QUINTA SARDONIA (RIB DEL D).

Toro r ★→★★★ Small DO w of Valladolid famed for rustic, overalc wines from Tinta del Toro (TEMPRANILLO). Today, best more restrained, but still with firm tannic grip. Try Maurodos (*see* MAURO), dense old-vine San Román. Glamour comes with VEGA SICILIA-owned Pintia, and LVMH property Numanthia. Also: Elias Mora, Estancia Piedra, PAGO la Jara from TELMO RODRÍGUEZ, Paydos, Teso la Monja.

Toro Albalá Mont-M ★→★★★★ From young dry FINOS to glorious sweet wines, a triumph for MONT-M. Among them lively AMONTILLADO Viejísimo. Seek out remarkable, sumptuous Don PX Convento Selección 1931.

Torres Cat, Pri, Rio r p w sw ★★→★★★★ With three members of family involved, Torres towers full of news and new vintages. Miguel Jr and sister Mireia are full-time, but Miguel Sr is busy on many fronts. Latest release is long-awaited Vardon Kennett, the oddly named but beautifully packaged traditional method sparkling (not CAVA). Ever-reliable DYA CAT Viña Sol never fails to please, nor does grapey Viña Esmeralda. Best reds: outstanding, elegant B'x-blend RES Real, top PEN CAB *Mas la Plana*; CONCA DE BARBERÀ duo (burg-like *Milmanda*, one of Spain's finest CHARDS, *Grans Muralles* blend of local varieties) is stunning. In RIB DEL D Celeste continues to improve as does RIO Ibéricos, and PRI Salmos. Owns JEAN LEON. Also pioneer in Chile.

Tradición Sherry ★★→★★★★ Young (1998) BODEGA assembled by the great José Ignacio Domecq from exceptional selection of fine old SOLERAS. Based on oldest-known Sherry house (1650) and revived by founding family. Use of letters CZ refers to original name of oldest Sherry brand. VOS, VORS Sherries, also a 12-yr-old FINO. Outstanding art collection, archives.

Txakolí / Chacolí P Vas (r) (p) w (sw) ★→★★ Basque, from DOS Getariako Txakolina, Bizkaiko Txakolina, Arabiako Txakolina. Many v'yds face chilly Atlantic winds and soaking rain, hence sharp crunchiness of *pétillant* whites, esp in Getaria where DYA Txakolí is poured into tumblers from a height to add to spritz. Bizkaya wines, with less exposed v'yds, can develop over time. Top: Ameztoi,

Sherry styles

Manzanilla: fashionable pale, dry, low-strength (15% alc): supposedly green-appley. The world's best-value dry white wine; sip it with almost any food, esp crustaceans. Matured by the sea at SANLÚCAR where the FLOR grows thickly and the wine grows salty. Drink cold and drink up; it fades when open like any top white. Eg. HEREDEROS DE ARGÜESO, San León RES.

Manzanilla Pasada: mature Manzanilla, where flor is fading; v. dry, complex. Eg. HIDALGO-LA GITANA's single-v'yd Manzanilla Pasada Pastrana.

Fino: pale, dry, biologically aged in JEREZ or EL PUERTO DE STANTA MARÍA; weightier than Manzanilla; 2 yrs age min (as Manzanilla). Eg. GONZÁLEZ BYASS 4-yr-old Tío Pepe. Serve as Manzanilla, don't keep more than one week once opened. Trend for mature Finos aged more than 8 yrs, eg. FERNANDO DE CASTILLA Antique, González Byass Palmas range.

Amontillado: Fino in which layer of protective yeast flor has died. Oxygen gives more complexity. Naturally dry. Eg. LUSTAU Los Arcos. Commercial styles sweetened.

Oloroso: not aged under flor. Heavier, less brilliant when young, matures to nutty intensity. Naturally dry. May be sweetened with PX and sold as Cream. Eg. EMILIO HIDALGO Gobernador (dr), Old East India (sw). Keeps well.

Palo Cortado: v. fashionable. Traditionally wine that had lost flor – between AMONTILLADO and v. delicate OLOROSO. Difficult to identify with certainty, though some suggest it has a keynote "lactic" or "bitter butter" note. Rich, complex; worth looking for. Eg. BARBADILLO Reliquía, FERNANDO DE CASTILLA Antique. Drink with meat or cheese.

Cream: blend sweetened with grape must, PX and/or MOSCATEL for a commercial medium-sweet style. Few great Creams as old VORS: EQUIPO NAVAZOS La Bota No. 21 is outstanding exception.

En Rama: Manzanilla or Fino bottled from BUTT with little or no filtration or cold stabilization to reveal full character of Sherry. More flavoursome, said to be less stable. Seasonal bottlings in small batches, sell out fast. *Saca* or withdrawal is typically when flor is most abundant. Keep in fridge, drink up quickly.

Pedro Ximénez (PX): raisined sweet, dark, from partly sun-dried PX grapes (grapes mainly from MONT-M; wine matured in Jerez DO). Concentrated, unctuous, decadent, bargain. Sip with ice-cream. Tokaji Essencia apart, world's sweetest wine. Eg. Emilio Hidalgo Santa Ana 1861, LUSTAU VORS.

Moscatel. aromatic appeal, around half sugar of PX. Eg. Lustau Emilín, VALDESPINO Toneles. Now permitted to be called "Jerez".

VOS / VORS: age-dated Sherries: some of treasures of Jerez BODEGAS. Exceptional quality. Wines assessed by carbon dating to be more than 20-yrs-old are called VOS (Very Old Sherry/Vinum Optimum Signatum); those over 30-yrs-old are VORS (Very Old Rare Sherry/ Vinum Optimum Rare Signatum). Also 12-yr-old, 15-yr-old examples. Applies only to Amontillado, Oloroso, PALO CORTADO, PX. Eg. VOS Hidalgo Jerez Cortado Wellington. Some VORS wines are softened with PX: sadly producers can be overgenerous with PX. VORS with more than 5 g/l residual sugar are labelled Medium.

Añada "Vintage": Sherry with declared vintage. Runs counter to tradition of vintage blended SOLERA. Formerly private bottlings now winning public accolades. Eg. Lustau Sweet Oloroso Añada 1997.

Astobiza, Doniene Gorrondona, Txomín Etxaníz. Also Gorka Izagirre, with Michelin three-star restaurant Azurmendi, nr Bilbao airport.

Utiel-Requena r p (w) ★→★★ Arid satellite of v'CIA, marriage of two towns, slowly forging its own identity with rustic but now improving Bobal grape. Tiny Cerrogallina been leader in quality.

Valdeorras Gal r w ★→★★★★ Most inland GAL DOS, named after gold Romans found in valleys. Exceptional GODELLO, potentially more interesting than ALBARIÑO, driving change. Best: A Tapada, Godeval, RAFAEL PALACIOS, TELMO RODRÍGUEZ, Valdesil.

Valdepeñas C-La M r (w) ★→★★ Large DO nr Andalucían border. Gd-value RIO-ish reds. Home to huge Félix Solís business and its ever-popular VIÑA Albali brand.

Valdespino Sherry ★★→★★★★ Home to Inocente FINO from top Macharnudo single v'yd, rare oak-fermented Sherry (EN RAMA version bottled by EQUIPO NAVAZOS). Terrific dry AMONTILLADOS Tío Diego, *Coliseo* VORS; vibrant SOLERA 1842 OLOROSO VOS; remarkable 80-yr-old *Toneles* MOSCATEL, JEREZ's best. Expertise of winemaker Eduardo Ojeda ensures quality. Owned by Grupo Estévez (also owns LA GUITA).

Valencia r p w sw ★→★★ Once known for anonymous bulk wine and cheap, fortified, sweet MOSCATEL, and still guilty. Nevertheless most reliable producer: Murviedro. Growing interest in higher-altitude old vines and min-intervention winemaking: eg. Aranleon, Celler del Roure, El Angosto, *garagiste* Rafael Cambra, Los Fraíles. Sumptuous roasted, treacly Cuva Vella from Valsangiacomo.

Txakolí wine named after C19 farmhouses that made/sold their own wine: Txakolís.

Vega Sicilia Rib del D r ★★★★ All change recently at Spain's "First Growth" with change of winemaker. Yet these wines take yrs to reveal best, so stylistic changes will be slow to show. Único, aged 6 yrs in oak; second wine *Valbuena* outstanding despite lesser status. Unique flagship: RES Especial, NV blend of three vintages, with up to 10 yrs in barrel. Neighbouring Alión shows modern take on RIB DEL D. Now working on a white. Owns TORO property Pintia, Oremus in Tokaji (Hungary), joint-venture project Macan in RIO with Rothschild.

Vendimia Harvest.

Vi de Finca Pri Single v'yd category: wine made for 10 yrs from same single v'yd and commercially recognized as such. Pioneered in PRI by ÁLVARO PALACIOS and colleagues, following Burgundian model of v'yd classification. Vi de Vila describes a village wine in Pri.

Viña Literally, a v'yd.

Vino de la Tierra (VDT) Table wine usually of superior quality made in a demarcated region without DO. Covers immense geographical possibilities; category incl many prestigious producers, non-DO by choice to be freer of inflexible regulation and use varieties they want.

Vivanco, Bodegas R Alt r p w sw ★→★★ Briones BODEGA. Gd collection single-variety RIO reds, rare sweet late-harvest Rio red blend. *Outstanding wine museum*.

Williams & Humbert Sherry ★→★★★★ BODEGA recently best known for private-label wines. Now rapidly improving with excellent selections, eg. vintage EN RAMA FINO 2006. Bestsellers incl Dry Sack, Winter's Tale AMONTILLADOS. V.gd mature wines incl *Dos Cortados* PALO CORTADO, *As You Like It* sweet OLOROSO, VOS Don Guido PX.

Ximénez-Spinola Sherry V. fine small producer only using PX. Grows PX in JEREZ, which is v. rare; most source PX from MONT-M. Top PX and brandy. Intriguing rarity is Exceptional Harvest, from overripe PX, unfortified.

Yecla Mur r (p) w ★→★★ Something stirs in the isolated enclave of Yecla. Only 11 producers, but a real focus on reviving MONASTRELL, esp CASTAÑO.

Zárate Gal (r) w ★★→★★★★ Based in Val de Salnés. Elegant, textured ALBARIÑOS with long lees ageing. El Palomar is from centenarian v'yd, one of RÍAS BAIXAS' oldest, on own rootstock, aged in *foudre* for texture, complexity. Ethereal reds.

Portugal

Portugal's wine revolution is not over yet. In the past decade we have been getting over our surprise to find, for example, wonderful fresh elegant reds and whites from places, above all the Douro Port country, where the textbooks said it couldn't be done. Cleverly, the Portuguese made no great fuss, didn't blow trumpets or charge show-off prices; they just offered tempting wines at tempting prices from first-class grape varieties that were all their own. Of course there are experiments with international bestsellers, but they somehow pulled off a nationwide upgrade with grapes no one had heard of. They simply did their own thing, and well. Over 300 native grapes are currently in use in Portugal. It is not uncommon to find 80-year-old vines, with field blends of over 30 varieties – growing, moreover, in regions to which they have long been adapted. For a small country, Portugal has many different terroirs: from the Atlantic seaside to the mountains, from sandy clay to schist soils, from cold and rainy to warm and dry. In the last 20 years there has been an educational revolution that has included new university viticulture and oenology courses and international internships. Family ownership often means knowledge has been smoothly passing from one generation to the next. The Portuguese language is not easy to learn; its wine is relatively easy.

Recent Port vintages

A vintage is "declared" when the wine is outstanding and meets the shippers' highest standards; something of a parallel to Champagne. In good but not quite classic years most shippers use the names of their quintas (estates) for single-quinta wines of real character but needing less ageing in bottle. The vintages to drink now are 63, 66, 70, 77, 80, 83, 85, 87, 92, 94, though very young Vintage Port, with chocolate cake, even with peppered steak, can be a delight.

2016 Patchy, challenging harvest. Many grapes took far longer than expected to reach maturity. Probably single-quinta year.

2015 Excellent, expected to be widely declared. Very dry, very hot; two days of refreshing September rain followed by ideal harvest weather.

2014 Excellent from vineyards that ducked September's rain; production low.

2013 Single-quinta year; mid-harvest rain. Stars: Vesuvio, Fonseca Guimaraens.

2012 Single-quinta year. Very low yield, drought-afflicted. Stars: Noval, Malvedos

2011 Classic year, widely declared. Inky, outstanding concentration, structure. Stars: Noval Nacional, Vargellas Vinha Velha, Fonseca.

2010 Single-quinta year. Hot, dry but higher yields than 2009. Stars: Vesuvio, Senhora da Ribeira.

2009 Controversial year. Declared by Fladgate, but not Symington's or Sogrape. Stars: Taylor, Niepoort, Fonseca, Warre.

2008 Single-quinta year. Low-yielding, powerful wines. Stars: Noval, Vesuvio, Terra Feita, Passadouro. Sandeman's LBV is v.gd.

2007 Classic year, widely declared. Deep-coloured, rich but well-balanced wines. Stars: Taylor, Vesuvio.

2006 Difficult; a few single quintas. Stars: Vesuvio, Roriz, Barros Quinta Galeira.

2005 Single-quinta year. Stars: Niepoort, Vargellas, Senhora da Ribeira – iron fist in velvet glove.

2004 Single-quinta year. Stars: Pintas, Vargellas Vinha Velha, La Rosa, Noval Nacional – balanced, elegant wines.

See **Portugal** map p.176.

See Portugal map p.176.

Recent table wine vintages

2016 Patchy, complicated year; very long harvest. Very good quality (red and white) for those who patiently waited.

2015 Great quality with quantity: aromatic, intense, balanced wines.

2014 Excellent fresh whites; bright, intense reds (provided picked before rain).

2013 Great for (most) whites, reds picked before rain; mixed results after rain.

2012 Concentrated wines, good balance, especially whites.

2011 Well-balanced year; outstanding Douro, Alentejo reds.

2010 Good quality and quantity all round. Bairrada had another excellent year.

2009 Good overall. Bairrada, Lisboa excellent. Douro, Tejo, Alentejo: big, high alcohol.

Açores / Azores w sw (r) ★→★★★ 15' Mid-Atlantic archipelago of nine volcanic islands with DOCS Pico, Biscoitos and Graciosa for whites and traditional *licoroso* (late-harvest/fortified). Pico landscape, incl vine-protecting *currais* (pebble walls), is UNESCO World Heritage Site. New dynamic winemakers, and arrival of budget flights, producing exciting volcanic-soil wines. Best: Arinto dos Açores, Terrantez do Pico, VERDELHO from Azores Wine Company, Cancela do Porco, Curral Atlantis, Insula.

Adega A cellar or winery.

Alenquer Lis r w ★★→★★★ 11' 12 13 14 15' Microclimatic DOC, home to LIS's best reds. Look for SYRAH pioneer MONTE D'OIRO, CHOCAPALHA, Pinto, and back on form, QUINTA de Pancas.

Alentejo r (w) ★→★★★★ 08' 09 10 11' 12 13 14 15' Reliably warm popular s region, divided into subregional DOCS Borba, Redondo, Reguengos, PORTALEGRE, Évora, Granja-Amareleja, Vidigueira (known for quality white), Moura. Ancient clay amphora technique Vinho de TALHA seeing a comeback. More liberal VR Alentejano preferred by many top estates. Rich, ripe reds, esp from Alicante Bouschet, SYRAH, TRINCADEIRA, TOURIGA N. Whites fast improving. CARTUXA, ESPORÃO, Herdade de São Miguel, JOÃO PORTUGAL RAMOS, MALHADINHA NOVA, MOUCHÃO, MOURO, Sonho Lusitano have potency, style. Watch: DONA MARIA, DO ROCIM, FITA PRETA, MONTE DE RAVASQUEIRA, SUSANA ESTEBAN, Terrenus.

Algarve r p w sp ★→★★ S coast producing mostly Vinho Regional, national and international varities. Recent advances means wines are progressing but still fall short of famed beaches and Michelin-starred gastronomy. Barranco Longo and QUINTA dos Vales honourable mentions.

Aliança Bair r p w sp ★→★★★ Large firm with gd reds and *sparkling*. Wines shown with art at Aliança Underground Museum. Interests in ALEN (QUINTA da Terrugem, Alabastro), DÃO (Quinta da Garrida), DOU (Quinta dos Quatro Ventos). Owner of popular Casal Mendes brand.

Ameal, Quinta do Vin w sw sp ★★★ 00 03 04 05 07' 09 11 14 15 Age-worthy, fine organic LOUREIRO incl oaked Escolha and, in top yrs (11 14) low-yield low-intervention Solo. Gd wine tourism project, incl accommodation.

Andresen Port ★★→★★★★ Family-owned house. Excellent wood-aged Ports, esp 20-yr-old TAWNY. Outstanding *Colheitas* 1900' 1910' (still bottled on demand) 68' 80' 91' 03'. Pioneered age-dated WHITE PORTS 10-, 20-, v.gd 40-yr-old.

Aphros Vin r p w sp ★★★ Bio pioneer, "natural" wine player. V.gd LOUREIRO and Vinhão (both sparkling and oak-aged Silenus) will age beautifully. New cellar frees up old "medieval cellar" for traditional winemaking without electricity (amphorae, *lagares*).

Aveleda, Quinta da Vin r p w ★→★★ DYA Home of Casal García, VIN's biggest seller since 1939. Regular range of estate-grown wines with special mention for Follies.

Bacalhôa Vinhos Alen, Lis, Set r p w sw sp ★★→★★★ Principal brand and HQ of billionaire and art-lover José Berardo's group. Also owns National Monument QUINTA da Bacalhôa (v.gd CAB SAUV 1st planted 1974), sparkling estate Quinta dos Loridos. Top MOSCATEL DE SETÚBAL barrels, incl rare Roxo. Owner of historic Quinta do Carmo brand making v.gd ALEN reds. Modern, well-made brands: Serras de Azeitão, Catarina, Cova da Ursa (SET), TINTO da Ânfora (ALEN). Also see his museum in Funchal.

Bágeiras, Quinta das Bair r w sp ★★★→★★★★ 04′ 05′ 08′ 09 10 11 Stunning, v. age-worthy range: whites (esp Avô Fausto barrique-aged 100% MARIA GOMES), BAGA reds (esp GARRAFEIRA – RES, Pai Abel and Avô Fausto blended with TOURIGA N), sparkling wines and fortified BAGA *Abafado*. Most made traditionally – fermented in open cement vats (reds 100 per cent whole-bunch fermentation) then matured in old *toneis* (wooden vats).

Bairrada r p w sw sp ★→★★★★ 03′ 04 05′ 06 07 08′ 09′ 10′ 11 12 13 14 Atlantic-influenced DOC and VINHO REGIONAL Beira Atlântico. Age-worthy, structured BAGA reds, sparklings (new Baga Bair designation for best). Top Baga specialists: Casa de Saima, CAVES SÃO JOÃO, FILIPA PATO, LUÍS PATO, QUINTA DAS BÁGEIRAS, Sidónio de Sousa. Watch: ALIANÇA, Campolargo, Colinas de S. Lourenço, Quinta de Baixo (NIEPOORT-owned), Vadio, V Puro.

Barbeito Mad ★★→★★★★ Innovative MADEIRA producer with standout labels. V.gd single-v'yd single-cask COLHEITAS. Outstanding 20-, 30-, 40-yr-old MALVASIAS. Excellent Ribeiro Real range with 20-yr-old BOAL, Malvasia, SERCIAL, VERDELHO, with dash of 50s TINTA NEGRA. Sublime use of hard-to-reach Fajã dos Padres v'yds. 96 Colheita 1st to mention Tinta Negra on front label. Historic Series: Madeira most coveted wine in US in C18 and C19.

Barca Velha Dou r ★★★★ 65 66 78 81 82′ 83 85 91′ 95′ 99 00 04 08′ Portugal's iconic red, created in 1952 by FERREIRA, forging DOU's reputation for world class. Released in exceptional yrs, only 18 times. Aged several yrs pre-release. Second label, also released in exceptional yrs from CASA FERREIRINHA's best barrels (when Barca Velha not made), *Res Especial*, v.gd, esp 62 80′ 84 86 89′ 94′ 97′ 01′ 07. Arguably 80′ 89′ 94′ 97′ could have been Barca Velha.

Barros Port ★★→★★★ Founded 1913, SOGEVINUS-owned since 2006, maintains substantial stocks of aged TAWNY and COLHEITA. V.gd Colheitas 35′ 38′ 41′ 44′ 50′ 57′ 60′ 66′ 63 66′ 74′ 78 80′ 97′. V.gd 20-, 30-, 40-yr-old Tawny, VINTAGE PORT: 95 87 03 07 11. Very Old Dry White and Colheita (35) White Ports.

Barros e Sousa Mad ★★→★★★ Acquired by neighbour PEREIRA D'OLIVEIRA (2013) who will bottle remaining stock under its name. Old lodge to be new visitor centre. Look for rare Bastardo Old RES.

One of every five bottles sold in Portugal is from the Alentejo.

Beira Interior Bei Int r p w ★→★★ DOC incl some of highest mtns in Portugal, between DÃO and Spanish border. Huge potential from old, high (up to 750m) v'yds, esp for white Siria, Fonte Cal. Gd-value Beyra, QUINTAS do Cardo. Watch: Quintas dos Currais, dos Termos.

Blandy Mad ★★→★★★★ Historic family firm with dynamic CEO Chris Blandy. *Funchal lodges* showcase history, incl vast library of FRASQUEIRA (BUAL 1920′ 1966′, MALMSEY 1988′, SERCIAL 1975′, VERDELHO 1979′). V.gd 20-yr-old Terrantez and COLHEITAS (Bual 1996 2008, Malmsey 1999, 2002 Sercial). New: superb 50-yr-old Malmsey, 1980′ Terrantez, 1995 TINTA NEGRA; Atlantis table wine: white Verdelho, rosé Tinta Negra.

Borges, HM Mad ★→★★★ Sisters Helena and Isabel Borges still hold tiny amounts of fine 1877 Terrantez demi-john from founding yr. V.gd 30-yr-old MALVASIA incl wine from 1932. V.gd 1990 SERCIAL.

Branco White.

Bual (or Boal) Mad Classic MADEIRA grape: medium-rich (sweet), tangy, smoky wines; less rich than MALVASIA. Perfect with harder cheeses and lighter desserts. Tends to be darkest in colour.

Buçaco Bei At r w ★★★ *Bussaco Palace hotel* lists wines back to 40s. Manueline Gothic architecture as frothy as wines are stern. Barriques and new oak since 2000 have slightly modernized style, esp whites and single-v'yd red Vinha da Mata (VM). Blends of two regions. Reds: BAGA (BAIR), TOURIGA N (DÃO). Whites: Encruzado (Dão), MARIA GOMES, Bical (Bair). Member of BAGA FRIENDS.

Bucelas Lis w sp ★★ Tiny DOC making crisp, dry, racy, min 75% ARINTO. Gd-value sparkling. Widely popular in C19 England as "Lisbon Hock". Best: QUINTAS da Murta, DA ROMEIRA.

Burmester Port ★→★★★ Est 1730, Sogevinus-owned since 2005. Elegant, wood-aged, gd-value Ports esp 20-, 40-yr-old TAWNY. 1890 1900' 37' 52' 55' 57' COLHEITAS. Age-dated WHITE PORTS, incl fine 30-, 40-yr-old. Gd Single-QUINTA VINTAGE PORT Quinta do Arnozelo.

Cálem Port ★→★★★ Est 1859, Sogevinus-owned since 1998. Popular entry-level fruity Velhotes. Best are COLHEITAS 61', 10-, 40-yr-old TAWNY. Lodge in Gaia gets over 100,000 visitors/yr.

Campolargo Bair r w sp ★→★★★ Large estate, pioneer with B'x varieties. V.gd native ARINTO, Bical, CERCEAL (w), Alvarelhão, PINOT N, Rol de Coisas Antigas blend, B'x blend Calda Bordaleza (r).

Canteiro Mad Method of naturally cask-ageing the finest MADEIRA in warm, humid lodges for greater subtlety/complexity than ESTUFAGEM.

Carcavelos Lis br sw ★★★ New toothsome fortified Villa Oeiras breathed life into v. old, tiny, ailing DOC, with v'yd area of 12.5 ha.

Cartuxa, Adega da Alen r w sp ★★→★★★★ C17 cellars, wine restaurant a tourist magnet, while flagship Pêra Manca red 98 01 03 05' 07 08' 09 11' and white draw connoisseurs. Gd-value volume Vinea and EA (organic version available) reds. Consistent best-buy Cartuxa RES 10 11' 12' 13. Scala Coeli, reputed single variety (different each yr).

Carvalhais, Quinta dos Dão r p w sp ★→★★★ SOGRAPE: home of Duque de Viseu and Grão Vasco. Polished estate-grown age-worthy range esp oak-aged Encruzado, RES (r w), TOURIGA N, TINTA RORIZ, Único. Unusual oxidative yet fresh "Branco Especial" (w) a delight.

Castro, Álvaro de Dão ★★→★★★★ Emblematic producer, characterful wines mostly under QUINTA names, Saes and Pellada. Excellent Primus (w), *Pape* (r). Carrocel 06 07 08' 10 11' (TOURIGA N) released in great yrs. Limited-release single-barrel/-v'yd Muleta, Dente d'Ouro preserve old field blend heritage.

Chocapalha, Quinta de Lis r p w ★★★ Family-run estate blending tradition and modernity, native and international varieties. Winemaker is WINE & SOUL'S Sandra Tavares da Silva. *Among Lisboa's best reds*, esp CASTELÃO, CAB SAUV and flagship TOURIGA N CH. Vibrant, fresh whites, esp new RES.

Chryseia Dou r ★★→★★★ 07 08' 09 11' 12' 13 14 B'x's Bruno Prats and SYMINGTON FAMILY ESTATES partnership. Polished TOURIGA-driven (Nacional and Franca) red. Fresher, finer since sourced from QUINTA de Roriz. Second label: *Post Scriptum*. Prazo de Roriz gd value.

Churchill Dou, Port r p w sw ★★→★★★ Port house est 1981 by John Graham whose family founded GRAHAM. V.gd DRY WHITE PORT (10 yrs old), 20-, 30-yr-old (new), unfiltered LBV, VINTAGE PORT 82 85 91 94 97 00 03 07' 11'. QUINTA da Gricha is source of old-vine, grippy Single QUINTA Vintage Port and v.gd single-v'yd DOU red. Gd Churchill's Estates label (esp TOURIGA N).

Cockburn Port ★★→★★★ Part of SYMINGTON FAMILY ESTATES and back on form, esp drier, fresher style of VINTAGE PORT in 11'. Extraordinary 1908' 27' 34 63 67.

Consistently gd Special RES aged longer in wood than others. Vibrant LBV aged 1 yr less. V.gd single-QUINTA dos Canais.

Colares Lis r w ★★ Historic coastal DOC (1908). Windswept ungrafted vines on sand produce Ramisco *tannic reds*, MALVASIA fresh, salty whites. Fundação Oriente and Casal Santa Maria bring modern flair to traditional style of ADEGA Regional de Colares and Viúva Gomes.

Colheita Vintage-dated Port or MADEIRA of a single yr. Cask-aged: min of 7 yrs for TAWNY Port (often 50 yrs+, some 100 yrs+); min 5 yrs for Madeira. Bottling date shown on label.

Conceito Dou, Port r w sp ★★★ Talented Rita Ferreira Marques does style and substance. Strikingly labelled DOU Superior wines (esp Conceito red and white) bring class and finesse to local grapes, incl traditional now-rare PINOT N-like Bastardo. Irreverent Dou GRÜNER V fizz.

Cortes de Cima Alen r w ★★★ Built from scratch by Danish/Californian couple in 1988. ALEN SYRAH pioneer with (v.gd, now more elegant, top red) Incógnito. Consistent range, esp v.gd RES and varietals (ARAGONEZ, Syrah, TRINCADEIRA). V.gd whites from new Alen coastal v'yds incl ALVARINHO, SAUV BL.

Cossart Gordon Mad MADEIRA WINE COMPANY-owned brand. Drier style than BLANDY eg. bracing BUAL 1962' is bottled electricity.

Crasto, Quinta do Dou, Port r w ★★★→★★★★ (r) 07' 08 09' 10 11' 12 13 One of DOU's most reputed estates. Striking hilltop location. Jewels in crown are two v. old field-blend single-v'yd reds Vinha da Ponte 03 04 07' 10' 12 13, Maria Teresa 05' 06 07 09' 11' 13. Great-value old-v'yd RES. Probably Portugal's best single-variety TINTA RORIZ. Great TOURIGA N. Dou Superior v'yds brought gd-value wines to market incl attractive red, innovative acacia-aged white and SYRAH with VIOGNIER dash. Gd VINTAGE PORT and unfiltered LBV.

Croft Port ★★★★ Fladgate-owned historic shipper with visitor centre in glorious v'yds nr Pinhão. Sweet, fleshy VINTAGE PORT 66 70 75 77 82 85 91 94 00 03' 07 09' 11'. Single-QUINTA da Roêda Vintage Port 03 04 07 08' 09 12' v.gd value. Popular: Indulgence, Triple Crown, Distinction and Pink rosé PORT.

Crusted Port Rare, traditional NV Port style. V.gd-value. Blend of two or more vintage-quality yrs, aged up to 4 yrs in casks, released 3 yrs after bottling. Unfiltered, forms deposit ("crust") so decant. Look for CHURCHILL, DOW, FONSECA, GRAHAM, NIEPOORT, NOVAL.

Dão r p w sp ★★→★★★ 05 06 07' 08' 09 10 11' 12 13 Historic mtn-fenced DOC. Modern pioneers ÁLVARO DEL CASTRO, CARVALHAIS, DÃO SUL, Falorca, MAIAS, Roques make elegant, perfumed, age-worthy reds, textured, balanced whites (Encruzado is king); 2nd wave CASA DA PASSARELLA, CASA DE MOURAZ, Julia Kemper. Watch: António Madeira, Druida, Lemos, MOB, NIEPOORT (QUINTA da Lomba), Ribeiro Santo, Vegia. Top Dão Nobre ("noble") designation now used. Superb, gd-value GARRAFEIRAS.

DOC / DOP (Denominação de Origem Controlada / Protegida) Quality-oriented protected designation of origin controlled by a regional commission. Similar to France's AC. *See also* VINHO REGIONAL.

Doce (vinho) Sweet (wine).

Cork benefits

Cork has been widely used as a wine stopper since the C18. It's as environmentally friendly as it gets: 100 per cent natural, easy to recycle and biodegradable. It's hand-harvested from cork trees every 9 yrs. Cork-oak trees are not cut down and can live up to 300 yrs. Portugal produces 55 per cent of all cork in the world. Cork is now one of the most important materials used in spacecrafts. What a waste to use it for stopping bottles of ordinary wine. Screwcaps are a far better idea for those.

Douro Dou, Port r p w sw ★★★→★★★★ World's 1st demarcated and regulated wine region (1756), named after its river. Dramatic UNESCO World Heritage Site. Formerly inaccessible, now wine-tourism ready. Famous for Port, now produces just as much quality table wine (Dou DOC). Three subregions (Baixo Corgo, Cima Corgo and fast-expanding Dou Superior) with great diversity of terroir. Over 100 native vines (often planted together, 80 yrs+) in terraces of unforgiving schist. Powerful, increasingly elegant, age-worthy reds; fine, characterful whites. Best: ALVES DE SOUSA, BARCA VELHA, CASA FERREIRINHA, CHRYSEIA, CRASTO, *Niepoort*, POEIRA, QUINTA Nova, RAMOS PINTO, *Vale Dona Maria*, *Vale Meão*, VALLADO, WINE & SOUL. To watch: Boavista, Foz Torto, Maria Izabel, Murças, NOVAL, POÇAS, Pôpa, Quanta Terra, REAL COMPANHIA VELHA, S. José, Vesuvio. VR is Duriense.

Schist layers in Dou almost vertical: vine roots can penetrate. Otherwise couldn't.

Dow Port ★★★→★★★★ Historic SYMINGTON owned shipper. Drier VINTAGE PORT 66' 70' 72 75 77' 80' 83 85' 91 94' 97 00' 03 07' 11'. Single-QUINTAS do Bomfim and Senhora da Ribeira in non-declared Vintage years. Beautiful riverside Bomfim winery visitor centre in Pinhão.

Duorum Dou, Port r w ★★→★★★ Consistent DOU Superior project of JOÃO PORTUGAL RAMOS and ex-FERREIRA/BARCA VELHA José Maria Soares Franco. Gd-value, fruity, entry-level *Tons*, COLHEITA. Fine RES and O. Leucura from v. old vines. V.gd dense, pure-fruited VINTAGE PORT 07 11' 12 from 100-yr-old vines. Fine second label Vinha de Castelo Melhor and gd-value LBV.

Esporão, Herdade do Alen r w sw ★★→★★★ Landmark estate, part certified organic, part sustainable. High-quality, fruit-focused, modern. Gd-value entry-level Monte Velho, well-regarded RES (r w). V.gd single-v'yd/variety range. New rammed-earth winery for top wines. Sophisticated GARRAFEIRA-like Private Selection and rare Torre. New TALHA (old clay amphora) red back to ALEN tradition. Auspicious DOU project (QUINTA das Murças).

Espumante Sparkling. Generally gd value. Best from BAIR (esp BÁGEIRAS, Colinas São Lourenço, Kompassus, lookout for BAGA Bairrada designation), DOU (esp Vértice), Távora-Varosa (esp MURGANHEIRA) and VIN (esp SOALHEIRO).

Esteban, Susana Alen r w ★★→★★★ Eponymous boutique label. Stunning flagship Procura (r w), from PORTALEGRE's v.old low-yield v'yds (red adds Alicante Bouschet from Évora). Gd-value second label Aventura. Innovative Sidecar blends winemakers (first Dirk NIEPOORT, second FILIPA PATO).

Estufagem Tightly controlled process of heating MADEIRAS for min 3 mths for faster ageing, characteristic scorched-earth tang. Used mostly on entry-level wines. Finer results with external heating jackets and lower max temperature (45°C).

Falua Tej r p w ★→★★ JOÃO PORTUGAL RAMOS' TEJO outpost. Well-made export-focused Tagus Creek blends native and international grapes. Gd-value entry-level Conde de Vimioso (RES a step up).

Favaios, Adega de Dou (r) (w) sw Sizeable 600-member co-op making over 70 per cent of DOU fortified MOSCATEL do Dou. Top aged vintage examples retain delicacy, freshness (80' 89').

Ferreira Port ★★→★★★ SOGRAPE-owned historic Port house. Winemaker Luis Sottomayor reckons LBV now as gd as last decade's VINTAGE PORT, both categories on the up here. Vintage 11' a standout. V.gd spicy TAWNY incl Dona Antonia RES, 10-, 20-yr-old Tawny (QUINTA do Porto, *Duque de Bragança*).

Ferreirinha, Casa Dou r w ★★→★★★★ SOGRAPE's remarkable array of age-worthy DOU wines. Gd-value entry-level Callabriga, Esteva, Papa Figos. Classy Dou QUINTA da Leda, Antónia Adelaide Ferreira. Rarely-released RES Especial, (iconic) BARCA VELHA.

Fita Preta Alen r w ★★ António Maçanita scored with populist Sexy sister-brand. Fita Preta label more serious, esp Palpite (v.gd w and Grande RES r). Signature

Series flirts with unusual techniques (skin contact, TALHA, unoaked TOURIGA N) and varieties eg. BAGA.

Fladgate Port Independent family-owned partnership. Owns leading Port houses (TAYLOR, FONSECA, CROFT, KROHN) and luxury wine hotels: The Yeatman (VILLA NOVA DE GAIA), Vintage House (Pinhão).

Fonseca Port ★★★ →★★★★ FLADGATE-owned Port house, founded 1815. Voluptuous Bin 27, organic Terra Prima RES. V.gd 20-,40-yr-old TAWNY. Excellence in VINTAGE PORT 27' 63' 66' 70 75 77' 80 83 85' 92 94' 97 00' 03' 07 09 11'. Second label Fonseca Guimaraens. Single-QUINTA Panascal.

Fonseca, José Maria da Lis r p w sw sp ★ →★★★★ Historic, c.200-yr-old, 7th-generation producer; extensive v'yds (650 ha) and dynamic portfolio. LANCERS, PERIQUITA: bread-and-butter brands. Cherry on cake: fortified MOSCATEL DE SETÚBAL, which mines aged stock to great effect (v.gd-value 20-yr-old Alambre, Roxo, remarkable SUPERIOR 11' 18 34' 35 42 55' 66 71). Innovative wine bar in Lisbon. Pioneer of modern TALHA wines under characterful ALEN José de Sousa label.

Frasqueira Mad Top MADEIRA category. Also called Vintage. Single-yr, single-noble-variety aged min 20 yrs in wood, usually much longer. Date of bottling required.

Garrafeira Label term for superior quality. Traditionally a merchant's "private RES". Must be aged for min 2 yrs in cask and 1 yr in bottle (often much longer). Whites need 6 mths in cask, 6 mths in bottle. Special use in Port by NIEPOORT.

Global Wines Dão r w sp ★★ →★★★ Also known as Dão Sul. One of Portugal's biggest producers, DÃO-based, with estates in many other regions. Great-value popular brands Cabriz (esp RES) and Casa de Santar (esp RES, superb Nobre). Classy Paço dos Cunhas single-v'yd Vinha do Contador. Modern wines, striking architecture, visitor centre at BAIR's QUINTA do Encontro. Other brands: Grilos, Encostas do Douro (DOU), Monte da Cal (ALEN), Quinta de Lourosa (VIN).

Graham Port ★★★ →★★★★ SYMINGTON-owned Port house. 1st division Ports from RES RUBY Six Grapes to VINTAGE PORT 45' 63' 66 70' 75 77' 80 83' 85' 91' 94' 97 00' 03' 07' 11', incl limited release Stone Terraces 11' and age-worthy single-QUINTA dos Malvedos. V.gd-value, attractive 20-, 30-, 40-yrs-old TAWNY, LBV. Fine Single-Harvest (COLHEITAS) esp 52' 69' 72'. Trumping them all, sublime Ne Oublie Very Old TAWNY, one of three 1882 casks laid down by AJ Symington.

Gran Cruz Port ★ →★★★ Owned by La Martiniquaise, runs Port's largest brand (Porto Cruz) with a focus on volume and cocktails. VILA NOVA DE GAIA museum, rooftop terrace bar tourist attraction. Dalva brand: gd VINTAGE PORT, excellent TAWNY stocks (esp COLHEITAS, white 52' 63' 73'). New QUINTA de Ventozelo project promising bet on quality.

Portugal's two (wine) UNESCO World Heritage Sites: Douro Valley, Pico (Azores)

Henriques & Henriques Mad ★★ →★★★★ Only MADEIRA shipper to own v'yds (incl rare Terrantez plot). Owned by rum giant La Martiniquaise. Unique extra-dry apéritif Monte Seco. Best are 20-yr-old MALVASIA and Terrantez, 15 yr-old (NB *Sercial*), Single Harvest (now aged in seasoned bourbon barrels, 1997', 1998', BUAL 2000'), Vintage (VERDELHO 1957, Terrantez 1954', SERCIAL 1971'). V.gd new TINTA NEGRA 50-yr-old.

Horácio Simões Set Innovative boutique producer. Dynamic range incl late-harvest and fortified MOSCATEL (esp single-cask Roxo and Excellent). Thrilling, rare fortified Bastardo. Table wines to watch (esp 100-yr-old vines Grande RES) BOAL (w), CASTELÃO (r).

Justino Mad ★ →★★★ Largest MADEIRA shipper, owned by rum giant La Martiniquaise, makes Broadbent label. Fairly large entry-level range. Some jewels: Terrantez Old Res (NV, probably around 50-yrs-old), Terrantez 1978' (oldest in cask), MALVASIA 1964', 1968', 1988'.

Kopke Port ★→★★★★ Oldest Port house, est 1638, now Sogevinus owned. Well-known for v.gd spicy, structured COLHEITAS 35' 41' 57' 64' 65' 66 78 80' 84 87 from middle/upper slopes of QUINTA S. Luiz. Standout WHITE PORT range, esp now-rare 1935' and 30-, 40-yr-olds.

Krohn Port ★→★★★ Now FLADGATE-owned. Exceptional stocks of aged TAWNY (rich 10-, 20-yr-old), COLHEITA 61' 66' 67' 76' 82' 83' 87' 91 97 dating back to 1863 (source of TAYLOR 1863 Single Harvest). VINTAGE PORTS improving.

Lancers p w sp ★ JOSÉ MARIA DA FONSECA's semi-sweet, semi-sparkling ROSADO, now white, sparkling (p w) and alc-free versions.

Lavradores de Feitoria Dou r w ★★→★★★ Well-run collaboration of 15 producers (19 v'yds). Gd whites, esp SAUV BL, Meruge (100% old vines Viosinho). Gd reds, incl Três Bagos RES. V.gd Grande Escolha (esp long-aged Estágio Prolongado), QUINTA da Costa das Aguaneiras, elegant Meruge (mostly TINTA RORIZ from a n-facing 400m v'yd).

LBV (Late Bottled Vintage) Port Affordable and ready-to-drink alternative to VINTAGE PORT. A single-yr wine, aged 4–6 yrs in cask, twice as long as VINTAGE PORT. Age-worthy unfiltered versions eg. FERREIRA, NIEPOORT, DE LA ROSA, NOVAL, RAMOS PINTO, Romaneira, SANDEMAN, WARRE.

Lisboa r p w sp sw ★→★★ Large, hilly region around capital; varied terroir, muddle of local and international grapes. Best-known DOCS: ALENQUER (pioneering boutique wineries CHOCAPALHA, MONTE D'OIRO for best reds) and traditional BUCELAS, COLARES. Fresh dry whites growing in strength, esp from limestone, coastal/elevated v'yds esp. Adega Mãe (Viosinho), Casal Figueira (Vital), Casal Sta Maria (COLARES), Quinta do Pinto (blends), Vale da Capucha (organic).

Madeira Mad r w ★→★★★★ Island and DOC, famous for fortifieds. Modest table wines (Terras Madeirenses VR, Madeirense DOC). VERDELHO best. Look for Atlantis, Barbusano, Moledo, Palmeira, Primeira Paixão, Terras do Avô.

Madeira Vintners Mad Brave producer, est 2012. Plans to release small-batch, terroir-driven wines, Listrão (aka PALOMINO Fino) and techniques (eg. cask fermentation, fermentation on skins, micro-oxygenation of ESTUFAGEM) to attain complexity, profile of 5- to 10-yr-old in 3 yrs. Promising 1st releases.

Madeira Wine Company Mad Association of all 26 British MADEIRA companies, est 1913. Owns BLANDY, COSSART GORDON, Leacock, MILES and accounts for over 50 per cent of bottled Madeira exports. Since BLANDY family gained control, almost exclusively focused on promoting Blandy brand.

Maias, Quinta das Dão r w ★★→★★★ Sister of QUINTA DOS ROQUES. V.gd organic entry-level, varietal wines, DÃO's only VERDELHO, distinctive Jaen. V.gd Flor das Maias red and white (oaked-aged, fresh Encruzado-dominated blend).

Malhadinha Nova, Herdade da Alen r p w sw ★★★ Family estate; fashionable country house hotel. Entry-level (Peceguina) and middle-tier wines increasingly single varietal. Top blends (Malhadinha and Marias) offer better complexity, balance.

Malvasia (Malmsey) Mad Sweetest and richest of traditional MADEIRA noble grape varieties, yet with Madeira's unique sharp tang. Perfect with rich fruit, chocolate puddings, or just dreams.

Mateus Rosé p (w) sp ★ World's bestselling, medium-dry, lightly carbonated rosé

What grows together goes together
Some local wine pairings: MADEIRA's dry SERCIAL with grilled limpets; fresh grilled fish with lively VIN or BUCELAS; suckling pig with red or white sparkling BAIR; any traditional combination of egg yolks with lots of sugar (eg. Torta de Azeitão) with MOSCATEL DE SETÚBAL; Rich MALVASIA with honey cake (bolo de mel); VINTAGE PORT with creamy, fat Serra da Estrela cheese. Finally, enjoy a glass of Very Old TAWNY with best company you can find.

now in transparent bottles and available in white (drier, no spritz) or fully sparkling (p w). Expressions range: (MARIA GOMES/CHARD) and three rosé blends (BAGA/SHIRAZ, Baga/MUSCAT; ARAGONEZ/ZIN).

Mendes, Anselmo Vin r w sw sp ★★→★★★★ Acclaimed winemaker and consultant. Several benchmark, age-worthy ALVARINHOS, incl gd-value (aged on lees) Contacto, excellent oaked voluptous Curtimenta, single-v'yd Parcela Única, classy Muros de Melgaço and vibrant new Expressões. Gd LOUREIRO, silky, modern red VIN (Pardusco). Orange VIN in works.

Many Galicians say they prefer Portugal to Spain. Must be Alvarinho-envy.

Minho Vin River between n Portugal and Spain, also VR covering same region as VIN. Some leading Vin producers prefer VR Minho label.

Monte de Ravasqueira Alen ★★→★★★ Great terroir (high-up amphitheatre, clay-limestone, granite), precision viticulture and experienced winemaker make gd range esp v.gd single-v'yd Vinha das Romãs, MR Premium (r p w).

Monte d'Oiro, Quinta do Lis r w p ★★→★★★ Cuttings from 60-yr-old Hermitage vines from Chapoutier (*see* France) now make age-worthy savoury, creamy SYRAH, gd VIOGNIER (Madrigal), fine TINTA RORIZ (Têmpera). Ex-Aequo is Bento & Chapoutier Syrah/TOURIGA N blend.

Moscatel de Setúbal Set sw ★★★→★★★★ DOC s of Lisbon. Prestigious fortified MOSCATEL dessert wines incl rare Roxo. "Superior" label for quality-approved wines. JOSÉ MARIA DA FONSECA (oldest) owns old stocks incl famous 100-yr-old Round Trip. Best: Adriano Tiago, António Saramago, BACALHÔA VINHOS and HÓRACIO DOS SIMÕES, QUINTA do Piloto. Gd value: ADEGA DE PEGÕES, Casa Ermelinda Freitas, SIVIPA.

Moscatel do Douro Dou The elevated Favaios region produces surprisingly fresh, fortified MOSCATEL Galego Branco (MUSCAT Blanc à Petit Grains) that rival those of SET. Look for: ADEGA FAVAIOS, POÇAS, Portal, NIEPOORT.

Mouchão, Herdade de Alen r w sw ★★★→★★★★ 05' 06 07 08' 09 10 11' Traditional family-run Alicante Bouschet-focused estate. V.gd museum release (COLHEITAS Antigas), *Tonel* 3–4 03 05' 08 11', fortified *licoroso*. Gd value: Ponte das Canas blend (incl SYRAH), Dom Rafael.

Mouraz, Casa do Dão r w ★★ Boutique organic (certified 1996) pioneer. Modern but characterful (esp Elfa) gd-value wines from family-owned v'yds (140–400m). AIR label from bought-in ALEN, DOU, VIN organic grapes.

Mouro, Quinta do Alen r w ★★→★★★★ Reliable ALEN wines with imposing reds blending native grapes with CAB SAUV (also single-variety). V.gd Mouro, excellent Gold label in top yrs 05 06' 07' 08 09 10 11. Vinha do Malhó is savoury Centurion/PETIT SYRAH blend. Gd-value Vinha do Mouro, Zagalos.

Murganheira, Caves sp ★★★ Largest ESPUMANTE producer; owns RAPOSEIRA. Blends and single varietal (native, French grapes) fizz: Vintage, Grande RES, Czar rosé.

Niepoort Dou, Port r p w ★★★→★★★★ Quality-focused family-owned Port shipper and DOU pioneer. Highlights: VINTAGE PORT, unique demijohn-aged GARRAFEIRA and single v'yd Bioma. V.gd TAWNY, esp bottle-aged (elegant) COLHEITAS. Age-worthy, increasingly elegant DOU range, esp *Redoma* (r p w Res w), Coche (superb w), Batuta, iconic Charme and unique 130-yr-old single-v'yd Turris. Exciting Projectos portfolio incl experimental, cross-region/winemaker wines esp António Madeira (Dão), DODA (DÃO), Ladredo (Ribeira Sacra, Spain), Navazos (Spain). Dirk Niepoort's vision now in BAIR (esp GARRAFEIRA, Poeirinho, VV), DAO (esp Conciso) and VIN.

Noval, Quinta do Dou, Port r w ★★★→★★★★ Historic AXA-owned (1993) estate. Elegantly structured VINTAGE PORT 63' 66 67 70 75 78 82 85 87 91 94' 95 97' 00' 03' 04 07' 08' 11' 12' 13' 14 is fraction of price of rare, compelling

Nacional 62 63' 66' 70 94' 96' 97' 00' 01' 03' 04' 11' from 2.5 ha ungrafted vines. Second vintage label: Silval. V.gd COLHEITAS, 20-, 40-yrs-old, unfiltered LBV. Plump Noval Black RES. Since 2004 making DOU wines incl gd-value Cedro (native/SYRAH blend), v.gd Noval, varietal TOURIGA N.

Offley Port ★→★★ Owned by SOGRAPE. Gd recent fruit-driven VINTAGE PORT, unfiltered LBV, TAWNY. Apéritif/cocktail styles: Cachuca RES WHITE PORT, ROSÉ PORT.

Palmela Set r w ★→★★★ Castelão-focused DOC. Best: Herdade Pegos Claros, HORÁCIO SIMÕES, QUINTA do Piloto. To watch.

Portugal's longest road, EN2, stretches 738km, crosses five wine regions.

Passarella, Casa da Dão r p w ★★→★★★ Steady revival of historic DÃO C19 estate. V.gd range recreated by Paulo Nunes esp flagship Villa Oliveira: Encruzado, TOURIGA N (selectively harvested from old field-blend v'yd), single v'yd Pedras Altas (r), Vinha do Província (w). Innovative new Black Label NV (twice-a-decade blend of best white barrels of previous 5 yrs). V.gd boutique Fugitivo range esp Enólogo, Enxertia (Jaen), Vinhas Centenárias (red blend of tiny 100-yr-old vines); new Curtimenta. Excellent (v.gd-value) GARRAFEIRA (w).

Pato, Filipa Bair r w sp sw ★★→★★★ "Wines with no make-up" motto puts terroir centre-stage for old-vine age-worthy Nossa Calcario flagship label: silky, perfumed BAGA (r) and complex Bical (w). V.gd old-vine, oak-*lagares* fermented Territorio Vivo. Tests boundaries (like her father, LUÍS PATO) esp with amphorae-aged Post Quercus (r w) and elegant Espirito de Baga fortified.

Pato, Luís Bair r w sw sp ★★→★★★★ Self-assured BAIR unconformist wine-grower. Made his "Mr BAGA" name with *seriously age-worthy, single-v'yd Baga* (Vinhas Barrio, Barrosa, Pan) and two Pé Franco wines from ungrafted vines (sandy-soil QUINTA do Ribeirinho, chalky-clay Valadas). Ready-to-drink, gd-value: Vinhas Velhas (r w), Baga Rebel, wacky red FERNÃO PIRES (fermented on Baga skins). V.gd whites incl Vinhas Velhas (single-v'yd Vinha Formal), sparkling (traditional MARIA GOMES Método Antigo, early-picked Informal).

Pegões, Adega de Set r p w sw sp ★→★★ Dynamic co-op. Stella label and low-alc Nico white offer gd clean fruit. COLHEITA Seleccionada (r w) gd value.

Península de Setúbal Set ★→★★ Formerly Terras do Sado. Atlantic-facing region s of Lisbon. VR wines mostly from chalky slopes or sandy soils of Sado and Tagus Rivers. Est: ADEGA DE PEGÕES, Bacalhôa Vinhos, Casa Ermelinda Freitas, JOSÉ MARIA FONSECA, SIVIPA. Watch: António Saramago, Herdade do Portocarro, Soberanas.

Pereira d'Oliveira Vinhos Mad ★★→★★★★ Family-run producer with vast stocks (1.6 million litres) of bottled-on-demand FRASQUEIRA, many available to taste at characterful 1619 cellar door. Best incl stunning C19 vintages (Moscatel 1875, Sercial 1875, Terrantez 1880) and rare Bastardo 1927.

Periquita Grape also known as CASTELÃO. Also trademark of JOSÉ MARÍA DA FONSECA's successful brand.

Poças Dou, Port ★★→★★★ Family-owned firm est 1918. V.gd COLHEITAS 64 67' 92 94 95 97 00 01. Old stocks allow for v.gd 20-, 30-, 40-yr-old TAWNY. Gd VINTAGE PORT. Table wines increasing in quality. New partnership between B'x-trained Jorge Pintão and B'x-owner (Angélus) Hubert de Bouard.

Poeira, Quinta do Dou r w ★★★ Consultant Jorge Moreira's own project. Age-worthy wines from cool, n-facing slopes, intense yet softly spoken, esp red, now more bottle age. Taut, keen, oaked ALVARINHO. Classy second label Pó de Poeira (r w).

Portalegre Alen r p w ★→★★★ Wine writers Richard Mayson (QUINTA do Centro) and João Afonso (Solstício/Equinócio), Lisbon chef Vitor Claro, consultant Rui Reguinga (Terrenus), SUSANA ESTEBAN, ESPORÃO have flocked to ALEN's most n subregion (DOC). Elevation, granite and schist, old vines (incl field blends), gd rainfall account for fresh, structured wines with depth. Region to watch.

Quinta Portuguese for "estate" (eg. CRASTO, QUINTA DO). "Single-quinta" denotes single-estate VINTAGE PORTS made in non-declared yrs (increasingly made in top yrs too by single-estate producers).

Ramos, João Portugal Alen r w ★→★★★ One of Portugal's most respected winemakers, now works under own name (VIN) and other brands (DUORUM, Falua, Foz de Arouce, QUINTA da Viçosa, Vila Santa). Recipe: gd-value, true-to-region wines, commercial appeal. Classy top wines: Estremus, Marqués de Borba RES.

Ramos Pinto Dou, Port ★→★★★★ 1880 pioneering Port and DOU producer owned by Champagne Roederer. Consistent, esp Duas Quintas RES (r), RES Especial (mainly TOURIGA N from Bom Retiro). V.gd age-worthy VINTAGE PORT incl single-QUINTA Vintage (de Ervamoira). Complex single-QUINTA TAWNY 10-yr-old (de Ervamoira) and v.gd 20-yr-old (Bom Retiro). Gd 30-yr-old incl a dash of centenarian TAWNY. Winemaker Ana Rosas now replacing (retired) João Nicolau de Almeida.

Raposeira Dou sp ★★ MURGANHEIRA-owned. Classic-method fizz. Flagship Velha RFS, CHARD/PINOT N lees-aged 4 yrs.

Real Companhia Velha Dou, Port r p w sw ★→★★★ Silva Reis family have renewed their Port (incl Royal Oporto and Delaforce) and DOU portfolio thanks to stellar precision viticulture (540 ha) and winemaking (led by POEIRA's Jorge Moreira). V.gd old-vine flagship QUINTA das Carvalhas (r w), VINTAGE PORT, 20-yr-old TAWNY. Gd-value brands Aciprestes, Evel. Quinta de Cidrô blends native and international grapes (v.gd CAB SAUV/TOURIGA N). Gd experimental project Séries. New, thrilling whites from Quinta do Síbio (esp rare Samarrinho). Grandjó is best late-harvest in Portugal. Fabulous 149-yr-old Carvalhas Memories Very Old Tawny.

Reserve / Reserva (Res) Port Higher quality than basic or ages before being sold (or both). In Port, bottled without age indication (used in RUBY, TAWNY). In table wines, ageing rules vary between regions.

Romeira, Quinta da r p w sp ★→★★ Historic BUCELAS estate. Consolidating pre-eminent position under new owner Wine Ventures. Extended v'yd (75 ha, mostly ARINTO) now offers s and n aspects for slightly different styles. V.gd Arinto (Prova Régia RFS, oaked Morgado Sta Catherina Res). Gd-value Prova Regia Arinto, Principium French/native grape blends (VR LISBOA).

Rosa, Quinta de la Dou, Port r p w ★★★ Delightfully located estate (riverside, Pinhão). Port and DOU's range rapidly increasing in quality under winemaker Jorge Moreira (POEIRA). V.gd VINTAGE PORT, LBV. Rich but elegant wines, esp RES (r w). DouROSA is entry level. Generous Passagem label.

Rosado Rosé. Growing category. Best incl Colinas São Lourenço Tête de Cuvée, Covela, QUINTA Nova, Monte da Ravasqueira, SOALHEIRO (sp), Vértice (sp).

Rosé Port Port Pioneered by Croft's Pink (2005) now made by other shippers (eg. POÇAS, KROHN). Quality variable. Serve chilled, on ice or, most likely, in a cocktail.

Rozès Port ★★★ Port shipper owned by Vranken-Pommery. VINTAGE PORT, incl LBV, sourced from DOU Superior QUINTAS (Grifo, Anibal, Canameira). Terras do Grifo Vintage is blend of all three; v.gd LBV from Grifo only.

Portugal has over 1001 ways of cooking *bacalhau* (dried, salted cod).

Ruby Port The most simple, young and cheap sweet Port style. RES better.

Sandeman Port Port ★★→★★★ Historic house owned by SOGRAPE. V.gd age-dated TAWNY, esp 20-, 30-, 40-yr-old (with attractive new bottle), unfiltered LBV. Great old VINTAGE PORT 07' 11' bring back quality. Second label: forward Vau Vintage. Superb Very Old Tawny Cask 33.

***São João*, Caves** Bair r w sp ★★→★★★ Traditional, family-owned firm known for v.gd, old-fashioned reds, esp *Frei João*, Poço do Lobo (BAIR), Porta dos Cavaleiros (DÃO). Regular museum releases from vast stock (back to 1963). Gd ARINTO/CHARD white, sparkling blends.

Sercial Mad White grape. Makes the driest of MADEIRAS. *Supreme apéritif*, gd with gravlax or sushi. *See* Grapes chapter (pp.16–26).

Smith Woodhouse Port ★★★ SYMINGTON-owned small Port firm est 1784. Gd unfiltered LBV; some v.gd drier VINTAGE PORT 66 70 75 77' 80 83 85 91 94 97 00' 03 07 11'. Single-quinta da Madelena.

Soalheiro, Quinta de Vin r p w sp ★★→★★★★ Leading ALVARINHO specialist with dynamic, age-worthy (partly organic) range. V.gd (subtly barrel-fermented) old-vine Primeiras Vinhas, oak-aged RES (w), chestnut barrel/partial malolactic fermentation Terramatter; 1st red, Oppaco, unique Vinhão/Alvarinho blend. V.gd sparkling (p w).

Sogrape Vin ★→★★★★ Portugal's most successful firm. MATEUS ROSÉ, BARCA VELHA jewels in crown for contrasting reasons. Portfolio encompasses ALEN (Herdade do Peso), DÃO (CARVALHAIS), DOU (Casa Ferreirinha, Legado), Port (FERREIRA, SANDEMAN, OFFLEY), VIN (incl gd-value Azevedo). Approachable multi-regional brands incl Grão Vasco, Pena de Pato.

Sousa, Alves de Dou, Port r w ★★→★★★★ Family-owned DOU pioneer. Characterful range from various QUINTAS incl bottle-aged late releases. Best: superb Abandonado ("abandoned" 90-yr-old vines), classy single-quinta da Gaivosa, original (oxidative, skin-contact) Pessoal (w), polished Vinha de Lordelo. Expanding Port range incl elegant VINTAGE PORT, 20-yr-old TAWNY.

Symington Family Estates Dou, Port r w ★★→★★★★ DOU's biggest landowner with 27 QUINTAS, a clutch of top Port houses (incl COCKBURN, DOW, GRAHAM, VESUVIO, WARRE); classy Dou range (CHRYSEIA, Vesuvio and well-made organic Altano).

Talha Large impermeable clay jar (c.1000 litres) traditionally used to ferment and age in ALEN. DOC Vinho de Talha (2012) preserves tradition of keeping wine on skins in *talha* until November 11. Other regions trying it (eg. FILIPA PATO, APHROS). Look for: do Rocim, dos Outeiros Altos, ESPORÃO, José da Sousa, Piteira.

Tawny Port Wood-aged Port (hence tawny colour), ready to drink on release. RES, age-dated (10-, 20-, 30-, 40-yr-old) wines go up in complexity, price. COLHEITAS can cost gd deal more than VINTAGE. Luscious Very Old Tawny Ports (min 40-yrs-old, most much older) rare, may cost more than Vintage.

Taylor Port ★★→★★★★ Historic Port shipper, FLADGATE's jewel in the crown. Imposing VINTAGE PORTS 66 70 75 77' 80 83 85 92' 94 97 00' 03' 07' 09' 11', incl single-QUINTAS (Terra Feita, Vargellas), rare Vargellas Vinha Velha from 70-yr-old+ vines. Market leader for TAWNY incl v.gd age-dated, 50-yr-old COLHEITAS and luscious Very Old Tawny (Scion, 1863).

Tejo r w DOC and VR around River Tagus. Quantity-to-quality shift but still little sets pulse racing. Solid: FALUA, QUINTAS da Alorna, da Lagoalva, da Lapa. More ambitious: Encosta do Sobral, Rui Reguinga/Tributo show potential of top terroir. Old vines produce gd results with stalwart CASTELÃO (Casal Branco), FERNÃO PIRES.

Tinto Red.

Trás-os-Montes Mountainous inland DOC, just n of DOU. Leader: Valle Pradinhos. Promising: Encostas de Sonim, QUINTA de Valle de Passos. (VR Transmontano.)

Vale Dona Maria, Quinta do Dou, Port r p w ★★→★★★ V.gd plush yet elegant reds incl two single parcel wines: Vinha do Rio, Vinha da Francisca. Smoky, oaky but

---

Poor man's Vintage Port

CRUSTED and LBVS often known as "Poor man's VINTAGE PORT" for their Vintage Port quality at fraction of cost. Crusted Ports blend at least two or more harvests, age in wood for up to 4 yrs and (normally) age at least another 3 yrs in bottle (before release). LBVs are single-harvest wines, released ready-to-drink after 4–6 yrs of cask ageing (hence "late bottled"). Both increasingly better in quality, age-worthiness, value for money.

brisk whites feature in labels made with bought-in fruit incl flagship CV, mid-range Van Zellers, new VVV and entry level Rufo. Gd Port.

Vale Meão, Quinta do Dou r w ★★★→★★★★ Leading DOU Superior estate; once source of BARCA VELHA. V.gd, age-worthy, elegant top red as is single-QUINTA VINTAGE PORT. Gd-value second label Meandro (also w). Single-varietal Monte Meão range.

Vallado, Quinta da Dou r p w ★★→★★★ Family-owned Baixo Corgo estate with modern hotel/winery. DOU Superior QUINTA do Orgal (boutique Casa do Rio) with new, fresh organic red. Strong, increasingly elegant range of Dou (r w) incl RES field blend. Gd 10-, 20-, 30-, 40-yr-old TAWNY. Adelaide designates top Dou red, VINTAGE PORT, thrilling Tributa Very Old (pre-phylloxera) Tawny.

Vin has over 19,000 wine-growers, many with less than 1 ha vines.

Vasques de Carvalho Dou, Port ★★★ New producer (2012) est by António Vasques de Carvalho (inherited family's wine cellars, stock, v'yd) and business partner Luís Vale (injected capital). V.gd, stylish 10-, 20-, 30- and 40-yr-old TAWNY blended by Jaime Costa (ex-BURMESTER).

Verdelho Style and grape of medium-dry MADEIRA; pungent but without austerity of SERCIAL. Gd apéritif or pair with pâté. Increasingly popular for table wines.

Vesúvio, Quinta do Dou, Port ★★★★ Magnificent QUINTA and Port on par with best VINTAGE PORT 00' 01 03' 04 05' 06 07' 08' 09 10 11' 12 13'. Only SYMINGTON FAMILY ESTATES Port still foot-trodden by people (not robotically). Single-parcel Capela da Quinta Vesúvio, DOU reds first made 2007.

Vila Nova de Gaia Dou, Port Home of major Port shippers' lodges. Cross double-decked metal D Luís bridge over River Douro from Oporto to visit and taste inside famous Port cellars.

Vinho Verde r p w sp ★→★★★ Portugal's biggest DOC in cool, rainy, verdant nw. Renaissance: fresh, better blends. Best: high-end, subregional, varietal QUINTA wines, incl ALVARINHO from Monção e Melgaço (eg. ANSELMO MENDES, da Pedra, do Regueiro, Luis Seabra, Reguengo de Melgaço, SOALHEIRO), LOUREIRO from Lima (eg. APHROS, Paço de Palmeira, QUINTA DO AMEAL). Red Vinhão grape now targeted for makeover by leading players (eg. Anselmo Mendes, Aphros, Soalheiro). Large brands are spritzy; DYA. Watch: Quintas de Santiago, de San Joanne.

Vintage Port Port Classic vintages are best wines declared in exceptional yrs by shippers between 1 Jan and 30 Sept in 2nd yr after vintage. Bottled without filtration after 2 yrs in wood, it matures v. slowly in bottle-throwing a deposit – always decant. Modern vintages broachable earlier (and hedonistic young) but best will last more than 50 yrs. Single-QUINTA Vintage Ports also drinking earlier, best can last 30 yrs+.

VR / IGP (Vinho Regional / Indicação Geográfica Protegida) Same status as French Vin de Pays. More leeway for experimentation than DOC/DOP.

Warre Port ★★★→★★★★ Oldest of British Port shippers (1670), now owned by SYMINGTON FAMILY ESTATES. V.gd, rich, age worthy VINTAGE 63 66 70' 75 77' 80' 83 85 91 94 97 00' 03 07' 09' 11' and unfiltered LBV. Elegant Single-QUINTA and 10-, 20-yr-old TAWNY Otima reflect Quinta da Cavadinha's cool elevation.

White Port Port Port from white grapes. Ranges from dry to sweet (*lágrima*); mostly off-dry and blend of yrs. Apéritif straight or drink iced with tonic and fresh mint. Growing, high-quality, niche: age-dated (10-, 20-, 30-, or 40-yr-old), eg. ANDRESEN, KOPKE, QUINTA de Santa Eufemia; rare COLHEITAS eg. C DA SILVA's Dalva.

Wine & Soul Dou, Port r w ★★★★ Sandra Tavares' and Jorge Serôdio Borges' intense wines incl stunning Guru (w), elegant QUINTA da Manoella Vinhas Velhas and denser (80-yr-old vine) Pintas. V.gd second labels: Pintas Character, Manoella. V.gd Pintas VINTAGE PORT. Oustanding 5G (120-yr-old barrel kept from five generations) Very Old TAWNY Port.

Switzerland

Abbreviations used in the text:

Aar	Aargau
Ber	Bern
Gris	Grisons
Luc	Lucerne
Neu	Neuchâtel
Schaff	Schaffhausen
Thur	Thurgau
Tic	Ticino
Val	Valais
Vd	Vaud
Zür	Zürich

Few outside Switzerland drink Swiss wine – or know what they are
missing, though skiers are well aware of Fendant and its deceptive
kick. The prices of most wines, with unfamiliar names, put them off, but
wine-lovers should persevere. The rare grape varieties of the Alps have
unique qualities, and remarkable variety. The most impressive are dense,
often sweet, golden-amber and live for years. The most useful are sharp
and full-bodied, great food wines such as Petit Arvine and Completer,
or the ubiquitous red Dôle the Swiss seem to drink every day – though
they have far better and more interesting reds: Cornalin, for example,
and Humagne Rouge, not to mention the Merlot of Ticino and some
impressive Syrah in Valais. The most prestigious are Burgundy varieties
from Bundner Herrschaft in German-speaking Switzerland. The best
advice to off-piste wine-lovers and ditto skiers is to employ a guide.

Recent vintages

2016 Frost in April, rainy summer then sun: late, healthy harvest; mostly
mid-weight wines.

2015 Great vintage, maybe best in 50 yrs: ripe fruit, perfectly balanced acidity.

2014 Dry, sunny September saved crop; a year of classically structured wines.

2013 Very small crop; eastern Switzerland outstanding, great freshness, purity.

2012 A winemaker's vintage. Difficult year with hail and rain.

2011 Very good vintage, from an unusually long, warm autumn.

Fine vintages: 2009, 2005 (all), 2000 (esp Pinot N, Valais reds), 1999
(Dézaley), 1997 (Dézaley), 1990 (all).

Aargau Wine-growing canton se of Basel, mainly PINOT N, MÜLLER-T. Gd growers incl Döttingen co-op, Haefliger, Hartmann, LITWAN, Meier (zum Sternen).

Aigle Vd ★★ Commune for CHASSELAS known for BADOUX' v. light Les Murailles. Try Terroir du Crosex Grillé.

AOC The equivalent of French Appellation Contrôlée, but unlike in France, it is not nationally defined and every canton has its own rules. 85 AOCs countrywide.

Bachtobel, Schlossgut Thur ★★★ Since 1784 owned by descendants of Kesselring family, known for refined PINOT N from slopes nr Weinfelden.

Bad Osterfingen Schaff ★★★ Michael Meyer is a PINOT specialist. Co-producer of ZWAA (with R BAUMANN). Restaurant too.

Badoux, Henri Vd ★★ Big producer, his CHASSELAS AIGLE les Murailles (classic lizard label) is most popular Swiss brand, though seldom convincing.

Baumann, Ruedi Schaff ★★★ Leading estate at Oberhallau; berry-scented, ageable PINOT N, esp -R-, Ann Mee. ZWAA: collaboration with nearby BAD OSTERFINGEN estate.

Bern Capital and homonymous canton. Wine villages on Lake Biel (esp Ligerz, Schafis, Twann) and Lake Thun (Spiez), mainly CHASSELAS, PINOT N. Top growers: Andrey, Johanniterkeller, Schlössli, Steiner.

Besse, Gérald et Patricia Val ★★★ Leading VAL family estate, mostly on steep-sloping terraces; elegant FENDANT Les Bans, superb old-vines Ermitage (MARSANNE) Les Serpentines planted 1945, 600m altitude, 08 09 13' 14.

Blattner, Valentin Grower and vine breeder in the Jura canton, known for crossings like Cabertin, Pinotin and Cabernet Jura, bringing together fungal resistance and high quality.

Bonvin Val ★★ →★★★ An old name of VAL, recently much improved, esp local grapes: *Nobles Cépages* series (eg. HEIDA, PETITE ARVINE, SYRAH).

Bovard, Louis Vd ★★ →★★★★ Family estate (ten generations) famous for its textbook DÉZALEY La Médinette 99' 00 03 05' 06 07 09 11 12' 13 14, old vintages back to 2000 available from the domaine.

Bündner Herrschaft Gris ★★ →★★★★ 05' 09' 10 11 12 13' 14 15' 16 Switzerland's Burgundy: PINOT N (BLAUBURGUNDER) with structure, fruit and age-worthiness, individualistic growers. But only four villages: FLÄSCH, Jenins, Maienfeld, MALANS. Climate balanced between mild s winds and cool climate from nearby mts. Severe frost April 2016.

Calamin Vd ★★★ GRAND CRU of LAVAUX, tarter CHASSELAS than neighbour DÉZALEY. Only 16 ha, growers incl BOVARD, Dizerens, DUBOUX.

Chablais Vd ★★ →★★★ Wine region at upper end of Lake Geneva, top villages: AIGLE, YVORNE. Name is derived from Latin *caput lacis*, head of the lake.

Chanton, Josef-Marie and Mario Val ★★★ Terrific Valais *spécialités*; v'yds up to 800m: Eyholzer Roter, Gwäss, HEIDA, Himbertscha, Lafnetscha, Resi.

Chappaz, Marie-Thérèse Val ★★★ →★★★★ Small bio estate at Fully, famous for magnificent sweet wines (GRAIN NOBLE CONFIDENCIEL) of local grape Petite ARVINE 00 02 03 04' 06' (430g/l residual sugar!) 09 10 and Ermitage (MARSANNE). Hard to find.

Côte, La Vd ★ →★★★ 2000-ha w of Lausanne on Lake Geneva, mainly CHASSELAS of v. light, commercial style. Best-known villages: FÉCHY, Mont-sur-Rolle, Morges.

Cruchon, Henri Vd ★★ →★★★ Bio producer of LA CÔTE known for a wide range of varieties incl SPECIALITIES like VIOGNIER, Altesse, Servagnin and BLATTNER-breedings. Top growth is refined, age-worthy PINOT N Raissennaz.

Dézaley Vd ★★★ 90' 97 99 00 03 05' 09' 10 11 12 13 14 15' 16 Celebrated LAVAUX GRAND CRU on steep slopes of Lake Geneva, 50 ha; planted in C12 by Cistercian monks. Potent CHASSELAS develops with age. Best: DUBOUX, *Fonjallaz*, *Louis Bovard*, Monachon, Ville de Lausanne. Tiny red production too, mostly blends.

Dôle Val ★★ This is VAL's answer to Burgundy's Passetoutgrains – PINOT N plus

SWITZERLAND

GAMAY. Try BESSE, Gilliard, MERCIER, PROVINS. Lightly pink Dôle Blanche pressed straight after harvest.

Domaine la Colombe Vd ★★→★★★ Family estate of FÉCHY, LA CÔTE, 15 ha, bio. Best known for range of ageable CHASSELAS, eg. La Brez.

Donatsch, Thomas Gris ★★★ Barrique pioneer (1974) at MALANS, rich, supple PINOT N, crisp CHARD. Family restaurant, zum Ochsen, gd place to have a bottle opened.

Duboux, Blaise Vd ★★★ 5-ha family estate in LAVAUX. Outstanding DÉZALEY *vieilles vignes* Haut de Pierre (v. rich, mineral), CALAMIN Cuvée Vincent.

Schaff town Diessenhofen: historical rights to make Swiss wine from German grapes.

Epesses Vd ★→★★★ 11' 12 13 14 15 (16) Well-known LAVAUX AOC, 130 ha surrounding GRAND CRU CALAMIN: sturdy, full-bodied whites. Growers incl BOVARD, DUBOUX, Fonjallaz, Luc Massy.

Féchy Vd ★→★★★ Famous though unreliable AOC of LA CÔTE, mainly CHASSELAS.

Federweisser / Weissherbst German-Swiss pale rosé or even Blanc de Noirs from BLAUBURGUNDER.

Fendant Val ★→★★★ Full-bodied VAL CHASSELAS, ideal for fondue or raclette. Try BESSE, Domaine Cornulus, GERMANIER, Provins, SIMON MAYE. Name derived from French *se fendre* (to burst) because ripe berries of local Chasselas clone crack open if pressed between fingertips.

Fläsch Gris ★★★→★★★★ Village of BÜNDNER HERRSCHAFT on schist and limestone, producing mineral, austere PINOT N. Lots of gd estates, esp members of Adank, Hermann, Marugg families. *Gantenbein* is outstanding, also for CHARD.

Flétri / Mi-flétri Late-harvested grapes for sweet/slightly sweet wine.

Fribourg 115 ha on shores of Lake Murten (Mont Vully): powerful CHASSELAS, elegant TRAMINER, round PINOT N. Try Château de Praz, Chervet, Cru de l'Hôpital, Derron.

Fromm, Georg Gris ★★★ 04 05' 08 09' 10 11 12 13' 14 15' 16 Top grower in MALANS, 4 ha, known for fragrant, subtle PINOT N from a range of single v'yds: Fidler, Schöpfi, Selfi. Constructing new cellar with architect Peter Zumthor.

Gantenbein, Daniel & Martha Gris ★★★★ 05 08 09' 10' 11 12 13' 14 15' 16 Country's most famous growers, based in FLÄSCH. Top PINOT N from DRC clones *(see* France), RIES clones from Loosen (*see* Germany), exceptional CHARD in v. limited quantity.

Geneva City and wine-growing canton, 1400 ha, mostly remote from lake. International varieties, PINOT N, GAMAY, CHASSELAS from Balisiers, Grand'Cour, Les Hutins, Novelle. Most v'yds on Lake Geneva belong to neighbouring canton VD.

Germanier, Jean-René Val ★★→★★★ Important VAL estate, reliable FENDANT Les Terrasses, elegant SYRAH Cayas, AMIGNE from schist at Vétroz (dr sw – "Mitis").

Glacier, Vin du (Gletscherwein) Val w dr ★★★ Fabled oxidized, (larch)-wooded white from rare Rèze grape of Val d'Anniviers. Find it at the Rathaus of Grimentz. A sort of Alpine Sherry.

Grain Noble ConfidenCiel Val Quality label for authentic sweet wines, eg. CHAPPAZ, DOMAINE DU MONT D'OR, Dorsaz (both estates), GERMANIER, Philippe Darioli, PROVINS.

Grand Cru Val, Vd Inconsistent term. VAL commune Salgesch has a local regulation (for PINOT N); in VD "Premier Grand Cru" may be used for wide range of single estate wines. Switzerland has only two Grands Crus in the sense of a classification of v'yd sites: CALAMIN, DÉZALEY.

Grisons (Graubünden) Mtn canton, mainly German-Swiss (and Rhaeto-Romanic). PINOT N king, CHARD v.gd, also MÜLLER-T. *See* BÜNDNER HERRSCHAFT. Best growers in other areas: Cicero, Manfred Meier, VON TSCHARNER.

Huber, Daniel ★★→★★★ Pioneering German Swiss immigrant to TIC, producing subtle reds from possibly historical sites Huber reclaimed from fallow in 1981. Bio since 2003. Reliable MERLOT Fusto 4, premium label Montagna Magica 03 05' 07 08 09 10 11.

Johannisberg Val VAL name for SILVANER, often off-dry or sweet; great with fondue. Excellent: *Domaine du Mont d'Or*.

Lavaux Vd ★★→★★★★ Best region on Lake Geneva; 30 km of steep s-facing terraces e of Lausanne; UNESCO World Heritage site. Rich, mineral CHASSELAS. GRANDS CRUS DÉZALEY, CALAMIN, several village AOCs.

Litwan, Tom Aar ★★★ Newcomer who studied in Burgundy. Delicate, fine-grained PINOT N Auf der Mauer ("on top of the wall") and Chalofe ("lime kiln").

Malans Gris Village in BÜNDNER HERRSCHAFT. Top PINOT N producers incl DONATSCH, FROMM, Liesch, Studach, Wegelin. Late-ripening local grape Completer gives a phenolic white. Monks used to drink it with day's last prayer (Compline). Adolf Boner is keeper of the Grail.

Maye, Simon et Fils Val ★★★ Perfectionist estate at St-Pierre-de-Clages. Dense SYRAH *vieilles vignes* 00 02 06 07 08 09 10 11'; spicy, powerful Païen (HEIDA); PINOT N. DÔLE, FENDANT v.gd too.

Mémoire des Vins Suisses Union of 57 leading growers in effort to create stock of Swiss icon wines, to prove their ageing capacities. Oldest wines from 1999.

Mercier, Anne-Catherine & Denis Val ★★★ Immigrant couple from BERN and VD at SIERRE, only 6 ha, meticulous v'yd management produces dense, aromatic reds, eg. rare CORNALIN 99 02 03 05' 07 09' 10' 11 12 13 14 and SYRAH.

Mont d'Or, Domaine du Val ★★→★★★★ Emblematic VAL estate for semi- and nobly sweet wines, esp JOHANNISBERG Saint-Martin 06 07 09 10 11.

Neuchâtel ★→★★★ 600 ha around city and lake on calcareous soil. V. light, slightly sparkling CHASSELAS, exquisite PINOT N from local clone (Cortaillod). Growers incl Château d'Auvernier, La Maison Carrée, Porret, TATASCIORE.

Oeil de Perdrix Neu PINOT N rosé, allegedly the colour of a partridge's eye. Originally from NEU, now found elsewhere.

Ottiger, Toni Luc ★★→★★★ Grower at Lake Lucerne, remarkable PINOT N, MÜLLER-T.

Pircher, Urs Zür ★★★→★★★★ Top estate at Eglisau, steep s-facing slope overlooking Rhine. Outstanding PINOT N Stadtberger Barrique 02 04 05' 08 09' 10 11 12 13' 14 15' from old Swiss clones. Whites of great purity.

Provins Valais Val ★→★★★ Huge co op and biggest producer: 4000+ members, 1500 ha, 34 varieties. Gd oak aged Maître de Chais range; reliable entry-level ARVINE, rare Crus des Domaines. Electus is ambitious B'x blend.

Rouvinez Vins Val ★→★★★ Famous producer at SIERRE, best known for cuvées La Trémaille (w) and Le Tourmentin (r). Controls also BONVIN, Caves Orsat, Imesch.

Ruch Schaff ★★★ Small producer at Hallau, only 2.5 ha, excellent PINOT N, eg. Chölle from 60-yr-old vines. Haalde from steep slope.

Schaffhausen Schaff ★→★★★ Canton/town on Rhine with famous falls, 482 ha. BLAUBURGUNDER, MÜLLER-T, spécialités. The best-known village is Hallau, but be v. careful. Top growers: BAD OSTERFINGEN, BAUMANN, RUCH, Strasser.

Schenk SA Vd ★→★★★ Wine giant with worldwide activities, based in Rolle, founded 1893. Classic wines (esp VD, VAL); substantial exports.

Schloss Salenegg Gris ★★★ Historic estate (since 1654) at Maienfeld, BUNDNER HERRSCHAFT, berry-scented PINOT N.

Schwarzenbach, Hermann Zür ★★★ Leading family estate on Lake Zürich. Best-known for crisp whites that match freshwater fish: local Räuschling, MÜLLER-T.

Wine regions

Switzerland has six major wine regions: VAL, VD, GENEVA, TIC, Trois Lacs (NEU, Bienne/BER, Vully/FRIBOURG) and German Switzerland, which comprises ZÜR, SCHAFF, GRIS, AAR, St Gallen, Thur and some smaller wine cantons. And contrary to Switzerland's reputation for making white wines, 60 per cent of wines are red, mostly PINOT N.

Breaking the Swiss bank
You can find top Swiss wines abroad, but they're expensive. Some examples: Unique PINOT N, DONATSCH, €350 in Singapore; GANTENBEIN CHARD, €254 in Hong Kong; Grain Noble, CHAPPAZ, €90 in Germany; Sassi Grossi TIC, Gialdi, €70 in the UK; Haut de Pierre DÉZALEY, Duboux, €50 in Hong Kong, or Dézaley la Medinette, BOVARD, €50 in the US.

Sierre Val ★★→★★★ VAL town on six hills, famously sunny, home of rich, luscious wines. Best-known names: Imesch, MERCIER, ROUVINEZ, Zufferey.

Sion Val ★★→★★★ Capital/wine centre of VAL, domicile of big producers: *Charles Bonvin* Fils, PROVINS VALAIS, Robert Gilliard, Varone.

Specialités / Spezialitäten Quantitatively minor grape varieties producing some of best Swiss wines, eg. Räuschling, GEWURZ or PINOT GR in German Switzerland, or local varieties (and grapes like JOHANNISBERG, SYRAH) in VAL.

Sprecher von Bernegg Gris ★★★ Historic estate at Jenins, BÜNDNER HERRSCHAFT, revived by young Jan Luzi, esp PINOT N: Lindenwingert, vom Pfaffen/Calander.

St. Jodern Kellerei Val ★★→★★★ VISPERTERMINEN co-op famous for unique HEIDA Veritas from ungrafted old vines: superb reflection of Alpine terroir.

St-Saphorin Vd ★→★★★ 10 11' 12 13 14 15' 16 Famous AOC in LAVAUX, neighbour of DÉZALEY, lighter, but equally delicate. Try Monachon's Les Manchettes.

Stucky, Werner Tic ★★★→★★★★ Pioneer of MERLOT del TIC now joined by son Simon. Three wines: Temenos (Completer/SAUV BL), Tracce di Sassi (Merlot), Conte di Luna (Merlot/CAB SAUV). Stucky's best v'yd is only accessible via a funicular.

Tatasciore, Jacques Neu ★★★★ Shooting star in NEU, refined PINOT N to show that Burgundy isn't far away.

Ticino ★★→★★★ 05' 08 09' 10 11 12 13 14 15' Italian-speaking; mainly MERLOT. Best are well-structured, far from "international" style, eg. Gialdi, HUBER, Kaufmann, Klausener, Kopp von der Crone Visini, STUCKY, Tamborini, Vinattieri, ZÜNDEL.

Tscharner, Gian-Battista von ★★→★★★ Family estate at Reichenau Castle, Graubünden; tannin-laden PINOT N (Churer Gian-Battista 99 00 05') to age.

Valais (Wallis) Largest wine canton, in dry, sunny upper Rhône Valley. Many local varieties, but also MARSANNE, SYRAH. Top: BESSE, CHANTON, CHAPPAZ, Darioli, Domaine Cornulus, DOMAINE DU MONT D'OR, Dorsaz, GERMANIER, Joris, MERCIER, PROVINS VALAIS, ROUVINEZ, SIMON MAYE, ST. JODERN KELLEREI, Zufferey (both estates).

Vaud (Waadt) Wine canton known for conservative spirit. Important big producers: Bolle, Hammel, Obrist, SCHENK. CHASSELAS is main grape – but only gd terroirs justify growers' loyalty.

Visperterminen Val w ★→★★★ Upper VAL v'yds, esp for HEIDA. One of highest v'yds in Europe (at 1000m+; called Riben). Try CHANTON, ST. JODERN KELLEREI.

Yvorne Vd (r) w ★★→★★★ Top CHABLAIS AOC for rich CHASSELAS. Best v'yd sites lie on detritus of 1584 avalanche. Try Château Maison Blanche, Commune d'Yvorne, Domaine de l'Ovaille.

Zündel, Christian Tic r w ★★★→★★★★ 02 05' 09 10 11 12 13 German Swiss geologist in TIC. Pure, age-worthy MERLOT/CAB SAUV Orizzonte. Recent emphasis on wonderful cool-climate CHARD.

Zürich Largest wine-growing canton in German Switzerland, 610 ha; for mainly BLAUBURGUNDER, MÜLLER-T. Räuschling a local speciality. Best growers: Gehring, Lüthi, PIRCHER, SCHWARZENBACH, Zahner.

Zwaa Schaff ★★★ Dialect expression for "two", naming a collaboration of two leading SCHAFF estates with complementary soils (BAUMANN – calcareous, deep soil – and BAD OSTERFINGEN – light, gravelly). PINOT N 94' 97 98 99 99 01 02 03 04 05 06 07 09' 10 11 12 13' 14 15', white counterpart a blend PINOT BL/CHARD 00' 04 05' 06 07' 08 09 10 11' 12 13 14.

Austria

NIEDERÖSTERREICH
KAMPTAL WEINVIERTEL
KREMSTAL
WACHAU
TRAISENTAL WAGRAM
Danube VIENNA Vienna
CARNUNTUM
THERMENREGION
Neusiedler See
WESTSTEIERMARK Graz
VULKANLAND
STEIERMARK
SÜDSTEIERMARK
Mur

Abbreviations used in the text:

Burgen	Burgenland
Carn	Carnuntum
Kamp	Kamptal
Krems	Kremstal
Nied	Niederösterreich
S Stei	Südsteiermark
Therm	Thermenregion
Trais	Traisental
V Stei	Vulkanland Steiermark
Wach	Wachau
Wag	Wagram
Wein	Weinviertel
W Stei	Westseiermark

There is a certain equivalence between Austria and Alsace. Both are makers of sterling white wines, clean, potent and (mainly) dry, excellent food wines, aromatic but not to excess. They have many devotees, without quite making the mainstream of critical acclaim – or having many imitators. Which makes them good value, and exciting places to hunt. Austrian wine is above all food friendly, with its combination of impressive flavour and acidic backbone. Few other countries can boast such a high general standard and such clean wines. The vast majority of producers are still small and family-run; hand-crafting individual, expressive wines. Vineyards are concentrated in the country's east and south, where Alpine mountains give way to soft hills. The climate is deeply continental, with marked seasons, giving freshness and fruit. Austria's flagship Grüner Veltliner remains the perennial favourite, while fine bracing Rieslings, and now Styrian Sauvignon Blanc and some terrific reds, especially Blaufränkisch, now share the limelight. Look out for new labelling: from 2016 it's compulsory to use the term *Ried* for single-vineyard wines, which will make them immediately recognizable. And in bubbles a new three-tier Sekt classification is now in force: Klassik, Reserve and Grosse Reserve all guarantee 100 per cent regional Austrian grapes, and the last two also indicate traditional bottle fermentation.

Recent vintages

2016 Spring frost, mildew and hail reduced yield. What's left is good.

2015 Very good quality. Summer heat spikes did little harm.

2014 Tricky weather necessitated scrupulous selection. Quality meant sacrificing quantity.

2013 Hot, dry summer, rain in September; very good for sweet wines.
2012 Quantities down from 2011. Quality satisfactory or better.
2011 One of finest vintages in living memory. Try it while you can.
2010 Hand-picking/meticulous work imperative, yields down up to 55 per cent.
2009 Uneven; some outstanding whites (Niederösterreich, Steiermark), reds
(Neusiedlersee, Mittelburgenland).

Achs, Paul Burgen r (w) ★★★ 10 12 13 14 15 Focused producer of individual reds. Esp BLAUFRÄNKISCH Edelgrund, Heideboden.

Allram Kamp w ★★★ 10 11 12 13 14 Reliable producer of GRÜNER V, esp Hasel Alte Reben and RIES, Res Heiligenstein.

Alphart Therm w ★★ Specialist for regional rarities ROTGIPFLER and ZIERFANDLER with HEURIGER.

Alzinger Wach w ★★★★ 06 08 09 10 11 12 13 14 15 Top estate. Long-lived, slow-burning RIES, GRÜNER V.

Arndorfer Kamp r w ★★★ Gifted, ambitious couple. Try top-level wines Leidenshaft ZWEIGELT and oaked RIES.

Ausbruch Prädikat wine with min must weight 27°KMW or 138.6°Oechsle, made from botrytized or dried grapes. Traditional; as of 2016 vintage restricted to RUST.

Ausg'steckt ("Hung out") Fresh greenery and bunting outside a HEURIGEN or Buschenschank to signal opening.

Bauer, Anton Wag r w ★★★ Est producer; obsessive quality focus. Notable GRÜNER V from single v'yds Rosenberg, Spiegel. Wonderfully ethereal, unforced PINOT N.

Beck, Judith Burgen r w ★★→★★★ Young bio winemaker of balanced indigenous reds and red blends.

Braunstein, Birgit Burgen r w ★★★ 11 12 13 15 Gifted, v. conscientious bio winemaker of poetic BLAUFRÄNKISCH LEITHABERG, PINOT N, ST-LAURENT. Experimental amphora-aged Magna Mater CHARD.

Bründlmayer, Willi Kamp r w sw sp ★★★★ 06 08 10 11' 12 13 14 15 Stellar producer. World-class GRÜNER V, RIES, esp Heiligenstein and Steinmassl. Beautiful *méthode traditionelle*, esp Extra Brut.

Burgenland r (w) Federal state and wine region bordering Hungary. Warmer than NIED, thus ideal for reds like BLAUFRÄNKISCH, ST-LAURENT. Also reliable conditions for botrytis around shallow NEUSIEDLERSEE, eg. at RUST.

Carnuntum Nied r w Dynamic region se of VIENNA specialized in reds, esp ZWEIGELT marketed as Rubin Carnuntum. Best: G Markowitsch, MUHR-VAN DER NIEPOORT, Netzl, TRAPL.

Christ Vienna r w ★★★ Dynamic VIENNA producer, Bisamberg v'yds. Influential GEMISCHTER SATZ and experimental red blends.

DAC (Districtus Austriae Controllatus) Origin- and quality-based appellation system for regionally typical wines. The first, WEIN DAC, created in 2001, marked a steep quality step. Currently nine DACs: EISENBERG, KAMP, KREMS, LEITHABERG, MITTELBURGENLAND, NEUSIEDLERSEE, TRAIS, Wein, Wiener GEMISCHTER SATZ. Most DACs are stratified into Klassik and RES with varietal and ageing stipulations.

Domäne Wachau Wach w ★★★→★★★★ Best Austrian co-op (formerly Freie Weingärtner) with impressive v'yds like Kellerberg, Achleiten, Bruck. Impressive across the board, producing a third of all WACH wines. Great-value SMARAGD.

Ebner-Ebenauer Wein w sp ★★★ Quality-focused youngsters determined to put WEIN on the map. Impressive single v'yd GRÜNER V Hermanschachern, Bürsting, Sauberg. Gorgeous Blanc de Blancs *méthode traditionelle* 08'.

Eichinger, Birgit Kamp w ★★★→★★★★ Gifted producer of consistently top RIES, esp Heiligenstein and exceptionally savoury GRÜNER V, esp Hasel.

Eisenberg Burgen Small DAC (since 2009). Elegant BLAUFRÄNKISCH grown on slate.

Erste Lage First Growth according to ÖTW v'yd classification, currently 62 v'yds in KAMP, KREMS, TRAIS, WAGRAM.

Esterhazy Burgen r (w) ★★★ Historic Schloss (Haydn was resident composer) in Eisenstadt (BURGEN) with quality-obsessed new management and winemaker.

Federspiel Wach Mid-level of VINEA WACHAU classification, min 11.5%, max 12.5% alc. Gastronomic wines of restrained power and elegance. Name refers to falconry.

Feiler-Artinger Burgen r w sw ★★★→★★★★ 06 07 08 09 10 11 12 13 14 15 One of the top RUST estates. Exquisite AUSBRUCH dessert wines and subtle BLAUFRÄNKISCH Umriss. Beautiful buildings in historic centre.

Gemischter Satz Vienna White field-blend of co-planted and co-fermented varieties. Historically a way to hedge frost risk to any one variety; now fashionable again. Prevalent in WIEN and VIENNA: determined producers achieved DAC status in 2013 for Vienna. No variety to exceed 50%. Look for CHRIST, LENIKUS, WIENINGER.

Gesellmann, Albert & Silvia Burgen r w (sw) ★★★ Full-bodied reds and red blends.

Geyerhof Krems r w ★★→★★★ Clean-cut, crunchy and zesty RIES, esp Sprinzenberg.

Gols Burgen r (w) Wine village on n shore of NEUSIEDLERSEE. Top producers: BECK, G HEINRICH, NITTNAUS, PITTNAUER, PREISINGER.

Gritsch Mauritiushof Wach w ★★→★★★ Fine SMARAGD, esp RIES from 1000-Eimberglm; new high-altitude GRÜNER V plantings.

Groiss, Ingrid Wein w ★★ Creative newcomer specializing in old v'yds and vines. Peppery GRÜNER V and GEMISCHTER SATZ from unusual varieties.

Gross S Stei ★★★ Producer of SAUV BL, esp Jakobi, fragrant Gelber MUSKATELLER.

Grosse Lage Stei Highest classification level in STEI, but not in use along Danube (*see* ERSTE LAGE).

Gsellmann Burgen r w sw ★★ Bio estate. Notable red blend Gabarinza.

Gumpoldskirchen Therm Popular HEURIGEN village s of VIENNA, centre of THERM. Day-trip destination and home to rarities ZIERFANDLER, ROTGIPFLER.

Gut Oggau Burgen r w ★★→★★★ Hipsterish and experimental bio producer.

Heinrich, Gernot Burgen r w dr sw ★★★ 08 09 10 11 12 13 15 PANNOBILE member. Subtle and elegant BLAUFRÄNKISCH, esp Alter Berg and LEITHABERG.

Heinrich, J Burgen r w ★★★ 08 09 11 12 13 14 15 Producer of rather full-bodied BLAUFRÄNKISCH, esp Goldberg. Also note Vitikult and Siglos.

Heuriger Wine of most recent harvest. Heurigen are taverns where growers by ancient decree can serve their own wines with rustic foods – integral to VIENNA life, haunted by Beethoven.

Silberweisse, Grauer, Weisser Vöslauer: rare indigenous grapes. Time for a comeback?

Hiedler Kamp w sw ★★★ Precise and exacting RIES Steinhaus, savoury GRÜNER V Thal and Kittmannsberg.

Hirsch Kamp w ★★★ 06 10 11 12 13 14 15 Great-value RIES and GRÜNER V from Heiligenstein, Lamm. Impressive entry-level GRÜNER V Hirschvergnügen.

Hirtzberger, Franz Wach w ★★★★ 06 07 08 10 11' 12 13 14 15 WACH beacon of world-class, long-lived RIES, GRÜNER V, esp Honivogl, Kirchweg, Singerriedel v'yds.

Huber, Markus Trais w ★★★ Dynamic, energetic TRAIS producer emphasizing region's inherent light-footedness.

Illmitz Burgen sw SEEWINKEL market town and region famous for BA, TBA (*see* Germany). Best from KRACHER, Opitz.

Jäger Wach w ★★★ Incisive GRÜNER V at FEDERSPIEL and SMARAGD level, esp Klaus.

Jamek, Josef Wach w ★★→★★★ WACH institution with long-est restaurant, now back with renewed vigour. RIES, GRÜNER V esp Klaus, Achleiten.

Johanneshof Reinisch Therm r w ★★★→★★★★ Three talented brothers specializing in PINOT N, ST-LAURENT, ZIERFANDLER, ROTGIPFLER. Notable single v'yds Frauenfeld, Holzspur, Satzing, Spiegel.

Jurtschitsch Kamp w sp ★★★ Re-invigorated estate; impeccable quality. Gd sparkling.

Kamptal Nied (r) w Wine region along River Kamp n of WACH; with softer style, less altitude. Top v'yds: Heiligenstein, Käferberg, Lamm. Best: BRÜNDLMAYER, EICHINGER, HIEDLER, HIRSCH, JURTSCHITSCH, LOIMER, SCHLOSS GOBELSBURG. Kamp is DAC for GRÜNER V, RIES.

Kerschbaum, Paul Burgen ★★★ 09 11 12 13 14 15 BLAUFRÄNKISCH specialist, notable single v'yd Hochäcker.

Look out for *Kellergassen* (cellar lanes): hobbit doors in a hillside, with cellars behind.

Klosterneuburg Wag r w Wine town in WAG with wine research institute and university founded in 1860. Best: Klosterneuburg, Stift. *See also* KMW.

KMW Abbreviation for *Klosterneuburger Mostwaage* ("must level"), Austrian unit denoting must weight, ie. sugar content of grape juice. 1°KMW = 4.86°Oechsle (*see* Germany).

Knoll, Emmerich Wach w ★★★★ 01 05 06 07 08 09 10 11 12 13 14 15 Iconic, world-class WACH producer. Exquisite, concentrated, long-lived RIES, GRÜNER V. Impressive from FEDERSPIEL via SMARAGD to Auslese. Best when mature.

Kollwentz Burgen r w ★★★ 09 10 11 12 13 15 Great reds and red blends.

Kracher Burgen sw ★★★★ 03 04 05 06 07 08 09 10 11 12 13 14 Famed ILLMITZ sweet wine producer. Auslese, Eiswein, BA, TBA (*see* Germany).

Kremstal (r) w Wine region and DAC for GRÜNER V, RIES. Top: Buchegger, MALAT, MOSER, NIGL, SALOMON-UNDHOF, WEINGUT STADT KREMS.

Krutzler Burgen r ★★★ 07 08 09 11' 12 13 14 15 Famous BURGEN producer of powerful, concentrated but nuanced, age-worthy BLAUFRÄNKISCH. Top wine: Perwolff.

Lagler Wach w ★★★ Clean-cut RIES from 1000-Eimerberg, GRÜNER V from Seinborz. Look out for rare NEUBURGER SMARAGD.

Laurenz V Kamp ★★★ Mainly internationally distributed range of GRÜNER V styles.

Leithaberg Burgen DAC on n shore of LAKE NEUSIEDL, based on limestone and mica schist of Leitha mtn.

Lenikus Vienna w ★★ Well-financed VIENNA project, clean-cut GEMISCHTER SATZ from Bisamberg.

Loimer, Fred Kamp (r) w sp ★★★→★★★★ 06 07 09 11 12 13 14 Famous and ever-inquiring KAMP bio pioneer. Authentic and expressive across board. Esp single-v'yds Heiligenstein, Steinmassl. Lovely rosé sparkling too.

Malat Krems w ★★★→★★★★ Thrillingly pure RIES, GRÜNER V, esp single v'yds Gottschelle and Silberbichl.

Mantlerhof Krems w ★★★ Thoughtful grower of rich but precise GRÜNER V from loess soils.

Mayer am Pfarrplatz Vienna (r) w ★★ VIENNA institution and HEURIGER.

Mittelburgenland Burgen r DAC (since 2005) on Hungarian border: structured, age-worthy BLAUFRÄNKISCH. Producers: GESELLMANN, J HEINRICH, KERSCHBAUM, WENINGER.

Moric Burgen ★★★→★★★★ 06 09 10 11 12 13 15 Stellar producer of supremely elegant BLAUFRÄNKISCH with deserved cult following.

Morillon Traditional designation for CHARD in STEI.

Moser, Lenz Krems ★→★★ Austria's largest producer (2700 ha), based nr Krems.

Muhr-van der Niepoort Carn r w ★★★ Innovative but elegant BLAUFRÄNKISCH Spitzerberg. Also try more approachable Liebeskind, Samt & Seide.

Neumayer Trais w ★★★ Est producer of expressive, aromatic, dry GRÜNER V, RIES.

Neumeister V Stei ★★★ 09 11 12 13 14 15 Great producer of sublime oak-aged SAUV BL from Klausen, Moarfeitl v'yds.

Neusiedlersee (Lake Neusiedl) Burgen Shallow BURGEN lake on Hungarian border, largest steppe-lake in Europe, important nature reserve. Lake mesoclimate instrumental for botrytis. Eponymous DAC limited to ZWEIGELT.

Niederösterreich (Lower Austria) Region in ne with 58 per cent of Austria's v'yds, divided in three parts: areas around the Danube (KAMP, KREM, TRAIS, WACH, WAGRAM), WIEN (ne) and CARN, THERM (s).

Nigl Krems w ★★★★ Outstanding estate at Senftenberg, great RIES esp from v'yds Pellingen and Piri.

Nikolaihof Wach w ★★★→★★★★ 06 07 08 09 10 11 12 13 14 15 Bio pioneer of incredible precision. Stellar RIES. Do not miss late releases under the Vinothek label.

Nittnaus, Anita & Hans Burgen r w sw ★★★→★★★★ Outstanding bio producer, top BLAUFRÄNKISCH Tannenberg, LEITHABERG. Note red PANNOBILE blend Comondor.

Ott, Bernhard Wag w ★★★ GRÜNER V specialist in WAG. Cult following for rich, rounded style, esp Fass 4, Rosenberg, Spiegel.

ÖTW (Österreichische Traditionsweingüter) Association engaged in classification of ERSTE LAGE v'yds. Currently 33 members, but no WACH estates.

Pannobile Burgen Union of nine NEUSIEDLERSEE growers centred on GOIS. Pannobile bottlings may only use indigenous reds (ZWEIGELT, BLAUFRÄNKISCH, ST-LAURENT), whites only PINOTS BL, GR, CHARD. Members: ACHS, BECK, GSELLMANN, G HEINRICH, NITTNAUS, PITTNAUER, PREISINGER.

Pfaffl Wein r w ★★→★★★ 11 12 13 14 15 Large WEIN player. Notable RES wines, esp Hommage, Hundsleiten. Creator of ultra-successful brand The Dot Austrian Pepper, Austrian Cherry, etc.

Pichler, Franz X Wach w ★★★★ 06 07 08 09 11 12 13 14 15 Thrilling, intense, *iconic Ries*, of world-class quality. GRÜNER V, esp Kellerberg.

Pichler, Rudi Wach w ★★★★ 06 09 10 11 12 13 14 15 World-class producer of RIES, GRÜNER V from single v'yds Achleiten, Hochrain, Kirchweg, Steinriegl.

Pichler-Krutzler Wach w ★★★ Two wine dynasties united, outstandingly pure, *thrilling Ries*.

Pittnauer, Gerhard Burgen r ★★★ Creative, intuitive BURGEN producer of Austria's finest ST-LAURENT esp Rosenberg; also quality entry-level Pitti.

Polz, Erich & Walter S Stei ★★★→★★★ 12 13 14 15 Large s STEI estate. Top v'yd Hochgrassnitzberg: SAUV BL, CHARD.

Prager, Franz Wach w ★★★★ 06 07 08 09 10 12 13 14 15 World-class RIES, GRÜNER V, impressive array of top v'yds. Some single-stake v'yds on steep al sites.

Preisinger, Claus Burgen r ★★★ Young, creative PANNOBILE member. Try fun, easy red Puszta Libre.

Prieler Burgen r w ★★★ BURGEN institution of long-lived BLAUFRÄNKISCH Goldberg, notable PINOT BL. Haidsatz and Seeberg.

Proidl, A & F Krems w ★★★ Pure, impressive RIES, GRÜNER V, both from Ehrenfels. Look for late RIES releases.

Reserve (Res) Attribute for min 13% alc and prolonged (cask) ageing.

Ried V'yd. As of 2016 compulsory term for single v'yd bottlings.

Rust Burgen r w dr sw Fortified C17th baroque town on LAKE NEUSIEDL. Look for noisy nesting storks in historic centre. Famous for Ruster AUSBRUCH. Top: FEILER-ARTINGER, SCHRÖCK, E TRIEBAUMER.

Rust in Burg sits on the same latitude (47.8°N) as Chablis in northern Burgundy.

Sabathi, Hannes S Stei w ★★★ Quality-focused grower of whistle-clean SAUV BL.

Salomon-Undhof Krems w ★★★→★★★★ Iconic, long-lived wines. GRÜNER V, RIES always in clean-cut style, esp from single v'yds Kögl and Pfaffenberg.

Sattlerhof S Stei w ★★★ 08 09 10 11' 12 13 15 STEI icon; clean, oak-aged SAUV BL, MORILLON from v. steep v'yds.

Schiefer, Uwe Burgen r ★★★ Characterful, edgy; elegant BLAUFRÄNKISCH in EISENBERG.

Schilcher W Stei Term for easy-drinking, thirst-quenching, peppery rosé from indigenous Blauer Wildbacher grapes, speciality of w STEI. Try: Hainzl-Jauk, Oswald, Langmann.

Schilfwein (Strohwein) Sweet wine made from grapes dried on reeds from NEUSIEDLERSEE. *Schilf* = reed, *Stroh* = straw.

Schloss Gobelsburg Kamp r w dr sw ★★★★ 08 09 10 11 12 13 14 15 Historic Cistercian estate now run by *wunderkind* Michael Moosbrugger. RIES, GRÜNER V of exceptional purity, esp Tradition and single v'yds Gaisberg, Heiligenstein, Lamm, Renner. Gd sparkling.

Heurigen taverns still governed by Josephinian Circular Decree of 1784.

Schlumberger sp Largest sparkling winemaker in Austria.

Schmelz Wach w ★★★ Fine, underrated producer, outstanding.

Schröck, Heidi Burgen (r) w sw ★★★ Est, intuitive RUST grower of expressive, evocative AUSBRUCH.

Schuster, Rosi Burgen r ★★★ 11 12 13 15 Young BURGEN specialist in BLAUFRÄNKISCH and ST-LAURENT.

Seewinkel Burgen ("Lake corner") Part of NEUSEIDLERSEE around ILLMITZ, ideal conditions for botrytis.

Smaragd Wach Highest category of VINEA WACHAU, min 12.5% alc but often up to 14%, dry, rich, age-worthy, expressive. Depending on producer sometimes even botrytis-influenced. Named after local emerald (=Smaragd) lizard.

Spätrot-Rotgipfler Therm Blend of ROTGIPFLER/Spätrot = synonym for ZIERFANDLER. Aromatic, weighty whites. Typical for GUMPOLDSKIRCHEN. *See* Grapes chapter.

Spitz an der Donau Wach w Picturesque town at the narrowest and coolest part of WACH. Famous v'yds Singerriedel and 1000-Eimerberg. GRITSCH MAURITIUSHOF, HIRTZBERGER, LAGLER.

Stadlmann Therm r w sw ★★→★★★ Exemplary, precise ZIERFANDLER/ROTGIPFLER. Also try ultra-delicate Gelber MUSKATELLER, and ethereal PINOT N.

Steiermark (Styria) Most s region of Austria, known for aromatic fresh dry whites, esp SAUV BL. *See* S STEI, V STEI, W STEI.

Steinfeder Wach Lightest VINEA WACHAU category for delicate, dry wines. Max 11.5% alc. Named after the fragrant Steinfeder grass.

Stift Göttweig w ★★→★★★ Baroque Benedictine monastery (=Stift) nr Krems; wines made by talented Fritz Miesbauer. Exemplary RIES and GRÜNER V from single v'yds Gottschelle, Silberbichl.

Südsteiermark (South Styria) Best STEI region close to Slovenian border, cool-climate whites (SAUV BL, MUSKATELLER) from steep slopes. Best growers: GROSS, POLZ, SABATHI, SATTLERHOF, TEMENT, WOHLMUTH. Look for MORILLON.

Tegernseerhof Wach w ★★→★★★ V. clean, zesty RIES, GRÜNER V. Lovely FEDERSPIEL.

Tement, Manfred S Stei w ★★★ 05 07 08 09' 10 11 12 13 15 World-class oaked SAUV BL, MORILLON from Zieregg, Grassnitzberg v'yds.

Thermenregion Nied r w Region of thermal springs e of VIENNA. Indigenous grapes (eg. ZIERFANDLER, ROTGIPFLER), serious reds (ST-LAURENT, PINOT N). Producers: ALPHART, JOHANNESHOF REINISCH, STADLMANN.

Tinhof, Erwin Burgen r w ★★★ Talented, thoughtful grower of fine BLAUFRÄNKISCH, esp Gloriette; ST-LAURENT, esp Feuersteig. Age-worthy PINOT BL Golden Erd.

Traisental Nied Small district s of Krems on Danube. Limestone soils dominate, thus delicate style. Top producers: HUBER, NEUMAYER.

Trapl, Johannes Carn r ★★→★★★ Talented newcomer; poised, floral BLAUFRÄNKISCH, esp Sitzerberg. Also vinifies some WACH RIES.

Triebaumer, Ernst Burgen r (w) (sw) ★★★★ 05 06 07 08 09 10 11' 12 13 14 15 Legendary RUST estate, credited with BLAUFRÄNKISCH revival, notably Mariental. V.gd AUSBRUCH.

Umathum, Josef Burgen r w dr sw ★★★→★★★★ Stellar bio producer. Poetic reds, incl PINOT N, BLAUFRÄNKISCH esp Kirschgarten. Stunning rosé Rosa.

Velich w sw ★★★ One of Austria's best CHARD winemakers. Some of top sweet wines in SEEWINKEL.

Veyder-Malberg Wach ★★★ 2008 start-up; cult following. Super-pure RIES, GRÜNER V.

Vienna (r) w Wine region with 612 ha within city limits. Ancient tradition, with reinvigorated drive for quality. As of 2013 DAC GEMISCHTER SATZ for locally famous white field-blends. *Heurigen visit a must.* Best producers: CHRIST, LENIKUS, WIENINGER, Zahel.

Vinea Wachau Wach WACH growers association founded 1983. No v'yd classification, but strict quality charter with important three-tier ripeness scale for dry wine: STEINFEDER, FEDERSPIEL, SMARAGD.

Vulkanland Steiermark (Southeast Styria) (r) Formerly called Süd-Oststeiermark, region famous for aromatic varieties. Best: NEUMEISTER, Ploder-Rosenberg, Winkler-Hermades.

Wachau Nied World-renowned Danube region, home to some of Austria's most expressive, long-lived RIES, GRÜNER V. Top: ALZINGER, DOMÄNE WACHAU, Donabaum, HIRTZBERGER, JAMEK, KNOLL, NIKOLAIHOF, F PICHLER, R PICHLER, PICHLER-KRUTZLER, PRAGER, TEGERNSEERHOF, VEYDER-MALBERG.

Wachter-Wiesler, Weingut Burgen r ★★★ Impressive, peppery BLAUFRÄNKISCH illustrative of EISENBERG DAC.

Wagentristl Burgen r (w) ★★★ Sensitive newcomer, feel for PINOT N. Gd BLAUFRÄNKISCH.

Wagram Nied (r) w Region w of VIENNA, incl KLOSTERNEUBURG. Giant bank of loess ideal for GRÜNER V. Best: Ehmoser, Fritsch, Leth, OTT.

Weingut Stadt Krems Krems i w ★★→★★★ Co-op blossoming under Fritz Miesbauer. He also vinifies for STIFT GÖTTWEIG.

Weinviertel (r) w ("Wine Quarter") Largest Austrian wine region, 13,356 ha between Danube and Czech border, eponymous DAC. Region formerly slaked Vienna's thirst, still grows base for sparkling but quality ethos now surging with GRÜNER V fame. Try. EBNER-EBENAUER, Graf Hardegg, GRÖISS, PFAFFL.

Weninger, Franz Burgen r (w) ★★★★ 08 09 11' 12 13 15 Young creatives crafting a nuanced array of BLAUFRÄNKISCH.

Weststeiermark (West Styria) Small wine region specializing in SCHILCHER. Best: Hainzl-Jauk, Langmann, Oswald.

Wien *See* VIENNA.

Wieninger, Fritz Vienna r w sp ★★★→★★★★ 11 12 13 14 15 Dynamic producer instrumental in creation of GEMISCHTER SATZ DAC. Viennese HEURIGEN institution. Best v'yds. Nussberg, Rosengartl.

Winzer Krems Krems w Quality-oriented co-op with 981 growers covering 990 ha. Gd RIES, GRÜNER V.

Wohlmuth S Stei w ★★★ Outstanding STEI producer of SAUV BL, esp from single v'yds Edelschuh, Steinriegl. *Do not miss* weightless, aromatic Gelber MUSKATELLER.

Zweigelt: arch-Austrian red

Just over a third of Austria's v'yds are now planted to red varieties. Chief among them, at least by area, is arch-Austrian ZWEIGELT. Created in 1922 by crossing ST-LAURENT with BLAUFRÄNKISCH, it is surprisingly versatile. With its cherry-like flavour it makes both light-bodied, easy-drinking reds perfect for the picnic basket, and more concentrated, long-lived reds when vinified in oak. It also makes sprightly base wines for Austrian Sekt. The 2011-created DAC NEUSIEDLERSEE is dedicated to Zweigelt but also look out for it in CARN where it finds supreme expression. Notable producers: Markowitsch, Netzl.

England

The big news is the decision of not one, but two Champagne houses to invest in English vineyards. Taittinger was the first to announce it had bought land in Kent to plant in 2017, shortly followed by Pommery which plans to do the same. If any confirmation that the UK's sparkling wines have arrived was needed – this must surely be it. In the past year the penny has well and truly dropped; exports are multiplying, supermarkets are launching their own brands, and we are all tasting the evidence and sharing the news; England has its own world-class wines. Vintage 2016 turned out to be quite small (at least for some producers) but very ripe, with the highest natural sugar levels ever being achieved. The best yields were in the east of the country, East Anglia, Kent and East Sussex. So far NV blends are in a minority; small vintages leave little for reserve wines for blending. Abbreviations: Berkshire (Berks), Buckinghamshire (Bucks), Cornwall (Corn), East/West Sussex (E/W S'x), Hampshire (Hants), Herefordshire (Heref).

Alder Ridge Berks New producer with award-winning Blanc de Noirs **13**.

Bluebell Vineyard Estates E S'x Est large-scale producer using Champagne varieties and SEYVAL BL. Hindleap Blanc de Blancs **11** best. Nr Bluebell Steam Railway.

Bolney Wine Estate W S'x ★★★ Est 1972 nr Haywards Heath, now 3rd generation, v.gd sparkling, and still. Best wines: Blanc de Blancs **11**, **14** and Cuvée Rosé **14**.

Breaky Bottom E S'x ★★★ Est 1974, same owner/winemaker. Best: SEYVAL BL-based Cuvée Koizumi Yakumo **10**, Champagne blend Cuvée Gerard Hoffnung **09**.

Bride Valley Dorset Steven and Bella Spurrier's v'yd nr coast. Fine Blanc de Blancs and Rosé a model of the new English fresh-fruit look.

Camel Valley Corn ★★★ One of England's largest and Cornwall's only major winery, dynamically run by the Lindo family. Many awards. Best wines DORNFELDER-based Cuvée Raymond Blanc Rosé **14**, CHARD Brut **14**.

Chapel Down Kent Set to be country's largest producer. Best: CHARD-based Blanc de Blancs **11**, Champagne-blend Three Graces **10** and Rosé Brut NV. Excellent visitor facilities. Wine looking a bit old-guard now.

Coates & Seely Hants ★★★ Ambitious young estate nr Winchester uses name Britagne. Best: Blanc de Blancs NV, Brut Res, Rosé **09**. Pure, balanced wines tend to be drier than some.

Check out WSTA English Wine Trail for details of v'yd tours, tastings, cellar doors.

Cottonworth Hants Newish, with small range. Best are Champagne-blend Classic Cuvée NV and Rosé NV, grown on chalk in Test Valley.

Court Garden E S'x ★★★ V'yd n of Brighton. Impressive range. Best: PINOTS N/M Ditchling Res **10** and CHARD Blanc de Blancs **10**.

Davenport E S'x One of few consistently gd UK organic producers (still and sparkling). Best: AUXERROIS **14**, Limney Estate **13** (1st CHARD/PINOTS N/M blend).

Denbies Surrey UK's largest single v'yd. Best sparklings CHARD/PINOTS N/M Greenfields Brut NV, CHARD Cubitt Blanc de Blancs **13**. Wines are commercial.

Digby ★★★ One of 1st négociant-style producers, using grapes bought from growers under contract. Stylish, esp Res Brut **09** in magnums and Leander Pink NV.

Exton Park Hants Large Meon Valley v'yd with ex-COATES & SEELY winemaker. NV wines (Brut, Blanc de Blancs, Rosé) v.gd. PINOT M-based rosé. Wines on dry side.

Gusbourne Kent, W S'x ★★★ Major Champagne-variety producer nr Ashford with 93 ha. Best: Brut Res **13**, Blanc de Blancs **13**. Still CHARD, PINOT N also gd.

Hambledon Vineyard Hants ★★★ England's oldest commercial v'yd now with big new investment, lots of knowhow and impressive gravity winery. Best is v. stylish NV Premier Cuvée.

Hart of Gold New négociant-style label owned by MW Justin Howard-Sneyd; impressive Champagne blend Hart of Gold 10, made with Heref grapes.

Hattingley Valley Hants ★★★ Impressive newcomer nr Alresford with v.-well-equipped winery. Best 11 Blanc de Blancs, 13 Classic Cuvée, Rosé. Makes wines for several other v'yds.

Herbert Hall Kent Nr Marden. One of few organic growers making gd (if quite dry, high-acid) sparkling from Champagne varieties. Best: Brut, Brut Rosé 14.

High Clandon Surrey Small high-quality producer starting to make an impression. Best: Celebration Cuvée 10, Rosé Aurora 11.

Hush Heath Estate Kent ★★★ One of England's best. Impressive v'yds nr Staplehurst, only Champagne varieties. Best: Balfour Brut Rosé 13, Leslie's Res 13, new 1503 NV range. Cider too.

Jenkyn Place Hants Well-sited v'yds nr Farnham, some gd wines. Best: Blanc de Noirs 10, Classic Cuvée 13.

Laithwaite's Berks, Bucks Major online retailer with own v'yds. Sells Ridgeview's South Ridge plus top-quality *Wyfold* wines from Henley. Now also Harrow & Hope (esp rosé) from Marlow and new Windsor Great Park, launched 2017 with 2013 vintage.

Langham Dorset ★★★ Regular award-winning producer nr Dorchester with gd value wines. Best: Classic Cuvée and Rosé 14, Blanc de Noirs 13 and Classic Cuvée 11 in magnum.

Nutbourne W S'x Large v'yd 1st planted in 1981, producing wide range of varities. Best sparkling is Nutty Brut 13. Also Nutty Wild.

Nyetimber W S'x ★★★★ UK's best-known quality producer with 171 ha v'yds and more being planted. Best: Classic Cuvée NV, Blanc de Blancs 09, (expensive) Tillington Single V'yd Brut 10.

Painshill Surrey Unique revival of v'yd 1st planted 1740 on steep s slope to lake in historic park. Fine clean all-SEYVAL sparkling made by BLUEBELL.

Plumpton College E S'x UK's only wine college; growing influence and now own wines. Gd still, sparkling. Best sparklers Dean Brut NV, Rosé NV.

Ridgeview E S'x ★★★ Still leader for consistency, range, value, although others are challenging. Best: Blanc de Blancs 13 and Rosé de Noirs 13. Founding Roberts family in charge.

Squerryes Kent 15-ha v'yd nr Westerham mainly supplying grapes to others but starting to produce own wines. Best is major award-winner Brut 10. 13 to come.

Westwell Kent New producer planted on favoured Kent chalk slopes just off the Pilgrim's Way. Best: Special Cuvée 14, Pelegrim NV.

Wiston W S'x ★★★ Estate with historic mansion on South Downs nr Brighton with fine range. Winemaker Dermot Sugrue has great track record. Best: Blanc de Blancs 10.

Wyfold Oxon Tiny (1-ha) Champagne-variety v'yd at 120m above sea level in the Chilterns, part-owned by hands-on LAITHWAITE family. Best: Brut 11, Rosé 14.

ENGLAND

Central & Southeast Europe

More heavily shaded areas are the wine-growing regions.

CZECH REPUBLIC
Prague

SLOVAK REPUBLIC
Bratislava
Danube
Budapest
MOLDOVA
Chişinău

SLOVENIA
Ljubljana
Zagreb
Drava
HUNGARY
ROMANIA
Timişoara
Olt
Prut

CROATIA
BOSNIA-HERZEGOVINA
Belgrade
Danube
Bucharest
Danube

Split
Adriatic Sea
Sarajevo
SERBIA
Varna

MONTENEGRO
Dubrovnik
Podgorica
BULGARIA
Sofia
Plovdiv
Black Sea

Skopje
MACEDONIA
Tirana
ALBANIA

Abbeviations used in the text:

Bal	Balaton	N Hun	North Hungary
Cri & Mar	Crişana & Maramures	N/S Pann	North/South Pannonia
Cro Up	Croatian Uplands	Pod	Podravje
Dalm	Dalmatia	Pos	Posavje
Dan P	Danubian Plain	Prim	Primorje
Dob	Dobrogea	Sl & CD	Slavonia & Croatian Danube
Is & Kv	Istria & Kvarner	Thr L	Thracian Lowlands
Mold	Moldova / Moldavia	Tok	Tokaj
Mun	Muntenia & Oltenia Hills	Trnsyl	Transylvania

HUNGARY

Hungary has been known up to now for its glorious sweet wine, Tokaji Aszú, its robust reds and pretty good budget whites. The next stage, now well on its way, is better-balanced reds in more variety, a wider choice of quality Tokaji producers and fine white wines from varieties hardly known to the world. Exposure to the world, and to their colleagues' ideas, is leading to finer interpretations of one of Europe's deepest and most original wine cultures and its mosaic of vine varieties.

Alana-Tokaj Tok w sw ★★ Rich, luscious ASZÚ and late harvest, most exported to US.

Árvay Tok w dr sw ★★ Family winery in TOK since 2009, 17 ha. Long-lived dry whites.

Aszú Tok Botrytis-shrivelled grapes and the resulting sweet wine from TOK. From 2014, legal minimum sweetness is 120 g/l residual sugar, equivalent to 5 PUTTONYOS. Option to label as 5 or 6 Puttonyos but not obligatory. 3 and 4 Puttonyos are no longer made though still allowed on labels provided wines meet new higher standards. Gd Aszú in 05 06 07 08 09 13. V. wet in 10, 14 so limited Aszú with careful selection; hot, dry in 11, 12, not much botrytis; 15, 16 look better but won't be universal Aszú yrs.

Aszú Essencia / Eszencia Tok Term for 2nd-sweetest TOKAJI level (7 PUTTONYOS+), permitted up to 2010. No longer. Do not confuse with ESSENCIA/ESZENCIA.

Badacsony Bal ★★→★★★ Volcanic slopes n of Lake BAL; full, rich whites. Look for *Szeremley* (age-worthy KÉKNYELŰ, SZÜRKEBARÁT), Villa Sandahl (esp 13 All of a kind, 12 Rake & scoop RIES), Villa Tolnay (esp GRÜNER V, RIES), Laposa (Bazalt Cuvée, KÉKNYELŰ, 4-Hegy OLASZRIZLING).

Balaton Region, and Central Europe's largest freshwater lake. Incl BADACSONY, CSOPAK, Balatonmelléke, Zala, SOMLÓ to n, BALATONBOGLÁR to s.

Balatonboglár Bal r w dr ★★→★★★ Wine district, also major winery of TÖRLEY, s of Lake BAL. Gd: Budjosó, GARAMVÁRI, IKON, KONYÁRI, Légli Otto, Légli Géza, Pócz, Varga.

Bardon Tok w sp ★★ 12 13 (15) New winery already impressing with Alpha and Omega dry FURMINTS.

Barta Tok w dr sw ★★★ 12 13' 15 Highest v'yd in TOK, producing impressive dry whites (esp Öreg Király FURMINT) with Vivien Újvári (ex-Degenfeld) as new winemaker. Also v.gd sweet SZAMORODNI, ASZÚ.

Béres Tok w dr sw ★★→★★★ 06 07 08 (sw) 12 13 15 (dr) Stunning winery producing v.gd ASZÚ and dry wines, esp Lőcse FURMINT, Diókút HÁRSLEVELŰ.

Bikavér r ★→★★★ 11' 12' 13 Means "Bull's Blood". PDO for two regions only, EGER and SZEKSZÁRD. Always a blend of min three varieties. In Szekszárd, KADARKA is compulsory, max 7%, with KÉKFRANKOS as base with no new oak. Look for: Eszterbauer Tüke, HEIMANN, Meszáros, Sebestyén Iván Völgyi, TAKLER. Egri Bikavér is majority Kékfrankos and no grape more than 50%, oak-aged for min 6 mths. Superior is min five varieties,12 mths in barrel, from restricted sites. Best for Egri Bikavér: Bolyki, DEMETER, GÁL TIBOR, Grof Buttler, ST ANDREA, Thummerer.

Bock, József S Pann r ★★→★★★ 11 12 13 (15) Leading family winemaker in VILLÁNY, making rich, full-bodied reds. Try: Bock CAB FR Fekete-Hegy, Bock & Roll SYRAH, Capella Cuvée, fruity DYA PORTUGIESER.

Csányi S Pann r ★→★★ 12 13 15 Largest winery in VILLÁNY with new winemaker and ambitious plans. Look for Chateau Teleki CAB FR, Kővilla Cuvée.

Csopak Bal N of Lake BAL with producer group Kodex for top OLASZRIZLING. Look for: Figula (v.gd Sáfránykert) Homola (with Atila HOMONNA), Jásdi (esp single v'yd selections), St Donát. Also Béla és Bandi, Feind.

Degenfeld, Gróf Tok w dr sw ★★→★★★ 08 (sw) 14 (15) dr Improved estate with luxury hotel and new manager from ROYAL TOKAJI. Sweet wines best: 6 PUTTONYOS, ASZÚ ESZENCIA, also late-harvest Andante, Fortissimo. Single-v'yd Dry FURMINT 14 is gd.

Demeter, Zoltán Tok w dr sw ★★★★ 12 13' 15 Benchmark for elegant, intense dry wines, esp Boda, Veres FURMINTS; excellent Szerelmi HÁRSLEVELŰ, lovely Oszhegy MUSCAT. V.gd 100% Furmint PEZSGŐ (sp), Eszter late-harvest cuvée 11, top ASZÚ 08.

Dereszla Tok w dr sw ★★→★★★ 07' 08' 09' for excellent ASZÚ. Gd DYA dry FURMINT and Kabar (grape). Also gd PEZSGŐ (sp). Rare flor-aged dry SZAMORODNI Experience.

DHC (Districtus Hungaricus Controllatus) Term for Protected Designation of Origin (PDO). Symbol is a local crocus and DHC on label.

Disznókő Tok w dr sw ★★→★★★★ 07' 08' 09 11' 13' 15 Benchmark estate with focus on long-lived sweet wines. Fine expressive ASZÚ, superb *Kapi* cru in top yrs incl 11. Also gd-value late-harvest and *Édes* (sw) SZAMORODNI.

Dobogó Tok (r) w dr sw ★★★ 08' 09 11 12 13' Impeccable small estate (name means "Clip Clop"). Benchmark ASZÚ and late-harvest Mylitta, superb Mylitta Álma, thrilling dry FURMINT, esp Betsek DŰLŐ and *pioneering Pinot N* Izabella Utca.

Dűlő Named single v'yd. Top names in TOK: Betsek, Király, Mézes-Mály, Nyúlászó, SZENT TAMÁS WINERY, Úrágya.

Duna Duna Great Plain. Districts: Hajós-Baja (try Sümegi, Koch – also VinArt in VILLÁNY), Csongrád (Somodi), Kunság (Frittmann: Font winery).

Eger N Hun ★→★★★ Top red region of n producing more burgundian-style reds and noted for Egri BIKAVÉR. Try: Bolyki (Bikavér Superior, Meta Tema), Gróf Buttler, DEMETER, *Gál Tibor*, Kaló Imre (noted for natural wines), KOVÁCS NIMRÓD, Pók Tamás, ST ANDREA, Thummerer.

Egri Csillag N Hun "Star of Eger". Dry white blend modelled on BIKAVÉR. Min 50% local Carpathian varieties.

Essencia / Eszencia Tok ★★★★ Syrupy, luscious free-run juice from ASZÚ grapes, rarely bottled. Residual sugar min 450g/l (but can be 800g/l), alc usually well below 5%. Reputed to have miraculous medicinal/aphrodisiac properties.

Etyek-Buda N Pann Dynamic region noted for expressive, crisp whites and fine sparklers, esp CHARD, *Sauv Bl*, PINOT GR and promising for PINOT N. Leading producers: Etyeki Kúria (esp Pinot N, SAUV BL), György-Villa (premium wines from TÖRLEY), Haraszthy (Sauv Bl, Sir Irsai, Oröghegy), Nyakas (v.gd Chard), Kertész, Rókusfalvy.

Gál Tibor N Hun r w ★★ Improving wines from son of late Tibor Gál, famed as winemaker at Ornellaia (*see* Italy). Try appealing EGRI CSILLAG DYA and vibrant, youthful TiTi BIKAVÉR 15.

Garamvári Bal r p w dr sp ★→★★★ Top Hungarian producer of bottle-fermented fizz (previously Chateau Vincent). Try Optimum Brut 11, FURMINT Brut Natur 11, PINOT N Evolution Rose 08. Also gd DYA IRSAI OLIVÉR, SAUV BL, PINOT N.

Gere, Attila S Pann r p ★★★→★★★★ 09' 11 12' 13 (15) (16) Leading light in VILLÁNY making some of country's best reds, esp rich Solus MERLOT, intense Kopar Cuvée, top Attila barrel selection. New Fekete-Járdovány is rare historic grape.

Grand Tokaj Tok w dr sw ★→★★ 13 15 New name for former Crown Estates, part of fresh-start strategy, incl new winemaker (Karoly Áts, ex-ROYAL TOKAJ), new winery and programme for sourcing better grapes. Appealing Arany Késői Late-Harvest 13, 15; Dry FURMINT Kővágó DŰLŐ 15; promising Szarvas ASZÚ 6 PUTTONYOS 13.

Heimann S Pann r ★★→★★★ 11' 12' 13 15 Impressive family winery in SZEKSZÁRD, esp superb Barbár and benchmark BIKAVÉR. Key focus is local grapes, esp v.gd KADARKA, KÉKFRANKOS.

Hétszőlő Tok w dr sw ★★ Historic "First Growth" TOK estate bought in 2009 by Michel Rebier, owner of Cos d'Estournel (B'x). Noted for lighter styles of Tokaji.

Heumann S Pann r w ★★→★★★ 12 13' 14 15 Small German/Swiss-owned estate in Siklós making great KÉKFRANKOS Res, CAB FR, fruity Kadar-O.

Hilltop Winery N Pann r p w dr ★★ In Neszmély. Meticulous, gd-value DYA varietal wines. V.gd Premium range (esp CHARD, PINOT GR).

Holdvölgy Tok w dr sw ★★→★★★ 12 13 (15) Aka Moon Valley. Young winery making mark with complex dry wines, v.gd Signature Late Harvest and luscious ASZÚ 08.

Homonna Tok w dr ★★★ 12 13 15 Fine, elegant dry FURMINTS, esp Határi and Rány.

Ikon Bal r w ★★ Gd-value, well-made wines from majority shareholder Janos KONYÁRI and former Tihany abbey v'yds. Try Evanglista CAB FR.

Kikelet Tok w dr sw ★★★ 08 09 (sw) 12 13 (15) One of TOK's inspiring group of leading women winemakers. Wonderful Váti FURMINT and fine, pure SZAMORODNI.

Királyudvar Tok w dr sw sp ★★★→★★★★ 07' 08 09 12' 13 (15) Bio TOK winery in old royal cellars at Tarcal. Excellent FURMINT Sec, Cuvée Ilona (late-harvest), flagship 6 PUTTONYOS Lapis ASZÚ and Henye PEZSGŐ (sparkling).

Konyári Bal r p w dr ★★→★★★ 12 13 15 High-quality estate wines at BALATONBOGLÁR: esp DYA rosé; Loliense (r w). Top: Jánoshegy KÉKFRANKOS, Páva (r), Szárhegy (w).

Hearts of oak

Arguably more widely exported than the wines, and found in wineries all over the world. Hungarian oak is v. high quality, less pricey than French. Cool growing conditions in Zemplen Hills nr TOK provide particularly fine, tight-grained oak from best species, *Quercus petraea*.

Kovács Nimród Winery N Hun r p w dr ★★→★★★ 09 11' 13 EGER producer, impressive v'yd selections: Grand Bleu (r), Blues KÉKFRANKOS, Battonage CHARD, Soul SYRAH.

Kreinbacher Bal w dr sp ★★→★★★ 12 13 Excellent new *sparkling* range based on FURMINT esp Classic Brut. Also v.gd dry wines incl Juhfark, HÁRSLEVELŰ, Öreg Tőkék (old vines).

Mád Tok Historic town in heart of TOK region with Mád Circle of leading producers: ALANA-TOKAJ, BARTA, Demetervin (gd dry FURMINT, sweet Elvezet), HOLDVÖLGY, KIKELET, Lenkey, Orosz Gabor, ROYAL TOKAJI, SZENT TAMÁS WINERY, SZEPSY, Tok Classic.

Feel like a spritzer in hot Hungarian summer? Ask for *fröccs* ("frurch", more or less).

Malatinszky S Pann r p w dr ★★★ 08' 09 11' 12 13' 15 Certified organic. Excellent long-lived Kúria CAB FR, Kövesföld (r). Gd: Noblesse rosé, CHARD, Serena (w).

Mátra N Hun ★→★★ Gd region for decent-value, fresh whites, rosé and lighter reds. Better producers: Balint, Benedek, Gábor Karner, NAG, NAGYRÉDE, Szőke Mátyás.

Mór N Pann w ★→★★ Small region, famous for fiery local *Ezerjó*. Also promising for CHARD, RIES, TRAMINI. Try Czelvei Winery.

Nagyréde N Hun (r) p w ★ Gd-value, commercial DYA varietal wines under Nagyréde and Mátra Hill labels.

Oremus Tok w dr sw ★★→★★★★ 06' 07 08 09 11 12 13 (15) Outstanding Tolcsva winery, owned by Spain's Vega Sicilia: 1st-rate ASZÚ; v.gd dry FURMINT *Mandolás*.

Pajzos-Megyer Tok w dr sw ★★→★★★ 99 06' 07 08 09 11 12 13' 15 Jointly managed properties. Megyer for gd-value, modern dry and late-harvest (sw) varietals. Pajzos focused on sweet styles, gd age-worthy ASZÚ, recently serious dry wines.

Pannonhalma N Pann r p w dr ★★→★★★ 13 15 800-yr-old Pannonhalma Abbey producing stylish, aromatic whites, esp RIES, SAUV BL, Tramini. Gd-value Tricollis, lovely top *Hemina* (w) and improving PINOT N.

Patricius Tok w dr sw ★★→★★★ 06' 07 08 09 11 12 13 15 Hungary's Winery of the Year 2016. Consistent dry FURMINT, late-harvest Katinka, ASZÚ.

Pendits Winery Tok w dr sw ★★ 06 08 09 11 13 Demeter-certified bio estate. Luscious long-ageing ASZÚ, pretty, dry DYA MUSCAT.

Pezsgő Hungarian for sparkling wine – v. trendy, esp from TOK, kick-started by cold, wet 2010 vintage.

Puttonyos (putts) Traditional indication of sweetness in TOKAJI ASZÚ. Optional since 2013 (see ASZÚ). Historically a *puttony* was a 25kg bucket or hod of Aszú grapes, sweetness determined by number of puttonyos added to a 136-litre barrel of base wine.

Royal Tokaji Wine Co Tok dr sw ★★→★★★★ 06 07' 08' 09 11' 13' 15 Pioneer winery at MÁD that led renaissance of TOK in 1990 (I am a co-founder). Mainly "First Growth" v'yds. 6-PUTTONYOS single-v'yd bottlings, esp Botrok, *Mézes-Mály*, Nyulászó plus 5 Puttonyos, Szent Tamás. Also v.gd dry FURMINT The Oddity, plus luscious, gd-value Late Harvest (MÁD Cuvée in US) and light, dry MUSCAT.

Sauska S Pann, Tok r p w ★★→★★★★ 11' 12 13 15 Immaculate winery in VILLÁNY. V.gd KADARKA, KÉKFRANKOS, CAB FR and impressive red blends, esp Cuvée 7 and Cuvée 5. Also Sauska-TOK with focus on v.gd dry whites, esp Medve and Birsalmás FURMINTS. Gd new PEZSGŐ *Extra Brut fizz.*

Somló Bal w ★★→★★★ 11 12 13 15 Dramatic volcanic hill famous for long-lived, austere white *Juhfark* ("sheep's tail"), FURMINT, HÁRSLEVELŰ, OLASZRIZLING. Region of small producers, esp Fekete (under new ownership), Györgykovács, Royal Somló, Somlói Apátsági, Spiegelberg. Bigger TORNAI (esp Grofi HÁRSLEVELŰ, JUHFARK), KREINBACHER also v.gd.

Sopron N Pann r ★★→★★★ Dynamic district on Austrian border overlooking Lake Fertő. KÉKFRANKOS most important, plus CAB SAUV, PINOT N, SYRAH. Top: bio *Weninger*; maverick Ráspi noted for natural wines. Watch: Luka, Pfneiszl, Taschner.

224 |

> **Tokaj runs dry**
> Dry wine has always existed in TOK, as a by-product when ASZÚ did not
> appear, but last decade has seen a new focus on deliberate production
> of serious dry wines. The combination of a world-class grape in FURMINT,
> with Tok's landscape of extinct volcanoes, is proving exciting. Producers
> to seek out: ever-pioneering ISTVÁN SZEPSY but also lovely wines from
> Balassa, BARDON, BARTA, Bott, Degenfeld, DEMETER ZOLTÁN, DOBOGÓ, HOMONNA,
> KIKELET, KIRÁLYUDVAR, OREMUS, ROYAL TOKAJI WINE CO, SZENT TAMÁS, TOKAJ-NOBILIS.

St Andrea N Hun r w p dr ★★★ 11' 12 13 15 Leading light in EGER for modern, high-quality BIKAVÉR (Áldás, Hangács, Merengő). Top white blends: Napbor, Örökké and delicious Szeretettel rosé. New flagships Mária (w) and Nagy-Eged-Hegy (r).

Szamorodni Tok Literally "as it was born"; for TOK produced from whole bunches with no separate ASZÚ harvest and 1 yr barrel ageing. Mini-renaissance led by SZEPSY for sweet (*édes*) version. Also try BARTA, HOLDVÖLGY, KIKELET, OREMUS, ST TAMÁS. Best dry versions are flor aged; try DERESZLA, Karádi-Berger, *Tinon*.

Szekszárd S Pann r p ★★→★★★ Ripe, rich reds. Increasing focus on BIKAVÉR, KÉKFRANKOS and reviving KADARKA. Look for: Dúzsi (rosé), Eszterbauer (esp Tüke Bikavér, Nagyapám Kadarka), HEIMANN, Mészáros, Remete-Bor (Kadarka), newcomer Schieber (CAB FR, Kékfrankos), Sebestyén (Ivan-Volgyi Bikavér), TAKLER, Vesztergombi (Csaba's Cuvée, Turul), Vida (Hidaspetre Kékfrankos, La Vida).

Szent Tamás Winery Tok w sw ★★★ 09 11 12' 13' 15 Important new winery in MÁD with ISTVÁN SZEPSY Jr. Excellent dry FURMINT esp Dongó and Percze. Sweet focus now on SZAMORODNI; Nyulászó and Dongó superb. Useful café.

Szepsy, István Tok w dr sw ★★★★ 08' 09 11' 12 13' 15 Brilliant, soil-obsessed, no-compromise (he destroyed nearly all his 2014 vintage) TOK producer in MÁD. Powerful, pure dry FURMINT, esp DŰLŐ Urágya, Betsek and Nyulászó blend. V.gd sweet SZAMORODNI 12. Superb ASZÚ.

Szeremley Bal w dr sw ★★→★★★ 09 11' 12 13 (15) Pioneer in BADACSONY. Intense, fine RIES, *Szürkebarát*, (aka PINOT GR), KÉKNYELŰ, appealing sweet Zeus.

Takler S Pann r ★★ 11' 12 13 (15) Super-ripe, supple reds. Best: Res selections of BIKÁVER, Cab Fr, KÉKFRANKOS, SYRAH. Excellent Kékfrankos Görögszó, rich Primarius MERLOT.

Tinon, Samuel Tok w dr sw ★★★ 04 05 07 09 Sauternais in TOK since 1991. Distinctive complex ASZÚ with v. long maceration and barrel-ageing. V.gd sweet and superb dry flor-aged *Szamorodni*. Fine dry FURMINTS, esp v'yd selections.

Tokaj Nobilis Tok w dr sw ★★★ V. fine small producer run by Sarolta Bárdos, one of TOK's inspirational women. Superb ASZÚ 08, dry Barakonyi HÁRSLEVELŰ, FURMINT 15.

Bor is "wine": *vörös* is red; *fehér* is white; *édes* is sweet, *száraz* is dry, *válogatás* is selected.

Tokaj / Tokaji ★★→★★★★ Tokaj is the town and wine region; Tokaji the wine. From 2014, PDO requires bottling in region. Recommended producers without standalone entry: Arvay, Balassa (Betsek FURMINT, Villő ASZÚ), Bott Pince (esp late-harvest Bott-rytis), Carpinus, Demetervin, Erzsébet, Füleky, Gizella, Karádi-Berger, Lenkey, Orosz Gábor.

Tolna S Pann Antinori-owned ★★Tűzkő is most important estate.

Törley r p w dr sp ★→★★ Innovative large company. Chapel Hill is major brand name. Well-made, gd-value DYA international and local varieties IRSAI OLIVÉR, Zenit, Zefir. Major fizz producer (esp *Törley*, Gala, Hungaria labels), v.gd classic method, esp François President Rosé Brut, CHARD Brut Natur. György-Villa for top selections (try JUHFARK, SYRAH).

Tornai Bal w dr ★★ 13 15 2nd-largest SOMLÓ estate. Gd-value entry-level varietals, excellent top Grofi HÁRSLEVELŰ, Juhfark.

Villány S Pann Most s wine region. Noted for serious ripe B'x varieties (esp CAB FR) and blends, also try juicy examples of *Kékfrankos*, PORTUGIESER. High quality: ATTILA GERE, *Bock*, CSÁNYI, Kiss Gabor, HEUMANN, Jackfall, Janus, *Malatinszky*, Polgar, Riczu-Stier, *Sauska*, Tamás & Zsolt Gere, Tiffán, *Vylyan*, WENINGER-GERE.

Villányi Franc S Pann New classification for CAB FR from VILLÁNY. Premium version has restricted yield, 1 yr in oak. Super-premium from 2015 is max 35hl/ha.

Furmint probably half-sibling of Chard, Ries, c.80 others. No clue in the taste.

Vylyan S Pann r p ★★→★★★ 12' 13 14 (15) Red specialist making v.gd v'yd selections, esp Gombás PINOT N, Mandolás CAB FR, Pillangó MERLOT. *Duennium Cuvée* is flagship red. Also delicious rare Csóka.

Weninger N Hun r ★★★ 11' 12 13' 14 (15) Benchmark winery in SOPRON run by Austrian Franz Weninger Jr. Bio since 2006. Single-v'yd *Spern Steiner Kékfrankos* is superb. SYRAH, CAB FR and red Frettner blend also impressive.

Weninger-Gere S Pann r p ★★→★★★ 11 12' 13' 15 Joint-venture between Austrian Franz Weninger Sr and ATTILA GERE. Excellent CAB FR, tasty Tinta (TEMPRANILLO), Cuvée Phoenix and DYA fresh rosé.

BULGARIA

The Bulgarian wine scene continues to evolve rapidly. There were 262 wineries by 2016 (up from 216 in 2012) and another 19 under construction. Many are small estates and boutique operations largely selling to the home market, which is prepared to pay higher prices than export markets. Still Bulgarians only drink 5.7 litres each, and while wine culture is growing, the limited market size means wineries are trying hard to sell abroad. As a result some premium wines are appearing, showing that the country has more to offer than bottom-shelf Cabernet.

Angel's Estate Thr L r p w 12 13 14 Ambitious quality-focused estate (previously Angelus) making ripe, oaky, polished reds from international grapes. New Angel range, Deneb varietals and impressive flagship Stallion Gold.

Bessa Valley Thr L r p ★★★ 10 11' 12 (13) Stephan von Neipperg (Canon la Gaffelière, B'x) and K-H Hauptmann's pioneering estate winery nr Pazardjik. Smooth, rich reds, plus tasty DYA Rosé. Try Enira, v.gd SYRAH and Enira Res, excellent BV by Enira and new Grande Cuvée.

Black Sea Gold Thr L r p w ★ Large winery with two sites and 600 ha nr coast. Better labels: Golden Rhythm, Salty Hills, Villa Ponte.

Borovitsa Dan P r w ★★★ 10 11 12 13 15 After tragic loss of co-founder Dr. Ognyan Tzvetanov, Adriana Srebırıova is continuing to focus on their joint vision of hand-crafted parcels of terroir wines – among Bulgaria's best. Dux is long-lived flagship. Also v.gd The Guardians MRV (Rhône white grapes), Cuvée Bella Rada (RKATSITELI), Granny's and Black Pack (both GAMZA), Orange Garden CHARD, Vox Dei PINOT N, Sensum (r) and Maxxima range.

Boyar, Domaine Thr L r p w ★→★★★ Produces everything from DYA entry-level labels via mid-range Ars Longa, Deer Point, Dom Boyar, Platinum, Quantum, Silver Rock to premium wines from Korten incl "Boutique" range and impressive Solitaire.

Bratanov Thr L r w ★★ 13 15 New family winery; v.gd Temjanika (w), charming MAVRUD, weighty CAB FR.

Burgozone, Chateau Dan P r w ★★ 13 14 15 Gd whites from family estate close to Danube esp VIOGNIER, SAUV BL and Iris Creation. Decent PINOT N.

Castra Rubra Thr L r w ★★→★★★ 08 09 10 11' 12 13 15 Michel Rolland from B'x consults. Try complex B'x blend Castra Rubra and impressive Butterfly's Rock.

> **Independents rule**
> It's not long since wine estates were non-existent in Bulgaria. Today it's hard to keep up with pace of change. Recommended: Alexandra Estate, Chateau Copsa (Karlovo Misket, Stradivarius), Eolis (GEWURZ, SYRAH), Gulbanis (CAB FR), Kamenki (CAB/MERLOT, MAVRUD), Kapatovo (red blend), Maryan (Res, Ivan Alexander Grand Cuvée), Medi Valley (EXcentric CHARD/SAUV BL, Incanto reds), Orbelus (Prima, MELNIK), Rumelia (Merul Merlot, Mavrud Res, Erelia), Salla (whites, Cab Fr), Villa Yustina (4 Seasons range, Monogram RUBIN/Mavrud).

Expressive Dominant blends from organic grapes, consistent Via Diagonalis and tasty Motley Cock blends for US.

Damianitza Thr L r w ★★ 10 11' 13 14 15 Struma Valley. Uniqato label features local grapes esp MELNIK, RUBIN. ReDark is robust blend with CAB SAUV, RUBIN and Ruen. Also gd: No Man's Land Kometa; No Man's Gold, skin-fermented ASSYRTIKO.

Dragomir Thr L r p w ★★ 11' 12 13 Garage winemaker making serious weighty reds, plus fresh Sarva (p w). V.gd Pitos, RUBIN, long-lived Res.

Ivo Varbanov Thr L r p w ★★ Concert pianist making super-ripe big reds, esp SYRAH, vinous rosé; best is sleek CHARD.

Katarzyna Thr L r p w ★★ 12 13 14 15 Large modern winery in "No Man's Land" border zone nr Greece, just celebrated 10th anniversary. V. ripe smooth reds: try Chopin Nocturne, Encore MALBEC, SYRAH, Question Mark, Res.

Logodaj Thr L r p w sp ★★ 12 13 14 15 Struma Valley. Interesting rosé and fizz from local broad-leaved MELNIK. Juicy vibrant Melnik 55 (r) and promising Incantesimo SYRAH. Riccardo Cotarella consults.

Lovico Suhindol Dan P r w ★ One of Bulgaria's most famous names – founded in 1909, noted for CAB SAUV and GAMZA. Ranges from entry-level Craftsman's Creek to top-end Gamza AOC, Lin 53, Lovico 100.

Midalidare Estate Thr L r p w ★★ 12 13 14 15 No-expense-spared boutique winery. Try SAUV BL/SÉM, Sauv Bl Premium, rosé. Gd Nota Bene red blend and Grand Vintages: MALBEC, SYRAH, CAB FR.

Minkov Brothers Thr L r p w ★★ 12 13' 15 Large estate reviving tradition dating back to 1875. Competent modern wines: Cycle, Ethno, Jamais Vu, Le Photografie, Minkov. Oak Tree is more structured flagship. Cuvée, Minkov CAB SAUV and Deja Vu SAUV BL/SEM 15 showing well.

Miroglio, Edoardo Thr L r p w sp ★★→★★★ 12 13 14 15 Italian-owned v'yds at Elenovo. Bulgaria's best bottle-fermented sparkling, esp Blanc de Blancs, Brut Rosé. Fine long-lived PINOT N Res, v.gd flagship Soli Invicto. Try Elenovo CAB FR, MAVRUD. EM varietals are reliable, interesting bio blends incl Bouquet, Mavrud/RUBIN.

Neragora Thr L r w ★★ 13 15 Organic estate producing v.gd MAVRUD and blends Ares (with MERLOT), Cherno (with CAB SAUV).

Peshtera, Vinprom r p w ★ 13 14 15 One of biggest in Bulgaria. Also owns Villa Yambol and boutique winery Saedinenie for modern, clean Pixels, Verano Azur labels, plus characterful F2F reds.

Fancy a glass? Bulgarians shake their heads for yes and nod for no. Careful...

Preslav, Vinex Thr L r w ★→★★ 12 13 14 15 Whites best here, esp long-lived Rubaiyat CHARD. Also try Novi Pazar PINOT GR, RIES. Golden Age range is decent. Shared ownership with Khan Krum winery, noted for whites and esp 1939 range.

Rossidi Thr L r p w ★★→★★★ 13 14 15 Boutique winery nr Sliven. Elegant concrete egg-fermented CHARD. V.gd rosé, RUBIN, PINOT N and Bulgaria's 1st "orange" CHARD.

Santa Sarah Thr L r w ★★★ 12 13 14 15 Pioneering *garagiste*; top reds, esp exciting Privat, Bin 40 CAB SAUV, Bin 49 CAB FR, RUBIN. Gd RIES, TRAMINER, Bin 44 SAUV BL.

Slavyantsi, Vinex Thr L r p w ★→★★ 13 15 1st Bulgarian company to receive "Fair for Life" certification for its work with local Roma community. Doing great job with budget varietal wines and blends, esp under Leva brand.

Bulgaria's version of mulled wine is *greyano vino*: honey, pepper, orange, apple.

Terra Tangra r w ★★ Large estate in Sakar: rich reds, sleek whites plus organic blend.
Yamantiev's Thr L r w ★★ 10 13 14 15 Best for Marble Land v'yd selections, esp buttery CHARD and excellent long-ageing Red 10'.
Zagreus Thr L r p w ★★ 12 13 14 15 MAVRUD in all styles from unusual white to complex Amarone-style Vinica from semi-dried grapes. Decent St Dimitar SYRAH.

SLOVENIA

$\mathbf{S}$lovenia is one of the stars of Central Europe, with her top winemakers gaining global recognition. The trend for orange (skin-fermented whites) and natural wines has helped, but Slovenia's wines range from aromatic, crisp and appetizing in the east, to rich and complex in the west. The gorgeous landscape and fantastic restaurants are increasingly making this tiny country a food-and-wine tourism hotspot.

Batič Prim r p w sw ★★ 09 11 13 15 Bio/natural wines in VIPAVA. Rosé is top seller. Also Angel Blends, Valentino (sw).
Bjana Prim sp ★★→★★★ V.gd traditional-method PENINA from BRDA, esp Brut Zero 10, Brut Rosé, NV.
Blažič Prim w ★★→★★★ 09 13 14 15 From BRDA. Long-ageing, complex REBULA, SAUVIGNONASSE and Blaž Belo (w) in top yrs.
Brda (Goriška) Prim Top-quality district in PRIM. Many leading wineries, incl BJANA, BLAŽIČ, EDI SIMČIČ, Dolfo (esp sparkling Spirito, SIVI PINOT, Škocaj), Erzetič, JAKONČIČ, KLET BRDA, KRISTANČIČ, MOVIA, Prinčič, Reya, ŠČUREK, SIMČIČ, ZANUT and orange wines from KABAJ and Klinec.

Slovenia's Lipica stud, home of Lipizzaners, operating continuously since 1580.

Burja Prim r w ★★★ 13 14 15 Bio VIPAVA estate, Petite Burja features local grapes Zelen and MALVAZIJA. Excellent Burja Bela, Burja Noir (PINOT N) and Burja Reddo based on Schioppettino.
Čotar Prim r w ★★ 09 11 12 13 Intriguing, long-lived organic/natural wines from KRAS, esp Vitovska (w), MALVAZIJA, SAUV BL, TERAN, Terra Rossa red blend.
Cviček Pos Traditional low-alc, sharp, light red blend of POS, based on Žametovka.
Dveri-Pax Pod r w sw ★★→★★★ 11 13 15 Benedictine-owned estate nr Maribor. Crisp, taut, v.gd-value whites in Benedict series (esp SAUV BL, FURMINT, RIES). V.gd v'yd selections: Sauv Bl Vajgen, Ries M, Furmint Ilovci. Superb sweet ŠIPON/Chard.
Guerila Prim r w ★★ 14 15 Bio producer in VIPAVA. V.gd local DYA PINELA and Zelen.
Istenič Pos sp ★→★★ Reliable PENINA in all forms. Try N°1, Gourmet Rosé 06, Prestige Extra Brut 11.
Istria Coastal zone extending into Croatia; main grapes: REFOŠK, MALVAZIJA. Best: Bordon (E Vin rosé, Malvazija), Korenika & Moškon (PINOT GR, REFOŠK, Kortinca red), Rodica, Rojac (Renero, Stari d'Or), Pucer z Vrha (Malvazija), SANTOMAS, Steras (Refošk Kocinski), VINAKOPER.
Jakončič Prim r w sp ★★★ 12' 13' 14 V.gd BRDA producer, esp Carolina Rebula, Bela (w), Red. Also gd PENINA.
Joannes Pod r w ★★ 10 12 13 14 15' RIES specialist nr Maribor, wines age well. Also fresh light PINOT N.
Kabaj Prim r w ★★★ 09 11 12 13 US top-100 winery on multiple occasions. Noted for orange Rebula, Amfora, Ravan (FRIULANO), Luisa Prestige (w).

Klet Brda Prim r w sp ★★→★★★12 13 14 15 Slovenia's largest co-op, surprisingly gd and forward-thinking. Bright modern DYA Quercus varietal whites, Krasno unoaked blends, v.gd Colliano for US. Bagueri is premium v'yd selections. Excellent A+ (r w).

Kobal Pod w ★★ 15 Former PULLUS winemaker gone solo. V.gd FURMINT, SAUV BL.

Kogl Pod r p w ★★ 15 Hilltop estate nr Ormož, dating from 1542. Vibrant precise whites: Mea Culpa AUXERROIS, SAUV BL, Yellow MUSCAT. Try PINOT N rosé, Rubellus.

Kras Prim Renowned district on Terra Rossa soil in PRIM. Best-known for TERAN, MALVAZIJA. Try Vinakras.

Slovenian wine consumption 4th highest in world: 44.07 l/head. More than France.

Kristančič Prim r w ★★ 11 12 13 14 15 Family winery in BRDA making gd CHARD, CAB SAUV, MERLOT. Pavó is top label.

Kupljen Pod r w ★★ 13 15 Dry wine pioneer nr Jeruzalem. Gd RENSKI RIZLING, SIVI PINOT, FURMINT, PINOT N. Top selections: Spirit of Jeruzalem, Star of Stiria.

Marof Pod r w ★★→★★★ 13 14 15 Exciting winery in Prekmurje. Bright DYA classic range, esp RIES, SYLVANER, LAŠKI RIZLING. Breg is selected old vines and barrel-fermentation, Cru is top range from single sites.

Movia Prim r w sp ★★★→★★★★ 08' 09 11 12 13 14 15 High-profile bio winery led by charismatic Aleš Kristančič. Excellent v. long-lived Veliko Belo (w), Veliko Rdeče (r); v.gd MODRI PINOT, showstopping Puro rosé (sp). Orange Lunar (esp CHARD) is notable.

P&F Pod r w sp ★★15' Former state producer, now family run, renamed P&F (Puklavec & Friends). Now v.gd-value, *consistent crisp aromatic whites* in P&F range. Selected Gomila wines are excellent esp FURMINT, SAUV BL. Jeruzalem Ormož label for local market.

Penina Name for quality sparkling wine (Charmat or traditional method). V. trendy: now being produced by many wineries.

Podravje Largest wine region covering Štajerska and Prekmurje in e. Best for crisp dry whites, gd sweet wines, reds typically lighter styles from MODRA FRANKINJA (aka BLAUFRÄNKISCH), PINOT N.

Posavje Region in se. Best wines are sweet, esp Mavretič (superb ★★★★SAUV BL Icewine, gd Yellow MUSCAT), PRUS, Šturm (★★★★Icewine, botrytized Muscat).

PRA-VinO Pod w sw 12 13 14 15 1970s pioneer of private wine production, son and grandson now in charge. World-class ★★★★ sweet wines, incl Icewine (*ledeno vino*) and botrytis wines from LAŠKI RIZLING, RIES, ŠIPON.

Primorje Region in w covering Slovenian ISTRIA, BRDA, VIPAVA, KRAS. Aka Primorska.

Prus Pos w sw Small family producer making stunning ★★★★ sweet wines, esp Icewines and botrytis wines from Rumeni MUŠKAT, RIES, SAUV BL.

Pullus Pod r w ★★→★★★13 14 15 V.gd crisp modern whites from Ptuj winery, esp Pullus SAUV BL, RIES. Excellent "G" wines (notable Sauv Bl). Superb sweet LAŠKI RIZLING, Rumeni MUSCAT.

Radgonske Gorice Pod sp ★→★★ Producer of bestselling Slovenian sparkler Srebrna (silver) PENINA, classic-method Zlata (golden) Penina and popular demi-sec black label TRAMINEC.

Try orange wines with fish or meat. If they're gd, they're versatile.

Santomas Prim r p w ★★→★★★ 12 13 14 15 Leading ISTRIAN estate, some of country's best *Refošk* and REFOŠK/CAB SAUV blends, esp Antonius from 60-yr-old vines and Grande Cuvée blend.

Ščurek Prim r w sw ★★→★★★ 12 13 14 15 Family estate in BRDA, five sons. Gd DYA varieties CAB FR, Jakot, PINOT BL, REBULA, plus Strune blends. Best wines from local grapes, esp Kontra, Pikolit, Stara Brajda (r w).

> **Slovenia's quality wines**
> 70 per cent of Slovenia's wines have a quality designation – reckoned to be one of highest percentages in world. Passing a tasting is obligatory. *Vrhunsko vino z zaščtenim geografskim poreklom*, or *Vrhunsko vino ZGP*, is term for top-quality PDO wines. *Kakovostno vino ZGP* is more common for quality wines. *Deželno vino PGO* is for PGI wines. For quality sweet wines, descriptions are: *Pozna Trgatev* (Spätlese), *Izbor* (Auslese), *Jagodni Izbor* (BA), *Suhi Jagodni Izbor* (TBA). *Ledeno Vino* is Icewine, *Slamno Vino* is straw wine from semi-dried grapes.

Simčič, Edi Prim r w ★★★→★★★★ 09 10 11' 12 13 Perfectionist in BRDA; red wine superstar with Duet Lex and barrel-selection Kolos. Excellent whites: MALVAZIJA, Rebula, SAUV BL, Triton Lex. Superb Kozana single v'yd CHARD.

Simčič, Marjan Prim r w sw ★★★ →★★★★ 11 12' 13' 14 Whites, esp CHARD, Rebula, SAUV BL, Selekcija, SIVI PINOT impress. Teodor blends always v.gd. MODRI PINOT is elegant. V. fine Opoka single v'yd range, esp Sauv Bl and Rebula. Sweet Leonardo is great.

Štajerska Pod Large eastern wine region incl important districts of Ljutomer-Ormož, Maribor, Haloze. Crisp, refined whites and top sweet wines. Best (without individual entries): Doppler, Gaube (Kaspar CHARD), Gross (FURMINT, SAUV BL Colles), Heaps Good Wine, Krainz (ŠIPON), Miro, M-vina (esp ExtremM Sauv Bl), Valdhuber, Zlati Grič (Rosé PENINA, Sauv Bl).

Steyer Pod w sw sp ★★ 13 14 15 TRAMINER specialist in Štajerska: dry, sparkling, oak-aged, Vaneja sweet.

Sutor Prim r w ★★★ 11' 12' 13 Excellent small producer from VIPAVA. Try Sutor White from REBULA/MALVAZIJA, also v.gd SAUV BL, fine CHARD, elegant MERLOT.

Tilia Prim r w ★★→★★★ 12 13 14 15 Self-styled "House of Pinots" in VIPAVA since co-owner gained PhD studying PINOT N, now in three qualities. Sunshine range for appetizing gd-value whites. Black label for more serious reds incl gd Pinot N, White label in top yrs.

Verus Pod r w ★★★ 13 14 15' Fine, focused, brisk whites, esp v.gd FURMINT, crisp SAUV BL, flavoursome PINOT GR, refined RIES. Promising PINOT N.

Vinakoper Prim r w ★ →★★ 13 14 15 Large producer in ISTRIA. Try DYA MALVAZIJA, REFOŠK, Capris Malvazija 14 (part-acacia-aged). Capo D'Istria Refošk 11 drinking well.

Vipava Prim Valley noted for cool breezes in PRIM, source of some fine wines. Recommended: BATIČ, Benčina (PINOT N), BURJA, GUERILA, Frlanova (BARBERA) Jangus (SAUV BL, MALVAZIJA), Lepa Vida (v.gd Malvazija, oOo orange wine), Miška (PINELA), Mlečnik, Pasji Rep (Jebačin), Štokelj (Pinela), SUTOR, TILIA, Vina Krapež (excellent Lapor Belo).

Zanut Prim r w ★★ 09 14 15 Family winery in BRDA; excellent SAUVIGNONASSE, intense SAUV BL and in top yrs single v'yd MERLOT Brjač.

CROATIA

Croatian wine is building a great reputation, but with around 500 commercial wineries and just 21,000 ha of vines, it is no simple matter. Over 200 varieties and more new "old" grapes appearing on the scene makes this country endlessly intriguing. A strong tourist industry has undoubtedly helped but this also brings a dark side of all-inclusive packages and cruise ships that do little to support local business – including wine.

Agrokor r p w ★ →★★ 13' 15' Ice-cream-to-supermarket conglomerate with multiple wineries. Best: Agrolaguna in ISTRIA with Vina Laguna Festigia (v.gd MALVAZIJA in all forms esp Vižinada, Akacija Riserva. Also MERLOT, CAB SAUV, Castello). Vina Belje nr Danube (esp Goldberg GRAŠEVINA, premium CHARD).

Arman, Franc Is & Kv r w ★★ **12** 13' 15' A 6th-generation family winery. V.gd DYA MALVAZIJA and skin-contact Malvazija Classic, MERLOT, TERAN.

Badel 1862 r w ★★ 13 14 15 Group of wineries. Best: Korlat SYRAH and Cuvée from Benkovac winery. Gd-value Duravar range esp SAUV BL, GRAŠEVINA. Gd PLAVAC and Ivan Dolac from PZ Svirče.

Benvenuti Is & Kv r w ★★ 13 15 ISTRIAN family winery. Benchmark fresh MALVAZIJA, complex Anno Domini (w), v.gd TERAN **12'**, sweet San Salvatore 09.

BIBICh Dalm r w ★★ 12 13 15 Well-regarded producer; focus on local grapes esp Debit (w). Try Lučica single-v'yd and sweet Ambra. Also R6 Riserva red blend.

Bolfan Cro Up p w dr ★→★★ 13 15 Bio/natural wine. RIES, SAUV BL, PINOT N rosé best.

Bura-Mrgudič Dalm r ★★→★★★ 10 11 Brother/sister, renowned DINGAČ, Mare POSTUP.

Cattunar Is & Kv r w dr ★★ 13' 15 Hilltop estate with gd range of MALVAZIJA from four soils, esp White Soil and Black Soil. V.gd late-harvest Collina.

Coronica Is & Kv r w ★★ 11 13 15 Notable ISTRIAN winery, esp barrel-aged Gran MALVAZIJA and benchmark Gran TERAN.

Dalmatia Rocky coastal zone and its lovely islands to s of Zadar. Tourism hotspot.

Dingač Dalm 10 11' 12 (13) 1st quality designation in 1961, now PDO, on Pelješac peninsula in s DALM. Full-bodied from PLAVAC MALI. Try: BURA-MRGUDIČ, Kiridžija, Lučič, Madirazza, Matuško, Milicic, SAINTS HILLS, Skarmuča, Vinarija Dingač.

Enjingi, Ivan Sl & CD w sw ★★ Pioneer in SLAVONIJA. V.gd sweet botrytis and dry whites, esp GRAŠEVINA barrique, Venje.

Feravino Sl & CD r p w ★ One of largest small producers with 160 ha. Entry-level wines modern, decent value.

Galić Sl & CD r w ★★ 12 13 14 15 Promising new producer in SLAVONIJA, esp GRAŠEVINA, red blend Crno 9.

Gerzinić Is & Kv r p w ★★ 13 14 15 Brothers making v.gd TERAN, MALVAZIJA. Decent SAUV BL and gd Teran rosé.

Gracin Dalm r p ★★→★★★ Small exciting winery with rocky coastal v'yds nr Primošten owned by Prof Leo Gracin, making country's *best Babić*, also Kontra (BABIČ/PLAVAC blend).

Croatia has 1246 islands and islets, and 39 indigenous grape varieties.

Grgić Dalm r w ★★→★★★ 10 11 13 Napa Valley legend for Montelena CHARD that beat French in 1976 Judgement of Paris. Returned to Croatian roots to make PLAVAC MALI, rich POŠIP on Pelješac peninsula with daughter and nephew.

Hvar Beautiful island with world's oldest continuously cultivated v'yd and UNESCO protection. Noted for PLAVAC MALI, incl Ivan Dolac designation. Gd: Carič, Plančič, PZ Svirče, TOMIČ, ZLATAN OTOK and new Ahearne Rosé from rare Darnekuša.

Iločki Podrumi Sl & CD r p w ★★→★★★ 14' 15 Now family owned; claims 2nd-oldest wine cellar in Europe: built in 1450. Superb Premium GRAŠEVINA, TRAMINAC, Principovac range.

Istria North Adriatic peninsula. MALVAZIJA is main grape. Gd also for CAB SAUV, MERLOT, TERAN. Look for: ARMAN FRANC, Banko Mario, BENVENUTI, Capo (Malvazija, Stellae range), CATTUNAR, Clai (orange wines esp Sveti Jakov), CORONICA, Cossetto, Degrassi (VIOGNIER, CAB FR), Elio Fakin, GERZINIČ, KABOLA, KOZLOVIČ, MATOŠEVIČ, MENEGHETTI, Novacco, Peršurič, PILATO, Radovan, ROXANICH, SAINTS HILLS, Sirotic, Tomaz (Avantgarde, Sesto Senso), TRAPAN, Zigante.

Kabola Is & Kv r p w ★★→★★★ 12 13' 14 15' Immaculate ISTRIAN estate. V.gd MALVAZIJA as fizz, young wine, cask-aged Unica **10**, Amfora **09**. Tasty DYA Rosé; v.gd TERAN.

Katunar Is & Kv r w ★★ 14 15 Leading producer of Žlahtina only found on island of Krk. Try Sv. Lucija.

> ### In the Opol
> Pink wine is the next big thing in DALM, often marketed as Opol. Better suited to holiday palates in the summer heat than the region's hefty reds. Try FRANO MILOŠ, SAINTS HILLS, Senjković, STINA, Suha Punta.

Korta Katarina Dalm r p w ★★ →★★★ 08 09 11 12 13 15 Modern winemaking from Korcula. Excellent POŠIP, PLAVAC MALI, esp Reuben's Res.

Kozlović Is & Kv r w ★★★ 13' 15 *Benchmark Malvazija* in all its forms, esp exciting, complex Santa Lucia 08. Also v.gd Santa Lucia Crna 12; sweet Sorbus 09' from dried MUŠKAT Momjanski, Violetta rosé.

Krauthaker, Vlado Sl & CD r w sw ★★★ 12 13 15 Top producer from KUTJEVO, esp CHARD Rosenberg, GRAŠEVINA Mitrovac, sweet Graševina Izborna Berba. PINOT N Selekcija shows promise.

Vrhunsko vino: premium quality wine; *Kvalitetno Vino:* quality wine; *Stolno Vino:* table wine. *Suho:* dry; *Polsuho:* semi-dry.

Kutjevo Cellars Sl & CD w dr sw ★★ 12 13 15' Producer in town of same name – noted for gd GRAŠEVINA esp De Gotho, Turkovič and lovely Icewine.

Maraština Alias of the common MALVAZIJA of the coast; often fair refreshment.

Matošević Is & Kv r w ★★ Benchmark MALVAZIJA, esp Alba 15, Alba Robinia (aged in acacia) 12, Antiqua 09. V.gd Grimalda (r w).

Meneghetti Is & Kv r w ★★ 10 13 15 Sleek blends (r w), fine precise MALVAZIJA.

Miloš, Frano Dalm r p ★★ 07 12 Reputed for the powerful Stagnum, but PLAVAC is more approachable.

Pilato Is & Kv r w ★★ 13 15 Family winery: v.gd MALVAZIJA, PINOT BL, TERAN, MERLOT.

Postup Dalm Famous v'yd designation nw of DINGAČ. Full-bodied rich red from PLAVAC MALI. Donja Banda, Miličič, Mrgudič Marija, Vinarija Dingač are noted.

Prošek Dalm Historic sweet wine made from dried grapes in DALM. Oldest bottle known is dated 1888. Gd versions: TOMIČ Hectorovich using Bogdanuša, Maraština, Prč. Also STINA made with PLAVAC MALI and POŠIP.

Roxanich Is & Kv r w ★★ →★★★ 08 09 10 Natural producer making powerful, intriguing orange wines (MALVAZIJA Antica, Ines U Bijelom) and impressive complex reds, esp TERAN Ré, Superistrian Cuvée, MERLOT

Saints Hills Dalm, Is & Kv r p w ★★ →★★★ 12 13 14 15 Two wineries and three locations with Michel Rolland. V.gd Nevina white from ISTRIA; richly fruity PLAVAC MALI St Roko, serious DINGAČ.

Slavonija Region in ne, famous for oak, and for whites, esp from GRAŠEVINA. Gd reds appearing now, cup PINOT N. Look for Adzič, Bartolovič, Belje, ENJINGI, GALIČ, KRAUTHAKER, KUTJEVO, Mihalj, Zdjelarevič.

Stina Dalm r p w ★★ →★★★ 12 13 14 15 Dramatic steep v'yds on Brač island, v.gd POŠIP, PLAVAC MALI, esp Majstor label. Gd Crljenak (AKA ZINFANDEL), Opol rosé, PROŠEK.

Tomac Cro Up r w sp ★★ Estate nr Zagreb with 200-yr history, famous for sparkling and pioneering amphora wines.

Tomić Dalm r w p ★★ 09 11 12 Outspoken personality on island of HVAR, with organic PLAVAC MALI v'yd. Gd reds, esp PLAVAC Barrique, Hectorovich PROŠEK.

Trapan, Bruno Is & Kv r w ★★ 12 13 14 15 Dynamic young producer. Try MALVAZIJA, incl aged Uroboros and fresh DYA Ponente. Also sleek modern Terra Mare TERAN, Revolution (r).

Veralda Is & Kv r p w ★★ 13 15 Award-winning winery impressing with rich polished reds, bright whites and orange amphora wine.

Zlatan Otok Dalm r p w ★★ →★★★ 10 11 12 Family winery from HVAR with v'yds also at Makarska. Famous for huge reds, esp Zlatan PLAVAC Grand Cru. Also look for easier-drinking Plavac Šibenik, BABIČ, gd DYA POŠIP.

BOSNIA & HERZEGOVINA, KOSOVO, MACEDONIA (FYROM), SERBIA, MONTENEGRO

A dynamic, rapidly changing wine scene across the Balkans as more and more quality-focused producers appear and volume-based former-state dinosaurs are forced to reinvent themselves.

Bosnia & Herzegovina has around 3500 ha and a well-organised wine route. Local grapes dominate, esp aromatic white Žilavka (Anđelić, Koža, Nuič, esp 15 Selection, Podrumi Andrija 15 Selection 13, Tvrdos, Vukoje) and vibrant red Blatina (Hercegovina Produkt, Koža, Nuič Premium 13, Podrumi Andrija Barrique 12, Zadro Selekcija 10). Vranac also gd from Tvrdos, Vukoje, Anđelić.

Kosovo has 3200 ha and 12 commercial wineries but winemaking lags behind rest of region. Stonecastle is biggest.

Macedonia (Republic of, or even Former Yugoslav Republic of Macedonia because of ongoing disagreements with Greece) remains dependent on cheap bulk though efforts continue to raise quality and focus on bottled wines. Many smaller investments have disappeared/ failing to find a market. Unusually, it's the bigger wineries driving quality and investing in research. Giant Tikveš has a French-trained winemaker and continues to impress with Bela Voda and Barovo single v'yd wines; gd Special Selection range (esp GRENACHE BLANC, Temjanika, Vranec) and rich oaky Domaine Lepovo CHARD, Grand Cuvée. Stobi sources only from its own 600 ha of v'yds; try Vranec Veritas, Vranec classic, Aminta (r), Žilavka and refined PETIT VERDOT. Château Kamnik is leading boutique winery, with gd CARMENÈRE, SYRAH 10 Barrels, Temjanika Premium, Vranec Terroir. Other wineries to look out for: Ezimit (Stardust range, Vranec Barrique), Popov, Popova Kula (Stanušina in three styles), Skovin (Markov Manastir Vranec, Temjanika).

Montenegro is EU candidate country. Its 4500 ha of v'yds are divided between the coastal zone and Lake Skadar basin. 13 Jul Plantaže major producer (2310 ha), indeed one of Europe's largest v'yds, but wines are pretty gd (try Procorde Vranac, Stari Podrumi, Vranac Barrique). Serious Vranac from tiny Sjekloča winery.

Serbia has largest wine industry, with around 18,000 ha planted to wine grapes (over two-thirds are international varieties) and around 235 commercial producers, but new names continue to appear as pace of wine revolution continues. Try: Aleksandrovič (Trijumf, Triumf Noir, Sparkling, Barrique, Regent and Rodoslav), Aleksič (Amanet), Budimir (Triada, Svb Rossa), Cilič, Despotika (Morava, Dokaz), Ivanovič (Prokupac), Janko (Vrtlog, Misija), Kovačevič (CHARD, Aurelius), Matalj (Kremen CAB SAUV, Kremen Kamen), Pusula (CAB FR), Radovanovič (Cab Res), Temet (Ergo, Tri Morave), Zvonko Bogdan (SAUV BL, Rosé Sec, Cuvée No.1). No one's going thirsty.

CZECH REPUBLIC

C zech and Moravian wine has a long history but few real champions. The Czech Republic has two wine regions, the tiny Bohemia (Boh) and 20-times larger Moravia (Mor), and a total vineyard area of 17,400 ha. Annual production accounts for less than half of annual consumption, which, given the patriotic tendencies of the drinking public, keeps the producers in a highly advantageous position, hence few bargains. Leading player on the market is the giant Bohemia Sekt Group, based near the beer capital of Pilsen (Boh), which also owns several sizeable Moravian wineries. It is followed by Vinselekt Michlovský, Znovín Znojmo, Vinné sklepy Valtice (Valtice Wine Cellars) and Zámecké vinařství Chateau Bzenec Winery (all in Mor).

Baloun, Radomil Mor ★→★★ One of 1st to go private in 1990. Investing and stylishly modernizing two dilapidated former wine co-ops with own (not EU) money.

Dobrá Vinice Mor ★★★ Maverick inspired by Slovenia's Aleš Kristančič. Undoubtedly best whites in country.

Dufek, Josef Mor ★★ Dynamic, modern family winery drawing on centuries-old tradition, cultivating more than 30 organically grown varieties.

Dva Duby Mor ★★★ Dedicated terroirist, mainly BLAUFRÄNKISCH, bio principles.

Lobkowicz, Bettina Boh ★→★★★ Outstanding PINOT N and classic-method sparkling RIES, Pinot N Blanc de Noirs, Cuvée CHARD/PINOT BL/PINOT GR.

Plešingr & Sons Mor ★★→★★★ Brothers Michal and Patrik follow in footsteps of father. Flagships PINOTS N, GR.

Stapleton & Springer Mor ★★ Joint-venture between Jaroslav Springer and ex-US ambassador Craig Stapleton with brother Benjamin. Emphasis on PINOT N.

Stávek, Richard Mor ★→★★★ Raw-wine devotee. His orange wine features in specialized NY wine bars and several European restaurants.

Tanzberg Mor ★★ Gd Pálava hills WELSCHRIESLING, PINOT N. Award-winning sparklers.

Žernoseky Cellars Boh ★★ Best RIES, PINOT BL, MUSCAT from great Elbe River Valley terroir.

SLOVAK REPUBLIC

Slovakia's vineyards start around Bratislava on the Danube, continue along the Carpathian foothills to the north and in the south run as far as the Slovak Tokaj region. Classic Central European vines dominate alongside international favourites; total area is c.12,000 ha. Big money continues to flow into swanky new wineries such as Elesko (Modra, Small Carpathians), a huge facility unrivalled in Central Europe with restaurant, art gallery (Warhol originals) and money from abroad. Other notable producers: Château Belá Riesling (Mužla, Southern Slovakia) with Mosel's Egon Müller involvement famous in NY, Tokyo; Golguz Hlohovec, Karpatská Perla (Šenkvice), Víno Matyšák (Pezinok), Malík & Sons (Modra), Miroslav Dudo (Modra), Château Modra (all Small Carpathians), Movino Veľký Krtíš and Pivnica Radošina (both Central Slovakia) and JJ Ostrožovič (Veľká Tŕňa, Tokaj), while Vinárske závody Topoľčianky and JE Hubert Sereď are, with their seven million bottles each, the country's largest wine and Sekt producers respectively.

ROMANIA

Changing times lie ahead for Romania. On one hand new, quality-focused wineries and vineyard investments continue apace, making Europe's 6th-largest producer one of the few to increase volumes in the tricky 2016 harvest. On the other hand, arrests for tax fraud at the country's biggest winery suggest all is not rosy, though this may create an opportunity for newer wineries fighting for market share. Exports are largely good-value international varietal wines but more interesting local grapes like Fetească (Albă, Regală and Neagră), and rarieties like Negru de Drăgăşani and Novac are now winning listings.

Avincis Mun r w ★→★★ 11' 12 13 15 In dynamic DRĂGĂŞANI region with Alsace winemaker. Try Cuvée Andréi (r), pretty Cuvée Amelie, Negru de Drăgăşani 13, PINOT GR/FETEASCĂ REGALĂ.

Balla Gèza Cri & Mar r p w ★ →★★ Aka Wine Princess. Leading producer in Minis. Best is Stone Wine range from v'yd.

Banat Wine region in w.

Bauer Winery Mun r w ★★ 13 15 Personal project from winemaker at PRINCE ȘTIRBEY, V.gd Crâmposie and FETEASCĂ NEAGRĂ.

Budureasca Mun r w ★→★★ 13 15 300-ha estate in DEALU MARE with British winemaker. Consistent mid-level Budureasca (esp classy Sec Fumé, Vine in Flames FETEASCĂ REGALĂ) and top Origini Res.

Corcova Mun r w ★→★★ 13 15 Renovated C19 royal cellar and v'yds. Try FETEASCĂ NEAGRĂ, CHARD Res, new CAB SAUV-based blend 13.

Cotnari Mold DOC region in MOLD, historic renown for sweet wines but today mostly dry-to-medium styles from FETEASCĂ ALBĂ, Frâncușă, GRASĂ, Tămâioasă.

Oldest modern human footprints found in cave in Romania: 37,000 yrs old.

Cotnari Wine House Mold p w ★ 14 (15) Next-generation producer in COTNARI, 350 ha, founded 2011. Focus is local varieties: Busuioaca de Bohotin, GRAȘA de Cotnari.

Cotnari Winery Mold w sw ★ One of Romania's largest producers with 1200 ha. Mostly dry and semi-dry whites from local grapes. Aged sweet Collection wines *can be long-lived and impressive.*

Crișana & Maramures Region in nw incl DOC Minis. Carastelec (Vinca label) and renovated Nachbil.

Davino Winery Mun r w ★★★ 12' 13 14 15 Top producer with 68 ha in DEALU MARE. Focus on blends for v.gd Dom Ceptura, superb Flamboyant and Rezerva. Local varieties featured in entry level Plai and v.gd Monogram for more complex FETEASCĂS NEAGRĂ and ALBĂ.

Dealu Mare / Dealul Mare Mun Means "The Big Hill". Historic quality zone and DOC on s-facing slopes. Location of promising new boutiques: Crama Basilescu (MERLOT, FETEASCĂ NEAGRĂ), LACERTA, Rotenberg (Merlot, esp Menestrel, Notorius).

Dobrogea Dob Black Sea region. Incl DOC regions of MURFATLAR, Badabag and Sarica Niculitel. Historically famous for sweet, late-harvest CHARD and now for full-bodied reds. New bio Bogdan estate.

DOC (Denumire de Origine Controlată) Romanian term for PDO. Sub-categories incl DOC-CMD for wines harvested at full maturity, DOC-CT for late-harvest and DOC-CIB for noble-harvest. *Vin cu indicatie geografică* (IG) term for PGI.

Domeniul Coroanei Segarcea Mun r w ★ Historic royal estate. Best for whites: FETEASCĂ ALBĂ, TĂMÂIOASĂ (also gd s/sw p). Prestige Marselan, VIOGNIER show promise.

Drăgășani Mun Dynamic region on River Olt. PRINCE ȘTIRBEY pioneered revival, joined by AVINCIS, Negrini, Isarescu, Via Sandu and recently BAUER. Gd for aromatic crisp whites, esp local Crâmposie Selectionată, TĂMÂIOASĂ, zesty SAUV BL. Distinctive local reds: Novac, Negru de Drăgășani.

Girboiu, Crama Mold r w ★→★★ 200 ha in earthquake-prone Vrancea, hence Tectonic label (try Sarba, FETEASCĂ NEAGRĂ) and Epicentrum blends. Only grower of rare Plavaie grape under DYA Livia brand and in Cuartz sparkling.

Halewood Romania Mun r p w ★→★★ 13 15 Smart female winemaker continues to raise quality at British-owned company. Best: Hyperion PINOT GR, CAB SAUV, Kronos PINOT N, Theia CHARD. V'yd selections also v.gd: Scurta VIOGNIER/TĂMÂIOASĂ, Sebes Chard. La Umbra: gd-value commercial range.

Jidvei Trnsyl w ★→★★ 15 Romania's largest v'yd with 2460 ha in Jidvei subregion in TRNSYL. Improved since new winery in 2014 and consultancy from Marc Dworkin (also Bulgaria's Bessa Valley). Stick to dry wines esp Classic SAUV BL, Owner's Choice CHARD Ana, PINOT GR Maria.

Lacerta Mun r w ★★ 12 13 (15) Quality estate in DEALU MARE, named after local lizards. Try Cuvée IX (r) and Cuvée X (w), SHIRAZ.

Liliac Trnsyl r p w ★★→★★★ 13' 15 V.gd Austrian-owned estate; name means "bat". Graceful, fresh whites esp FETEASCĂ REGALĂ, FETEASCĂ ALBĂ, delicious sweet Nectar. Excellent PINOT N red and rosé. Intriguing orange CHARD 14.

Metamorfosis, Viile Mun r w ★★ 13 15 Antinori-owned (*see* Italy) estate in DEALU MARE. Top: Cantvs Primvs CAB SAUV **09** and new FETEASCĂ NEAGRĂ 12. V.gd Via Marchizului Negru de DRĂGĂŞANI 13' and gd Metamorfosis range.

Moldova Largest wine region ne of Carpathians. Borders Republic of Moldova.

Muntenia & Oltenia Hills Major wine region in s covering DOC areas of DEALU MARE, Dealurile Olteniei, DRĂGĂŞANI, Pietroasa, Sâmbureşti, Stefaneşti, Vanju Mare.

Murfatlar Winery Dob r w Major domestic producer in region of same name, but watch this space following management arrests.

Oprişor, Crama Mun r p w ★★→★★★ 13' 15 Exciting Crama Oprişor CAB SAUV, Smerenie red blend and top cuvée Ispita 11'. Consistent La Cetate range. Gd Caloian Rosé, vibrant Rusalca Alba 15.

Petro Vaselo Ban r p w ★★ 13 15 Italian investment in BANAT, organic approach. Gd Bendis (sp), Melgris FETEASCĂ NEAGRĂ, Ovas (r). V.gd entry-level Alb, Roşu, Rosé.

Prince Ştirbey Mun r p w sp ★★→★★★ 13 15 Pioneering estate in DRĂGĂŞANI. V.gd dry whites, esp local Crâmposie Selectionată (still and sparkling), SAUV BL, FETEASCĂ REGALĂ, TĂMÂIOASĂ Sec. V.gd local reds (Novac, Negru de Drăgăşani).

Recaş Winery Ban r p w ★★→★★★ 13 15' Large (980 ha) progressive, consistent estate with longstanding Australian and Spanish winemakers. V.gd-value, bright varietal wines sold as Calusari, Dreambird, Frunza, I heart, I am, Paparuda, Werewolf. Mid-range: La Putere, Sole. Excellent premium wines, esp Cuvée Uberland, Selene reds, Solo Quinta (white blend).

Sahateni, Domeniile Mun r w ★→★★ 12 13 (15) 70-ha estate in DEALU MARE. Try Anima Fete Negre 3, Artisan Alb (w), Rosu (r) and TĂMÂIOASĂ.

Senator Mold r w ★ 850 ha across four regions. Monser and Glia (try Sarba, Babească Neagră) ranges feature Romanian varieties, Omnia is organic, Varius for international grapes.

S.E.R.V.E. Mun r p w ★★→★★★ 12 13 15 Pioneering DEALU MARE winery founded by the much-missed Corsican Count Guy de Poix – new 100% FETEASCĂ NEAGRĂ Cuvée named in his honour. Reliable entry-point Vinul Cavalerului label, excellent Terra Romana range. *Cuvée Charlotte* quality red benchmark.

Transylvania Cool mtn plateau, central Romania. Mostly whites with gd acidity.

Villa Vinea Trnsyl r w ★★ 13 (15) Young Italian-owned estate. Gd whites, esp GEWURZ, SAUV BL, FETEASCĂ REGALĂ and red blend Rubin (not made from Bulgaria's grape).

Vinarte Winery Mun r w ★★ 11 12 13 Italian-led investment with three estates: Villa Zorilor in DEALU MARE, Castel Bolovanu in DRĂGĂŞANI, Terase Danubiane in Vanju Mare. Best: Soare CAB SAUV, Prince Matei MERLOT.

Vincon Winery Mold r w dr sw ★ Major domestic-focused producer with 1500 ha in Vrancea.

MALTA

Malta and Gozo have just over 300 ha of vineyards, mostly owned by growers who sell their crop to the large wineries, including Delicata, Marsovin, and Antinori-owned Meridiana. In addition wines are produced from imported Italian grapes. If you want something typically Maltese, look for local grapes Gellewza (light red, also makes acceptable fizz) and white Girgentina, which is often blended with Chardonnay to produce a succulent full-fruited wine. Malta's most celebrated wine is Marsovin's Grand Maître, an equal blend of Cabernets Sauvignon and Franc, aged in new oak, costly but hardly good value. There are a handful of boutique wineries, some rustic, but others, such as San Niklaw, making high quality but in very limited quantities. San Niklaw's Vermentino, Sangiovese and Syrah are noteworthy.

Greece

The economic misfortunes of Greece would be enough on their own to make the kind-hearted want to offer sympathy and support to a country with such problems. Happily sentiment is not needed in assessing where Greek wine fits in to our diet; the answer is high on the list of tasty, invigorating alternatives. The best new wines of Greece are not aping anyone; they come from original indigenous vines with characters and flavours of their own. The fact that for most wine-lovers Greek wine is still left-field stuff is all the more reason to choose it. The industry is a great success story in troubled times – though you'll need to refer to Grape Varieties pp.16–26 to sort out some of the unfamiliar names, from Agiorgitiko to Xinomavro. Abbreviations: Aegean Islands (Aeg), Central Greece (C Gr), Ionian Islands (Ion), Macedonia (Mac), Peloponnese (Pelop), Thessaloniki (Thess).

Alpha Estate Mac ★★★ Highly acclaimed estate in AMYNTEO with outstanding v'yds. Excellent MERLOT/SYRAH/XINOMAVRO blend, exotic MALAGOUSIA, Xinomavro Res from old, ungrafted vines is New World in style.

Amynteo Mac (POP) The coolest appellation of Greece, XINOMAVRO-dominated. Fresh reds, excellent rosés, both still and sparkling.

Argyros Aeg ★★★★ Top SANTORINI producer; exemplary VINSANTO aged 20 yrs+ in cask (★★★★). Exciting KTIMA (w), age for a decade. Vareli (w) is solid, balanced. Spicy, rare MAVROTRAGANO (r) is a top example.

Avantis C Gr ★★★ Boutique winery in Evia, v'yds in Boetia too. SYRAH specialist with exquisite Aghios Chronos Syrah/VIOGNIER, Rhône-like Collection Syrah and rich MALAGOUSIA. New Delfinia project in SANTORINI, at GAVALAS winery, is v. promising.

Biblia Chora Mac ★★★ Big success: benchmark SAUV BL/ASSYRTIKO. Ovilos range (r w), could rival top B'x at triple the price. Try Vidiano. Sister estate of GEROVASSILIOU.

Boutari, J & Son ★ →★★★★ Historic producer across regions but with heart in NAOUSSA. Excellent value, esp *Grande Res Naoussa* to age for decades. Top wines: Oropedio MOSCHOFILERO and 1879 Legacy Naoussa.

Carras, Domaine Mac ★★ History-making estate at Halkidiki, with own red and white POP (Côtes de Meliton). Chateau Carras has been a trailblazer, ambitious SYRAH, floral MALAGOUSIA; LIMNIO (r) might be *best value* of all.

Cephalonia Ion Important island with three POPs: mineral ROBOLA (w), rare MUSCAT (w sw) and excellent MAVRODAPHNE (r sw). Dry Mavrodaphne is a trend here (as elsewhere in Greece).

Dalamaras ★★★ Stellar producer in NAOUSSA. XINOMAVROS of great purity.

Dougos C Gr ★★★ Excellent reds, incl Châteauneuf-like Methymon, but focus is now on RAPSANI, esp Old Vines.

Driopi Pelop ★★★ Venture of TSELEPOS in NEMEA. Top wine: single-v'yd Res but try also Tavel-like Driopi rosé.

Economou Crete ★★★ One of great artisans of Greece, with brilliant, hard-to-find Sitia (r). Burgundian in style but truly Greek.

Gaia Aeg, Pelop ★★★ Top NEMEA and SANTORINI producer. Great Thalassitis Santorini (Submerged is a version aged underwater) and elegantly oaked *wild-ferment Assyrtiko*. Top wine: *Gaia Estate* from NEMEA keeps 15+ years. Dazzling "S" red (AGIORGITIKO with a touch of SYRAH).

Gavalas Aeg ★★→★★★★ Rising SANTORINI producer. Must-try v. rare Katsano variety (w).

Gentilini Ion ★★→★★★ Leading Cephalonia producer, incl *steely Robola*. Marvellous rare dry MAVRODAPHNE Eclipse (r), serious SYRAH.

Gerovassiliou Mac ★★★ Quality (and trend) leader. The original ASSYRTIKO/MALAGOUSIA and a top oaked Malagousia, a grape of which he is the leading light. Top reds Avaton from indigenous varieties, and SYRAH. Linked with BIBLIA CHORA, Kokkalis wineries (and Escapades in Stellenbosch).

Goumenissa Mac (POP) ★→★★★ XINOMAVRO/Negoska red, lighter than NAOUSSA. Esp Chatzyvaritis (★★★), Tatsis (★★★), Aidarinis (single v'yd ★★★), BOUTARI (Filiria).

Hatzidakis Aeg ★★★ Top-class producer redefining SANTORINI appellation; extremely powerful, single-v'yd wines. Nihteri, Mylos, Louros (★★★★) ASSYRTIKOS age decades.

Helios Pelop Umbrella name for Semeli, Nassiakos and Orinos Helios wines, gd value across the range. Top Nassiakos MANTINIA.

Karydas Mac ★★★ Tiny family estate and amazing v'yd in NAOUSSA with great attention to detail, crafting classic, compact but always refined XINOMAVRO.

Katogi-Strofilia Att, Pelop ★★→★★★ Initially from mountainous Epirus. Katogi was the original cult Greek wine. Top: KTIMA Averoff and Rossiu di Munte range from plots at 1000m+. Charming Strofilia (w).

Katsaros Thess ★★★ Small winery on Mt Olympus. KTIMA (CAB SAUV/MERLOT) is Greek classic. Tight XINOMAVRO Valos is the latest addition to the range.

Kir-Yanni Mac ★★→★★★ V'yds in NAOUSSA, AMINTEO. Scion of the BOUTARIS family. Trendsetting, age-worthy reds incl Ramnista Naoussa, Diaporos, Blue Fox. Try Akakies sparklings (p w) to wash away the tannins.

Ktima Estate Some insist on using the term Ktima in Latin script on labels. They are correct.

Lazaridi, Nico Mac ★→★★★ Wineries in Drama, Kavala. Gd Château Nico Lazaridi (r w), interesting Cavalieri range. Top: Magiko Vouno red (CAB SAUV), white (SAUV BL).

Lazaridis, Kostas Att, Mac ★★★ Wineries in Drama, Attika (under Oenotria Land label). Popular Amethystos label. Top wine: amazing Cava Amethystos CAB SAUV, followed by Oenotria Land Cab Sauv/AGIORGITIKO. V. trendy, Provence-like Julia (p).

Lyrarakis Crete ★★→★★★ Producer from Heraklio, reviving old Cretan varieties like Plyto, Dafni and Melissaki, practically saving these from extinction. Hard-to-find *single-v'yd versions* are extraordinary. Extremely interesting ASSYRTIKO.

Manoussakis Crete ★★★ Great estate with Rhône-inspired blends but Greek varieties on way. Solid Nostos range, led by age-worthy, powerful ROUSSANNE, SYRAH.

Mantinia Pelop (POP) w High-altitude, cool region. Fresh, crisp, low alcohol, almost Germanic styles from the charming, MUSCAT-scented *Moschofilero*. Sparklers are allowed now under POP designation.

Mercouri Pelop ★★★ One of the most beautiful estates in Greece, on w coast. V.gd KTIMA (r), delicious RODITIS (w), complex dry MAVRODAPHNE (r), classy REFOSCO (r).

Monemvassia-Malvasia Pelop Latest POP (2010), Monemvassia, ASSYRTIKO and Kydonitsa varieties re-create legendary sun-dried, sweet whites of Middle Ages: original Malmsey. So far, only one eg, in market, by Monemvassia Winery (★★★).

Naoussa Mac ★★→★★★ (POP) Top-quality region for sophisticated, fragrant XINOMAVRO. Best examples on a par in quality and style (but not price) with Barolo. Top producers incl DALAMARAS, KARYDAS, KIR-YIANNI, THIMIOPOULOS.

Nemea Pelop ★★→★★★ (POP) AGIORGITIKO reds. Huge potential for quality; styles from fresh to classic to exotic. (*see* DRIOPI, GAIA, HELIOS, NEMEION, PAPAÏOANNOU, SKOURAS). High-altitude v'yds are increasing in importance, new oak less so.

Nemeion Pelop ★★★ A KTIMA in NEMEA, high prices (esp Igemon red), opulent style.

Greek appellations

Terms are changing in line with other EU countries. The quality appellations of OPAP and OPE are now fused together into the POP (or PDO) category. Regional wines, known as TO, will now be PGE (or PGI). Don't you love it?

GREECE

> **The different faces of Xinomavro**
>
> XINOMAVRO is multifaceted red king of north, with no fewer than four appellations dedicated to it: NAOUSSA, AMYNTEO, GOUMENISSA, RAPSANI. It can produce excellent still rosés (THIMIOPOULOS), white and pink fizz (KIR-YIANNI, Karanikas makes a great BdN), reds that can be traditional (BOUTARI, Foundis), heavyweights (ALPHA ESTATE, Chatzivaritis), v. linear (DALAMARAS, KARYDAS) or just wild (Kokkinos, Tatsis). Great value all round.

Palyvos Pelop ★★→★★★ Excellent producer in NEMEA making modern, big-framed reds. Single-v'yd selections are excellent. Most interesting VIOGNIER.

Papaïoannou Pelop ★★★ If NEMEA were Burgundy, Papaïoannou would be Jayer. Benchmark range: excellent value KTIMA, Palea Klimata (old vines), Microklima (micro-single-v'yd), top-end Terroir. Most vintages need at least a decade.

Pavlidis Mac ★★★ Outstanding estate at Drama. Trendy Thema (w) ASSYRTIKO/SAUV BL. Emphasis range: varietals incl classy Assyrtiko, AGIORGITIKO, TEMPRANILLO. Thema (r) from Agiorgitiko/SYRAH is dazzling.

Rapsani Thess ★★★ POP on Mt Olympus. Made famous in 90s by TSANTALIS (try Grande Res); new producers, ie. DOUGOS and new venture by THIMIOPOULOS, have different interpretations. XINOMAVRO, Stavroto, Krasato. High-altitude v'yds best.

Retsina Seen by many as the nail in the coffin of Greek wine, but new Retsinas (eg. GAIA or Kechris), packed with freshness are a great alternative to Fino Sherry. Yes, great, even age-worthy Retsinas exist.

Samos Aeg ★★→★★★★ (POP) Island famed for sweet MUSCAT Blanc. Esp (fortified) Anthemis, sun-dried Nectar. Rare old bottlings are ★★★★ in all but price, ie. hard-to-find Nectar 75 or 80.

Santo Aeg ★★→★★★ Most successful SANTORINI co-op. Vibrant portfolio with dazzling Grande Res, rich yet crisp VINSANTOS. ASSYRTIKO and Nyhteri are great value. Sparklers are recent (and exciting) development. Restrained in style.

Santorini Aeg ★★★→★★★★ Dramatic volcanic island n of CRETE and POP for white (dr sw). Luscious VINSANTO, salty, *bone-dry Assyrtiko*. Top producers: GAIA, HATZIDAKIS, SIGALAS, SANTO. Possibly cheapest ★★★★ dry whites around, able to age for 20 yrs. World class. Reds from MAVROTRAGANO (not incl in POP) can be sublime. Apex of Greek wine.

Sigalas Aeg ★★★★ Leading light of SANTORINI. Stylish VINSANTO, excellent MAVROTRAGANO. Nyhteri, Cavalieros (dr w) out of this world. Seven Villages microcuvées range breaks new ground.

Skouras Pelop ★★→★★★ V. consistent range. Lean, wild-yeast Salto MOSCHOFILERO rewards keeping. Top reds: high-altitude Grande Cuvée NEMEA, Megas Oenos. Solera-aged, multi-vintage Labyrinth is weird but beautiful.

Tatsis Mac ★★★ Experimental producer in GOUMENISSA, wide range of styles, incl orange. Top Old Roots XINOMAVRO.

Thimiopoulos Mac ★★★★ New-age NAOUSSA with spectacular export success, sold as Earth and Sky or Uranos. Must try. New project in RAPSANI. Young Vines is an interesting intro to this winery.

Tsantalis Mac ★→★★★ Long-est producer. Huge range. Gd Metoxi (r), RAPSANI Res, Grande Res, gd-value wines from Thrace. Made monastery wines from Mount Athos famous, eg. excellent Avaton.

Tselepos Pelop ★★★ Top MANTINIA and NEMEA (see DRIOPI) producer, with an intriguing range of MOSCHOFILEROS. Greece's best MERLOT (★★★★ Kokkinomylos) and single-v'yd Avlotopi CAB SAUV not far behind. Venture in SANTORINI with Canava Chrysou.

Vinsanto Aeg ★★★→★★★★ Sun-dried, cask-aged luscious ASSYRTIKO and Aidani from SANTORINI can age forever.

Zitsa ★★ Mountainous, cool POP. Delicate Debina (w sp). Top: Glinavos, Zoinos.

Eastern Mediterranean & North Africa

EASTERN MEDITERRANEAN

A wine-lover from 2000 years ago would not be surprised to see wines produced here, including what is today Cyprus, Israel, Lebanon and Turkey. They were well known in their day. In the last 20 years the Eastern Mediterranean has gone through a wine renaissance. Perfect climates, high altitudes, modern technology and internationally trained winemakers have made the difference. Each country is making far better wines than it did even only ten years ago. A fascinating region for wine historians, but a new region for many wine-lovers today.

Cyprus

Cyprus is a two-speed wine country today – on the one hand all-inclusive holidays and cheap imports are putting pressure on volume producers, while on the other hand the island's leading producers are making better wines than ever before and often selling out. A focus on rare local varieties like Yiannoudi, Promara and Morokanella continues, along with improving Xynisteri and Maratheftiko.

Aes Ambelis r p w br ★→★★ 13 14 15 (16) Consistent, appealing XYNISTERI-based whites and rosé. V.gd modern version of COMMANDARIA.

Argyrides Estate (Vasa) r w ★★ 13 14 15 Immaculate pioneering estate winery. Excellent MARATHEFTIKO, MOURVÈDRE. V.gd VIOGNIER, Agyrides MERLOT/CAB SAUV, VLASSIDES consults.

Ayia Mavri w sw ★→★★ 13 14 15 Stick to gd sweet MUSCAT, plus new COMMANDARIA 10.

Commandaria Rich, sweet PDO wine from sun-dried XYNISTERI and MAVRO grapes undergoing revival. Claims to be most ancient named wine still in production. New-generation producers: AES AMBELIS, Anama, Ktima Gerolemo, KYPEROUNDA, TSIAKKAS. Traditional styles: St Barnabas (Sodap), St John (KEO), Centurion (ETKO).

Constantinou r w ★→★★ In Lemesos region; Ayioklima XYNISTERI DYA and CAB SAUV.

ETKO & Olympus r w br ★→★★ Former big producer, improving since move to Olympus winery. Best for St Nicholas COMMANDARIA 12 and superior Centurion 00.

K&K Vasilikon Winery r p w ★★ 12 13 14 15 Family winery owned by three brothers. Gd DYA XYNISTERI, Finalia rosé and consistent reds: Ayios Onoufrios, Methy.

Kamanterena (SODAP) r p w ★→★★ 13 14 15 Winery name of large SODAP co-op in Pafos hills. Gd-value competent DYA whites and rosé esp LEFKADA/SHIRAZ. V.gd COMMANDARIA St Barnabas 02.

KEO r w br ★ 13 15 Winemaking now moved to Mallia Estate in hills. Ktima Keo range is best esp Heritage (r). Classic St John ★★COMMANDARIA.

Kyperounda r w br ★★→★★★ 13' 14 15' Some of Europe's highest v'yds at 1450m. Petritis is standard-setting XYNISTERI. Excellent CHARD esp new own-v'yd Epos. Reds v.gd: SHIRAZ, Andessitis, top-red Epos. Excellent modern COMMANDARIA 08.

Cyprus is still phylloxera-free, and some vines may be centuries old.

Makkas r p w ★→★★ 12 13 14 15 Former economist with garage winery in Pafos region. Gd XYNISTERI, MARATHEFTIKO, SYRAH, Red.

Tsiakkas r p w br ★★→★★★ 13 14 15 Banker turned winemaker. Expressive whites esp SAUV BL, XYNISTERI. Also v.gd Yiannoudi, Vamvakada (aka MARATHEFTIKO), new modern COMMANDARIA 08.

Vlassides r w ★★→★★★ 13' 14 15 UC Davis-trained Vlassides makes benchmark SHIRAZ, v.gd Grifos white (XYNISTERI/SAUV BL), CAB SAUV, excellent long-ageing Private Collection.

Cyprus has possibly the longest harvest anywhere – from late July to November.

Vouni Panayia r p w ★→★★ 13 14 15 Pioneer with local grapes. Try Promara, Spourtiko, MARATHEFTIKO.

Zambartas r p w ★★→★★★ 13' 14 15 Top family winery making intense CAB FR/LEFKADA rosé, v.gd SHIRAZ/Lefkada red, excellent MARATHEFTIKO, zesty XYNISTERI, esp exciting new single v'yd version. Promising local Yiannoudi.

Israel

Israeli wine has moved northwards and eastwards in search of higher altitudes. The original vineyards were in the hot and humid coastal regions. Now the best wines may be found from the Upper Galilee, Golan Heights and Judean Hills. Israeli winemakers are young, dynamic and inventive. Wines are becoming more elegant and terroir-led. Abbreviations: Galilee (Gal), Golan (Gol), Judean Hills (Jud), Negev (Neg), Samson (Sam), Shomron (Shom); Upper Galilee (Up Gal).

Abaya Gal p r ★★ Terroirist. CARIGNAN Pét-Nat (*see* A Little Learning) rosé. Moving towards natural.

Agur Jud r w ★→★★ Elegant reds. Complex barrel-aged rosé.

Barkan-Segal Gal, Sam r w ★→★★ Israel's largest winery and largest exporter. Barkan, Segal are marketed separately. Assemblage gd, and interesting blends.

Bar-Maor Shom r ★★ Min-intervention winemaking. Intriguing reds. Lilith best.

Carmel Up Gal r w sp ★★ Historic winery. Complex Kayoumi v'yd RIES, Fruity, flavourful 4 Vats (r). Gd value Selected. New bold MALBEC.

Congrats to Israel's 1st MW, Eran Pick (Tzora). Only 2nd from East Med.

Château Golan Gol r (w) ★★→★★★ Geshem (r w) V.gd Mediterranean blends. Eliad is bold, concentrated.

Clos de Gat Jud r w ★★★→★★★★ Classy estate exuding quality, style, individuality. Powerful Sycra SYRAH 06 07' 09 11, rare MERLOT and traditional, buttery CHARD are remarkable. Fresh entry-level Chanson (r w) gd value.

Cremisan Jud r w ★→★★ Palestinian wines made in a monastery from indigenous grapes: Baladi, Dabouki, Hamdani, Jandali.

Dalton Up Gal r w ★→★★ Family winery. New young winemaker. Alma blends of interest.

Domaine du Castel Jud r w ★★★→★★★★ Pioneer of Jud. Set standards in Israel for style, quality. Characterful, supple Grand Vin 08' 09' 10 11 12 13' 14. Plush Petit Castel. Quality CHARD. New La Vie (r w) gd value.

Feldstein Gal r w ★★ Artisan. Excellent Anu red blend and GRENACHE. Also Dabouki.

Flam Jud, Gal r (w) ★★★★ Founded by brothers. Superb, elegant B'x blend Noble 08' 09 10' 11' 12. Fruit-forward SYRAH, deep MERLOT. Classico great value. Excellent, fresh, fragrant white (SAUV BL/CHARD), crisp rosé.

Galilee Quality region in n, esp higher altitude Up Gal.

Galil Mtn Up Gal r w ★★ Pioneering draught wine in Israel. Yiron always gd value.

Golan Heights High-altitude plateau, with volcanic tufa and basalt soil.

Gush Etzion Jud r w ★→★★ Central mtn v'yds. Aromatic SAUV BL, gd CAB FR.

Jezreel Valley Shom ★→★★ Gd single-v'yd old-vine Israeli variety Argaman.

Judean Hills Quality region rising towards Jerusalem. Terra rossa on limestone.

Kishor Gal ★→★★ Part of village for adults with special needs. Elegant Savant (r).

Kosher A designation that is not relevant to quality; and some can be v.gd.

Remember not all kosher wines are Israeli and not all Israeli wines are kosher.

Lewinsohn Gal r w ★★★ Quality *garagiste* in a garage. Exquisite, lean CHARD. Red a chewy Mediterranean blend of SYRAH/CARIGNAN/PETITE SIRAH.

Maia Shom r w ★★ Innovative Mediterranean-style wines. Mare Nostrum chewy, refreshing. Greek consultants.

Margalit Gal, Shom r ★★★→★★★★ Israel's first cult wine. Father-and-son-owned. B'x blend Enigma 11' 12 13' 14. Complex CAB FR. Fine, well defined CAB SAUV. Wines with gd ageing potential. New GSM blend.

Mia Luce Gal ★★→★★★ *Garagiste*. SYRAH with stems: smooth, Northern Rhône feel.

Montefiore Jud r w ★★ Fruity, chewy unoaked red and fresh white gd value. Complex, quality PETITE SIRAH. Adam M, same family, contributes to this book.

Negev Neg Desert region in s of country. V'yds at high elevations.

Pelter Gol r w (sp) ★★ Fresh whites with gd acidity. Kosher label Matar.

Recanati Gal r w ★★★ Quality from prestige Special Res 09' 11' 12' 13, to entry-level Yasmin. Complex, wild CARIGNAN. First ever Israeli wine from Marawi grape.

Recanati Marawi: result of cooperation between Palestinian grower, Israeli maker, Holy Land variety.

Samson Central region incl the JUD plain and foothills, se of Tel Aviv.

Sea Horse Jud r (w) ★★ Idiosyncratic, artistic winemaker. V.gd James CHENIN BL.

Shomron Shom Region with v'yds mainly around Mt Carmel and Zichron Ya'acov.

Shvo Up Gal r w ★★★ Non-interventionist grower-winemaker. Super-rustic Mediterranean red. Rare Gershon SAUV BL, racy CHENIN BL. Characterful rosé.

Sphera Jud w ★★★ White Concept RIES, CHARD, SAUV BL and White Page blend quality with crispness. Outstanding, rare Signature.

Tabor Gal r w sp ★★→★★★ V.gd whites, incl SAUV BL, RIES, Har CHARD. Adama (r) v.gd value. Complex, elegant Malkiya: single v'yd CAB SAUV.

Teperberg Jud, Sam r w sp ★→★★ Large family winery. Gd value at every price point.

Tulip Gal r (w) ★★ Rich, opulent Black Tulip. Racy, refreshing Net SAUV BL.

Tzora Jud r w ★★★★ Terroir-led; talented winemaker. Crisp Shoresh (SAUV BL). JUD Red great value. Complex, elegant prestige Misty Hills (CAB SAUV/SYRAH) 09 10' 11 12' 13'. Luscious Or dessert.

Vitkin Jud r w ★★→★★★ Pioneering CARIGNAN. Entry-level gd honest wines.

Yaacov Oryah Sam ★★→★★★ Creative artisan. V.gd orange wines. Superb bottle-aged EFM.

Yarden Gol r w sp ★★→★★★ Brought New World technology to Israel. Rare, prestige Katzrin 07 08' 11' 12. Big-selling brand Hermon Red. Gd Blanc de Blancs and Brut Rosé. Delicious sw Heights Wine. New crisp PINOT GR.

Yatir Jud r (w) ★★★ Desert winery with high-altitude v'yds. Velvety, concentrated Yatir Forest 09 10 11' 12. Powerful PETIT VERDOT.

Lebanon

Problems never seem to leave poor Lebanon, but nor does the indomitable spirit of the Lebanese winemakers. More money is being invested in wineries, and new regions other than the Bekaa Valley are being explored. Interesting times.

Atibaia r ★★ *Garagiste*. Elegant red blend with soft tannins. One to watch.

Chateau Belle-Vue r (w) ★★★ Le Château a plush blend of B'x grapes and SYRAH.

Château Ka r w ★→★★ Great-value, fruity cherry-berry Cadet de Ka.

Château Kefraya r w ★★→★★★ Fine, ripe, concentrated *Comte de M* 08 09' 10' 11'. Full, oaky Comtesse de M (CHARD/VIOGNIER).

Chateau Ksara r w ★★ Founded 1857. Res du Couvent is fruity, easy drinking and full of flavour.

Château Marsyas r (w) ★★ Crisp CHARD, SAUV BL; deep, powerful red. Owner of complex, savoury ★★★Dom Bargylus (Syria). Stéphane Derenoncourt consults.

Chateau Musar r w ★★★→★★★★ Icon wine of the e Med, in family of late legend Serge Hochar. CAB SAUV/CINSAULT/CARIGNAN 02 03 04 05' 07' 08 09. *Unique recognizable style*. Best after 15–20 yrs in bottle. Indigenous Obaideh and Merwah (w) age indefinitely; younger, fruitier Hochar (r) now higher profile.

Bekaa Valley part of same faults system as Sea of Galilee, Dead Sea, Great Rift Valley.

Clos St. Thomas r w ★→★★ Soft, plummy reds. Ch St. Thomas intense but rounded.

Domaine de Baal r (w) ★★ Powerful, heady estate red from organic v'yd.

Domaine des Tourelles r w ★★→★★★ Blockbuster SYRAH, outstanding Marquis des Beys, fragrant white. Maybe Lebanon's fastest improving winery.

Domaine Wardy r w ★→★★ Gd value. Whites with good acidity and typicity.

IXSIR r w ★★ Inky, full-bodied reds, quality floral whites and fresh rosé.

Massaya r w ★★→★★★ Entry-level v.gd-value, prestige wine full-bodied and high-quality. Best are Rhône-style blends: sun and spice of Lebanon.

Turkey

Government strictures and growers who prefer to grow raisins are just two of the problems here. But grape varieties like Boğazkere, Oküzgözü, Narince are original, characterful, and quality gets better all the time: less oak, more elegance.

Büyülübağ r (w) ★★ One of the new small, quality wineries. Gd CAB SAUV.

Corvus r w ★★ Boutique winery, Bozcaada island (ancient Tenedos). Powerful Corpus.

Doluca r w ★→★★ DLC label showcases local varieties. Gd rounded OKÜZGÖZÜ.

Kavaklidere r w sp ★→★★★ Pendore estate is best, esp ÖKÜZGÖZÜ, SYRAH. Gd value at every price. Stéphane Derenoncourt consults.

Narince vine leaves (for stuffing with rice) v. popular; cost even more than grapes.

Kayra r w ★→★★ Spicy SHIRAZ, fresh NARINCE. Rustic *Buzbag* from OKÜZGÖZÜ, BOĞAZKERE. Californian winemaker.

Sevilen r w ★→★★ International variety specialist. Deep SYRAH, aromatic SAUV BL.

Suvla r w ★→★★ Full-bodied B'x blend Sur, and fruity SYRAH backed by oak.

Urla r w ★★ Tempus is red blend with complexity, depth and length.

Vinkara r w ★ Charming NARINCE and cherry-berry KALECIK KARASI.

NORTH AFRICA

Once one of world's biggest wine producers, reduced to a sad little rump, Algeria gone, Morocco the one survivor with aspirations, still attracting some French investment. Tourists need not despair.

Bernard Magrez Mor r ★★ Tannic and spicy SYRAH/GRENACHE in Southern Rhône style. Meaty.

Castel Frères Mor r p ★ Gd-value brands like Bonassia, Halana, Larroque, Sahari.

Celliers de Meknès, Les Mor r p w ★→★★ Virtual a monopoly in Mor. Château Roslane is best.

Domaine Neferis Tun r p w ★→★★ Calastrasi joint venture. Selian CARIGNAN best.

Ouled Thaleb Mor r p w ★★ Medaillon generous blend of CAB SAUV/MERLOT/SYRAH. Lively Syrah Tandem (Syrocco in US): Alain Graillot (Rhône) joint venture.

Val d'Argan Mor r p w ★→★★ At Essaouira. Gd value: Mogador. Best: Orients.

Vignerons de Carthage Tun r p w ★ Best from UCCV co-op: Magon Magnus (r).

Vin Gris ★ Pale pink resort of the thirsty. Castel Boulaouane brand best known.

Volubilia Mor r p w ★→★★ Best delicate pink *vin gris* in Morocco.

Asia & Old Russian Empire

Perhaps a curious appellation, but how else to describe this historic, wide-ranging bit of geography?

ASIA

China Wine production has taken a dip as a result of China's anti-corruption drive, but some producers are focusing on quality and value. China is still the world's 5th-largest producer and 4th-largest v'yd, with around 680,000 ha of vines, though mostly for table grapes and raisins; only c.15 per cent goes to making wine. Most v'yds are n of the Yangtze River, from far-flung nw Xinjiang province (c.20 per cent plantings) to n-central Ningxia and Shanxi, and the e-coastal provinces of Liaoning and Hebei. Around 60 per cent is CAB SAUV, followed by MERLOT, CHARD, Cab Gernischt and SYRAH. There's some RIES, WELSCHRIESLING, UGNI BL, SEM, PINOT N, PETIT VERDOT, GAMAY and, more recently, Marselan, Petit MANSENG and VIDAL. One of the biggest challenges in the n is the harsh winters: temperatures can fall to -20°C. Vines have to be buried in autumn to survive. Coastal Shandong province has summer rain and typhoons. Newer high-altitude (2200–2700m) sites in s Yunnan province (bordering Laos and Myanmar) are promising, although remote. Moët-Hennessy Shangri-La Winery's Ao Yun Cab/Merlot has been well received, but is expensive. Ningxia is the "Bordeaux of China". Gd reds: Jia Bei Lan, Silver Heights, Legacy Peak, Domaine Helan Mountain (Pernod Ricard), Leirenshou; sparkling: Moët Hennessy's Dom Chandon. Also Sha Po Tou Cab Gernischt, Fontaine Sable Fragrance Merlot and late-harvest Chard, Cuvée No. 61. The future? More and, in some instances, better, with more foreign involvement.

India's challenges incl monsoons, heat, humidity and high duties. Out of 115,000 ha of vines, only 2000 ha make wine, mainly SAUV BL, CHENIN BL, VIOGNIER (w) and SYRAH, CAB SAUV, MERLOT, GRENACHE (r). There is some CHARD and a little TEMPRANILLO, ZIN, SANGIOVESE. Main regions: Maharashtra, Karnataka, Andhra Pradesh. Sauv Bl remains the best white: Sula, Grover (esp Zampa Art Collection), Charosa. Labruyère family (Domaine Jacques Prieur, Burgundy; Château Rouget, Pomerol; Champagne JM Labruyère) have invested in Grover. Gd reds: Myra Res Shiraz, Grover Zampa La Res Cab Sauv/SHIRAZ. Moët Hennessy's Chandon is gd sparkling; also York Sparkling Cuvée (Chenin Bl), Fratelli Wines Gran Cuvée Brut and still Sangiovese Bianco.

Japan is now making more Koshu than all its reds put together.

Japanese wine consumption continues to grow, even though only about a 3rd is "domestic" wine (regulations are so lax that only about a quarter of that 3rd is from domestically grown grapes). Yamanashi Prefecture in Honshu island is the heart of Japanese wine-growing, with a tradition going back to the mid-1870s; 40 per cent of Japan's 19,000 ha are here. Japan's 200+ wineries are mainly in Yamanashi, Nagano and Hokkaido. Annual production is now c.800,000hl. Most small to mid-sized wineries combine wine with table grapes. Large brewers dominate: Sapporo, Kirin, Suntory. The most ambitious, though, are small family wineries using 100 per cent homegrown grapes, esp hybrid Muscat Bailey for light red, and indigenous, fashionable, high-acid white Koshu (which has quite a fan club). Top: Grace Winery (Blanc de Blancs sparkling also outstanding), Chateau Mercian, Lumiere, Haramo and Soryu. Chitose Winery in Hokkaido in far n, famous for ski resorts, produces a superb PINOT N.

THE OLD RUSSIAN EMPIRE

Russians are buying more domestic wine. Crimea, whose historic winemaking was established on the orders of the last tsars, once again attracts attention for quality. Other important areas are located around the Black Sea and in the Caucasus. Internationally Georgia is suited to be a new darling of the wine world, both for its ancient vine varieties and production methods (especially clay amphorae, locally called *kwevri*). A boom of private investment in Armenia, another country with a real wine heritage, makes it an exciting place to watch.

Armenia vies with Georgia as a birthplace of winemaking (the most ancient winery dates back 6100 yrs). Its remote mountainous v'yds are phylloxera-free. Indigenous white Voskeat and Garandamak, red Areni, Hindogny and Kakhet can give high quality. ArmAs, Tierras de Armenia, Zorah Karasi use internationally renowned consultants.

Georgia Private households own 90 per cent of Georgia's 48,000 ha of v'yds. Wine is deeply rooted in culture, linked with Christianity. With over 7000 yrs of viticultural history, Georgia has preserved its unique grapes (around 500), production techniques, wine styles. The two principal varieties are red SAPERAVI (anything from easy and semi-sweet to robust, tannic, age-worthy and white RKATSITELI (lively, refreshing). Handmade *kwevris* (amphorae), now with UNESCO World Heritage status, are a symbol of Georgian winemaking and inspire winemakers worldwide. Another heritage is production of skin-macerated whites, known as Kakheti method, and more fashionably as "orange" wine. Leading large and small producers incl Badagoni, Château Mukhrani, GWS, Tbilvino, Kindzmarauli Marani, Marani (TWC), Pheasant's Tears, Schuchmann.

Kwevri School & Academy open 2017. Does what it says. (*Kwevri* = clay amphorae).

Moldova Squeezed between Ukraine and Romania, Moldova has over 110,000 ha of v'yds. Wine is vital to the economy, employing 10 per cent of the population. The quality bar is rising. European grapes are historically grown along with typically Romanian (w) FETEASCĂ ALBĂ, Fetească Regală, (r) Rară Neagră, Fetească Neagră and others. Historic red blends Roşu de Purcari (CAB SAUV, MERLOT, MALBEC) and Negru de Purcari (Cab Sauv, Rara Neagră, SAPERAVI) can be seriously interesting. Along with flagship Vinăria Purcari, producers of note are Asconi, Château Vartely, Cricova (sparkling), Et Cetera, Fautur, Gitana, Lion Gri, Vinăria Bostavan, Vinăria din Vale.

Russia Winemaking is on the increase. Reliable quality remains the problem, as well as a legal loophole that allows any wine bottled inside the country to be called Russian. V'yds stretch from the Black Sea coast to the River Volga; the Krasnodar region is the biggest producer. Harsh climate is a hazard for inland v'yds: they have to be covered for winter. Mostly international grapes are grown: reds fare better than whites. For authentic Russian try red Krasnostop (tannic, rustic) or Tsimliansky (pleasant fizzy red). Château le Grand Vostock and Lefkadia perform consistently; look for top ranges of Abrau Durso (sparkling) and Fanagoria. Burnier, Gai-Kodzor, Rayevskoye are worthy smaller producers.

Ukraine Natural conditions are favourable, but most production is industrial. International grapes (r w) dominate. For gd quality seek wineries with estate-grown grapes, eg. Guliev Wines, Oleg Repin, Pavel Shvets, Prince Trubetskoy Winery, Veles. Historically the best (often excellent) wines were modelled on Sherry, Port, Madeira and Champagne. Also, curiously, Cahors. Gd fortifieds have long been made by Koktebel, Magarach, Massandra, Solnechnaya Dolina. For traditional-method fizz try Artyomovsk Winery, Novy Svet, Zolotaya Balka.

United States

NORTH COAST Mendocino Sierra Foothills
Anderson Redwood Valley
Valley Clear Lake
  Clear Lake

onoma Coast
Northern
Sonoma Napa Valley El Dorado Shenandoah Valley
  Carneros Amador
Sonoma Coombsville/Oak Knoll **CENTRAL**
Valley Lodi Calaveras **VALLEY**
  Clarksburg

San Francisco

Livermore Valley

Santa Clara Valley

Santa Cruz
Mountains

Monterey *Salinas*

Carmel Valley/Arroyo Seco
Santa Lucia
Highlands San Lucas

NEVADA

Lake Tahoe

Sacramento

San Joaquin

O Fresno

CENTRAL COAST

Pacific Ocean

Abbreviations used in the text
(see also Principal Vineyard/
Viticultural Areas p.247, p.264, p.268):

Paso Robles

CALIFORNIA

San Luis Obispo
Edna Valley/Arroyo GV
Santa Maria Valley
Santa Barbera
Sta Rita Hills
Santa Ynez Valley

CA	California
Clark	Clarksburg, CA
Coomb	Coombsville, CA
Mad	Madera, CA
Mend	Mendocino, CA
Mont	Monterey, CA
Oak Knoll	Oak K, CA
San LO	San Luis Obispo, CA
Santa B	Santa Barbera, CA
Santa Cz Mts	Santa Cruz Mountains, CA
Son	Sonoma, CA
ID	Idaho
NJ	New Jersey

Santa Barbara

OH	Ohio
OR	Oregon
PA	Pennsylvania
PNW	Pacific Northwest
TX	Texas
VA	Virginia
WA	Washington

O Los Angeles

California is not about to get crowded out. It (or is it she?) makes 90 per cent of US wine and will always dominate the picture. But there's no ignoring the other states – which is most of them – elbowing their way in. In my earliest editions in the 70s California had nine pages, New York State two. Oregon? Washington? They hardly made wine. Not a mention. Oregon reached 1000 acres in 1980 and Washington shortly after. Today a new winery opens in Washington every 15 days. The equivalent figure for the whole of the US would be scary. In past editions we divided the country into regions, but now we list all the most wine-aspirational states in alphabetical order. It's states, not regions, that have patriotic pride. It has been a struggle to fit all the local leaders in, even in our dreadful condensed style. One thing's sure: next year it will be tighter still.

Arizona

Arizona Stronghold: ★ flagship red Rhône blend Nachise and excellent white blend Tazi. **Alcantara Vineyards:** elegant and earthy reds, esp Confluence IV and Grand Rouge, a six-wines blend. **Burning Tree Cellars:** artisanal, small batch, intense red blends. **Caduceus Cellars:** ★★ →★★★ owned by Tool frontman Maynard James Keenan; excellent white blend Dos Ladrones (limited), top reds Sancha, Nagual del Marzo (limited quantities). **Callaghan Vineyards:** ★★ high marks for TANNAT and red blends; top-rated Caitlin B'x blend made by vintner's daughter. **Page Springs Cellars:** GSM, other white Rhône single-varietal, esp Dragoon MARSANNE, and blends. **Pillsbury Wine Company:** ★ film producer Sam Pillsbury makes excellent dessert wine Symphony "Sweet Lies", PETITE SIRAH Special Res, also v.gd CHENIN BL, award-winning "Guns & Kisses" SHIRAZ. **Sand-Reckoner Vineyards:** well-priced; v.gd MALVASIA and "z" a ZIN-led blend.

Verde Valley Wine Trail: high-altitude Arizona v'yds in volcanic rock/limestone soil.

California

While we've seen periods of high activity in CA wine in the past, it's not a stretch to suggest that none have been as manic and widespread as today's. Mainstay producers continue to plug along and, with vine age (and evolving sensibilities), improve. But it's the explosion of new winemakers that's radically expanding the state's repertoire of regions, grapes and styles. No longer is it possible to stereotype CA wine. The push into new, cooler regions continues, seeing expanded v'yds in the coolest reaches of Santa B County, Son and even Humboldt County. Conversely, old, overlooked vines in existing places like Lodi and the Sierra F'hills are being rediscovered and recuperated. Hipster winemakers seek out forgotten plantings (or create new ones) of esoteric grapes like Trousseau and FIANO. More and more wines demonstrate evolving winemaking, as well, moving into the realms of carbonic maceration, skin contact and beyond.

Recent vintages

California is too diverse for any off-the-rack summary to stack up. But the main thing to know is that there have been no "bad" vintages in over a decade. So this year we've taken a different approach to recommending vintages in the entries that follow, and instead of listing every vintage, we've focused on vintages that we're drinking now.

2016 Good quality, quantity, early harvest. Wines look balanced.
2015 Another dry year, quality very good. Mild winter, early bud-break/harvest.
2014 Despite a 3rd year of drought, quality high.

2013 Another large harvest with excellent quality prospects.
2012 Cab Sauv looks oustanding. Very promising for most varieties.
2011 Difficult year. Those who picked later reported very good Cab Sauv/Pinot N.
2010 Cool, wet. But some outstanding bottlings, esp Rhône varieties, Zin.
2009 Reds/whites good balance, ageing potential. Napa Cab Sauv excellent.
2008 Uneven quality. Acid levels low; some areas' grapes may not have ripened.
2007 Rain; results mixed, especially for Cab Sauv.

Principal vineyard areas

There are well over 100 AVAs in CA. Below are the key players.

Alexander Valley (Alex V) Son. Warm region in upper RRV. Gd Sauv Bl nr river; Cab Sauv, Zin on hillsides.

Anderson Valley (And V) Mend. Pacific fog and winds follow Navarro River inland; gd Ries, Gewurz, Pinot N; v.gd Zin on benchlands.

Arroyo Seco Mont. Warm AVA; gd Cab Sauv, Chard.

Atlas Peak Napa. Exceptional Cab Sauv, Merlot.

Calistoga (Cal) Warmer n end of Napa V. Red wine territory, esp Cab Sauv.

Carneros (Car) Napa, Son. Cool AVA at n tip of SF Bay. Gd Pinot N, Chard; Merlot, Syrah, Cab Sauv on warmer sites. V.gd sparkling.

Coombsville (Coomb) Napa. Cool region nr SF Bay; top Cab Sauv in B'x pattern.

Diamond Mountain Napa. High-elevation vines, outstanding Cab Sauv.

Dry Creek Valley (Dry CV) Son. Outstanding Zin, gd Sauv Bl; gd hillside Cab Sauv end Zin.

Edna Valley (Edna V) San LO. Cool Pacific winds; v.gd Chard.

Howell Mtn Napa. Classic Napa Cab Sauv from steep hillside v'yds.

Livermore Valley (Liv V) Alameda. Historic gravelly white-wine district mostly swallowed by suburbs but regaining some standing with new-wave Cab Sauv and Chard.

Mt Veeder Napa. High mtn v'yds for gd Chard, Cab Sauv.

Napa Valley (Napa V) Cab Sauv, Merlot, Cab Fr. Look to sub-AVAs for meaningful terroir-based wines. NB Napa V is area within Napa County.

Oakville (Oak) Napa. Prime Cab Sauv territory.

American Viticultural Areas

I'm not sure AVAs will ever catch on with the public as USPs. They're not exactly (or even approximately) like Appellations Contrôlées. One thing they do is stimulate local feelings and claims for specialness, which is, overall, a gd thing. Federal regulations on appellation of origin in the US were approved in 1977. There are two categories. First is a straightforward political AVA, which can incl an entire state, ie. CA, WA, OR and so on. Individual counties can also be used, ie. Santa B or Son. When the county designation is used, all grapes must come from that county. The 2nd category is a geographical designation, such as Napa V or Will V, within the state. These AVAs are supposed to be based on similarity of soils, weather, etc. In practice, they tend to be inclusive rather than exclusive. Within these AVAs there can be further sub-appellations, eg. the Napa V AVA contains Ruth, Stags L and others. When these geographical designations are used, all grapes must come from that region. A producer who has met the regulatory standards can choose a purely political listing, such as Napa, or a geographical listing, such as Napa V. It will probably be many yrs before the public recognizes the differences, but there is no doubt that some AVAs already fetch hefty premiums.

Paso Robles (P Rob) San LO. Excellent Zin, Rhône varieties.

Pritchard Hill (e of St Helena, Napa). High, dry and excellent, esp for Cab Sauv.

Red Hills Lake County. Promising for Cab Sauv, Zin.

Redwood Valley Mend. Warmer inland region; gd Zin, Cab Sauv, Sauv Bl.

Russian River Valley (RRV) Son. Pacific fog lingers; Pinot N, Chard, gd Zin on benchland.

Rutherford (Ruth) Napa. Outstanding Cab Sauv, esp hillside v'yds.

Saint Helena Napa. Lovely balanced Cab Sauv.

Santa Lucia Highlands (Santa LH) Mont. Higher elevation with gd Pinot N, Syrah, Rhônes.

Santa Maria Valley (Santa MV) Santa B. Coastal cool; gd Pinot N, Chard, Viognier.

Sta Rita Hills (Sta RH) Santa B. Excellent Pinot N.

Santa Ynez (Santa Y) Santa B. Rhônes (r w), Chard, Sauv Bl best bet.

Sierra Foothills (Sierra F'hills) Zin, Sauv Bl, Rhônes best.

Sonoma Coast (Son Coast) V. cool climate; edgy Pinot N, Chard.

Sonoma Valley (Son V) Gd Chard, v.gd Zin; excellent Cab Sauv from Sonoma Mountain (Son Mtn) sub-AVA. Note Sonoma V is area within Sonoma County.

Spring Mtn Napa. Terrific Cab Sauv; v.gd Sauv Bl.

Stags Leap (Stags L) Napa. Classic Cab Sauv; v.gd Merlot.

Abreu Vineyards Napa V ★★★→★★★★ 05 07 09 10 11 12 13 (14) Supple CAB SAUV-based wines from selected v'yds. Madrona v'yd leads the way with powerful, balanced opening, long, layered finish. V.gd cellar choice for 10–15 yrs.

Acacia Car ★★★ Cool-climate pioneer in Car offers consistently outstanding CHARD, PINOT N from single v'yds. Also classic SYRAH, all smoke and fruit.

Acaibo r ★★★ B'x-like estate of Gonzague and Claire Lurton in Chalk Hill is called Trinité (CAB SAUV, MERLOT, CAB FR). Acaibo is top wine; a winner. Also seductive *G&C Lurton* blend.

Ackerman Family Coomb ★★★ Small family v'yd from cooler, rising-star region. Dense CAB SAUV, Le Chatelaine B'x blend 13, burly SANGIOVESE Alavigna Tosca.

Alban Vineyards Edna V ★★★→★★★★ 10 11 12 13 14 (15) John Alban, a SYRAH frontiersman and original Rhône Ranger, still making great wine. Top VIOGNIER, GRENACHE, splendid Syrah capable of extended ageing.

Albatross Ridge Mont ★★★ Young producer, beautifully balanced PINOT NS, finely etched CHARDS from cool v'yd in Carmel Valley, seven miles from Pacific, on rare CA limestone. Wines have unmistakably calcareous lift.

Alder Springs Vineyard Mend ★★★ All-star roster of grape buyers made fruit from this rugged, remote v'yd famous. Now makes own excellent CHARD, PINOT N, SYRAH.

Alma Rosa Sta RH ★★★→★★★★ Richard Sanford, Central Coast PINOT N master, continues to craft high-level, harmonious *Pinot N*. CHARD is superb. Also v.gd *vin gris* (Pinots N/GR).

AmByth P Rob ★★→★★★ Ambitious natural wine producer, min intervention. Dry farming on P Rob's dry, hot e side is no joke. Some vinifications in amphora. GRENACHE, SANGIOVESE gd.

Anaba Son V ★★★ Ross COBB and Katy Wilson (LARUE WINES) were lured here to share winemaking duties. Together they make sharp, expressive CHARD, PINOT N, SYRAH at terrific prices.

Ancient Oak RRV, Son ★★★ Unheralded family-owned winery whose generic name belies v.gd wines. Brilliance in v'yd and cellar: winemaker Greg Lafollette ensures Son V CAB SAUVS, RRV PINOT N, ZINS are balanced, complex.

Andrew Murray Santa B ★★→★★★ Rhônes around the clock and hits keep coming. SYRAH is a favourite but don't overlook VIOGNIER, ROUSSANNE, esp tasty GRENACHE BL.

Antica Napa V ★★★ 09 10 11 12 13 (14) It took a few yrs to sort out Piero Antinori's (see Italy) Napa v'yds, but wines at last meeting expectations, with bright, balanced CAB SAUV, rounded, zesty CHARD. Lively rosé a treat.

Araujo Napa V *See* EISELE VINEYARD.

Arnot-Roberts N Coast ★★★★ Pioneer of "new California", made early picking, low alc fashionable, turning idiosyncratic single-v'yd wines into sensations. Gamey SYRAH, brambly Trousseau, penetrating CAB SAUV not to be missed. CHARDS racy.

A Tribute to Grace N Coast ★★★ Kiwi Angela Osborne's homage to Rhône red is all GRENACHE, all the time. Fruit from exceptional v'yds, diverse terroirs all over state, none more exciting than 975m, mtn-ringed Santa Barbara Highlands.

Au Bon Climat Santa B ★★★★ Jim Clendenen made PINOT N before it was cool, and fought for the balanced wine style now coming round. Fomented rise of Central Coast with burg-style CHARD, PINOT. Try small lots under Clendenen Family label.

Banshee Wines Son Coast ★★★ Three wine industry vets used insider connections to buy unsold barrels of juice from other wineries and reblend into PINOT N gold, selling it for reasonable prices. Now also line of well-crafted single-v'yd wines.

Beaulieu Vineyard Napa V ★→★★★ 09 10 11 For yrs, this historic estate's flagship, Georges de Latour Private Res CAB SAUV, seemed behind times, but now its graceful, finessed style is back, and wine seems fresh. Budget wines under Beaulieu Coastal Estate label gd gulps.

Beckmen Vineyards Santa B ★★★ A passionate farmer, Steve Beckmen's Purisima Mtn v'yd become icon of warm Santa Y zone. SYRAH, GRENACHE esp gd.

Bedrock Wine Co. Son V ★★★ Morgan Peterson (son of RAVENSWOOD founder Joel) follows in father's footsteps with brand dedicated to CA heritage v'yds. Model is old-school, but wines aren't heavy or hot. Style is (relatively) restrained, elegant. Go for Heirloom Field Blends and SYRAHS.

Benziger Family Winery Son V ★★ Heart's in right place with this family-run pioneer of bio/organic farming, but wines often lack character. Tribute, CAB SAUV-based blend, complex and structured for ageing.

Beringer Blass Napa ★→★★★ (CAB SAUV) 05 06 07 Yes, a big producer of many grocery-level wines, but Private Res Cab Sauv, single-v'yd Cabs are massive and age-worthy. Howell Mtn wines strong, but best kept secret is Knights Valley Cab.

Bokisch Lodi ★★ →★★★ Markus B state's leader when it comes to Spanish varieties. V.gd TEMPRANILLO leads list backed by superb GARNACHA, *Albariño*; flirty rosado.

Bonny Doon Mont ★★★→★★★★ 07 08 10 12 13 (Le Cigare Volant) Terroirist Randall Grahm's marketing is playful and witty, but wines are serious. Flagship Châteauneuf-style *Le Cigare Volant* moved into ★★★★ territory. Vin Gris de Cigare one of CA's top rosés.

Bonterra *See* FETZER.

Brassfield Lake ★★→★★★ One of emerging leaders of Lake County. Gd varietal wines but it's blends that compel: Eruption (MALBEC, SYRAH, MOURVÈDRE, PETITE SIRAH) and Serenity (PINOT GR, RIES, GEWURZ). Winemaking legend David Ramey consults.

Brewer Clifton Santa B ★★★ Following a recent sale, one of CA's original cult PINOT N brands back on game: bold, ripe Pinot; CHARD that never fails to impress with balance, verve.

Broc Cellars N Coast ★★ →★★★★ Berkeley-based urban winery, leader of modern CA

> **Grenache growing**
> CA's Rhône obsession goes back more than 30 yrs, but strangely, GRENACHE was never a big focus. That's changing as more and more winemakers see this heat-loving grape is a CA natural. A TRIBUTE TO GRACE is devoted to Grenache, but other producers also take it seriously. For fine examples, check out DASHE CELLARS, NEYERS, Pax, Stolpman.

> **Chenin Blanc on the rise**
> If CA CHENIN BL plantings are only growing slowly – just 12 per cent up in
> 10 yrs – its profile is growing much faster, thanks to young winemakers.
> For examples of hipster Chenins, look to Habit, KUNIN, Lo-Fi, SANDLANDS.
> CHAPPELLET a long-term star.

wine, not striving for critics' points, but making delicious, quaffable wine like
Vine Star Red, Carbonic CARIGNAN. Great visit for Bay Area weekend.

Bronco Wine Company Famous for "Two-Buck Chuck", scores of commercial labels.

Buehler Napa ★★★ 07 09 10 11 12 13 14 So old-school that even prices seem unraised
in decades, underrated family-run Napa treasure delivers balanced CAB SAUV in
pleasing brambly style with gd structure.

Cain Cellars Spring Mtn ★★★ 07 09 10 11 12 Proprietor Chris Howell one of Napa's
most inquisitive, opened-minded vintners, obsessed with expressing place. Cain
Five, layered blend of five B'x varieties, a CA classic. Consistent, designed to age.

Cakebread Napa V ★★★ CAB SAUV remains gold standard, structured for ageing but
delicious after 4 or 5 yrs in bottle.

Calera ★★★ →★★★★ 08 09 10 11 12 13 14 (PINOT N) Josh Jensen is CA Pinot hero,
devoting his life to it before it was cool. Makes single-v'yd Pinot old-fashioned
way: savoury, spicy. Don't miss excellent Central Coast CHARD or intense VIOGNIER.

Caymus Napa V ★★★ →★★★★ 04 05 06 07 09 After more than 30 yrs, Special
Selection CAB SAUV remains Napa icon: strong, intense, slow to mature. Regular
Napa bottling no slouch. Conundrum, second label, offers gd value, touch sweet.

Ceritas Son Coast ★★★ Nuanced, ethereal PINOT NS, CHARDS from husband-wife team
in Son unique in delicacy and highly sought by sommeliers. Buy if you see.
(Winemaker also makes LIOCO.)

Chalone Mont ★★★ A *sui generis* v'yd in Gavilan mts, e of Mont, with limestone (rare
in CA), giving PINOT N, CHARD decisive, stony lift.

Chappellet Napa V ★★★ →★★★★ 08 09 10 11 12 To its great credit, this pioneer
(1969) on Pritchard Hill is still family-owned and run. *Signature label* CAB SAUV
for serious ageing; NB *dry Chenin Bl*. Chappellet owns SONOMA-LOEB.

Charles Krug Napa V ★★ →★★★ Historically important winery made a comeback in
recent yrs, demanding it be recognized for role in modern Napa V. Late owner
Peter Mondavi (Feb 16) Robert's estranged brother. Supple CAB SAUV, gd SAUV BL.

Chateau Montelena Napa V ★★★ →★★★★ (CHARD) 10 11 12 13 14 (CAB SAUV) 01 03 05
06 07 Balanced, supple Cab Sauv for drinking young or putting away for at
least a decade. Chard outstanding, as is delicious estate ZIN.

Chateau St Jean Son V ★★ For decades, one of top names in Son, with slew of
gd varietals. But top bottle is bland Cinq Cépages.

Chimney Rock Stags L ★★★ 03 04 05 07 08 Underrated Stags L stalwart doesn't
shout, but under longtime guidance of Doug Fletcher, makes balanced CAB SAUV
that ages with grace, complexity.

Cliff Lede Stags L ★★★ 10 11 12 Brilliant Stags L CAB SAUV manages to be fruity and
big, but holds together with tightly knit tannins, acid. Also v.gd Cab Sauv series
from Howell Mtn, Diamond Mtn, Oak.

Clos du Val Napa V ★★★ Despite changes in ownership, Gallic spirit of former
winemaker Bernard Portet persists in consistently outstanding, balanced CAB
SAUV and intense, full-bodied CHARD. SEM/SAUV BL blend Ariadne a charmer.

Clos Pegase Napa V ★★★ Look-at-me winery; v.gd MERLOT from Car v'yd, gd CAB SAUV.

Cobb Wines Son Coast ★★★ Ross Cobb is captain of family ship, making wonderful
Son Coast PINOT N, CHARD from select v'yds. Restrained, balanced, lovely. Pinots
improve with few yrs; when ready, they're some of CA's best. Emaline Ann,
Coastlands top sites. *See also* ANABA.

Conn Valley Napa V ★★★ 12 13 14 Throwback winery just s of Howell Mtn district channels Napa from an earlier, simpler time. Wines proudly unflashy, full of balanced, earthy character. Delicious, rich blends Right Bank, Eloge.

Constellation ★→★★★ World's biggest wine company. Produces 90+ million cases/yr. Owns wineries in CA, NY, WA, Canada, Chile, Australia, NZ. Once a bottom-feeder, now going for top, incl ROBERT MONDAVI, FRANCISCAN V'YD, Estancia, MT VEEDER WINERY, RAVENSWOOD, Simi, among others.

Continuum Napa V ★★★ 08 09 10 11 12 Tim Mondavi broke with family tradition by leaving benchland for heights of Pritchard Hill. He's spared no expense or energy to make this single, exactingly crafted wine from B'x varieties. Needs time, but impeccably dense, complex, profound.

Copain Cellars And V ★★★ One of 1st chic wineries to invest deeply in And V. Wells Guthrie spurned his high Parker points and changed style to low alc, less ripeness. Sold to KENDALL-JACKSON in 2016. PINOT N is strong suit here, esp Kiser v'yd, elegant, spicy, bright; also gd Halcon SYRAH.

Corison Napa V ★★★★ 99 00 01 02 05 06 07 09 10 Cathy Corison is national treasure. While many in Napa V follow $iren call of powerhouse wines for big scores and little pleasure, Corison continues to make flavoursome, *age-worthy Cab Sauv*. Top choice is luscious, velvety Kronos V'yd.

Cornerstone Cellars Howell Mtn ★★★ 05 07 09 10 11 Impressive CAB SAUV from rugged Howell Mtn, always focuses on harmony, balance; v.gd Cab Sauv from valley floor; bright SAUV BL, SYRAH rosé.

Cuvaison Car ★★★ Quiet top estate, making great wine yr after yr, Top marks to PINOT N, CHARD from Car estate; gd SYRAH, superb CAB SAUV from Mt Veeder. Single Block bottlings incl lovely rosé, v.gd SAUV BL.

Dashe Cellars Dry CV, N Coast ★★★ RIDGE veteran Tom Dashe indulges his obsession from urban winery in Oak with Dry CV ZIN, with single-v'yd bottlings in classic Dry CV brambly style. Don't overlook excellent GRENACHE rosé, marvellous old-vine CARIGNANE.

Davis Bynum RRV ★★→★★★ Early RRV PINOT pioneer still makes big, juicy single-v'yd RRV Pinot N and rounded CHARD. Almost too generous in fruit and alc.

Dehlinger RRV ★★★→★★★★ PINOT N master still at top of game after more than four decades. Also v.gd CHARD, SYRAH and balanced, elegant CAB SAUV.

Diamond Creek Napa V ★★★★ 05 06 07 09 One of Napa's jewels, overshadowed in recent yrs by more glitzy cult CABS, but should not be overlooked. Prices v. high for wonderful, austere Cab Sauv from famous hillside v'yds on Diamond Mtn. Wines age beautifully.

Dirty and Rowdy N Coast ★★★ Part of changing face of CA wine, this sommelier darling specializes in high-quality, small-production lots of MOURVÈDRE, SÉM, along with sparkling PINOT BL, CHENIN BL. Wines have a wild, unpredictable bent and lots of energy.

Domaine Carneros Car ★★★ Taittinger outpost in CA offering consistently gd sparklers, esp Vintage Blanc de Blancs La Rêve; v.gd NV bubbly rosé. Vintage brut also v.gd. Outstanding range of PINOT N, CHARD led by The Famous Gate Pinot.

Uber Wine service will take you round Napa, Santa B or San LO for the day.

Domaine Chandon Napa V ★★→★★★ Popular destination (great restaurant) in Yountville, but fruit comes from cooler bay-side Car. Top bubbly is NV Res Étoile; v.gd rosé sparkler. Still PINOT M a delight.

Domaine de la Côte Sta RH ★★★ Exacting, burgundy-style estate PINOT N from coolest w reaches of Sta RH by brilliant wine mind and former sommelier Rajat Parr and renowned winemaker Sashi Moorman. *See also* SANDHI.

Dominus Estate Napa V ★★★★ 02 04 05 06 07 Christian Moueix of Pomerol's foray into Napa remains one of valley's great treasures, singular in its restrained design as place and wine. Don't rush; amply repays cellar time with supple layers of intense flavours, long wraparound finish. Napa superstar, yr after yr.

Donum N Coast ★★★ Anne Moller-Racke has passionately worked Car soils since 1981, and her fruit is pure. PINOT N from four sites is focus: generous, complex.

Drew Family And V ★★★ Wonderful single-v'yd PINOT N from sites only few miles from Pacific and Yorkville Highlands. Look for Morning Dew V'yd Pinot N from Mend Ridge; also excellent SYRAH from Valenti V'yd. Lovely ALBARIÑO too.

Dry Creek Vineyard Dry CV ★★→★★★ Long-term leader in Heritage ZIN movement: v. impressive line-up of single-v'yd bottlings. V.gd *Sauv Bl*, CHENIN BL.

Duckhorn Vineyards ★★→★★★ CA classic, known for dark, tannic, plummy-ripe single-v'yd MERLOTS (esp Three Palms) and CAB SAUV-based Howell Mtn. Also Goldeneye PINOT N, Excellent RRV CHARD, Pinot N added to Migration label. Decoy label is drink-me-now, esp red blend.

Dunn Vineyards Howell Mtn ★★★★ Randy Dunn makes superb, *intense Cab Sauv* from this estate. Older vintages may take 20, 30 yrs to come around; more restrained bottlings from valley floor for short-term drinking. One of few Napa V winemakers to resist stampede to jammy, lush wines to curry critics' favour.

Dutton-Goldfield RRV ★★★ Powerful, potent vision of PINOT N: lush, structured, terroir-based from Son Coast and RRV. Modern CA classics. Limited bottling of ZIN also worth a glass or two.

Edna Valley Vineyard Edna V ★★★ Easy-drinking varietals from gentle Central Coast. Lovely, lilting SAUV BL, crisp but tropical CHARD. Impressive SYRAH, gd CAB SAUV from top v'yd.

Eisele Vineyard Napa V ★★★★ In 2016 this canonical CAB SAUV's name changed from Araujo to Eisele V'yd (effective 2013 vintage), after historic planting from which it comes. Also, refreshing SAUV BL, v.gd VIOGNIER, SYRAH. Now a Pinault (*see* Château Latour, B'x) property.

Ernest Vineyards Son ★★★ Who would've thought we need more PINOT N, CHARD in the state, but this newcomer brings verve, acidity and style to a roster of excellent regional and single v'yd wines. Complex, racy, addictively drinkable.

Etude Car ★★★ Winery started by Tony Soter now belongs to a giant corp, but team remains true to his vision, issuing artful PINOT NS from many terroirs. Heirloom Grace v'yd bottling is special. Napa CAB SAUVS better than most Cab specialists.

Failla Son Coast ★★★ One of savviest, most talented winemakers in CA, Ehren Jordan effortlessly tempers CA fruit to make savoury, compelling, complex PINOT N, SYRAH, CHARD from cool coastal sites.

Farella Coomb ★★★ Excellent portfolio from cool Coomb AVA. Excellent La Luce SAUV BL, cherry-bright MERLOT, elegant CAB SAUV. Estate MALBEC outstanding.

Far Niente Napa V ★★★★ Historic winery (1885), revived only in last 20 yrs. Pioneer of single-v'yd CAB SAUVS, CHARDS in big, generous, Napa style. Hedonism with soul. Dolce: celebrated botrytized sweet wine.

Fetzer Vineyards N Coast ★★→★★★ Pioneer in organic/sustainable viticulture. Consistent value from least expensive range (Sundial, Valley Oaks) to well-made Res. Owns BONTERRA v'yds (organic grapes) where *Roussanne and Marsanne shine*.

Field Recordings P Rob ★★★ No one knows coastal vyds better than Andrew Jones, who vinifies small lots from most expressive sites. Best are blends Neverland and Barter & Trade, but don't miss Alloy and Fiction, delicious in 500ml cans.

Firestone Santa Y ★★→★★★ From same family fortune as tyre empire, reliable Central Coast producer makes esp gd SAUV BL, SYRAH. Also respected brewer.

Flowers Vineyard & Winery Son Coast ★★★ Son Coast pioneer (1st CHARD planted 1991) sold in 2009 to Huneeus corporation, but wines remain great. Now farming organically to make intense PINOT N, Chard.

Foppiano Son ★★→★★★ Classic CA table wine, esp ZIN and rich, deep PETITE SIRAH.

Forlorn Hope N Coast ★★★ Name says it all: Matthew Rorick's devotion to overlooked, forgotten grapes in old v'yds. From VERDELHO, Alvarelão to unique Portuguese-variety field blends, all compelling and v.gd.

Forman Vineyard Napa V ★★★ Ric Forman is a dedicated, even fanatic terroirist making elegant, age-worthy CAB SAUV-based wines from hillside v'yds. Also v.gd CHARD with nod to Chablis.

Freeman RRV, Son Coast ★★★→★★★★ Elegant terroir-driven PINOT N, CHARD from cool-climate Son Coast and RRV, with nod to Burgundy. The Ryo-fu Chard ("cool breeze" in Japanese) is amazing, as is Akiko's Cuvée Pinot N.

Freemark Abbey Napa V ★★★ Veteran overlooked for quality of CAB SAUV, esp single-v'yd Sycamore, Bosché bottlings.

Freestone Son Coast ★★★ Fine expression of Son Coast. Intense, racy CHARD, PINOT N from vines only few miles from Pacific show gd structure, long finish, esp Chard. Owned by Napa's JOSEPH PHELPS.

Frog's Leap Ruth ★★★ 07 08 09 10 (CAB SAUV) John Williams, leader in organic and bio movement, now in historic Ruth building, says all starts in v'yd and he means it. Cab Sauv and MERLOT both supple, balanced, capable of ageing; toasty CHARD, lean, bright *Sauv Bl*, zesty ZIN all excellent.

Gallo of Sonoma Son ★→★★★ Jug-wine giant GALLO launched this to prove it can make quality too. CAB SAUV and ZIN can be v.gd, while Gina Gallo signature wines always terrific.

CA Pét-Nat (single fermentation fizz) increasing every yr. Nothing to do with dogs.

Gallo Winery, E & J ★→★★ CA's biggest winery has done more to open up the American palate to wine than any other company. Basic commodity wines, plus regional varieties: Anapauma, Marcellina, Turning Leaf and more, all wines of modest quality, perhaps, but predictable and affordable. Recent shopping spree has tripled production capacity in Napa; now 15 wineries in CA and WA.

Gary Farrell RRV, Son Coast ★★★ Excellent PINOT N, CHARD from cool-climate v'yds. Rocholi v'yd Chard superb. Don't overlook stylish ZIN, splendid SYRAH. New Inspiration series features small lots, eg. Gap's Crown V'yd from Son Coast.

Gloria Ferrer Car ★★→★★★ Gd bubbly; also spicy CHARD and bright, silky PINOT N. Owned by Spanish Cava giant Freixenet. Royal Cuvée best.

Grace Family Vineyard Napa V ★★★★ 03 05 06 07 09 10 Stunning CAB SAUV shaped for long ageing. One of few cult wines that might actually be worth price.

Green and Red Napa V ★★★ Named for colours of its v'yd soils (iron red and green serpentine), winery founded 1977 still specializes in old-school, savoury, balanced ZINS (no high-alc fruit bombs here), SYRAH, SAUV BL. All estate fruit, three v'yds.

Grgich Hills Cellars Napa V ★★★ 07 08 09 10 11 Mike Grgich (now retired) made 1973 Montelena CHARD that won 1976 Judgement of Paris tasting. Still going, his winery, now bio, is outstanding; CAB SAUV supple, age-worthy Chard.

Gundlach Bundschu Son V ★★★ CA's oldest family-operated winery (2nd oldest overall). Welcoming vibe makes it popular tasting destination. Like atmosphere, CAB SAUV, MERLOT round, friendly, well-priced. Quaffable *Gewurz* a throwback.

Hahn Santa LH ★★→★★★ Once known for decent PINOT N at bargain prices, has upped game. Value still gd, but quality soaring. Single-v'yd releases on Lucienne label are fantastic; basic level wines better than ever.

Hall Napa V ★★★ Solid Napa CABS, though somewhat bewildering in number, worth sorting; Kathryn Hall Signature outstanding with full-palate layers of flavour and gd ageing potential. Delicious, tense SAUV BL.

Hanna Winery Son ★★★ Son classic with outstanding SAUV BL, PINOT N; Res CAB SAUV, MERLOT superb. Merlot-based rosé a treat.

Hanzell Son V ★★★★ PINOT pioneer of 50s still making CHARD *and Pinot N* from estate vines. Both repay few yrs' cellar time. Deserves to be ranked with best of CA. Sebella Chard, from young vines, all bright crisp fruit.

Harlan Estate Napa V ★★★★ Concentrated, robust CAB SAUV – one of original cult wines only available via mailing list at luxury prices. Still all those things today.

HdV Wines Car ★★★ Underrated Son gem makes fine complex *Chard* with a honed edge and v.gd PINOT N, from grower Larry Hyde in conjunction with Aubert de Villaine of DRC (*see* France). V.gd CAB SAUV, SYRAH.

Heitz Cellar Napa V ★★★→★★★★ Everyone focuses on iconic, age-worthy Martha's V'yd CAB SAUV; basic Napa Cab always poised, delicious. Gd SAUV BL, even GRIGNOLINO.

Heller Estate Mont ★★★ Founded Carmel V AVA and still prevails there with signature CHENIN BL, supple CAB SAUV, v.gd MERLOT and rosé.

Hess Collection, The Napa V ★★★ Great Napa V visit with world-class art gallery, also makes gd wine. CAB SAUV from MOUNT VEEDER WINERY hits new quality level, esp exceptional 19 Block Cuvée, blockbuster with gd manners.

Hirsch Son Coast ★★★★ Pioneer of Son Coast, David Hirsch's v'yd won acclaim as premier seller of grapes. Now family label gets best of that. Gorgeous, lithe PINOT N, CHARD of startling character, vitality from towering ridge above Pacific.

Honig Napa V ★★★ Easy to find, mainstay Napa winery still offers consistent quality, esp Campbell V'yd CAB SAUV, rich and deep, shoud age well. *Sauv Bl* standard bearer for grape in Napa V.

Inglenook Oak ★★★★ FF Coppola's Rubicon, now under Inglenook label, marks return to classic Napa CAB SAUV: balanced, elegant, true to great tradition. Also CHARD, MERLOT.

Iron Horse Vineyards Son ★★★ Too easily forgotten in category of CA bubbles. Amazing selection of 12 sparklings, all vintage, all wonderfully made. Ocean Res Blanc de Blancs is v.gd, Wedding Cuvée a winner. V.gd CHARD, PINOT N.

Jolie-Laide Son ★★★ Outstanding voice of "new California" makes distinctive wines from unusual grapes: Melon (MUSCADET), GAMAY, Trousseau Gris. In San Francisco's hippest restaurants.

Jordan Alex V ★★★ Changes in grape sourcing has led to brilliant revival of balanced, elegant wines from showcase Alex V estate. CAB SAUV homage to B'x: and it lasts. Zesty, delicious CHARD.

Joseph Phelps Napa V ★★★★ (Insignia) 05 06 07 08 09 10 11 Napa "First Growth" Phelps CAB SAUV, esp *Insignia* and Backus, always nr top: intense, for long ageing. Ovation CHARD is v.gd. *See* FREESTONE.

Joseph Swan Son ★★★ Long-time RRV producer of intense old-vine ZIN and single-v'yd PINOT N. Often overlooked Rhône varieties also v.gd, esp ROUSSANNE/MARSANNE blend and orange GRENACHE BL.

Kendall-Jackson ★★★ Huge player, still focuses on quality. Market-driven CHARD, CAB SAUV. Even more noteworthy for developing a diversity of wineries under umbrella of Jackson Family Wines with international cast from Australia, Chile, France, Italy as well as homegrown CA, OR brands.

Kenwood Vineyards Son V ★★→★★★ Landmark Son V producer reinvented itself with focus on finer quality. CAB SAUV leads way: epic Jack London v'yd bottling.

Kistler Vineyards RRV ★★★★ Change in style: buttery CHARD, potent PINOT N become better, more lean and racy. Still from a dozen designated v'yds in any given yr. Still highly sought.

Kongsgaard Napa ★★★→★★★★ There are few more delightful personalities than 5th-generation Napa-ite John Kongsgaard. He also makes incredible wine, notably CHARD from Judge v'yd and excellent CAB SAUV, SYRAH.

Korbel ★★ Cheap fizz sold in grocery stores, but all traditional method and remarkably decent for price. Also, fun visit in Son.

Kunin ★★★ One-time ZIN specialist Seth Kunin found his true calling in Rhône vines, incl beefy SYRAH and delightful Pape Star, an ode to Châteauneuf. Dalliances in Loire headlined by spirited CHENIN BL.

Lagier-Meredith Mt Veeder ★★★ Wine from renowned UC Davis vine researcher Carole Meredith and oenologist husband Steve Lagier. Handmade, tiny production of beautiful, pure SYRAH, MONDEUSE, MALBEC and ZIN (whose genetic ancestry in Croatia Meredith famously decoded).

Lamborn Family Vineyards Howell Mtn ★★★★ Superstar winemaker Heidi Barrett makes intense, age-worthy CAB SAUV and big full-flavoured ZIN from estate v'yd.

Lang & Reed Mend, Napa ★★★ No one in CA has flown CAB FR banner more passionately. Wines capture perfume, litheness with Napa generosity. Also delicious Mend CHENIN BL.

Larkmead Napa V ★★★ 10 11 13 14 Historic Cal estate revived; *outstanding Cab Sauv*, supple, balanced; bright, delicious SAUV BL. New release Tocai FRIULANO a delight. *See also* MASSICAN.

Larue Wines Son Coast ★★★ Katy Wilson has special touch that lifts elegant PINOT N, CHARD above ordinary. Serious wines that provoke a smile. *See also* ANABA.

Laurel Glen Son ★★★ 03 05 06 09 13 14 Supple, age-worthy CAB SAUV from hillside v'yd on Son Mtn rated nr top for more than three decades. New owners keeping bar high. Counterpoint Cab Sauv a drink-now bargain.

Lewis Cellars Napa V ★★★★ For those who embrace Napa largesse, CAB SAUVS, CHARDS, SYRAH from former racing driver Randy Lewis can only be described as full-throttle. Unapologetic Napa hedonism at its best.

Lieu Dit Sta RH ★★★ Oft overlooked varieties of Loire: tangy SAUV BL, crisp CHENIN BL, appealingly crunchy CAB FR.

Lioco N Coast ★★★ Intended to prove that CA can make lean, mineral CHARD. Mission accomplished. Now also excellent PINOT N, scrumptious red and rosé Indica CARIGNAN from Mend. Winemaker is John Raytek of CERITAS.

Littorai Son Coast ★★★ Quietly and steadily, Burgundy-trained Ted Lemon become one of CA's iconic names; ethereal, site-driven PINOT N, CHARD age beautifully.

Lohr, J ★★→★★★ Prolific producer of Central Coast makes CAB SAUV, PINOT N, CHARD for balance and $$ value. Cuvée Pau and Cuvée St E pay homage to B'x. Don't miss Valdigue, CA rarity.

Long Meadow Ranch Napa V ★★★→★★★★ Smart, holistic vision incl destination winery with restaurant, beef cattle and organic working farm. Supple, age-worthy CAB SAUV has reached ★★★★ status; lively Graves-style SAUV BL.

Louis M Martini Napa ★★★ Classic brand revitalized with Mike Martini at helm. Now sappy, potent wines from historic CAB SAUV, ZIN v'yds. Look esp for Cab Sauv from *Monte Rosso*.

MacPhail Son Coast ★★→★★★ Hardworking PINOT N, CHARD brand. good, but risk-averse. Ripe fruit will only take you so far. But there's potential. Mardikian (estate PINOT) is excellent: intense, tightly-wound.

MacRostie Son Coast ★★★ Easy-drinking PINOT N, CHARD from Son Coast and RRV. Delicious Pinot N rosé.

Marimar Torres Estate RRV ★★★ Great Catalan family's CA outpost issues several bottlings of CHARD, PINOT N. V'yds now all bio. Chards are excellent, long-lived, esp Acero (unoaked, *fresh, expressive)*. Pinot N from Doña Margarita v'yd nr ocean is intense, rich.

Massican Napa V ★★★ LARKMEAD winemaker Dan Petroski's homage to Italian whites: SAUV BL, blends Annia (FRIULANO/RIBOLLA/CHARD), Gemina (PINOT GR/GRECO) are delights.

Matthiasson ★★★ Experimental wines have become cult hits. Racy CHARD, elegant CAB SAUV, epic white blend, plus esoterica like RIBOLLA GIALLA, Schioppetino.

Mayacamas Vineyards Mt Veeder ★★★ Under new ownership (Charles Banks, former partner in SCREAMING EAGLE), CA classic has not changed classic style, only improved. Age-worthy CAB SAUV, CHARD recall great bottles of 70s, 80s.

Melville ★★★ Family-run anchor of Sta RH, with bold, v.gd CHARD, PINOT N, but estate SYRAH steals show. Worth tasting too is SamSara, Chad and Mary Melville's personal label.

Meritage Basically a B'x blend (r or w). Term invented for CA but has spread. It's a trademark, and users have to belong to The Meritage Alliance. It's supposed to rhyme with heritage but often doesn't.

Merry Edwards RRV ★★★★ One of great CA winemakers, and PINOT N pioneer. Single v'yds from Son always wildly popular. Ripe, plummy, rounded, layered with flavour, edged with dark spice. Slightly off-dry SAUV BL also trendy.

Meteor Coomb ★★★ Another rising name from suddenly fashionable Coomb. Coolish site produces wonderfully dense CAB SAUV from estate v'yd. Second wine, Perseid, v.gd for earlier drinking.

Mount Eden Vineyards Santa Cz Mts ★★★★ V'yd high up in Santa Cz Mts, one of CA's 1st boutique wineries, superlative CAB SAUV, PINOT N, CHARD since 1945. Current ownership since 1981.

Mount Veeder Winery Mt Veeder ★★★ Classic CA mtn CABS SAUV, FR grown at 500m on rugged, steep hillsides. Big, dense wines with ripe, integrated tannins.

Mumm Napa Valley Napa V ★★★ Stylish bubbly, esp *delicious Blanc de Noirs* and rich, complex DVX single-v'yd fizz to age a few yrs in bottle; v.gd Brut Rosé.

Nalle Son ★★★ ZIN is star turn here, a pleasure to drink young, but will age. Excellent PINOT N, CHARD.

Marijuana now legal in CA: what effect on wine industry? Workers might prefer it.

Newton Vineyards Spring Mtn ★★→★★★★ 40 yrs old in 2017, Newton's rigorous quality control and push toward ripeness fuelled Napa's rise in 80s. "Unfiltered" series introduced many to the word; still compelling, esp CAB SAUV.

Neyers Napa V ★★★ Complex CHARD, floral GRENACHE, silky CAB SAUV French in sensibility, looking for substance beyond grape variety. Prices more than fair.

Niebaum-Coppola Estate *See* Inglenook.

Obsidian Ridge Lake ★★★ Bargain prices for sophisticated, intense CAB SAUV. True mtn wine, from sloping v'yd at 780m with iron-rich soils and scattering of obsidian. Res Cab Half Mile is excellent.

Ojai Santa B ★★★ Successfully navigating a change of style from big, super-ripe to leaner, finer, former AU BON CLIMAT partner Adam Tolmach making best wines of his career. V.gd PINOT N, CHARD, Rhône styles. SYRAH-based rosé is delicious.

Opus One Oak ★★★★ Still standard bearer for fine Napa CAB SAUV, Mondavi-Rothschild collaboration is in great form today. Current vintage is 2013, but wines best with at least 10 yrs age.

Ovid St Helena ★★★ Cult-styled, ultra-luxurious organic estate on Pritchard Hill. Supple B'x blends star turn but SYRAH also fine.

Pahlmeyer Napa V ★★★ Fashionable estate from decades of CA's 1st ascent. Wines massive, jammy, but supple. B'x blend most famous, gd for short ageing.

Palmina Santa B ★★★ Accurate Italian styles, unusual vines. CA flair: sumptuous, meant for food. FRIULANO, VERMENTINO, NEBBIOLO, LAGREIN.

Parador Napa V ★★★ Napa's TEMPRANILLO specialist: luscious, age-worthy versions inspired by Ribera del Duero. CAB SAUV savoury, suave.

Patz & Hall N Coast ★★★ Jim Hall one of CA's most thoughtful winemakers, with over decade of devotion to single-v'yd PINOT N, CHARD. Basic Son Coast bottlings incredibly reliable.

Paul Hobbs N Coast ★★★ Entrepreneurial winemaker with one foot in Argentina,

Hobbs' bread still buttered in CA. Bottlings of single-v'yd CHARD, PINOT N, CAB SAUV, SYRAH: depth, intensity, jamminess. V. popular with those who like that style.

Peay Vineyards Son Coast ★★★ Standout brand from one of coast's coldest zones, PINOT N, CHARD. SYRAH might be greatest. Second label, Cep, also v.gd, esp rosé.

Pedroncelli Son ★★ Old school Dry CV winery updated v'yds, winery; still makes bright, elbow-bending ZIN, CAB SAUV, solid CHARD.

Peju Napa V ★★★ Immensely popular showcase winery on tasting-room circuit; quality underrated, esp balanced, supple CAB SAUV.

Peter Michael Winery Mont, Son ★★★★ *Sir* Peter Michael to you. Brit in Knight's Valley sells mostly to restaurants, mailing list. Quality outstanding: rich, dense CHARD, B'x blend Les Pavots (r), hedonist's PINOT N

Philip Togni Vineyards Spring Mtn ★★★★ 99 00 03 05 07 Living link to classic, early Napa, Togni, a student in B'x of Emile Peynaud, arrived in Napa in 1959. Outstanding estate CAB SAUV-based wine looks to Margaux for guidance. Balanced, powerful, will age for decades.

Pine Ridge Napa V ★★★ 03 04 05 06 07 09 10 11 12 13 14 (15) Outstanding CAB SAUV made from several Napa v'yds. Stags L bottling is silky, graceful. Epitome, made only in best yrs, can be superb. Gd CHARD, lively rosé.

Pisoni Vineyards Santa LH ★★★ Family winery in Santa LH became synonymous with PINOT N explosion and big, jammy wines. Still, Pinot N is and always was v. well made and remains popular.

Presqu'ile Santa MV ★★★ New Central Coast winery, elegantly styled PINOT N, SYRAH.

Quintessa Ruth ★★★ Since debut in 90s, this red blend from Agustin Huneeus been star of Napa's upper, non-cult tier. Pricey, but in reach.

Qupé Santa B ★★★ One of original SYRAH champions, brilliant range of Rhônes, esp X Block, from one of CA's oldest v'yds. Hillside Estate also epic; don't miss unshakeable MARSANNE, ROUSSANNE.

Ravenswood *See* CONSTELLATION.

Red Car Son Coast ★★★ Move from Central Coast to Son Coast brought change of style in small, artsy producer: now crisp, finely drawn. Precise CHARD, lacy, fruit-forward PINOT N, killer rosé.

Ridge N Coast, Santa Cz Mts ★★★★ Saintly founder Paul Draper is retired, but his spirit lives on. Supple, harmonious estate *Montebello Cab Sauv* is superb. Outstanding single-v'yd ZIN from Son, Napa V, Sierra F'hills, P Rob. Don't overlook *outstanding Chard.*

Robert Mondavi ★★→★★★ After sale to Constellation brands in 2004 quality dipped, but returning to gd form with classic Napa CAB SAUV, esp Oak, Res, To Kalon.

Robert Sinskey Vineyards Car ★★★ Great, idiosyncratic Napa estate favouring balance, restraint. Great CAB SAUV and Car PINOT N. Racy Abraxas white blend and Pinot rosé excellent.

Roederer Estate And V ★★★→★★★★ Owned by Champagne Roederer, style favours restraint, elegance, esp in luxury cuvée l'Ermitage.

Saintsbury Car ★★★ Potent, balanced PINOT N, CHARD from Car No-nonsense approach, not afraid of tannin or extract.

Sandhi Sta RH ★★★→★★★★ *See* DOMAINE DE LA CÔTE. Same winemaking team, grapes bought from top local v'yds. Must for lovers of white burgundy: racy, intense CHARD, gd PINOT N.

Sandlands N Coast ★★★ Tegan Passalaqua, also winemaker for TURLEY WINE CELLARS, made name as CA's premier v'yd bloodhound. For his own label he finds old, forgotten vines. Great CHENIN BL, Trousseau Noir, CARIGNANE.

Scharffenberger Mend Best-known as a chocolate brand, made wine since 1981. V.gd, affordable NV Brut Rosé. New ownership (Champagne Roederer) revived quality. Look for gd things to come.

Schramsberg Napa V ★★★★ Best bubbles in CA. Quality in every cuvée; J Schram, creamy luxury bottling, been called CA's Krug.

Schug Vineyards Car, Son Coast ★★★ Hard not to think about late Walter Schug, PINOT N master, when drinking this. Carried Pinot banner before it was cool. Wines still v.gd.

Screaming Eagle Napa V Even young vintages of this cultest of cult CAB SAUVs sell for c.$1500... if you can find it.

Scribe Son ★★★ Appealing to millennial set, tasting room is gentleman-farmer chic, serving well-made esoterica like SYLVANER, ST-LAURENT and lots of PINOT N rosé.

Sea Smoke Sta RH ★★★ Used to make big PINOT N and earned cult following. Wines still lush, generous, but now more balanced, farming is bio and precise. Sea Spray is hard-to-find sparkling.

Seghesio Son ★★★ Synonymous with ZIN. Rich, strong, but graceful. Old Vine bottling is benchmark.

Selene Napa V ★★★ Simply a wonderful brand: superb, small lots of B'x grapes from selected Napa v'yds. Excellent CAB FR, balanced and elegant CAB SAUV and fine SAUV BL.

Sequoia Grove Napa V ★★★ Rutherford staple for more than 30 yrs, still v.gd. Flagship Cambium is stunning CAB SAUV blend, balanced, age-worthy. CHARD v.gd.

Ser Mont ★★★ Longtime Randall Grahm associate Nicole Walsh has launched Ser to standing ovation. CHARD is superb, intensity, firmness; PINOT N offers bright fruit, gd structure.

Shafer Vineyards Napa V ★★★→★★★★ Hillside Select remains emblematic full-on Napa. Also v.gd MERLOT; fine CHARD from Car grapes.

Silverado Vineyards Stags L ★★★ Belongs to Disney family, made lovely CAB SAUV for decades. Single-v'yd Solo is powerful, but smooth; new release of Geo from Coomb AVA is dark, dense. CAB FR v.gd.

Silver Oak Alex V, Napa V ★★★ So popular in 90s that sommeliers in 2000s turned backs on it. Yet wines never changed, remain classic expressions. Napa is classic CAB SAUV, Alex V is supple, can be drunk younger.

Smith-Madrone Spring Mtn ★★★ Serious, purist producer, daring to dry-farm in hot climate. Superb RIES with brilliant floral briskness. Also v.gd powerful CAB SAUV from high-elevation v'yd.

Sonoma-Cutrer Vineyards Son ★★★ Flagship CHARD a classic, still by glass at restaurants all over country, rich but zesty and bright. Owsley PINOT N from RRV lush with black fruit.

Sonoma-Loeb Car, RRV ★★★ Precise, cool-climate PINOT N, CHARD. Made by CHAPPELLET's winemaker at its winery for 20 yrs, so 2011 sale to Napa brand made sense.

Spottswoode St Helena ★★★★ CA "First Growth". ***Outstanding Cab Sauv*** built old-fashioned way, to drink well and age with dignity. Brilliant SAUV BL. RIP founder Mary Novak, 2016

Spring Mountain Vineyard Spring Mtn ★★★→★★★★ 04 05 07 08 Top-notch estate that has ignored trends in favour of site driven wines. Signature Elivette CAB SAUV blend, concentrated, will age. Estate Cab Sauv v.gd, as is SAUV BL.

St Francis Son ★★→★★★ Commercial estate, but reliable, gd fruit-friendly wines

---

Rhône-style Syrahs

SYRAH is quietly emerging as one of CA's best grapes, esp suited to cool-climate areas like Son Coast and Sta RH. Ten great cool-climate Syrahs: Anthill Farms Son Coast, ARNOT-ROBERTS Clary Ranch, Baker Lane, BEDROCK WINE CO Griffin's Lair, Failla, Landmark Steel Plow, PEAY VINEYARDS La Bruma, Piedrasassi, QUPÉ Hillside Estate, WIND GAP Son Coast.

mostly from Son County grapes, esp gd CHARD, VIOGNIER, CAB SAUV; outstanding old-vine ZIN.

St-Supéry Napa ★★★ Bought by owners of Chanel 2015, estate has large holdings in Ruth, Napa V, making gd, balanced wines with elegance. Flagship may be excellent, gd-value SAUV BL.

Staglin Family Vineyard Ruth ★★★★ Wonderful estate, family run, gd natured, wines that focus on elegance. CAB SAUV is fluid, balanced, while estate CHARD shows complexity, intensity.

Stag's Leap Wine Cellars Stags L ★★★→★★★★ Gd to see quality maintained since founder sold to large corp. Flagships still silky, seductive CAB SAUVS (top-of-line Cask 23, Fay, SLV), but don't sleep on excellent CHARD.

Sterling Napa V ★★→★★★ Always a fun visit, winery (at 90m above Cal, accessible by cable car) offers commanding view of n Napa V.

Stone Edge Farms Son V ★★★ Up-and-comer has holistic approach to food, wine, life. Excellent CAB SAUV from Mayacamas range. Second wine, Surround, also great.

Stony Hill Vineyard Spring Mtn ★★★★ Famous antidote to oaky, buttery CA CHARD complaint; always been crisp. Restrained, balanced CAB SAUV. Gd RIES, GEWURZ.

Sutter Home *See* TRINCHERO FAMILY ESTATES.

Tablas Creek P Rob ★★★ Joint venture between Beaucastel (*see* France) and importer Robert Haas with v'yd cuttings from Châteauneuf. Côtes de Tablas Red and White amazingly gd, as is Tablas Creek Esprit.

Tatomer Santa B ★★★ Graham T learned to make exceptional dry RIES, GRUNER V in Austria. Now he's state leader in these grapes and on every list in LA and SF.

Thomas Fogarty Santa Cz Mts ★★★ Bright light from sparse region. Single-v'yd bottlings of CHARD, PINOT N top list. Estate Chard is esp gd. New fruity NEBBIOLO.

Trefethen Family Vineyards Oak K ★★★ Great Napa *Ries* reminds of life beyond CAB SAUV, which, from this historic family winery, is also splendid and will age. Top Cab: Halo.

Trinchero Family Estates ★→★★★ Foundational Napa producer with bewildering number of labels; ahead of pack is affordable, v. pleasing CAB SAUV under Napa Wine Company label.

Trione Alex V, RRV ★★★ From warm, dry Alex V, bold CAB SAUV-based blend tops list.

Truchard Car ★★★ Brilliant bottlings of TEMPRANILLO, ROUSSANNE. Also tangy, lemony CHARD; flavourful MERLOT. CAB SAUV, SYRAH v.gd too. All Car grapes.

Turley Wine Cellars N Coast ★★★★ Selling mostly to mailing list, so rare in market. Known for big, brambly old-vine ZIN from century-old v'yds. True CA treasures. Buy on sight.

Turnbull Napa V ★★★ Still making great CAB SAUV after 35 yrs: powerful yet supple, balanced. Pierra V'yd bottling should be cellared for 10 yrs+.

Tyler Santa B ★★★ Boutique brand became a sommelier darling, thanks to austere CHARDS and elegant, finely etched PINOT N. *See also* LIEU DIT.

Unti Dry CV ★★★ Feels old-school, but is perhaps Dry CV's most dynamic producer, always refining range of luscious wines like tasty BARBERA, MONTEPULCIANO, ZIN.

Varner Santa Cz Mts ★★★→★★★★ Too long under radar, Varner brothers make elegant, terroir-driven CHARD (among CA's best), also v.gd, site-driven PINOT N.

Viader Estate Howell Mtn ★★★★ Ripe, powerful expression of Howell Mtn still turns heads. "V" is marvellous B'x blend based on PETIT VERDOT. V.gd CAB FR.

Vina Robles San LO ★★→★★★ Swiss-owned winery looks for Euro style in warm P Rob climate. Gd CAB SAUV, SAUV BL; excellent ALBARIÑO, great prices.

Vineyard 29 Napa V ★★★ Located at 2929 Hwy 29, just outside St Helena, one of most technologically advanced in California; high-level CAB SAUV and blends.

Vino Noceto Sierra F'hills ★★★ Showcasing potential of Amador County, all about SANGIOVESE with multiple expressions, all tasty.

Vin Roc Napa V ★★★ Producers now figuring out Atlas Peak, historically tricky; exemplified here with outstanding CAB SAUV, silky, deep with lingering finish.

Volker Eisele Family Estate Napa V ★★★ 01 03 05 07 09 10 11 12 13 14 (15) Supple, luscious CAB SAUV-based blends, esp Terzetto bottling; new offering is Alexander, 100% Cab. Gemini is lovely, lively SAUV BL/SEM blend. All from organic grapes.

Wente Vineyards ★★→★★★ Oldest continuing family winery in CA makes better whites than reds. Outstanding gravel-grown SAUV BL leads way.

Wind Gap Son Coast ★★★ Pax Mahle one of CA's most talented winemakers, esp in cool climates. PINOT N, CHARD v.gd but SYRAH top. Single v'yds excellent, but basic Son Coast tremendous.

Wine Group, The Central V ★ By volume 2nd-largest producer in world; brands like Almaden, Cupcake, Franzia.

Colorado

Some of highest-altitude v'yds in nation and climate similar to Rhône and Central Coast make this a rising star of a region. Grand Valley and West Elks AVAs. Wines are coming into their own identity. **Bookcliff:** ★★ excellent MALBEC, SYRAH, Res CAB FR, CAB SAUV, VIOGNIER. **Boulder Creek:** ★ gd Cab Sauv, Syrah, MERLOT, v.gd RIES. **Canyon Wind:** excellent Anemoi Lips Syrah, gd PETIT VERDOT/Syrah Notus and B'x blend IV. **Carlson:** small winery with whimsical names but well-made, value-priced wines, esp award-winning Ries. **Creekside:** v.gd Cab Sauv, Petit Verdot. **Grande River:** focus on traditional B'x- and Rhône-style wines, but intense and floral Viognier shines here too. **Guy Drew:** ★★★ nicely priced wines incl Viognier, dry Ries from Russell Vy'd, unoaked CHARD, Metate, Cab Fr. **Infinite Monkey Theorem:** v.gd red blend 100th Monkey and Viognier/ROUSSANNE Blind Watchmaker White, also wines on tap and by the can. **Jack Rabbit Hill:** bio/organic, M&N v.gd PINOT M/PINOT N. **Plum Creek:** superb Ries, v.gd Merlot. **Snowy Peaks (Grande Valley):** v.-high-altitude vines, v.gd Petit Verdot. Oso blend uses hybrid grapes. **Sutcliffe:** v.gd Cab Fr, Syrah, Merlot. **Turquoise Mesa:** ★ award-winning Syrah. **Two Rivers:** ★ excellent Cab Sauv, v.gd Chard, Ries. **Whitewater Hill Vineyards:** exceptional red blend Ethereal. **Winery at Holy Cross:** ★ excellent Cab Fr, v.gd Res Merlot.

Georgia

Expanding region with increasingly sophisticated wines, incl CHARD, CAB, MERLOT, TANNAT, TOURIGA N, also native muscadine. Top estates: **Château Élan, Crane Creek, Engelheim, Frogtown, Habersham, Sharp Mountain, Stonewall Creek, Three Sisters, Tiger Mountain, Wolf Mountain, Yonah Mountain.**

Idaho

ID, along with OR and WA make up the PNW. Compared to its neighbours, it's still early days in the ID wine industry with just over 50 wineries. The state has three appellations, Snake River Valley, Eagle Foothills and Lewis-Clark Valley, two of which were recently approved. Varietal exploration, with B'x and Rhône varieties currently in lead, but no single grape has as yet est itself.

Cinder Wines Snake RV ★★ Standout ID winery making limited amounts of VIOGNIER, a unique TEMPRANILLO blend, v.gd SYRAH.

Coiled Snake RV ★★★ Owner Leslie Preston makes some of state's best wines. The Coiled Dry RIES is pitch-perfect; Sidewinder SYRAH a winner.

Ste Chapelle Snake RV ★ ID's 1st and largest winery. Wide range, dry and off-dry, incl quaffable RIES, budget bubbly, Icewines.

> **What's in a name?**
> Would you drink Enchantment and Opportunity? They're new grape
> varieties developed by the University of Arkansas, bred for hot, humid
> summers, cold winters. Flavour might be better than the names. Or not.

Maryland

Roughly the size of Belgium, with 80 wineries. Leaders: pioneering **Boordy**,
plus **Big Cork**, **Black Ankle**, **Bordeleau**, **Knob Hall**, **Old Westminster**, **Sugarloaf**.
Rising stars: **Dodon** (for SAUV BL and red B'x blends), **Port of Leonardtown**
(notable ALBARIÑO, BARBERA, PETIT VERDOT). Chesapeake Bay, which plays a critical
role in moderating the climate, cuts through state from top to bottom.

1st post-Prohibition commercial wine in e US: 1945 Baco Noir (French hybrid) from
Maryland's Boordy V'yds.

Michigan

124 wineries, mostly nr Lake Michigan, which moderates climate. PINOT N now
most widely planted red, with RIES, GEWURZ, PINOT GR, CAB FR also strong. Current
leaders: **Bel Lago**, **Black Star**, **Boathouse**, **Bowers Harbor**, **Brys**, **Chateau
Chantal**, **Chateau Fontaine**, **Chateau Grand Traverse**, **12 Corners**, **Fenn Valley**,
Hawthorne, **2 Lads**, **Laurentide**, **Lawton Ridge**, **Left Foot Charley**, **L Mawby**,
Mari, **45 North**, **St Julian**, **Tabor Hill**, **WaterFire**.

Ries is Michigan's most-planted vinifera variety, only state with that distinction.

Missouri

The University of Missouri has a new experimental winery to test techniques
and grape varieties in local conditions, which are warm and humid. Best so far:
Chambourcin, SEYVAL BL, VIDAL, Vignoles (sweet and dry). **Stone Hill** in Hermann
produces v.gd Chardonel (frost-hardy hybrid, Seyval Bl x CHARD), Norton and
gd Seyval Bl, Vidal. **Hermannhof** is notable for Vignoles, Chardonel, Norton.
Also: **St James** for Vignoles, Seyval, Norton; **Mount Pleasant** in Augusta for rich
fortified and Norton; **Adam Puchta** for fortifieds and Norton, Vignoles, Vidal;
Augusta Winery for Chambourcin, Chardonel, Icewine; **Les Bourgeois** for
SYRAH, Norton, Chardonel, Montelle, v.gd Cynthiana, Chambourcin.

Nevada

Limited commercial wineries. Churchill Vineyards: gd SEM/CHARD. **Pahrump
Valley**: v.gd PRIMITIVO, ZIN. Sanders Family, former owners of Pahrump Winery.

New Jersey

Cool in n, warmer in s. 50 wineries; leaders incl **Alba**, **Beneduce**, **Cape May**,
Unionville Vineyards. CHARD, RIES, PINOT N esp successful in recent vintages.

Alba ★★★ 14 15 16 Exceptional CHARD, gd RIES, GEWURZ; one of largest PINOT N
plantings on East Coast.
Unionville Vineyards ★★ 14 15 16 Large estate with five separate v'yds. UC-Davis-
trained winemaker produces excellent CHARD, RIES, PINOT N.

New Mexico

Capuchin monks planted grapevines in the 1600s. Arid, with a mix of mts and
high plains; lower-alc wines. Sparkling excels here. **Black Mesa:** ★★ excellent

SYRAH, v.gd PETITE SIRAH, CHARD. **Casa Abril:** family-owned, high-altitude. Spanish and Argentine varieties. **Gruet:** ★★★ renowned for excellent sparkling, esp Blanc de Noirs and Grand Rosé, also excellent Chard, PINOT N. **La Chiripada:** ★ top-notch Res CAB SAUV and v.gd Petite Sirah, VIOGNIER. **Noisy Water:** ★ excellent Cab Sauv, v.gd SHIRAZ. **Vivác:** ★★ excellent red blends Divino (Italian grapes) and Diavolo (French) and Port-style Amante.

New York (NY)

Largest and fastest-growing East Coast wine state with more than 400 wineries in 59 of 62 NY counties, and ten AVAs: Champlain Valley, FINGER LAKES ([Finger L] incl Cayuga and Seneca Lakes), HUDSON RIVER, LAKE ERIE, LONG ISLAND ([Long I] incl NORTH FORK and THE HAMPTONS), Niagara Escarpment.

21 Brix ★★ 14 15 16 Exceptional estate on Lake Erie shores; stylish dry CHARD, GEWURZ, Noiret, RIES, Icewine.

Anthony Road Finger L ★★★★ **13** 14 15 16 Superb wines incl some of best dry and semi-dry RIES in US, also outstanding GEWURZ, PINOT GR, CAB FR/LEMBERGER blend.

Bedell Long I ★★→★★★ **10** 13 14 15 16 Prominent North Fork estate since 1980. Influential winemaker makes balanced ALBARIÑO, CHARD, SAUV BL, VIOGNIER, plus noteworthy CAB FR, MALBEC AND MERLOT. Artist labels, eg. Chuck Close and April Gornik.

Boundary Breaks Finger L ★★★ 14 15 16 Excellent estate, only RIES, bone-dry to dessert.

Casa Larga Finger L ★ ★ 14 15 16 Fine family-run estate with notable GEWURZ, RIES, Pinot N, VIDAL Icewine.

Channing Daughters Long I ★★★ 14 15 16 Innovative South Fork producer for Bianco Pétillant Naturel, Rosato di Refosco, other light, refreshing rosés; also v.gd Tocai FRIULANO, PINOT GRIGIO, CAB-based red blends.

Finger Lakes One of most exciting wine regions in US, with 129 wineries today. While RIES undoubtedly est its reputation, other varieties incl GEWURZ, GRÜNER V, CAB FR, SYRAH gaining stature. Up-and-coming wineries: Atwater, Billsboro, Domaine Leseurre, Hector, Kemmeter, Ventosa.

Fox Run Finger L ★★★ 13 14 15 16 Excellent RIES, plus gd CHARD, rosé, CAB FR, PINOT N. Café overlooking Lake Seneca.

Frank, Dr. Konstantin (Vinifera Wine Cellars) Finger L ★★★★ **12** 14 15 16 One of country's leading RIES producers. Also fine GEWURZ, GRÜNER V, PINOT N, RKATSITELI, plus classy Château Frank (sp). Est 1961, with 4th generation now involved.

Hamptons, The (aka South Fork) Long I Fashionable seaside destination for Manhattanites, with three wineries: CHANNING DAUGHTERS, Duckwalk, WÖLFFER.

Heart & Hands Finger L ★★★ 14 15 16 On shores of Cayuga Lake; classic cool-climate RIES, delicate PINOT N.

Hermann J Wiemer Finger L ★★★ **13** 14 15 16 Est 1976 by German winemaker. One of best RIES producers in US, plus fine sparkling, CHARD, GEWURZ, CAB FR, PINOT N.

Hudson River Region Scenic region 90 minutes from Manhattan with 42 wineries. Leaders: Benmarl, Hudson-Chatham, MILLBROOK, Robibero, Tousey, Whitecliff. Oldest is Brotherhood, est 1839.

Long Island

Jutting e into the Atlantic some 80 km from Manhattan, Long I's relatively mild climate let vintners concentrate on classic vinifera grapes, esp CAB FR, MERLOT, CHARD, SAUV BL. With 30 wineries and three AVAs: Long I, North Fork of Long I, THE HAMPTONS (aka South Fork). Leaders: BEDELL, CHANNING DAUGHTERS, MACARI, MARTHA CLARA, PAUMANOK, SHINN, SPARKLING POINTE, WÖLFFER.

Lake Erie Tri-state AVA. Standout producers: 21 BRIX and Mazza Chautauqua Cellars. Look for CHARD, PINOT GR, RIES, Icewine, high-quality eau de vie.

Lamoreaux Landing Finger L ★★★ 12 14 15 16 Greek Revival building overlooking Lake Seneca; excellent *Chard*, RIES, dry white blend (MUSCAT/CHARD/Ries), Icewine, plus CAB FR, MERLOT.

Macari Long I, North F ★★★ 13 14 15 16 Set on Macari family's 500-acre waterfront estate. Topnotch SAUV BL; premium reds incl CAB FR, MERLOT and B'x-style blends.

Martha Clara Long I, North F ★★★ 14 15 16 Gd Crémant Blanc, excellent MERLOT, fine MALBEC, CHARD, SAUV BL.

Paumanok, native name for Long I, was home to 13 different Indian tribes in 1643.

McCall Long I, North F ★★★ 13 14 15 16 V.gd red blends from CAB FR, MERLOT, other Bd'x varieties, plus serious PINOT N and gd CHARD. Also pure-bred Charolais cattle.

McGregor Finger L ★★ 14 15 16 On scenic Keuka Lake, with gd RIES, PINOT N and exciting SAPERAVI/Sereksiya Charni blend.

Millbrook Hudson ★★ ★ 14 15 16 Most important Hudson Valley winery with CHARD, RIES, Tocai (FRIULANO), CAB FR.

North Fork Long I One of longest growing seasons in ne. Top estates: BEDELL, MACARI, MARTHA CLARA, MCCALL, PAUMANOK, SHINN ESTATE, SPARKLING POINTE .

Paumanok Long I ★★★ 10 13 14 15 16 Top-notch winery; father and son produce noteworthy wines, esp CHENIN BL and red B'x-style blends; fine CHARD, RIES, MERLOT.

Ravines Finger L★★★ 14 15 16 Exceptional dry and dessert *Ries* plus CAB FR, PINOT N.

Red Newt Finger L ★★★ 13 14 15 16 Elegant GEWURZ, PINOT GR, RIES; gd CAB FR, MERLOT, PINOT N. Homey bistro.

Red Tail Ridge Finger L ★★★ 14 15 16 Highest quality; incl dry and dessert CHARD, Ries, PINOT N, TEROLDEGO.

Shinn Estate Long I ★★★ 12 14 15 16 Lively SAUV BL, earthy CAB FR, fine MERLOT, crisp Blanc de Blancs sparkler. Attractive farmhouse inn.

Silver Thread Finger L ★ ★★ 14 15 16 Super-dry and semi-dry RIES; gd PINOT N, rosé, CHARD, B'x-style red blend.

Sparkling Pointe Long I ★★★ *Notable sparkling* crafted by French-born winemaker.

Swedish Hill Finger L ★★★ 14 15 16 Historic FINGER L estate est 1969; consistently gd CHARD, RIES, sparkling, PINOT GRIGIO, Vignoles late-harvest.

Wölffer Estate Long I ★★★ 12 13 14 15 16 Esteemed South Fork estate where German-born winemaker makes fine CHARD, rosé, fine CAB SAUV, superior MERLOT.

North Carolina

Humid, sub-tropical s state with 155 wineries, incl **Biltmore**, **Childress**, **Cypress Bend** (for muscadine), **Duplin** (likewise for muscadine), **Grandfather**, **Hanover Park**, **Laurel Gray**, **McRitchie**, **Old North State**, **Ragapple Lassie**, **RayLen**, **Raffaldini**, **Shelton**. Top varieties: CHARD, VIOGNIER, CAB FR and native muscadine.

Ohio

Extreme cold in winter is moderated by Lake Erie. 254 wineries, five AVAs. PINOT GR, RIES, PINOT N, Icewine can be excellent, plus Pinot Gr and CAB FR in s OH. Top: **Breitenbach**, **Debonné**, **Ferrante**, **Firelands**, **Harpersfield**, **Laurentia**, **M Cellars**, **Markko**, **Paper Moon**, **St Joseph**, **Valley Vineyards**.

Oklahoma

Only one AVA, Ozark Mtn. Mostly reds, esp CAB SAUV. **Chapel Creek:** gd TEMPRANILLO, Norton; **Clauren Ridge:** gd PETITE SIRAH, VIOGNIER, Meritage; **Durso Hills:** Norton, **Redbud Ridge:** SYRAH; **Sand Hill:** wide range, esp Cab Sauv. **Stable Ridge:** v.gd Bedlam CHARD. **The Range Vineyard:** gd white blend Jackwagon.

Oregon

PINOT N is king in OR, and particularly in the Will V AVA, the 1st New World region to impress the Burgundians in the 80s. No big firms have emerged here; small scale is part of the appeal of this tricky, often rainy region. But wines can be elegant in the French way. Lately there has been strong interest in the state from outside investors, buying v'yd land and wineries.

Principal viticultural areas

Southern Oregon (S OR) Warm-climate region incl AVAs Rogue, Applegate (App V) and Umpqua Valleys (Um V). Tempranillo, Syrah, Viognier are v.gd; lots of experimentation.

Willamette Valley (Will V) Oregon's home for cool-climate Pinot N, Pinot Gr, plus v.gd Chard, dry Ries. Important child AVAs incl Dundee Hills, Chehalem Mts, Yamhill-Carlton (Y-Car), Eola-Amity Hills.

Abacela S OR ★★★ Pioneer of Spanish varieties; consistent leader in ALBARIÑO, TEMPRANILLO; v.gd SYRAH, VIOGNIER. Paramour is excellent Rioja-style blend.

Adelsheim Vineyard Will V ★★★ 10' 11 12' 13 14 15 One of OR's founding wineries, producer of top-notch single-v'yd PINOT N, v.gd Res CHARD.

Anam Cara Cellars Will V ★★★ 11' 12' 13 14 15 Small, family winery crafting 1st-class PINOT N: grace, depth. Nicholas Estate a standout; ditto Dry RIES.

Antica Terra Will V ★★★→★★★★ 10 11' 12' 13 14 15 Maggie Harrison left CA's Sine Qua Non to make Will V PINOT N; now has cult-like following. Recently added highly touted Aurata CHARD. Botanica Pinot N consistent standout.

Archery Summit Will V ★★★ 10 11 12' 13 14' 15 Part of Crimson Wine Group, producer of outstanding, age-worthy PINOT N from estate v'yds in Dundee Hills and Ribbon Ridge AVAs, esp Red Hills and Arcus Estate. Whites incl v.gd concrete-fermented PINOT GR.

Argyle Will V ★★→★★★ 10 11 12' 13 14 15 Winery known for well-priced PINOT N, CHARD, dry and sweet RIES, multiple styles of *v.gd bubbly*.

Beaux Frères Will V ★★★→★★★★ 10 11' 12' 13' 14 15 Part-owned by critic Robert M Parker, Jr, this prestige bio estate makes increasingly refined, collectible PINOT N. Beaux Frères V'yd is outstanding.

Bergström Wines Will V ★★★→★★★★ 10 11' 12' 13 14 15 Josh Bergström's PINOT NS from bio estate are elegant yet powerful. Small-lot Sigrid CHARD is sublime. Le Pré Du Col V'yd Pinot N otherworldly.

Bethel Heights Will V ★★→★★★ 11' 12' 13 14 15 2nd-generation family winery and OR legend. Spicy PINOT N, *v.gd Chard*, PINOTS GR, BL. Æolian Pinot N a standout.

Brick House Will V ★★★ 09' 10 11 12' 13 14' 15 Bio leader producing earthy, powerful estate PINOT N (esp Cuvée du Tonnelier and Evelyn's), elegant, stylish CHARD.

Broadley Vineyards Will V ★★ 10' 11' 12 13 14 15 Family winery; characterful PINOT N from older estate vines and select v'yds. Basic Will V PINOT N a steal, Claudia's Choice a top-end winner.

Brooks Winery Will V ★★★ 10 11' 12' 13 14 15 Leading bio producer and RIES champion with zesty dry, balanced sweet RIES. Superb PINOT N, esp estate Rasteban. Basic Will V Pinot N gd value.

Chehalem Will V ★★★ 10 11' 12' 13 14 15 Highly regarded PINOT N producer, equally strong RIES, CHARD, PINOT GR. Ridgecrest Pinot N is age-worthy; unoaked *INOX Chard great value*. Three V'yd Pinot N v.gd value.

Cowhorn S OR ★★★ 11 12' 13 14 15 App V AVA bio purist makes top-quality SYRAH, VIOGNIER. Spiral 36 ROUSSANNE/Viognier sensational.

Cristom Will V ★★★ 10 11' 12' 13 14 15 Consistently high-quality PINOT N. Jessie V'yd has fresh savouriness, Sommers Res truffle overtones.

Dobbes Family Estate Will V ★★→★★★ 09 10' 11' 12' 13 14 15 Winemaker Joe Dobbes makes prestige Will V PINOT N; plus SYRAH, GRENACHE BL. Sundown VIOGNIER a standout. Second label Wine by Joe: great bargain Pinot N, PINOT GR.

Domaine Drouhin Oregon Will V ★★★→★★★★ 10 11' 12' 13 14 15 OR branch of Burgundy's Joseph Drouhin. Top-quality PINOT N, crisp, complex Arthur CHARD. Barrel-select Laurène Pinot N stunning. Purchase of Roserock estate in Eola-Amity Hills brings another 122 acres of Pinot N, Chard. Winery to watch.

Domaine Serene Will V ★★★ 10 11 12' 13 14 15 Premium PINOT N consistently wins rave reviews. Small-production Evenstad Res CHARD worth seeking out.

Elk Cove Vineyards Will V ★★→★★★ 10 11 12' 13 14 15 2nd-generation winemaker; excellent value wines. PINOT GR, RIES perennially tops; seven estate-v'yd PINOT NS deliver delectable array of Will V terroirs. Entry-level Will V Pinot N v.gd value.

Erath Vineyards Will V ★★→★★★ 10 11 12' 13 14 15 Founding OR winery now owned by WA's Ste Michelle Wine Estates. Diverse array of value-priced Pinot-family wines but also standout single v'yd PINOT NS. La Nuit Magique top cuvée.

Evening Land Will V ★★★→★★★★ 11 12' 13 14' 15 Prestige producer; Seven Springs Summum PINOT N, CHARD are rare, but among best on either side of Atlantic. La Source Seven Springs Estate Pinot N also tops.

Eyrie Vineyards Will V ★★★→★★★★ 10 11' 12 13 14 15 Founder David Lett planted 1st Will V PINOT N in 1965. Today son Jason extends legacy with terrific Pinot N in graceful, classically OR style. Also unique, v.gd CHARD, PINOT GR.

Gran Moraine Y-Car ★★ 12' 13 14 15 1st PINOT NS from OR estate of CA giant Jackson Family Wines terrific, esp lithe, polished Estate Res, La Première. To watch.

Hyland Estates Will V ★★★ 10 11 12' 13 14 15 OR veteran Laurent Montalieu uses some of oldest PINOT N vines in Will V for succulent, polished wines. Also top-notch CHARD, GEWURZ, RIES.

Ken Wright Cellars Will V ★★★ 10 11' 12' 13 14 15 Renowned winemaker for top-quality single-v'yd PINOT N, showing range of Will V terroirs. Freedom Hill dense, firm; Guadalupe balanced, expressive.

King Estate ★★→★★★ 11 12' 13 14 15 One of state's largest wineries makes PINOT GR a speciality along with PINOT N. Some Will V wines. Gd value at multiple price-points. NxNW label for WA wines incl Red Blend, RIES.

Lange Estate Winery Will V ★★★ 10' 11 12' 13 14 15 2nd generation winemaker Jesse Lange makes sumptuous PINOT N (esp Lange Estate), barrel-aged Res PINOT GR. CHARD gaining reputation.

Ponzi Vineyards Will V ★★★→★★★★ 10' 11 12' 13 14 15 2nd generation, legendary PINOT N specialist, outstanding wines. Aurora PINOT N knockout; Res CHARD standout. Don't miss brilliant ARNEIS. Entry Tavola Pinot N v.gd value.

Quady North S OR ★★→★★★ Standout winemaker Herb Quady crafts delicious CAB FR from cooler Rogue Valley AVA sites, also intriguing SYRAHS. Winery to watch.

Rex Hill Will V ★★★ 11' 12' 13 14 15 Highly regarded, bio farmer hand-crafts superb estate PINOT NS; notable CHARD. A to Z Wineworks is value label.

Scott Paul Wines Will V ★★★ 10 11' 12 13 14 15 PINOT N-only producer emphasizes elegance, grace with Burgundy-inspired character. Audrey gd for cellaring.

Sokol Blosser Will V ★★★ 11 12' 13 14 15 2nd-generation maker of consistently high-

OREGON

Two states share a border but not much else

Growing regions in OR and neighbouring WA could not be more different. Will V in OR has a wet, maritime climate. WA's Col V meanwhile is e part of state and has a dry, continental climate. Most of Will V v'yds are dry-farmed whereas irrigation is a necessity in arid e WA. In Will V, cool-climate PINOT N is king; in Col V, heat-loving CAB SAUV is increasingly popular.

quality PINOTS N, GR from Dundee Hills; v.gd-value white blend and Pinot N Evolution. Innovative tasting venue worth the stop.

Soter Vineyard Will V ★★★★ 10 11' 12' 13 14 15 CA legend Tony Soter moved to OR to make PINOT N. Estate *Mineral Springs Ranch Pinot N* is sublime. Fizz is PNW's best.

Stoller Family Estate Will V ★★★ 10 11 12' 13 14 15 Beautifully balanced PINOT NS exemplify Dundee Hills. Also v.gd CHARD. Helen's and Nancy's Pinot N standouts. Entry Dundee Hills Pinot N v.gd value.

Teutonic Wine Company ★★★ 11 12' 13 14 15 Iconoclastic, Mosel-inspired RIES, crisp white blends, Germanic-styled PINOT N. Up-and-comer generating buzz.

Trisaetum Will V ★★★ 11 12' 13' 14' 15 Owner, artist, winemaker James Frey makes cool-climate RIES, PINOT N from Coast Range estate vines and other sources. Ribbon Ridge Estate Pinot N tops. New project titled 18401 uses Walla fruit.

Willamette Valley Vineyards Will V ★★→★★★ 10 11 12' 13 14 15 Publicly owned producer makes high-quality estate PINOT NS, CHARD; v.gd RIES. New Elton V'yd project. Now in Walla too.

Pennsylvania

220+ wineries. Some exploration now with GRÜNER V and other Austrian varieties. Top estates: **Allegro** (red B'x blend), **Blair** (PINOT N, CHARD), **Briar Valley** (RIES, CAB FR), **Galen Glen** (Grüner V, Ries), **Galer Estate** (Chard, Rosé), **Karamoor** (Cab Fr, red blends), **Manatawny Creek** (Meritage), **Mazza** (VIDAL Icewine), **Nimble Hill** (Ries), **Penns Wood** (Chard, Cabs), **Pinnacle Ridge** (B'x blend), **Seven Mountains** (Ries), **The Vineyard at Grandview** (red B'x blends), **Waltz** (Chard, CAB SAUV), **Va La** (Italian varieties).

30,000 acres Concord grapes on Lake Erie shoreline and PA. Mostly juice and jam.

Texas

The 1st vines were planted by missionaries in 1650s, TX now main wine-growing state of the sw with steady innovations; maturing all the time with less oak and lower alc. Warm-climate grapes excel here: B'x and Rhône varieties, SANGIOVESE, TEMPRANILLO, ZIN, VERMENTINO and VIOGNIER, and there are even experiments in orange wines. There are more than 300 bonded wineries of record but not all are producing TX-appellation wines (75 per cent or more grown in state). Best wines often available only through direct sales at winery because of price margins. Be selective on wine route, as some more touristic destinations than serious producers. TX High Plains showing promise with talented producers.

Becker Vineyards ★★★ Wide range, some wines from out-of-state grapes. Try: TEMPRANILLO Res, Prairie Rotie, MALBEC/PETIT VERDOT blend called Raven. CAB SAUV Res Canada Family, Res Newsom V'yd Cab Sauv, Res Malbec, rosé Provençal.

Bending Branch ★★ Pioneering sustainable winery in picturesque setting nr San Antonio; Mediterranean varieties; TANNAT a signature grape. ROUSSANNE, Newsom V'yds TEMPRANILLO, v.gd Single Barrel Picpoul Blanc aged in used bourbon barrels.

Bingham Family Vineyards Should be gathering stars over the next few yrs. In meantime, enjoy excellent VIOGNIER, v.gd VERMENTINO.

Massive Texas Hill Country, one of the state's eight AVAs, 2nd largest in US.

Brennan Vineyards ★★ Excellent dry VIOGNIER; Lily is white Rhône blend; award-winning Res TEMPRANILLO; v.gd MOURVÈDRE Dry Rosé and MONTEPULCIANO.

Cap Rock ★★→★★★ Much-medalled High Plains winery, esp MERLOT, *Roussanne*.

Dotson Cervantes ★★ Outstanding dessert wine Gotas de Oro.

Duchman ★★★ →★★★ Nr Austin. Specializes in Italian varietals and blends. Awards for DOLCETTO and VERMENTINO. Nr-perfect TEMPRANILLO, refreshing Bianco, v.gd Salt Lick Cellars GSM and BBQ White.

Fall Creek Vineyards ★★★ One of TX's oldest, bolstered by new winemaker from Chile. Gorgeous Salt Lick TEMPRANILLO and GSM, consistently excellent B'x blend.

Haak Winery ★★ Gd dry Blanc du Bois; top "Madeira" copies: Spanish winemaker.

Inwood Estates ★★★ Exceptional TEMPRANILLO and Mericana CAB SAUV, v.gd PALOMINO/CHARD blend and Dallas County Chard. Small but well worth checking out.

Lewis Wines ★★ Young winemakers infusing scene with TEMPRANILLO, plus v.gd Rosé, Texas White, Portuguese Tinta Cão.

Llano Estacado ★→★★★ Huge historic winery, often exceptional, occasionally plain. Excellent MALBEC, 1836 (r w), V.gd Viviana (w), Viviano (r) mimics a Super Tuscan.

Lost Draw Vineyards ★★ Small-batch wines from Kim McPherson, specializing in Mediterrnean varieties: VIOGNIER, award-winning PICPOUL Blanc. V.gd TEMPRANILLO.

McPherson Cellars ★★★ Delicious Les Copains (r p w), excellent Res ROUSSANNE. One of TX's best winemakers.

Messina Hof Wine Cellars ★→★★★ Large range. Excellent RIES, esp late-harvest. V.gd Papa Paolo Port-style, Res CAB FR, unoaked CHARD.

Pedernales Cellars ★★★→★★★★ Top VIOGNIER Res, excellent TEMPRANILLO, GSM. Old-world style; 100 per cent TX grapes.

Perissos Vineyard and Winery ★★ Excellent AGLIANICO, PETITE SIRAH, TEMPRANILLO.

Spicewood Vineyards ★★→★★★ Estate-grown; exceptional Sancerre-like SAUV BL, v.gd SEM. Gd TEMPRANILLO, dry MOURVÈDRE rosé, Portuguese varieties.

Virginia

Rapidly expanding, with 285 wineries. Climate and growing conditions seem closer to s/sw France and n Italy than to other US regions. CHARD performs well in cooler locations. VIOGNIER still popular though yields can be a problem. PETIT VERDOT seems to be outshining CAB FR as up-and-coming variety; future looks bright for TANNAT, PETIT MANSENG. 2016 had ideal growing conditions, esp in Aug and Sept.

Barboursville ★★★★ 12 13 14 15 16 One of best and earliest estates in e (founded 1976 by Italy's Zonin family) with excellent B'x-style reds, CAB SAUV and NEBBIOLO, plus Paxxito, a luscious VIDAL/MOSCATO Ottonel blend. Superb restaurant, inn on historic site frequented by Thomas Jefferson.

Boxwood ★★★ 13 14 15 16 Reds from five B'x grapes; 80 km w of Washington DC.

Breaux ★ 14 15 Hilltop v'yd, 1 hour from Washington DC. Gd Meritage, CAB FR, CHARD.

Chrysalis ★★★ 13 14 15 16 Leading VIOGNIER producer, plus ALBARIÑO, PETIT VERDOT, TEMPRANILLO, VA native Norton.

Delaplane ★★★ 12 13 14 15 16 Fine, scenic hillside estate, incl CHARD, PETIT MANSENG, B'x style reds, CAB FR, TANNAT.

Gabriele Rausse ★★ 14 15 16 Small estate nr Jefferson's Monticello; owned by VA's 1st commercial grape-grower. CHARD, CABS SAUV, FR, MERLOT, NEBBIOLO.

Glen Manor Vineyards ★★★ 13 14 15 16 In Blue Ridge Mtns; crisp SAUV BL, excellent red B'x-style blend, gd rosé, CAB FR, PETIT MANSENG, Petit Verdot.

Grace Estate ★★ 14 15 16 Estate in central VA; impressive VIOGNIER, fine CHARD, VIDAL/Viognier blend, TANNAT, PETIT VERDOT and B'x-inspired red blends.

Horton ★★ 14 15 16 Pioneering estate (est 1991); gd VIOGNIER, also PETIT MANSENG, CAB FR, TANNAT, and SYRAH/Viognier blend.

King Family Vineyards ★★★ 13 14 15 16 Serious, age-worthy MERITAGE, gd CHARD, VIOGNIER, CAB FR, luscious *vin de paille*-style PETIT MANSENG dessert wine.

Linden ★★★★ 12' 14 15 16 Just 105 km w of Washington DC. Leading VA estate with notable high-altitude wines incl rich CHARD, vivacious SAUV BL, savoury PETIT VERDOT, elegant, complex B'x-style red blends, superb late-harvest VIDAL.

Michael Shaps Wineworks ★★★★ 12 13 14 15 16 Richly textured VIOGNIER, toothsome CHARD and PETIT MANSENG, also tasty TANNAT, gd PETIT VERDOT, exceptional Meritage and unique, concentrated late-harvest Raisin d'Etre.

Pollak ★★★ 12 13 14 15 16 Top VIOGNIER, CABS SAUV, FR, MERLOT, PETIT VERDOT, Meritage.

More than 2.3 million people visited VA wineries last yr. A lot of tasting samples.

RdV Vineyards ★★★★ 10 12 13' 14 15 One of best in e, focusing solely on B'x-inspired red blends characterized by elegance, complexity and power.

Sunset Hills ★★ 14 15 16 Scenic winery in renovated barn; gd CHARD, VIOGNIER, CAB SAUV, outstanding B'x-style red blend.

Upper Shirley Vineyards ★★★ 13 14 15 16 Promising young estate (since 2013) in Tidewater region. Nice VIOGNIER, serious high-quality PETIT VERDOT, MERLOT, TANNAT.

Veritas ★★ 14 15 16 Gd sparkling, opulent VIOGNIER, gd CHARD, CAB FR, MERLOT, PETIT VERDOT and B'x-inspired red blend.

Washington

This is a time of grand exploration in WA, as growers and winemakers alike consider varieties, sites and, increasingly, clones. There are over 40 varieties planted and no single vine dominates. However, RIES, CHARD, CAB SAUV, MERLOT and SYRAH make up over 75 per cent of state's production. Rhône varieties are on rise, with some turning heads. Keep an eye out for GRENACHE and MOURVÈDRE.

Principal viticultural areas

Columbia Valley (Col V) Huge AVA in central and e WA with a touch in OR. Quality Cab Sauv, Merlot, Ries, Chard, Syrah. Key sub-divisions incl Yakima Valley (Yak V), Red Mtn, Walla AVAs.

Red Mountain (Red Mtn) Child AVA of Col V and Yak V. Hot region known for Cab Sauv and B'x blends.

Walla Walla Valley (Walla) Child AVA of Col V with own identity and vines in WA and OR. Home of important boutique brands and prestige labels focusing on quality Cab Sauv, Merlot, Syrah.

Yakima Valley (Yak V) Child AVA of Col V. Focus on Merlot, Syrah, Ries.

Abeja Walla ★★★ Producer of top Col V CAB SAUV, CHARD. Estate SYRAH v.gd.

Andrew Will ★★★→★★★★★ 10' 11 12' 13' 14 Winemaker Chris Camarda made name for top-quality single-v'yd red blends from outstanding Col V v'yds. Sorella is flagship but no misses in line-up.

WA has no phylloxera: almost all vines on their own roots.

Avennia ★★★ 12' 13' 14' (15) Young winery from Microsoft alum Marty Taucher and winemaker Chris Peterson, formerly of DeLille, turning heads with B'x, Rhône styles. Sestina B'x blend and Arnaut SYRAH worth seeking out.

Betz Family Winery ★★★→★★★★ 09' 10 11 12' 13 14' (15) Maker of Rhône, B'x styles from top Col V v'yds. La Côte Patriarche comes from state's oldest SYRAH vines. Pére de Famille CAB SAUV consistent standout and one for cellar.

B Leighton Col V New project from Brennon Leighton, winemaker for K Vintners. Rhône blend Gratitude, SYRAH, PETIT VERDOT all standouts.

Brian Carter Cellars ★★★ 09 10 11' 12' 13 Focus on blends, with wines aged before release. Try unconventional PETIT VERDOT-driven Trentenaire, Byzance Rhône blend or aromatic Oriana (w).

Cadence ★★★ 10' 11 12' 13' (14) B'x-style blends from Red Mtn fruit. Age-worthy wines, incl spicy CAB FR-dominant Bel Canto and CAB SAUV-heavy Camerata.

Cayuse Walla ★★★★ 09' 10 11 12' 13' 14 (15) One of state's top wineries that consistently receives stratospheric scores for its estate v'yd wines. Spellbinding, earthy SYRAH (esp Cailloux and Bionic Frog) and GRENACHE, but you have to be on mailing list with yrs-long wait to get any. Sister wineries No Girls and Horsepower also top notch.

Charles Smith Wines Walla ★★→★★★ Sold to Constellation in 2016 for $120 million. Focus on value wines. Look for Kung Fu Girl RIES.

Chateau Ste Michelle ★★→★★★★ Largest single producer of RIES in world; all prices/ styles: v.gd quaffers (excellent Col V Ries) to TBA-style rarities (Eroica Single Berry Select). Gd-value Col V label, premium Ethos Res. Turned 50 in 2017.

Chinook Wines Col V ★★★ 09' 10 11 12' 13' (14) Husband (vines) and wife (wines) have a history of fine, value CAB FR (rosé is delightful), MERLOT, CHARD, SAUV BL.

Col Solare Col V ★★★→★★★★ 07 08 09' 10 11' 12' 13 (14) Partnership between Ste Michelle Wine Estates and Tuscany's Antinori. Focus on single CAB SAUV-dominant Red Mtn red blend, complex, long-lasting.

Columbia Crest Col V ★★→★★★ By far WA's largest winery makes oodles of v.gd, affordable wines under Grand Estates, H3, Res labels. Res wines offer v.gd value, esp CAB SAUV; H3 wines all from Horse Heaven Hills AVA: great value.

Much WA soil derives from Ice Age floods: inundated everything up to 365m.

Corliss Estates Col V ★★★ 08' 09' 10 11 12 (13) Producer of high-end CAB SAUV, B'x blend and SYRAH. Wines released after substantial time in barrel and bottle.

Côte Bonneville Yak V ★★★ 08 09' 10 11 12' 13 14 Estate winery for DuBrul V'yd, said to be one of best in state. *Carriage House* v.gd value. Don't overlook CHARD, SYRAH.

DeLille Cellars ★★★→★★★★ 09 10' 11 12' 13 14' (15) Est producer of sophisticated, age-worthy reds. Celebrated 25th vintage in 2016.

Doubleback Walla ★★★ 09 10' 11 12' 13' 14 (15) Footballer Drew Bledsoe makes one wine, CAB SAUV, a feminine expression of Walla fruit with cellaring potential.

Dusted Valley Vintners Walla ★★★ 10 11 12' 13 14 (15) Impressive line-up. Popular for Stained Tooth SYRAH; beautiful Old Vine CHARD. Stoney Vine Syrah from estate plantings v. impressive.

Efesté ★★★ 09 10 11 12' 13 14 (15) Everything is gd here. Best known for zesty RIES, racy CHARD from cool Evergreen V'yd, also v.gd SYRAHS and old-vine CAB SAUV.

Fidelitas Col V ★★★ 09 10 11' 12' 13 14 (15) Former CHATEAU STE MICHELLE winemaker Charlie Hoppes makes fine B'x-style blends, CAB SAUV. Ciel du Cheval V'yd Cab shows power of Red Mtn AVA fruit. Quintessence V'yd Cab Sauv also top notch.

Fielding Hills Col V ★★★ Focuses on estate v'yd on Wahluke Slope. CAB SAUV and MERLOT outstanding.

Figgins Walla ★★★ 10 11 12' 13' 14 (15) Chris Figgins is also winemaker at famed LEONETTI. Focus on age-worthy, estate B'x blend, RIES. New OR PINOT N project.

Force Majeure ★★★ Young winery uses exclusively Red Mtn fruit. Estate v'yd crawls up hillside. CAB SAUV, B'x blends, VIOGNIER standouts. Cult winery in making.

Gramercy Cellars Walla ★★★→★★★★ 10 11 12' 13 14' (15) Sommelier Greg Harrington worked at top restaurants before making wine. Speciality juicy, earthy SYRAHS (esp Lagniappe), herby CAB SAUV. GRENACHE also consistent winner.

Hedges Family Estate Red Mt ★★★ Venerable Red Mtn family winery; polished, reliable wines, esp estate red blend and DLD SYRAH.

Hogue Cellars, The Col V ★★ Long-time winery owned by Constellation Brands; stylish, value, single variety wines. Genesis, Res labels more focused, smaller production.

Januik ★★★ 10 11 12' 13 14 (15) Artisan wines from a CHATEAU STE MICHELLE veteran. Wide selection varietals, single v'yds. Champoux V'yd CAB SAUV consistent standout.

K Vintners Col V, Walla ★★★ Top quality SYRAH, incl Col V single v'yds. Walla SYRAHS consistent standouts, esp Klein, Rock Garden. The Boy GRENACHE also tops.

L'Ecole No 41 Walla ★★★ 10 11 12' 13 14 (15) One of Walla's founding wineries; wide range of Col V and Walla wines. Apogee, Perigee and Ferguson (each from a different v'yd) top B'x blends. CHENIN BL v.gd value.

Leonetti Cellar Walla ★★★★ 09 10' 11 12' 13 14 (15) Founding Walla winery now in hands of 2nd-generation winemaker Chris Figgins. Has cult status winery for elegant, refined, collectable CAB SAUV, MERLOT, SANGIOVESE. Res B'x blend flagship.

Day and night temperatures in WA can vary by 40°F. Best take a pullover.

Long Shadows Walla ★★★→★★★★ Former Ste Michelle Wine Estates CEO Allen Shoup brings a group of globally famous winemakers to WA to each make a single wine from Col V fruit.

Maison Bleue Col V ★★★ 11' 12' 13 14 (15) Rhône-focused winery from winemaker Jon Meuret turning heads with GRENACHE, SYRAH. Domaine J Meuret impressive new CHARD, PINOT N project.

Mark Ryan ★★★ Woodinville-based producer of bold, fruit-filled B'x and Rhône styles largely from Red Mtn fruit. MERLOT-based Long Haul and Dead Horse CAB SAUV tops. Also VIOGNIER. Board Track Racer second label.

Milbrandt Vineyards Col V ★★ Focus on value. The Estates is higher-tier, single-v'yd wines from Wahluke Slope and Ancient Lakes. Look for RIES, PINOT GR.

Northstar Walla ★★★→★★★★ 09 10' 11 12' 13 14 Ste Michelle Wine Estates' MERLOT-focused winery, with Col V and Walla. Premier Merlot (made to age) is gorgeous.

Pacific Rim Col V ★★ RIES specialist making oceans of tasty, inexpensive yet eloquent Dry to Sweet and Organic. For more depth *single v'yd releases*.

Pepper Bridge Walla ★★★ 09 10' 11' 12 13 (14) Winemaker Jean François Pellet's CAB SAUVS are sensuous, rich, MERLOT spicy, aromatic. B'x Estate Pepper Bridge and Seven Hills V'yds among WA's best.

Quilceda Creek ★★★★ 03' 04' 05' 06 07 09 10 11' 12' 13 (14) One of state's oldest wineries and one of its flagships. Producer of top quality, often 100-point *Cab Sauvs*: dense, intense, tremendously long-lasting. One of most lauded producers in US. Sold by allocation. Find it if you can.

Reynvaan Family Vineyards Walla ★★★→★★★★ 09 10' 11 12' 13 14 (15) Family winery dedicated to SYRAH, CAB SAUV, Rhône-style whites. Has developed cult following and high critical scores. Wait-list winery but worth it.

Seven Hills Winery Walla ★★★ 09 10 11 12' 13 14 (15) One of Walla's oldest, most respected wineries, esp for silky CAB SAUV (Ciel du Cheval V'yd an age-worthy delight). Pentad top B'x blend. Recently bought by Crimson Wine Group.

Sparkman Cellars ★★★ 09 10 11 12' 13 14 (15) Woodinville producer of diverse grapes and styles, with a focus on power. Most notable: Stella Mae and Ruby Leight B'x blends. Look out for Evermore Old Vines CAB SAUV.

Spring Valley Vineyard Walla ★★★ 09 10' 11' 12' 13 14 Ste Michelle Wine Estates owned; estate Walla wines. Uriah MERLOT blend a perennial winner. Katherine Corkrum CAB FR also standout in superb lineup.

Syncline Cellars ★★★ Winery making excellent Rhône styles from Col G and Col V fruit. Subduction Red is v.gd value. NB the MOURVÈDRE.

Woodward Canyon Walla ★★★★ 06 07 09 10 11 12' 13 14 (15) Venerable Walla winery. *Old Vines Cab Sauv* is refined, complex, age-worthy. Estate Res for cellar; CHARD consistent winner. Nelms Road value label.

In Alaska you may not legally serve alc to a moose.

Wisconsin

Wollersheim Winery (est 1840s) is one of best estates in midwest, with hybrid and Wisconsin-native American hybrid grapes. Look for Prairie Fumé (SEYVAL BL) and Prairie Blush (Marechal Foch).

Mexico

Vines brought from Europe by the Spanish in the C16 make this the oldest wine-growing region in the Americas. Now there are 54,000 acres of wine grapes, with 90 per cent of production coming from Baja California. Quality small producers are clustered in the Valle de Guadalupe, about 100 km southeast of Tijuana. High altitudes and a reasonably cool climate present good ripening conditions. In recent decades there has been an upsurge of boutique wineries, fuelled by Hugo d'Acosta's wine incubator in Baja – a wine school and custom-crush facility called La Escuelita ("little school"). Wines are produced with international varieties. Though the wines have improved and are even trendy, the region is not quite the equivalent of Napa. Baja's rough roads require navigation by SUV. And underground is an issue, too: the ocean-influenced groundwater, used for irrigation, can get to the wines so they occasionally have a saline quality. The better wines are produced on hillsides where the water comes from mountain springs.

Adobe Guadalupe ★★→★★★ Baja's high-profile winemaker Hugo Acosta consults here. Wines, incl B'x blends, are named after archangels. Often v.gd quality, balanced, flavourful. Also a gd restaurant, B&B.

Bibayoff Vinos ★★→★★★ Outstanding ZIN and v.gd Zin/CAB SAUV blend. Zesty CHENIN BL all from dry-farmed hillside vines.

Casa de Piedra ★★→★★★ Artisanal winemaker Hugo Acosta makes Vino de Piedra, v.gd blend of CAB SAUV/TEMPRANILLO; Piedra del Sol, CHARD, three sparklers still seeking identity.

Château Camou ★★→★★★ CAB SAUV-based blend Gran Vino Tinto is velvety, balanced with a supple, elegant finish. Companion wine, Gran Vino Tinto ZIN, is powerful statement of variety.

Hacienda La Lomita ★★ Est 2009 by a Mexicali family heir and La Rioja (Spain)-trained winemaker using ultra-modern technology. Pagan GRENACHE (r) and bold red blends of CAB SAUV/MERLOT, v.gd fruit-forward Tinto de la Hacienda.

Boutique wineries with cutting-edge design reflect a new wave of young growers.

Monte Xanic ★★→★★★ Speakeasy-like setting with excellent CAB SAUV; v.gd MERLOT. Delightful apéritifs in the unoaked CHARD and fresh CHENIN BL.

Paralelo ★★ Cutting-edge project by Hugo Acosta and designed by his star-architect brother. Small production. Emblema SAUV BL; and two versions of Ensamble, red B'x blends.

Rincón de Guadalupe ★★→★★★ Oldest TEMPRANILLO vines in Mexico; v.gd SAUV BL and excellent red blend, Viejo Tinto.

Rognato ★★→★★★ Small new winery making excellent CAB SAUV and super red blend, Tramonte, with layers of flavour, lasting finish, potential for ageing.

Tres Mujeres ★★→★★★ Rustic co-op owned by women reflects new wave of artisan producers in Baja. Top TEMPRANILLO; v.gd GRENACHE/CAB SAUV, La Mezcla del Rancho.

Tres Valles Powerful reds from Guadalupe, Santo Tomas, San Vincente Valleys. Jala (Guadalupe) blend of CAB SAUV/GRENACHE powerful but clean.

Vena Cava ★★ Hip winery owned by a former US music exec and constructed from reclaimed fishing boats. Modern, organic wines. Complex oak-aged CAB SAUV and TEMPRANILLO. Signature is Res CAB SAUV/SYRAH blend. Farm-to-table restaurant.

Viñas Pijoan *Garagista* in spirit and style with a small tasting room manned by the winemaker. Domenica is pleasant Rhône blend.

Canada

Canadian wine is hot, and that's not easy to do in a country that defines cool climate. Interest has never been higher at home and exports are building. With a helpful hand from a warming planet, nothing seems impossible. There are 700+ wineries and 12,000 ha under vine, and a new generation of winemakers is pushing the boundaries of production from coast to coast. Generous acidity and moderate alcohol are the recipe for fresh, food-friendly wines that are capturing the imagination of wine-drinkers here and abroad. Chardonnay, Riesling and sparkling wine lead the white brigade, while the most talked-about reds are Pinot Noir and Syrah, with Cabernet Franc and Meritage red blends on the upswing.

Ontario

Three prime appellations of origin: Niagara Peninsula (Niag), Lake Erie North Shore, Prince Edward County (P Ed). Within the Niagara Peninsula: two regional appellations – Niagara Escarpment (Niag E) and Niagara-on-the-Lake (Niag L) – and ten sub-appellations.

Bachelder Niag r w ★★★ 11 12' 13 14' Thomas Bachelder is also in Burgundy and Oregon. Leads Niag with pure, precise, elegant, age-worthy CHARD, PINOT N grown on Dolomitic limestone and clay.

Cave Spring Niag r w sw sp ★★★ 13 14' 15' (16') Respected RIES pioneer; CSV (old vines). Estate labels age gracefully. Elegant CSV CHARD, top late-harvest, Icewine.

Château des Charmes Niag r w sw ★★ 12' 13 14' 15' (16') The 114-ha Bosc family farm is a charter member of Sustainable Winegrowing Ontario; RIES from bone-dry to Icewine, sparkling and Equuleus: flagship red blend.

Creekside Niag r w ★★★ 12' 13 14' 15' (16') Eclectic group defying convention, focused on SAUV BL and SYRAH; NB organic, single-barrel Undercurrent lots. Wonderful tasting/visitor experience.

Flat Rock Niag r w ★★ 11 12' 13 14' 15' (16') 32 ha on Twenty Mile Bench; a rich selection of juicy, crisp RIES, PINOT N, CHARD. Top picks Single-block Nadja's Ries, Rusty Shed Chard. All screwcapped.

Okanagan Lake is said to be bottomless: 750m+ sediment sits under 232m of water.

Henry of Pelham Niag r w sw sp ★★ 12' 13 14' 15' (16') Speck brothers make CHARD, RIES, exceptional Cuvée Catherine Brut fizz, Speck Family Res (SFR), unique Baco Noir, Ries Icewine.

Hidden Bench Niag r w ★★★★ 12' 13 14' 15' (16') Beamsville Bench artisanal producer. RIES, PINOT N, CHARD and top Terroir Series Roman's Block Ries and Nuit Blanche and La Brunate blends.

Huff Estates P Ed r w ★★ 12' 15 16 9-ha South Bay v'yd planted over clay/shale loam over limestone. Making name with CHARD, traditional-method sparkler; new PINOT N.

Inniskillin Niag r w sw ★★ 13 14' 15' (16') Canada Icewine pioneer evolving under winemaker Bruce Nicholson. Juicy Res RIES, PINOT GR, PINOT N, super CAB FR; Single V'yd Series in best yrs only.

Malivoire Niag r w ★★★ 12' 13 14' 15' (16') Shiraz Mottiar (yes, really) makes eco-friendly GAMAY, plus CAB FR, CHARD; tasty PINOT N, GEWURZ and a cult Rosé from four Niag Esc v'yds.

Norman Hardie P Ed r w ★★★ 11 12' 13 14' 15' (16') Iconic P Ed Cty pioneer hand-crafting on-the-edge CHARD, PINOT N, RIES on limestone-clay soils. Buy Cuvée L Chard, Pinot N in best yrs.

Pearl Morissette Niag r w ★★★ 13 14' 15' François Morissette (winemaker/partner) trained under Frédéric Mugnier in Burgundy makes original RIES aged in *foudre*, CHARD, CAB FR, PINOT N with concrete eggs and *foudres*.

Ravine Vineyard Niag r w ★★★ 13 14' 15' (16') Organic 14-ha St David's Bench v'yd spans early Niagara River watercourse. Top Res CHARD and CAB FR; drink-now label: Sand and Gravel.

Stratus Niag r w ★★★ 12' 13 14' 15' 16' Iconoclast JL Groux works 25 ha of Niagara Lakeshore fruit at LEEDS-certified green winery. Blends (r w) reflect a quest for somewhereness; v.gd RIES, SYRAH.

Tawse Niag r w ★★★★ 12' 13 14' 15' (16') Winemaker Paul Pender runs this eco-friendly 2016 Canadian Winery of the Year making outstanding CHARD, RIES, gd PINOT N, CAB FR, MERLOT, v'yds certified organic and bio.

British Columbia

BC has identified five appellations of origin: Okanagan Valley (Ok V), Similkameen Valley, Fraser Valley, Vancouver Island and the Gulf Islands.

Blue Mountain Ok V r w sp ★★★ 12' 13' 14' (15) (16') Next generation continue traditional-method fizz incl smart RD versions; age-worthy PINOT N, CHARD, PINOT GR, GAMAY. Outstanding Res Pinot N.

Burrowing Owl Ok V r w ★★★ 12' 13' 14' (15) (16') Pioneer estate; excellent CAB FR, v.gd PINOT GR, SYRAH on Black Sage Bench; successful boutique hotel/restaurant.

CedarCreek Ok V r w ★★★ 12' 13' 14' (15) (16') A new innovative Amphora Project leads CedarCreek's stellar line-up of aromatic RIES, GEWURZ, Ehrenfelser and Platinum single-v'yd blocks PINOT N, CHARD.

Church & State Wines Ok V r w ★★★ 13' 14' (15) (16') Stylish Coyote Bowl winery making delicious blends Trebella (Rhône white), Quintessential (B'x red); excellent CHARD, VIOGNIER, SYRAH.

Haywire Ok V ★★★ 14' (15) (16') Hipster Summerland producer working with Alberto Antonini and Pedro Parra on natural, Pét-Nat (*see* A Little Learning), organics, concrete ferments, amphora. CHARD, PINOT GR, PINOT N, GAMAY, sparkling.

Mission Hill Ok V r w ★★★ 12' 13' 14' (15) (16') Darryl Brooker (ex-CedarCreek) takes over to polish Legacy Series: Oculus, Perpetua, Quatrain, Compendium. Benchmark visitor centre/outdoor restaurant.

Nk'Mip Ok V r w ★★★ 14' (15) (16') Steady fresh RIES, PINOT N; top-end Qwam Qwmt Pinot N, SYRAH. Part of $25 million aboriginal resort/Desert Cultural Centre.

Osoyoos Larose Ok V r ★★★ 12' 13' 14' (15) B'x-based Groupe Taillan owns this 33-ha single v'yd. Age-worthy Le Grand Vin echoes B'x. Second label Pétales d'Osoyoos.

Painted Rock Ok V r w ★★★ 14' (15) (16') Skaha Bench, steep-slope, 24 ha. B'x consultant Alain Sutre; v.gd SYRAH, CAB FR, CHARD, signature red blend Icon.

Quails' Gate Ok V r w ★★★ 13 14' (15) (16') New inspired style under winemaker Nikki Callaway mixes fruit and complexity. Excellent PINOT N, CHARD, aromatic RIES, CHENIN BL and all-new Collector Series.

Road 13 Ok V r w ★★★ 13' 14' (15) (16') Star on Golden Mile Bench; 1st Ok V sub-appellation. Fabulous old-vine CHENIN BL (w sp) and VIOGNIER, SYRAH, PINOT N, CAB FR.

Stag's Hollow Ok V ★★★ 14' (15) (16') Winemaker Dwight Sick fuses Old and New Worlds creating Next World Okanagan Falls. Delicious, affordable ALBARIÑO, VIOGNIER, GRENACHE, PINOT N, SYRAH.

Tantalus Ok V r w ★★★ 13' 14' (15) (16') Natural wine-growing is at root of terroir-driven RIES. PINOT N, CHARD from oldest (1927) continuously producing Ok V v'yds.

Nova Scotia

Benjamin Bridge ★★★ 07' 08 09 10 11 Gaspereau Valley is home to this noteworthy traditional-method sparkling. Excellent age-worthy vintage and NV brut made from CHARD/PINOTS N/M blends.

South America

Abbreviations
used in the text:

Aco	Aconcagua
Bío	Bío-Bío
Cach	Cachapoal
Casa	Casablanca
Cata	Catamarca
Cho	Choapa
Col	Colchagua
Coq	Coquimbo
Cur	Curicó
Elq	Elqui
Ita	Itata
La R	La Rioja
Ley	Leyda
Pat	Patagonia	Lim	Limarí
Rap	Rapel	Luján	Luján de Cuyo
Río N	Río Negro	Mai	Maipo
Sal	Salta	Mal	Malleco
San A	San Antonio	Mau	Maule
San J	San Juan	Men	Mendoza
Uco V	Uco Valley	Neu	Neuquén

CHILE

A question I have had to field more than once recently is "Which do you prefer, Chile or Argentina?" (It's wine they're talking about, of course. At least I hope so.) I have to fumble the answer. Argentina for Malbec, of course, and Chile for Cabernet and its cousins, most of the time. There is something that can creep into Chilean Cab, though, a taste of the earth, which is a bit too earthy for me. For sheer enjoyment Malbec is hard to beat, and not necessarily the de luxe versions. Chile is generally a happier hunting ground for white wines, both Chardonnay and Sauvignon. Sadly I don't find much room for Torrontés in my life; perhaps my diet is too bland. I've had delicious Pinot Noir from both countries – and hope for more. Syrah, too. Most recent Chilean surprise: a sparkling wine made from the practically disenfranchised País, the old Mission grape. Behind all the developments is the most basic of all: the search for the best terroirs. It is going on apace in both countries. In Chile you'll find the best Cabernet Sauvignon and bold Bordeaux blends from the sometimes mountainous midlands of Aconcagua, Maipo, Colchagua, Cachapoal; Sauvignon Blanc and Chardonnay come to life in the cooler coastal regions of San Antonio, Casablanca, Limarí; the warm spice of Carmenère finds its home in the heart of the Central Valley in Curicó, Colchagua; old-vine Carignan and País are best in Maule, Itata. You just have to learn the geography.

Recent vintages

Chile is fairly consistent, but vintage variation does have a role to play.
2016 was a bit cool and wet for Bordeaux red varieties, with lower production.
2011 remains the best Cab Sauv vintage in recent years.

Aconcagua Known for red mtn blends, and coastal sites are increasingly recognized for gd CHARD, SYRAH and PINOT N.

Almaviva Mai ★★★→★★★★ Costly B'x-style blend made by CONCHA Y TORO/Baron Philippe de Rothschild joint venture. One of Chile's top wines, from Puente Alto region in MAI.

Altaïr Wines Rap ★★★ Show pony of the SAN PEDRO group of wineries. A de luxe CAB SAUV blend; second label is Sideral.

Antiyal Mai ★★★ Alvaro Espinoza is Chile's top bio consultant. His family project: understated, elegant reds with a cult following.

Apaltagua ★★ An ever-evolving portfolio of wines from Central Valley and coast. Gd CARMENÈRE, CARIGNAN.

Aquitania, Viña Mai ★★★ French-Chilean joint venture with top-notch CAB SAUV Lazuli from MAI and elegant CHARD, PINOT N from Mal.

Arboleda, Viña Aco ★★★→★★★ ERRÁZURIZ brand picking up pace under young winemaker Emily Faulconer. Fresh SAUV BL, vibrant CHARD, juicy reds. Coastal v'yds.

Aristos Cach ★★★→★★★★ Dream-team project with Chilean and Burgundian expertise, making classy CAB SAUV and stellar CHARD.

Bío-Bío Region in S with long history and deep roots. Mild, cool climate, gd for crisp RIES, SAUV BL, PINOT N, CHARD.

Bouchon ★★→★★★ Traditional MAU producer reinvented. Generous reds with typical fruit character of region. V.gd Canto blends; PAIS Salvaje is natural wine from wild vines.

Caliboro Mau ★★→★★★ Property of Italian Count Francesco Cinzano. Juicy red blends and rare Torontel (MUSCAT family) Late Harvest.

Caliterra Casa, Col, Cur, Ley ★★→★★★ MALBEC has always been the flagship, but a range of juicy reds is made. Cenit is top blend. Part of ERRÁZURIZ stable.

Calyptra Cach ★★★ Some of Cach's highest v'yds. Not only altitude, but attitude. Classy CAB SAUV, CHARD; complex barrel-aged SAUV BL. François Massoc winemaker

Carmen, Viña Casa, Col, Mai ★★→★★★ Part of SANTA RITA group. Winemaker Sebastián Labbé makes host of wines from major valleys. Gd CAB SAUV, esp Gold, and Winemaker's labels.

Casablanca Casa Chile's first and still foremost cool-climate coastal region. Top CHARD, zesty SAUV BL, fresh PINOT N, peppery SYRAH.

Casa Marin San A ★★★ Felipe Marin followed his mother's footsteps into winemaking at family property in Lo Abarca, just 2.5 miles from coast. Excellent RIES, SAUV BL, SYRAH, and one of Chile's only Sauvignon Gris.

Casas del Bosque Casa, Mai ★★→★★★ In heart of CASA. Cool, sloped site making v.gd SAUV BL, SYRAH, CHARD.

Casa Silva Col, S Regions ★★→★★★ Renowned producer. Large portfolio of solid

---

Top ten Chilean Syrahs

Casa Marin, Miramar savoury, cool climate; **Concha y Toro, Gravas** voluptous MAI rendition; **Cono Sur, 20 Barrels** marked acidity from LIM; **De Martino, Alto Los Toros** electric, high-altitude ELQ; **Errázuriz, Aconcagua Costa** fresh, vibrant coastal; **Errázuriz, La Cumbre** ACO fruit bomb; **Lapostolle, The Collection Pirque** top of tasty terroir series; **Matetic, Matetic** silky, complex. Bio; **Maycas del Limarí, Los Acacios** intense Lim, tension; **Ventisquiero, Pangea** generous, ripe Apalta.

> **Chilean fizz**
> The boom of Chilean sparkling wine (both Charmat and traditional method) has sparked a think tank to create a special name for it. Any guesses what it could be? Think-tank Method?

CARMENÈRE and juicy reds, with fresher whites from Paredones region. Try unique Lago Ranco SAUV BL and PINOT N from Pat.

Clos des Fous Cach, Casa, S Regions ★★→★★★ "Dr Terroir" Pedro Parra and winemaker François Massoc join forces in terroir-chase around Chile. Excellent red blends; PINOT N.

Clos Ouvert Mau ★★ "Natural" wine project of French expat Louis Antoine Luyt. Focus on PAÍS, CARIGNAN, CINSAULT from MAU. Luyt also has his own label.

Concha y Toro Cent V ★→★★★★ Unsurprisingly for one of world's largest producers, Concha y Toro has wines from all major valleys in Chile. Highlights incl Terrunyo SAUV BL, CAB SAUV; Maycas de LIMARÍ CHARD, PINOT N, Sauv Bl, SYRAH from LIM; Gravas Syrah from MAI, and top Cab Sauv in Marques and *Don Melchor*. Lion's share of production goes into classic and consistent Casillero del Diablo brand. *See also* ALMAVIVA, Trivento (Argentina).

Cono Sur Casa, Col, Bio ★★→★★★ Biggest PINOT N producer in S America; great quality at all levels (esp 20 Barrels). Bicicleta is popular Pinot N; rest of range offers gd-value weekday wines. Top CAB SAUV Silencio is excellent, gd RIES.

Cousiño Macul Mai ★★→★★★ One of Chile's oldest wineries, in outskirts of Santiago. Reliable wines in Antiguas line leads up to top blend, *Lota*.

De Martino Cach, Casa, Elq, Mai, Mau, Ita ★★→★★★ Winemaker Marcelo Retamal is one of Chile's best. Diverse portfolio, but all with fresh-fruit focus and sensitive to oak. Single-v'yd range has some treats: 2000m ELQ SYRAH, limestone LIM CHARD, old-vine MALBEC, CARIGNAN. Viejas Tinajas is amphora-aged from ITA.

Elqui Region known for starry skies and steep slopes. Chile's most n commercial valley with v.gd mtn SYRAH, gd SAUV BL, interesting PX (better known for Pisco).

Emiliana Casa, Rap, Bio ★→★★★ Organic/bio specialist involving Alvaro Espinoza (*see* ANTIYAL). Complex, SYRAH-heavy G and Coyam show almost Mediterranean-style wildness; cheaper Adobe, Novas ranges v.gd for affordable complexity.

Errázuriz Aco, Casa ★★→★★★★ Top ACO producer with coastal and mtn v'yds. Superb Pizarras CHARD and PINOT N. V.gd wild-ferment SAUV BL, Chard, Pinot N, SYRAH. Rich CAB SAUV blend Don Maximiliano, perfumed CARMENÈRE KAI. Winemaker Francisco Baettig is one of Chile's best. *See also* VIÑA ARBOLEDA, CALITERRA, SEÑA, VIÑEDO CHADWICK.

Falernia, Viña Elq ★★→★★★ Intrepid Italian cousins, first commercial producer in ELQ. Excellent Rhône-like SYRAH, herbaceous SAUV BL, complex reds, uncommon PX. Labels incl Alta Tierra, Mayu.

Fournier, Bodegas O Ley, Mau ★★ Spaniard's Chilean outpost (*see* Spain, Argentina) focusing on old-vine CARIGNAN in MAU and fresh coastal Ley SAUV BL.

Garcés Silva, Viña San A ★★→★★★ Amayna is rich, opulent collection of SAUV BL, CHARD, PINOT N, SYRAH. Boya is fresher version, from same vines in SAN A.

García & Schwaderer Casa, Mau ★★→★★★ Delicious reds from ITA and MAU, racy whites and PINOT N from CASA. Part of MOVI crowd.

Haras de Pirque Mai ★★→★★★ MAI breeder of fast horses and rich reds. Albis is top blend (CAB SAUV/CARMENÈRE). Consistent Cab Sauv, v.gd SYRAH, smoky SAUV BL.

Itata Mainly dry-farmed old vines, but this s region is seeing new development too. Best for CINSAULT, PAÍS, MUSCAT.

Lapostolle Cach, Casa, Col ★★→★★★ No-expense-spared bio estate in Apalta (Col). Rich reds (lush CARMENÈRE-based Clos Apalta), bold whites. Highlight is Collection range: single-site SYRAHS and fresher Carmenères from around the country.

Leyda, Viña Col, Mai, San A ★★→★★★ Specializing in eponymous coastal region in SAN A. Zesty, concentrated coastal whites (CHARD, SAUV BL, Sauvignon Gris), spicy SYRAH, juicy PINOT N. Lot is top-of-line range.

Limarí Drought is always a problem in this arid, coastal region in n Chile. But the limestone soils make it worth the risk. V.gd CHARD, SAUV BL, SYRAH, PINOT N.

Loma Larga Casa ★★ Hillside reds from CASA showing region can make more than SAUV BL. Top MALBEC, CAB FR.

Maipo The CAB SAUV cradle of Chile, nr Santiago. Ranges from warmer flat v'yds to cooler mtn v'yds. Best Cab sites are Pirque, Puente Alto.

Matetic Casa, San A ★★★ Large bio estate spread across CASA and SAN A. Always consistent and sometimes superb. Try SYRAH, **Sauv Bl**, PINOT N.

Maule Chile's biggest wine region is also oldest. Renowned for old-vine CARIGNAN (see VIGNO) and PAÍS.

Maycas del Limarí Lim ★★→★★★ Crisp, sappy LIM **Sauv Bl**, CHARD, PINOT N, SYRAH in this smaller CONCHA Y TORO project led by winemaker Marcelo Papa.

Montes Casa, Col, Cur, Ley ★★→★★★★ Aurelio Montes Jr. is now winemaker at this modern Col operation. Intense, complex reds (Alpha CAB SAUV, **Folly Syrah**, Purple Angel CARMENÈRE) are complemented by fresher coastal wines incl v.gd Outer Limits range (SAUV BL, PINOT N) from Zapallar and CINSAULT from ITA.

Montes stopped irrigating 300 ha, saved water to supply 20,000 people for 1 yr.

MontGras Col, Ley, Mai ★★ Col winery with gd-value reds and pink ZIN. Intriga CAB SAUV from MAI, excellent Amaral SAUV B, v.gd CHARD from LEY.

Montsecano Casa ★★★ Cool, high-altitude, small-scale, bio PINOT N made by five Chileans and Frenchman André Ostertag. **Top stuff**.

Morandé Casa, Mai, Mau ★★→★★★ Diverse portfolio of wines from all over Chile. Solid wines in classic line and more intriguing blends in Limited Edition. Brut Nature NV (CHARD, PINOT N) is a top Chilean **bubbly**.

Neyen Col ★★★ Complex, old-vine CARMENÈRE/CAB SAUV blend from vines dating back to 1889. VERAMONTE's Apalta project.

Odfjell Mai, Mau ★→★★★ French winemaker Arnaud Hereu produces v.gd red blends and single varieties incl excellent CARIGNAN from MAU.

Pérez Cruz, Viña Mai ★★→★★★ Family-owned estate producing B'x varieties and blends in MAI. Interesting Chaski PETIT VERDOT.

Polkura Col ★★ Small producer of gd SYRAH from Marchigue. Also SAUV BL, MALBEC.

Quebrada de Macul, Viña Mai ★★→★★★ Excellent CAB SAUV Domus Aurea. Elegant and capitivating reds from Macul MAI.

Rapel Largest Central Valley denomination incl CACH, COL. Incl warm valley floor and mtn v'yds.

RE Mai ★★★→★★★★ Pablo Morandé Jr.: "natural" wines, clay amphorae, offbeat blends and orange wines. Unorthodox and exciting for Chile.

Ribera del Lago Mau ★★→★★★ Excellent SAUV BL and Laberinto PINOT N from personal project of Rafael Tirado.

San Antonio San A Coastal region next to CASA, but cooler. SAUV BL, CHARD, SYRAH, PINOT N do best. LEY is subregion.

San Pedro Cur ★→★★★ Flagship brand of Chile's second largest wine group. Eco-friendly Cur-based winery makes everyday wines 35 South (35 Sur) and Castillo de Molina; and premium 1865 Limited Edition with single v'yd wines. Top of

---

Itata: where it's at

Interested in old vines (up to 200 yrs), cool conditions and forgotten varieties? ITA in far s is your region. Home to mainly small producers, but with TORRES buying up 230 ha, the big guns are moving in.

> **Mountains to coast**
> When you think Chile, forget North to South, think East to West. Chile's
> wine regions and appellation system are divided into Andes (East),
> Entre Valles (Central Valleys) and Costa (West, Coastal). Division marks
> impact of mtns and coast – more important than latitude in Chile's case.

range is elegant Cabo de Hornos. ALTAÏR, Viña Mar, Missiones de Rengo, Santa
Helena, TARAPACÁ owned by same group.

Santa Carolina, Viña ★★→★★★ Big traditional brand with a few ventures into the
less explored. Try Specialities range and Luis Pereira CAB SAUV; new, but follows
old winemakers' instructions from 50s. V.gd Herencia (CARMENÈRE).

Santa Rita Mai ★★→★★★ Large, historic MAI winery, big portfolio from around
country. Try Bougainville PETITE SIRAH, *Casa Real Cab Sauv* for classic richness,
Pehuèn CARMENÈRE, Triple C (CAB SAUV/CAB FR/Carmenère), Floresta range, gd-
value Medalla Real CHARD.

Seña Aco ★★★★ Single-label wine made by Chadwick/ERRÁZURIZ. Deluxe and
splendid CAB SAUV-based B'x blend from ACO valley.

Tabalí Lim ★★→★★★ One of most renowned LIM wineries. Top coastal CHARD, SAUV BL,
PINOT N, SYRAH on coastal limestone, some mtn reds. Try v.gd Talinay range.

Tarapacá, Viña Casa, Ley, Mai ★★ Steadily improving historic winery, part of the
VSPT group. Top wines: Tara-Pakay (CAB SAUV/SYRAH) and Etiqueta Negra Gran
Res (Cab Sauv).

Torres, Miguel Cur ★★→★★★★ Long-est, still-innovative, Cur-based winery with v'yds
all over Chile. V.gd CAB SAUV (esp *Manso de Velasco* from old vines), gd everyday
SAUV BL, delightful sparkling PAÍS. Latest focus is big-investment PINOT N, Escaleras
de Empedrado: v'yd cost $4-million+ to plant.

Undurraga Casa, Ley, Lim, Mai ★→★★★ Head winemaker Rafael Urrejola's TH
(Terroir Hunter) series is a highlight in Undurraga's large Chile-wide portfolio.
Some top CAB SAUV, CARIGNAN and plethora of party fizz.

Valdivieso Cur, San A ★→★★★ Major producer impressing with Res and Single V'yd
range (esp CAB FR, MALBEC) from top terroirs around Chile (*Ley Chard* esp gd). V.gd
red blend Caballo Loco, wonderful CARIGNAN-based Éclat.

Vascos, Los Rap ★→★★★ B'x-style red blends coming from joint venture by Lafite-
Rothschild. Top: Le Dix, Grande Res.

Chile's v'yds go from Atacama to Osorno: 2000 km+ = London to Sicily.

Ventisquero, Viña Casa, Col, Mai ★→★★★ Classic wine brand revamped. Daring
ventures in Atacama produce top Tara PINOT N, CHARD. V.gd Enclave CAB SAUV,
Pangea SYRAH. Kalfu is popular weekday range.

Veramonte Casa, Col ★★→★★★ Now under guidance of winemaker Rodrigo Soto,
CASA estate turning bio, wines are more juicy. Ritual PINOT N, SYRAH, SAUV BL v.gd.

Vigno Mau Old-vine CARIGNAN movement in MAU. Wines must be 65% Carignan,
30-yr+ v'yds and dry-farmed to get Vigno seal of approval.

Villard Casa, Mai ★★ Sophisticated wines made by French-born Thierry Villard. Gd
MAI reds, esp PINOT N, MERLOT, Equis CAB SAUV, CASA whites.

Viñedo Chadwick Mai ★★★→★★★★ Stylish CAB SAUV made from Puente Alto v'yd that
used to be polo field. Owned by Chadwick/ERRÁZURIZ.

Viu Manent Casa, Col ★★ MALBEC specialist (totally different from Argentine
Malbec) with lots more to offer. Top CARMENÈRE-based El Incidente and zesty
SAUV BL from CASA).

Von Siebenthal Aco ★★→★★★ Smaller producer with rich, luscious reds (esp
CARMENÈRE), full-bodied VIOGNIER. Parcela 7 is top-value blend, Toknar is one of
Chile's few 100% PETIT VERDOT.

ARGENTINA

Argentina has been making wine for over 500 years, and with a strong Italian inheritance, Italianate red wine in a straw-covered *fiasco* was once the Argentine norm. There where hardly any exports until the 90s, when low costs and tasty Malbec led the way. By 2010 there was such an export boom, especially to the US, that supply was the problem. Chronic economic disarray is Argentina's bugbear; the only profitable way is up – in quality, and in altitude, planting ever higher into the Andes. Mendoza province has almost three-quarters of the vines, but Salta to the north and Patagonia to the south are gaining. Malbec still leads, followed by Bonarda for everyday wines and Cabernet and Syrah for exports. Recently Sauvignon Blanc has caught on, joining Chardonnay in the export boom. There are also new vineyards south of Buenos Aires and even in the Pampas – anywhere there is a sniff of quality potential.

Achaval Ferrer Men ★★→★★★ MALBEC specialist no longer limited to Malbec. Single-v'yd philosophy still strong but portfolio now extends to CAB SAUV and blends.

Aleanna Men ★★→★★★★ Complex wines by CATENA winemaker Alejandro Vigil and youngest Catena daughter, Adrianna. V.gd single-v'yd range incl top CHARD, CAB FR, MALBEC. El Enemigo is name on bottle.

Alta Vista Men ★→★★★ French investment in Luján. First to work on single-v'yd concept in Argentina. Top MALBECS, gd sparkling and TORRONTÉS.

Altocedro Men ★★→★★★ Winemaker Karim Mussi focuses on La Consulta in Uco V. Distinctive style with v.gd TEMPRANILLO, MALBEC.

Altos las Hormigas Men ★★★ Italians Alberto Antonini and Attilio Pagli join with Chileans for this terroir-driven MALBEC venture. Excellent single-v'yd range. Try BONARDA (sparkling and still) in Colonia Las Liebres.

Antucura Men ★★ Boutique Vista Flores production with Michel Rolland (*see* France) as consultant. Focused on bigger B'x varieties.

Atamisque Men ★→★★★ Great value, consistently gd wines from large estate in Uco V. Catalpa range has v.gd CHARD, PINOT N. Serbal CAB FR, SAUV BL top value.

Benegas Men ★★→★★★ Old World-style producer in historic winery using old vines for top-notch CAB FR and Meritage Benegas Lynch label. Interesting SANGIOVESE.

Bressia Men ★★→★★★ Consultant Walter Bressia's family winery. Complex red blends age-worthy; v.gd Monteagrelo SYRAH, CAB FR and Lagrima Canela CHARD.

Caelum Men ★★ If you thought Argentina was all about reds, Caelum's Italian winemaker will try to persuade you otherwise with gd CHARD, FIANO.

Callia San J ★→★★ Gd-value wines based on SYRAH in hotter SAN J region.

Canale, Bodegas Humberto Rio N ★→★★★ Historic RÍO N specialists with top old vine RIES and distinctly s style of MALBEC.

Caro Men ★★★→★★★★ Luxury B'x-style blend made in joint venture by CATENA and Rothschilds of Lafite (France). Top blend is Caro followed by Amancaya.

Casa Bianchi Men ★→★★★ V. traditional winery and sparkling producer in San Rafael. Gd value. Look for Leo brand, joint venture with Lionel Messi's Foundation.

Casarena Men ★★→★★★ Modern producer with v.gd single-v'yd range of MALBEC, CAB FR, CAB SAUV; Ramanegra is gd-value everyday range. Try sparkling cider.

Catena Zapata, Bodega Men ★★→★★★★ Nicolas Catena was a pioneer of quality in modern Argentina. Today his family and winemaking team carry on pioneering in the large Luján winery. Highlights: Adrianna Gualtallary MALBEC, CHARD (White Bones, White Stones), CAB FR. Alamos (distributed by Gallo) is worthy workhorse.

Chacra Rio N ★★★ **Superb Pinot N** from old vines in bio estate in RÍO N, Pat. Piero Incisa della Rocchetta of Sassicaia (*see* Italy) is one of best, and most expensive, PINOT N producers in Argentina.

Top-altitude Malbecs
Cafayate started the high-altitude trend, but winemakers in MEN are planting higher into the mts too, seeking that fresher style with higher acidity. Top-altitude MALBECS: ZUCCARDI (San Pablo; 1400m), ALTOS LAS HORMIGAS (Gualtallary; 1300m), PASSIONATE WINE (Gual.; 1600m), CATENA ZAPATA (Gual.; 1450m), ZORZAL (Gual.; 1350m).

Clos de los Siete Men ★★ Michel Rolland's B'x-style blend made from cluster of wineries in Uco V (*see* DIAMANDES, MONTEVIEJO).

Cobos, Viña Men ★★★ Flying winemaker Paul Hobbs' label. CAB SAUV stands out (top Volturno, premium Bramare, entry-level Felino). Don't miss v.gd MALBEC and CHARD from Uco V.

Colomé, Bodega Sal ★★→★★★ Seriously high-altitude wines: up to 3100m in Calchaquí. Intense MALBEC-based reds, lively TORRONTÉS, smoky TANNAT. Owned by California's Hess Collection.

Decero, Finca Men ★★→★★★ Modern operation with Swiss owners, and precise wines. Try PETIT VERDOT, top red blend Amano.

DiamAndes Men ★★★ Bonnie family of Château Malartic-Lagravière (B'x) own this state-of-the-art winery in CLOS DE LOS SIETE neighbourhood. Rich red wines and lively VIOGNIER, CHARD.

Dominio del Plata Men ★★→★★★ Family winery of Susana Balbo. Frontrunner in TORRONTÉS (excellent barrel-aged Signature line, Crios is everyday brand). V.gd MALBEC, CAB SAUV in Ben Marco, Nosotros.

Doña Paula Men ★→★★★ Innovative winery in Luján, always delivers on quality. Excellent single-v'yd MALBECS (try Parcel range), also some of best SAUV BL, RIES in MEN. Owned by Santa Rita (*see* Chile) group.

Etchart Sal ★→★★ Leading TORRONTÉS in high-altitude Cafayate. Historical producer with gd-value wines.

Fabre Montmayou Men, Rio N ★★→★★★ French-owned, started in 90s, bought old v'yds in Luján, RÍO N (Infinitus). Gd second label Phebus; gd-value Viñalba, top *Malbec*, CAB SAUV, Grand Vin.

Fin del Mundo, Bodega Del Neu ★→★★ Big producer in Neu. Entry-level Postales, Ventus, Newen gd value. Top: Special blend; try single-v'yd Fin range (esp CAB FR).

Flichman, Finca Men ★★→★★★ MAI winery making wines from all over MEN. Dedicado is top terroir red blend, Paisaje has two single-v'yd red blends from Uco V and MAI, and CHARD. Caballero de la Cepa everyday brand.

Fournier, O Men ★→★★★ Large estate in San Carlos (Uco V) making top TEMPRANILLO blend (A Crux), SAUV BL (B Crux), v.gd Urban Uco entry-level range. Stunning, Spanish-owned winery; *see* Chile.

Kaikén Men ★★→★★★ Owned by Montes (*see* Chile); top Mai MALBEC, also Ultra CAB SAUV and Malbec, Corte blend.

La Anita, Finca Men ★★→★★★ Boutique winery in Luján with attractive, deep reds. Try Varúa CAB SAUV and unusual FRIULANO white. Gd SYRAH, MALBEC.

La Riojana La R ★→★★ Big Fairtrade producer. *Raza Ltd Edition Malbec* is top wine, but quality and value at all levels, esp TORRONTÉS.

Las Moras, Finca San J ★→★★ Gd-value SAN J label owned by TRAPICHE. Bright, fruit-forward SYRAH, BONARDA staples.

Luca / Tikal / Tahuan / Alma Negra / Animal Men ★★→★★★ Family of boutique wineries owned by Nicolas CATENA's children Laura (Luca) and Ernesto (T/T/A/A). Excellent red blends, v.gd sparkling, sophisticated PINOT N.

Luigi Bosca Men ★★→★★★ Large Luján winery with popular domestic following. Finca La Linda is everyday range (gd sparkling). Finca Las Nobles are special occasion wines; v.gd old-vine MALBEC. Icono is top of range (Malbec/CAB SAUV).

Manos Negras / Tinto Negro / TeHo / ZaHa ★★→★★★ Sister labels focusing on site-specific wines. V.gd MALBEC, PINOT N, excellent CAB FR from Uco V and beyond.

Marcelo Pelleriti Men ★★→★★★ Personal label from MONTEVIEJO winemaker with concentrated MALBEC and blends. Special releases with Argentine musicians incl v.gd Abremundos Malbec/CAB FR.

Masi Tupungato Men ★★→★★★ Masi (Italy) heads s. Passo Doble, fine *ripasso*-style MALBEC/CORVINA/MERLOT; *Corbec* even-better Amarone lookalike (Corvina/Malbec).

Matias Riccitelli Men ★★→★★★ Expanding portfolio by promising winemaker. Juicy, fresh Hey MALBEC; Republica Malbec more serious; young Apple Doesn't Fall Far From The Tree range homage to father, renowned winemaker Jorge Riccitelli.

Mendel Men ★★★ Roberto de la Motta makes top MALBECS (Finca Remota) and attractive Unus blend. Classy SÉM from 70-yr-old vines, and gd Lunta range.

Mendoza Argentina's main wine province and city split into three: historic Maipú in warmer city outskirts; traditional Luján, known for its top MALBEC; exciting Uco V (incl Gualtallary, Altamira, La Consulta) with high elevation and high investment winemaking.

Michel Torino Sal ★★→★★★ Historic and big Cafayate producer. Gd table wine, and finer wines under El Esteco brand (try Fincas Notables CAB SAUV).

Moët-Hennessy Argentina Men ★→★★ Known simply as Chandon. Biggest sparkling wine house in South America with Charmat-method party fizz, and traditional-method Baron B. *See* TERRAZAS DE LOS ANDES.

Monteviejo Men ★★→★★★ Flagship winemaker of CLOS DE LOS SIETE estate. Superb, tiny La Violeta; Lindaflor MALBEC; v.gd Lindaflor CHARD. V.gd-value Petite Fleur range.

Neuquén Pat's biggest wine region. Known for hearty reds (esp MALBEC, CAB FR) and fruity PINOT N. Watch out for dinosaur fossils.

Nieto Senetiner, Bodegas Men ★→★★★ Large winery given fresh approach with new-generation winemaker Santiago Mayorga. V.gd single-v'yd Cadus MALBEC, gd fresh SÉM and big portfolio of sparkling wines.

Noemia ★★★→★★★★ Top Pat MALBEC producer with old vines in RÍO N. Winemaker Hans Vinding-Diers also makes beautiful D'n style blend.

Norton, Bodega Men ★→★★★ Long-est winery, classic style and consistency. Gd-value entry-level wines, excellent single-v'yd MALBEC Lot range, top Gernot Lange blend. Lots of gd sparkling.

Passionate Wine Men ★★→★★★ One of Argentina's most experimental winemakers, Matias Michelini has growing Uco V based portfolio. Highlights: Demente (MALBEC/CAB FR), fresh Agua de Roca SAUV BL, juicy PINOT N, host of orange wines.

Peñaflor Men ★→★★★ Argentina's biggest wine group, incl Finca Las Moras, Andean V'yds (SAN J), MICHEL TORINO (SAL), Santa Ana, TRAPICHE (MEN).

Piatelli Sal ★★ Modern operation, v'yds in Cafayate, MEN. Gd TORRONTÉS, rich reds.

Piedra Negra Men ★→★★ B'x winemaker François Lurton's Argentina outpost. V.gd white blends (PINOT GR base), concentrated MALBEC.

70 per cent of world's Malbec is in Argentina: almost 40,000 ha.

Poesia Men ★★→★★★ Same owner as Clos l'Église, B'x. Dedicated to reds: Poesia (CAB SAUV/MALBEC); Clos des Andes (Malbec); Pasodoble Malbec/SYRAH/Cab Sauv.

Porvenir de Cafayate, El Sal ★★→★★★ Young team in Cafayate make modern wines. Top TORRONTÉS and attractive TANNAT, MALBEC, CAB SAUV. Laborum is varietal range, Amauta blends.

Pulenta Estate Men ★★→★★★ Modern Luján winery owned by 3rd-generation wine family (ex-PEÑAFLOR). Excellent single v'yd range, top CAB FR, MALBEC, SAUV BL. La Flor range v.gd value.

Renacer Men ★★→★★★ Chilean-owned (with SAUV BL from Casa). Flagship Renacer mostly MALBEC; v.gd Punto Final (Malbec, CAB SAUV); try Amarone-style Enamore.

Riglos Men ★★→★★★ Uco V producer based in Tupungato. Gran Corte (MALBEC/CAB SAUV/CAB FR) is top of portfolio of concentrated reds. Also Quinto SAUV BL.

Río Negro Rio N Old pear-growing region, now top spot for Pat PINOT N. Also gd for old-vine SÉM, RIES and new vine MALBEC, MERLOT.

Ruca Malén Men ★★ Busty reds from Luján. Top blend Don Raul (MALBEC/CAB SAUV/ PETIT VERDOT), Kinean range offers gd value and consistency. Try Petit Verdot too.

Salentein, Bodegas Men ★★→★★★ Stunning Dutch-owned winery in Uco V. Gd-value El Portillo; v.gd PINOT N, MALBEC, CHARD, CAB SAUV in Primus range.

Salta Home of high-altitude winemaking and TORRONTÉS. Top wines from Cafayate (esp Calchaquí) where vines planted over 2300m produce fresh acidity and intense colour in reds incl TANNAT, MALBEC.

San Juan Ripe SYRAH, BONARDA are renowned from this large, warm region n of MEN. Look for Barreal subregion.

San Pedro de Yacochuya Sal ★★★ Cafayate collaboration between Michel Rolland (see France) and ETCHART family. Ripe but fragrant TORRONTÉS, dense MALBEC SPY, powerful Yacochuya (Malbec from oldest vines).

Schroeder, Familia Neu ★★ Pat winery focusing on bubbly and PINOT N (try Saurus Select, named for dinosaur fossils found in cellar).

Sophenia, Finca Men ★★→★★★ Uco V producer in Gualtallary. Solid SAUV BL, v.gd MALBEC, BONARDA. Synthesis is top range.

Tapiz Men ★★ Luján winery has llamas as residents. Attractive varietal wines with Black Tears MALBEC at the top of the range.

Terrazas de los Andes Men ★★→★★★★ A wide portfolio of MEN wines makes up the still-wine sister company of Chandon (MOËT-HENNESSY). V.gd single-v'yd MALBEC series. Joint venture with Cheval Blanc (B'x): superb *Cheval des Andes* blend.

Toso, Pascual Men ★★→★★★ Winery with century-long history in MEN. Wide range is MALBEC-dominated. Top Magdalena Toso also Malbec-based. Gd SYRAH, CAB SAUV.

Trapiche Men ★→★★★ One of largest and oldest producers in Argentina. Immense portfolio. Look for *Medalla* CAB SAUV; Iscay MALBEC/CAB FR blend; single-v'yd Finca range Malbec; Costa & Pampa range from coast.

Trivento Men ★→★★ Owned by Concha y Toro of Chile. Eolo MALBEC is pricey flagship, but Golden Malbec, SYRAH, CHARD top value.

Val de Flores Men ★★★ Michel Rolland owns this old (and bio) MALBEC v'yd in Vistaflores. Deep, elegant, earthy, with firm tannins. For ageing. Also try Mariflor line (single varieties and excellent Camille blend).

Viña Alicia Men ★★★ Part-owned by LUIGI BOSCA family. Small production: seductive white blend Tiara (RIES/ALBARIÑO/SAVAGNIN) and racy NEBBIOLO among others.

Vines of Mendoza / Winemaker's Village Men ★★ Cluster of boutique wineries in Vista Flores and Uco V. Labels to look for: Recuerdo, Super Uco, Abremundos (see MARCELO PELLERITI), Corazon del Sol.

Zorzal Men ★★★ Focused on energetic wines from Gualtallary. Juan Pablo Michelini makes top Eggo line with no oak, just cement eggs. V.gd CAB FR, SAUV BL.

Zuccardi Men ★★→★★★★ State-of-the-art winery in Altamira is filled with hundreds of cement eggs and amphorae. Vision of 3rd-generation winemaker Sebastian Zuccardi. Excellent terroir-driven Alluvional range (MALBEC), v.gd Emma BONARDA, Q TEMPRANILLO. Santa Julia is everyday brand, made in larger Maipú winery.

BRAZIL

Brazil might be better known for its beaches, but its bubbly is turning heads in the wine world. The top spot for sparkling is Pinto Bandeira and the mecca for Merlot is Vale dos Vinhedos. Both are in the cooler southern region of Serra Gaúcha where over 1000 small growers share a mainly Italian heritage. Italian varieties feature alongside Portuguese, but most popular are Bordeaux varieties. Other southern regions include Campanha, Serra do Sudeste, Planalto Catarinense and Campos de Cima de Serra, and in the tropical north Vale do São Francisco stands alone.

Aurora ★ →★★ V. large co-op; long tradition in Serra Gaucha. Mostly value table wines.

Casa Valduga ★ →★★★ Well-known historical producer with gd traditional-method sparklers, a top MERLOT (Storia) and own production of grappa.

Cave Geisse ★★★ Top sparkling producer in Pinto Bandeira. Chilean Mario Geisse makes excellent traditional-method Nature bubblies.

Lidio Carraro ★ →★★ Boutique family winery with v'yds in Vale dos Vinhedos and Serra do Sudeste. Gd Quorum blend of B'x varieties.

Miolo ★ →★★★ Largest premium producer; landmark winery in Vale dos Vinhedos, production in all major regions. V.gd MERLOT, CHARD, TOURIGA N, and top sparkling Millésime.

Pizzato ★ →★★★ Flavio Pizzato makes v.gd MERLOT (try DNA 99), CHARD, sparkling in Vale dos Vinhedos. Younger Fausto wines from other v'yds in Serra Gaucha.

Salton ★ →★★ One of Brazil's most historic and largest producers. Plenty of Prosecco-style party fizz. Try Salton Gerações blend.

URUGUAY

Uruguay's wine is unique in South America for its Atlantic maritime influence, more similar to the Old World than New. Wine production is concentrated in Canelones, just outside the capital Montevideo, but new plantings are spreading up the coast to Punta del Este. Pockets of vineyards have spread inland too, including the Brazilian border. Tannat is king in Uruguay, but Albariño and Sauvignon Blanc are interesting counterparts.

Alto de la Ballena ★ →★★ Boutique family winery that pioneered the Punta del Este region. V.gd SYRAH, CAB FR and juicy TANNAT/VIOGNIER blend.

Bouza ★★ →★★★ State-of-the-art winery in Canelones with v'yds in Pan de Azucar too. First to make ALBARIÑO in Uruguay; still one of best. V.gd single v'yd TANNAT.

Garzón, Bodega ★ →★★★ Ambitious winery in Maldonado with big budget and Alberto Antonini leading way. Try fresh, maritime ALBARIÑO and rich reds.

Juanico Establecimiento ★ →★★★ Leader in Uruguay with largest production. Lots of gd-value wines, incl fresh SAUV BL. Paul Hobbs consults on top Familia Deicas range with excellent Preludio CHARD blend and single-v'yd TANNAT collection.

Marichal ★ →★★ Boutique family producer in Canelones. Try PINOT N/TANNAT blend.

Pisano ★ →★★★ Pisano family were at forefront of quality revolution in Uruguay. V.gd TORRONTÉS, VIOGNIER, TANNAT.

Viñedo de los Vientos ★★ →★★★ Independent winemaker Pablo Fallabrino makes playful white blends, solid TANNAT (try *ripasso* method), indulgent dessert wines.

OTHER SOUTH AMERICAN WINES

Bolivia No one can boast about high-altitude winemaking quite like Bolivia. All v'yds are above 1800m and some top 3000m. Result is racy acidity and most impressive colour. SYRAH grows particularly well; CAB SAUV, MERLOT too. Bolivian MUSCAT is unique, but most of it goes to Singani brandy. Look for Campos de Solana, Kohlberg, Kuhlmann (sparkling), La Concepción and Sausini.

Peru has a long heritage of winemaking, but the majority of grapes go for Pisco production today. Warm region of Ica is heart of Pisco, but producers also making rich TANNAT, Ancellota, unique wines from Quebranta grapes. Look for Intipalka, Mimo, Quebrada de Ihuanco, Tacama and Vista Alegre.

Australia

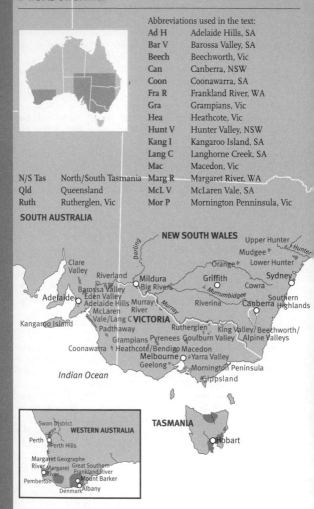

Abbreviations used in the text:

Ad H	Adelaide Hills, SA
Bar V	Barossa Valley, SA
Beech	Beechworth, Vic
Can	Canberra, NSW
Coon	Coonawarra, SA
Fra R	Frankland River, WA
Gra	Grampians, Vic
Hea	Heathcote, Vic
Hunt V	Hunter Valley, NSW
Kang I	Kangaroo Island, SA
Lang C	Langhorne Creek, SA
Mac	Macedon, Vic
N/S Tas	North/South Tasmania
Marg R	Margaret River, WA
Qld	Queensland
McL V	McLaren Vale, SA
Ruth	Rutherglen, Vic
Mor P	Mornington Penninsula, Vic

Given that for many years Australia was synonymous with the sunshine-in-a-bottle richness of its Chardonnay and its rum-swigger's Shiraz, it's quite telling that debate now rages over whether Australian wine styles have swung too far the other way. Instead of harpooning drinkers with flavour, many Oz wines now wish to spin you in on a fly. This is especially true, ironically, of its Chardonnay, which nowadays treasures tightness, complexity, line and length as much as it does bold-faced power (more Glenn McGrath than Jeff Thompson). This is further evidenced by the inexorable creep towards spicier, "bunchier", lighter reds. Or as some people say, reds built on acid and tannin rather than on old-fashioned fruit and oak. If Australian wine once resembled an episode of an *Asterix* comic, it now has more in common with the *Diary of a Wimpy Kid*. Of course, both representations are exaggerations, written with tongue in cheek. They leave a nagging question, though: which tone of voice has the Sense of Place we're always looking for? Truth is Australian wine has gone from the expected to the unexpected. Next goal is finding perfect balance. I sense it won't be too long now.

Recent vintages

New South Wales (NSW)

2016 Challengingly wet in the Hunter but good/excellent everywhere else.
2015 Difficult in most parts, but Orange and Canberra excellent; Hilltops very good.
2014 Hunter Shiraz will be exceptional. Canberra Ries, Shiraz right up there.
2013 Rich reds, whites. Hunter Sem and Canberra Ries especially good.
2012 Wet, cold. Sem may be okay, perhaps Cab Sauv, generally disappointing.
2011 Hunter Valley escaped floods of further south, still a cold, damp year.

Victoria (Vic)

2016 Dry but otherwise average year. No disasters but no raves either.
2015 Strong year across the board.
2014 Frost damage galore but very good red vintage for most.
2013 Wet winter followed by a hot, dry summer. Quality surprisingly high.
2012 Turning out better than first expected. Red/white very good to exceptional.
2011 Wet; lots of disease pressure. Generally better for whites. Be cautious.

South Australia (SA)

2016 Hopes are high that this is a special vintage for both reds and whites.
2015 Standout Clare Ries; Adelaide Hills excellent; warm regions coped well with wild climate swings.
2014 Hot, low-yield year has produced generous whites, reds.
2013 Water a problem so yields generally well down. Streaky vintage.
2012 Yields down but a brilliant year. Great for Ries; excellent Cab Sauv.
2011 Cool, wet. Lean whites, herbal/spicy reds. Some interesting results.

Western Australia (WA)

2016 Ries (generally) and Margaret River (specifically) pulled rabbits out of a difficult, humid hat.
2015 Challenging, mixed results; pays to be selective, but gems will be found.
2014 The luck continues; almost getting monotonous. Another tiptop year.
2013 Both Cab Sauv, Chard very strong. Some rain but, again, gods were kind.
2012 Drought continued, so too the run of beautiful, warm/hot vintages.
2011 Warm, dry, early vintage. Very good Cab. Delicate whites less successful.

Accolade Wines r w Name for wines/wineries previously under the once-mighty CONSTELLATION, HARDYS groups. Resurgent new era is the tomorrow that never quite comes.

Adelaide Hills SA Best SAUV BL region: cool 450m sites in Mt Lofty ranges. CHARD, SHIRAZ outgun PINOT N. ASHTON HILLS, HENSCHKE, JERICHO, MIKE PRESS, MURDOCH HILL, SC PANNELL, SHAW & SMITH all in excellent form.

Alkoomi Mt Barker, WA r w (RIES) 05′ 10′ 13′ 16 (CAB SAUV) 04′ 10′ 12′ 13 14 Veteran maker of fine Ries; rustic reds; more accessible young than previously.

All Saints Estate Ruth, Vic br ★ Great fortifieds, past and present. Hearty table wines.

Alpine Valleys Vic In the valleys that stem from the Victorian Alps. Best producers: Billy Button, MAYFORD, Ringer Reef. TEMPRANILLO the star, though aromatic whites have come up swinging.

Andevine Hun V, NSW r w ★ Shot from blocks with initial SHIRAZ, SEM, CHARD releases from mature HUNT V v'yds; 2nd album blues since but still firing gd shots.

Andrew Thomas Hun V, NSW r w ★★ Alpha producer. Old-vine SEM; silken SHIRAZ. Reds particularly gutsy in HUNTER context.

Angove's SA r w (br) ★★ MURRAY V family business. Cheapies (r w) often the standouts of a broad range, but if you want organically grown wine, you'll find one to your liking here.

Annie's Lane Clare V, SA r w Part of TWE. Boldly flavoured wines. Flagship Copper Trail (can be) excellent, esp RIES, SHIRAZ. Doldrums, sadly.

Arenberg, d' McL V, SA r w (br) (sw) (sp) ★★→★★★ Sumptuous SHIRAZ, GRENACHE. Many varieties, wacky labels (incl The Cenosilicaphobic Cat SAGRANTINO). The Elton John of Oz wineries.

A.Rodda Beech, Vic r w ★★ Bright CHARD from est v'yds; whole bunch-fermented TEMPRANILLO grown at high altitude is savoury (and delicious) to its back teeth.

Ashton Hills Ad H, SA r w (sp) ★★ (PINOT N) 05′ 10 12 13 Totemic AD HILLS producer. Compelling Pinot N from 30-yr-old+ v'yds. Bought in 2015 by WIRRA WIRRA. Jury out on new era.

Bailey's NE Vic r w br ★★ Rich SHIRAZ, magnificent dessert MUSCAT (★★★★) and TOPAQUE. Largely unloved part of TWE but performs against the odds. V'yds all organic. PETIT VERDOT a gd addition.

Balgownie Estate Bendigo, Vic, Yarra V, Vic r w ★→★★ At its best it makes medium-bodied, well-balanced, minty CAB of elegance, finesse, character from its BENDIGO heartland. Separate YARRA V arm. Hits and misses.

Balnaves of Coonawarra SA r w ★★★ Family-owned COON champion. Lusty CHARD; v.gd spicy, medium-bodied SHIRAZ, full-bodied Tally CAB SAUV flagship. New "joven-style" Cab v.gd.

Bannockburn Vic r w ★★★ (CHARD) 10′ 12′ 14 (PINOT N) 08′ 10′ 12′ 14 Intense, complex Chard and spice-shot Pinot N. Full box and dice styles for now; new winemaker recently installed.

Sparkling Shiraz anyone?

If it wasn't for BEST'S GREAT WESTERN and MOUNT LANGI GHIRAN in the GRAMPIANS region of nw Vic you might wonder whether anyone cares about sparkling SHIRAZ anymore. It's not in general favour. Which is a shame, because it's not only more-or-less uniquely Australian (full-bodied red with bubbles in it) but when done well, it has a useful place at the table. There are two styles: rich, sweet and power-packed, usually from the warmer regions. And peppery and spicy, often from cooler Vic regions (eg. Grampians). Particularly once they've had time to mellow/soften both styles can be wonderful with poultry of all descriptions (with Christmas Day turkey is the norm, but if you can drag yourself away from PINOT N an aged sparkling red is terrific with roast or Peking duck) and as these styles are typically given a sizeable dosage, they are particularly gd with spicy-but-hearty dishes. What to drink with an Indian curry? Enter, sparkling Shiraz. Look out for: BEST'S GREAT WESTERN, CASTAGNA, HENTLEY FARM, MOUNT LANGI GHIRAN, SEPPELT (historically the doyen), TURKEY FLAT.

Banrock Station Riverland, SA r w ★★ 1600 ha property on Murray River, 243 ha v'yd, owned by ACCOLADE. Partial eclipse of its star in market-prominence terms.

Barossa Valley SA Ground zero of Aussie red wine. V-old-vine SHIRAZ, MOURVÈDRE, CAB SAUV, GRENACHE. Can produce bold, black, beautiful reds with its eyes closed, and has done for just about ever. The best bits are known, but often blended (eg. Grange).

Bass Phillip Gippsland, Vic r ★★★ (PINOT N) 10' 12' 14 Ultimate soloist. Tiny amounts of variable but mostly exceptional Pinot N. Gives idiosyncrasy a gd name.

Bay of Fires N Tas r w sp ★★→★★★ Pipers River outpost of ACCOLADE empire. Stylish table wines and Arras *super-cuvée sparkling(s)*. Complex PINOT N. Arguably Oz's top sparkling house.

All Saints Estate has released a Tawny "Port" in a hip bottle, "Hip Sip".

Beechworth Vic The rock-strewn highlands of ne Vic. Tough country. CHARD, SHIRAZ best performing varieties. NEBBIOLO rising from the (winter) fog. A.RODDA, CASTAGNA, DOMENICA, FIGHTING GULLY ROAD, GIACONDA, SAVATERRE, Schmölzer and Brown, Sorrenberg essential producers.

Bendigo Vic Hot central Vic region. BALGOWNIE ESTATE the stalwart, but numerous handy performers, if rarely more than that. Home of rich SHIRAZ, CAB SAUV.

Best's Great Western Gra, Vic r w ★★★ (SHIRAZ) 05' 10' 11' 12' 13' 14 Conservative family winery; *v.gd mid-weight reds*. Thomson Family Shiraz from 120-yr-old vines superb. Sparkling Shiraz worth tracking down.

Bindi Mac, Vic r w ★★★★ (PINOT N) 04' 06' 10' 12' 13' 15' Ultra-fastidious maker of outstanding, long-lived Pinot N (esp), CHARD. Beg, borrow or steal territory.

Bortoli, De Griffith, NSW, Yarra V, Vic r w (br) dr sw ★★★ (Noble SEM) Both irrigation-area winery and leading YARRA V producer. Excellent cool-climate PINOT N, SHIRAZ, CHARD, SAUV BL and gd sweet, botrytized, Sauternes-style Noble Sem. YARRA V arm is where sparks fly.

Brand's of Coonawarra Coon, SA r w Custodian of 100-yr-old vines. Quality struggles at top end but fighting range (CAB SAUV, SHIRAZ, CHARD) delivers gd fruit/oak flavour.

Brash Higgins McL V, SA ★★★ Brad Hickey has degrees in English and botany but as a former brewer, baker, sommelier and now maker of radical expressions of MCLAREN V (r w), it's fair to guess that he knows most of all about yeast. Creativity and quality in harmony here.

Bremerton Lang C, SA r w ★★ Silken CAB, SHIRAZ with mounds of flavour.

Brokenwood Hun V, NSW r w ★★ (ILR Res SEM) 03' 05' **06'** 09' (Graveyard SHIRAZ) **00'** 06' 09' 13'. Outside of the Cricket Pitch Sem/SAUV BL can be hard to find value, but quality generally gd.

Brookland Valley Marg R, WA r w ★ Volume (and value) producer of v.gd SAUV BL, CHARD, CAB SAUV. ACCOLADE-owned.

Brown Brothers King V, Vic r w br dr sw sp ★ Family firm with wide range of crowd-pleasing styles, varieties. General emphasis on sweetness.

By Farr / Farr Rising Vic r w ★★★★ 10' 12' 13' 14 (PINOT N) Superb producer. CHARD, Pinot N can be minor masterpieces.

Campbells Ruth, Vic r (w) br ★★ Smooth ripe reds (esp Bobbie Burns SHIRAZ); extraordinary Merchant Prince Rare MUSCAT, Isabella Rare TOPAQUE (★★★★).

Canberra District NSW Both quality and quantity rising; site selection important; cool climate. CLONAKILLA best known. New guns: COLLECTOR WINES, EDEN ROAD, RAVENSWORTH.

Cape Mentelle Marg R, WA r w ★★★ (CAB SAUV) 01' 10' 11' 12' 13' Pioneer in excellent form. Robust Cab has become more elegant (with lower alcohol), CHARD v.gd; also ZIN, v. popular SAUV BL/SEM. SHIRAZ on rise. Owned by LVMH Veuve Clicquot.

Casella Riverina, NSW r w Yellow Tail's budget reds, whites hit sweet spot in US over a decade ago and have continued to milk the market, and beyond, since.

Castagna Beech, Vic r w ★★★ (SYRAH) 05' 06' 08' 10' 12' 14 Julian C leads the Oz bio brigade. Estate-grown SHIRAZ/VIOGNIER, SANGIOVESE/Shiraz excellent. Non-estate range named Adam's Rib.

Chambers Rosewood NE Vic (r) (w) br ★★★ Viewed with MORRIS as greatest maker of sticky TOPAQUE, *Muscat*.

Adelaide Botanic Garden now makes own wine: drink at Garden's restaurant.

Chapel Hill McL V, SA r (w) ★★ Leading MCLAREN V producer. SHIRAZ, CAB the bread and butter but TEMPRANILLO and esp GRENACHE on rise.

Charles Melton Bar V, SA r w (sp) ★ Tiny winery with bold, ripe, traditional reds, esp Nine Popes, an old-vine GRENACHE/SHIRAZ blend. Low key.

Chatto Tas r ★★★★ Jim C's (MOUNT PLEASANT winemaker) secret TAS assignment. Tiny producer; PINOT N of fruit, spice and all things nice. Ultra savoury. Ultra gd.

Clarendon Hills McL V, SA r ★★ Full-Monty reds (high alc, intense fruit) from grapes grown on hills above MCLAREN V. Knife-and-fork territory.

Clare Valley SA Small, pretty, high-quality area 145-km n of Adelaide. Best toured by bike, some say. Australia's most prominent RIES region. Gumleaf-scented SHIRAZ; earthen, tannic CAB SAUV. GROSSET, KIRRIHILL, KILIKANOON, MOUNT HORROCKS, TIM ADAMS, WENDOUREE lead way.

Clonakilla Can, NSW r w ★★★★ (SHIRAZ) 05' 06' 07' 09' 10' 13' 14' 15 *Deserved leader of the Shiraz/Viognier brigade.* RIES, VIOGNIER excellent. Has put CANBERRA on wine map. Varietal SYRAH may well be best of lot.

Clyde Park Vic r w ★★ Single-v'yd CHARD and PINOT N in stellar form. SHIRAZ too turning heads.

Coldstream Hills Yarra V, Vic r w (sp) ★★★★ (CHARD) 10' 11' 12' 13' 14' 15 (PINOT N) 06' 10' 12 13' 14' 15 Est 1985 by critic James Halliday. Delicious PINOT N to drink young, *Res to age*. V.gd Chard (esp Res). Recent *single-v'yd releases* are quite something. Part of TWE.

Collector Wines Can, NSW r ★★ 07' 09' 12' 13' Res SHIRAZ is the one. Layered, spicy, perfumed and complex.

Constellation Wines Australia (CWA) *See* ACCOLADE WINES.

Coonawarra SA Most s v'yds of state: home to some of Australia's best (value, quality) CAB SAUV; land of richest red soil (on limestone). WYNNS is senior, and champion, name. BALNAVES, KATNOOK, LINDEMANS, MAJELLA, RYMILL, YALUMBA all key.

Coriole McL V, SA r w ★★★ (Lloyd Res SHIRAZ) 98' 02' 04' 10' 12' 13 To watch, esp for SANGIOVESE and old-vine Shiraz Lloyd Res. Interesting Italians: FIANO, SAGRANTINO, NERO D'AVOLA. Back in town.

Craiglee Mac, Vic r w ★★★ (SHIRAZ) 00' 08' 10' 12' 13' Salt-of-the-earth producer. Northern Rhône inspired. Fragrant, peppery Shiraz, age-worthy CHARD.

Crawford River Hea, Vic w ★★★ Could well be Australia's best RIES producer; undeniably top three. Cool, cold, scintillating (dry) style, wild with seafood.

Cullen Wines Marg R, WA r w ★★★★ (CHARD) 09' 10' 11' 12' 13' 14 (CAB SAUV/MERLOT) 04' 05' 09' 11 12 13' 14 2nd-generation star Vanya Cullen makes substantial but subtle SEM/SAUV BL, outstanding Chard, elegant, sinewy Cab/Merlot. Bio in all she does. Strength to strength.

Curly Flat Mac, Vic r w ★★★ (PINOT N) 10' 11' 12' 13' 14 Robust but perfumed Pinot N on two price/quality levels. Full-flavoured CHARD. Both age-worthy, excellent.

Dalwhinnie Pyrenees, Vic r w ★ (CHARD) 07' 10' (SHIRAZ) 06' 07' 08' 10' Rich Chard, CAB SAUV, Shiraz. Stunning site.

Dawson & James Tas r w ★★ Two old stagers of SA wine now produce delicious CHARD, PINOT N from s TAS. Miniscule production.

Deakin Estate Vic r w ★ Top marks for value. V.-low-alcohol MOSCATO. Spicy SHIRAZ, CAB SAUV. Keeps delivering goods.

Devil's Lair Marg R, WA r w ★★ Opulent CHARD, CAB SAUV/MERLOT. Fifth Leg gd second label. Owned by TWE.

Domaine A S Tas r w ★★ Swiss owners/winemakers Peter and Ruth Althaus are perfectionists; v.gd oak-matured SAUV BL. Polarizing cool-climate CAB SAUV. Charismatic, let's say.

Domaine Chandon Yarra V, Vic r (w) sp ★★ Cool-climate sparkling and table wine. Owned by Moët & Chandon (*see* France). Known in UK as Green Point. NV cuvées in best ever shape.

Domenica Beech, Vic ★★★ Flashy new BEECH producer with est v'yds. Exuberant, spicy SHIRAZ. Textural MARSANNE.

Eden Road r w ★★★ Elite young producer winning prizes for wines from Hilltops, TUMBARUMBA, CANBERRA DISTRICT regions. Excellent SHIRAZ, CHARD, CAB SAUV. Metronomic line and length.

Eden Valley SA Hilly region home to Chris Ringland, HENSCHKE, PEWSEY VALE, Radford, TORZI MATTHEWS and others; cutting RIES, (perfumed, bright) SHIRAZ and CAB SAUV of top quality.

Elderton Bar V, SA r w (br) (sp) ★★ Old vines; rich, oaked CAB SAUV, SHIRAZ. All bases covered. Some organics/bio. Rich reds in form of their life.

Eldridge Estate Mor P, Vic r w ★★★ Winemaker David Lloyd is a fastidious experimenter. PINOT N, CHARD worth the fuss. Varietal GAMAY really quite special.

Epis Mac, Vic r w ★★ (PINOT N) Long-lived Pinot N; elegant CHARD. Cold climate. Powerful at release; complexity takes time.

Evans & Tate Marg R, WA r w ★★ Owned by MCWILLIAM'S since 2007. Quality has taken an upward leap. SHIRAZ, CAB SAUV, CHARD. Value too.

Faber Vineyards Swan V, WA r ★★★ (Res SHIRAZ) 07' 09' 11' 12' 13 John Griffiths is a guru of WA winemaking. Home estate redefines what's possible for SWAN V Shiraz.

Fighting Gully Road Beech, Vic r w ★ Touchstone producer of the BEECH region. CHARD, TEMPRANILLO, AGLIANICO kicking goals.

Flametree Marg R, WA r w ★★★ Exceptional CAB SAUV; spicy, seductive SHIRAZ; occasionally compelling CHARD.

Fraser Gallop Estate Marg R, WA r w ★★ Concentrated CAB SAUV, CHARD, (wooded) SEM/SAUV BL. Threatens to become top tier.

Freycinet Tas r w (sp) ★★★ (PINOT N) 09' 10' 11 12' 13 Pioneer family winery on e coast producing dense Pinot N, gd CHARD, excellent Radenti sparkling. A beacon.

Geelong Vic Region w of Melbourne. Cool, dry climate. Best names: BANNOCKBURN, Bellarine Estate, BY FARR, CLYDE PARK, LETHBRIDGE, Provenance.

Gemtree Vineyards McL V, SA r (w) ★★ Warm-hearted SHIRAZ alongside TEMPRANILLO and other exotica, linked by quality. Largely bio.

Giaconda Beech, Vic r w ★★★★ (CHARD) 08' 10' 11 12' 13' 14 (SHIRAZ) 08' 10' 13' 14 In mid-80s Rick Kinzbrunner walked up a steep, dry, rock-strewn hill and came down a winemaking legend. In the process he unearthed the BEECH region. Arguably Oz's best Chard producer. Tiny production of powerhouse wines.

Australia edges 7 cm north each yr. Cool-climate Barossa, here we come.

Giant Steps / Innocent Bystander Yarra V, Vic r w ★★★ Buoyant producer. Top single-v'yd CHARD, PINOT N. Vintages 12' 13' 14' 15 are all exciting for both the main varieties. Innocent Bystander brand sold off to BROWN BROTHERS.

Glaetzer-Dixon Tas r w ★★★ GLAETZER clan famous in Oz for cuddly warm-climate SHIRAZ. Then Nick Glaetzer turned all this on its head by setting up shop in cool TAS. Euro-style RIES, Rhône Shiraz, meaty PINOT N. Never a dull wine.

Glaetzer Wines Bar V, SA r ★★ Big, polished reds with (eye-catching) packaging to match. V.-ripe old-vine SHIRAZ led by iconic Amon-Ra.

Goulburn Valley Vic Temperate region in mid-Vic. Full-bodied, earthen table wines. MARSANNE, CAB SAUV, SHIRAZ the pick, MITCHELTON, TAHBILK perpetual flagbearers. Aka Nagambie Lakes.

Grampians Vic Region previously known as Great Western. Temperate region in nw Vic. High-quality spicy SHIRAZ, sparkling Shiraz. Home to SEPPELT (for now), BEST'S, MOUNT LANGI, The Story.

Granite Belt Qld High-altitude, (relatively) cool, improbable region just n of Qld/ NSW border. Spicy SHIRAZ, rich SEM, eg. Boireann, Golden Grove. Works mostly at tourism end of wine.

Grant Burge Bar V, SA r w (br) (sw) (sp) ★ Smooth reds, whites from best grapes of Burge's large v'yd holdings. Acquired by ACCOLADE in 2015.

Great Southern WA Remote cool area in s; Albany, Denmark, Frankland River, Mount Barker, Porongurup are official subregions. 1st-class RIES, SHIRAZ, CAB SAUV.

Grosset Clare V, SA r w ★★★★ (RIES) 05' 10' 12' 13' 15' 16 (Gaia) 04' 05' 12' 13 Fastidious winemaker. Foremost Oz Ries, lovely CHARD, v.gd *Gaia* CAB SAUV/ MERLOT. Beetrooty PINOT N on the improve.

Harcourt Valley Vineyards Bendigo, Vic r ★ Has sprung thoroughly to life in recent yrs. Dense, syrupy, seductive SHIRAZ, MALBEC, CAB SAUV, with help from American oak. Hard not to use the word "smooth".

Hardys r w (sw) sp ★★ (Eileen CHARD) 02' 06' 10' 12' 13 (Eileen SHIRAZ) 04' 06' 10' 12' 13 Historic company now part of ACCOLADE. Chard excellent. Shiraz (now) not far off. New Eileen PINOT N a curious career move but decent.

Heathcote Vic The region's 500-million-yr-old Cambrian soil has great potential for high-quality reds, esp SHIRAZ; judging by number of external producers now lining up to buy region's grapes – the time to realize that potential is now.

Henschke Eden V, SA r w ★★★★ (SHIRAZ) 90' 91' **96'** 04' 06' 09' 12 (CAB SAUV) 86' 90' **96'** 02' 04' 06' 09' 10 Pre-eminent 150-yr-old family business known for delectable Hill of Grace (Shiraz), v.gd Cab Sauv, red blends, gd whites and genuinely scary prices.

Hentley Farm Bar V, SA r ★★ Consistently produces SHIRAZ of immense power and concentration – wall-of-flavour territory – though importantly in a (generally) fresh, almost frisky, context.

Hewitson SE Aus r (w) ★★ (*Old Garden Mourvèdre*) 05' 06' 09' 10' 12' 13 Dean Hewitson sources parcels of v. old vines. SHIRAZ and varietal release from "oldest MOURVÈDRE vines on the planet".

Houghton Swan V, WA r w ★★ (Jack Mann) 08' 11' 12' **13** Once-legendary winery of Swan Valley nr Perth. Part of ACCOLADE. Inexpensive white blend once considered *a national classic*. V.gd CAB SAUV, SHIRAZ, etc. sourced from MARG R, GREAT SOUTHERN. Jack Mann Cab blend is seriously underappreciated.

Howard Park WA r w ★★★ (RIES) 08' 11' 12' 13' 14' 15 (CAB SAUV) 01' 05' 09' 10' 11' 12' **13' 14** Scented Ries, CHARD; earthy Cab. Second label *MadFish* oft superb value. PINOT N the new plaything.

Hunter Valley NSW It makes no sense but it works. Sub-tropical coal-mining area 160-km n of Sydney. Mid-weight, earthy SHIRAZ, gentle SEM can live for 30 yrs. Arguably most terroir-typical styles of Oz. ANDREW THOMAS, BROKENWOOD, MOUNT PLEASANT, TYRRELL'S the pillars.

Inkwell McL V, SA r (w) ★★ All wines highly opinionated, much like owner/maker Dudley Brown himself. Wines of character, flavour, polish, poise.

Jacob's Creek (Orlando) Bar V, SA r w (br) (sw) sp ★ Owned by Pernod Ricard. Almost totally focused on various tiers of uninspiring-but-reliable Jacob's Creek wines, covering all varieties, prices.

Jamsheed Pyrenees, Vic, Yarra V, Vic r w ★★ Exciting producer, esp SHIRAZ from BEECH, GRAMPIANS, PYRENEES, YARRA V. Complex, savoury wines that both seduce and stir your imagination.

Jasper Hill Hea, Vic r w ★★ (SHIRAZ) 04' 06' 10' 13 Emily's Paddock Shiraz/CAB FR blend, Georgia's Paddock Shiraz from dry-land estate are intense, burly, long-lived and bio.

Jericho Ad H, SA, McL V, SA r w ★★★ Excellent fruit selection and skilled/ consistent winemaking combine to produce a suite of thoroughly modern, tasty wines, esp SHIRAZ, TEMPRANILLO.

Jim Barry Clare V, SA r w ★★★ Great v'yds provide v.gd RIES, McCrae Wood SHIRAZ and richly robed, pricey, oaked-to-the-devil The Armagh SHIRAZ.

John Duval Wines Bar V, SA r ★★ John Duval – former chief red winemaker for PENFOLDS (and Grange) – makes *delicious Rhôney reds* of great intensity, character.

Kaesler Bar V, SA r (w) ★★ If you're looking for a heroic, full-on red then this is a gd place to strike gold. Old vines put, at least most of the time, to gd use.

Kalleske r ★★ Old family farm at Greenock, nw corner of BAROSSA, makes rather special single v'yd Shiraz.

Katnook Estate Coon, SA r w (sw) (sp) ★★ (Odyssey CAB SAUV) 00' 04' 05' 10 Pricey icons Odyssey, Prodigy SHIRAZ. Concentrated fruit, oak.

Kilikanoon Clare V, SA r w ★★★ RIES, SHIRAZ excellent performers in recent yrs. Luscious, beautifully made. Generosity (of flavour) in a glass.

King Valley Vic Altitude between 155–860m has massive impact on varieties, styles. 20+ brands headed quality-wise by BROWN BROTHERS, Chrismont, Dal Zotto, PIZZINI.

Kirrihill Clare V, SA r w ★ V.gd CAB SAUV, SHIRAZ, RIES at, often, gd prices. Affordable way to stock mid-term cellar.

Knappstein Wines Clare V, SA r w ★★ Reliable RIES, CAB SAUV/MERLOT, SHIRAZ, Cab Sauv. Sold by LION NATHAN to ACCOLADE in 2016. New medium-bodied, perfumed Shiraz/MALBEC and skin-contact Ries adds much-needed charm to range.

Kooyong Mor P, Vic r w ★★★ PINOT N, *superb Chard* of harmony, structure. PINOT GR of charm. Single v'yd wines. Clearly among Australia's finest

Lake Breeze Lang C, SA r (w) ★★ Maker of succulently smooth, gutsy, value SHIRAZ, CAB SAUV. Struggles to produce top-end wine but has mid-range licked.

Lake's Folly Hun V, NSW r w ★★ (CHARD) 09' 13' 14 (CAB SAUV) 05' 13' 14 Founded by surgeon Max Lake, pioneer of HUNTER V Cab Sauv. Chard often better than Cab Sauv blend. Idiosyncratic.

Langmeil Bar V, SA r w ★★ Owns v. old block of SHIRAZ (planted mid-1800s) plus other old v'yds, often producing opulent full-throttle Shiraz, GRENACHE, CAB SAUV.

Larry Cherubino Wines Fra R, WA r w ★★★★ Intense SAUV BL, RIES, *spicy Shiraz*, polished CAB SAUV. Ambitious label now franking its early promise in full. Kicking goals from all angles.

Leasingham Clare V, SA r w ★ Once-important brand now a husk of its former self. Owned by ACCOLADE.

Leeuwin Estate Marg R, WA r w ★★★★ (CHARD) 06' 08' 10' 12' 13 Iconic producer. All about Chard. Full-bodied, age-worthy Art Series rendition. SAUV BL, RIES less brilliant. *Cab Sauv* can be v.gd.

Leo Buring Bar V, SA w ★→★★ 02' 05' 13' 14' 15 Part of TWE. Exclusively RIES; Leonay top label, *ages superbly*. Maybe a half-step behind where it once was.

Lethbridge Vic r w ★★★ Small, stylish producer of CHARD, SHIRAZ, PINOT N, RIES. Forever experimenting. Cool climate but wines have ample meat on their bones.

Limestone Coast Zone SA Important zone, incl Bordertown, COON, Mt Benson, Mt Gambier, PADTHAWAY, Robe, WRATTONBULLY.

Lindemans r w ★ Owned by TWE. Low-price Bin range now main focus, far cry from former glory. Lindeman's COON Trio reds still gd but shadow of former self.

Lion Nathan Sold its Oz wine holdings (KNAPPSTEIN, PETALUMA, ST HALLETT, STONIER, Tatachilla) to ACCOLADE in 2016.

Luke Lambert Yarra V, Vic r ★★★ SHIRAZ, PINOT N, NEBBIOLO of real distinction. Operates at point where personality meets power.

Macedon and Sunbury Vic Adjacent regions: Macedon higher elevation, Sunbury nr Melbourne airport. Quality from BINDI, CRAIGLEE, CURLY FLAT, EPIS, Granite Hills, Hanging Rock.

Mac Forbes Yarra V, Vic ★★★ Myriad (in both number, styles) single-v'yd releases, mainly PINOT N, CHARD, RIES. Building enviable reputation.

Main Ridge Estate Mor P, Vic r w ★★★ Rich, age-worthy CHARD, PINOT N. Founder Nat White is legend of MOR PEN wine; impossible to imagine this place without him. Changed hands in 2015.

Majella Coon, SA r (w) ★★ Opulent SHIRAZ, CAB SAUV. Essence of modern COON. Never puts a foot wrong.

Margaret River WA Temperate coastal area s of Perth. Powerful CHARD, structured CAB SAUV, spicy SHIRAZ. CULLEN, DEVIL'S LAIR, FLAMETREE, FRASER GALLOP, LEEUWIN, MOSS WOOD, VOYAGER ESTATE and many others. Great touring (and surfing) region.

Marius McL V, SA r ★★★ Varietal SHIRAZ and blends of dramatic concentration. Quality in inverse proportion to fuss; latter kept to a minimum.

Mayford NE Vic, Vic r w ★★★ Tiny v'yd in private, hidden valley. Put Alpine Valleys on map. SHIRAZ, CHARD, exciting spice-shot TEMPRANILLO.

McHenry Hohnen Marg R, WA w ★★★ If you wanted to compile the best examples of MARG R CHARD you would be remiss not to call here. Slowly building into one of the region's best producers.

McLaren Vale SA Beloved maritime region on outskirts of Adelaide. Big-flavoured reds in general but BRASH HIGGINS, CORIOLE, CHAPEL HILL, GEMTREE, INKWELL, MARIUS, SC PANNELL, WIRRA WIRRA and growing number of others show elegance as well as flavour.

McWilliam's SE Aus r w (br) (sw) ★★ Family-owned. BRAND'S, EVANS & TATE, Hanwood, MOUNT PLEASANT (esp SEM) key pillars. Focusing increasingly on home NSW state.

Meerea Park Hun V, NSW r w ★ Brothers Garth and Rhys Eather create age-worthy SEM, SHIRAZ often as single v'yd expressions.

Mike Press Wines Ad H, SA r (w) ★ Tiny production, tiny pricing. SHIRAZ, CAB SAUV, CHARD, SAUV BL. Crowd favourite of bargain hunters.

Mitchelton Goulburn V, Vic r w (sw) ★ Stalwart producer of RIES, SHIRAZ, CAB SAUV, plus speciality of *Marsanne*, ROUSSANNE.

Mitolo r ★ Quality SHIRAZ, CAB SAUV. Heroically styled.

Montalto Mor P, Vic r w ★★★ For some yrs it was a nice restaurant, gallery. Recently, wine quality has sky rocketed. Now a "must try" of MORN PEN region.

Moorilla Estate Tas r w (sp) ★★ Pioneer nr Hobart on Derwent River. Gd RIES, CHARD; PINOT N. Superb restaurant, extraordinary art gallery.

1st vines planted in Marg R: Fragola grape, 1915, wine sold for two shillings/flagon.

Moorooduc Estate Mor P, Vic r w ★★★ Long-term producer of stylish, sophisticated CHARD, PINOT N. Just a bit special.

Moppity Vineyards Hilltops, NSW r w ★★★ Making a name for its SHIRAZ/VIOGNIER, CAB SAUV (Hilltops), CHARD (TUMBARUMBA). Stern, tannic, spice-drenched reds.

Mornington Peninsula Vic Coastal area 40-km se of Melbourne. Quality boutique wineries abound. Cool climate. PINOT N, CHARD and PINOT GR. Wine/surf/beach/ food playground.

Morris NE Vic (r) (w) br ★★★★ RUTH producer of Australia's greatest dessert *Muscats* and TOPAQUES.

Moss Wood Marg R, WA r w ★★★ (CAB SAUV) 01' 04' 05' 12' 13 MARG R's most

> **Whose family?**
> MORRIS WINES is finally back in family hands. Or is it? Owned by Pernod
> Ricard since 1970, in 2016 it was announced that the family had finally
> bought back the farm, only for it later to be revealed that CASELLA (YELLOW
> TAIL, PETER LEHMANN) were the real buyers.

opulent wines. SFM, CHARD and super-smooth *Cab Sauv*. Oak-and-fruit-rich.

Mount Horrocks Clare V, SA r w ★★ Fine dry RIES, sweet Cordon Cut Ries. SHIRAZ, CAB SAUV in fine form.

Mount Langi Ghiran Gra, Vic r w ★★★★ (SHIRAZ) 04′ 08′ 09′ 10′ 12′ 13′ 14 Rich, peppery, *Rhône-like Shiraz*. Excellent Cliff Edge Shiraz. Special patch of dirt.

Mount Mary Yarra V, Vic r w ★★★★ (PINOT N) 05′ 10′ 12′ 13′ 14 (Quintet) 00′ 04′ 10′ 12′ 13′ 14 Late Dr. Middleton made tiny amounts of suave CHARD, vivid PINOT N, elegant CAB SAUV blend. All age impeccably. Remarkably, post-Dr. era is improvement, if anything.

Mount Pleasant Hun V, NSW ★★★★ Old HUNTER producer owned by MCWILLIAM'S, now thoroughly re-invigorated. One of best stories in Oz wine today. NB single-v'yd SEMS (csp Lovedale), SHIRAZ.

Mudgee NSW Region nw of Sydney. Earthen reds, fine SEM, full CHARD.

Murdoch Hill Ad H, SA r w ★★ Few wineries in Oz have risen so far, so fast. Stunningly peppery PINOT N; SYRAH.

Murray Valley SA Vast irrigated v'yds. Key figure in climate-change discussions.

Ngeringa Ad H, SA r w ★★ Perfumed PINOT N and NEBBIOLO. Rhôney-style SHIRAZ. Savoury rosé. BIO.

Ninth Island Tas *See* PIPERS BROOK (Kreglinger).

Ochota Barrels Bar V, SA r w ★★ Quixotic producer making hay with (mostly) old-vine GRENACHE, SHIRAZ from MCLAREN V, BAROSSA.

O'Leary Walker Wines Clare V, SA r w ★★ Low profile but excellent quality. CLARE V RIES, CAB SAUV standout. MCLAREN V SHIRAZ oak-heavy but gd.

Orange NSW Cool-climate, high-elevation region. Lively SHIRAZ (when ripe) but best suited to (intense) aromatic whites and CHARD.

Padthaway SA V.gd SHIRAZ, CAB SAUV. Soil salinity ongoing issue.

Paringa Estate Mor P, Vic r (w) ★★★ Maker of irresistible PINOT N, SHIRAZ. Fleshy, fruity, flashy styles.

Passing Clouds Bendigo, Vic r ★★ Pioneer of the modern era of Vic wine though off the radar for many yrs. Burst back this yr with a gloriously elegant, textured release of its signature CAB blend.

Paxton McL V, SA r ★★ One of Australia's most prominent organic/bio grower/producers. Ripe but elegant SHIRAZ, GRENACHE.

Pemberton WA Region between MARG R and GREAT SOUTHERN; initial enthusiasm for PINOT N replaced by RIES, CHARD, SHIRAZ.

Penfolds r w (br) ★★★→★★★★ (Grange) 55′ 60′ 62′ 63′ 66′ 71′ 76′ 86′ 90′ 96′ 98′ 99′ 02′ 04′ 05′ 06′ 08′ 10′ 12 (CAB SAUV Bin 707) 91′ 96′ 98′ 02′ 04′ 06′ 10′ 12′ 14 and of course *St Henri*, "simple" SHIRAZ. Originally Adelaide, now SA. Oz's best warm-climate red wine company. *Yattarna* CHARD, Bin Chard now of comparable quality to reds.

Petaluma Ad H, SA r w sp ★★ (RIES) 02′ 11′ 12′ 13′ 16 (CHARD) 12′ (CAB SAUV COON) 04′ 05′ 07′ 08′ 12 Seems to miss ex-owner/creator Brian Croser. Gd but low-key now.

Peter Lehmann Wines Bar V, SA r w (br) (sw) (sp) ★★ Well-priced wines incl easy RIES. Luxurious/sexy Stonewell SHIRAZ among many others (r w). Peter died 2013; company sold 2014 to CASELLA (YELLOW TAIL).

Pewsey Vale Ad H, SA w ★★ Excellent RIES, standard and (aged-release) The Contours, grown on lovely tiered v'yd.

Piano Piano Beech, Vic r w ★★ V'yd in next paddock along from GIACONDA. Powerful CHARD, SHIRAZ.

Pierro Marg R, WA r w ★★ (CHARD) 12' 13' 14' 15 Producer of expensive, tangy SEM/SAUV BL and full-throttle Chard.

Pipers Brook Tas r w sp ★★★ (RIES) 09' 13' (CHARD) 13' Cool area pioneer, gd Ries, *restrained Chard and sparkling* from Tamar Valley. Second label: Ninth Island. Owned by Belgian Kreglinger family.

Pizzini King V, Vic r ★★ (SANGIOVESE) 13' 14 A leader of Italian varieties in Oz, esp NEBBIOLO, SANGIOVESE (recently stepped up a gear). Dominant KING VALLEY producer.

Primo Estate SA r w dr (sw) ★ Joe Grilli's many successes incl rich MCLAREN V SHIRAZ, tangy COLOMBARD, potent Joseph CAB SAUV/MERLOT.

Punch Yarra V, Vic r w ★★★ Lance family ran Diamond Valley for decades. When they sold, they retained the close-planted PINOT N v'yd. It can grow detailed, decisive, age-worthy wines.

Pyrenees Vic Central Vic region making rich, often minty reds. Blue Pyrenees, DALWHINNIE, Dog Rock, Mount Avoca, TALTARNI leading players.

Ravensworth Can, NSW r w ★★ Suddenly in hot demand for various wine experiments. SANGIOVESE best-known but there's a buzz over skin-contact whites and GAMAY NOIR.

Richmond Grove Bar R, SA w ★ Gd RIES at bargain prices. Owned by JACOB'S CREEK.

Riverina NSW Large-volume irrigated zone centred on Griffith.

Robert Oatley Wines Mudgee, NSW r w ★★ Ambitious venture of ROSEMOUNT ESTATE creator Robert Oatley. Appointment of group winemaker LARRY CHERUBINO is paying dividends.

Rockford Bar V, SA r (w) sp ★★ Sourced from various old, low-yielding v'yds; reds best; also iconic sparkling Black SHIRAZ.

Rosemount Estate r w ★ Periodically loses its way but reds can be gd.

Ruggabellus Bar V, SA r ★★ Causing a stir. Funkier, more savoury version of BAROSSA. Old oak, min sulphur, wild yeast, whole bunches/stems. Blends of GRENACHE, SHIRAZ, MATARO, CINSAULT.

Rutherglen & Glenrowan Vic Two of four regions in ne Vic zone, justly famous for sturdy reds, magnificent fortified dessert wines.

Rymill Coon, SA r ★★ Well-est. Just when its mark seemed well set it has taken CAB SAUV quality up a gear.

Saltram Bar V, SA r w ★ Value Mamre Brook (SHIRAZ, CAB SAUV) and (rarely sighted) No 1 Shiraz are leaders. One of TWE's many "where are they now?" brands.

Samuel's Gorge McL V, SA r ★★ Justin McNamee makes (at times) stunning SHIRAZ, TEMPRANILLO, GRENACHE of character and place.

Savaterre Beech, Vic r w ★★ (PINOT N) 04' 06' 10' 12' 13 Fine producer of full-bodied CHARD, meaty Pinot N, close-planted SHIRAZ.

Scarborough Hunt V, NSW w ★ Just to prove the baby hasn't been thrown out with the bathwater: Yellow Label CHARD is old-school rich in fruit and oak, done well.

China buying more Australian wine than ever: exports risen 64 per cent in past yr.

SC Pannell McL V, SA r ★★★ Excellent (spicy, whole-bunch-fermented) SHIRAZ (often labelled SYRAH) and (esp) GRENACHE-based wines. NEBBIOLO to watch. Get on board.

Seppelt Gra, Vic r w br sp ★★★ (St Peter's SHIRAZ) 02' 04' 08' 10' 12' 13' 14 Historic name owned by TWE. Impressive RIES, CHARD, (esp) SHIRAZ. Brand remains as a husk; winery shut down.

Seppeltsfield Bar V, SA r br ★★ National Trust Heritage Winery bought by KILIKANOON in 2007. Fortified wine stocks back to 1878.

Serrat Yarra V, Vic r w ★★★ Micro v'yd of noted winemaker Tom Carson (YABBY LAKE) and wife Nadege. Complex, powerful, precise SHIRAZ/VIOGNIER, PINOT N, CHARD.

Seville Estate Yarra V, Vic r w ★★★ (SHIRAZ) 05' 06' 10' 13 Excellent CHARD, spicy Shiraz, delicate PINOT N. YARRA V pioneer still showing 'em how it's done.

Shadowfax Vic r w ★★ More than just a tourist adjunct to the historic Werribee Park. V.gd CHARD, PINOT N, SHIRAZ. Never a bad wine.

Shaw & Smith Ad H, SA r w ★★★ Savvy outfit, black turtlenecks and all. Crisp *harmonious* SAUV BL, complex M3 CHARD and, surpassing them both, *Shiraz*. Daylight to PINOT N but it's improving.

Check out Uber for on-demand wine tours: Ad Hills trialling first.

Simao & Co Ruth, Vic r w ★ Young Simon Killeen, of STANTON & KILLEEN family, released an undeniably scrumptious TEMPRANILLO in 2015. New range but rich in story, personality, interest.

Southern NSW Zone NSW Incl CANBERRA, Gundagai, Hilltops, TUMBARUMBA. Savoury SHIRAZ; lengthy CHARD. Ascendant.

Spinifex Bar V, SA r w ★★★ Bespoke BAROSSA producer. Complex SHIRAZ, GRENACHE blends. Routinely turns out rich-but-polished reds.

Stanton & Killeen Ruth, Vic (t) br ★ Fortified vintage the main attraction.

Stefano Lubiana S Tas r w sp ★★★ Beautiful v'yds on Derwent River, 20 mins from Hobart. Excellent PINOT N, sparkling, MERLOT, CHARD. Homely but driven, ambitious.

Stella Bella Marg R, WA r w ★★★ Humdinger wines. CAB SAUV, SEM/SAUV BL, CHARD, SHIRAZ, SANGIOVESE/Cab Sauv. Sturdy, characterful.

St Hallett Bar V, SA r w ★★★ (Old Block) 02' 04' 06' 08' 12' 13 Old Block SHIRAZ the star; rest of range is smooth, sound, stylish. LION NATHAN-owned.

Stoney Rise Tas r w ★★★ Joe Holyman was wicketkeeper for TAS; holds 1st-class record for highest number of catches on debut; now looks after all winemaking tasks for his outstanding PINOT N, CHARD.

Stonier Wines Mor P, Vic r w ★★ (CHARD) 12' 13' (PINOT N) 12' 13' 15 Consistently gd; Res notable for elegance. PINOT N in particularly fine form.

Sunbury Vic *See* MACEDON AND SUNBURY.

Swan Valley WA as minor n of Perth. Birthplace of wine in the w. Hot climate makes strong, low-acid wines. FABER V'YDS leads way.

Tahbilk Goulburn V, Vic r w ★★★ (MARSANNE) 06' 08' 13' 14' 16 (SHIRAZ) 04' 06' 10' 12' Historic Purbrick family estate; long-ageing reds, also some of Oz's best old-vine *Marsanne*. Res CAB SAUV can be outstanding. Rare 1860 Vines Shiraz.

Taltarni Pyrenees, Vic r w sp ★★ SHIRAZ, CAB SAUV in best shape in yrs. Long-haul wines but jack hammer no longer required to remove tannin from your gums. Crowbar still helps.

Tamar Ridge N Tas r w (sp) Big fish in the small TAS pond. Acquired in 2010 by BROWN BROTHERS. Unexciting thus far.

Tapanappa SA r ★★★ WRATTONBULLY collaboration between Brian Croser, Bollinger, J-M Cazes of Pauillac. Splendid CAB SAUV blend, SHIRAZ, MERLOT, CHARD. Surprising *Pinot N* from Fleurieu Peninsula.

Tar & Roses Hea, Vic r w ★★ SHIRAZ, TEMPRANILLO, SANGIOVESE of impeccable polish, presentation. Modern success story.

Tarrawarra Estate Yarra V, Vic r w ★★★ (Res CHARD) 10' 12' 13' (Res PINOT N) 04' 06' 10' 12' 13' Moved from hefty and idiosyncratic to elegant and long. Res far better than standard.

Tasmania Cold island region with hot reputation. Outstanding sparkling, PINOT N, RIES. V.gd CHARD, SAUV BL, PINOT GR.

Taylors Wines Clare V, SA r w ★ Large-scale production led by RIES, SHIRAZ, CAB SAUV. Exports under Wakefield Wines brand.

Ten Minutes by Tractor Mor P, Vic r w ★★★ Wacky name, smart packaging, even better wines. *Chard, Pinot N both excellent* and will age. Style meets substance.

Teusner Bar V, SA r ★★★ Old vines, clever winemaking, pure fruit flavours. Leads a BAROSSA V trend towards "more wood, no good".

Tim Adams Clare V, SA ★★ Ever-reliable RIES, CAB SAUV/MALBEC blend, SHIRAZ and (full-bodied) TEMPRANILLO.

Tolpuddle Tas ★★★ SHAW & SMITH bought this outstanding 1988-planted v'yd in the Coal River Valley in 2011. Scintillating PINOT N, CHARD in lean, lengthy style.

Topaque Vic Replacement name for iconic RUTH sticky "Tokay", thanks to EU. Still provokes a double-take.

Torbreck Bar V, SA r (w) ★★★ Dedicated to (often old-vine) Rhône varieties led by SHIRAZ, GRENACHE. Ultimate expression of rich, sweet, high-alcohol style.

Torzi Matthews Eden V, SA r ★★ Aromatic, stylish SHIRAZ. Combines excellence with value.

Tumbarumba NSW Cool-climate NSW region nestled in the Australian Alps. Sites 500–800m. CHARD the star.

Turkey Flat Bar V, SA r p ★★★ Top producer of bright-coloured rosé, GRENACHE, SHIRAZ from core of 150-yr-old v'yd. Controlled alcohol and oak. New single-v'yd wines. Old but modern.

TWE (Treasury Wine Estates) Aussie wine behemoth. Dozens of well-known brands, BAILEYS, COLDSTREAM HILLS, DEVIL'S LAIR, LINDEMANS, PENFOLDS, SALTRAM, WYNNS among them.

Tyrrell's Hun V, NSW r w ★★★★ (SEM) 10' 11' 13' 14' 15' 16 (Vat 47 CHARD) 10' 12 13' 14' 15' 16 Oz's greatest maker of Sem, Vat 1 now joined with series of individual v'yd or subregional wines. *Vat 47*, Oz's 1st Chard, continues to defy climatic odds. Outstanding old-vine 4 Acres SHIRAZ, Vat 9 Shiraz. One of greats.

Vasse Felix Marg R, WA r w ★★★ (CAB SAUV) 08' 09' 10' 11' 12' **13' 14** With CULLEN, pioneer of MARG R. Elegant Cab Sauv for mid-weight balance. Complex/funkified CHARD creating waves. Returning to estate-grown roots.

Old Grenache, new panache

One of the great reveals of Australian wine in recent yrs is the complete turnaround of MCLAREN V GRENACHE. It's as if the workhorse has gone out and won the Grand National. The vines are often (v.) old, dry-grown and as a result, they look the part: all twisted, thick-trunked and craggy. But save for particularly enthusiastic souls, they've been widely and largely unloved. McLaren V Grenache is one of the great blenders: it adds sweet red-berried flavour to inkier SHIRAZ; it makes the broody dude in the corner seem like fun. In single-varietal form, until recently, it was almost universally high in alc, sweet and simple. The words "delusions of grandeur" often sprang to mind. And then things changed. "The perceived problem," winemaker Steve Pannell says, "was that it is medium-bodied when compared to Shiraz. So in order to compensate for the lighter weight, it tended to be made overripe. It was made in more of a faux-Shiraz style.

"But the increase in popularity of lighter reds and the influx of imported wines – many of which are Grenache-based – is having an impact. I like to think of Grenache as a warm-climate Pinot Noir."

Low-oaked, modest alc, complex, nuanced Grenache is suddenly in vogue. Terrific examples incl: Yangarra Estate Small Pot Ceramic Egg 2014, OCHOTA BARRELS 186 2016, Bekkers 2014, Marmont Single V'yd 2015, Samuel's Gorge 2014, Longline Albright 2014, Bondar Wines Rayner V'yd 2015, SC PANNELL Old McDonald 2014 and Dub Style No2 2014. All can be thrown into a large-bowled glass and allowed to run wild.

Voyager Estate Marg R, WA r w ★★★ Sizeable volume of (mostly) estate-grown, rich, powerful SEM, SAUV BL, (esp) CHARD and CAB SAUV/MERLOT.

Wantirna Estate Yarra V, Vic r w ★★★★ Regional pioneer showing no sign of slowing down. CHARD, PINOT N, B'x blend all terrific. Tiny production; just the way they like it.

Wendouree Clare V, SA r ★★★ Treasured maker (tiny quantities) of powerful, tannic, concentrated reds, based on SHIRAZ, CAB SAUV, MOURVÈDRE and MALBEC. Recently moved to screwcap; the word "longevity" best defined with a picture of a Wendouree red.

West Cape Howe Denmark, WA r w ★ Affordable, flavoursome reds the speciality.

Westend Estate Riverina, NSW r w ★ Thriving family producer of tasty bargains, esp Private Bin SHIRAZ/Durif. Recent cool-climate additions gd value.

Willow Creek Mor P, Vic r w ★★ Gd gear. Impressive producer of CHARD, PINOT N in particular. Power and poise.

Wirra Wirra McL V, SA r w (sw) (sp) ★★★ (RSW SHIRAZ) 04' 05' 10' 12' 13' (CAB SAUV) 05' 10' 12' 13 '14 High-quality, concentrated wines in flashy new livery. The Angelus Cab Sauv named Dead Ringer in export markets.

Wolf Blass Bar V, SA r w (br) (sw) (sp) ★★ (Black Label CAB SAUV blend) 04' 05 10' 12 Owned by TWE. Not the shouty player it once was but still churns through an enormous volume of clean, inoffensive wines.

Woodlands Marg R, WA r (w) ★★★ 7 ha of 35-yr-old+ CAB SAUV among top v'yds in region, plus younger but still v.gd plantings of other B'x reds. Reds of brooding impact.

Wrattonbully SA Important grape-growing region in LIMESTONE COAST ZONE; profile lifted by activity of TAPANAPPA, Peppertree.

Wynns Coon, SA r w ★★★★ (SHIRAZ) 04' 05' 06' 10' 12 13' 14' 15 (CAB SAUV) 91' 98' 00' 04' 05' 06' 10' 12' 13' 14 TWE-owned COON classic. RIES, CHARD, Shiraz, *Cab Sauv* all v.gd, esp Black Label Cab Sauv, *John Riddoch Cab Sauv*. Recent single-v'yd releases add finishing touches.

Yabby Lake Mor P, Vic r w ★★★ CHARD, PINOT N and SHIRAZ are all generally and routinely sensational.

Yalumba Bar V, SA, SA r w sp ★★★ 167 yrs young, family-owned. *Full spectrum of high-quality wines*, from budget to elite single v'yd. Entry level Y Series v.gd value.

Yangarra Estate McL V, SA r w ★★★ It just goes to show that wild, free-thinking, inventive winemaking can sit hand-in-glove with clean, conventional, structured thinking – and wines. You get full box and dice here.

Yarraloch Yarra V, Vic r w ★★★ CHARD "to die for", basically. But often exceptional PINOT N too.

Yarra Valley Vic Historic area just ne of Melbourne. Growing emphasis on v. successful PINOT N, CHARD, SHIRAZ, sparkling. Understated, elegant CAB SAUV.

Yarra Yering Yarra V, Vic r w ★★★ (Dry Reds) 00' 04' 05' 06' 08' 10' 12' 15 YARRA V pioneer. Powerful PINOT N; deep, herby CAB SAUV (Dry Red No 1); SHIRAZ (Dry Red No 2). Luscious, daring flavours (r w).

Yellow Tail NSW *See* CASELLA.

Yeringberg Yarra V, Vic r w ★★★★ (MARSANNE/ROUSSANNE) 06' 09' 12' 13' (CAB SAUV) 00' 04' 05' 06' 10' 12' 13 Dreamlike historic estate still in hands of founding (1862) Swiss family, the de Purys. Small quantities of v.-high-quality Marsanne, Roussanne, CHARD, Cab Sauv, PINOT N.

Yering Station / Yarrabank Yarra V, Vic r w sp ★★★ On site of Vic's 1st v'yd; it was replanted after an 80-yr gap. Snazzy table wines incl Res CHARD, PINOT N, SHIRAZ and VIOGNIER; Yarrabank – sparkling wines in joint venture with Champagne Devaux.

New Zealand

Abbreviations used
in the text:

Auck   Auckland
B of P   Bay of Plenty
Cant   Canterbury
N/C Ot   North/Central Otago
Gis   Gisborne
Hawk   Hawke's Bay
Hend   Henderson
Marl   Marlborough
Mart   Martinborough
Nel   Nelson
Waih   Waiheke Island
Waip   Waipara
Wair   Wairarapa

The heart of New Zealand's wine industry can be summed up in just five words – Sauvignon Blanc, Pinot Noir, Marlborough. Kiwi Sauvignon conquered by being pungent, aromatic, assertive, instantly recognizable. Its Pinot Noir then made that tricky variety seem easy. Marlborough, in the north of the South Island, is the country's biggest and best-known vineyard area. So much for the obvious. What happens in other areas with other grapes is potentially more interesting. Certainly more complicated. In Hawke's Bay NZ has a region capable of making superb Cabernets, Chardonnays and Syrahs of huge potential. Gisborne further north has excellent Chardonnay. Waiheke Island, near Auckland, makes glorious Cabernet, Syrah and Chardonnay and there are several other fine regions. Some ambitious producers are working on versions of Sauvignon Blanc with less stridency and more subtlety, but such wines are more expensive and thus harder to sell. New Zealand's best wines can give France a run for her money – and her standard lines masses of uncomplicated pleasure.

Recent vintages

2016 Huge harvest, warm growing season. Ripe, tropical Marlborough Sauv Bl. In Hawke's Bay, excellent Chard but autumn rain hit Merlot.
2015 Aromatic, vibrant Marlborough Sauv Bl. Fragrant, charming, rather than powerful, reds in Hawke's Bay.
2014 Hawke's Bay: weighty, ripe, well-rounded Chard and reds. Marlborough: those who picked early fared best.
2013 Especially good in North Island, Marlborough. Hawke's Bay reds will age.

Akarua C Ot r (p) (w) (sp) ★★★ Thriving producer of consistently outstanding, Bannockburn PINOT N 12 13' 14'; delicious Rua (briefly oak-aged). Stylish CHARD; scented PINOT GR. Vivacious sparkling, esp fragrant Vintage Brut 11.

Allan Scott Marl (r) (p) w (sp) ★★ Medium-sized family firm. Light RIES; tropical SAUV BL. New, upper-tier Generations range: Sauv Bl, CHARD, dry Ries, PINOT N.

Alpha Domus Hawk r w ★★ Harmonious First Solo CHARD; peachy VIOGNIER. Rich B'x-style reds, esp savoury MERLOT-based The Navigator 10' 13' and notably dark AD CAB SAUV The Aviator 13'. Powerful Barnstormer SYRAH 15. AD is top range.

Amisfield C Ot r (p) (w) ★★→★★★ Fleshy PINOT GR; tensely acidic RIES (dry and medium-sweet); ripe, tangy SAUV BL; classy Pinot Rosé; v. floral, savoury PINOT N 14' (RKV Res is Rolls-Royce model 13'). Lake Hayes is lower-tier label.

Ara Marl r (p) w ★★ Huge v'yd in Waihopai Valley. Best-known for weighty SAUV BL; generous PINOT N. Top tier: Resolute, followed by Select Block, then Single Estate, then Pathway. Ara brand (although not site) purchased by GIESEN in 2016.

Astrolabe Marl (r) w ★★ Classy wines from Simon Waghorn (ex-WHITEHAVEN). Herbaceous Province SAUV BL; full PINOT GR; dry and medium-dry RIES; peachy CHARD; crisp ALBARIÑO; vivacious dry rosé. Supple PINOT N.

Ata Rangi Mart r (p) (w) ★★★→★★★★ Small, highly respected. Seductive, long-lived PINOT N 10' 11 12 13' 14' is one of NZ's greatest (oldest vines planted 1980). Delicious younger-vine Crimson Pinot N 13 14'. Rich, complex Craighall CHARD 13' 14' 15' from vines planted in 1983; off-dry Lismore PINOT GR.

Auckland Largest city (n, warm, cloudy) in NZ with 1.1 per cent of v'yd area. Nearby wine districts: Hend, Kumeu/Huapai/Waimauku (both long est); newer (since 80s): Matakana, Clevedon, WAIH (island v'yds, popular with tourists). Stylish MERLOT/CAB blends in dry seasons 10' 13', 14; peppery SYRAH 13' 14 is fast-expanding (rivals HAWK for quality); rich, underrated CHARD; promising ALBARIÑO.

Auntsfield Marl r w ★★ Consistently gd wines with strong personality, from site of the region's 1st v'yd, planted on s side of Wairau Valley in 1873 (replanted 1999). Intense, partly barrel-fermented SAUV BL 16; fleshy CHARD; dense PINOT N 13' 14' (Heritage esp lush 10').

Awatere Valley Marl Key subregion (pronounced *Awa-terry*), v. few wineries but huge v'yd area (more than HAWK), pioneered in 1986 by VAVASOUR. YEALANDS: key producer. Slightly cooler and drier than the WAIRAU VALLEY, with herbaceous ("tomato stalk") SAUV BL; tight RIES, PINOT GR; scented, often slightly herbal PINOT N. (Earthquake in late 2016 damaged some v'yds and winery equipment.)

Babich Hend r w ★★→★★★ Medium-to-large family firm (1916), now 3rd generation. HAWK, MARL v'yds; wineries in AUCK and Marl. Refined, v. age-worthy Irongate wines, from GIMBLETT GRAVELS: CHARD 10' 13' 14'; B'x-like Irongate CAB/MERLOT/CAB FR 10' 14'. Marl SAUV BL is biggest seller. Top red The Patriarch (B'x style) 13' 14'.

Bell Hill Cant r w ★★★ Tiny (2 ha), elevated, inland v'yd on limestone, with family link to GIESEN. Rare but strikingly rich CHARD and gorgeously scented, velvety PINOT N. Second label: Old Weka Pass Road.

Blackenbrook Nel r w ★★ Small winery with impressive aromatic whites, esp highly perfumed, rich, Alsace-style GEWURZ 16; PINOT GR 16 and (rarer) off-dry MUSCAT. Punchy, dry SAUV BL 16; v. bold Family Res PINOT N 15. Second label: St Jacques.

Black Estate Cant r w ★★ Small Waip producer with some vines over 30 yrs old. Concentrated CHARD; slightly honeyed RIES; graceful, harmonious PINOT N.

Borthwick Wair r w ★★ V'yd at Gladstone with Paddy Borthwick brand (mostly exported). Lively SAUV BL; rich RIES; toasty CHARD; dry PINOT GR; perfumed PINOT N.

Brancott Estate Marl r (p) w ★→★★★ Major brand of PERNOD RICARD NZ that replaced Montana worldwide. Top wines: Letter Series eg. fleshy, rich "B" Brancott SAUV BL; rich, complex "O" CHARD. Huge-selling, ripely herbaceous, v.gd-value Sauv Bl 16; floral, easy-drinking South Island PINOT N. Terroir Series: mid-tier, subregional whites. Living Land: organic. Flight: plain, low alc. Chosen Rows: v. classy, long-lived Sauv Bl 13. Top value HAWK MERLOT 15.

Brightwater Nel (r) w ★★ Impressive, gd-value whites: weighty SAUV BL 16; fresh, medium-dry RIES; gently oaked CHARD; rich, sweetish PINOT GR. V. charming PINOT N **14**. Top: Lord Rutherford (incl fleshy, intense Sauv Bl **15**').

Canterbury NZ's 4th-largest wine region; most v'yds are in relatively warm, sheltered, n Waip district. Greatest success with aromatic, vibrant RIES (since mid-80s) and later dark, rich PINOT N. Emerging strength in Alsace-style PINOT GR. SAUV BL is widely planted but often goes into regional blends.

Carrick C Ot r w ★★★ Bannockburn winery with intense RIES (dry, medium C OT; sweetish Josephine); elegant CHARD **14**', esp EBM **13**'; partly oak-aged, organic PINOT GR; dense PINOT N, built to last **13**'. Delicious, drink-young Unravelled Pinot N **14**'. Top Excelsior Pinot N **13**', v. fragrant, silky.

Central Otago (r) **13**' **14** 16 (w) **13**' **14** 16 Cool, sunny, v. low-rainfall, high-altitude inland region (now NZ's 3rd largest) in s of South Island; many v. small producers. Most vines in Cromwell Basin. Scented RIES, PINOT GR; famous PINOT N (over 75 per cent v'yd area) is perfumed, with drink young charm; older vines yield more savoury wines. V.gd Pinot N rosé and traditional method sparkling.

Chard Farm C Ot r w ★★ Pioneer winery with precipitous access road. Oily, dry PINOT GR; citrus RIES; mid-weigh PINOT N (charming River Run; single-v'yd The Tiger; The Viper more complex). Light Rabbit Ranch Pinot N. Mata-Au Pinot N is sweet-fruited, silky, signature red.

Church Road Hawk r w (p) ★★→★★★ PERNOD RICARD NZ winery with historic HAWK roots. Rich barrel-aged CHARD; ripe, partly oak-aged SAUV BL; weighty, Alsace-style PINOT GR; full MERLOT/CAB/MALBEC (all great value). Impressive Grand Res wines. McDonald Series, between standard and Grand Res ranges, offers eye-catching quality, value (incl SYRAH **14**' Cab Sauv **14**' Merlot **13**'). Prestige, high-priced TOM selection: classy Cab Sauv/Merlot **13**'; deep Chard **13**'; smooth Syrah **13**'.

Albariño is most talked about of NZ's emerging white grapes: 20+ producers.

Churton Marl r w ★★ Elevated Waihopai Valley site; bone-dry SAUV BL **16**; oak-aged Best End Sauv Bl **15**; sturdy VIOGNIER; harmonious PINOT N **13**' (esp The Abyss: oldest vines, greater depth **13**'). Steely, compelling PETIT MANSENG **15**'.

Clearview Hawk r (p) w ★★ →★★★ Coastal v'yd at Te Awanga (also drawing grapes from inland) renowned for hedonistic, oaky Res CHARD **15**' (Beachhead Chard is excellent junior version **15**'); gd oak-fermented Res SAUV BL; dark Enigma (MERLOT-based **14**), Old Olive Block (CAB SAUV/CAB FR/Merlot blend **14**').

Clos Henri Marl r w ★★→★★★ Founded 2001 by Henri Bourgeois of Sancerre. V. lightly-oaked SAUV BL (stony soils) one of NZ's best; sturdy PINOT N (clay). Second label: Bel Echo (reverses variety/soil match). Third label Petit Clos, from young vines. Distinctive, satisfying wines, priced right.

Cloudy Bay Marl r w sp ★★★ Large-volume but still classy SAUV BL (some barrel ageing since 2010) is NZ's most famous wine (**16**'). CHARD (robust), PINOT N (rich **14**') both classy. Elegant, Chard-led Pelorus NV sparkling. Te Koko (oak-aged Sauv Bl) is full of personality. Expanding involvement in C OT for Te Wahi Pinot N (**14**'). Owned by LVMH.

Constellation New Zealand Auck r (p) w ★→★★ Largest producer of NZ wine, previously Nobilo Wine Group, now owned by US-based Constellation Brands. Strong in US market. Strength mainly in solid, moderately priced wines (esp SAUV BL) under KIM CRAWFORD, Monkey Bay, NOBILO and SELAKS brands.

Cooper's Creek Auck r w ★★→★★★ Innovative medium-sized producer, gd-value from four regions, flavoury, home-v'yd MONTEPULCIANO **14**'. Excellent Swamp Res Hawk CHARD; gd SAUV BL, RIES; MERLOT; top-value VIOGNIER; easy-drinking PINOT N; rich SYRAH. SV (Select V'yd) range is mid-tier. NZ's 1st: ARNEIS (2006), GRÜNER V (08), ALBARIÑO (11), MARSANNE (13).

Craggy Range Hawk r (p) w ★★★→★★★★ High-profile winery, large v'yds in HAWK,

MART. Top restaurant. Stylish CHARD 15', PINOT N 13'; excellent mid-range MERLOT 14', SYRAH 14' from GIMBLETT GRAVELS; dense Sophia (Merlot) 14'; show-stopping Syrah Le Sol 14'; complex Aroha (Pinot N) 14'. Value Te Kahu (Merlot-based blend).

Delegat Auck r w ★★ Large, listed company (over two million cases/yr), still controlled by Delegat family. Owns v'yds (2000 ha) in HAWK, MARL; three wineries (incl AUCK). Hugely successful OYSTER BAY brand, esp SAUV BL. Delegat range: citrus CHARD; herbaceous Sauv Bl; vibrant MERLOT; smooth PINOT N.

Delta Marl ★★→★★★ Partnership between top winemaker Matt Thomson and UK importer David Gleave. Supple PINOT N; weighty, sweet-fruited SAUV BL.

Destiny Bay Waih r ★★→★★★ Expatriate Americans make classy, high-priced B'x-style reds, brambly, silky. Flagship is deep Magna Praemia 08' 09 10' 13' (mostly CAB SAUV). Mid-tier: Mystae 09 10' 13'. Destinae: for earlier drinking 10' 13'.

Deutz Auck sp ★★★ Champagne house gives name to refined sparklings from MARL by PERNOD RICARD NZ. V. popular Brut NV is citrus, yeasty (min 2 yrs on lees, incl res wines). Much-awarded Vintage Blanc de Blancs is vivacious (13'). Rosé is crisp, toasty (14). V. rich Prestige (disgorged after 3 yrs) is mostly CHARD 12'.

Dog Point Marl r w ★★★ Grower Ivan Sutherland and winemaker James Healy (both ex-CLOUDY BAY) make minerally, oak-aged SAUV BL (Section 94) 14'; CHARD (v. elegant, age-worthy) 14; rich, fine PINOT N 10' 11 12' 13', 14', one of region's greatest. Also larger volume, but v.gd, weighty, unoaked Sauv Bl 16'.

Dry River Mart r w ★★★ Small pioneer winery, now US-owned. Reputation for elegant, long-lived CHARD 13' 14; intense, age-worthy RIES 13' 14' 15', PINOT GR (NZ's 1st outstanding Pinot Gr 14' 15'), GEWURZ 14' 15'; late-harvest whites; slowly evolving PINOT N 13' 14'.

Elephant Hill Hawk r (p) w ★★→★★★ Stylish winery/restaurant at coastal Te Awanga site, also draws grapes from inland. Rich CHARD 15'; dense MERLOT/MALBEC 14'; generous SYRAH 14'. Excellent Res range. Top pair: Airavata Syrah (powerful 13'); Hieronymus (blended red 13').

Escarpment Mart r (w) ★★★ Known for complex PINOT N. Top label: Kupe. Single-v'yd, old-vine reds esp gd. MART Pinot N is regional blend. Lower-tier: The Edge.

Esk Valley Hawk r p w ★★→★★★ Owned by VILLA MARIA. Acclaimed MERLOT-based reds (esp Winemakers Res blend 10' 11 13' 14); great-value Merlot/CAB SAUV/MALBEC 13' 14' 15. Floral SYRAH (Res 13' 14'). Lovely dryish Rosé 16; buttery CHARD is superb value 15'; crisp CHENIN BL, VERDELHO. Striking flagship red Heipipi The Terraces: spicy, single-v'yd blend, Malbec/Merlot/CAB FR 06' 09' 13' 14'.

Fairbourne Marl ★★★ NZ's only SAUV BL specialist. Tightly structured, bone-dry wines from single v'yd on s side of WAIRAU VALLEY.

Felton Road C Ot r w ★★★★ Star winery at Bannockburn, famous for PINOT N, but RIES, CHARD classy too. Bold Pinot N Block 3 and 5 12' 13' 14' 15' from The Elms V'yd, light, intense Ries (dr s/sw) outstanding 16'; long-lived Chard (esp Block 2 13' 14' 15') is key label is perfumed Bannockburn Pinot N 13' 14' 15, blended from three v'yds. V. fine single-v'yd Pinot N: Cornish Point 13' 14' 15', Calvert 13' 14' 15'.

Forrest Marl r (p) w ★★ Mid-size winery. Gd SAUV BL (full-bodied, ripe, dry) and RIES (medium); gorgeous botrytized Ries; rich HAWK Newton/Forrest Cornerstone (B'x blend 13'). Distinguished flagship range, John Forrest Collection, released several yrs after vintage. Popular low-alc (9%) Ries and Sauv Bl The Doctors'. Impressive C OT and WAITAKI VALLEY range: Tatty Bogler.

Framingham Marl (r) w ★★→★★★ Owned by Sogrape (see Portugal). Strength in aromatic whites: intense RIES (esp rich Classic) from mature vines. Lush PINOT GR, GEWURZ. Elegant CHARD. Subtle SAUV BL. Lush Noble Ries. Silky PINOT N. Rare F Series wines (incl Old Vine Ries, botrytized sweet whites) full of personality.

Fromm Marl r w ★★★ Distinguished PINOT N, esp organic, hill-grown, Clayvin V'yd (perfumed, supple 10' 11 12' 13' 14). V. stylish Clayvin CHARD 13', RIES Dry. Earlier-drinking La Strada range incl ripely herbaceous SAUV BL 15'; fleshy, oak-aged PINOT GR; excellent dry rosé.

Gibbston Valley C Ot r (p) w ★★ →★★★ Pioneer winery with original v'yd at Gibbston. Most v'yds now at Bendigo. Strong reputation for PINOT N, esp rich GV Collection regional blend 14' 15' and exuberantly fruity Res 09' 12' 13' 15'. Scented Le Maitre 13' 14' 15' mostly from 1st (1984) vines. Racy, medium-dry RIES, full PINOT GR, classy CHARD (China Terrace 15). Gold River Pinot N: drink young charm.

Giesen Cant (r) w ★★ Large family winery heading for top quality. Most is ripe, tangy MARL SAUV BL. Light, distinctly medium RIES 15' (value). Bold The Brothers (mid-tier) Sauv Bl, barrel-fermented The August Sauv Bl 13'. Fast-improving PINOT N, Single V'yd bottlings. Recently leased famous Clayvin V'yd (Pinot N 13').

Soil in Gimblett Gravels is 150 yrs old. In nearby Bridge Pa Triangle it's 10,000.

Gimblett Gravels Hawk Defined area (800 ha planted) of old riverbed, mostly free-draining, low-fertility soils noted for rich B'x-style reds (mostly MERLOT-led, but stony soils also suit CAB SAUV – arguably better). Flavour-packed SYRAH. Best reds world-class. Also age-worthy CHARD.

Gisborne (r) 13' 14 (w) 13' 14' 15 NZ's 5th-largest region (biggest in 70s/80s), on e coast of North Island. Abundant sunshine but often rainy; v. fertile soils. Key is CHARD (deliciously fragrant, soft in youth, best mature well.) Excellent GEWURZ, VIOGNIER; MERLOT, PINOT GR more variable. Interest in ALBARIÑO (rain resistant).

Gladstone Vineyard Wair r w ★★ Largest producer in n WAIR. Tropical SAUV BL (incl barrel-fermented Sophie's Choice 14'); smooth PINOT GR; gd medium-dry RIES; classy VIOGNIER; graceful PINOT N under top label, Gladstone 14'; 12,000 Miles is lower-priced brand.

Grasshopper Rock C Ot r ★★ →★★★ Estate-grown at Alexandra by specialist PINOT N producer. Subregion's finest red 13 14' 15: v. graceful, with strong cherry, spice, dried-herb flavours. V. age-worthy; great value.

Greenhough Nel r w ★★ →★★★ One of region's top producers: immaculate RIES; organic SAUV BL 16; consistent CHARD, PINOT N. Top label: Hope V'yd (complex, organic Chard 14'; old-vine PINOT BL NZ's finest 13; mushroomy Pinot N 14').

Greystone Waip (r) w ★★★ Star producer (also owns MUDDY WATER); perfumed whites (RIES 15', GEWURZ 15', PINOT GR 15'); classy CHARD 15', SAUV BL (complex oak-aged 15'), PINOT N (fragrant 15'). Thomas Brothers is top, seductive Pinot N 13'.

Greywacke Marl r w ★★ →★★★ Distinguished wines from Kevin Judd, ex-CLOUDY BAY. Flavour-packed SAUV BL 16'; complex CHARD 14; fleshy PINOT GR 15'; gently sweet RIES 15'; savoury PINOT N 12 13 14'. Barrel-fermented, age-worthy Wild Sauv 14'.

Grove Mill Marl r w ★★ Attractive whites: punchy SAUV BL 16'; generous WAIRAU VALLEY CHARD; weighty, oily PINOT GR; slightly sweet RIES. Moderately complex PINOT N. Value, lower-tier Sanctuary brand.

Hans Herzog Marl r w ★★★ Warm, stony v'yd at Rapaura; dense MERLOT/CAB SAUV 07'; PINOT N earthy, organic. Rich CHARD 13; oak-aged PINOT GR 15', SAUV BL 15'. Classy TEMPRANILLO 13', MONTEPULCIANO 13'. Sold under Hans brand in Europe, US.

Hawke's Bay (r) 10' 13' 14' (w) 13' 14' 15 NZ's 2nd-largest region. Long history (since 1850s) of wine in sunny, warm, dryish climate. Classy MERLOT and CAB SAUV-based reds in favourable vintages; SYRAH (vibrant plum and black pepper) a fast-rising star; peachy CHARD; ripe, round SAUV BL (suits oak); NZ's best VIOGNIER. Alsace-style PINOT GR and promising PINOT N from cooler, elevated, inland districts, esp Mangatahi and Central Hawk. *See also* GIMBLETT GRAVELS.

Huia Marl (r) w (sp) ★★ V.gd, partly oak-aged, organic SAUV BL; bold GEWURZ; rich CHARD; vibrant PINOT N. Complex vintage Brut. Gd-value range: Hunky Dory.

Hunter's Marl (r) (p) w (sp) ★★ →★★★ Pioneer winery with strength in whites. Classic, tropical SAUV BL 16; Kaho Roa is ripe, oak-aged style. Vibrant CHARD (new

Succession Chard 13' is smoky). Excellent sparkling Miru Miru (Res is disgorged later). RIES (off-dry), GEWURZ, PINOT GR (dry) all gd value. PINOT N is easy-drinking. Second label: Stoneburn.

Invivo Auck r w ★★ Fast-expanding young producer: strong, nettley MARL SAUV BL 16'; full, medium-dry MARL PINOT GR; savoury C OT PINOT N 14'. Recent focus on celebrity labels, esp Graham Norton (*see* box, below).

Johanneshof Marl (r) w sp ★★ Small winery acclaimed for perfumed, gently sweet GEWURZ (one of NZ's finest 14' 15). Crisp Blanc de Blancs; v.gd RIES, PINOT GR.

Jules Taylor Marl (r) (p) w ★★ Stylish, gd-value MARL (mostly) and GIS. Refined, partly barrel-aged Marl CHARD 15'; classy Marl SAUV BL 16'; fragrant Marl PINOT N 15'.

Kim Crawford Hawk ★→★★ Brand owned by CONSTELLATION NEW ZEALAND. Easy-drinking (with "Res" on capsule, but not label): punchy MARL SAUV BL (huge seller in US); floral PINOT GR; fresh HAWK MERLOT; generous PINOT N (blend of Marl/C OT grapes). Low-alc range: First Pick.

Kumeu River Auck (r) w ★★★ Rich Estate CHARD 14' 15' is multi-site blend; value. Single-v'yd Mate's V'yd Chard (planted 1990) is more opulent 13' 14' 15'; single-v'yd Hunting Hill Chard 13' 14' 15' a rising star: notably refined, tight-knit. Lower-tier Village Chard is great value. Floral PINOT GR; earthy PINOT N.

Lake Chalice Marl (r) (p) w ★★ Medium-sized producer, purchased by Saint Clair in 2016 (will preserve brand). Vibrant CHARD; dryish PINOT GR; slightly sweet RIES; crisp SAUV BL. Solid PINOT N. Lower-tier: The Nest.

Lawson's Dry Hills Marl (r) (p) w ★★→★★★ Gd-value wines. Best-known for faintly oaky MARL SAUV BL, exotically perfumed GEWURZ 15. Medium-dry, bottle-aged RIES 15'. Fast-improving PINOT N. Top range: The Pioneer (outstanding GEWURZ 14'.) New Res range: Sauv Bl, CHARD, Pinot N. Lower-tier: Mount Vernon.

Lindauer Auck ★→★★ Hugely popular, low-priced sparkling brand, esp bottle-fermented Lindauer Brut Cuvée NV, owned by Lion. Latest batches offer lively, easy drinking. Special Res (disgorged after 2 yrs) offers gd complexity, value.

Lowburn Ferry C Ot r ★★→★★★ PINOT N specialist, top reputation. Flagship is The Ferryman Res (savoury, complex 14'). Home Block (fleshy 12 13 14' 15'), Skeleton Creek (not entirely estate-grown, but concentrated 13 14).

Mahi Marl r w ★★ Stylish, complex wines. Fine SAUV BL (part oak-aged); gd-value CHARD (Twin Valleys V'yd 14); dry PINOT GR 16; Rosé 15'; mushroomy PINOT N 13' 14.

Man O' War Auck r w ★★★ Largest v'yd on WAIH. Tight CHARD; slightly-sweet Exiled PINOT GR 15' (from adjacent Ponui Island). Generous MERLOT/CAB/MALBEC/PETIT VERDOT 14; delicious Death Valley Malbec 14', firm Dreadnought SYRAH 12' 14'.

Marisco Marl r w ★★ Fast-expanding Waihopai Valley producer with two brands, The Ned and Marisco The King's Series. Impressive, ripe, rich Marisco The King's Favour SAUV BL; punchy The Ned Sauv Bl. Gd CHARD, PINOT GR, PINOT N. Owned by Brent Marris, founder of WITHER HILLS.

Marlborough (r) 13' 14 15 16' (w) 15' 16 NZ's major region (two-thirds of plantings) at top of South Island; 1st vines in modern era planted 1973 (SAUV BL in 1975.) Warm, sunny days and cold nights give aromatic, crisp whites. Intense Sauv Bl,

---

Fame in a glass

A host of celebrities own v'yds and wineries, or have linked their names to brands. Now it's a trend in NZ. INVIVO, one of fastest-growing NZ companies, makes Graham Norton's Own MARL SAUV BL; the flamboyant Irish TV presenter also has a stake in the company. Paul Henry's Own PINOT N, named after one of NZ's highest-profile TV and radio personalities, also from Invivo. Leighton Smith, a prominent radio talkback host, owns Clevedon Hills v'yd, in S AUCK, and everyone wants to drink actor Sam Neill's Pinot N, grown in his TWO PADDOCKS v'yds (C OT).

from green capsicum to tropical fruit (some top wines faintly oak-influenced). Fresh, medium-dry RIES (recent wave of sweet, low-alc wines); some of NZ's best PINOT GR, GEWURZ; CHARD leaner than HAWK but can mature well. V. high-quality sparkling and botrytized Ries. PINOT N underrated, top eg. (from n-facing clay hillsides) among NZ's finest. Interest stirring in ALBARIÑO, GRÜNER V.

Martinborough Wair (r) 13' 14 15 16 (w) 13' 14 15 16 Small, prestigious district in s WAIR (foot of North Island). Warm summers, dry autumns, gravelly soils. Success with several white grapes (SAUV BL, PINOT GR both widely planted), but esp acclaimed since mid- to late 80s for sturdy, savoury, long-lived PINOT N (higher percentage of mature vines than other regions).

Martinborough Vineyard Mart r (p) (w) ★★★ Pioneer winery; famous savoury PINOT N (Home Block 13' 14'). Biscuity CHARD; partly barrel-fermented SAUV BL; intense RIES (dr s/sw); medium-dry PINOT GR. Gd-value, drink-young Te Tera range (Pinot N 14'). Purchased in 2014 by Foley Family Wines. Lower-tier: Russian Jack.

Matawhero Gis r (p) w ★★ Former star GEWURZ producer of 80s, now different ownership. Gd unoaked CHARD; Gewurz (fleshy, soft); ripe PINOT GR; plummy MERLOT; promising ALBARIÑO, ARNEIS, GRÜNER V. Top range: Church House (Chard rich, upfront style 15').

Matua Auck r w ★→★★★ Producer of NZ's 1st SAUV BL in 1974 (from AUCK grapes). Now owned by TWE. Long known as Matua Valley. Most are pleasant, easy drinking. Lands & Legends is mid-tier. Impressive, luxury *range of Single V'yd wines*, incl pure, searching Sauv Bl; v. classy ALBARIÑO; powerful CHARD; dense MERLOT/MALBEC 14'; SYRAH 14'.

NZ's 1st grapevines were planted in 1819; 1st recorded wine flowed in 1840.

Maude C Ot r w ★★ Consistently gd, scented, dryish PINOT GR; floral, fine PINOT N; outstanding RIES, CHARD, PINOT N from Mt Maude V'yd, at Wanaka.

Mills Reef B of P r w ★★ →★★★ Consistent easy-drinking wines from estate v'yds in GIMBLETT GRAVELS and other HAWK grapes. Top Elspeth range incl generous, tight CHARD; fine B'x-style reds, esp lovely CAB SAUV 13' and SYRAH 13' (latest vintages more floral, supple). Res range reds typically gd value.

Millton Gis r (p) w ★★ →★★★★ Region's top wines from NZ's 1st organic producer. Hill-grown single-v'yd Clos de Ste Anne range (CHARD, CHENIN BL, VIOGNIER, SYRAH, PINOT N) is strikingly complex, characterful. Long-lived, partly barrel-fermented **Chenin Bl** (honeyed in wetter vintages), is NZ's finest 15'. Drink-young range: Crazy by Nature (gd value). Classy, new La Cote Pinot N 14 15'.

Misha's Vineyard C Ot r w ★★ Large v'yd at Bendigo; top winemaker Olly Masters (ex-Ata Rangi.) Harmonious GEWURZ, PINOT GR, RIES (dry Lyric, slightly sweet Limelight); partly oak-aged SAUV BL; complex PINOT N (Verismo is oak-aged longer).

Mission Hawk r (p) w ★★ NZ's oldest wine producer; 1st vines 1851; 1st sales 1890s; still owned by Catholic Society of Mary. Wide range of decent regional varietals, with V'yd Selection next up the scale. Res range incl excellent MERLOT, CAB SAUV, SYRAH, MALBEC, CHARD, SAUV BL. Top label: Jewelstone (v. classy Chard 15', Syrah 13', 14). Purchased large AWATERE VALLEY v'yd in 2012 (crisp, incisive MARL Sauv Bl).

Mondillo C Ot r w ★★ Rising star at Bendigo with scented dry RIES 15; rich PINOT N 13' 14' 15'; rare scented Bella Pinot N 13'.

Mount Edward C Ot r w ★★ Small, respected producer; gently oaked CHARD, racy RIES, complex PINOT N.

Mount Riley Marl r (p) w ★★ Medium-sized family firm. Punchy SAUV BL; fine PINOT GR 15', citrus, off-dry RIES 15, drink-young CHARD, gd-value PINOT N. Top range: Seventeen Valley (Chard 14', barrel-fermented Sauv Bl 14, Pinot N 14).

Mt Beautiful Cant r w ★★ Large v'yd at Cheviot, n of Waip, with biscuity CHARD; spicy PINOT GR; scented RIES; herbaceous SAUV BL; moderately complex, smooth PINOT N.

Mt Difficulty C Ot r (p) w ★★→★★★ Quality producer; popular restaurant in warm Bannockburn district. Powerful PINOT N 14'. Roaring Meg is slightly lighter, but still moderately complex, Cromwell Basin blend for early consumption; single-v'yd Pipeclay Terrace dense 13'; Target Gully graceful 13'; Mansons Farm strapping 13'. Classy whites (esp RIES, PINOT GR).

Mud House Cant r w ★★→★★★ Large, Australian-owned, MARL-based producer of South Island wines (incl Waip, c OT). Brands incl Mud House, Waipara Hills, Hay Maker (lower tier). Regional blends: punchy, gd-value Marl SAUV BL 16'; oily Marl PINOT GR; lively, medium-dry Waip RIES; v. charming, gd-value C Ot PINOT N. Excellent Estate selection (single v'yds) and Single V'yd range (from growers). New Sub Region Series: smooth CHARD 15'; fragrant Pinot Gr 16'.

Muddy Water Waip r w ★★→★★★ Small, high-quality organic producer, now owned by GREYSTONE. James Hardwick RIES (medium-dry, among NZ's best 13' 15'), youthful CHARD 15'; complex PINOT N 15 (esp Slowhand, based on oldest, low-yielding vines 12').

Nautilus Marl r w sp ★★→★★★ Medium-sized, rock-solid range of distributors Négociants (NZ), owned by S Smith & Sons (*see* Yalumba, Australia). Top wines incl dry SAUV BL 16; v. classy CHARD (complex, subtle 15'); elegant Southern Valleys PINOT N 14, mouthfilling PINOT GR 15'; yeasty NV sparkler (min 3 yrs on lees), one of NZ's best. Excellent new GRÜNER V, ALBARIÑO. Mid-tier: Opawa (fruit driven). Lower tier: Twin Islands.

Nelson (r) 13' 14 (w) 13 14 Smallish region w of MARL; climate wetter but equally sunny. Clay soils of Upper Moutere hills (full-bodied wines) and silty WAIMEA plains (more aromatic). SAUV BL is most extensively planted, but also strength in aromatic whites, esp RIES, PINOT GR, GEWURZ; also gd (sometimes outstanding) CHARD, PINOT N. Too often underrated.

Neudorf Nel r (p) w ★★★→★★★★ Smallish winery with big reputation. Zesty Moutere CHARD 13' 14' 15', one of NZ's greatest; excellent, drink-young Rosie's Block Chard 15'. Superb Moutere PINOT N 13' 14; lightly oaked SAUV BL; off-dry PINOT GR 15; RIES (dr s/sw) top flight. Delightful dry Pinot Rosé. Classy new ALBARIÑO 15'.

Ngatarawa Hawk r w ★★ Mid-sized producer, owned by Corban family. Easy-drinking Stables Res range (HAWK): mouthfilling CHARD; firm MERLOT/CAB; supple SYRAH. Outstanding Proprietors Res selection: fragrant Chard; dark, v. rich Merlot/Cab; dense Syrah; ravishing Noble RIES. Glazebrook: 2nd tier.

No. 1 Family Estate Marl sp ★★ Family-owned company of regional pioneer Daniel Le Brun, ex-Champagne. No longer controls Daniel Le Brun brand (owned by Lion). Specialist in often v.gd sparkling wine, esp top-end, yeasty, v. lively NV Blanc de Blancs, Cuvée No 1.

Nobilo Marl *See* CONSTELLATION NEW ZEALAND.

Obsidian Waih r (p) w ★★ V'yd in Onetangi. stylish B'x blend Res The Obsidian 16' 11 12 13'; toasty Res VIOGNIER 14; delicious Res CHARD 15', dense Res SYRAH 13'. 2nd tier (formerly Weeping Sands) now labelled Obsidian.

Oyster Bay Marl r w sp ★★ From DELEGAT, this is a marketing triumph – huge sales in UK, US, Australia. Vibrant, easy-drinking wines with a touch of class, from MARL, HAWK. Marl SAUV BL is biggest seller, 1.5 million cases/yr (full, passion fruit/lime), gently oaked Marl CHARD), medium-bodied, Grigio-style Hawk PINOT GR; plum/spice Marl PINOT N, fragrant Hawk MERLOT, easy-drinking fizz (Cuvée Rosé).

Palliser Mart r w ★★→★★★ One of district's largest and best. Excellent SAUV BL; fragrant, v. elegant CHARD 14'; slightly sweet RIES 15'; rounded PINOT GR 15'; bubbly (best in MART), perfumed PINOT N 13' 14. Top wines: Palliser Estate. Lower tier: Pencarrow (great value, majority of output).

Pask Hawk r w ★★ Mid-size winery (for sale in 2016), with extensive v'yds in GIMBLETT GRAVELS. CAB SAUV, MERLOT, SYRAH well-priced, full-flavoured, can be green-edged. Vibrant, gently oaked CHARD. Top Declaration range: toasty Chard 15'; concentrated Merlot 13' 14'; complex Cab/Merlot/MALBEC 13' 14', smooth Syrah 14'. Lower tier: Roys Hill, Kate Radburnd.

Passage Rock Waih r w ★★ Show-stopping, powerful, opulent SYRAH, esp Res 14'; non-res fine value 14'. Gd B'x-style reds, esp Res CAB SAUV/MERLOT 14.

Pegasus Bay Waip r w ★★★ Pioneer family firm with superb range: taut CHARD 12 13'; partly oak-aged SAUV BL/SEM 14'; zingy, medium RIES (big seller) 14'; exotically perfumed GEWURZ 13' 14; silky PINOT N 10' 11 12 13, esp mature-vine Prima Donna 10' 11 12'. Lovely sweet whites, from Ries, Sem. Second label: Main Divide, v.gd value, esp PINOT GR.

Peregrine C Ot r w ★★ Crisp whites (esp RIES, dry, slightly sweet Rastaburn); v. finely balanced CHARD 13'. Yeasty sparkling, simply called Vintage 12. Silky PINOT N 11 12 13. Saddleback Pinot N gd value. (Legal battle between owners in 2016.)

Pernod Ricard NZ Auck r (p) w sp ★→★★★ One of NZ's largest producers, formerly Montana. Wineries in AUCK, HAWK, MARL. Extensive co-owned v'yds for Marl whites: punchy, huge-selling BRANCOTT ESTATE SAUV BL 16. Strength in sparkling, esp DEUTZ Marl Cuvée. Classy, wonderful value CHURCH ROAD reds and CHARD. Other key brands incl STONELEIGH (tropical Sauv Bl).

Pisa Range C Ot r (w) ★★→★★★ Small v'yd with enticingly scented Black Poplar PINOT N 13' 14'; v.gd young-vine Pinot N 14; Run 245; PINOT GR; RIES 14.

Prophet's Rock C Ot r w ★★ Fleshy PINOT GR; barrel-aged dry RIES; savoury PINOT N. Drink young: Rocky Point.

Puriri Hills Auck r (p) ★★→★★★ V. classy, complex, silky, long-lived MERLOT-based reds (blended with CAB FR, CARMENÈRE, CAB SAUV, MALBEC) from Clevedon 08' 09 10'. Res esp fragrant, with more new oak. Top label, outstandingly lush Pope 10'. Second label: Mokoroa.

Pyramid Valley Cant r w ★★★ Tiny elevated limestone v'yd at Waikari. Estate-grown, increasingly generous PINOT N (Angel Flower, Earth Smoke 10' 12 13); tight CHARD 13'. Classy Growers' Collection wines (incl PINOT BL, CAB FR) from other regions. Not universally admired, but strong personality. For sale in 2017.

Quartz Reef C Ot r w sp ★★→★★★ Small, quality, bio producer with peachy dry PINOT GR 14 15'; perfumed PINOT N 13' 14' 15', Bendigo Estate esp concentrated 10' 12 14'; intense, yeasty, *racy sparkling* (vintage esp gd 09 10').

Rapaura Springs Marl ★★ Consistently gd, value CHARD, PINOT GR, SAUV BL, esp Res.

Rippon Vineyard C Ot r w ★★→★★★ Stunning pioneer v'yd on shores of Lake Wanaka; arresting wines. Scented Rippon PINOT N 10' 12' from mature vines; Jeunesse Pinot N 12' is younger vines. Powerful, complex Tinker's Field Pinot N (from oldest vines 10' 12'). Tinker's Bequest Pinot N 13' was made with "no adjustment or additions": sense of unlocked power. Slowly evolving whites, esp outstanding, steely RIES 10' 11' 12' 13.

Rockburn C Ot r (p) w ★★ Lively PINOT GR; v.gd light, medium-sweet RIES 14' 15. Fragrant PINOT N 13' 14' 15 blended from Cromwell Basin (mostly) and GIBBSTON grapes; Eleven Barrels, deep 13'. Second label: Devil's Staircase.

Rod McDonald Hawk r (p) w ★★ Highly experienced winemaker (ex-VIDAL 1993–2006), several brands: Te Awanga, Two Gates, Quarter Acre. Top CHARD, MERLOT.

Sacred Hill Hawk r w ★★→★★★ Mid-size producer. Acclaimed Riflemans CHARD 13' 14' 15', powerful but v. refined, from inland, elevated site. Long-lived Brokenstone MERLOT 10' 11 13 14', Helmsman CAB/Merlot 10' 11 13 14 and Deerstalkers SYRAH 10' 12 13' 14', from GIMBLETT GRAVELS. Punchy MARL SAUV BL 16; gd-value HAWK Merlot/Cab Sauv 15. Halo and Res: mid-tier. Other brands: Gunn Estate, Wild South (gd-value Marl range).

Saint Clair Marl r (p) w ★★ →★★★ Largest family-owned producer in region, 1st vintage 1994. Acclaimed for pungent SAUV BL from lower WAIRAU VALLEY – esp great-value regional blend and strikingly rich, slightly salty Wairau Res. Easy-drinking RIES, PINOT GR, GEWURZ, CHARD, MERLOT, PINOT N. Res is top range; then array of 2nd-tier Pioneer Block wines (classy Pinot N, Sauv Bl); then gd-value regional blends; 4th tier is Vicar's Choice. Recent investment in HAWK for reds.

Seifried Estate Nel (r) w ★★ Region's 1st and biggest winery, family-owned. Long respected for gd, medium-dry RIES 14' 15', GEWURZ 16; now gd-value, often excellent SAUV BL 16, CHARD V 14. Spicy GRÜNER V 14. Best: Winemakers Collection (esp Sweet Agnes Ries 15' 16'). Old Coach Road: 3rd tier. Whites better than reds.

Selaks Marl r w ★→★★ Old producer of Croatian origin, now a brand of CONSTELLATION NEW ZEALAND. Solid, easy-drinking Premium Selection range. Gd Res HAWK CHARD, MERLOT/CAB, SYRAH. Recently revived top Founders range: esp gd Chard.

Seresin Marl r w ★★ →★★★ Quality organic producer. Sophisticated, age-worthy SAUV BL 15' (partly oak-aged), one of NZ's finest; rich, barrel-fermented Marama Sauv Bl from oldest vines 13'. Classy Res CHARD 13'. Savoury PINOT N and dry, oak-aged PINOT GR; 3rd tier Momo (gd quality/value). Overall, complex, fine wines.

Sileni Hawk r (p) w ★★ Large producer, strong focus on PINOT N. Top: powerful Exceptional Vintage CHARD 13', SYRAH 13', MERLOT 13'. Mid-range Estate Selection incl lush The Lodge Chard 14 15', rich Triangle Merlot 14', Springstone 15' and Parkhill 15' Pinot N, then Cellar Selection (Merlot, off-dry PINOT GR). Rich, smooth MARL SAUV BL (esp Straits 16'). Other brands: Greyrock, Overstone, Satyr.

It still trails dairy, lamb, but in dollar terms, wine is NZ's 6th most important export.

Spy Valley Marl r (p) w ★★ →★★★ High achievers; extensive v'yds. Flavoury aromatic whites (RIES 15', GEWURZ 15', PINOT GR 15'), superb value; impressive SAUV BL 16, CHARD 15', PINOT N 14. Satisfying Pinot N Rosé 16. Classy top selection: Envoy (subtle Chard 14'; Alsace-style Pinot Gr, oak-aged, dry Ries; complex Outpost Pinot N 14). Second label: Satellite.

Staete Landt Marl r w ★★ V'yd at Rapaura (WAIRAU VALLEY): refined, biscuity CHARD; top-flight Annabel part-oak-aged SAUV BL; graceful PINOT N. V. promising VIOGNIER. Second label: Map Maker (gd value).

Starborough Family Estates Marl (r) w ★★ Family-owned, v'yds in AWATERE and WAIRAU VALLEYS. SAUV BL aromatic, weighty, vibrant, deep-flavoured 16. Scented PINOT GR; supple PINOT N. NB: Starborough Family Estates not to be confused with Starborough brand controlled by Gallo.

Stonecroft Hawk r w ★★ Small winery. NZ's 1st serious SYRAH (1989); dense Res 13' 14'; lighter Serine Syrah. Fragrant Ruhanui (MERLOT/CAB SAUV) 14'. V. rich Old-Vine GEWURZ 15'. Oak-aged SAUV BL 16'. NZ's only ZIN (medium-bodied, spicy 14).

Stoneleigh Marl r (p) w ★★ Owned by PERNOD RICARD NZ. Based on relatively warm Rapaura v'yds. Gd large-volume MARL whites, incl punchy SAUV BL; floral, slightly sweet PINOT GR; full-bodied RIES, slightly buttery CHARD. Top wines: Rapaura Series (Sauv Bl 15', Chard 14' 15, Pinot Gr 15', PINOT N 14').

Stonyridge Waih r w ★★★ →★★★★ Boutique winery, famous since mid-80s for exceptional CAB SAUV based red, Larose 10' 11 12 13' 14' 15', one of NZ's greatest, matures superbly. Airfield is little brother of Larose. Rhône-style Pilgrim 15', super-charged Luna Negra MALBEC 15'. Fallen Angel: non-WAIH.

Te Awa Hawk r w ★★ →★★★ GIMBLETT GRAVELS v'yd known for MERLOT-based reds. Purchased 2012 by VILLA MARIA and site of its key new winery. Elegant CHARD 15'; fleshy SAUV BL 15; fragrant Merlot/CAB 13' 14'; floral SYRAH 14. Savoury TEMPRANILLO 13' 14'. Left Field range: easy-drinking, gd value.

Te Kairanga Mart r w ★★ One of district's largest wineries, much improved since purchase by American Bill Foley in 2011. V.gd CHARD 14', dry PINOT GR 16', SAUV BL 16', finely-poised PINOT N 15' (value); gd slightly sweet RIES 14' 15. Runholder is mid-tier (Pinot N 14'). Res is John Martin: Chard 14', Pinot N 14'.

Te Mania Nel ★★ Small, gd-value producer with lively CHARD, GEWURZ, PINOT GR, RIES, racy SAUV BL (organic). Top Res range: organic PINOT N 14' and Chard 15'.

Te Mata Hawk r w ★★★→★★★★ Prestigious winery (1st vintage 1895) run by Buck family since 1974. Coleraine (CAB SAUV/MERLOT/CAB FR blend) 09' 10' 13' 14' has rare breed, great longevity; much lower-priced Awatea Cabs/Merlot 13' 14 also classy, more forward. Bullnose SYRAH 10' 13' 14' among NZ's finest. Rich, elegant Elston CHARD 13' 14' 15'. Estate V'yds range for early drinking (v.gd Chard, SAUV BL, GAMAY NOIR, Merlot/Cabs, Syrah).

"Te Mata", in Spanish, means "it kills you". Won them a marketing award in Spain.

Terra Sancta C Ot r (p) (w) ★★ Bannockburn's 1st v'yd, founded 1991 as Olssens, new owner in 2011. V.gd-value, generous, drink-young Mysterious Diggings PINOT N 15'; Bannockburn Pinot N is mid-tier 13' 14'; dense, savoury Slapjack Block Pinot N from oldest vines 13' 14'. Excellent RIES, PINOT GR, outstanding, vivacious Pinot N Rosé 16' (one of NZ's best).

Te Whare Ra Marl r w ★★ Label: TWR. Some of region's oldest vines, planted 1979. V. perfumed, spicy, organic GEWURZ; vibrant SAUV BL, RIES (dry "D", medium "M").

Te Whau Waih ★★→★★★ Tiny, acclaimed seaside v'yd (pronounced Tay Fow) and restaurant. Classy, complex CHARD 13' 14' 15' is best wine. Savoury, mostly CAB SAUV blend, The Point 10' 12 13 14'. Complex SYRAH 10 12 13 14'.

Tiki Marl (r) w ★★ McKean family owns extensive v'yds in MARL and Waip; SAUV BL (Single V'yd 16'); PINOT GR 16'; Koru C OT PINOT N 14'. Second label: Maui.

Tohu r w ★★ Maori-owned venture with extensive v'yds in MARL, NEL. Racy Single V'yd SAUV BL 16'; rich, oak-aged Mugwi Res Sauv Bl 15; strong, dry RIES; full, dryish PINOT GR 16, increasingly complex PINOT N 15'.

Trinity Hill Hawk r (p) w ★★→★★★ Highly regarded, US-owned since 2014. B'x-style blend, The Gimblett, refined 13 14'; stylish GIMBLETT GRAVELS CHARD 13' 14' 15'. Exceptional Homage SYRAH w. floral 09' 10' 13' 14'. Impressive TEMPRANILLO 14' 15'; delicious MONTEPULCIANO 14'. Scented VIOGNIER among NZ's best. Lower-tier, "white label" range gd value, esp drink-young MERLOT 15'.

Two Paddocks C Ot r (w) ★★ Actor Sam Neill makes light, racy, off-dry RIES 14' and several PINOT NS. Excellent regional blend 13' 14'. Single-v'yd range: First Paddock (more herbal, from cool Gibbston district 13'), Last Chance (riper, from warmer Alexandra 12' 13'). Latest is The Fusilier, grown at Bannockburn, complex 14'. Picnic: gd drink-young, regional blend 14.

Two Rivers Marl r (p) w ★★ Convergence SAUV BL: incisive wine from WAIRAU and AWATERE VALLEYS 16. V.gd CHARD (mouthfilling) 15', PINOT GR, RIES. Pale-pink, delicate dry rosé. Tributary PINOT N, savoury 15'. Second label: Black Cottage (gd value).

Urlar Wair r w ★★ Small organic producer; creamy PINOT GR 14'; mouthfilling, dry RIES; partly oak-aged SAUV BL; lovely Noble RIES 15'; complex PINOT N 14.

Valli C Ot ★★→★★★ Excellent range of complex, single-v'yd PINOT N (Gibbston 13' 14' 15', Bendigo 13' 14' 15', Bannockburn 13 14' 15', WAITAKI 13 14' 15') and strikingly intense, dry Old-Vine RIES 13' (vines planted 1981).

Vavasour Marl r w ★★→★★★ Planted 1st vines in AWATERE VALLEY (1986). Rich, creamy CHARD 14' 15' (Anna's V'yd 15', from oldest vines, esp elegant, complex), best-known for nettley SAUV BL 15; v. promising PINOT N; off-dry PINOT GR 15'. Owned by Foley Family Wines.

Vidal Hawk r w ★★→★★★ Est 1905, owned by VILLA MARIA since 1976. Top Legacy range: tight-knit CHARD 15'; silky SYRAH 14'; superb CAB SAUV 14'; great-value mid-tier Res range: Chard 15'; MERLOT/Cab Sauv 14'; Syrah 14'; MARL PINOT N 15'. Top-value Marl SAUV BL 16'.

Villa Maria Auck r (p) w ★★→★★★ NZ's largest fully family-owned winery, headed by Sir George Fistonich. Also owns ESK VALLEY, TE AWA, VIDAL. Wine-show focus, with glowing success. Top ranges: Res (express regional character) and Single V'yd (reflect individual sites); Cellar Selection: mid-tier (less oak) excellent, great value; 3rd-tier, volume Private Bin wines can also be v.gd (esp SAUV BL, also CHARD, GEWURZ, PINOT GR, RIES, VIOGNIER, MERLOT, PINOT N.) Small volumes of v.gd ALBARIÑO, ARNEIS, VERDELHO, GRENACHE. New icon red, Ngakirikiri The Gravels 13': CAB SAUV-based, v. youthful, pure, rich.

Waiheke Island r (w) Lovely, sprawling island in Auckland's Hauraki Gulf (temperatures moderated by sea). Pioneered by Goldwater (1978). Initial acclaim for stylish CAB SAUV/MERLOT blends; more recently bold SYRAH. Also rich CHARD.

Waimea Nel r (p) w ★★ One of region's largest and best-value producers. Punchy SAUV BL 16, rounded PINOT GR 16, GEWURZ 15', vibrant VIOGNIER 14'. V.gd RIES (Classic is honeyed, medium style 16), weighty, rich CHARD 14'. Scented, dry GRÜNER V 16, steely ALBARIÑO 16. Supple PINOT N 14'. Spinyback is 2nd tier.

Wairarapa NZ's 7th-largest wine region (not to be confused with Waip, CANT). *See* MART. Also incl Gladstone subregion in n (slightly higher, cooler, wetter). Driest, coolest region in North Island; strength in whites (SAUV BL, PINOT GR most widely planted, also gd RIES, GEWURZ, CHARD, VIOGNIER) and esp PINOT N (full-bodied, warm, savoury from relatively mature vines). Strong sales in nearby capital, Wellington.

Wairau River Marl r (p) w ★★ Gd whites: tropical SAUV BL 16; full PINOT GR 16; gently sweet Summer RIES 16; tangy ALBARIÑO 16. Res is top label: concentrated Sauv Bl 16; peachy VIOGNIER 15; powerful CHARD 15'; weighty PINOT N 15'.

Wairau Valley MARL's largest subregion (1st v'yd planted 1873; modern era since 1973). Vast majority of region's cellar doors. Three important side valleys to s: Brancott, Omaka, Waihopai (known collectively as Southern Valleys). SAUV BL thrives on stony, silty plains; PINOT N on clay based, n-facing slopes. Limited scope for further planting.

Waitaki Valley C Ot Slowly expanding subregion in N Ot, with cool, frost-prone climate. V. promising PINOT N (but can be leafy); racy PINOT GR, RIES. Several producers, only one winery.

Whitehaven Marl r (p) w ★★ Medium-sized producer. Flavour-packed, harmonious SAUV BL is top value, big seller in US. Rich GEWURZ; slightly buttery CHARD; oily PINOT GR; off-dry RIES, v.gd dry rosé from PINOT N 16'; savoury Pinot N. Gallo (*see* California) is part-owner. Top range: Greg.

Wither Hills Marl r w ★★ Large producer, once small and prestigious, now owned by Lion. Popular, gooseberry/lime SAUV BL. Fleshy PINOT GR; gently oaked CHARD; fragrant PINOT N. Savoury Single V'yd Taylor River Pinot N 13'.

Wooing Tree C Ot r (p) w ★★ Single-v'yd, mostly reds. Bold, dark PINOT N 14' 15' (Beetle Juice less new oak 14' 15'). Powerful Sandstorm Res Pinot N 14'. Creamy CHARD 14' 15. Less "serious" wines, all from Pinot N: delicious Rosé 16', Blondie (basically white 16), Tickled Pink (sweet, light, raspberry/plum 15').

Yealands Marl r (p) w ★★ NZ's biggest "single v'yd", at coastal site in AWATERE VALLEY. Partly estate-grown, mostly MARL wines. High profile for sustainability, but most wines not certified organic. Single V'yd range: SAUV BL, vibrant; RIES, refined, off-dry; GRÜNER V is NZ's best, lemony, spicy, dry. PINOT N, generous. Impressive Single Block Sauv Bls. Lower-priced range: Peter Yealands: v.gd value. Other key brands: The Crossings, Crossroads, Babydoll.

Deus dat incrementum

... as they say at Marlborough College, Wiltshire. Over 90 per cent of NZ's total plantings of SAUV BL are clustered in MARL. It also has more CHARD than anywhere else (just ahead of HAWK); more GEWURZ (well ahead of GIS); and – surprise! – more PINOT N (far ahead of C OT). God gives the increase, indeed.

South Africa

"South Africa is on a roll," we noted last edition, and the 8th-largest wine country shows every sign of continuing its upward spiral. Styles are evolving, and with every year SA develops a stronger personality of its own. These aren't lookalikes: the grapes might be international (how could they not be?) but they are handled with subtlety and understanding. There's no such thing as a single South African style, but wines here are balanced and utterly drinkable, with depth, concentration and lovely freshness. Look to Swartland for original white blends of great complexity, Stellenbosch for classic reds and cool coastal regions for exemplary Pinot Noir and Sauvignon Blanc – never forgetting the country's USP, its super-versatile Chenin Blanc. Experimentation and risk-taking are flourishing alongside rigorous scientific research and the newest technology; and everywhere there are more and more forays into neglected, forgotten and, most excitingly, as-yet-unexplored wine territories.

Recent vintages

2016 Unusually hot and dry; year for later-ripening varieties and cooler areas.
2015 Exceptional across the board, perhaps better even than stellar 2009.
2014 Challenging; needed good judgement and timing; lighter, elegant wines.
2013 Bumper harvest, in both size and quality, with bonus of moderate alcohol.
2012 Good to very good vintage for reds and whites alike; lower alcohol levels.
Note: Most dry whites are best drunk within 2–3 years.

AA Badenhorst Family Wines Swa r (p) w (sp) ★★→★★★★ Old vines, heritage varieties, natural yeasts, whole-bunch fermentations – cousins Adi and Hein Badenhorst are cutting-edge producers. Mostly Med grapes and CHENIN BL handled with imagination and joy.

Alheit Vineyards W Cape (r) w ★★★ Old-vine and heirloom-variety specialist with highly rated multi-region CHENIN BL/SEM Cartology, various single-site wines and field-blend from HEM home farm.

Anthonij Rupert Wyne W Cape r (p) w (br) sp ★→★★★ Portfolio named for owner Johann Rupert's late brother, from own v'yds in DARLING, SWA, Overberg and stately home farm (and cellar-door) L'Ormarins nr FRAN. Best of the five wine ranges are flagship Anthonij Rupert and site-specific Cape of Good Hope.

Ataraxia Wines W Cape r w ★★★ Vaunted CHARD, SAUV BL, Serenity red and newer PINOT N by grower and co-owner Kevin Grant. To see: chapel-like cellar door on promontory overlooking HEM.

Avondale Paarl r p w sp ★→★★★ Family-owned eco-pioneer, embracing organics, bio, science for impressive B'x and Rhône reds, rosé, white blend, CHENIN BL, MCC.

Babylonstoren W Cape r (p) w (sp) ★★ Media mogul Koos Bekker's showpiece cellar and lifestyle venue nr PAARL, B'x reds, CHARD, CHENIN BL and newer MCC.

Bartho Eksteen W Cape r p w sw sp ★★★ Now HEM-based, Bartho E specializes in Rhône varieties and CHENIN BL; runs mentoring programme for young growers/distillers under Trees of Knowledge/Wijnskool banner.

Bartinney Private Cellar Stell r (p) w (sp) ★→★★★ Rising star on precipitous Banhoek Valley slopes, Jordaan family-owned; increasingly impressive CAB SAUV, CHARD, SAUV BL. Noble Savage "lifestyle" range.

Bayten *See* BUITENVERWACHTING.

Beau Constantia Const r w ★→★★ Elegant B'x/Rhône varieties and blends from steep mtn v'yds planted by Du Preez family in early 2000s.

Beaumont Family Wines Bot R r (p) w (br) (sw) ★★→★★★ Historic family estate; expressive CHENIN BL (varietal, top new blend, Vitruvia), PINOTAGE, MOURVÈDRE, SYRAH.

Beeslaar Wines Stell r ★★★ KANONKOP winemaker's own take on one of that celebrated estate's signature grapes, PINOTAGE. Refined and rather special.

Bellingham W Cape r (p) w ★→★★★ Enduring DGB brand; fascinating low-production, high-class Bernard Series and quartet of bigger volume easy-drinking ranges.

Beyerskloof W Cape r (p) (w) (br) ★→★★★ SA's PINOTAGE champion, nr STELL. Ten versions of the grape on offer, incl varietal Diesel 06 07' 08' 09 10 11 12 13' 14 15 16, CAPE BLENDS, Port style. Even PINOTAGE burgers at cellar-door bistro. Also classic CAB SAUV/MERLOT Field Blend 01 02 03' 04 05 07 08 09' 10 11 12 13 14 15.

Black Economic Empowerment (BEE) Initiative aimed at increasing wine-industry ownership and participation by previously disadvantaged groups.

BLANKbottle W Cape r (p) w ★→★★ Pieter Walser travels around 13,000 km harvesting special parcels for his limited bottlings, most with beguiling backstory, quirky name and label ("Family Murder").

Boekenhoutskloof Winery W Cape r (p) w sw ★★→★★★★ Consistently excellent; spicy SYRAH 01' 02' 03 04' 05 06' 07 08 09' 10 11 12' 13 14 15 16; intense CAB SAUV 01' 02' 03 04' 05 06' 07' 08' 09' 10 11' 12 13 14 15 16; *fine Sem* and Med-style red Chocolate Block; organic PORSELEINBERG; value Porcupine Ridge, Wolftrap lines.

Bon Courage Estate Rob r (p) w (br) sw (s/sw) sp ★→★★★ Broad family-grown range led by Inkará reds; stylish trio of brut MCC; aromatic desserts (RIES, MUSCAT).

Boplaas Family Vineyards W Cape r w br (sp) (sw) ★→★★★ Nel family vintners at C'DORP, known for Port styles, esp Vintage Res 01 03 04' 05' 06' 07' 08 09' 10 11 12' 13 14 15 and Tawny. Recently more emphasis on unfortified Port grapes.

Boschendal Wines W Cape r (p) w (sw) sp ★→★★★ Famous, photogenic old estate nr FRAN under DGB ownership, noted for SHIRAZ, SAUV BL, CHARD and MCC.

Botanica Wines W Cape r (p) w ★★→★★★★ Debut CHENIN BL from old w-coast bush vines joined more recently by equally superlative PINOT N, SEM and *vin de paille*, by American Ginny Povall. Own STELL vines coming onstream.

Bot River *See* WALKER BAY.

Bouchard Finlayson Cape SC r w ★★→★★★★ V. fine PINOT N grower in HEM. Galpin Peak 01 02' 03 04 05 07 08 09 10 11 12 13' 14 15; barrel selection Tête de Cuvée 99 01' 03' 05' 07 09 10 12 13. Also impressive CHARD and exotic Hannibal red.

Breedekloof Large (c.13,000 ha) inland mostly bulk- and entry-level wine DISTRICT; pockets of high quality: Dagbreek, Deetlefs, Olifantsberg, OPSTAL ESTATE, Silkbush.

Buitenverwachting W Cape r (p) w sw (sp) ★★→★★★ Classy family winery in CONST. Standout CHARD, SAUV BL, CAB FR, B'x blend Christine (r) 01' 02 03 04 06 07 08 09' 10 11 12. Labelled Bayten for export.

B Vintners Vine Exploration Co Stell r w ★★★ RAATS FAMILY members showcase heirloom varieties and special terroirs around STELL.

Calitzdorp DISTRICT climatically similar to the Douro and known for Port styles eg. Axe Hill, BOPLAAS, DE KRANS, Peter Bayly. Newer unfortified Port-grape C'dorp Blends and varietals.

Cape Agulhas *See* ELIM.

Cape Blend Usually a red blend with PINOTAGE component. Masters of the genre: Alvi's Drift, Clos Malverne, Idiom, Môreson, OPSTAL ESTATE, Paul Roos.

Cape Chamonix Wine Farm Fran r w (sp) ★★→★★★ Excellent winemaker-run mtn property. Distinctive PINOT N, PINOTAGE, CHARD, SAUV BL, B'x blends (r w) and newer CAB FR, all worth keeping.

Capensis W Cape w ★★★ SA-US venture between GRAHAM BECK WINES' Antony Beck and Jackson Family Wines' Barbara Banke. To date, stylish multiregion CHARD.

Cape Peninsula Maritime DISTRICT covering Cape Town and its peninsula; c.440 ha, mainly SAUV BL, MERLOT, CAB SAUV, SHIRAZ. Hout Bay and CONST are WARDS.

Cape Point Vineyards W Cape (r) w (sw) ★→★★★ Consistent producer of complex, age-worthy SAUV BL/SEM blends, CHARD. Gd-value label Splattered Toad.

Cape Rock Wines W Cape r (p) w ★→★★ OLI R's leading boutique grower. Personality-packed, strikingly presented Rhône and Port-grape blends (r w).

Cape South Coast Cool-climate "super REGION" comprising DISTRICTS of CAPE AGULHAS, ELG, Overberg, Plettenberg Bay, Swellendam and WLK B, plus standalone WARDS Herbertsdale, Napier, Stilbaai East and new Lower Duivenhoks River.

Cape Winemakers Guild (CWG) Independent, invitation-only association of 47 top growers. Stages benchmarking annual auction of limited premium bottlings.

Catherine Marshall Wines W Cape r w (br) ★★ Cool-climate specialist Cathy M and partners, focus on PINOT N, MERLOT, SAUV BL, CHENIN BL (mostly from ELG).

Cederberg High-altitude standalone WARD in Cederberg mts. Mainly SHIRAZ, SAUV BL. Driehoek and CEDERBERG PRIVATE CELLAR are sole producers.

Cederberg Private Cellar Ced, Elim r (p) w (sp) ★→★★★ Nieuwoudt family with among SA's highest (CED) and most southerly (ELIM) v'yds. Elegant intensity in CAB SAUV, PINOT N, SHIRAZ, rare BUKETTRAUBE, CHENIN BL, SAUV BL, SEM.

Central Orange River Standalone Northern Cape "mega WARD" (c.10,000 ha).

Grenache rising

Though its vine-print remains tiny (less than one per cent of SA's total ha) GRENACHE as a category is growing fast, with red, pink and white versions appearing in over 50 solo bottlings (twice the number of 5 yrs ago) and many more blends. Top varietals to try: **AA Badenhorst** Raaigras Grenache Noir, **David & Nadia** Grenache Noir, **Neil Ellis Wines** Piekenierskloof Grenache Noir, **Maanschijn** Easy, Tiger (Grenache Gris), **The Foundry** Grenache Blanc, **Rall Wines** Grenache Blanc.

Hot, dry and irrigated; mainly whites and fortified. Major producer is Orange River Cellars.

Charles Fox Cap Classique Wines Elg sp ★★★ Traditional-method bubbly specialist; classic and delicious Vintage Brut, Brut Rosé and newer best-yrs-only Cipher.

Coastal Largest REGION (c.45,000 ha), incl sea-influenced DISTRICTS of CAPE PENINSULA, DARLING, Tygerberg, STELL, SWA, but confusingly also non-coastal FRAN, PAARL, TUL, WELL.

Colmant Cap Classique & Champagne W Cape sp ★★★ Belgian family *méthode traditionnelle* sparkling specialists at FRAN. Brut Res, Rosé, CHARD and newer Sec Res; all MCC, NV and excellent.

Constantia Cool, scenic CAPE PENINSULA WARD, SA's 1st and among most famous fine-wine-growing areas, revitalized in recent yrs by GROOT, KLEIN CONSTANTIA *et al.*

Constantia Glen Const r w ★★★ Waibel-family-owned gem on upper reaches of Constantiaberg. Superb B'x blends (r w) and varietal SAUV BL.

Constantia Uitsig Const r w br sp ★→★★★ Premium v'yds; new owners; high ambitions. Visitor venue and cellar to come (vinification currently at neighbour STEENBERG). Mostly white wines and MCC.

Creation Wines Wlk B r w ★★→★★★ Elegant modernity in family-owned/-vinified range of B'x, Rhône and Burgundy varieties and blends.

Crystallum W Cape r w ★★★ Peter-Allan Finlayson sources from cool HEM and Overberg sites for excellent PINOT N and CHARD.

Dalla Cia Wine & Spirit Company W Cape r w ★★→★★★ Reputable 3rd-generation family vintners/distillers at STELL. Flagship wine is pricey "Supertuscan" Teano.

Darling DISTRICT around eponymous w-coast town. Best v'yds in hilly Groenekloof WARD. Cloof, Darling Cellars, Groote Post/Aurelia, Ormonde, Mount Pleasant, Withington bottle under own labels; most other fruit goes into 3rd-party brands.

David & Nadia Swa r w ★★★→★★★★ D&N Sadie follow natural winemaking principles of SWARTLAND Independent Producers. Exquisite Rhône-style red, GRENACHE Noir, CHENIN BL (varietals, blend), SEM, new PINOTAGE, mostly old vines.

De Krans W Cape r (p) w br (sw) (sp) ★→★★★ Nel family at C'DORP noted for Port styles (esp Vintage Rev 01 02 03' 04' 05' **06' 07** 08' 09' 10' 11' 12' 13' 14 15) and fortified MUSCAT. Recent success with unfortified Port grapes.

Delaire Graff Estate W Cape r (p) w (br) (sw) (sp) ★★→★★★ Diamond merchant Laurence Graff's eyrie v'yds, winery and tourist destination nr STELL. Gem-encrusted portfolio headed by Laurence Graff Res CAB SAUV.

Delheim Wines Coast r (p) w sw (s/sw) ★★→★★★ Eco-minded family winery nr STELL. Vera Cruz SHIRAZ and PINOTAGE; cellar-worthy CAB SAUV-driven Grand Res 00 01 03 04' 05 06 07' 08 13 14, scintillating Edelspatz botrytis RIES.

DeMorgenzon W Cape r (p) w (sp) ★★→★★★ With baroque music piped to vines 24/7, Hylton and Wendy Appelbaum's property is not your average STELL spread. Focus on B'x and Rhône varieties and blends, CHARD, CHENIN BL.

De Toren Private Cellar Stell r ★★→★★★ Consistently flavourful B'x red Fusion V 02 03' 04 05' 06' 07 08 09' 10 11 12 13 14 15 and earlier-maturing MERLOT-based Z; light-styled red La Jeunesse Délicate.

De Trafford Wines Cape SC r w sw ★★→★★★ Boutique grower David Trafford with track record for bold yet harmonious wines. B'x/SHIRAZ blend Elevation 393 01 03' 04 05 06 07 08 09 10 11 12, CAB SAUV 01 03' 04 05 06 07 08 09 10 11 12 13 14 15, Shiraz, CHENIN BL Straw Wine. See also SIJNN.

De Wetshof Estate Rob r w sw sp ★→★★★ Danie de Wet is famed CHARD pioneer and exponent; nine versions (oaked/unwooded, varietal/blended, still/sparkling), in De Wetshof, Danie de Wet and Limelight tiers.

DGB W Cape Long-est WELL-based producer/wholesaler, with brands like BELLINGHAM, BOSCHENDAL, Brampton, Douglas Green.

Diemersdal Estate W Cape r (p) w ★→★★★ DUR family farm; younger generation excelling with various site and row-specific SAUV BL (new, fashionably skin-fermented Wild Horseshoe), red blends, PINOTAGE, CHARD and SA's 1st/only commercial GRÜNER V.

Diemersfontein Wines Well r w ★★★★ Family wine estate, restaurant and guest lodge, esp noted for full-throttle Carpe Diem range. PINOTAGE created much-emulated "coffee style". BEE brand is Thokozani.

Distell W Cape SA's biggest drinks company, in STELL. Owns many brands, spanning styles/quality scales. Has interests in BEE/organic Earthbound label and in DURBANVILLE HILLS, and via Lusan Premium Wines, various top Stell estates.

District See GEOGRAPHICAL UNIT.

Dorrance Wines W Cape r w ★★★ French-toned, family-owned, with one of only two cellars in Cape Town city (reason to visit). Gorgeous SYRAH, CHARD, CHENIN BL.

Durbanville Cool, hilly WARD nr Cape Town, best known for pungent SAUV BL. Corporate co-owned DURBANVILLE HILLS, resurgent Bloemendal, many family farms.

Durbanville Hills Dur r (p) w (sw) (sp) ★★★★ Maritime winery owned by DISTELL, local growers and staff trust, with awarded PINOTAGE, CHARD, SAUV BL. V.gd new Tangram B'x red and MCC.

Eagles' Nest Coast r (p) w ★★★★ Consistently superior MERLOT, VIOGNIER; also elegant SHIRAZ, vibrant SAUV BL. Classicist Martin MEINERT advises.

Edgebaston W Cape r w (sw) ★★→★★★ Finlayson family winery nr STELL. V.gd GS CAB SAUV 05' 06 07 08 10 11 12 13 14; handsomely packaged old-vines series Camino Africana; classy early-drinking white.

Eikendal Vineyards W Cape r w ★→★★★ Resurgent Swiss-owned property nr STELL. Historic strong suits (B'x red Classique, MERLOT, CHARD) back to form.

Elgin Cool-climate DISTRICT recognized for SAUV BL, CHARD, PINOT N. Recently also exciting SYRAH and MCC. Mostly family boutiques, eg. bio Elgin Ridge.

Elim Sea-breezy WARD in S-most DISTRICT, CAPE AGULHAS, producing aromatic SAUV BL, white blends and SHIRAZ. Also grape source for majors like DISTELL.

Ernie Els Wines W Cape r (p) (w) ★★★★ SA's star golfer's wine venture at STELL, driven by big-ticket B'x Ernie Els Signature (r) 01 02' 03 04' 05 06 07' 08 09' 10 11 12 13 14. Earlier-ready Big Easy range.

Estate Wine Official term for wine grown, made and bottled on "units registered for the production of estate wine". Not a quality designation.

Fable Mountain Vineyards Coast r p w ★★★→★★★★ Bio TUL grower and sibling of MULDERBOSCH, owned by California's Terroir Selections. Exceptional SHIRAZ (varietal and blend), white blend and Rhône-grape rosé.

Fairview Coast r (p) w (sw) (s/sw) (sp) ★→★★★ Dynamic, innovative owner Charles Back with smorgasbord of varietal, blended, single-v'yd and terroir-specific bottlings incl Fairview, Spice Route, Goats do Roam, La Capra and Leeuwenjacht.

FirstCape Vineyards W Cape r p w sp DYA Hugely successful export joint-venture of five local co-ops and UK's Brand Phoenix, with entry-level wines in more than a dozen ranges, some sourced outside SA.

Flagstone Winery W Cape r w (br) ★→★★★ High-end winery at Somerset West, owned by Accolade Wines, with impressive PINOTAGE, SAUV BL, B'x white. Sibling to mid-tier Fish Hoek and entry-level KUMALA. Winemaker Bruce Jack the driver behind his family's Overberg boutique, The Drift, for exotic reds (varietal and blended), singular TOURIGA FRANCA rosé.

Fleur du Cap W Cape r (p) w sw ★→★★★ DISTELL premium label, incl v.gd Unfiltered Collection, always-stellar botrytis CHENIN BL and B'x-blend Laszlo (r).

Foundry, The Stell, V Pa r w ★★★ MEERLUST winemaker Chris Williams' own brand, with wine-partner James Reid; v.gd varietal Rhônes, esp GRENACHE BLANC, VIOGNIER.

Franschhoek Valley Huguenot-founded DISTRICT; CAB SAUV, CHARD, MCC. Characterful portfolio: Black Elephant, Môreson, Rickety Bridge, French-owned Topiary.

Free State Province and wo area pending official demarcation. The Bald Ibis is sole producer, in e highlands.

Fryer's Cove Vineyards W Cape (r) w (sw) ★★ SAUV BL (fumé, unoaked, botrytized) specialist boutique on w coast; 1st/only v'yds in tiny (6 ha) Bamboes Bay WARD.

Geographical Unit (GU) Largest of the four main wo demarcations. Currently five GUs: Eastern, Northern and Western Cape, KwaZulu-Natal and Limpopo. The other WO delineations (in descending size): REGION, DISTRICT, WARD.

Glen Carlou W Cape r (p) w (sw) (sp) ★→★★★ 1st-rate Donald Hess-owned winery, v'yds, art gallery, restaurant nr PAARL, hailed for B'x reds, single/multisite CHARD.

Glenelly Estate Stell r w ★★→★★★ Former Château Pichon-Lalande (*see* B'x) owner May-Eliane de Lencquesaing's v'yds and cellar. Impressive flagships Lady May (B'x red) and Estate Res duo (B'x/SHIRAZ and CHARD).

GlenWood Coast r w (sw) ★★→★★★ Assiduous FRAN grower recently stepping up a level with prestige label Grand Duc (SYRAH, CHARD and new botrytis SEM).

Graham Beck Wines W Cape sp ★★★ Front-ranker now focused exclusively on MCC bubbly. Seven variants led by superb Cuvée Clive (CHARD/PINOT N).

Grangehurst Stell p ★★→★★★ Top small-batch specialist (r p). CAPE BLEND Nikela 98 99 00 01 02 03' 05 06 07' 08 and PINOTAGE 97 98 99 01 02 03' 05 06 07 08.

Groot Constantia Estate Const r (p) w (br) sw (sp) ★→★★★★ Historic property and tourist mecca in SA's original fine-wine-growing area, with suitably serious wines, esp Grand Constance, reviving CONST tradition of world-class desserts.

Guardian Peak *See* RUST EN VREDE ESTATE.

Hamilton Russell Vineyards Hem V r w ★★★→★★★★ Cool-climate pioneer, enduring Burgundy-style specialist at Hermanus, recently embracing bio. Elegant PINOT N 01' 03' 04 05 06 07 08 09' 10 11 12' 13 14 15' 16 17; exceptional CHARD. Super SAUV BL, PINOTAGE and blends (r w) under Southern Right and Ashbourne labels.

Local Syrah beat Aussie icon Grange in tasting: SA loved Syrah ever since.

Hartenberg Estate Coast r w ★★→★★★ Consistent top performer. Outstanding SHIRAZ: quintet: extrovert single-site The Stork 03 04' 05' 06 07 08 09' 10 11 12 13 14, savoury Gravel Hill, serious Estate Shiraz 02 03 04' 05 06 07 08 09 10 11 12 13 14 15, recent entry-level Doorkeeper. Gd-value Alchemy blends (r w).

Haskell Vineyards W Cape r w ★★→★★★ American-owned v'yds and cellar nr STELL receiving rave notices for trio of monosite SYRAH, single-v'yd CHARD and red blends. Ever-improving sibling label Dornbeya.

Hemel-en-Aarde Trio of cool-climate WARDS (Hem V, Up Hem, Hem Rdg) in WLK B DISTRICT, producing outstanding PINOT N, CHARD, SAUV BL.

Hermanuspietersfontein Wynkelder W Cape r (p) w ★→★★★ Leading SAUV BL and B'x/Rhône blend (r w) specialist; creatively markets physical and historical connections with seaside resort Hermanus.

Iona Vineyards Elg r (p) w ★→★★★ Co-owned by staff, with high-altitude v'yds converting to bio. Hailed for CHARD, SAUV BL, PINOT N. New SYRAH and B'x white,

Jardin *See* JORDAN WINE ESTATE.

JC le Roux, The House of W Cape sp ★★ SA's largest specialist bubbly house at STELL, DISTELL-owned. Best labels are PINOT N, Scintilla and Brut NV, all MCC.

Jean Daneel Wines W Cape r w ★★→★★★ Family winery at Napier producing outstanding Director's Signature series, esp CHENIN BL and new SAUV BL.

Joostenberg Wines Paarl r w (sw) ★→★★ Ever-improving family estate, organically farmed. SYRAH, CHENIN BL; some gems in experimental Small Batch Collection.

Jordan Wine Estate W Cape r (p) w (sw) ★★→★★★★ Family winery nr STELL offering consistency, quality, value, from entry Bradgate and Chameleon lines to immaculate CWG Auction bottlings. Flagship Nine Yards CHARD; B'x Cobblers Hill (r) 01 03 04' 05' 06 07 08 09 10 11 12 13 14 15 16.

Julien Schaal U Hem, Ela w ★★★ Alsace couple Julien Schaal and Sophie Bollaert make thrilling CHARD from cool pockets in ELG, HEM and Overberg.

Kaapzicht Wine Estate Stell r w (br) (sw) ★·★★★ Family winery; widely praised top range Steytler: Vision CAPE BLEND 01' 02' 03' 04 05' 06 07 08 10 12' 15, PINOTAGE, B'x blend Pentagon (r). Superb old-vines The 1947 CHENIN BL and new CINSAULT.

Kanonkop Estate Stell r (p) ★★→★★★★ Grand local status for three decades, mainly with PINOTAGE 01 02 03' 04 05 06 07 08 09' 10' 11 12 13 14 15 16, B'x blend Paul Sauer (r) 01 02 03 04' 05 06' 07 08 09 10 11 12 13 14 15 and CAB SAUV. Second tier is Kadette (red, dry rosé and newer PINOTAGE).

Keermont Vineyards Stell r w sw ★★·★★★ Recently nearing heights of neighbour DE TRAFFORD with mostly SHIRAZ, CHENIN BL (single-v'yd and blended); new CAB FR.

Ken Forrester Wines W Cape r (p) w sw (s/sw) (sp) ★·★★★ Now with international drinks giant AdVini as partner, STELL-based vintner/restaurateur Ken Forrester concentrates on Mediterranean varieties and CHENIN BL (dry, off-dry, botrytis). Unputdownable budget line-up, Petit.

Klein Constantia Estate W Cape r (p) w sw sp ★★→★★★★ Iconic property, recently re-energized and focused on SAUV BL, with nine different varietal bottlings, and on luscious, cellar-worthy Vin de Constance 00' 01 02' 04 05 06' 07' 08 09 11 12' 13 14 15 (non-botrytis MUSCAT DE FRONTIGNAN), a convincing re-creation of the legendary C18 CONST sweet dessert.

Kleine Zalze Wines W Cape r (p) w sp ★→★★★ STELL-based star with brilliant CAB SAUV, SHIRAZ, CHENIN BL, SAUV BL in Family Res and V'yd Selection ranges. Exceptional value in Cellar Selection series.

Klein Karoo Mainly semi-arid REGION known for fortified, esp Port-style in C'DORP. Revived old blocks beginning to feature in young-buck bottlings eg. Ronnie B Wines' CHENIN BL (varietal) and COLOMBARD blend.

Krone W Cape (p) sp ★·★★★ Refined and classic MCC, incl newly released RD 2001. Made at revitalized Twee Jonge Gezellen Estate in TUL.

Two more grapes now debuting as solo commercial bottlings: Carmenère, Albariño.

Kumala W Cape r p w s/sw ★ DYA Major entry-level export label and sibling brand to premium FLAGSTONE and mid-tier Fish Hoek. All owned by Accolade Wines.

KwaZulu-Natal Province and demarcated GEOGRAPHICAL UNIT on SA's e coast; summer rain; sub-tropical/tropical climate in coastal areas; cooler, hilly central Midlands plateau home to nascent fine-wine industry, led by Abingdon Estate.

KWV W Cape r (p) w br (sw) sp ★→★★★ Formerly national wine co-op and controlling body, today one of SA's biggest producers and exporters, based in PAARL. Reds, whites, sparkling, Port-styles and other fortified under more than a dozen labels, headed by serially decorated The Mentors.

Lammershoek r w (br) (sp) (sw) ★→★★★ Influential winery in recent SWA/SA evolution, through early emphasis on old vines, organics, "natural" winemaking etc. Lots happening in The Mysteries range, eg. ultra-rare HÁRSLEVELÜ.

La Motte W Cape r w sw sp ★★★ Graceful winery and cellar door at FRAN owned by the Koegelenberg-Rupert family. Old World-styled B'x and Rhône varietals and blends, CHARD, SAUV BL, MCC, VIOGNIER *vin de paille*.

Le Riche Wines Stell r (w) ★★★ Fine CAB SAUV-based boutique wines, hand crafted by respected Etienne le Riche and family. Also elegant CHARD.

MCC (Méthode Cap Classique) EU-friendly name for bottle-fermented sparkling, one of SA's major success stories; c.300 labels and counting.

Meerlust Estate Stell r w ★★★★ Historic family-owned v'yds and cellar. Elegance and restraint in flagship Rubicon 00 01' 03' 04 05 06 07' 08 09' 10' 12 13 14 15, one of SA's 1st B'x reds; excellent MERLOT, CAB SAUV, CHARD, PINOT N.

Meinert Wines Elg, Dev V r (p) w (sw) ★→★★★ Thoughtful producer/consultant/

collaborator Martin Meinert esp noted for fine CAPE BLEND Synchronicity.

Miles Mossop Wines Coast r w sw ★★→★★★ TOKARA wine chief Miles Mossop's own brand; consistently splendid red and white blend, botrytized CHENIN BL.

Morgenster Estate Stell r (p) w (sp) ★★→★★★ Prime Italian-owned wine, olive farm nr Somerset West, advised by Bordelais Pierre Lurton (Cheval Blanc). Classically styled Morgenster Res 00 01 03 04 05' 06' 08 09 10 11' 12 13 and second label Lourens River Valley (both B'x-blends). New MCC, unusually from CAB FR.

Mount Abora Vineyards Swa r w ★★ "SWARTLAND chic" epitomized in naturally fermented, old-vine CINSAULT, Rhône red blend and bush-vine CHENIN BL, vinified by non-interventionist rising star Johan Meyer.

Mulderbosch W Cape r p w (sw) ★★→★★★ Highly regarded STELL winery owned by California's Terroir Capital: SAUV BL, single-site CHENIN BL, CHARD.

Mullineux & Leeu Family Wines Coast r w sw ★★★→★★★★ Chris and Andrea M with investor Analjit Singh specialize in smart, carefully made SYRAH (single-site, multisite 08 09' 10' 11 12 14 15 16), Rhône blends (r w), **Chenin Bl** (all SWA) Wider-sourced new Leeu Red, CHARD; California boutique brand Fog Monster.

Mvemve Raats Stell r ★★★ Mzokhona Mvemve, SA's 1st qualified black winemaker, and Bruwer Raats (RAATS FAMILY): stellar best-of-vintage B'x (r), MR de Compostella.

Nederburg Wines W Cape r (p) w sw s/sw (sp) ★→★★★★ Among SA's biggest (2.8 million cases) and best-known brands, PAARL based, DISTELL owned. Excellent II Centuries flagship, Manor House, Heritage Heroes ranges. Exceptional Ingenuity Red Italian Blend 05 06 07' 08 09 10 11 12 13, White Blend. Low-priced quaffers (still, sparkling). Small Private Bins for annual Nederburg Auction: CHENIN BL botrytis Edelkeur 02 03' 04' 05 06 07' 08 09' 10' 11 12' 13 14.

Neil Ellis Wines W Cape r w ★★→★★★★ Pioneer STELL-based négociant Neil Ellis and son Warren source cooler-climate parcels for site expression. Masterly V'yd Selections, esp CAB SAUV 00' 01 03 04' 05 06 07 09 10' 11 12 13 14 15.

Newton Johnson Vineyards Cape SC r (p) w (sw) ★→★★★ Acclaimed family winery in Up HEM. Top Family V'yds PINOT N 08' 09' 10' 11' 12' 13' 14' 15' 16, **Chard**, SAUV BL, **Granum** SYRAH/MOURVÈDRE, from own and partner v'yds; SA's 1st commercial ALBARIÑO. Lovely botrytis CHENIN BL, L'illa, ex-ROB; entry-level brand Felicité.

Olifants River W-coast REGION (c.10,000 ha). Warm valley floors, conducive to organic cultivation, and cooler, fine-wine-favouring sites in mtn WARD Piekenierskloof, and, nr the Atlantic, Bamboes Bay and Kockenaap.

Opstal Estate Bre, Sla r p w (sw) ★→★★★ Emerging as BRE's leader; family-owned in stunning mtn amphitheatre. Fine CAPE BLEND, old-vines CHENIN BL and SÉM.

Orange River Cellars See CENTRAL ORANGE RIVER.

Paarl Town and demarcated wine DISTRICT 30 miles+ ne of Cape Town. Diverse styles and approaches; best results with Mediterranean varieties (r w), CAB SAUV, PINOTAGE, CHENIN BL. Kleine Draken among handful of SA kosher portfolios.

Painted Wolf Wines Coast r (p) w ★★ Personality-laden PINOTAGE, CHENIN BL and Mediterranean varieties and blends by Jeremy Borg and his "pack", passionate about conserving the African Wild Dog (aka Painted Wolf).

Paul Cluver Estate Wines Elg r w sw s/sw ★★→★★★ ELG's standard bearer, Cluver family-owned; convincing PINOT N, elegant CHARD, gorgeous GEWURZ, knockout RIES (botrytis 03' 04 05' 06' 07 08' 09 10 11' 12 14 17 and two drier versions).

Porseleinberg Swa r ★★★ BOEKENHOUTSKLOOF-owned, partly bio v'yds and cellar with expressive SYRAH 10 11 12' 13 14 15 16. Handcrafted, down to ethereal front label, printed on-site by winemaker.

Raats Family Wines Stell r w ★★→★★★ CAB FR, pure CHENIN BL (oaked and unwooded), vinified by STELL-based Bruwer Raats, also partner in B VINTNERS, MVEMVE RAATS.

Rall Wines Coast r w ★★★→★★★★ Donovan R among original SWA "revolutionaries" with modulated SYRAH-based Red, CHENIN BL-led White. Vinifies STELL's Vuurberg.

Region *See* GEOGRAPHICAL UNIT.

Reyneke Wines W Cape r w ★★→★★★ Leading organic/bio producer nr STELL; apt Twitter handle (and newer wine brand) "Vine Hugger". SHIRAZ, CHENIN BL, SAUV BL.

Richard Kershaw Wines Elg r w ★★★→★★★★ UK-born MW Richard Kershaw at top of SA firmament with refined, cool-climate CHARD, SYRAH, PINOT N. Wines' consituent sites showcased separately in new Deconstructed bottlings.

Rijk's Coast r w sp ★★→★★★ TUL pioneer with multiple tiers of varietal SHIRAZ, PINOTAGE, CHENIN BL. V.gd CHARD MCC.

Robertson Valley Low-rainfall inland DISTRICT; c.14,000 ha; lime soils; historically gd CHARD, desserts; more recently SAUV BL, SHIRAZ, CAB SAUV. Major cellars eg. GRAHAM BECK and many small family concerns incl organic Solara.

Robertson Winery Rob r (p) w (br) sw s/sw sp ★→★★ Consistency, value throughout extended portfolio. Best: Constitution Rd SHIRAZ; also v.gd V'yd Selections.

Rupert & Rothschild Vignerons W Cape r w ★★★ Top v'yds and cellar nr PAARL owned by Rupert family and Baron Benjamin de Rothschild. B'x blend Baron Edmond (r) 01 03' 04 05 07 08 09 10' 11 12 13 14 15; CHARD Baroness Nadine.

Rust en Vrede Estate Stell r (p) (w) sw ★★→★★★★ Owner Jean Engelbrecht's powerful, pricey offering incl Rust en Vrede red varietals, blends; Cirrus SYRAH joint-venture with California's Silver Oak; STELL Res; Donkiesbaai CHENIN BL, PINOT N; v.gd Guardian Peak wines.

Sadie Family Wines Stell, Swa, Oli R r w ★★★→★★★★ Organically grown, traditionally made Columella (SHIRAZ/MOURVÈDRE) 01 02' 03 04 05' 06 07' 08 09' 10' 11 12 13 14 15 16, a Cape benchmark; complex, intriguing multivariety white Palladius; ground-breaking Old Vines series, celebrating SA's wine heritage.

Saronsberg W Cape r (p) w (sw) (sp) ★→★★★ Art-adorned TUL family estate with awarded B'x-blends (r), Rhône (r w) varieties, blends; newer CHARD MCC.

Savage Wines W Cape r w ★★★ CAPE POINT V'YDS' former cellar chief Duncan Savage's own wines from selected cooler parcels; thrillingly understated Mediterranean reds, white blend, CWG Auction bottlings.

Saxenburg Wine Farm Stell r (p) w (sp) ★★→★★★ Swiss-owned v'yds and cellar with roundly oaked reds, SAUV BL, CHARD in high-end Private Collection; premium-priced flagship SHIRAZ Select 00 01 02 03' 05' 06' 07' 09 11.

Shannon Vineyards Elg r w (sw) ★★★ Exemplary MERLOT, PINOT N, SAUV BL, SEM, rare botrytis PINOT N, by brothers James and Stuart Downes, vinified at NEWTON JOHNSON.

Sijnn Mal r (p) w ★★→★★★ DE TRAFFORD co-owner/winemaker David Trafford and partners' pioneering venture on CAPE SOUTH COAST. Pronounced "Seine". Stony soils, maritime climate, distinctive and unusual varieties, blends.

Simonsig Estate W Cape r w (br) (sw) (s/sw) sp ★→★★★ Malan family estate nr STELL admired for consistency and lofty standards. Powerful pinnacle wine The Garland (CAB SAUV); Merindol SYRAH 01 02' 03 04 05 06 07 08 10' 11 12 13 14 15, Red Hill PINOTAGE 01 02 03' 04 05 06 07' 08 09 10 11 12 13 14 15 16; excellent MCC.

Solms-Delta W Cape r (p) w (br) (sp) ★→★★★ Delightfully different wines from historic FRAN estate, partly staff-owned; Amarone-style red Africana, sparkling SHIRAZ, new VERDELHO/ROUSSANNE.

Southern Right *See* HAMILTON RUSSELL.

Spice Route Winery *See* FAIRVIEW.

Spier W Cape r (p) w (sp) ★→★★★ Large, multi-awarded winery and tourist magnet nr STELL. Flag-bearer is brooding B'x/SHIRAZ Frans K Smit 04 05' 06' 07 08 09 10 11' 12. Creative Block, 21 Gables and Collaborative series, in particular, show meticulous wine-growing.

Spioenkop Wines Elg r w ★★→★★★ Ebullient Belgian Koen Roose and family on estate named for Second Boer War battle zone. V.gd individual PINOTAGE, CHENIN BL, (rare in SA) RIES.

> **Unstoppable Syrah**
> The rise and rise of SYRAH as a player on the SA stage in the past few decades is remarkable. Overwhelmingly a solo performer, with well over 700 varietal bottlings, Syrah also has the lead in excess of 300 blends and a bit part in many more. It's made into rosé, Port-style, MCC sparkling, distilled into pomace brandy and given all sorts of vogueish treatments (early picking, amphora ageing, extended barrel-maturation). At the cellar door, Syrah is paired with everything from Belgian chocolate to pâté to steak lunches. There is even an annual Syrah festival, where the star shares the limelight with charcuterie.

Springfield Estate Rob r w ★★→★★★ Cult grower Abrie Bruwer with traditionally vinified CAB SAUV, CHARD, SAUV BL, B'x-style red, PINOT N. Quaffable white blend.

Stark-Condé Wines Elg, Stell r w ★★→★★★ Meticulous boutique winemaker José Conde in STELL's Alpine Jonkershoek. Super CAB SAUV, SYRAH in Three Pines and eponymous ranges; earlier-drinking Postcard Series from ELG and Overberg.

Steenberg Vineyards W Cape r (p) w sp ★→★★★ Top CONST winery, v'yds and chic cellar door. SAUV BL, Sauv Bl/SEM blends, MCC; polished reds (rare varietal NEBBIOLO).

Stellenbosch University town, demarcated wine DISTRICT (c.13,000 ha), heart of wine industry – Napa of SA. Many top estates, esp for reds, tucked into mtn valleys and foothills; extensive wine tasting, accommodation and fine-dining options.

Stellenbosch Vineyards W Cape r (p) w (sp) ★→★★ Big-volume winery; impressive Flagship (PETIT VERDOT, CAB FR), new Limited Release (GRENACHE, VERDELHO).

Storm Wines U Hem, Hem V r ★★★ PINOT N and CHARD specialist Hannes Storm (ex-HAMILTON RUSSELL) expresses his favoured HEM sites with marvellous precision and sensitivity.

Sumaridge Wines U Hem r (p) w ★★→★★★ UK-owned cool-climate v'yds and cellar recently showing improved form; fine PINOT N, CHARD, Maritimus white.

Swartland Fashionable, mainly warm-climate DISTRICT; c.11,000 ha of mostly shy-bearing, unirrigated bush vines producing concentrated, hearty but fresh wines. Increasingly source of fruit for others, with some stellar results.

Testalonga Swa r w ★★→★★★ Out-there SYRAH, GRENACHE N, CARIGNAN, HÁRSLEVELŰ, CHENIN BL by extreme non-interventionist Craig Hawkins. Every sip a surprise.

Thelema Mountain Vineyards W Cape r (p) w (s/sw) (sp) ★→★★★★ STELL-based pioneer of SA's modern wine revival. CAB SAUV 00' 03 04 05 06 07 08 09 10 11 12 13 14; The Mint Cab Sauv 05 06' 07 08 09 10 11 12 13 14 (v'yd being replanted). Sutherland (ELG) v'yds broaden repertoire (eg. rare VIOGNIER/ROUSSANNE blend).

Thorne & Daughters Wines W Cape w ★★★→★★★★ John Seccombe and wife Tasha's single-site SEM and multiregion blends, some from old, coddled vines, are marvels of purity and refinement.

Tokara W Cape r (p) w (sw) ★★→★★★★ Wine, food and art showcase nr STELL. V'yds also in ELG, WLK B. Gorgeous Director's Res blends (r w); elegant CHARD, SAUV BL. New CAB SAUV Res. Winemaker MILES MOSSOP's eponymous bottlings also superb.

Tulbagh Inland DISTRICT historically produced white, bubbly, latterly also beefy reds, some sweeter styles, organic; c.1100 ha.

Uva Mira Mountain Vineyards Stell r w ★★→★★★ Helderberg eyrie v'yds and cellar resurgent under owner Toby Venter, CEO of Porsche SA. Expanded line-up incl brilliant SYRAH plus longtime performers CHARD, SAUV BL.

Vergelegen Wines W Cape r w (sw) (sp) ★★★→★★★★ Historic mansion, immaculate v'yds/wines, stylish cellar-door at Somerset West; owned by Anglo American, advised by top French consultants. Powerful CAB SAUV r 01' 03 04 05 06 07 08 09' 11 12 13, sumptuous B'x blend GVB Red, perfumed SAUV BL/SEM White.

Vilafonté Paarl r ★★★ California's acclaimed Zelma Long (ex-Simi winemaker)

> **The avant-garde: adventurous, ethereal, spiritual**
> Ready for something different? These passion-fuelled, mostly young avant-garde producers deliver in spades: **Blackwater** fresh wines, rare varietal CARIGNAN. **Bryan MacRobert** organic-cultivated old-vine CHENIN BL, PINOTAGE (SWA). **Charla Haasbroek** thrilling amphora-vinified Chenin Bl. **City on a Hill Wine Co** naturally made, reviving neglected vines. **Craven Wines** fresh, drinkable. **Dagbreek** BRE exotic reds eg. CARMENÈRE, TINTA AMARELA; Chenin Bl. **Elemental Bob** Cosmic Hands Red/White. **Fram Wines** in search of best, most interesting parcels. **Hogan Wines** assured, charismatic. **Illimis/Eendevanger** lets sites speak by min interference. **Intellego** serious, light-textured Swa wines. **JC Wickens Wines** textured, mineral "Swerver" ("Wanderer"). **JH Meyer Signature Wines/Mother Rock/Force Majeure** hard-core new-generation winemaking. **Momento** exceptional GRENACHE NOIR, TINTA BAROCCA, Chenin Bl blend. **Queen of Africa** exciting, nr Swellendam. **Ronnie B Wines** reviving special sites, incl old Chenin Bl (KLEIN KAROO). **Silwervis/Smiley/ Terracura** Swa standout Chenin Bl. **Skinny Legs** twinkle-toed orange/ amber wines. **The Blacksmith** minuscule quantities. **Tim Martin Wines** in Cape Town city. **Trizanne Signature Wines** rare varietal BARBERA.

and Phil Freese (ex-Mondavi viticulturist) partnering WARWICK's Mike Ratcliffe. Superb B'x blends incl newer Seriously Old Dirt.

Villiera Wines Elg, Stell r w (sw) sp ★→★★★ Grier family v'yds and winery nr STELL with excellent quality/value range, esp brut MCC bubbly quintet (incl low-alcohol). Also boutique-scale Domaine Grier nr Perpignan, France.

Vondeling V Pa r (p) w sw sp ★→★★★ UK-owned, sustainability-focused estate in Perdeberg foothills. Eclectic offering: one of SA's few *méthode ancestrale* bubblies.

Walker Bay Highly regarded maritime DISTRICT (c.1000 ha). WARDS HEM, Bot River, Sunday's Glen, Stanford Foothills. PINOT N, SHIRAZ, CHARD, SAUV BL standout. Look out for Benguela Cove, La Vierge, Paardenkloof, Seven Springs, Springfontein.

Ward Smallest of the WO demarcations. *See* GEOGRAPHICAL UNIT.

Warwick Estate W Cape r (p) w ★★→★★★ Tourist-cordial Ratcliffe family farm (STELL). Fine CAB FR, opulent CHARD, new CAB SAUV with celebrity DJ Thabo "Touch" Molofe.

Waterford Estate W Cape r (p) w (sw) (sp) ★→★★★ Classy family winery nr STELL, with awarded cellar door. Savoury Kevin Arnold SHIRAZ 01 02' 03 04 05 06 07 08 09 10 11 12 13, elegant CAB SAUV 01 02 03' 04 05 06 07 08 09 10 11 12 13 14 15, intricate Cab Sauv-based flagship The Jem.

Waterkloof Elg, Stell r (p) w ★→★★★ British wine merchant Paul Boutinot's bio v'yds, winery and cantilevered cellar door nr Somerset West. Top tiers: Waterkloof, Circle of Life, Seriously Cool and new Astraeus MCC.

Wellington Warm-climate DISTRICT abutting PAARL with growing reputation for PINOTAGE, SHIRAZ, chunky red blends and CHENIN BL. Must visit: Mischa (also a major vine nursery) with next-gen Nutrition Farming practices, and Imbuko, for gd-value wines and warm-hearted cellar door.

Wine of Origin (WO) SA's "AC" but without French restrictions. Certifies vintage, variety, area of origin. Opt-in sustainability certification additionally aims to guarantee eco-sensitive production from grape to glass. *See* GEOGRAPHICAL UNIT.

Winery of Good Hope, The W Cape r w (sw) ★→★★★ STELL winery with portfolio as eclectic as its Australian-French-SA-UK ownership. Creative, compatible blend of styles, influences, varieties and terroirs. Instant hit with newer Thirst range – juicy, lower-alcohol CINSAULT, Gamay Noir, CLAIRETTE BL blend.

Worcester DISTRICT with mostly co-ops producing bulk wine. Family-run Arendskloof/New Cape/Eagle's Cliff, Alvi's Drift, Conradie, Leipzig aim higher.

Together, apart

Syrah, Grenache and friends

Why these grapes? Syrah and Grenache are by no means the world's most-planted red vines, but each is under the spotlight now. Syrah, the star of the Northern Rhône, is proving to be an adept traveller, making wines of freshness and violet aromas in regions as different as NZ and Chile, South Africa and Washington State. Grenache (which we should, and sometimes will, call Garnacha because of its Spanish origins) is less widely travelled but is the focus of scrupulous attention. It can speak eloquently of its origins; its terroir. Why look at them together? Because they are frequent blending partners – in the Rhône, in Australia, in the US. And yet (if you're going to contradict yourself, do it quickly) in the Rhône they have found their greatest fame in different places. There's no Grenache in the Northern Rhône appellations, which make wines of aromatic depth and presence from (usually) Syrah only; in the south Syrah is a blending grape. So it's only when they go abroad that they really learn to love each other. "GSM" has become Australian shorthand for Grenache, Syrah, Mourvèdre blends, and Rhône Ranger winemakers in the US often blend the same trio, with or without other Southern Rhône grapes like Cinsault or Carignan. This is where the "friends" in our subtitle comes in. You can't look at either on its own; each so often gains from the presence of others. Each, though, has a solo career. You'll find Garnacha in Priorat, Navarra and elsewhere in Spain, though in Rioja it often plays second fiddle to Tempranillo. In the Languedoc it's taken seriously on its own, as it is in Sardinia as Cannonau, and there is wonderful old-vine Grenache in Australia – where Shiraz, to give it its local name, is an institution.

The wheel of fortune
Syrah, Grenache and fashion

Few grapes have had as dramatic changes in fortune as Syrah and Grenache. They've both been in huge demand in the past, though not always for the best reasons, and they've both gone out of fashion to the point where you could hardly give them away. If you wanted reasons why no vine should ever be dismissed as hopeless, Grenache and Syrah are two of them. More often than not it's not the vine that's at fault, but fashion, or lack of imagination – they can be related.

Both are probably quite old. Garnacha is probably the older of the two, and probably originated in Aragón, Spain (in Portugal it is still known as Aragonez). It appears in written records certainly from 1678 and perhaps earlier; it arrived in France in the late C18, spreading eastwards from Roussillon, and arrived in Australia early on: it was one of the first vines to be planted there.

Syrah has spawned more hypotheses about its origins than most grapes, but the truth is mundane: it's a crossing of Mondeuse Blanche and Dureza, and it was probably born in the Rhône-Alpes region, from where it was taken to Australia by James Busby in 1832. Until the late C20 those are the only two places it was found in any quantity.

So they were both early arrivals in Australia. This is key to understanding their rise and fall and rise there: they became workhorse grapes, able to oblige with any style you wanted, especially fortifieds. But fortifieds went out of fashion and modern table wines came in. A government vine-pull scheme began in 1986: get rid of it! Uproot it, burn it! Plant something modern, something international, something fashionable!

World classics

That something was of course Cabernet Sauvignon. Cabernet, in the 1980s, almost took over the world. But at the same time that it was taking over Australia, a few Australians began to look again at the ancient vines that were being tossed on bonfires. They began to wonder what was being lost. And they wondered so loudly that people began to listen – and think again. Old vines in Australia are now the subject of a form of ancestor worship. The Barossa classifies its old vineyards as Old Vines (35 years+), Survivor Vines (70+), Centenarian Vines (100+) and Ancestor Vines (125+). Barossa Shiraz – dark, chewy and with flavours of black olive, soy, chocolate and raisins, is acknowledged as one of the classic wine styles of the world.

Grenache returned to favour in Australia at about the same time, and for the same reasons. (*See* box, p.296.) And in the Rhône? It's a parallel story. In the Southern Rhône it originally rose to dominance

Shiraz in the Barossa, where the older you are, the more you'll be photographed

because of demand from Burgundian négociant houses, who liked Grenache because it bolstered the then pallid, poorly made wines of the Côte d'Or. (I said it was popular for bad reasons.) But as Southern Rhône wines began to be better appreciated, so growers there took their raw materials more seriously. They realized that if you cut its yields, Grenache behaves very differently. (*See* box, p.58.) By the end of the 20th century it was fast becoming a cult grape across the South of France. Its rise to prominence in Spain's Priorat didn't hurt, of course. This was always a predominantly Garnacha area, and the wines were a bit dowdy, but pioneers moving in from 1986 onwards added Cabernet Sauvignon and Merlot to the blend and started making big, chewy, tarry, blackberry-ish wines that attracted a following.

But Syrah in the Rhône, you might think, has inbuilt glamour. How could it ever have been unfashionable? Yet in the early C20 Rhône Syrah was so little regarded that it was seldom even domaine-bottled. That's why you won't find old bottlings of Hermitage or Côte-Rôtie to equal Bordeaux. The revival started in the 1970s; and it hasn't faltered since.

Roses and chocolate raisins
The flavours of Syrah

Can red grapes be aromatic? Yes, certainly. Syrah can smell of roses and autumn flowers, or black olives and herbs, or – yes – chocolate raisins. If you put your nose into a glass and get soy and black olives, that's Syrah. It has acidity and it's happy with oak ageing – though these days none of us wants to feel we're chewing on oak. Obvious new-oak aromas – those notes of vanilla and (heaven forfend) coconut are out, out, out.

But hang on – Syrah, as we've seen, flourishes in climates as diverse as the northern Chilean desert (cool climate, believe it or not, if it's near the sea. Though those who call it such have perhaps never spent much time in England) and the desert that is inland Washington State, the flat grey vineyards of Gimblett Gravels in NZ or the steep slopes of the Northern Rhône. Surely it doesn't taste the same everywhere?

No, it doesn't. Think of the list of flavours above as progressive: the hotter the climate, the more the wine will tend towards chocolate raisins; the cooler, the more floral it will be. The soil is part of it. Richer soils will give fleshier wines, poorer soils more leanly structured. But the real dichotomy in flavour is between Syrah and Shiraz.

Syrah is (of course) what the grape is called in the Rhône. Shiraz is its Australian moniker, and Barossa Shiraz – chewy, chocolatey and pruney – is its archetype. Elsewhere in the New World growers choose which name to use according to which style they seek – that choice of name is a reliable guide to style, better than any back label.

Dichotomy in flavour

In the Northern Rhône there's something wild about Syrah. If it's possible to taste rock you taste it here: rock with thyme and fennel growing in the crevices, and wild roses with a dash of soy, and black olives. Co-ferment it with a dash of Viognier and you get some white fruits in there as well.

In the Barossa you get soy and black olives, but what is ripe here would be considered overripe in the Rhône, and the palate gives that away. The fruit is wrinkling, getting squashy inside. At its most extreme you get what Australians call "dead fruit" flavour, but that's not admired. Too much heat is not good, any more than too little. Barossa Shiraz is getting fresher, more elegant these days – stand-a-spoon-up wines are starting to look like the past.

And in between? NZ's Hawke's Bay, perhaps. Here cooler years make wines that Côte-Rôtie growers would be proud of; warmer years tend more towards Shiraz. Cooler-climate Chile (think coastal Limarí, Leyda) is a bit like this too: a cassis sweetness of fruit and a note of violets tempered by freshness. Syrah always has acidity – more acidity than, say, the Bordeaux varieties at the same pH. In Australia, working back from the black-chocolate Barossa style, McLaren Vale is more milk chocolate; the Hunter Valley broader, quite chewy; Eden Valley precise and black-fruited; Heathcote aromatic and supple. In the Rhône, Hermitage is the biggest and most powerful and tannic, Côte-Rôtie aromatic, Cornas robust. Crozes-Hermitage and St-Joseph are where the clever Rhône money goes: slightly earlier maturing, they have benefited from warmer summers and better winemaking.

Providing it's warm enough for the grapes to ripen but not too hot, Syrah seems to succeed in many places. It's become an extremely successful traveller, able to flourish on most soils providing they're well drained and not overrich. Clay gives fine tannins; the free-draining gravel of Gimblett Gravels gives a lean masculinity; richer, deeper soils give more flesh and prettiness. The Northern Rhône's granite, gneiss and schist – well drained, all of them – retain the heat in what was and still can be a marginal region for Syrah.

Wild fennel and *garrigue* herbs and a lick of rock characterize Rhône Syrah

Violets and dried figs
The flavours of Grenache

If the archetypal Syrah is dark, glossy and travel-friendly, the archetypal Grenache is the opposite: low in acidity, oxidative, paler in colour, high in alcohol. It can taste of toffee as well as lavender and violets, rosemary and thyme – the plants that surround its vineyards. With age it smells of aromatic leather; big, chewy Garnachas taste of deep, powerful blackberries, the sort of blackberries you could build a wall with.

But to taste of anything at all it has to be carefully cultivated. Let it run riot and yield prolifically, and it will churn out vast quantities of alcoholic liquid that can be blended with something more structured to satisfy the lowest end of the market. That's what it was used for for years. And as a result Spanish growers increasingly replaced it with something else: by Cabernet and Merlot in the 90s and in this century by Tempranillo. In southern France it was Cabernet, Merlot and Syrah. Yet even while EU subsidies were being deployed in its destruction, Grenache was reinventing itself. In southern France and in Spain's Priorat and Montsant, Campo de Borja and Calatayud, and in the scattered vineyards around Madrid, gathered under the (unofficial) name of Gredos, a new fan club of Garnacha producers has

Lavender and violets: just add herbs and a touch of toffee

refined winemaking, focusing on higher-altitude vineyards, low yields and old vines to produce wines that are less oxidative and therefore have a longer life expectancy. And they do something that Garnacha/ Grenache does supremely well: they have the texture of silk.

Texture is crucial to Garnacha. It can taste of herbs and violets (sunshine develops the violet notes, and Garnacha loves sunshine) and that, combined with the sensation of silk in your mouth, is unique. They have alcohol: it's rare (though not impossible) to find a good Garnacha under 14% alc. They don't have the look-at-me attention-seeking quality of Syrah, but they have subtlety and complexity. They're wines that make their own rules. The newest Priorats are in a lighter style than before, and show the red-fruit flavours that Garnacha gains from schist. Older-style Priorat, full of blackberry fruit in youth and ageing to tarry, figgy flavours, is still around, though, and is achieved by overripeness and heavy extraction: raisined fruit gives more raisiny flavours, and when that is combined with new oak the result is pretty massive.

Grenache reinvented

The newer Garnachas are suited to old oak much more than to new. Old oak sits better with the tannins, offers perfect transparency and frees the wine to reflect its site: schist, clay or stones in Priorat and Montsant, and vineyards at perhaps 500m+, limestone, sand, clay and red slate at every altitude you can think of in Campo de Borja. The vineyards of Gredos, varied as they are, have in common very old bush vines and altitudes of 600–1200m; burgundy-lovers will find wines they love here, all transparency and silk. (*See* box, p.181.)

In southern France, too, from the Rhône to Roussillon, Grenache is being properly appreciated now – not least because it's ideally suited to the climate. It tolerates drought in a way that Syrah does not, and its long growing season gives it far more room to manoeuvre in a world of climate change than the earlier-ripening Syrah. Châteauneuf-du-Pâpe, Gigondas and Vacqueyras can all be burly in youth – varietal Grenaches are rare here – but age to notes of perfumed leather and herbs. (*See* box, p.58.)

Grenache doesn't have the travel bug in quite the same way as Syrah. In Sardinia, where it is called Cannonau and regarded as a native, it produces rich, earthy flavours; in Australia where, as we've seen, old vines are treated with the reverence of an elderly woman who has yet to make her will, Grenache can be chewy, figgy, but is now brighter and fresher with it: the change of direction of Australian wines has taken Grenache with it.

Is it better in a blend than on its own? Not always. But for that subject, *see* pp.328–9.

Mutual attraction
Syrah and Grenache in blends

It's so easy to assume that varietal wines are better than blends – perhaps an idea that blends are just using up the leftovers, or that a grape that works on its own is a better grape than one that needs help. One could compare it to the sort of singing voice that works in a choir to one that demands a solo career: no prizes for guessing which brings fame.

A blend, like a choir, shouldn't have bits jutting out; it should be seamless, and more than the sum of its parts. And putting one together is so challenging that winemakers often construct a blend first, taking their pick of all the wines at their disposal, and then worry about the varietals later.

Grenache and Syrah are not automatically a marriage made in heaven. Not with each other, anyway: each can make perfectly happy partnerships with other grapes. But what is ideal terrain for one is probably not ideal terrain for the other; and when they are hitched together the driver is often fashion.

Take the South of France. Syrah is fashionable here, and sells. That recognizable word on a label is reassuring. But in fact it's seldom as delicious here as it is further north; it's often too hot and too dry, and Syrah can lose its *élan*. (*See* p.98 for a list of successful ones.) Yet Grenache loves the heat and the drought, and provided its yields are restricted it gives the blend much-needed perfume, flesh and texture. Grenache-based blends are often more interesting. (There's a list on p.80.) Acidity can come from a shot of Mourvèdre in the

The terraces of Priorat: hot and dry enough for the most demanding Garnacha vine

blend; and Carignan, from low-yielding old-vines, can be a brilliant blending partner, offering structure and lovely herby fruit.

A tempering subtlety

In Rioja, Garnacha has fallen to just eight per cent of the red vineyard: Tempranillo has won hands down. Here again, it's darker, more suited to extraction, more suited to new oak – and here again, Garnacha adds its silky texture and its subtlety to temper Tempranillo's bounciness. Even in those parts of Spain where Garnacha flourishes, like Priorat and Montsant, Campo de Borja and Calatayud, it's seldom made as a varietal.

So what of Australia's GSM blends – Grenache, Shiraz, Mourvèdre, though not necessarily in that order? The New World styles of each are somewhat different, and the bigger, more forward fruit, the rich juiciness and the presence of Mourvèdre as matchmaker all help them to combine differently. More widespread use of irrigation too can protect Shiraz from drought.

Before GSM became fashionable, Shiraz/Cabernet blends were the norm in Australia; this was until there were enough Cabernet vines in the country to satisfy demand. It's a happy blend, though seldom seen now. Now, when Shiraz is blended in Australia, it's with Viognier: just two or three or five per cent, in direct imitation of Côte-Rôtie. Add too much Viognier and you get an ice-cream note that detracts from the Shiraz, but just a little highlights the floral flavours and adds finesse.

But what of that earlier blend, the addition of Syrah, in the form of Hermitage, to C18 claret? Château Palmer (*see* p.118) is experimenting with doing just that.

The age question
When to drink?

Today's ideal wine is one that can be drunk young, but will improve over time – if time, and a cellar, are what you have. You're on safe ground with many, though not all, Syrahs and Grenaches. The ones that really do deserve to be kept are top Rhônes, North and South: they change enormously with time, and can last, and improve, for 20 years or more. But as a rule of thumb, drink Grenache before Syrah; it oxidizes far more easily.

That's one reason, in fact, why Grenache is so often blended with something less oxidative – like Tempranillo, Syrah, or Mourvèdre. Once you get a note of perfumed leather in the wine, it's a sign that while it's delicious now, it won't keep forever. Most commercial-to-good Châteauneufs and Gigondas are best drunk within six to ten years, depending on the vintage. There are now varietal Garnachas from across Spain that are beautifully expressive at two or three years. They will keep, and evolve, and the best, most concentrated and poised examples will keep for ten years or more, but mostly there is no real need to keep them. If you like youth in your wines, Garnacha will oblige.

Priorat is usually best drunk young. Yes, it's big, concentrated and dense, but with age it tends to lose its blackberry fruit and go baked and figgy. Overripeness and overextraction are seldom a recipe for long life.

Rioja can age famously well, though traditionally does its ageing in the cellar, whether in barrel or bottle, before release. Reservas and Gran Reservas don't need any further ageing; more "modern" wines, often without those designations because they don't fit into the standard categories, may need a few years, or at least benefit from a few years; but again, if youth is what you like, don't be deterred.

Life-long friends

Australian GSM blends and similar can usually age, however, it all depends on structure and concentration – and balance. Fine, poised examples should see out ten years with no trouble; blending other grapes, particularly Syrah and Mourvèdre, with Grenache tends to lengthen a wine's life. Syrah on its own, or with a touch of Viognier? Hermitage is the longest-living Rhône red, tight for ten years or so and good for 20, at least. Côte-Rôtie, at the top level, is not hugely different, and nor is Cornas, though a lot is ready sooner. Crozes-Hermitage and St-Joseph are ACs to look for if you want to drink your wine at about three years old.

Syrahs from elsewhere may well last very well, though styles are evolving so fast that it would be a brave person who gave a definitive figure. Cool-climate Chilean examples are wonderfully aromatic, though quite tight, in youth; give them a couple of years. NZ's Hawke's Bay probably needs a bit longer.

And those classic top old-vine Barossa Shiraz? They don't need a lot of ageing – a couple of years to allow them to soften a bit – but then they'll go for 15 years before fading slowly. If you're lucky enough to have some Grange, it'll last even longer. But as ever, opening a bottle to find it's past its best always feels more of a loss than opening it while it's a fraction too young.

Onwards and upwards: Côte-Rôtie needs some years in bottle

Food to flatter
Syrah and Grenache at table

These are not complicated wines to drink. Their breadth of flavour means that they will obligingly partner many different dishes; in fact, if you want all-purpose reds in your cellar, these are they.

Successful matching, if we're going to look at the detail, becomes a matter of weight. Hefty food needs weightier wines; that's pretty obvious. These are not wines for lettuce soup. But structure is also key. Does the wine feel linear, with plenty of acidity, or broad and open, or four-square? A linear, tight wine with acidity is good with roast meat – how's that for a rule of thumb? So with top Rhône or NZ Syrah you might think of roast venison, grouse or other strongly flavoured game – hare, perhaps. With partridge, more delicate in flavour, choose a lighter wine – something of comparable weight. Barbecued meat is a good bet too, particularly with Australian or South African Shiraz – it should be a natural match, and it is. Broader wines (Grenache tends to be broader than Syrah; hotter climates are broader than cooler) are often better with slow-cooked meat with a sauce, be that a tagine, a casserole or whatever variant on that sort of dish you have in mind. Don't worry about holding back on the spice. Chilli may not be ideal because it emphasizes tannin, but chilli is always tricky.

Barbecued steak: break out the Aussie Shiraz

Careful consideration

A soft, perfumed Garnacha can be brilliant with vegetable dishes, especially those with some Middle Eastern spicing, or those wonderful Spanish vegetable stews. And fresh, light Garnachas, without obtrusive tannins, can even match well-flavoured fish like sardines. If Pinot Noir will go with something then a Garnacha of similar structure will also go. And Grenache has one more advantage too: it complements food, but seldom takes over. Flavours like tarragon, anise, fennel, garlic (chicken with 40 cloves of wet garlic, perhaps): anything aromatic with herbs and spices, will suit Garnacha/Grenache.

The next thing to remember is that rules of thumb are very often wrong. Rioja with a barbecue? Of course. Though perhaps not a very old, fragile wine; roast shoulder of baby lamb might be better here, and is what they'd choose in Logroño (you might have to go to Logroño to source the baby lamb, but that's a small problem). South African Syrah with jerk-marinated pulled beef brisket? Nothing nicer. Australian GSM with kangaroo? Perfect.

But when it comes to very top wines, you want to choose the food to flatter what's in the glass. In which case keep it simple. Roast duck, guinea fowl, pheasant or well-matured beef will love pretty much any of these wines, and will sing with pleasure.

Light Garnacha will be perfect with grilled sardines

Fizz – and fortifieds
From one extreme to the other

It sounds like a contradiction in terms. Lots of table wine grapes can be coaxed into making sparkling wine. Some can be coerced into fortification, but they're not usually the same ones. Syrah and Grenache are possibly the only grapes in the world that can stretch from one extreme to the other, and convince you that actually, this is what they're made for.

It's only fair to say, though, that the fizz is not as fashionable as it once was. It comes from Australia (where else?) and it's red, assertive, tasting of blueberries and blackberries, damson jam and herbs and often some vanilla oak. It looks amazing in the glass: purple-red, topped with white froth. A bottle of Aussie sparkling Shiraz or Grenache will, if nothing else, attract attention. A list of attention-getting red Aussie fizz is on p.286.

Fortifieds, you could argue, are equally unfashionable – or probably even more so. Yet there are wonderful wines to be had, from the South of France, from Australia, from South Africa – all those places with a long history of making fortifieds. Most take their original inspiration from Port, and often Tawny Port, so are aged for some years in big old barrels. They taste like Port to the extent that they're sweet, rich, with flavours of nuts and spice, dried fruit and toast, if the inspiration is Tawny, damsons and spice if they're inspired by Vintage Port, and they're always blends – some Shiraz, some Grenache, some Mourvèdre, maybe something else. They're

wines from the great age of blending, before any of us started looking for grape names on labels. The old Australian companies, like Seppeltsfield, McWilliams, All Saints, De Bortoli, Penfolds, Peter Lehmann, all make them; if you want a top example, try Seppelt's Grenache-based 100-Year-Old Para Liqueur.

Keeping tradition alive

In France's Roussillon, down by the Spanish border, there's another tradition. In 1299 the king of Mallorca granted a patent to one Arnaldus de Villanova for a process that stopped fermentation by the addition of grape spirit. The kingdom of Mallorca included what is now Roussillon; these dry, rocky vineyards have kept the tradition alive ever since. The wines are *vins doux naturels* from Banyuls, Maury, Rasteau and Rivesaltes. The wines may be aged in barrel or in glass demi-johns; none need further ageing once bottled. And this is where the word *rancio* enters the vocabulary.

Rancio is the savoury and sour, leather, nuts and cheese flavour developed by these wines when they're aged in the presence of oxygen – in other words, for a long time in big old oak barrels. This *rancio* flavour is the key to these wines – indeed, it's almost the point. You'll find it too in very old Sherry and in very old Tawny Port, and in old Madeira. It's pungent, even austere, with age. Young wines will have brighter fruit flavours, but for real *rancio* character go for the very old wines, and drink them with chocolate or blue cheese; or even black chocolate and blue cheese, with a touch of cherry jam. It works.

Banyuls ageing in barrel in the old cellars of the Knights Templar

Pale, paler, palest
Gather ye rosés

Who cares, in the end, what rosé is made of? It's pink, and that's what counts. Most of us find that colour is a reasonable guide to style: darker rosés are jammier, paler ones crisper.

But that crispness, that jamminess, are matters of winemaker choice, and this is where grapes, and climate, come into play. Grenache will give different results to Syrah. Not just in flavour but in texture too – texture matters in rosé. You don't want a raw edge of tannin, but a faint grippiness can be nice, and adds to the sensation of freshness.

Blends of grapes usually work best for rosés. You're not looking for a paler, less ripe version of a red wine. You want harmony, some complexity, some fruit, be it raspberry or strawberry, watermelon or grapefruit; a touch of spice; acidity but not too much; a lively brightness and enough snap on the finish to bring you back for more. Provence rosé is pale – sometimes you wonder if flavour has been sacrificed in the search for paleness. But if you want your rosé delicate and relatively expensive, Provence is where to look. Quality is high, and this is one of the few places where growers plant and pick their vineyards specifically for rosé. Other southern French rosés may be less obsessed with paleness; Tavel is darker, structured, and can age, though will turn into a different animal – toastier and less fresh. Grenache and Cinsault are the main grapes; Syrah is often part of the blend.

Spanish Garnacha-based rosado often has a nice creaminess underlining its bright fruit; look in Navarra for good value. And elsewhere? Wherever makes rosé. Syrah-based wines are more upfront, sometimes a bit too punchy; Grenache/Garnacha more subtle, sometimes too jammy. Drink them young, nearly always, and perhaps from a magnum; magnums of rosé have a certain panache.

Provence is where they take rosé most seriously

A little learning...

A few technical words

The jargon of laboratory analysis is often seen on back-labels. It creeps menacingly into newspapers and magazines. What does it mean? This hard-edged wine-talk, unsympathetic as it is to most lovers of wine, is very briefly explained below.

Acidity is both fixed and volatile. Fixed: mostly tartaric, malic and citric, all from the grape, and lactic and succinic, from fermentation. Acidity may be natural or (in warm climates) added. Volatile (VA): acetic acid, formed by bacteria in the presence of oxygen. A touch of VA is inevitable, can add complexity. Too much = vinegar. Total acidity is fixed + VA combined.

Alcohol content (mainly ethyl alcohol) is expressed as per cent (%) by volume of the total liquid. (Also known as "degrees".) Table wines are usually between 12.5–14.5%; too many wines go as high as 16% these days.

Amphora the fermentation vessel of the moment, and the last 7000 years. Remove lid, throw in grapes, replace lid, return in six months. Risky: can be wonderful or frankly horrible.

Barriques small (225-litre) oak barrels, as used in Bordeaux and across the world for fermentation and/or ageing. The newer the barrel the stronger the smell and taste of oak influence; French oak is more subtle than American. The fashion for overpowering wine of all sorts with new oak has waned: oak use is now far more subtle across most of the globe.

Biodynamic (Bio) viticulture uses herbal, mineral, organic preparations in homeopathic quantities, in accordance with the phases of the moon and the movements of the planets. Sounds like voodoo, but some top growers swear by it. "Bio" in French means organic too, but in this book it means bio.

Malolactic fermentation occurs after the alcoholic fermentation, and changes tart malic acid into softer lactic acid. Can add complexity to red and white alike. Often avoided in hot climates where natural acidity is low and precious.

Micro-oxygenation is a widely used bubbling technique, allowing controlled contact with oxygen during maturation. Softens flavours, helps stabilize wine.

Minerality a tasting term to be used with caution: fine as a descriptor of chalky/stony flavours; often wrongly used to imply transference of minerals from soil to wine, which is impossible.

Natural wines are undefined, but start by being organic or biodynamic, involve minimal intervention in the winery and as little SO_2 as possible; sometimes none. Can be excellent and characterful, or oxidized and/or dirty. An element of Emperor's New Clothes may creep in.

Old vines give deeper flavours. No legal definition: some "vieilles vignes" turn out to be c.30 years. Should be 50+ to be taken seriously.

Orange wines are tannic whites fermented on skins, perhaps in amphorae. Caution: like natural wines, some are good, some not.

Organic viticulture prohibits most chemical products in the vineyard; organic wine prohibits added sulphur and must be from organically grown grapes.

Pét-Nat (*pétillant naturel*) bottled before end of fermentation, which continues in bottle. Slight residual sugar, quite low alcohol. Dead trendy.

pH is a measure of acidity: the lower the pH the sharper the acidity. Wine is normally 2.8–3.8. High pH can be a problem in hot climates. Lower pH gives better colour, helps stop bacterial spoilage and allows more of the SO_2 to be free and active as a preservative. So low is good in general.

Residual sugar is that left after fermentation has ended or been stopped, measured in grams per litre (g/l). A dry wine has almost none.

Sulphur dioxide (SO_2) added to prevent oxidation and other accidents in winemaking. Some combines with sugars, etc., and is "bound". Only "free" SO_2 is an effective preservative. Trend worldwide is to use less. To use none is brave.